5,50

D1083728

PUBLIC PAPERS OF THE PRESIDENTS

OF THE UNITED STATES

R
353.03 p

PUBLIC PAPERS OF THE PRESIDENTS

OF THE UNITED STATES

Harry S. Truman

Containing the Public Messages, Speeches, and

Statements of the President

APRIL 12 TO DECEMBER 31, 1945

1945

UNITED STATES GOVERNMENT PRINTING OFFICE

WASHINGTON : 1961

38026

PUBLISHED BY THE
OFFICE OF THE FEDERAL REGISTER
NATIONAL ARCHIVES AND RECORDS SERVICE
GENERAL SERVICES ADMINISTRATION

For sale by the Superintendent of Documents, U.S. Government Printing Office
Washington 25, D.C. — Price $5.50

FOREWORD

THE IMPORTANCE OF this series lies in the extraordinary character of the office of President of the United States.

A President's written and spoken words can command national and international attention if he has within him the power to attract and hold that attention. It is partly through the use of this power that leadership arises, events are molded, and administrations take their shape.

It is this power, quite as much as powers written into the Constitution, that gives to the papers of Presidents their peculiar and revealing importance.

Harry Truman

PREFACE

IN THIS VOLUME are gathered most of the public messages and statements of the President of the United States that were released by the White House during the period April 12–December 31, 1945. Similar volumes covering the remaining years of President Truman's administration are under preparation.

Annual volumes covering the administration of President Eisenhower are also available. Current plans call for the publication of volumes containing the public messages and statements of President Kennedy shortly after the beginning of each calendar year.

This series was begun in 1957 in response to a recommendation of the National Historical Publications Commission (44 U.S.C. 393).

An extensive compilation of the messages and papers of the Presidents, covering the period 1789 to 1897, was assembled by James D. Richardson and published under congressional authority between 1896 and 1899. Since that time various private compilations were issued, but there was no uniform, systematic publication comparable to the *Congressional Record* or the *United States Supreme Court Reports*. Many Presidential papers could be found only in mimeographed White House releases or as reported in the press. The National Historical Publications Commission therefore recommended the establishment of an official series in which Presidential writings and utterances of a public nature could be made promptly available.

The Commission's recommendation was incorporated in regulations of the Administrative Committee of the Federal Register issued under section 6 of the Federal Register Act (44 U.S.C. 306). The Committee's regulations, establishing the series and providing for the coverage of prior years, are reprinted at page 614 as "Appendix D."

Preface

The text of this book is based on Presidential materials issued during the period April 12–December 31, 1945. A list of White House releases from which final selections were made is published at page 591 as "Appendix A."

The full text of President Truman's news conferences is here published for the first time, since direct quotation of the President's replies usually was not authorized. Four meetings with special groups—numbered in source materials as News Conferences 11, 13, 36, and 39—were not in fact news conferences and are not included in this volume.

Proclamations, Executive orders, and similar documents required by law to be published in the *Federal Register* and *Code of Federal Regulations* are not repeated. Instead, they are listed by number and subject under the heading "Appendix B" at page 603.

The President is required by statute to transmit numerous reports to Congress. Those transmitted during the period covered by this volume are listed at page 613 as "Appendix C."

The items published in this volume are presented in chronological order, rather than being grouped in classes. Most needs for a classified arrangement are met by the subject index. For example, a reader interested in veto messages will find them listed in the index under the heading "veto messages."

The dates shown at the end of item headings are White House release dates. In instances where the date of the document differs from the release date that fact is shown in brackets immediately following the heading. Other editorial devices, such as text notes, footnotes, and cross references, have been held to a minimum.

Remarks or addresses were delivered in Washington, D.C., unless otherwise indicated. Similarly, statements, messages, and letters were issued from the White House in Washington unless otherwise indicated.

Preface

Original source materials, where available, have been used to protect against substantive errors in transcription. In maintaining the integrity of the text, valuable assistance was furnished by Dr. Philip C. Brooks and Philip D. Lagerquist of the Truman Library. David D. Lloyd, former Administrative Assistant to President Truman, assisted in the selection and annotation of materials.

The planning and publication of this series is under the direction of David C. Eberhart of the Office of the Federal Register. The editor of the present volume was Warren R. Reid, assisted by Mildred B. Berry and Dorothy M. Jacobson. Frank H. Mortimer of the Government Printing Office developed the typography and design.

WAYNE C. GROVER
Archivist of the United States

JOHN L. MOORE
Administrator of General Services
October 7, 1961

CONTENTS

CONTENTS

LIST OF ITEMS

List of Items

List of Items

List of Items

List of Items

List of Items

List of Items

List of Items

List of Items

List of Items

List of Items

List of Items

List of Items

List of Items

List of Items

Harry S. Truman

1945

63931—61——3

1 Statement by the President After Taking the Oath of
   Office. *April* 12, 1945

THE WORLD may be sure that we will prosecute the war on both
fronts, east and west, with all the vigor we possess to a successful
conclusion.

NOTE: The oath of office was administered by Chief Justice Harlan F. Stone
at 7:09 p.m. in the Cabinet Room at the
White House. Shortly thereafter the
President announced through an assistant that the United Nations Conference would be held in San Francisco on
April 25 as President Roosevelt had
directed.

   The foregoing statement was released
at 8:10 p.m.

2 Address Before a Joint Session of the Congress.
   April 16, 1945

Mr. Speaker, Mr. President, Members of the Congress:

It is with a heavy heart that I stand before you, my friends and colleagues, in the Congress of the United States.

Only yesterday, we laid to rest the mortal remains of our beloved
President, Franklin Delano Roosevelt. At a time like this, words are
inadequate. The most eloquent tribute would be a reverent silence.

Yet, in this decisive hour, when world events are moving so rapidly,
our silence might be misunderstood and might give comfort to our
enemies.

In His infinite wisdom, Almighty God has seen fit to take from us a
great man who loved, and was beloved by, all humanity.

No man could possibly fill the tremendous void left by the passing
of that noble soul. No words can ease the aching hearts of untold millions of every race, creed and color. The world knows it has lost a
heroic champion of justice and freedom.

Tragic fate has thrust upon us grave responsibilities. We *must* carry
on. Our departed leader never looked backward. He looked forward

1

and moved forward. That is what he would want us to do. That is what America *will* do.

So much blood has already been shed for the ideals which we cherish, and for which Franklin Delano Roosevelt lived and died, that we dare not permit even a momentary pause in the hard fight for victory.

Today, the entire world is looking to America for enlightened leadership to peace and progress. Such a leadership requires vision, courage and tolerance. It can be provided only by a united nation deeply devoted to the highest ideals.

With great humility I call upon all Americans to help me keep our nation united in defense of those ideals which have been so eloquently proclaimed by Franklin Roosevelt.

I want in turn to assure my fellow Americans and all of those who love peace and liberty throughout the world that I will support and defend those ideals with all my strength and all my heart. That is my duty and I shall not shirk it.

So that there can be no possible misunderstanding, both Germany and Japan can be certain, beyond any shadow of a doubt, that America will continue the fight for freedom until no vestige of resistance remains!

We are deeply conscious of the fact that much hard fighting is still ahead of us.

Having to pay such a heavy price to make complete victory certain, America will never become a party to any plan for partial victory!

To settle for merely another temporary respite would surely jeopardize the future security of all the world.

Our demand has been, and it *remains*—Unconditional Surrender!

We will not traffic with the breakers of the peace on the terms of the peace.

The responsibility for making of the peace—and it is a very grave responsibility—must rest with the defenders of the peace. We are not unconscious of the dictates of humanity. We do not wish to see unnecessary or unjustified suffering. But the laws of God and of man have been violated and the guilty must not go unpunished. Nothing shall shake our determination to punish the war criminals even though we must pursue them to the ends of the earth.

Lasting peace can never be secured if we permit our dangerous opponents to plot future wars with impunity at any mountain retreat—however distant.

In this shrinking world, it is futile to seek safety behind geographical barriers. Real security will be found only in law and in justice.

Here in America, we have labored long and hard to achieve a social order worthy of our great heritage. In our time, tremendous progress has been made toward a really democratic way of life. Let me assure the forward-looking people of America that there will be no relaxation in our efforts to improve the lot of the common people.

In the difficult days ahead, unquestionably we shall face problems of staggering proportions. However, with the faith of our fathers in our hearts, we do not fear the future.

On the battlefields, we have frequently faced overwhelming odds—and won! At home, Americans will not be less resolute!

We shall never cease our struggle to preserve and maintain our American way of life.

At this moment, America, along with her brave Allies, is paying again a heavy price for the defense of our freedom. With characteristic energy, we are assisting in the liberation of entire nations. Gradually, the shackles of slavery are being broken by the forces of freedom.

All of us are praying for a speedy victory. Every day peace is delayed costs a terrible toll.

The armies of liberation today are bringing to an end Hitler's ghastly threat to dominate the world. Tokyo rocks under the weight of our bombs.

The grand strategy of the United Nations' war has been determined—due in no small measure to the vision of our departed Commander in Chief. We are now carrying out our part of that strategy under the able direction of Admiral Leahy, General Marshall, Admiral King, General Arnold, General Eisenhower, Admiral Nimitz and General MacArthur.

I want the entire world to know that this direction must and will remain—*unchanged and unhampered!*

Our debt to the heroic men and valiant women in the service of our

3

country can never be repaid. They have earned our undying gratitude. America will never forget their sacrifices. Because of these sacrifices, the dawn of justice and freedom throughout the world slowly casts its gleam across the horizon.

Our forefathers came to our rugged shores in search of religious tolerance, political freedom and economic opportunity. For those fundamental rights, they risked their lives. We well know today that such rights can be preserved only by constant vigilance, the eternal price of liberty!

Within an hour after I took the oath of office, I announced that the San Francisco Conference would proceed.[1] We will face the problems of peace with the same courage that we have faced and mastered the problems of war.

In the memory of those who have made the supreme sacrifice—in the memory of our fallen President—*we shall not fail!*

It is not enough to yearn for peace. We must work, and if necessary, fight for it. The task of creating a sound international organization is complicated and difficult. Yet, without such organization, the rights of man on earth cannot be protected. Machinery for the just settlement of international differences must be found. Without such machinery, the entire world will have to remain an armed camp. The world will be doomed to deadly conflict, devoid of hope for real peace.

Fortunately, people have retained hope for a durable peace. Thoughtful people have always had faith that ultimately justice *must* triumph. Past experience surely indicates that, without justice, an enduring peace becomes impossible.

In bitter despair, some people have come to believe that wars are inevitable. With tragic fatalism, they insist that wars have always been, of necessity, and of necessity wars always will be. To such defeatism, men and women of good will must not and can not yield. The outlook for humanity is not so hopeless.

During the dark hours of this horrible war, entire nations were kept going by something intangible—hope! When warned that abject sub-

---

[1] See note to Item 1.

mission offered the only salvation against overwhelming power, hope
showed the way to victory.

Hope has become the secret weapon of the forces of liberation!

Aggressors could not dominate the human mind. As long as hope
remains, the spirit of man will *never* be crushed.

But hope alone was not and is not sufficient to avert war. We must
not only have hope but we must have faith enough to work with other
peace-loving nations to maintain the peace. Hope was not enough to
beat back the aggressors as long as the peace-loving nations were unwilling to come to each other's defense. The aggressors were beaten back
only when the peace-loving nations united to defend themselves.

If wars in the future are to be prevented the nations must be united
in their determination to keep the peace under law.

Nothing is more essential to the future peace of the world than continued cooperation of the nations which had to muster the force necessary to defeat the conspiracy of the Axis powers to dominate the
world.

While these great states have a special responsibility to enforce the
peace, their responsibility is based upon the obligations resting upon all
states, large and small, not to use force in international relations except
in the defense of law. The responsibility of the great states is to serve
and not to dominate the world.

To build a foundation of enduring peace we must not only work in
harmony with our friends abroad, but we must have the united support
of our own people.

Even the most experienced pilot cannot bring a ship safely into
harbor, unless he has the full cooperation of the crew. For the benefit
of all, every individual must do his duty.

I appeal to every American, regardless of party, race, creed, or color,
to support our efforts to build a strong and lasting United Nations
Organization.

You, the Members of the Congress, surely know how I feel. Only
with your help can I hope to complete one of the greatest tasks ever
assigned to a public servant. With Divine guidance, and your help, we

will find the new passage to a far better world, a kindly and friendly world, with just and lasting peace.

With confidence, I am depending upon all of you.

To destroy greedy tyrants with dreams of world domination, we cannot continue in successive generations to sacrifice our finest youth.

In the name of human decency and civilization, a more rational method of deciding national differences *must* and *will* be found!

America must assist suffering humanity back along the path of peaceful progress. This will require time and tolerance. We shall need also an abiding faith in the people, the kind of faith and courage which Franklin Delano Roosevelt always had!

Today, America has become one of the most powerful forces for good on earth. We must keep it so. We have achieved a world leadership which does not depend solely upon our military and naval might.

We have learned to fight with other nations in common defense of our freedom. We must now learn to live with other nations for our mutual good. We must learn to trade more with other nations so that there may be—for our mutual advantage—increased production, increased employment and better standards of living throughout the world.

May we Americans all live up to our glorious heritage.

In that way, America may well lead the world to peace and prosperity.

At this moment, I have in my heart a prayer. As I have assumed my heavy duties, I humbly pray Almighty God, in the words of King Solomon:

"Give therefore thy servant an understanding heart to judge thy people, that I may discern between good and bad; for who is able to judge this thy so great a people?"

I ask only to be a good and faithful servant of my Lord and my people.

NOTE: The President spoke in the House chamber shortly after 1 p.m. The address was broadcast over the major radio networks.

3   Statement by the President Upon Signing Bill Extending
    the Lend-Lease Act.   *April 17, 1945*

THIS IS the third time that the Lend-Lease Act has been extended by
the Congress—each time by overwhelming majorities.

This mighty instrument for victory is one of the growing monu-
ments to the boldness, imagination and effective statesmanship of
Franklin Roosevelt.

At a critical time in the history of this country, he saw the vital need
for aiding those who were fighting against Axis aggression and oppression all over the world.

The wisdom and effectiveness of that vision are being shown every
day on the battlefronts all over the world.

On the Western European front—the British, the French, the Dutch,
the Belgians and other Allied forces have been equipped in part with
lend-lease guns and other munitions; and, shoulder to shoulder with
our men are fighting their way into the heart of Nazi Germany.

In Italy—American, British, Polish, Brazilian and other Allied armed
forces are joined in a common effort to speed final victory.

On the eastern front—the Soviet forces, aided by lend-lease supplies,
are striking blows which are breaking the back of Nazi military power.

In the Far East—the Chinese, the British, the Australians, the New
Zealanders, the Dutch and other fighting Allies, have joined with us
in a combined attack which is now beating at the doors of Tokyo.

Lend-lease has been an effective instrument to help assure a complete
United Nations victory with the least cost in American and Allied
lives.

Lend-lease will be carried on until the unconditional surrender or
complete defeat of Germany and Japan.

NOTE: As enacted, the bill (H.R. 2013) is Public Law 31, 79th Congress (59
Stat. 52).

4 The President's News Conference of *April* 17, 1945

THE PRESIDENT. [1.] The first thing I want to do to you is to read the rules.

"News emanating from the President's conferences with the press will continue to be divided in categories already known to you, and in keeping with the practice of President Roosevelt's news meetings with the press.

"These categories are: first, off the record, confidential announcements which are to be kept secret by the newspapermen attending the conferences and not passed on by them to outsiders.

"Background—or not for attribution—information which may be given to the press for its guidance and use, the source of which cannot be published nor disclosed. In other words, it cannot be attributed to the President.

"News information which may be attributed to the President, when it is given to the press by the President at his conferences, but which cannot be directly quoted.

"Statements by the President cannot be directly quoted, unless he gives special permission."

[2.] Now, I have asked Mr. Early and Mr. Hassett, Mr. Daniels and Judge Rosenman, and they have offered to stay and help me get things organized, for which I am very grateful. And my staff will stand the training with those gentlemen.

I have asked Mr. Connelly to be my Confidential Secretary. Mr. Reinsch is going to help me with press and radio affairs.

Q. Mr. President, can you give us that full name?

THE PRESIDENT. Matthew J. Connelly.

Q. How do you spell it?

THE PRESIDENT. Leonard Reinsch. Connelly spells it the Irish way. [*Laughter*]

Q. How does Mr. Reinsch spell his name?

THE PRESIDENT. How is that?

Q. Reinsch—how does he spell his name?

THE PRESIDENT. R-e-i-n-c-h—S-c-h—there's an S in there. I forgot the S.

Q. Can we have something about where he is from?

THE PRESIDENT. He has been a radio executive for Governor Cox. Mr. Connelly has been with me all the time. Mr. Reinsch was connected with the National Committee during the last campaign as the radio expert for the National Committee. So I got acquainted with him. And he is efficient, I will tell you that. And so is Mr. Connelly. So are all these other gentlemen. That is no reflection on anybody, you understand? [*Laughter*]

[3.] I received a communication from Mrs. Roosevelt which I want to read to you. You will be given a mimeographed copy of it as you go out. This is dated April 16, 1945.

"My dear Mr. President:

"There have been many thousands of letters, telegrams and cards sent to me and my children which have brought great comfort and consolation to all of us. This outpouring of affectionate thought has touched us all deeply and we wish it were possible to thank each and every one individually.

"My children and I feel, in view of the fact that we are faced with the paper shortage and are asked not to use paper when it can be avoided, that all we can do is to express our appreciation collectively. We would therefore consider it a great favor if you would be kind enough to express our gratitude for us.

"Sincerely, Eleanor Roosevelt."

[4.] Now, there has been some question as to where I stand on various things, particularly Bretton Woods.

And I am for it. We need an international monetary setup. And I would have supported that proposition had I stayed in the Senate, and I would have done everything I possibly could as Vice President to help the President get it through the Senate.

I am for it all the way. I hope that is plain enough.

Q. Does that include also the monetary fund—stabilization——

THE PRESIDENT. It includes the program as sent to the Congress by the President. That is as plain as I can make it.

And I believe that's all.

If you want to ask me anything, I will try to answer; and if I don't know, I will tell you.

[5.] Q. Mr. President, in that same connection, would you say, just for the record, on reciprocal trade, has the President requested——

THE PRESIDENT. Yes. That was the other thing I wanted to mention.

Q. ——about the Export-Import Bank?

THE PRESIDENT. I am for the reciprocal trade agreements program. Always have been for it. I think you will find in the record where I stood before, when it was up in the Senate before, and I haven't changed.

[6.] Q. What about the Johnson Act repeal?

THE PRESIDENT. You mean the Johnson Act now pending for repeal?

Q. No, the Johnson Act which prohibits loans by private individuals to the defaulted governments.

THE PRESIDENT. Well, that is a matter I will have to look into and study. I haven't given it any thought. I can't answer that question at this time. I will answer it for you later.

[7.] Q. Mr. President, are you going ahead with the public power ambitions of your predecessor?

THE PRESIDENT. Wherever it is possible and necessary, I am.

Q. Mr. President, in that connection the term of TVA Chairman Lilienthal will be expiring in a few months——

THE PRESIDENT. I am not discussing appointments this morning of any sort. I am—when it comes to me to meet that situation, I will meet it; and you will know about it.

Q. Mr. President, could you tell us how you feel about the Missouri Valley Authority?

THE PRESIDENT. I think I made a speech in New Orleans endorsing the Missouri Valley Authority. I advise you to read that speech.

[8.] Q. Mr. President, probably as much as any group, the passing of President Roosevelt is very keenly felt by the Negroes in America, as they looked upon him as sort of a symbol of justice and equal opportunity. I wonder if you would comment on the things that they were so specifically interested in and felt they knew where the President stood: on the fair employment practice, the right to vote without being hampered by poll taxes, and all that?

THE PRESIDENT. I will give you some advice. All you need to do is to read the Senate record of one Harry S. Truman.

[9.] Q. Mr. President, do you mind discussing a companion piece to the Missouri Valley Authority, about the St. Lawrence? Can you tell us anything about that?

THE PRESIDENT. I don't want to discuss that this morning.

[10.] Q. Mr. President, is there any possibility that you will go to the United Nations Conference at San Francisco near the end?

THE PRESIDENT. There is not.

Q. Will you send a message, Mr. President, to the San Francisco Conference?

THE PRESIDENT. I shall probably welcome the delegates by an opening statement, when they arrive for their first meeting.

Q. Over the radio?

THE PRESIDENT. Yes.

Q. Could you tell us, Mr. President, some of the considerations that led to your decision not to go to San Francisco?

THE PRESIDENT. I have a competent delegation going to San Francisco to negotiate and represent the interests of the United States. I shall back them up from this desk right here—[*knocking on it*]—where I belong.

[11.] Q. Do you expect to see Mr. Molotov before he goes across——

THE PRESIDENT. Yes, I do.

Q. ——before he goes to San Francisco?

THE PRESIDENT. Yes. He is going to stop by and pay his respects to the President of the United States. He should.

Q. When do you expect him to arrive?

[12.] Q. Can you tell us something about your visit with the American delegation this morning?

THE PRESIDENT. I have told you—I have already told you exactly what I said to them.

[13.] Q. Mr. President, will Mr. Byrnes go to San Francisco in any capacity?

THE PRESIDENT. He will not. Mr. Byrnes is going back to South Carolina, and when I need his advice I shall send for him.

Q. Have you any plans for Mr. Byrnes to take any public office?

THE PRESIDENT. I have not.

[14.]   Q. Mr. President, do you have a desire, as soon as possible, to meet the other Allied leaders—Marshal Stalin and Prime Minister Churchill?

THE PRESIDENT. I should be very happy to meet them, and General Chiang Kai-shek also. And General de Gaulle; if he wants to see me I will be glad to see him. I would like to meet all of the Allied heads of governments.

Q. Have you initiated any move towards that end, Mr. President?

THE PRESIDENT. I have not.

[15.]   Q. Mr. President, do you approve of the work of the Truman Committee? [*Laughter*]

[16.]   THE PRESIDENT. There was another announcement I wanted to make. It was about these press conferences. Due to the fact that I have such a terrific burden to assume, I am going to have only one press conference a week. I shall have one in the morning and one in the afternoon—turnabout—week about. And I shall have that press conference on the days in the middle of the week as soon as I think I have something to say, or news to give out; and you will be notified in plenty of time so that you can come right down here Tuesday, Wednesday, or Thursday of each week; but I am not setting any specific day nor any specific hour, but to say that one will be in the morning and the next one will be in the afternoon.

[17.]   Q. Mr. President, will Mrs. Truman have a press conference?

THE PRESIDENT. Beg your pardon?

Q. Will Mrs. Truman have a regular press conference?

THE PRESIDENT. I would rather not answer that question at this time. Mrs. Roosevelt is having her last meeting with the ladies of the press on Thursday, and that question will be answered at a later date.

[18.]   Q. Mr. President, there are published reports that your administration plans to lift the ban on horseracing. Can you comment on that?

Voices: Louder—louder.

THE PRESIDENT. Say it again, so that they can hear it. [*Laughter*]

Q. There are published reports that your administration plans to lift the ban on horseracing. Can you comment on that?

THE PRESIDENT. I do not intend to lift the ban.

[19.] Q. Mr. President, can you give us your views on the disposal of synthetic rubber plants?

THE PRESIDENT. No, I cannot. That is not a matter for discussion here. It will be discussed at the proper time.

[20.] Q. Mr. President, can you say anything about the Cabinet?

THE PRESIDENT. No. Of course, I asked the Cabinet to remain. That is as much as I want to say.

Q. Mr. President——

Q. Mr. President, what is your feeling——

THE PRESIDENT. Let this fellow have a chance back here. *You're* in the front row. [*Laughter*]

[21.] Q. Does that statement of yours on horseracing apply to the ban on the brownout and the curfew too?

THE PRESIDENT. I think they have done a lot of good for the morale all over the country, and I have no intention of pushing Mr. Byrnes' office.

Somebody over here? [*Indicating another questioner*]

Q. Started to ask you if that applied after V-E Day?

THE PRESIDENT. Let's wait for V-E Day to come, and I will take care of the situation at that time.

Now, what was your question? I beg your pardon, the lady wants to ask a question. [*Laughter*]

[22.] Q. Mr. President, there is a story out that Stalin had reached an agreement with the new Polish Government approved by the United States and Britain. Can you comment?

THE PRESIDENT. I don't want to discuss that at this conference.

Now, what was your question?

Q. It has been asked, sir. [*Laughter*]

Q. Thank you, Mr. President.

NOTE: President Truman's first news conference was held in his office at the White House at 10:30 a.m. on Tuesday, April 17, 1945.

5 Address Broadcast to the Armed Forces.
   April 17, 1945

To the Armed Forces of the United States throughout the world:

After the tragic news of the death of our late Commander in Chief, it was my duty to speak promptly to the Congress, and the Armed Forces of the United States.

Yesterday, I addressed the Congress. Now I speak to you.

I am especially anxious to talk to you, for I know that all of you felt a tremendous shock, as we did at home, when our Commander in Chief fell.

All of us have lost a great leader, a far-sighted statesman and a real friend of democracy. We have lost a hard-hitting chief and an old friend of the services.

Our hearts are heavy. However, the cause which claimed Roosevelt, also claims us. He never faltered—nor will we!

I have done, as you would do in the field when the Commander falls. My duties and responsibilities are clear. I have assumed them. These duties will be carried on in keeping with our American tradition.

As a veteran of the first World War, I have seen death on the battlefield. When I fought in France with the 35th Division, I saw good officers and men fall, and be replaced.

I know that this is also true of the officers and men of the other services, the Navy, the Marine Corps, the Coast Guard, and the Merchant Marine.

I know the strain, the mud, the misery, the utter weariness of the soldier in the field. And I know too his courage, his stamina, his faith in his comrades, his country, and himself.

We are depending upon each and every one of you.

Yesterday I said to the Congress and I repeat it now:

"Our debt to the heroic men and valiant women in the service of our country can never be repaid. They have earned our undying gratitude. America will never forget their sacrifices. Because of these sacrifices, the dawn of justice and freedom throughout the world slowly casts its gleam across the horizon."

14

At this decisive hour in history, it is very difficult to express my feeling. Words will not convey what is in my heart.

Yet, I recall the words of Lincoln, a man who had enough eloquence to speak for all America. To indicate my sentiments, and to describe my hope for the future, may I quote the immortal words of that great Commander in Chief:

"With malice toward none; with charity for all; with firmness in the right, as God gives us to see the right, let us strive on to finish the work we are in; to bind up our nation's wounds; to care for him who shall have borne the battle, and for his widow, and his orphan—to do all which may achieve and cherish a just and lasting peace among ourselves, and with all nations."

NOTE: The President spoke at 10 p.m. from the White House. His address was broadcast over the Armed Forces Radio Service and was carried over the major networks.

6 Statement by the President on the Death of Ernie Pyle.
   April 18, 1945

THE NATION is quickly saddened again by the death of Ernie Pyle. No man in this war has so well told the story of the American fighting man as American fighting men wanted it told. More than any other man he became the spokesman of the ordinary American in arms doing so many extraordinary things. It was his genius that the mass and power of our military and naval forces never obscured the men who made them.

He wrote about a people in arms as people still, but a people moving in a determination which did not need pretensions as a part of power.

Nobody knows how many individuals in our forces and at home he helped with his writings. But all Americans understand now how wisely, how warm-heartedly, how honestly he served his country and his profession. He deserves the gratitude of all his countrymen.

7   Statement by the President on the Senate's Approval of the Water Utilization Treaty With Mexico.
April 18, 1945

IN VOTING its approval of the water treaty with Mexico, the Senate today gave unmistakable evidence that it stands firmly in support of the established policy of our Government to deal with our Good Neighbors on the basis of simple justice, equity, friendly understanding and practical cooperation. By this action of the Senate, the United States and Mexico join hands in a constructive, business-like program to apportion between them and develop to their mutual advantage the waters of the rivers that are in part common to them.

NOTE: The treaty and supplementary protocol are printed in the U.S. Statutes at Large (59 Stat. 1219). After rati- fication the treaty entered into force November 8, 1945.

8   The President's News Conference of
April 20, 1945

THE PRESIDENT. Well, I've got a telegram I will read to you. Is everybody in?

Mr. Early: Yes, sir.

[1.]   THE PRESIDENT. This is dated Miami, Florida, April 19, addressed to me here.

"Dear Mr. President: Some time ago, you made an appeal——

Voices: Little slower—slow!

Mr. Early: You will get copies of it later.

THE PRESIDENT. I will read it to you first. Then I will see that you get copies.

[*Reading, not literally*] "Dear Mr. President: Some time ago you made an appeal to me which I think I responded to at the moment in good spirit. Now I am going to make an appeal to you. Please let us have Leonard Reinsch back. When we gave our consent we were not sufficiently mindful of the tremendous tasks ahead of us in radio in connection with Television, Frequency Modulation and what not.

16

On special occasions for your personal uses his services could be availed of without embarrassment to us. It might not seem a patriotic impulse which prompts this message, and yet I am sure on reflection you will see it is justified. Kindest regards, James M. Cox."

And he is my friend. I think he will do anything in the world for me, so as to make Leonard available to me for the radio jobs that he has always done. Leonard will be on call just as Jimmy Byrnes is for anything that I want. And I am going to comply with Governor Cox's request.

[2.]   And the reason I am calling you in to give this to you is because I called in Charlie Ross last night after this happened, and Charlie agreed to come with me after this San Francisco Conference, on May 15th.

Then Charlie and I got sentimental, and called up our old schoolteacher in Independence last night, and I am afraid that there is a leak in Independence—[*laughter*]—and Charlie also called up his son. I didn't want you fellows to be scooped on it, so that's why I am doing this.

Q. Did you say he called his old schoolteacher——

THE PRESIDENT. He and I called her together. She is the only schoolteacher that is living, and so we called her up. We used to go to school together. I asked Mr. Pulitzer to give Charlie 2 years' leave, and Mr. Pulitzer very kindly complied with that; and I hope he won't do the same to me that has happened here. I hope not. He said he wouldn't.

Q. What is the schoolteacher's name?

THE PRESIDENT. Miss Tilly Brown. Matilda Brown. We always called her Tilly. Matilda—M-a-t-i-l-d-a—Brown. We always called her Tilly.

Q. That is at Independence?

THE PRESIDENT. At Independence.

Q. How old is she, Mr. President?

THE PRESIDENT. Well, I don't think she would object to her age being told—[*laughter*]—but I don't know. She is somewhere between 75 and 80.

Q. Was that grade school?

THE PRESIDENT. High school. She taught Charlie and me English.

Q. Were you in the same class?

THE PRESIDENT. Charlie and I graduated in the same high school class.

Q. What was that year, sir?

THE PRESIDENT. 1901. Do your own figuring. [*Laughter*] That covers everything, doesn't it?

[3.] Oh, yes. I almost forgot something. Jonathan [Daniels] has agreed to stay with me. He is going to stay with me until Charlie comes. Does that take care of everything? I am appreciative of that, too, just as I am of all these things; and I am exceedingly happy to have these people on call when I need them.

Q. When are you—when is Mr. Reinsch leaving?

THE PRESIDENT. At his convenience. The telegram is specific.

Q. Mr. Ross will come in about the 15th of May, sir?

THE PRESIDENT. Yes.

[4.] Q. Mr. President, what about the reports that Leslie Biffle will come down here?

THE PRESIDENT. They have no foundation in fact.

Q. Mr. President, ——

THE PRESIDENT. Les is literally of much more use to me as Secretary to the Senate than he would be down here at the White House—much more use to the Senate. I don't want to cripple the Senate by taking Les Biffle away from them.

What did you start to say?

Q. I started to say, sir, that means that you didn't even ask for him to come down. The report is going around that you and Mr. Barkley were arguing over who was going to get Les.

THE PRESIDENT. Oh, that is—no argument—[*inaudible words*]—only in fun. Don't quote that, though. There was never any thought on my part that Biffle be brought down here.

Q. Nothing serious?

THE PRESIDENT. No. I wouldn't say there was no kidding—[*inaudible words*]—Barkley, you know, and I like to rib each other. I was worrying him a little bit, and he was trying to worry me.

Q. You'd say he was a good man in almost any job he worked?

THE PRESIDENT. Biffle? They don't make them any better than Biffle.

And you can quote me on that.

Q. Mr. Ross will be the Press Secretary?

THE PRESIDENT. Press Secretary.

Reporter: Thank you, sir.

NOTE: President Truman's second news conference was held in his office at the White House at 11:45 a.m. on Friday, April 20, 1945.

9 Joint Statement With Allied Leaders Warning Against Mistreatment of Prisoners in Germany. *April 23, 1945*

THE GOVERNMENTS of the United Kingdom, United States of America and U.S.S.R., on behalf of all the United Nations at war with Germany, hereby issue a solemn warning to all commandants and guards in charge of Allied prisoners of war, internees or deported citizens of the United Nations in Germany and German occupied territory and to members of the Gestapo and all other persons of whatsoever service or rank in whose charge Allied prisoners of war, internees or deported citizens have been placed, whether in battle zones, on lines of communication or in rear areas. They declare that they will hold all such persons, no less than the German High Command and competent German military, naval and air authorities, individually responsible for the safety and welfare of all Allied prisoners of war, internees or deported citizens in their charge.

Any person guilty of maltreating or allowing any Allied prisoners of war, internees or deported citizens to be maltreated, whether in battle zone, on lines of communication, in a camp, hospital, prison or elsewhere, will be ruthlessly pursued and brought to punishment.

They give notice that they will regard this responsibility as binding in all circumstances and one which cannot be transferred to any other authorities or individuals whatsoever.

NOTE: This statement was made public at 6 p.m. The White House release accompanying the text states that Allied planes began distributing the warning in leaflet form at 6 p.m. over those portions of German territory still in German control. The leaflets bore facsimile signatures of the President, Prime Minister Churchill, and Marshal Stalin.

10   Address to the United Nations Conference in San
    Francisco.   *April 25, 1945*
[Delivered from the White House by direct wire]

Delegates to the United Nations Conference
on International Organization:

The world has experienced a revival of an old faith in the everlasting
moral force of justice. At no time in history has there been a more important Conference, or a more necessary meeting, than this one in San
Francisco, which you are opening today.

On behalf of the American people, I extend to you a most hearty
welcome.

President Roosevelt appointed an able delegation to represent the
United States. I have complete confidence in its Chairman, Secretary
of State Stettinius, and in his distinguished colleagues, former Secretary Cordell Hull, Senator Connally, Senator Vandenberg, Representative Bloom and Representative Eaton, Governor Stassen and Dean
Gildersleeve.

They have my confidence. They have my support.

In the name of a great humanitarian—one who surely is with us today
in spirit—I earnestly appeal to each and every one of you to rise above
personal interests, and adhere to those lofty principles, which benefit
all mankind.

Franklin D. Roosevelt gave his life while trying to perpetuate these
high ideals. This Conference owes its existence, in a large part, to the
vision, foresight, and determination of Franklin Roosevelt.

Each of you can remember other courageous champions, who also
made the supreme sacrifice, serving under your flag. They gave their
lives, so that others might live in security. They died to insure justice.
We must work and live to guarantee justice—for all.

You members of this Conference are to be the architects of the better
world. In your hands rests our future. By your labors at this Conference, we shall know if suffering humanity is to achieve a just and lasting
peace.

Let us labor to achieve a peace which is really worthy of their great sacrifice. We must make certain, by your work here, that another war will be impossible.

We, who have lived through the torture and the tragedy of two world conflicts, must realize the magnitude of the problem before us. We do not need far-sighted vision to understand the trend in recent history. Its significance is all too clear.

With ever-increasing brutality and destruction, modern warfare, if unchecked, would ultimately crush all civilization. We still have a choice between the alternatives: the continuation of international chaos—or the establishment of a world organization for the enforcement of peace.

It is not the purpose of this Conference to draft a treaty of peace in the old sense of that term. It is not our assignment to settle specific questions of territories, boundaries, citizenship and reparations.

This Conference will devote its energies and its labors exclusively to the single problem of setting up the essential organization to keep the peace. You are to write the fundamental charter.

Our sole objective, at this decisive gathering, is to create the structure. We must provide the machinery, which will make future peace, not only possible, but certain.

The construction of this delicate machine is far more complicated than drawing boundary lines on a map, or estimating fair reparations, or placing reasonable limits upon armaments. Your task must be completed first.

We represent the overwhelming majority of all mankind. We speak for people, who have endured the most savage and devastating war ever inflicted upon innocent men, women and children.

We hold a powerful mandate from our people. They believe we will fulfill this obligation. We must prevent, if human mind, heart and hope can prevent it, the repetition of the disaster from which the entire world will suffer for years to come.

If we should pay merely lip service to inspiring ideals, and later do violence to simple justice, we would draw down upon us the bitter wrath of generations yet unborn.

We must not continue to sacrifice the flower of our youth merely to check madmen, those who in every age plan world domination. The sacrifices of our youth today must lead, through your efforts, to the building for tomorrow of a mighty combination of nations founded upon justice—on peace.

Justice remains the greatest power on earth.

To that tremendous power alone will we submit.

Nine days ago, I told the Congress of the United States, and I now repeat it to you:

"Nothing is more essential to the future peace of the world, than continued cooperation of the nations, which had to muster the force necessary to defeat the conspiracy of the axis powers to dominate the world.

"While these great states have a special responsibility to enforce the peace, their responsibility is based upon the obligations resting upon all states, large and small, not to use force in international relations, except in the defense of law. The responsibility of the great states is to serve, and not dominate the peoples of the world."

None of us doubt that with Divine guidance, friendly cooperation, and hard work, we shall find an adequate answer to the problem history has put before us.

Realizing the scope of our task and the imperative need for success, we proceed with humility and determination.

By harmonious cooperation, the United Nations repelled the onslaught of the greatest aggregation of military force that was ever assembled in the long history of aggression. Every nation now fighting for freedom is giving according to its ability and opportunity.

We fully realize today that victory in war requires a mighty united effort. Certainly, victory in peace calls for, and must receive, an equal effort.

Man has learned long ago, that it is impossible to live unto himself. This same basic principle applies today to nations. We were not isolated during the war. We dare not now become isolated in peace.

All will concede that in order to have good neighbors, we must also be good neighbors. That applies in every field of human endeavor.

For lasting security, men of good-will must unite and organize.

22

Moreover, if our friendly policies should ever be considered by belligerent leaders as merely evidence of weakness, the organization we establish must be adequately prepared to meet any challenge.

Differences between men, and between nations, will always remain. In fact, if held within reasonable limits, such disagreements are actually wholesome. All progress begins with differences of opinion and moves onward as the differences are adjusted through reason and mutual understanding.

In recent years, our enemies have clearly demonstrated the disaster which follows when freedom of thought is no longer tolerated. Honest minds cannot long be regimented without protest.

The essence of our problem here is to provide sensible machinery for the settlement of disputes among nations. Without this, peace cannot exist. We can no longer permit any nation, or group of nations, to attempt to settle their arguments with bombs and bayonets.

If we continue to abide by such decisions, we will be forced to accept the fundamental concept of our enemies, namely, that "Might makes right." To deny this premise, and we most certainly do deny it, we are obliged to provide the necessary means to refute it. Words are not enough.

We must, once and for all, reverse the order, and prove by our acts conclusively, that Right Has Might.

If we do not want to die together in war, we must learn to live together in peace.

With firm faith in our hearts, to sustain us along the hard road to victory, we will find our way to a secure peace, for the ultimate benefit of all humanity.

We must build a new world—a far better world—one in which the eternal dignity of man is respected.

As we are about to undertake our heavy duties, we beseech our Almighty God to guide us in the building of a permanent monument to those who gave their lives that this moment might come.

May He lead our steps in His own righteous path of peace.

NOTE: The President spoke at 7:35 p.m. The address was broadcast over the major networks.

11 Letter to Secretary Wallace Requesting a Study of the Patent Laws. *April 26, 1945*

[Released April 26, 1945. Dated April 20, 1945]

My dear Mr. Secretary:

Much has lately been said and written to suggest that the patent statutes do not in all respects serve the constitutional purpose to promote the progress of science and useful arts, and that patents have been misused to support unlawful monopolies in contravention of the purposes of the anti-trust laws.

I believe the Congress would welcome such assistance as the executive branch of the government might be able to give in presenting the results of a full and objective study of the operation and effectiveness of the patent laws and their relation to the purposes of the anti-trust laws and to the post-war economy, together with specific proposals for such legislation as may seem to be appropriate. Thus far the several departments of the government have made no concerted effort to formulate a policy upon this subject.

Will you please undertake such study and submit to me your report and recommendations respecting the legislative proposals you think I should lay before the Congress. In so doing will you please consult with the Attorney General, the Director of Economic Stabilization, the Director of the Office of Scientific Research and Development, and the Chairman of the National Patent Planning Commission.

Very sincerely yours,

HARRY S. TRUMAN

NOTE: On April 26, 1945, a Department of Commerce release announced that Secretary Wallace had invited the officials listed in the President's letter to serve as a committee to make a full and objective study of the patent system, and that the Director of Economic Stabilization had consented to serve as chairman. The study, completed in 1947, was first published in 1960, with minor revisions, as Study No. 26 of the Subcommittee on Patents, Trademarks, and Copyrights of the Senate Committee on the Judiciary (Government Printing Office, 1960).

12   Statement by the President Announcing the Junction of
     Anglo-American and Soviet Forces in Germany.
     April 27, 1945

THE ANGLO-AMERICAN armies under the command of General
Eisenhower have met the Soviet forces where they intended to meet—
in the heart of Nazi Germany. The enemy has been cut in two.

This is not the hour of final victory in Europe, but the hour draws
near, the hour for which all the American people, all the British peoples
and all the Soviet people have toiled and prayed so long.

The union of our arms in the heart of Germany has a meaning for
the world which the world will not miss. It means, *first,* that the last
faint, desperate hope of Hitler and his gangster government has been
extinguished. The common front and the common cause of the powers allied in this war against tyranny and inhumanity have been demonstrated in fact as they have long been demonstrated in determination.
Nothing can divide or weaken the common purpose of our veteran
armies to pursue their victorious purpose to its final triumph in
Germany.

Second, the junction of our forces at this moment signalizes to ourselves and to the world that the collaboration of our nations in the cause
of peace and freedom is an effective collaboration which can surmount
the greatest difficulties of the most extensive campaign in military
history and succeed. Nations which can plan and fight together
shoulder to shoulder in the face of such obstacles of distance and of
language and of communications as we have overcome, can live together
and can work together in the common labor of the organization of the
world for peace.

Finally, this great triumph of Allied arms and Allied strategy is such
a tribute to the courage and determination of Franklin Roosevelt as
no words could ever speak, and that could be accomplished only by
the persistence and the courage of the fighting soldiers and sailors of
the Allied Nations.

But, until our enemies are finally subdued in Europe and in the
Pacific, there must be no relaxation of effort on the home front in sup-

25

port of our heroic soldiers and sailors as we all know there will be no pause on the battle fronts.

NOTE: The President's statement was released at 12 noon. Simultaneous (although not identical) statements were issued in London and in Paris.

13 Letter to Edwin W. Pauley Appointing Him as the President's Personal Representative on the Reparations Commission. *April 27, 1945*

My dear Mr. Pauley:

I hereby designate you to act as my personal representative, with the rank of Ambassador, to represent and assist me in exploring, developing and negotiating the formulae and methods for exacting reparations from the aggressor nations in the current war.

In this matter, you will represent me in dealing with the other interested nations.

At the Crimea Conference, it was agreed that Germany would be obliged to the greatest extent possible to make reparations in kind for the damage caused by her to the Allied countries. It was further agreed that a commission would be established to consider the question of the extent and methods for collecting such reparations.

I wish you also to represent the United States and me personally as a member of that commission.

In all matters within your jurisdiction you will report to me personally and directly.

May I express my gratification at your willingness to assume this important but arduous mission.

Very sincerely yours,

HARRY S. TRUMAN

NOTE: A statement by Mr. Pauley concerning reparations was released by the White House on the same day.

14 Statement by the President Announcing the Appointment
of Dr. Isador Lubin to the Reparations Commission.
April 27, 1945

I WISH, also, to announce that I have asked Dr. Isador Lubin, Commissioner of Labor Statistics, to serve with and accompany Mr. Pauley as his associate.

Dr. Lubin will be given the personal rank of Minister. I am very grateful to Dr. Lubin for accepting this post.

15 The President's News Conference of
April 27, 1945

[President Truman's third news conference was not recorded and no copy of the text has been found.

[The Official Reporter's notes state that he was notified too late and that he came in on the President's last words. They also state that the conference was held about 4:15 p.m., and that the President announced the appointment of Edwin W. Pauley as his Personal Representative on the Reparations Commission, with the rank of Ambassador, and of Dr. Isador Lubin as an Associate, with the rank of Minister.]

16 The President's News Conference on the Rumor of
German Surrender. *April 28, 1945*

THE PRESIDENT. Well, I was over here, as you can see, doing a little work, and this rumor got started. I had a call from San Francisco, and the State Department called me. I just got in touch with Admiral Leahy and had him call our Headquarters Commander in Chief in Europe, and there is no foundation for the rumor. That's all I have to say.

Q. May we quote you?

THE PRESIDENT. Yes.

Q. Are you going to stand by?

THE PRESIDENT. I'm going to finish this work.

NOTE: President Truman's fourth news conference was held in his office at the White House at 10 p.m. on Saturday, April 28, 1945.

17   Statement by the President Commending the Office of
Price Administration. *May 1, 1945*

I WANT TO SAY a word of deserved commendation for an organization which has been subjected to much criticism in recent weeks. I refer to the OPA. Probably no other government agency comes into such intimate contact with every citizen during wartime.

Our price control and rationing machinery enters into every home and affects directly the daily life of the housewife and her family. Naturally, things must be done which displease many people. No businessman, no farmer, no merchant likes to be told how much he can charge for his wares. No housewife likes to be told that she may have only a limited supply of meat, or sugar, or canned goods with which to feed her family.

As the war proceeds toward a victorious climax, shortages become more acute. The requirements of our military and naval forces are great. We must supplement the economic resources of our fighting allies, such as Britain, Russia, China and France, who have suffered great devastation in this war. We must do our part in helping to prevent anarchy, riot and pestilence in the areas liberated from Axis domination. These requirements place a greater and greater strain on our resources.

I suppose that OPA, like the rest of us, has made a few mistakes. But when we look at the whole record, I think that our price control and stabilization program has been one of the most remarkable achievements of this war. Had it not been for OPA and the stabilization program we should have had run-away inflation. In other countries, run-away inflation has sown the seeds of tyranny and disorder. In this country, we have kept inflation under control. OPA has helped to make it possible for our fighting men to come home to a stable and prosperous economy.

Our price control and stabilization program could not have been successful without a good law and good administration. Congress has given us a good law and I hope Congress will extend that law for at least another year.

28

OPA has been well administered by Mr. Chester Bowles. Its thousands of employees and hundreds of thousands of volunteer workers in local price and rationing boards have worked faithfully for long hours doing difficult jobs. Many able men from business and other walks of life have patriotically contributed their services to OPA, often at distinct financial sacrifice.

Irresponsible criticism should not be permitted to break down the confidence of the people in an essential wartime program and a hard-working wartime agency.

18 Letter to the Director, Office of War Mobilization and Reconversion, Concerning Key Personnel of the War Agencies. *May 1, 1945*

Dear Fred:

As V–E Day approaches, many of our wartime agencies will face a most critical personnel problem. Under the impact of war, these agencies have recruited many splendid executives from private life. In every grade and rank today the government is served by splendid personnel. These men and women have rendered faithful, patriotic and effective service for the country in meeting the critical problems of war on the home front.

These agencies cannot afford to relax their efforts or to disband their trained staffs after V–E Day. We still have a tremendous job ahead in bringing the entire war to a victorious conclusion. Beyond that, we must reconvert our domestic economy to the production of peacetime goods and services. The tasks which lie ahead are no less important, no less urgent, no less vital to the future stability of our free institutions than the tasks which are behind us.

In the months ahead, our government simply cannot afford to lose the services of its key personnel. Through you, I am calling upon these men and women to stick to their posts until the battle is won and the ship of state is safe in the harbor again. I want you to write to the head of each one of our important home front agencies and ask him to canvass his key personnel, informing him of my request that these key workers stay on the job. I want the head of each agency, insofar as possible, to secure a pledge from these essential employees that they will not go home on V–E Day, but will stay and help to finish the task. When the heads of the agencies have done this, I should like for them to report to you as to their success.

These patriotic citizens who have devoted themselves unstintingly to the nation's welfare in time of war have earned the lasting gratitude of the American people. They have helped to pay that debt which every citizen in the Democracy owes to his country and its institutions. But that debt is unpaid at least until we have finished the war and solved those urgent problems which war leaves in its aftermath. I reiterate with all the emphasis at my command that the nation cannot yet allow any man to leave his post of duty.

Sincerely yours,

HARRY S. TRUMAN

[The Honorable Fred M. Vinson, Director, Office of War Mobilization and Reconversion]

19 Statement by the President Concerning the Termination of the Office of Civilian Defense. *May 2, 1945*

THIS CHANGE does not in any respect lessen the need for volunteer efforts in our states and communities. State and local governments are fully aware of their continuing responsibilities, and I am sure that we can depend upon their knowledge and the patriotism of the millions of volunteers to continue the war jobs in which the whole nation has had to be trained. Protection volunteers, such as auxiliary firemen and policemen, working with state and local governments have done a magnificent job through their defense councils in organizing to protect the nation against the threat of enemy action, sabotage, and other war hazards. Civilian War Services volunteers have likewise rendered invaluable assistance.

The millions of volunteer workers throughout the nation, giving freely of their time, have been basic to the strength of our democracy. I know they will willingly continue to serve. Under General Haskell's able direction the OCD has provided needed assistance to the defense councils and volunteers in carrying on their important work in advancing the war effort on the home front.

NOTE: This statement was made public as part of a White House release stating that the President had that day written to the Congress announcing the forthcoming termination of the Office of Civilian Defense and withdrawing its proposed budget for the next fiscal year. The release further stated that developments in the European war and the efficient operation of community volunteer forces made possible the decision that Federal supervision of civilian defense was no longer needed.

The Office of Civilian Defense was terminated by Executive Order 9562, effective June 30, 1945 (3 CFR, 1942–1948 Comp., p. 388).

20   Statement by the President on the Surrender of German Forces in Italy.   *May 2, 1945*

THE ALLIED ARMIES in Italy have won the unconditional surrender of German forces on the first European soil to which, from the West, we carried our arms and our determination. The collapse of military tyranny in Italy, however, is no victory in Italy alone, but a part of the general triumph we are expectantly awaiting on the whole continent of Europe. Only folly and chaos can now delay the general capitulation of the everywhere defeated German armies.

I have dispatched congratulatory messages to the Allied and American officers who led our forces to complete defeat of the Germans in Italy. They deserve our praise for the victory. We have right to be proud of the success of our armies.

Let Japan as well as Germany understand the meaning of these events. Unless they are lost in fanaticism or determined upon suicide, they must recognize the meaning of the increasing, swifter-moving power now ready for the capitulation or the destruction of the so-recently arrogant enemies of mankind.

21 Messages to Allied Commanders on the Surrender of German Forces in Italy. *May 2, 1945*

To Field Marshal Alexander:

On this momentous occasion of the surrender of the German Armed Forces in Italy, I convey to you from the President and the people of the United States congratulations on the signal success of the Allied Armies, Navies and Air Forces under your command, gained only by persistent heroic effort through many months of a most difficult campaign.

I send also to you personally our appreciation of the high order of your leadership which conducted our Armies to their complete victory.

HARRY S. TRUMAN

To General Mark Clark:

On the occasion of the final brilliant victory of the Allied Armies in Italy, in imposing unconditional surrender upon the enemy, I wish to convey to the American forces under your command, and to you personally, the appreciation and gratitude of the President and of the people of the United States. No praise is adequate for the heroic achievements and magnificent courage of every individual under your command during this long and trying campaign.

America is proud of the essential contribution made by your American Armies to the final Allied victory in Italy. Our thanks for your gallant leadership and the deathless valor of your men.

HARRY S. TRUMAN

22 The President's News Conference of *May 2, 1945*

THE PRESIDENT. First, I want to read you a couple of letters, which will be distributed as you go out, so if I get a little too fast for you, why——

[1.] [*Reading, not literally*]: "My dear Mr. President: I hereby tender you my resignation as Postmaster General,[1] to become effective at a time that best meets with your convenience.

"I have in the stage of preparation a report of my stewardship, together with certain suggestions concerning a reorganization of the Postal Department. This report will be completed within thirty days. If agreeable to you, Mr. President, I would like to have the resignation made effective at that time.

"The mantle of a great President has fallen upon you. Statesman and humanitarian, Franklin D. Roosevelt had a heart which beat with true compassion for all who suffered or bore heavy burdens. The Nation, so sorely bereft of his leadership, has found unity as well as strength and courage in the pledge of faith which you gave to all the world in the address to the Congress in joint session this afternoon.

"Franklin D. Roosevelt now takes his place with the great men of the ages. May his noble spirit guide and inspire you as you take up the fight for the ideals in defense of which he gave all of his strength, his very life.

"It remains for me only to add that I have full confidence in your leadership. Although I relinquish public office, I am yours to command if ever I can be of service to you in the heavy tasks which lie ahead."

And this is my reply.

[2.] [*Reading, not literally*]: "Dear Frank: I have learned in a very short time that the President of the United States all too often has to act in ways that please others and which are very different from the personal wishes and feelings of the President himself. Full realization of this is brought home to me very forcibly by your request that I accept your resignation as Postmaster General.

"It goes without saying that your request is reluctantly and grudgingly granted, effective as of the close of business on June 30, 1945. I must warn you, however, that I confidently expect to take advantage of your offer to return to me whenever there is need of your services in the future.

---

[1] Frank C. Walker served from September 11, 1940, through June 30, 1945.

"We sever only the official ties between us. The warm friendship and close association which has been ours through many years goes on as before.

"The splendid service you have rendered your Country, and your Government, will long be remembered by a grateful people. I count myself one of them, and thank you for your statement of confidence in my Administration."

[3.]   I am sending down to the Senate the nomination of Robert E. Hannegan, of Missouri, to be Postmaster General, effective July 1, 1945.

Q. Sending it down tomorrow, probably?

THE PRESIDENT. It will go to Mr. Biffle this afternoon, who will present it to the Senate tomorrow.

[4.]   I nominate Mr. David E. Lilienthal, of Wisconsin, to be a member of the Board of Directors of the Tennessee Valley Authority, for the term expiring 9 years after May 18, 1945. That will go down at the same time as Mr. Hannegan's does.

[5.]   I issued an Executive order today, appointing Mr. Justice Jackson to be the representative of the United States—I will just read you this, this statement which I am issuing, which you will also receive as you go out, in mimeographed form.

[*Reading, not literally*]: "At my request, Mr. Justice Robert H. Jackson, in addition to his duties as Justice of the Supreme Court, has accepted designation as Chief of Counsel for the United States in preparing and prosecuting charges of atrocities and war crimes against such of the leaders of the European Axis powers, and their principal agents and accessories, as the United States may agree with any of the United Nations to bring to trial before an international military tribunal.

"Pursuant to the Moscow Declaration of November 1, 1943, all war criminals, against whom there is a sufficient proof of personal participation in specific atrocities, are to be returned to the countries where their crimes were committed, to be judged and punished by those countries themselves. These cases are not involved in this assignment.

"There are left, however, the cases of other war criminals—particularly the major war criminals and their principal agents and accessories, whose offenses have no particular geographical localization.

"I hope and expect that an international military tribunal will soon be organized to try this second category of war criminals. It will be Justice Jackson's responsibility to represent the United States in preparing and presenting the case against these criminals before such military tribunal.

"Justice Jackson has assembled a staff from within the War, Navy, and other departments concerned, which has already begun work, so that there will be no delay on the part of the United States. It is desirable that preparation begin at once, even though details of the military court are not yet determined.

"I have just signed an Executive order designating Justice Jackson to this post. He and his staff will examine the evidence already gathered and being gathered by the United Nations War Crimes Commission in London and by the various allied armies and other agencies; he will arrange for assembling the necessary additional evidence. He will begin preparation for the trial.

"It is our objective to establish as soon as possible an international military tribunal; to provide a trial procedure which will be expeditious in nature and which will permit no evasion or delay—but one which is in keeping with our tradition of fairness towards those accused of crime. Steps to carry this out are actively under way.

"Arguments in the Supreme Court for the current term will conclude this week, and the Court has ordered adjournment on May 28th. It is hoped that the trial of these war crimes cases will have been completed next October when the Court reconvenes."

I am ready for questions! [*Laughter*]

[6.] Q. Mr. President, have the negotiations which the State Department just told us about, being carried on by the Swedish Government and the German Government—have they broken down completely?

THE PRESIDENT. I can't answer that.

[7.] Q. Mr. President, with reference here to Mr. Hannegan, your understanding is he will continue as chairman of—National Chairman?

THE PRESIDENT. Yes.

[8.]   Q. Mr. President, when you were Vice President, a CIO delegation asked you to help in revising the Little Steel formula. You told
them, somewhat firmly, that you were against upsetting any formula
that would put us into a spiral of inflation. Can you elaborate on that?

THE PRESIDENT. My position on that hasn't changed a bit. Well, after
all, the reason for all these war agencies which have been established—
that is, price control and wage control—and agreements which we have
had with industry and with union labor have been with the one object
in view: to prevent wild inflation. I am just as strong for that now as I
was when I was Vice President.

[9.]   Q. Mr. President, we heard today that you might go up to
address a joint session of Congress on V-E Day. Is there anything to
that?

THE PRESIDENT. I haven't made any program of that nature. Haven't
had it in mind.

[10.]   Q. Mr. President, have you sent a new message to Mr. Stalin
regarding the Polish problem?

THE PRESIDENT. No, not any new one.

Q. Well, in the last—since Mr. Molotov came here, sir?

THE PRESIDENT. I have been in communication with Mr. Stalin since
Mr. Molotov came here.[1]

[11.]   Q. Mr. President, do you favor the Morgenthau plan designed
to use Germany as an agricultural country?

THE PRESIDENT. I don't know anything about the Morgenthau plan.
I haven't studied it at all, so I can't answer you.

[12.]   Q. Mr. President, did you mean to put a period at the end of
that sentence, or were you hoping for a question—

THE PRESIDENT. No, I wasn't hoping for a question.

Q. ——referring to your communication with Mr. Stalin?

---

[1] A White House release of April 23 announced that the President had twice received
V. M. Molotov, Vice Chairman, Council of People's Commissars and People's Commissar for
Foreign Affairs, USSR, during his short stay in Washington. The release also stated that
the Secretary of State had conferred with Mr. Molotov and with Anthony Eden, Secretary
of State for Foreign Affairs of the United Kingdom, on the Polish situation and on matters
connected with the San Francisco Conference. The release further stated that discussion of
the Polish situation would be continued by the three foreign secretaries at San Francisco.

THE PRESIDENT. I had a period at the end of the sentence—intended to have.

[13.] Q. Mr. President, did you have lunch today with the new Ambassador from the Argentine?

THE PRESIDENT. Yes, I did. I had a very pleasant visit with him, and he and his wife are coming to call on us tomorrow or the next day.

[14.] Q. Mr. President, it may not be a part of the addenda—whatever it's called—in connection with Justice Jackson, but there is before Congress—before the people—the question of war criminals who may evade or try to evade by escaping to neutral countries, or some other form. Have you anything particular to say about policy, in that respect?

THE PRESIDENT. Well, most of the neutral countries, I think, are on record as against protecting any war criminals, and I think we will succeed in getting all of the rest of the neutral countries into the same frame of mind. At least I hope so.

Q. Mr. President, that would be your desire?

THE PRESIDENT. Yes.

Q. Mr. President, can you tell us whether Admiral Doenitz is on the list of war criminals?

THE PRESIDENT. No sir, I can't.

[15.] Q. Mr. President, do you have any views on tax reductions after V-E Day?

THE PRESIDENT. I am discussing tax problems with the Secretary of the Treasury now, and I would prefer to discuss that in the press conference particularly devoted to taxes.

[16.] Q. Mr. President, this morning you made public a number of cuts that you are recommending in general. Would you give us any sort of figure on how much you expect to lop off altogether?

THE PRESIDENT. No, I didn't total it. It is somewhere in the neighborhood of 7 or 8 billion.[1]

Q. It is now, and I thought maybe there are additional cuts.

[1] On May 2 the White House announced that the President had sent letters to Congress recommending (1) a reduction in ship construction funds of more than $7 billion, and (2) a reduction of more than $80 million in the 1946 budget estimates for eight war agencies. A third release stated that the President had informed Congress that the Office of Civilian Defense would be terminated and that he had withdrawn its proposed budget of $369,000 for the next fiscal year.

THE PRESIDENT. Well, there will be additional cuts, but they are still under consideration, and that will be done circumspectly, so I don't want now to prophesy.

[17.] Q. Mr. President, is there any change in Army operation of Montgomery Ward contemplated?

THE PRESIDENT. None whatever. The policy on Montgomery Ward will be followed as it has been started.

[18.] Q. Mr. President, can you say anything on your attitude toward the full employment bill of Senator Murray?

THE PRESIDENT. I would—I am not familiar with Senator Murray's full employment bill, but I am for full employment, and shall do everything in my power to create full employment as soon as hostilities end and we start back on the civil program.

[19.] Q. Mr. President, in this 7 or 8 billion reduction in budget, has that been in any way translated into the numbers of civilian employees of the Government who will be dropped?

THE PRESIDENT. No. These are anticipated expenditures—on ship construction, and things of that sort.

Q. It does imply, sir——

THE PRESIDENT. It does imply, of course——

Q. ——obvious reductions?

THE PRESIDENT. ——it will imply some reductions. Studies are being made to meet that situation.

[20.] Q. The State Department recapitulation of the peace negotiations ends on the note that the Swedish Count Bernadotte came back from Germany yesterday, after having delivered the last message to Himmler and had no reply. Has there been a reply since yesterday?

THE PRESIDENT. There has not been a reply. The release of the State Department stands just as it is.

[21.] Q. Mr. President, would you care to comment on the death of Adolf Hitler reported, or Mussolini?

THE PRESIDENT. Well, of course, the two principal war criminals will not have to come to trial; and I am very happy they are out of the way.

Q. Well, does that mean, sir, that we know officially that Hitler is dead?

THE PRESIDENT. Yes.

Q. Do we know how he died, Mr. President?

THE PRESIDENT. No, we do not.

Q. Mr. President, I didn't quite get that. Is it official? This is confirmation that Hitler is dead?

THE PRESIDENT. We have the best—on the best authority possible to obtain at this time that Hitler is dead. But how he died we are not— we are not familiar with the details as yet.

Q. Could you name the authority, Mr. President?

THE PRESIDENT. I would rather not.

Q. Mr. President, do you mean that the—you are convinced that authority you give is the best possible, but it is—but that it is true?

THE PRESIDENT. Yes.

[22.] Q. Mr. President, do you care to comment at all on the situation in Germany today; that is, would you care to make any extension of your remarks on the surrender of the German army in Italy?

THE PRESIDENT. No, I would not.

Q. Mr. President, do you contemplate a radio broadcast imminently?

THE PRESIDENT. No, I do not.

Q. Mr. President, there have been reports late—later today, following the Italian announcement, that other groups of Germans are on the point of surrendering in the Dutch pockets?

THE PRESIDENT. I hope that is true. I don't know that it is.

[23.] Q. Mr. President, is there anything you can give us in the way of background, regarding last Saturday's situation and announcement?

THE PRESIDENT. What was *that*? [*Laughter*]

Q. I think that was the one——

THE PRESIDENT. I can't give you anything further on it, I am sorry to say.

Reporter: Thank you, Mr. President.

NOTE: President Truman's fifth news conference was held in his office at the White House at 4:02 p.m. on Wednesday, May 2, 1945.

23 Veto of Bill Providing for the Deferment of Additional
      Agricultural Workers. *May* 3, 1945

To the House of Representatives:

I return herewith, without my approval, H.J. Res. 106, "To amend
section 5(k) of the Selective Training and Service Act of 1940, as
amended, with respect to the deferment of registrants engaged in
Agricultural occupations or endeavors essential to the war effort."

The joint resolution would amend section 5(k) of the Selective
Training and Service Act of 1940, as amended, which provides for the
deferment of registrants determined to be necessary to and regularly
engaged in an agricultural occupation or endeavor essential to the war
effort. The indicated purpose of the amendment is to cause the deferment of larger numbers of registrants engaged in agricultural
production.

In time of war it is the paramount obligation of every citizen to
serve his country to the best of his ability. Under our democratic
system male citizens are selected for service in the armed forces pursuant to an Act of Congress which prescribes a fair and impartial
method of selection. It is the essence of that act, the Selective Service
and Training Act of 1940, that no one shall be placed in a favored
position, and thus safeguarded from the hazards of war, because of
his economic, occupational or other status. The sole test under the
law is whether the individual can better serve his country in the armed
forces or in an essential activity in support of the war effort.

The Congress, when it passed the Selective Training and Service
Act of 1940, wisely provided that no deferment from service in the
armed forces should be made in the case of any individual "except
upon the basis of the status of such individual, and no such deferment
shall be made of individuals by occupation groups * * *." This provision is the foundation stone of our selective service system under which
over 10 million men have been selected for the colors to make the
greatest military force in the history of this nation.

I do not believe that it was the real intent of Congress that agricultural workers should be given blanket deferment as a group, or that

Congress intended to enact legislation formulating the national policy that agricultural employment was more essential than any other type of employment, including service in the armed forces of the United States in the protection of our country. Nevertheless, the legislation now passed by the Congress and presented for my approval would appear to have that result and to constitute a departure from the sound principle hereinbefore stated on which we have erected our military manpower mobilization system. It would apparently provide that, in determining an individual deferment, the relative essentiality of the agricultural occupation cannot be gauged against an industrial occupation or against military service itself. Thus in practical effect it would single out one special class of our citizens, the agricultural group, and put it on a plane above both industrial occupation and military service.

Enactment of such a law would not only be an injustice to the millions already inducted into our armed forces and those yet to be inducted. It would do violence to the basic principle embodied in Section 5(e)(1) of the Selective Training and Service Act which prohibits deferment by occupational groups or groups of individuals, a principle which was incorporated into the present law because of the deferment scandals of the last war, particularly in shipyards. The resolution would also limit the authority now vested in the President by Section 5(1) to make final determination of all questions of exemption or deferment under the Act, and would deprive him of the right to determine the relative essentiality of the needs of agriculture and the armed forces.

In my opinion no group should have any special privileges, and, therefore, I am returning the joint resolution without my approval.

HARRY S. TRUMAN

24 Statement by the President Concerning Philippine Independence. *May 5, 1945*

I HAVE HAD several discussions with President Osmeña on the subject of Philippine independence. These discussions were started by President Roosevelt.

As a result of the discussions I have had with the President of the Philippines, I am prepared to endorse and carry through to their conclusion the policies laid down by President Roosevelt respecting the Islands and the independence of the Filipino people.

The date of independence will be advanced as soon as practicable in pursuance of the policy outlined by Congress in S.J. Resolution 93. The Filipino people whose heroic and loyal stand in this war has won the affection and admiration of the American people, will be fully assisted by the United States in the great problem of rehabilitation and reconstruction which lies ahead.

In view of the special relationship between the United States and the Philippines as created by S.J. Resolution 93, I believe that suitable reciprocal trade between the two countries should continue for such time, after independence, as may be necessary to provide the new Republic with a fair opportunity to secure its economic freedom and independence—a permanent blessing for the patriotic people of the Philippines.

To assist me in the attainment of these objectives and with concurrence of President Osmeña, I am asking Senator Millard Tydings, of Maryland, Chairman of the Filipino Rehabilitation Commission, to proceed to Manila as my special envoy to examine conditions there and report his recommendations to me.

I have also designated the following to accompany Senator Tydings and to assist him in the accomplishment of this mission:

Vice Admiral W. T. Tarrant, United States Navy;
Brigadier General Frank E. Lowe, United States Army;
Colonel Julian Baumann, United States Army;
George E. Ijams, Veterans Administration;
E. D. Hester, Interior Department;
J. Weldon Jones, Bureau of the Budget;
Ben D. Dorfman, United States Tariff Commission;
Daniel S. Brierley, United States Maritime Commission; and
C. H. Matthiessen, Consultant, War Production Board.

It will be my constant endeavor to be of assistance to the Philippines. I will be only too happy to see to it that the close friendship between our two peoples, developed through many years of fruitful association, is maintained and strengthened.

I hope to be able to accept the invitation of President Osmeña to visit Manila at the inauguration of the Philippine Republic.

NOTE: S.J. Res. 93 is Public Law 380, 78th Congress (58 Stat. 625).

25 Statement by the President on the Timing of the Announcement of the German Surrender.   *May 7,* 1945

I HAVE AGREED with the London and Moscow governments that I will make *no* announcement with reference to surrender of the enemy forces in Europe or elsewhere until a simultaneous statement can be made by the three governments. Until then, there is nothing I can or will say to you.

NOTE: Later in the day a White House release stated that on the basis of reports received the President "confidently expects to make an announcement to the nation by radio at 9 o'clock tomorrow morning." The release added that unless unforeseen developments caused a change in plans a press conference would be called at 8:30 a.m. at which time the press and radio would be given in confidence the text of the President's radio remarks.

26 The President's News Conference on V–E Day.   *May* 8, 1945

THE PRESIDENT. Well, I want to start off by reading you a little statement here. I want you to understand, at the very beginning, that this press conference is held with the understanding that any and all information given you here is for release at 9 a.m. this morning, eastern war time. There should be no indication of the news given here, or speculation about it, either in the press or on the radio before 9 o'clock this morning.

The radio—my radio remarks, and telegrams of congratulation to the Allied military leaders, are for release at the same time. Mr. Daniels has copies of my remarks, available for you in the lobby as you go out, and also one or two releases here.

[1.] Now, for your benefit, because you won't get a chance to listen over the radio, I am going to read you the proclamation, and the principal remarks. It won't take but 7 minutes, so you needn't be uneasy. You have plenty of time. [*Laughter*]

"This is a solemn but glorious hour. General Eisenhower informs me that the forces of Germany have surrendered to the United Nations. The flags of freedom fly all over Europe."

It's celebrating my birthday, too—today, too.

Voices: Happy birthday, Mr. President! [*Laughter*]

THE PRESIDENT. "For this victory, we join in offering our thanks to the Providence which has guided and sustained us through the dark days of adversity. Our rejoicing is sobered and subdued by a supreme consciousness of the terrible price we have paid to rid the world of Hitler and his evil band. Let us not forget, my fellow Americans, the sorrow and the heartache which today abide in the homes of so many of our neighbors—neighbors whose most priceless possession has been rendered as a sacrifice to redeem our liberty.

"We can repay the debt which we owe to our God, to our dead, and to our children, only by work, by ceaseless devotion to the responsibilities which lie ahead of us. If I could give you a single watchword for the coming months, that word is work, work, and more work. We must work to finish the war. Our victory is only half over."

[2.] Now, we have got another little release here, which doesn't go into the speech, but it informs the Japanese what they can expect. We are going to be in a position where we can turn the greatest war machine in the history of the world loose on the Japanese; and I am informed by the Chiefs of Staff, by the Secretary of State, and the Secretary of the Navy, that Japan is going to have a terrible time from now on. This release here, I will read it.

"The Japanese people have felt the weight of our land, air, and naval attacks. So long as their leaders and the armed forces continue the war, the striking power and intensity of our blows will steadily increase, and will bring utter destruction to Japan's industrial war production, to its shipping, and to everything that supports its military activity.

"The longer the war lasts, the greater will be the suffering and hardships which the people of Japan will undergo—all in vain. Our blows will not cease until the Japanese military and naval forces lay down their arms in *unconditional surrender*.

"Just what does the unconditional surrender of the armed forces mean for the Japanese people?

"It means the end of the war.

"It means the termination of the influence of the military leaders who brought Japan to the present brink of disaster.

"It means provision for the return of soldiers and sailors to their families, their farms, and their jobs.

"And it means not prolonging the present agony and suffering of the Japanese in the vain hope of victory.

"Unconditional surrender does not mean the extermination or enslavement of the Japanese people."

Now, you will have copies of that when you go out.

Mr. Daniels: Mr. President, will you point out that that is marked immediate release, but that it is for 9 o'clock?

THE PRESIDENT. That is for 9 o'clock. It is marked immediate release, but it was to be released after the proclamation this morning. But I thought it was so important that we released it at the same time; and while this release is marked immediate release, it wants to be released at 9 o'clock, after the other release.

[3.] [*Continues reading his address*]: "The West is free, but the East is still in bondage to the treacherous tyranny of the Japanese. When the last Japanese division has surrendered unconditionally, then only will our fighting job be done.

"We must work to bind up the wounds of a suffering world—to build an abiding peace, a peace rooted in justice and in law."

You remember, it has been emphasized here all the time that we want a peace of justice and law. That's what we are trying to get, at San Francisco—what we are going to get—the framework for a peace in justice and law. We have got terrific problems facing us. While we have been prepared for this thing for several days, I think ever since last Saturday night, if I remember correctly—[*laughter*]—we have had other things to think about, besides this formal proclamation which we are issuing this morning. We are facing a situation that we can either go the whole way and make the world the happiest place it has ever been in which to live, or we can go the wrong way and spoil the whole thing. So we are thinking all the time of the problems which we have to face.

[*Continues reading his address*]: "We can build such a peace only by hard, toilsome, painstaking work—by understanding and working with our Allies in peace as we have worked with them in war.

"The job ahead is no less important, no less urgent, no less difficult than the task which now happily is done.

"I call upon every American to stick to his post until the last battle is won. Until that day, let no man abandon his post or slacken his efforts."

[4.] Now, I want to read to you the formal proclamation.

"A Proclamation—The Allied armies, through sacrifice and devotion and with God's help, have wrung from Germany a final and unconditional surrender. The western world has been freed of the evil forces which for five years and longer have imprisoned the bodies and broken the lives of millions upon millions of free-born men. They have violated their churches, destroyed their homes, corrupted their children, and murdered their loved ones. Our Armies of Liberation have restored freedom to these suffering peoples, whose spirit and will the oppressors could never enslave.

"Much remains to be done. The victory won in the West must now be won in the East."

I want that emphasized time after time, that we are only half through.

"The whole world must be cleansed of the evil from which half the world has been freed. United, the peace-loving nations have demonstrated in the West that their arms are stronger by far than the might of dictators or the tyranny of military cliques that once called us soft and weak."

I would like to know what the Germans think about that now. [*Laughter*]

"The power of our peoples to defend themselves against all enemies will be proved in the Pacific war as it has been proved in Europe.

"For the triumph of spirit and of arms which we have won, and for its promise to peoples everywhere who join us in the love of freedom, it is fitting that we, as a nation, give thanks to Almighty God, who has strengthened us and given us the victory.

"Now, therefore, I, Harry S. Truman, President of the United States of America, do hereby appoint Sunday, May 13, 1945, to be a day of prayer."

And it's exceedingly fitting that that is Mother's Day, too.

"I call upon the people of the United States, whatever their faith, to unite in offering joyful thanks to God for the victory we have won and to pray that He will support us to the end of our present struggle and guide us into the way of peace.

"I also call upon my countrymen to dedicate this day of prayer to the memory of those who have given their lives to make possible our victory.

"In witness whereof, I have hereunto set my hand and caused the seal of the United States of America to be affixed."

[5.]   And I have sent messages to Prime Minister Churchill, Marshal Stalin, and General Eisenhower and General de Gaulle. This is the message to—to General Eisenhower, and I will let you read the rest of them from the release which will be given you. I want you to read every one of them.

Mr. Daniels: Mr. President—the time is getting late, Mr. President.

THE PRESIDENT. I'll just read the one [to General Eisenhower]:

"In recognition of the unconditional surrender—unconditional and abject surrender of the Nazi barbarians, please accept the fervent congratulations and appreciation of myself, and of the American people, for the heroic achievements of your Allied Army, Navy, and Air Forces. By their sacrifices, skill, and courage they have saved and exalted the cause of freedom throughout the world. All of us owe you, and to your men of many nations, a debt beyond appraisal for their high contribution to the conquest of Naziism.

"I send also my personal appreciation of the superb leadership shown by you and your commanders in directing the valiant legions of our own country, and of our Allies, to this historic victory.

"Please transmit this message to the appropriate officers of your command, and publish it to all Allied forces in your theaters of operation."

And in the message to Marshal Stalin, we asked him to do the same thing for the Russian commanders and Russian troops.

Reporter: Thank you, Mr. President.

NOTE: President Truman's sixth news conference was held in his office at the White House at 8:35 a.m. on Tuesday, May 8, 1945. The White House Official Reporter noted that members of the Cabinet, Mrs. Truman and Margaret Truman, high United States and British Army and Navy officials, and Senate and Congressional leaders were grouped in chairs around the President's desk.

27 Broadcast to the American People Announcing the Surrender of Germany. *May 8*, 1945

[Delivered from the Radio Room at the White House at 9 a.m.]

THIS IS a solemn but a glorious hour. I only wish that Franklin D. Roosevelt had lived to witness this day. General Eisenhower informs me that the forces of Germany have surrendered to the United Nations. The flags of freedom fly over all Europe.

For this victory, we join in offering our thanks to the Providence which has guided and sustained us through the dark days of adversity.

Our rejoicing is sobered and subdued by a supreme consciousness of the terrible price we have paid to rid the world of Hitler and his evil band. Let us not forget, my fellow Americans, the sorrow and the heartache which today abide in the homes of so many of our neighbors—neighbors whose most priceless possession has been rendered as a sacrifice to redeem our liberty.

We can repay the debt which we owe to our God, to our dead and to our children only by work—by ceaseless devotion to the responsibilities which lie ahead of us. If I could give you a single watchword for the coming months, that word is—work, work, and more work.

We must work to finish the war. Our victory is but half-won. The West is free, but the East is still in bondage to the treacherous tyranny

48

of the Japanese. When the last Japanese division has surrendered unconditionally, then only will our fighting job be done.

We must work to bind up the wounds of a suffering world—to build an abiding peace, a peace rooted in justice and in law. We can build such a peace only by hard, toilsome, painstaking work—by understanding and working with our allies in peace as we have in war.

The job ahead is no less important, no less urgent, no less difficult than the task which now happily is done.

I call upon every American to stick to his post until the last battle is won. Until that day, let no man abandon his post or slacken his efforts.

And now, I want to read to you my formal proclamation of this occasion:

"A Proclamation—The Allied armies, through sacrifice and devotion and with God's help, have wrung from Germany a final and unconditional surrender. The western world has been freed of the evil forces which for five years and longer have imprisoned the bodies and broken the lives of millions upon millions of free-born men. They have violated their churches, destroyed their homes, corrupted their children, and murdered their loved ones. Our Armies of Liberation have restored freedom to these suffering peoples, whose spirit and will the oppressors could never enslave.

"Much remains to be done. The victory won in the West must now be won in the East. The whole world must be cleansed of the evil from which half the world has been freed. United, the peace-loving nations have demonstrated in the West that their arms are stronger by far than the might of the dictators or the tyranny of military cliques that once called us soft and weak. The power of our peoples to defend themselves against all enemies will be proved in the Pacific war as it has been proved in Europe.

"For the triumph of spirit and of arms which we have won, and for its promise to the peoples everywhere who join us in the love of freedom, it is fitting that we, as a nation, give thanks to Almighty God, who has strengthened us and given us the victory.

"Now, therefore, I, Harry S. Truman, President of the United States of America, do hereby appoint Sunday, May 13, 1945, to be a day of prayer.

"I call upon the people of the United States, whatever their faith, to unite in offering joyful thanks to God for the victory we have won, and to pray that He will support us to the end of our present struggle and guide us into the ways of peace.

"I also call upon my countrymen to dedicate this day of prayer to the memory of those who have given their lives to make possible our victory.

"In Witness Whereof, I have hereunto set my hand and caused the seal of the United States of America to be affixed."

28   Statement by the President Calling for Unconditional Surrender of Japan.   *May 8, 1945*

NAZI GERMANY has been defeated.

The Japanese people have felt the weight of our land, air and naval attacks. So long as their leaders and the armed forces continue the war the striking power and intensity of our blows will steadily increase and will bring utter destruction to Japan's industrial war production, to its shipping, and to everything that supports its military activity.

The longer the war lasts, the greater will be the suffering and hardships which the people of Japan will undergo—all in vain. Our blows will not cease until the Japanese military and naval forces lay down their arms in *unconditional surrender*.

Just what does the unconditional surrender of the armed forces mean for the Japanese people?

It means the end of the war.

It means the termination of the influence of the military leaders who have brought Japan to the present brink of disaster.

It means provision for the return of soldiers and sailors to their families, their farms, their jobs.

It means not prolonging the present agony and suffering of the Japanese in the vain hope of victory.

Unconditional surrender does not mean the extermination or enslavement of the Japanese people.

29   Messages to Allied Leaders and to General Eisenhower on the Surrender of Germany.   *May 8, 1945*

To Prime Minister Churchill:

With the unconditional surrender of all the armies of Nazidom and the liberation of the oppressed people of Europe from the evils of barbarism, I wish to express to you, and through you to Britain's heroic Army, Navy and Air Forces, our congratulations on their achievements. The Government of the United States is deeply appreciative of the splendid contribution of all the British Empire forces and of the British people to this magnificent victory. With warm affection, we hail our comrades-in-arms across the Atlantic.

HARRY S. TRUMAN

To Marshal Stalin:

Now that the Nazi armies of aggression have been forced by the coordinated efforts of Soviet-Anglo-American forces to an unconditional surrender, I wish to express to you and through you to your heroic Army the appreciation and congratulations of the United States Government on its splendid contribution to the cause of civilization and liberty.

You have demonstrated in all your campaigns what it is possible to accomplish when a free people under superlative leadership and with unfailing courage rise against the forces of barbarism.

HARRY S. TRUMAN

To General Eisenhower:

In recognition of the unconditional and abject surrender of the Nazi barbarians, please accept the fervent congratulations and appreciation of myself and of the American people for the heroic achievements of your Allied Army, Navy and Air Forces. By their sacrifices, skill and courage they have saved and exalted the cause of freedom throughout the world. All of us owe to you and to your men of many nations a debt beyond appraisal for their high contribution to the conquest of Naziism.

I send also my personal appreciation of the superb leadership shown by you and your commanders in directing the valiant legions of our own country and of our allies to this historic victory.

Please transmit this message to the appropriate officers of your command and publish it to all allied forces in your theaters of operation.

HARRY S. TRUMAN

To General de Gaulle:

The Nazi forces of barbarian aggression having now been driven into an unconditional surrender by our allied armies, this is an appropriate time to send through you America's congratulations to the people of France on their permanent liberation from the oppression they have endured with high courage for so long.

I wish also to send to you this expression of our appreciation of the contribution made by valiant soldiers of France to our Allied victory.

HARRY S. TRUMAN

30 Statement by the President Upon Signing Bill Extending
the Selective Training and Service Act of 1940.
May 9, 1945

I AM reluctantly giving my approval to this legislation. I do not wish this approval to be interpreted as expressing my concurrence in Section 2 of the Bill, which places added restrictions on the War and Navy Departments in their management of the fighting forces. I sign the legislation only because the immediate extension of the Selective Service Act is of compelling necessity in the continuance of military operations against Japan.

NOTE: As enacted, the bill extending the   1940 is Public Law 54, 79th Congress
Selective Training and Service Act of   (59 Stat. 166).

31 The President's News Conference of
May 15, 1945

THE PRESIDENT. I am very sure that the first thing you are principally interested in is the free press in Germany. I would like to read a little statement here, and if you want to ask me some questions about it, I will try to answer them.

Q. Will you read slowly, Mr. President?

THE PRESIDENT. I will read it very slowly.

[1.] "General Eisenhower has advised me that he has issued no policy or order dealing with the importation of publications into Germany. The General has expressed the personal opinion that a free press and a free flow of information and ideas should prevail in Germany in a manner consistent with military security.

"General Eisenhower has emphasized, however, that there can be no restoration of a free German press in Germany until the elimination of Nazi and militarist influence has been completed. We are not going to lose the peace by giving license to racialist Pan-Germans, Nazis and militarists, so that they can misuse democratic rights in order to attack Democracy as Hitler did."

Now I agree with General Eisenhower on that.

And if you want to ask me some questions, why fire away.

Q. Mr. President, is that any reversal of the position taken last week by——

THE PRESIDENT. Yes, it is.

Q. ——Elmer Davis?

THE PRESIDENT. Yes, it is. Mr. Davis was in Europe, in conference with SHAEF on the lower level, and Mr. Davis thought he had reached a policy with them on this. After that was released, I got in touch with General Eisenhower himself, and he informed me of just what I told you. Mr. Davis acted in good faith. Mr. Davis thought he was outlining the policy which had been agreed on. Apparently, from General Eisenhower's statement, there had been no policy agreed on, and it has not yet been agreed on. But as you see, General Eisenhower is for a free press in Germany, when the time arrives to give it to them.

Mr. Davis was acting in good faith, be sure and get that.

[2.] Q. Mr. President, speaking of the military situation, as mentioned in the statement, have you decided what our position is going to be on the handling of the German general staff, and the militarist influences in Germany?

THE PRESIDENT. No, I haven't. That is in the hands of Mr. Jackson—
Mr. Justice Jackson, I should say.

[3.] Q. Mr. President, at your first press conference you said you
would give us your views on the repeal of the Johnson Act.

THE PRESIDENT. On that repeal, I will read you a statement of President Roosevelt's as to why it is necessary, if you like.

"At present, our foreign investment programs—" this is direct quotes
from the statement issued by President Roosevelt—

"At present our foreign investment programs are impeded by legislation which restricts loans to those countries which are in default on
loans arising out of the First World War. For both the International
Bank and the Export-Import Bank to operate effectively, as well as
to achieve an adequate flow of private investment, it is essential that
these restrictions be removed."

That is just as true as it can be. I never was for the Johnson Act
in the first place.

Q. Mr. President, is that his Message to Congress——

THE PRESIDENT. I think this—let's see—yes, in the Budget Message to
Congress of January 3, 1945—just the recent Budget Message, the one
which we are in now.

[4.] Q. Do you plan any early meeting with either Prime Minister
Churchill and/or Marshal Stalin?

THE PRESIDENT. Well, Mr. Eden was in to see me yesterday to discuss
that question and our hope that there will be a possibility for the three
of us to meet and discuss the coming peace program around the table.
I can't say anything about the date, or how soon that will be. It depends
on business right here. As you know, I am a very busy person.

Q. Mr. President, is it possible that General de Gaulle might be
included in this meeting?

THE PRESIDENT. The Big Three will have the meeting.

Q. Is there any possibility that may be at San Francisco, before the
present thing breaks up?

THE PRESIDENT. No, there isn't any possibility of its being at San
Francisco.

Q. Did you say the Big Three will have the meeting? In other words, there will be a meeting? It's just the——

THE PRESIDENT. I hope so. I am not saying there will be a meeting. I am saying I hope there will be one.

Q. Mr. President, I am not trying to pin you down on the time element, but are you looking into it in terms of *soon?*

THE PRESIDENT. Well, it won't be in the very distant future. It won't be immediately. [*Laughter*]

[5.] Q. Mr. President, can you tell us yet when you will have your press conference on taxes?

THE PRESIDENT. No, I can't. We are still working on that, and we will have one very shortly.

Q. Did you see Senator George's statement this morning?

THE PRESIDENT. Yes, I saw Senator George's statement—not this morning, I saw the other the other day—I didn't see the one this morning.

Q. He was foreseeing a 5-year plan for gradual reduction of taxes until they reached the prewar level.

THE PRESIDENT. Well, I want it distinctly understood that there can be no reduction in taxes until the war is over. I want that thoroughly understood. There is no possible way to reduce taxes until this war is over, and we still have a war to win in the Pacific. So you can talk about taxes all you want to, but we have got to meet obligations to make the United States of America good, and you can only make them good by taxation. And every man in this country is a partner in the Government of the United States. There are 85 million individual bondholders in the United States, and they must be protected; and in order to protect them, you have got to collect the money to make those bonds good. And that has to be done by taxes. And you can do it no other way.

Does that answer your question? [*Laughter*]

[6.] Q. Mr. President, there is a report that you were about to shake up the Veterans Administration, and that part of the shakeup will be to appoint Bennett Champ Clark. Do you plan such a shakeup?

THE PRESIDENT. I can't—I didn't hear the question—I am not planning a shakeup, but I didn't know what it was about.

Q. Veterans Administration.

THE PRESIDENT. No, I am not planning any immediate shakeup in the Veterans Administration. The Veterans Administration, of course, will have to be expanded to meet the situation which we will face as soon as the soldiers return in large numbers. And the Veterans Administration, of course, will have to be put on a basis to meet this situation, just as it was put on a basis to meet the situation after the First World War. That will be done. I don't think it necessitates any serious shakeup.

Q. You said you did not see any *immediate* shakeup?

THE PRESIDENT. That's what I meant.

Q. Can we quote that word *immediate?*

THE PRESIDENT. No, I wish you wouldn't, for this reason, because I don't want it to appear in any way that I have any intention of immediately discharging anybody. I am trying to get this "mess" to operate, and I want you to be as lenient with me as you possibly can. The Veterans Administration will be modernized; let's put it that way. That should be done as soon as possible, but I can't do it immediately.

Q. The second part of my question, Mr. President, was, do you intend to appoint Bennett Champ Clark——

THE PRESIDENT. I do not.

[7.] Q. Mr. President, is it true that you are going to send Dr. R. G. Sproul of the University of California to Moscow on a mission?

THE PRESIDENT. Yes. He is going with Mr. Pauley. I want to say to you, since you brought that subject up, that I think we have the finest layout here on this reparations thing that has ever been gotten together. It is headed by Mr. Pauley and Dr. Lubin, and we have Dr. Sproul——

Q. What's that first name, sir?

Mr. Daniels: Pauley.

Q. I mean Sproul.

THE PRESIDENT. Robert Gordon. And here is a fellow that must be descended from a Civil War veteran. His name is Jubal R. Parten. [*Laughter*]

Q. Steve Early!

Q. Steve's relative!

56

THE PRESIDENT. Jubal Early, as you remember. [*Laughter*]

Q. What is Parten going to do?

THE PRESIDENT. He is industrial adviser. I am going to give you all this—I think there's a release for you on this, but I will read the last sentence of that release: [1]

"The men chosen for this vital mission should inspire the confidence of all Americans. They are eminently qualified to do the job."

And I believe that, with everything that is in me.

And it's as fine a list as I ever saw. I don't know what we are going to do for experts for the peace conference, if Pauley takes them all. [*Laughter*]

[8.] Q. Mr. President, can you tell us what further steps are planned in the anthracite strike?

THE PRESIDENT. Whatever steps are necessary to get coal out. Coal is what we want, and coal is what we are going to have.

Reporter: Thank you, Mr. President.

NOTE: President Truman's seventh news conference was held in his office at the White House at 10:50 a.m. on Tuesday, May 15, 1945.

32 Statement by the President on German Reparations. *May 15, 1945*

A FAIR and workable settlement of reparations poses some of the most difficult problems of the entire post-war adjustment. These questions are closely related to the task of insuring a lasting peace. For that reason, the right answers will be vital to the security of America and the world.

I personally concur in the general view of our own objectives as shared by Ambassador Pauley and Dr. Lubin. Absolute insurance against German or Japanese rearmament—ever again—comes first with us.

I believe, further, that our allies are of one mind with us on this point, and that with such a basic agreement, the way will be clear for a just and equitable schedule of German reparations—reparations "in kind"

[1] For the full text of the statement by the President, see Item 32.

which will provide the maximum of rehabilitation and restoration of overrun territory.

The men chosen for this vital mission should inspire the confidence of all Americans. They are eminently qualified to do the job.

NOTE: At the time this statement was made public the White House also released a list of members of the staff selected by Mr. Pauley and Dr. Lubin to accompany them to Germany.

33 Statement by the President Following a Discussion With Foreign Minister Bidault of France. *May 18, 1945*

THE PRESIDENT had the pleasure today of conversing with the French Foreign Minister, M. Bidault, upon his arrival from San Francisco and of discussing with him a number of problems of primary interest to France and the United States.

The President took the occasion at the outset to express the gratification of the entire American Delegation at San Francisco for M. Bidault's cooperation and helpfulness and for the important and continuing contribution of the French Delegation to the work of the Conference.

The President made it abundantly clear that the American people and the American Government realize that the French nation has emerged with renewed strength and vigor from the catastrophe which it suffered and that it has demonstrated its determination and its ability to resume its rightful and eminent place among the nations which will share the largest measure of responsibility in maintaining the future peace of Europe and the world.

He expressed his desire to meet General de Gaulle and indicated that there was a full appreciation by the United States Government of the part which France could and should play in the settlement of questions of world and European interest.

In this connection, the President indicated that the United States was moved by the strongest ties of friendship, dating back to the founding of this nation. A strong France represents a gain to the world. As a consequence, the people of the United States have accepted reductions in their requirements of certain essential food items in order to permit increased shipments to the liberated countries of Europe, including France, where they are so urgently needed. Also the Government of the United States has taken extraordinary measures, despite American shortages of essential supplies and shipping, to arrange priorities for French procurement of such supplies and to provide shipping for their transportation to France. The people and Government of the United States will continue to take such measures as will lie within their power to facilitate the recovery of France and of her people.

The President confirmed to M. Bidault this Government's complete willingness to relinquish to France a part of the American zone of occupation in Germany. Details have already been conveyed informally to the French Government and are now in the process of being formalized.

The President emphasized that we are faced with a still strong and deadly enemy in the Far East to whose defeat the total resources of this country, both in manpower and material, are pledged. He indicated that such assistance as France and our other Allies may bring to that struggle and which may be synchronized with operations already planned or underway, will be welcomed.

The discussion was on the most friendly and cordial plane and afforded the President a welcome opportunity to emphasize the bonds of friendship and mutual interest between the two countries.

34 Remarks Before the Congress on Presenting the Medal of Honor to Sergeant Jake W. Lindsey. *May 21, 1945*

Mr. Speaker, Mr. President, Members of the Congress:

We are assembled here today to confer the Nation's highest decoration on a young American soldier. It so happens that Technical Sergeant Jake W. Lindsey of Lucedale, Mississippi, is the one hundredth Infantryman to receive the Medal of Honor in this war for bravery above and beyond the call to duty. Through him, we pay a grateful Nation's tribute to the courage of all our fighting men.

The history of this war is filled with countless acts of valor by our soldiers and sailors and marines under fire. Those who win the Medal of Honor have displayed the highest quality of courage.

We have heard in the citation what Sergeant Lindsey did. His inspiring deeds on the battlefield require no further praise from any man. They stand—with the deeds of the others on whom this decoration has been conferred—in the finest tradition of American heroism.

This Medal, to repeat, is given for gallantry at the risk of life *beyond the call to duty*. No officer ordered Sergeant Lindsey to stand alone against a company of the enemy. No officer ordered him when wounded to engage eight Germans in hand-to-hand combat. Those decisions came from his own heart. They were a flash of the nobility which we like to think is a part of every American. They were the unselfish valor which can triumph over terrible odds. They were the very essence of victory.

Since the beginning of this war, 223 Medals of Honor have been awarded to members of the Armed Forces. Of these, 162 have gone to the Army, 33 to the Navy, 27 to the Marine Corps, and one to the Coast Guard. One hundred of the men so decorated have been Infantrymen, and of them 50 died in performing the acts for which they were honored.

It seems fitting that in this symbolic ceremony we should honor an infantryman. There is little glamor in his service. He faces not only the enemy before him, but the cold and the heat, the rain and the snow, the dust and the mud, which so often makes his life miserable. These things he endures, and rises above them to such deeds as those we celebrate today.

This is a proud and moving occasion for every American. It follows the complete victory of our Allied Forces over a powerful enemy in Europe. It finds us striking devastating blows in the Pacific. We are preparing to strike them later in overwhelming force.

Before the battle against Japan is won, we shall have other men to honor—men whose deeds, like those we celebrate today, will have brought closer our inevitable victory.

I hope that every man and woman in our Nation today will reverently thank God that we have produced such sons as these. With their high courage as an inspiration, we cannot fail in the task we have set for ourselves.

It is with gratitude and pride that as President of the United States, and in the name of the Congress, I have presented this Medal of Honor to Technical Sergeant Jake W. Lindsey.

35   Letter to Heads of War Agencies on the Economic
     Situation in the Liberated Countries of Northwest Europe.
     May 22, 1945

Dear ————:

Judge Rosenman's report of which you have a copy has pointed out the extremely serious economic situation in the liberated countries of Northwest Europe. The report confirms in strong terms the need for action on the part of this Government.

In brief the report points out the following:

(1) A dangerously low level of nutrition exists generally in these liberated countries except in the rural, food raising areas. The production of coal is not meeting even minimum requirements. The means of internal transportation by rail, canal and highway have suffered substantially from looting and destruction. What are left have been largely devoted to Allied military use. Ports have suffered extensive damage from bombing and demolition. Manufacturing has been paralyzed by destruction or damage, lack of raw materials, and inadequate plant maintenance.

(2) The needs of the liberated countries of Northwest Europe are grave—not only from a humanitarian point of view, but also because they necessarily involve many internal and international political considerations. To a great extent the future permanent peace of Europe depends upon the restoration of the economy of these liberated countries, including a reasonable standard of living and employment. United States economy, too, will be deeply affected unless these areas again resume their place in the international exchange of goods and services. A chaotic and hungry Europe is not fertile ground in which stable, democratic and friendly governments can be reared.

(3) Just as the United States has been the largest producer of the United Nations in wartime, so will it naturally be looked to as the principal source of civilian supplies for these countries.

It is the established policy of this Government to accept this responsibility as far as it is possible to do so.

As a matter of national policy, therefore, I request your agency to grant the priority necessary to meet the minimum civilian requirements of those of our Allies who have been ravaged by the enemy to the fullest extent that the successful prosecution of military operations and the maintenance of our essential domestic economy permit.

Very sincerely yours,

HARRY S. TRUMAN

NOTE: This is the text of identical letters addressed to J. A. Krug, Chairman, War Production Board; Marvin Jones, Administrator, War Food Administration; Harold L. Ickes, Administrator, Solid Fuels Administration for War; and Leo Crowley, Chairman, Foreign Shipments Committee.

A summary of Judge Rosenman's report to President Truman on the problem of civilian supplies for the liberated areas of Northwest Europe, released by the White House on April 30, 1945, is published in the Department of State Bulletin (vol. 12, p. 860).

36 Letter Accepting Resignation of Francis Biddle as the Attorney General. *May 23, 1945*

Dear Francis:

In accepting your resignation, I desire to express my appreciation of the patriotic services which you have rendered to your country during the war and during the days when we were preparing for the war.

I shall always look back with pleasure upon my association with you while I was in the Senate as well as during the past months.

I hope that you will have continued happiness and success in your future work, and I trust that I may have the privilege of consulting you in the future whenever occasion arises.

I am making your resignation effective July 1, 1945.

Very sincerely yours,

HARRY S. TRUMAN

NOTE: Attorney General Biddle served from September 5, 1941, through June 30, 1945. His letter of resignation, dated May 21, 1945, was released with the President's reply.

37   Letter Accepting Resignation of Frances Perkins as Secretary of Labor.   *May 23, 1945*

Dear Frances:

I accept your resignation as Secretary of Labor with great regret and with deep appreciation for all of the untiring service which you have rendered to our country.

During your administration unsurpassed progress in position, influence and prestige has been made by American organized labor.

During this period, such far reaching legislation as the Fair Labor Standards Act, the National Labor Relations Act, and the Social Security Act have been enacted—carrying out the social philosophy you have so often expressed.

The rights of labor as a partner in the system of private enterprise in the United States have been more firmly established than ever before. There has been created a cooperative relationship between industry and labor in the United States which has been largely instrumental in turning out the weapons of war—weapons which brought about the unconditional surrender of the Axis powers in Europe, and will inevitably bring the same defeat to the Japanese.

You have certainly carried out the principle of the basic act creating your office—"to promote the welfare of the wage earners of the United States".

I am grateful to you for the leadership and energy and hard work which you have shown in this difficult and important field of human relations during the past twelve years.

I should like to make your resignation effective July 1, 1945.

With kindest personal regards,

Very sincerely yours,

HARRY S. TRUMAN

NOTE: Secretary Perkins served from March 4, 1933, through June 30, 1945. Her letter of resignation, dated May 21, 1945, was released with the President's reply.

38 Letter Accepting Resignation of Claude R. Wickard as Secretary of Agriculture. *May 23, 1945*

Dear Claude:

With great personal regret I am accepting your resignation as Secretary of Agriculture to take effect on the appointment and qualification of your successor.

You have served more than four years in that office. During that time the agricultural output of the United States reached unprecedented levels. Under your administration the farmers of the nation have performed miracles of production of foods and fibres which did so much to win the war in Europe and to place us on the road to victory in the Pacific.

It is a record from which, I am sure, you must derive much satisfaction and pride.

On behalf of our Government, I desire to thank you for your patriotic and devoted service.

I also wish to thank you for consenting to remain in government as the Administrator of the Rural Electrification Administration. The work of this agency means much for the comfort and efficiency of our rural dwellers. I am delighted that it will be in the hands of one who has so competently and tirelessly worked for their welfare.

As problems arise in the field of agriculture, I expect to call upon you for advice and assistance.

Very sincerely yours,
HARRY S. TRUMAN

NOTE: Secretary Wickard served from September 5, 1940, through June 29, 1945. His letter of resignation, dated April 17, 1945, was released with the President's reply.

39 Letter Accepting Resignation of Marvin Jones as War Food Administrator. *May 23, 1945*

Dear Marvin:

In view of your desire expressed to me last month to return to your place on the Court of Claims, I regretfully accept your resignation. I understand that the Chief Justice of the Court is now anxious that you resume your judicial work as soon as possible.

Let me express my own appreciation, and also the thanks of the people of the United States for the hard, conscientious and efficient work you have done as War Food Administrator.

It was a most difficult assignment. The needs of our armed forces, of our Allies, and of our own civilian population called for the highest degree of competence in food production, management and distribution. It is to the everlasting credit of the War Food Administration that even after supplying the great demands made upon us from all over the world, the American people as a whole not only did not go hungry but actually enjoyed a better diet than in the days before the war.

It is an accomplishment of which you can be very proud.

With best wishes for continued success and happiness in your work,

Very sincerely yours,

HARRY S. TRUMAN

NOTE: Mr. Jones served as War Food Administrator from June 28, 1943, through June 30, 1945. His letter of resignation, dated May 22, 1945, was released with the President's reply.

40   The President's News Conference of *May 23, 1945*

THE PRESIDENT. Everybody here?

[1.] Well, I have some Cabinet changes I wanted to tell you about. Mr. Biddle's resignation has been accepted, and Tom Clark of Texas will be appointed in his place as Attorney General.

Q. C-l-a-r-k—no E?

THE PRESIDENT. Tom C. Clark, no E.

I will read you the first paragraph of the letter I wrote to Mr. Biddle. It says, "In accepting your resignation, I desire to express my appreciation of the patriotic services which you have rendered to your country during the war, and during the days when we were preparing for the war."

And in the last paragraph, "I hope you will have continued happiness and success in your future work, and I trust that I may have the privilege of consulting you in the future when occasion arises."

I am accepting the resignation of Miss Perkins as Secretary of Labor, and am appointing Judge Lewis B. Schwellenbach of Washington to be Secretary of Labor. Miss Perkins wrote me a very fine letter, and I wrote her a good one. You will receive copies of it.

Mr. Wickard's resignation is being accepted, and he is being appointed REA Administrator; and Congressman Clinton P. Anderson of New Mexico is being appointed Secretary of Agriculture.

Q. Clinton *B.* Anderson?

THE PRESIDENT. Clinton *P.* Anderson.

Q. *D,* sir?

THE PRESIDENT. *P.* Anderson, Congressman from New Mexico. He has been Chairman of the War Food Committee in the House of Representatives.

Q. Are all these effective immediately——

THE PRESIDENT. No——

Q. ——effective immediately, or June 30th?

THE PRESIDENT. ——the last of the fiscal year. These are all effective on June 30, except Mr. Wickard's. His takes effect as soon as he is confirmed as REA Administrator.

I have the resignation of Marvin Jones as War Food Administrator, and I would like to read you the last two paragraphs of Mr. Jones's letter and comment on it.

"While the war was being fought on both fronts, there was considerable logic in having an independent War Food Administration. It has worked well. In each of the war years there has been an outstanding record of production. There has been complete cooperation between the Secretary of Agriculture and myself.

"Now, however, that victory in Europe has been achieved, I feel that the work of the Department and the War Food—and War Food could well be carried on by the Secretary of Agriculture, probably with somewhat less expenditure of funds."

Now Judge Jones is going back to the Claims Court on June 30th, and when he goes back and relinquishes the Office of War Food Administrator, I expect to make the Secretary of Agriculture War Food Administrator.

And I think that's about all, unless you have got some questions to ask me. [*Laughter*]

Q. I might say that is pretty good.

Q. Mr. President, the—Clinton Anderson has been—made two or three good reports——

THE PRESIDENT. I think so.

Q. ——and have you read them, and have they——

THE PRESIDENT. Yes.

Q. ——led you to any consideration on your part?

THE PRESIDENT. No, it didn't. I had him in mind before I read his reports, but his reports helped.

Q. Mr. President, did Mr. Morgenthau offer his resignation this morning?

THE PRESIDENT. No, he did not, and if he had, I wouldn't accept it.

Q. Mr. President, do you contemplate——

Q. Who was that?

Q. We didn't hear that.

THE PRESIDENT. Morgenthau.

Q. What was the reply, Mr. President?

THE PRESIDENT. He did not offer his resignation, and if he had, I wouldn't accept it.

Q. Sir, do you contemplate any change in the State Department?

THE PRESIDENT. I do not.

Q. Mr. President, were any of the resignations requested by you?

THE PRESIDENT. They were not. I have the resignation of every member of the Government who *can* resign since I have been President! [*Laughter*] I can accept them or not as I choose.

[2.] Q. Mr. President, would you clarify, please, the future status of Russia under lend-lease, now that the war in Europe is over?

THE PRESIDENT. The—I don't care to discuss that. I think I covered it very thoroughly in the statement that was issued.[1]

------

[1] For the President's statement upon signing the bill extending the Lend-Lease Act, see Item 3.

Q. It left open one question, and that is whether or not Russia is getting any lend-lease now?

THE PRESIDENT. Russia is getting the lend-lease that she has contracted to receive during the month of May.

Q. How about, sir, when the protocol expires at the end of June?

THE PRESIDENT. Well, let's wait and see what is necessary to be done at that time, then we will take care of it in a way which we think will be all right for the peace of the world.

Q. When did cancellation of orders begin on lend-lease to Russia?

THE PRESIDENT. The cancellation of lend-lease began as soon as the war ceased. It was not a cancellation, it was a readjustment because of the new conditions as they came about due to the collapse of Germany. The whole thing has to be gone into completely and thoroughly for all the nations, and I think it would be handled in a way that the country and the world will be helped by it.

Q. Have you any estimates of the amount of savings resulting from the readjustment?

THE PRESIDENT. No, I have not, because I don't know just how much of a readjustment has taken place at the present time.

Q. Mr. President, under the law can lend-lease equipment be sent to Russia, or to any country, when it is not engaged in the war against Japan?

THE PRESIDENT. Yes, it can. When it has been allocated to Russia by protocol and treaty, we have to carry out our commitments.

[3.] Q. Mr. President, now that the war in Europe is over, has any arrangement been made for early release of the Italian armistice terms?

THE PRESIDENT. I know nothing about it.

[4.] Q. Mr. President, have you—can you inform us at all, on this status of German war prisoners, as to when they will cease being prisoners? Have you any plans——

THE PRESIDENT. No, I can't.

Q. ——to make any statement on it?

THE PRESIDENT. No, I can't. I can't do anything about that until we have an established government in Germany.

Q. That might be for a generation.

THE PRESIDENT. Well, your guess is as good as mine. [*Laughter*]

[5.]   Q. Mr. President, a couple of weeks ago you told us you knew Hitler was dead, but you wouldn't give us very much detail about it. Can you give us any now?

THE PRESIDENT. Yes, I think I can tell you why I thought Hitler was dead. Himmler had told our Minister in Sweden, through the—I think Prince Bernadotte of Sweden—that Hitler had had a stroke and that he wouldn't have but 24 hours to live. And I understood that whenever Himmler said anybody had just 24 hours to live, that's about all—[*remainder of sentence inaudible*]. That's what I based my statement on.

Q. What—does it still hold true? Is that the way you think he died—when he died?

THE PRESIDENT. I don't know a thing about his death more than you do—only what I have seen in the papers.

Reporter: Thank you, Mr. President.

NOTE: President Truman's eighth news conference was held in his office at the White House at 4 p.m. on Wednesday, May 23, 1945.

41   Special Message to the Congress on the Organization of the Executive Branch. *May 24, 1945*

To the Congress of the United States:

The Congress has repeatedly manifested interest in an orderly transition from war to peace. It has legislated extensively on the subject, with foresight and wisdom.

I wish to draw the attention of the Congress to one aspect of that transition for which adequate provision has not as yet been made. I refer to the conversion of the Executive Branch of the Government.

Immediately after the declaration of war the Congress, in Title I of the First War Powers Act, 1941, empowered the President to make necessary adjustments in the organization of the Executive Branch with respect to those matters which relate to the conduct of the present war. This authority has been extremely valuable in furthering the prosecution of the war. It is difficult to conceive how the executive agencies could have been kept continuously attuned to the needs of the war without legislation of this type.

The First War Powers Act expires by its own terms six months after the termination of the present war. Pending that time, Title I will be of very substantial further value in enabling the President to make such additional temporary improvements in the organization of the Government as are currently required for the more effective conduct of the war.

However, further legislative action is required in the near future, because the First War Powers Act is temporary, and because, as matters now stand, every step taken under Title I will automatically revert, upon the termination of the Title, to the pre-existing status.

Such automatic reversion is not workable. I think that the Congress has recognized that fact, particularly in certain provisions of section 101 of the War Mobilization and Reconversion Act of 1944. In some instances it will be necessary to delay reversion beyond the period now provided by law, or to stay it permanently. In other instances it will be necessary to modify actions heretofore taken under Title I and to continue the resulting arrangement beyond the date of expiration of the Title. Automatic reversion will result in the re-establishment of some agencies that should not be re-established. Some adjustments of a permanent character need to be made, as exemplified by the current proposal before the Congress with respect to the subsidiary corporations of the Reconstruction Finance Corporation. Some improvements heretofore made in the Government under the First War Powers Act, as exemplified by the reorganization of the Army under Executive Order No. 9082, should not be allowed to revert automatically or at an inopportune time.

I believe it is realized by everyone—in view of the very large number of matters involved and the expedition required in their disposition— that the problems I have mentioned will not be met satisfactorily unless the Congress provides for them along the general lines indicated in this message.

Quite aside from the disposition of the war organization of the Government, other adjustments need to be made currently and continuously in the Government establishment. From my experience in the Congress, and from a review of the pertinent developments for a period of forty years preceding that experience, I know it to be a positive fact that, by and large, the Congress cannot deal effectively with numerous organizational problems on an individual item basis. The Congressional Record is replete with expressions of members of the Congress, themselves, to this effect. Yet it is imperative that these matters be dealt with continuously if the Government structure is to be reasonably wieldy and manageable, and be responsive to proper direction by the Congress and the President on behalf of the people of this country. The question is one that goes directly to the adequacy and effectiveness of our Government as an instrument of democracy.

Suitable reshaping of those parts of the Executive Branch of the Government which require it from time to time is necessary and desirable from every point of view. A well organized Executive Branch will be more efficient than a poorly organized one. It will help materially in making manageable the Government of this great nation. A number of my predecessors have urged the Congress to take steps to make the Executive Branch more business-like and efficient. I welcome and urge the cooperation of Congress to the end that these objectives may be attained.

Experience has demonstrated that if substantial progress is to be made in these regards, it must be done through action initiated or taken by the President. The results achieved under the Economy Act (1932), as amended, the Reorganization Act of 1939, and Title I of the First War Powers Act, 1941, testify to the value of Presidential initiative in this field.

Congressional criticisms are heard, not infrequently, concerning deficiencies in the Executive Branch of the Government. I should be less than frank if I failed to point out that the Congress cannot consistently advance such criticisms and at the same time deny the President the means of removing the causes at the root of such criticisms.

Accordingly, I ask the Congress to enact legislation which will make it possible to do what we all know needs to be done continuously and expeditiously with respect to improving the organization of the Executive Branch of the Government. In order that the purposes which I have in mind may be understood, the following features are suggested: (a) the legislation should be generally similar to the Reorganization Act of 1939, and part 2 of Title I of that Act should be utilized intact, (b) the legislation should be of permanent duration, (c) no agency of the Executive Branch should be exempted from the scope of the legislation, and (d) the legislation should be sufficiently broad and flexible to permit of any form of organizational adjustment, large or small, for which necessity may arise.

It is scarcely necessary to point out that under the foregoing arrangement (a) necessary action is facilitated because initiative is placed in the hands of the President, and (b) necessary control is reserved to the Congress since it may, by simple majority vote of the two Houses, nullify any action of the President which does not meet with its approval. I think, further, that the Congress recognizes that particular arrangement as its own creation, evolved within the Congress out of vigorous efforts and debate extending over a period of two years and culminating in the enactment of the Reorganization Act of 1939.

Therefore, bearing in mind what the future demands of all of us, I earnestly ask the Congress to enact legislation along the foregoing lines without delay.

HARRY S. TRUMAN

42 Special Message to the Congress on Unemployment Compensation. *May 28, 1945*

To the Congress of the United States:

The Congress and the Executive Branch of the Government have already moved to prepare the country for the difficult economic adjustments which the Nation will face during the transition from war to peace.

1. The Congress has created the Office of War Mobilization and Reconversion to coordinate the reconversion activities of all Federal agencies, and that Office has established basic reconversion policies.

2. Specific laws have been enacted by the Congress setting forth the

policies and providing the administrative machinery for contract termination, plant clearance, financial aid to business, and the disposition of surplus property.

3. Our military and civilian agencies have prepared themselves to expedite industrial reconversion and reemployment.

4. As part of an over-all program for returning veterans the GI Bill of Rights provides "readjustment allowances," weekly cash benefits to veterans until they are able to obtain jobs.

5. Congress has permitted business to carry back postwar losses against excess profits tax payments during the reconversion period.

6. Congress has established support prices for agricultural products so that farmers will be protected against a postwar collapse of income.

There remains, however, a major gap in our reconversion program: the lack of adequate benefits for workers temporarily unemployed during the transition from war to peace. I urge the Congress to close this gap.

I am confident that, with appropriate measures, we can avoid large-scale and lengthy unemployment during the transition period. However, some temporary unemployment is unavoidable, particularly when total demobilization becomes possible. Even if reconversion proceeds rapidly, no amount of planning can make jobs immediately available for all displaced personnel. We must provide maximum security to those who have given so fully of themselves on the fighting and production fronts. The transition from war to peace is part and parcel of the war and we cannot shirk our obligation to those temporarily unemployed through no fault of their own.

To produce what is needed for the Pacific war, we must appeal to the workers to accept and remain in jobs which they ultimately must lose when munitions production ceases. The Government has thus incurred a moral obligation to these workers and to those who have stuck faithfully to their posts in the past.

To fulfill this obligation, we must rely principally upon our existing system of unemployment insurance. However, the existing State laws embrace three major defects:

1. Only about 30 million of our 43 million non-agricultural workers

are protected by unemployment insurance. The absence of protection for Federal Government employees—in Navy Yards, arsenals and Government offices—is particularly inequitable, since these workers are subject to risks of unemployment similar to the risks of those who work for private employers. Lack of protection for employees in small establishments and for maritime workers also constitutes a serious shortcoming in the present programs.

2. The weekly benefit payments provided under many of the State laws are inadequate to maintain purchasing power and to provide a reasonable measure of economic security for the workers. Most States fix a maximum rate of $15 to $18 a week. This is clearly inadequate to protect unemployed workers against ruthless cuts in living standards, particularly if they have families.

3. The length of time for which benefits are paid is too short. In nearly one-third of the States, no worker can receive more than 16 weeks of benefits in any year, and many workers do not qualify even for this length of time.

Therefore, I recommend specifically that Congress take emergency action to widen the coverage of unemployment compensation and to increase the amount and duration of benefits—at least for the duration of the present emergency period of reconversion. Basically this can be accomplished only by amending the Social Security Act so as to induce State laws to provide more adequately for anyone who is unemployed.

To be sure, the States have large sums in the Unemployment Trust Fund. But since changes of State laws cannot be effected overnight, I propose that the Congress, during this emergency period, extend the coverage of unemployment compensation to include Federal employees, maritime workers, and other workers not now insured. Moreover, I see no feasible way to make benefits payable to such workers, unless they are financed entirely by the Federal Government during the present emergency. The benefits should appropriately be administered by the States.

I also recommend that Congress provide, through supplementary Federal emergency benefit payments, minimum standards for the weekly rate and duration of unemployment benefits. Every eligible worker should be entitled to 26 weeks of benefits in any one year, if his unemployment continues that long. The maximum payment, at least for the worker who has dependents, should be raised from present levels to not less than $25 per week. In this connection, Congress will no doubt wish to reexamine the readjustment allowance provisions of the GI Bill of Rights. All payments should be made through the existing unemployment compensation machinery of the several States, just as payments to veterans are now made.

These provisions are essential for the orderly reconversion of our wartime economy to peacetime production. They are badly needed for the duration of the reconversion emergency.

Decent unemployment benefits would serve as a bulwark against postwar deflation. By assuring workers of a definite income for a definite period of time, Congress will help materially to prevent a sharp decline in consumer expenditures which might otherwise result in a downward spiral of consumption and production. Adequate unemployment insurance is an indispensable form of prosperity insurance.

Congress will soon deal with the broader question of extending, expanding and improving our Social Security program, of which unemployment insurance is a part. Although such improvement is fundamental, congressional deliberations on the broad issues will take time. On the specific issue of unemployment benefits, we may not have time available. We are already entering the first phase of reconversion; we must be prepared immediately for the far larger problems of manpower displacement which will come with the end of the war in the Pacific.

I earnestly hope, therefore, that the appropriate Committees of Congress will undertake immediate consideration of the emergency problem.

Harry S. Truman

43 Letter Accepting Resignation of Stephen T. Early as Secretary to the President. *May 31, 1945*

Dear Steve:

I am very loath to see June first come around because, as you state in your very kind letter of the twenty-eighth, it means that you are definitely leaving your official post at the White House.

You know that it is no mere politeness for me to say that I hate to see you go. During these recent difficult weeks you have been such a help to me in getting acclimated to my new duties and responsibilities that I shall miss you very much—officially as well as personally. You have given me the benefit not only of your long experience in the White House, but of your innate wisdom and sound judgment; and I am sure that, without you, my task would have been much more difficult.

The quality and quantity of your work during the past twelve years are well known to all of us who have been in Washington. I know from the lips of President Roosevelt how much you meant to him, and how much he relied upon you. And I now know from personal experience how greatly your assistance, cooperation and association can lighten the burdens of high office.

I have been willing to let you go—but not without strings. You are to be subject to frequent calls to help me in many ways. You have been most gracious in offering whatever future help you can render; and I assure you that I shall take advantage of that offer to the fullest.

My best wishes go with you in your new venture and in anything you undertake.

Very sincerely yours,

HARRY S. TRUMAN

NOTE: Mr. Early served as Assistant Secretary from March 4, 1933, to July 1, 1937, and then as Secretary to June 1, 1945. His letter of resignation was released with the President's reply.

44   The President's News Conference of
  June 1, 1945

THE PRESIDENT. Well, I have got two short statements I want to read to you to start things off with.

[1.] [*Reading, not literally*]: "Secretary Morgenthau has told me about the shocking cases of tax evasion his men have discovered, and I am thoroughly in sympathy with his plan to enlarge the Bureau of Internal Revenue forces to whatever extent is required to insure full compliance with the law.[1]

"Yesterday, I acquainted the top officials of the Civil Service Commission with our special tax drive and the necessity for an accelerated program of recruitment. Arrangements have been made with the Civil Service Commission to have placed at every Army discharge center in the United States a qualified recruitment officer from the Civil Service Commission, fully versed in our recruitment requirements, who will steer to us the qualified veterans as they are discharged."[2]

I think there will be enough discharged veterans, probably, with the qualifications to meet this 10,000-man-program that Mr. Morgenthau is asking for.

It is a crime to—a terrible crime, in my opinion, to find these people who are hoarding money and living off the black markets, and things of that sort, when the sons of the rest of the population are out getting killed to save the country.

And we are going to try to put a stop to it.

I have another short statement I would like to make, with regard to prisoners of war.

[2.] [*Reading*]: "I wish to express my very deep sympathy for the

---

[1] At this point the statement, as released by the White House, continues as follows: "It will be good business for the Government, because every dollar we spend in collection and enforcement will produce $20 or more in revenue. And much more important is the matter of good morals. We are not fighting this war to make millionaires, and certainly we are not going to allow the black market operators or any other racketeers to be in a favored class, when the men in the armed forces, and our citizens generally, are sacrificing so heavily."

[2] The following final paragraph appears in the White House release of the statement: "The American people understand that sacrifices are necessary. They know the war is still far from being over. The one thing that might break down their will to keep on to complete victory would be a feeling that a few were profiting from the sacrifices of the many. We must see that there is no justification for any such feeling, and that is just what we are going to do."

relatives of those members of our armed forces who have the misfortune still to be held as prisoners of war by the enemy. The welfare of these men is a matter of deep concern to me, and I am determined to do everything possible to help them and to bring about their release as soon as possible.

"To this end, every effort is being made to get relief supplies and mail through to them. At the same time, definitive information is being sought concerning the names of those men who are still held as prisoners of war. The eventual liberation of these prisoners will be the result of the victory of our armed forces, and depends upon unrelenting prosecution of the war effort by every American."

These prisoners, of course, are the ones that are held by the Japanese. There are still a great many of our men who were captured in the Philippines, who are held in Manchuria and other places. We are trying our best to do what we can for them under the circumstances. And I hope we will really get something done for them.

Now, if you have any questions you want to ask, I will try to answer them.

[3.] Q. Mr. President, will you talk to us about universal military training this morning, and your views on it?

THE PRESIDENT. I have made a—I have had a conference on universal military training with some Members of the House and the Senate, and we are now trying to work out a policy on it. I would rather not discuss it at length this morning, although when I have the thing really in form, I will be glad to give it to you.

And I have got a few views on universal military training of my own, which don't agree with the Army, and don't agree with the Navy, and don't agree with the House or Senate, so I will try to get them in shape so that we will—. I would rather wait for another time and give you a complete statement on that.

[4.] Q. Mr. President, have you been receiving a great deal of mail on the subject of these war prisoners?

THE PRESIDENT. Yes, yes. We have received an enormous amount of mail. The House and Senate are receiving a lot of mail, particularly those Members of the House and Senate from the States where the men came from that were in the Philippines at the time the Japs got the Philippines.

[5.] Q. How about the Big Three meeting? Has it moved along any?

THE PRESIDENT. It is getting closer. It isn't yet definitely decided. But I think I can say definitely that it will take place in the not far distant future.

[6.] Q. Mr. President, you told us that Secretary Wickard's resignation would be effective when he was confirmed as REA Administrator. What will be the situation if the Senate rejects his nomination?

THE PRESIDENT. His term will end when the fiscal year ends, with the others.

[7.] Q. Can you tell us, sir, have you been following in the last 24 hours the Syrian controversy?

THE PRESIDENT. Yes. I have been following it for more than 24 hours.

Q. Have you been in communication with Prime Minister Churchill?

THE PRESIDENT. Yes. By wire.

Q. How recently, sir, could you tell us?

THE PRESIDENT. Well, every day. I had a message from him this morning, and a message I sent to him this morning; and yesterday, and the day before, and the day before that. We are in constant communication all the time.

Q. Does that mean by telephone?

THE PRESIDENT. No, no. By cable.

Q. Mr. President, have you any word that the French have agreed to Mr. Churchill's request?

THE PRESIDENT. The French have ceased firing as a result of the message which Mr. Churchill sent to De Gaulle, with the approval of the American Government.

Q. Have we had any message from the French?

THE PRESIDENT. None whatever. But the firing ceased, so I am reliably informed.

Q. Sir, has the American Government also given approval to the proposal for a tripartite meeting in London, to discuss this Syrian question?

THE PRESIDENT. No. I have not——

Q. Sir, some rather informal responses were given to us yesterday at the State Department, indicating that we would be interested in such a meeting.

THE PRESIDENT. I think we would, but there has been no arrangement for such a meeting officially. Not to me, at any rate.

Q. Mr. President, could you tell us what effect this Syrian crisis may have had on your plans to meet with General de Gaulle?

THE PRESIDENT. No, I don't think they have had any effect. There has been no definite date set for General de Gaulle's meeting.

[8.] Q. Mr. President, have you heard from Mr. Hopkins or Mr. Davies as to when they are likely to return?[1]

THE PRESIDENT. No. I haven't any definite date on that.

Q. Do you expect them soon?

THE PRESIDENT. Yes, I do.

Q. Could you——

THE PRESIDENT. But don't know just yet, of course,——

Q. That's what I was going to ask.

THE PRESIDENT. ——how soon; but I could say within a week or 10 days they will be back, I am sure.

[9.] Q. Was it planned for Justice Jackson to return at this time, or is it—his return a result of the fact that—

THE PRESIDENT. No. He expected to return at this time to finish up some—wind up some of his own business. He went over there for a preliminary meeting. He is expecting to return.

[10.] Q. Mr. President, have you had any conference with the leaders up on the Hill on the unemployment benefit program?

THE PRESIDENT. No, I haven't. No, I haven't.

Q. Do you expect to do anything of that kind?

THE PRESIDENT. I have had a conference with the Leaders of the House

---

[1] On May 23 the White House announced that the President had requested Harry Hopkins and Joseph E. Davies to undertake special missions for him. Mr. Hopkins, it was stated, would proceed to Moscow for conversations with Marshal Stalin on matters in discussion between the Governments of the Soviet Union and the United States. Mr. Davies, it was announced, would go to London to discuss with Prime Minister Churchill and other members of the British Government certain matters of common interest to the United States and Great Britain arising out of the war.

and Senate every Monday morning, and we will do it next Monday.

[11.] Q. Mr. President, there are reports from the Coast that indicate that the United Nations Conference might run on for a while yet. Do you—can you give us any light on that?

THE PRESIDENT. No. I don't think it will be unduly prolonged. I have been looking for it to end within the next 10 days.

[12.] Q. Mr. President, when Mayor Kelly of Chicago and Mayor LaGuardia of New York left Monday, they told us you talked about the civilian defense material that is around this country.

THE PRESIDENT. They talked to me about it. I have been giving it some consideration. We are trying to work out a policy and a plan for its disposal.

Q. That hasn't come to its conclusion?

THE PRESIDENT. That hasn't been worked out as yet. I think it will be worked out very shortly.

[13.] Q. Can you tell us about the resignation of Mr. Gillette from the Surplus Property office?

THE PRESIDENT. One of the first callers I had, after I came down here, was Senator Gillette; and he told me that he was not happy in his position and wanted to quit the Surplus Property Board. I asked him to stay on until I got more familiar with the situation, and he came up yesterday and told me that he would like to quit within the next month; in fact, not later than July 15.

[14.] Q. Mr. President, is it possible that the Big Three meeting will become a Big Four, or even a Big Five meeting?

THE PRESIDENT. The only meeting I have ever discussed has been a Big Three meeting.

Q. Is it possible, Mr. President, it may be held in this country?

THE PRESIDENT. There is a possibility, but I don't think it's very probable. [*Laughter*]

[15.] Q. Mr. President, despite your assertion last week regarding the State Department, there are persistent reports that we will have a new Secretary of State. Could you say anything on that?

THE PRESIDENT. I can't make it any more emphatic than I did last week.

[16.]   Q. Mr. President, can you tell us whether you will support, or are in sympathy with the Wagner-Dingell bill that was introduced, to expand social security?

THE PRESIDENT. I am in favor of the principal parts of it. In fact, I think I was one of the authors of that bill in the last Congress. I haven't studied the present draft of the bill, and I am not familiar with its details, but in principle I am for it.

[17.]   Q. Mr. President, getting back to the Big Three and the United Nations meeting, would a delay of a couple of weeks in concluding the United Nations Conference affect your plans for the Big Three meeting?

THE PRESIDENT. No. Not the slightest.

[18.]   Q. Mr. President, could you give—provide any more details about Mr. Hopkins's mission to Russia?

THE PRESIDENT. I will give you more details when Mr. Hopkins comes home.

Reporter: Thank you, Mr. President.

[*The President recalled the newsmen as they started to leave and continued the news conference.*]

THE PRESIDENT. Oh—Oh—I have got an announcement to make——

Voices: Just a minute—just a minute!

[19.]   THE PRESIDENT. I forgot something. I have persuaded Sam Rosenman to stay with me for another year, and I am very happy that he is going to do it.

Q. What will be his job?

THE PRESIDENT. The same as he has always had.

Q. Special Assistant, sir?

THE PRESIDENT. Special Assistant to the President.

Q. Thank you.

[20.]   THE PRESIDENT. Oh, yes. I am releasing a message to the Congress this morning, which will have—[*laughter*]—a summary on the war. It will be released at noon. Read that summary very carefully. You can't read the message, it's too thick! [*Laughter*]

NOTE: President Truman's ninth news conference was held in his office at the White House at 10:40 a.m. on Friday, June 1, 1945.

45 Special Message to the Congress on Winning the War
    With Japan. *June 1, 1945*

To the Congress of the United States:

The primary task facing the Nation today is to win the war in Japan —
to win it completely and to win it as quickly as possible. For every
day by which it is shortened means a saving of American lives.

No one can recount the success of the forces of decency in this war
without thinking of the one man who was more responsible for victory
than any other single human being—Franklin D. Roosevelt.

Under his guidance, this great Nation grew to be the most powerful
military force in all history.

Under his leadership, the Allied strategy was developed which broke
down Hitler's fortress, crumbled Germany itself into ruins and unconditional surrender, and has brought us within striking distance of
Tokyo.

But there can be no peace in the world until the military power of
Japan is destroyed—with the same completeness as was the power of
the European dictators.

To do that, we are now engaged in a process of deploying millions of
our armed forces against Japan in a mass movement of troops and
supplies and weapons over 14,000 miles—a military and naval feat
unequalled in all history.

I think it appropriate at this time to inform the Congress and my
countrymen of some of the problems, difficulties, and dangers which
confront us in finishing this war—and how we expect to meet them.

Those who have the heavy responsibility of directing the Nation's
military efforts do not underestimate the difficulties of crushing an
enemy defended by vast distances and animated by desperate fanaticism.

And yet, we have adopted what is a new development in military
history. In the face of a conflict with a numerous and fanatical enemy
we have undertaken during the next twelve months to discharge approximately two million of the best soldiers the world has ever seen.

The program for the defeat of Germany was accomplished with an
accuracy seldom attained in war—yet we had but little margin at the

finish. On April 1, 1945, the last American division to arrive in France entered the battle line.

The strategy of the war in Europe was to have all the men that could be effectively deployed on land and sea to crush the German military machine in the shortest possible time.

That is exactly what we plan to do to Japan.

———————

Up to the time of the collapse of Germany the United States Navy, under the superb leadership of Fleet Admiral King, was carrying on two great campaigns thousands of miles apart from each other—one in the Atlantic and one in the Pacific.

These campaigns were distinctly different. The Atlantic campaign consisted essentially of anti-submarine and amphibious operations. Even as the war nears the end, our Navy had to cope with a submarine blitz which was intended to hit our coast in April.

The Pacific campaign has involved to a major degree all the surface, air, amphibious, and submarine aspect of Naval warfare; but anti-submarine operations have played only a subordinate role.

At one time in 1943, the United States Navy was employing over 1100 planes in its anti-submarine warfare in the Atlantic; and, in mid 1944, over 900 ocean-going escort vessels.

All of our escort vessels have been, or will be, sent to the Pacific, except for a very few to be retained in the Atlantic for training purpose or to meet any remotely possible emergency.

Our Navy, in addition to the miraculous job of convoying our endless stream of men and materials to Europe, did its full share, under over-all British naval command, in amphibious operations in that theatre. The use of its landing craft and carriers, and the fire support of its battleships, cruisers, and destroyers, made possible the landings in North Africa in 1942, in Sicily and Italy in 1943, and in Normandy and southern France in 1944.

Even before the invasion of France, some of our Atlantic naval force had already been sent to the Pacific. After our troops were firmly established ashore, fighting ships were moved to the Pacific as rapidly as they could be released from the requirements of the European and Mediterranean theatres and from anti-submarine warfare. The Japanese have already felt the presence of those ships—and will continue to feel it more and more.

In the Pacific the naval campaign has gone through four major phases.

The first was the defensive of 1941 and of the first half of 1942, when we fought in the Philippines and the East Indies, in the Coral Sea, at Midway and in the Aleutians.

The second was the offensive-defensive in late 1942 at Guadalcanal.

The third was the limited offensive in 1943 when we advanced slowly through the Solomons and re-took the Aleutians.

The fourth was the full offensive of 1944 and 1945 when the forces of the Southwest Pacific Area under General of the Army MacArthur and those of the Central Pacific Area under Fleet Admiral Nimitz made their great seaborne sweeps to the Philippines and Okinawa.

During this time the Navy has fought four full-scale sea battles; the Coral Sea, Midway, the Philippine Sea last summer off Saipan, and the three-pronged Battle for Leyte Gulf last October.

The Japanese surface Navy has now been reduced to a fraction of its former self. We have driven their ships into hiding and their naval aircraft back to their shore bases.

A large part of this success is due to our present carrier-based air power, which has permitted us to carry forward, for many hundreds of miles at a time, the air cover that is needed for a successful amphibious attack. The carriers that made possible these enormous strides were laid down in 1940—a year and a half before we entered the war. Had they not been started then, our fast advances in the Pacific could not have occurred until much later.

The Japanese merchant marine, in spite of a large program of building, has now been reduced to less than a quarter of its pre-war size. In fact we have sunk more Japanese merchant tonnage than they had at the time of Pearl Harbor.

For this and for the reduction of the Japanese Navy, we can thank our submarines, our Army and Navy shore-based aircraft, and our fast carrier task forces. Today, no enemy ship can proceed between Japan and her southern conquests without running the most serious risk.

The outstanding feature of the Pacific war—the one which sets it apart from all previous wars—has been the number of the amphibious operations.

We have constructed a great fleet of special vessels for this purpose: attack transports, attack cargo ships, landing ships and landing craft. These ships make it possible to put troops and equipment ashore on open beaches in the minimum of time.

The Navy has a great share in every amphibious attack. For instance, one attack which involved landing 45,000 troops required the use of 125,000 naval personnel. In general it may be said it takes two to three sailors to put one soldier or Marine ashore. It takes half a million tons of naval shipping for each division in an amphibious operation.

The Navy is now engaged in a series of grim tasks: a battle of attrition with the Japanese Air Force in the waters around Japan and Okinawa; a tightening of the blockade of Japan; redeploying its own forces from Europe; aiding the Army to redeploy; and preparing for the climactic operations yet to come.

As we approach the enemy's homeland, the density of his air power naturally becomes greater and greater. A year and a half ago, the enemy had more than 5000 operating airplanes to guard perhaps eighteen million square miles of area. We could attack wherever we saw that the defense was thinly spread. Since then, we have reduced his total air power very much, but the area he is now forced to defend has been shrunk so much more quickly by our rapid advance, that the density of his air power is four or five times as great as it was.

This means tough fighting in the air. It means the loss of ships. It means damaged ships that must be replaced or brought back thousands of miles for repair.

We at home can hardly imagine either the delirium of Japanese suicide attacks on our troops, airfields and ships, or the heroism of our men in meeting them. As we approach the main islands of the enemy the damage to our ships and the loss of our men are becoming more severe.   In the future we shall have to expect more damage rather than less.

In carrying out its future tasks the Navy will need not only all of its present great fleets, it will need additional vessels.   These vessels are now being built—partly to replace anticipated losses in future operations and partly to reinforce the fleet for the final operations it will have to conduct in enemy home waters.

The Navy is deploying all but a handful of its men from Europe to the Pacific.   But unlike the Army, the Navy, after the collapse of Germany, did not have a surplus of personnel.   There cannot be even a partial naval demobilization—until the Japanese are defeated.

The Navy still needs civilian laborers, particularly in the yards where ships are repaired.   Working continuously under the concentrated air effort of the enemy, the fleet suffers daily damage.   Many vessels have come back wounded in varying degree.   To tell the number would give information to the enemy but the number is substantial.   The Navy must get these ships back into the fight with the least possible delay.

We have in our Navy yards the machinery and mechanical equipment to deal with the mounting load of battle damage.   But civilian workers are needed now in ever increasing numbers.   I know that the patriotic workers of the nation will rally to the aid of the Navy in this emergency as they have rallied in past emergencies.   For they know that every day saved in getting a damaged ship back into service shortens the war and saves American lives.

In the air, we have shown what America can do with land-based planes and with carrier-based planes—in strategic bombing and in tactical bombing.

We are now able in Germany to investigate and examine the results of our strategic bombing.   In spite of the most desperate resistance of the Luftwaffe and in spite of murderous barrages from anti-aircraft guns, the American and British Air Forces smashed at German industry day after day and night after night until its support of the German armies caved in.

Our strategic bombardment did a complete and masterly job of destroying the sources of strength of the German Air Force and the German military machine. Our bombers dried up the flow of vital oil and gasoline supplies not only to the German Air Force, but to the rest of the German Army and to German industry as well.

We have had experience too—deadly experience for the Nazis—with our tactical air forces as distinguished from strategic bombing. They wrecked the bridges and roads, the railroads and canals on which the German army counted. Germany's best panzer divisions—entire Army Corps, in fact—were immobilized.

The air force of Japan is not as strong an opponent as the Luftwaffe. Japanese industry is neither as great nor as scattered as Germany's. The planes we are using and will continue to use against Japan will be larger in size and more powerful in action than our bombers in Europe.

Our Army planes and our Navy ships and planes are now driving Japan out of the air, and when our strategic air force reaches the Pacific in full might it will demolish the enemy's resources of production. Our strategic bombardment of Japan is now well beyond its initial phase. The missions of the Twentieth Air Force are mounting in size and intensity. Substantial portions of Japan's key industrial centers have been levelled to the ground in a series of record incendiary raids. What has already happened to Tokyo will happen to every Japanese city whose industries feed the Japanese war machine. I urge Japanese civilians to leave those cities if they wish to save their lives.

Our tactical air forces, experienced and battle-wise, will soon be ranging over the Japanese homeland from nearby bases.

The Japanese air force will be shattered by our Army and Navy fliers as surely and relentlessly as the Luftwaffe. The concentration of Japanese industry, so long an advantage, will now contribute materially to Japan's downfall.

The Army Air Forces began its redeployment last December when a heavy bomber group returned to this country from Europe, and received B–29 training before moving to the Pacific. The following month a B–25 medium bomber group came to this country and pro-

88

ceeded, after training, to fly A–26 attack bombers against the Japanese.

During the last month twenty bombardment groups have received orders to move from Europe to the Far East by way of the United States.

———————

Our ground armies, our corps and our divisions have followed the best traditions of the American soldier for courage and skill; and their leadership has been of the uniformly high quality which results in victory.

The United States has been fortunate in having as the Chief of Staff to the Commander in Chief of the Army and Navy a man of so great experience and ability as Fleet Admiral Leahy.

We have also been fortunate in having at the head of our land and air forces men like General Marshall, General Eisenhower, General MacArthur and General Arnold. They have provided the inspiration and the leadership for all our Army operations.

The American soldier of this war is as brave and as magnificent as the American soldier has always been. He has the initiative and ingenuity he has always had. But in this war he is a better soldier and a more successful soldier than he has ever been before. For in this war he has gone into battle better trained, better equipped, and better led than ever before.

In the face of the formidable Nazi hordes which had secured a stranglehold on Western Europe, our armies, shoulder to shoulder with those of our Allies, forced a landing on the shores of France. In the short space of eleven months they drove the enemy from France, Belgium, Luxembourg and Holland and forced him to unconditional surrender in the heart of his own homeland.

To the south our troops and those of the Allies wrested North Africa from the Axis, fought a dogged advance through Italy from Sicily to the Alps, and pinned down a force that otherwise could have brought substantial aid to the enemy on the eastern and western fronts.

The heroism of our own troops in Europe was matched by that of the armed forces of the nations that fought by our side. They and

the brave men in the underground movements of the occupied countries—all gave their blood to wipe the Nazi terror from the face of the
earth. They absorbed the blows of the German military machine
during the many months in which we were building up our expedi-
tionary forces, and they shared to the full in the ultimate destruction
of the enemy.

The same courage and skill which brought about the downfall of the
Nazis are being displayed by our soldiers now fighting in the Pacific.
Many of them are veterans of the grim months following Pearl Harbor.

Since 1942 our Army troops and Marines in the south Pacific have
thrown the enemy back from his furthermost advances in New Guinea
and the Solomons, have traveled 1500 miles up the New Guinea coast-
line, have conquered the Admiralty Islands, Biak and Morotai. Meanwhile, Marines and Army troops have been cleaning up in the Solomons
and the Palaus. In October of last year these magnificent achievements
culminated in the landing of our troops in Leyte. Four months later
they freed Manila.

Westward across the Central Pacific other Marines and Army units,
in hard fought battles, have forced the Japanese back four thousand
miles. Tarawa, Kwajalein, Saipan, Guam, Iwo Jima have been the
stepping stones. Today Army and Marine divisions are slowly but
steadily sweeping the Japanese from Okinawa.

All of our campaigns in Europe and in the Pacific have depended on
long lines of communications and upon quantities of supply unheard
of in prior warfare. One of the marvels of Allied achievements has
been the organization, guarding and operation of these world-girdling
supply lines.

For this we have to thank management and labor in our war industries, our farmers and miners and other Americans—who produced the
equipment and supplies for ourselves and our Allies; the gallant members of our Merchant Marine—who transported them overseas under
the guns of our Navy; and the men of our Army Service Forces—upon
whose work in clearing ports, rushing up supplies, and constructing

roads, railroads, bridges, highways, and gasoline pipe lines, the fate of battle often depended.

There are also included in our experience in this war miracles of saving human life as well as miracles of destruction of the enemy. Since the invasion of Africa in November, 1942, in all our operations in Europe and in Africa, we have lost about 1600 soldiers from sickness. In the Civil War the Union forces, never more than a third as large as our forces in Europe, had 224,000 deaths from sickness. In the three years since April, 1942, the Army forces in the disease-infected islands of the Pacific lost fewer than 1400 men from sickness.

Surgery in this war has reduced the percentage of death from wounds in the Army from 8.25% in the last war to 4% in this one. This is due to many factors: the high professional skill of the surgeons and nurses, the availability of blood and blood plasma, penicillin and other new miracles of medicine; the devotion of the Medical Corps men who rescue the wounded under fire, the advanced position of surgical staffs right up behind the front lines.

Shifting our ground and air strength from Europe to the Far East presents transportation problems even greater and more complicated than those involved in the initial deployment of our forces to all parts of the world. Millions of men and millions of tons of supplies must be moved half way around the globe.

The movement of troops from Europe has been swift in getting under way. They are coming by ship and they are coming by air. Every day the process of transfer gains momentum.

After the first World War—when the only problem was getting men home and there was no bitter, powerful enemy left to fight—it took nearly a year to complete the evacuation of 1,933,156 men. This time the Army Transportation Corps and the Air Transport Command plan to move 3,000,000 troops out of Europe before a year passes.

It is not easy to visualize the volume of supplies that must precede, accompany, and follow the soldiers going from Europe and the United States into the Pacific. To maintain our forces in Europe the Army shipped across the Atlantic 68 million tons of equipment and food—nearly eight times the total shipped in all the first World War.

Now we must reclaim all of this equipment that is still serviceable. We must supplement it with new production. And we must make shipments of comparable size to the Pacific over supply lanes which are three times as long as those to Europe.

The initial requirement of equipment for each man fighting against Japan is about six tons and an additional ton is needed each month for maintenance.

Finding the ships to transport these supplies is not the only difficulty. We must continue to develop in the Pacific new harbors and bases out of practically nothing, install roads and build power systems.

Great as these problems of redeployment are, we are not losing sight of the human aspect in shifting men from one side of the world to the other. Wherever it can be done without slowing down the pace of our projected operations in the Pacific, we are deploying our soldiers by way of the United States so that they may have a chance to visit their homes and loved ones before they go on to tackle the Japanese.

On the basis of present estimates, only a small fraction of the men now in Europe will have to go directly to the Far East without first stopping off at home.

The remainder of our present European force will go to the Pacific through the United States, will be assigned to necessary military duties in this country, will be discharged, or will be kept in Europe for occupation duty. Most of those who will go directly to the Pacific are in supply and service units whose presence in the new theater is essential to the immediate construction of harbors, bases, communications and airfields—from which to step up our blows against Japan.

The Army is mindful that those who come through this country want to get home with the least possible delay once their ship docks or their plane lands. Everything is geared for speed to accomplish this at the air and sea ports. Within twenty-four hours in most cases they are aboard a train at government expense bound for one of the nineteen Army Personnel Centers, where the men immediately eligible for discharge are separated from those who are destined for further service.

Men who are to remain on active duty are promptly "ordered" home from the Personnel Center at government expense, for a period up to thirty days, plus travel time, for rest and recuperation.

The period spent at home is not charged against the man's furlough time nor is it classed as leave of absence. It is "temporary duty", and the soldier draws full pay for the period. His only instructions are to have the best time he knows how until he reports back to the Personnel Center. That is what I mean when I say that we have not forgotten the human side of redeployment.

Relatives and friends of servicemen can do their part in this program by not crowding around the ports and personnel Centers through which the men pass. The men will get home as soon as is humanly possible. Troop movements on the nation's railroads will become increasingly heavy from now on. I ask for full public cooperation in preventing any aggravation of this burden on domestic transportation, for it would slow down the rate at which soldiers can be reunited with their loved ones.

At the same time as we step up the movement of men and munitions to the Far East, we have been exerting every effort to increase the number of ships available to return men to this country for discharge.

Three hundred and sixteen cargo ships are being converted to help soldiers get out of Europe faster. They are not the most luxurious ships ever seen, but they will get the men home. In addition, the British are letting us use their three proudest passenger liners—the Queen Elizabeth, the Queen Mary and the Aquitania.

These, added to fifty of our own transport vessels, eight hundred bombers and transport planes, and such ships as we are able to use out of the German merchant fleet, will make it possible to bring men home for discharge without interfering with the main job of transferring troops and equipment to the war against Japan.

The Army's system for selecting the soldiers for release to civilian life represents a democratic and fair approach to this most difficult problem. A poll was taken among enlisted men in all parts of the world. They were asked what factors they believed should be taken into consideration in deciding who should be released from the Army first. More than 90 per cent said that preference should go to those who had been overseas and in combat longest, and to those with children.

The Army spent two years developing a program of point credits designed to carry out these views expressed by the soldiers. It checked and rechecked its program, and made comprehensive surveys in order to make sure that the plan would achieve the objectives.

The system applies equally to the members of our Army in all parts of the world. It embodies the principle of impartial selection that we applied in drafting our citizen Army and that we shall continue to apply in meeting the manpower requirements of our armed forces until Japan is defeated.

By reducing the strength of the Army from 8,300,000 to 6,968,000 and by maintaining the Army calls on Selective Service at a level substantially higher than requirements for actual replacements, it will be possible to restore to their homes during the next year a total of two million officers and men, including those who will leave because of wounds, sickness, age and other specific causes, as well as those who will leave under the point system.

To accomplish this while continuing to be liberal in the deferment of men thirty years of age and over, it is the Administration's policy to induct all non-veterans under thirty years of age who can be replaced and who can qualify for the armed forces. Many of such men who have thus far been irreplaceable will become available for induction when the plants in which they are working are cut back or when they can be replaced from time to time by cutback-production workers and returning veterans.

In the three weeks since the point system became effective 2500 officers and 33,000 enlisted men and women from every theater of war have received final discharge papers at Army Separation Centers. During June, 50,000 high-score men are scheduled to leave Europe for this country, and 33,000 are scheduled to come from the Pacific and Asia. The great majority of these, a few days after they arrive, will be civilians again.

Let no one be under the delusion that these discharges are being authorized because the war is nearing an end or because we feel the Japanese are easy to beat. They are being made because our military leaders believe that we can reduce the overall strength of our Army at this time without jeopardy to our cause in the Pacific or to the lives of the men fighting there.

The Joint Chiefs of Staff, after consultation with General MacArthur and Admiral Nimitz, have decided that our Army can deliver its heaviest blows in the Pacific and win final victory most quickly with a strength which a year from now will be about seven million.

By maintaining our Army at this size, we shall be able to more than double the force we now have in the Pacific and hurl against the Japanese an overseas force larger than the 3,500,000 men who united with our Allies to crush the Wehrmacht and the Luftwaffe.

These are the men who will be carrying the fight to the enemy, but obviously they cannot operate effectively unless there are adequate reserve troops in training in the United States, and also an adequate base from which our advance troops can be supplied and serviced.

It is our plan that every physically fit soldier in the United States who has not yet served overseas be assigned to foreign duty when he completes his training or, if he is fulfilling an essential administrative or service job, as soon as he can be replaced by a returning veteran. This has been the Army's policy since the beginning of the war. It will be rigidly adhered to in the redeployment period.

If it were not for the overwhelming ascendancy established by our air and fleet units, we should have to send many more men to the Pacific than we now intend. The Japanese have more than four million troops under arms—a force larger than the Germans were ever able to put against us on the Western Front. To back up this Army, they have several million additional men of military age who have not yet been called to the colors. We have not yet come up against the main strength of this Japanese military force. The Japanese army is organized into 100 combat divisions. Its air force, despite the heavy losses it has suffered, still comprises over 3,000 combat planes. We are cutting heavily into Japanese aircraft production through our Superfortress raids, but Japan remains capable of producing planes at the rate of 1,250 to 1,500 a month.

Army casualties on Okinawa from March 18 to May 29 totaled 3,603 killed and missing and 14,661 wounded. The Marines in the same period reported 1,880 dead and missing and 8,403 wounded. Navy and Coast Guard losses were 4,729 killed and missing and 4,640 wounded, an overall total for all services of 10,221 killed and missing and 27,704 wounded. Japanese deaths were nearly six times as great as our own. On May 29, the total of Japanese killed on Okinawa was 61,066.

That is an example of the increasing toughness of this war as our troops get closer to Tokyo.

It is this kind of fighting we must be prepared for in our future campaigns. All of our experience indicates that no matter how hard we hit the enemy from the air or from the sea, the foot soldier will still have to advance against strongly entrenched and fanatical troops, through sheer grit and fighting skill, backed up by all the mechanical superiority in flamethrowers, tanks and artillery we can put at his disposal. There is no easy way to win.

Our military policy for the defeat of Japan calls for:

(1) Pinning down the Japanese forces where they now are and keeping them divided so that they can be destroyed piece by piece.

(2) Concentrating overwhelming power on each segment which we attack.

(3) Using ships, aircraft, armor, artillery and all other materiel in massive concentrations to gain victory with the smallest possible loss of life.

(4) Applying relentless and increasing pressure to the enemy by sea, air and on the land, so that he cannot rest, reorganize or regroup his battered forces or dwindling supplies to meet our next attack.

Of course the differences between the war in Europe and the war in the Pacific will cause differences in war production. The composition of the army will be different, as will the equipment issued to troops. There will be changes in strategic plans and in replacement factors.

Until the expanded pipelines for the Pacific war are filled, and until equipment arrives in substantial amounts from the European theatre, war production must continue at a high rate.

The Navy program will continue on an even keel.

There has been a sharp reduction in the program of the Army Air Forces.

Similar sharp cuts in the program of supplies for our ground troops are now being put into effect. Some new items of equipment will be added. The emphasis will be shifted in others.

Thus, there will be a decreased production in heavy artillery, artillery ammunition, trucks, tanks and small arms.

There will be increased production in aircraft bombs, atabrine, steel barges, wire and insect screening cloth, combat boots, cotton uniforms, amphibious trucks, raincoats, distillation units, radio relay units, special railway equipment, and motorized shop equipment.

In a number of important items there will be little change in demand for an indefinite period. These include food, clothing, petroleum products, lumber, and certain chemicals. It is likely that all these will remain on the critical list. Leather is tight. So are textiles. There is a shortage of cotton duck and fabrics for clothing. The food problem has been accentuated by the steadily increasing numbers the Army has been called upon to feed.

Accordingly, production for the Japanese war cannot be taken as a matter of course. It will require a high percentage of our resources.

War Production Board Chairman Krug has stated that during the balance of this year, our munitions production will run at an annual rate of $54,000,000,000, which is almost equal to the rate of 1943, and more than nine-tenths the rate during the peak of 1944.

With these production objectives before us, we must not slacken our support of the men who are now preparing for the final assault on Japan. War production remains the paramount consideration of our national effort.

————————

These then are our plans for bringing about the unconditional surrender of Japan. If the Japanese insist on continuing resistance beyond the point of reason, their country will suffer the same destruction as Germany. Our blows will destroy their whole modern industrial plant and organization, which they have built up during the past century and which they are now devoting to a hopeless cause.

We have no desire or intention to destroy or enslave the Japanese people. But only surrender can prevent the kind of ruin which they have seen come to Germany as a result of continued, useless resistance.

The job ahead for this Nation is clear.

We are faced with a powerful Japanese military machine. These are the same Japanese who perpetrated the infamous attack on Pearl Harbor three and one-half years ago; they are the same Japanese who ordered the death march from Bataan; they are the same Japanese who carried out the barbarous massacres in Manila.

They now know that their dreams of conquest are shattered. They no longer boast of dictating peace terms in Washington.

This does not mean, however, that the Japanese have given up hope. They are depending on America tiring of this war—becoming weary of the sacrifices it demands. They hope that our desire to see our soldiers and sailors home again and the temptation to return to the comforts and profits of peace will force us to settle for some compromise short of unconditional surrender.

They should know better.

They should realize that this Nation, now at the peak of its military strength, will not relax, will not weaken in its purpose.

We have the men, the materiel, the skill, the leadership, the fortitude to achieve total victory.

We have the Allies who will help us to achieve it. We are resolute in our determination—we will see the fight through to a complete and victorious finish.

To that end, with the help of God, we shall use every ounce of our energy and strength.

HARRY S. TRUMAN

46 Letter Declining To Accept Resignation of Samuel I. Rosenman as Special Counsel to the President.
June 1, 1945

Dear Sam:

I am finally taking action on your letter of resignation dated April 14, 1945. I am declining to accept it.

I understand fully your wish to retire to private life. President Roosevelt told me that you had forcibly expressed such a desire to him several times since last November, but that he had refused to let you go. The reasons which moved him are the same as those which now prompt this action by me.

The self-effacing zeal and patriotic devotion with which you have served your country and your President in recent years cannot yet be spared. I know the kind of work which you have been doing for the Chief Executive day in and day out during that time—seldom, if ever, with any public credit or acclaim.

And yet I know not only from President Roosevelt, but from my own personal experience during these recent months, how much your efforts have meant to the Chief Executive and to the welfare of our country. Some day when accurate history is written, you will receive the credit which is due you.

I want you to stay at your post at least until V–J Day in order that I may have your continued assistance.

Very sincerely yours,

HARRY S. TRUMAN

[The Honorable Samuel I. Rosenman, The White House]

NOTE: Judge Rosenman's letter of resignation was released with the President's reply.

47 Citation Accompanying Presentation of the Legion of Merit to Prince Abdul Ilah of Iraq. *June 1, 1945*

CITATION FOR THE LEGION OF MERIT
DEGREE OF CHIEF COMMANDER

DURING the course of the present war His Royal Highness, Prince Abdul Ilah, Commander-in-Chief, Field Marshal of the Iraqi Army, Regent and Heir Apparent to the Throne of Iraq, has never wavered in his loyalty to the cause of the United Nations. In combating enemy efforts to create misunderstanding and hostility against the Allied Nations among the peoples of the Near East, he has risked his life and position without hesitation.

By his loyal and steadfast devotion to the Allied cause he has contributed materially to the success of the war effort of the United Nations.

NOTE: The President read the citation to Prince Abdul Ilah and presented him with the Legion of Merit, Degree of Chief Commander, at a ceremony in the White House.

48 Letter to the Chairman, House Civil Service Committee, Concerning Reduction in Hours of Work. *June 1, 1945*

Dear Mr. Congressman:

It is my understanding that your Committee, in connection with the Overtime Pay provisions of H.R. 2497, has expressed an interest in learning about the plans of the executive branch for reductions in hours of work.

Within the near future I intend to advise the heads of the departments and agencies that whenever they have offices which are located in labor market areas classified in Groups II, III, and IV by the War Manpower Commission they may reduce the hours of work from 48 per week.

Very sincerely yours,

HARRY S. TRUMAN

[The Honorable Robert Ramspeck, Chairman, Civil Service Committee, House of Representatives]

49   Statement by the President on the Continued Need for
     Food. *June 2, 1945*

IN THIS FOURTH YEAR of war the need for every ounce of food
which the American people can produce and preserve is greater than
ever before.

The supply lines to feed our troops and the millions fighting and
working with them are the longest in the history of warfare. Along
the thousands of miles of these lines, food must be kept moving. Our
soldiers in Europe are eating more canned fruits and vegetables because
they are changing from combat rations to regular meals.

Beyond our tremendous military requirements lies the task of working with other nations to help liberated peoples regain their strength
and rebuild their countries. There can be no lasting peace in a hungry
world.

We Americans must do our part to help swell the nation's food
supply.

I call upon every American to help discharge this obligation in every
way possible:

By growing a victory garden—whether it be in the backyard, in a
community or company employe plot, or on the farm. There is still
plenty of time to plant in most parts of the country.

By dedicating ourselves to growing larger and better gardens and
seeing them through to the harvest.

By preserving our food at home or in a community canning center.
Civilian supplies of commercially canned fruits and vegetables are now
at the lowest point of the war, and next winter will be one-fourth less
than last year.

By conserving food in every possible way—wasting not an ounce. In
anything so hazardous and difficult as growing food, we cannot afford
to take chances. We must always reckon with the weather, which in
some parts of the country delayed plantings and damaged some fruit
crops. We must plan for maximum production.

With millions of American men and women dedicated to this task,
our food will make a real contribution to the final victory and the peace.

50   Letter to the Speaker of the House of Representatives on
     the Defense Aid Program.   *June 4, 1945*

The Speaker of the House of Representatives:

I have the honor to transmit for the consideration of the Congress
an estimate of appropriation for defense aid for the fiscal year 1946,
exclusive of aid authorized to be transferred by the War and Navy
Departments and the Maritime Commission, as follows:

Defense Aid........................... $1, 975, 000, 000

This recommended appropriation, together with unobligated balances
of about $2,400,000,000 from the current year, will provide a total pro-
gram of $4,375,000,000. Since Germany has been defeated, the proposed
new program of defense aid and the appropriation required are less
than for the current year. This program, however, reflects our resolution to give fully effective aid in order to shorten the war and thereby
reduce the cost in allied lives and materials.

The war against Japan, like the war against Germany, is a cooperative allied effort. Through lend-lease and reverse lend-lease we shall
continue to pool our resources with those of our allies so that the crushing weight of our combined might may be thrown against our remaining enemy. Where lend-lease funds will make the efforts of our allies
more effective, we shall use them. Where the redeployment of our
troops from Europe or our control over enemy areas require aid from
other nations, lend-lease will be available to enable their maximum participation. Similarly, through reverse lend-lease we can expect our
allies to give us all the assistance possible.

In the light of changed war conditions, a preliminary review of lend-
lease assistance to individual nations has been made. Further review
will be necessary from time to time in the coming year as the war
progresses and the needs and the wartime roles of our allies vary. For
this reason any programs proposed must be considered as most tentative.

Our recent lend-lease agreements with France, Belgium and the
Netherlands will be carried out by lend-lease funds to the fullest extent
consistent with changed war conditions and the basic wartime purposes
of lend-lease aid. Beyond this I propose that these allies be assisted in

financing necessary equipment and supplies by the Export-Import Bank.

Such assistance is consistent with the enlarged role which the Bank should be given in providing certain types of industrial equipment and supplies which other nations may wish to obtain from us for reconstruction. Some aspects of reconstruction are of particular interest to this nation and can most appropriately be financed by our own instrumentality.

Accordingly there will be transmitted to the Congress at an early date, a proposal providing for adequate legal authorization and expanded lending capacity for the Bank.

The lend-lease and Export-Import Bank programs represent unilateral efforts of this country. They are not intended to duplicate the work of international agencies.

The United Nations Relief and Rehabilitation Administration, for example, has been created to meet the more immediate needs of relief and rehabilitation where nations are unable to meet their needs from their own resources. Legislation is now before the Congress to allow participation by the United States in the International Bank for Reconstruction and Development and the International Monetary Fund. This legislation merits early consideration and approval.

In contrast to these devices, however, lend-lease is a positive weapon of waging war. The appropriation estimate herein submitted provides for its full use to bring the conflict with Japan to a quick and decisive end.

The details of the defense aid estimate are set forth in the letter of the Director of the Bureau of the Budget, transmitted herewith, in whose observations and recommendations I concur.

Respectfully yours,

HARRY S. TRUMAN

NOTE: The letter from the Director of the Bureau of the Budget, dated June 1, 1945, and also released, is printed with the message in House Document 224 (79th Cong., 1st sess.).

51 Letter to the Chairman, House Rules Committee,
    Concerning the Committee on Fair Employment
    Practice. *June 5, 1945*

Dear Mr. Congressman:

I understand that the House Appropriations Committee has deleted
from the War Agencies Appropriation Bill for the fiscal year beginning
July 1, 1945, all appropriations for the Fair Employment Practice
Committee.

This action will have the effect of abolishing the Committee and
terminating its work without giving the Members of the House of
Representatives an opportunity to vote on the question.

The Fair Employment Practice Committee was originally established
before the attack upon us at Pearl Harbor, and was an integral part of
our defense production program. It has continued since then in one
form or another; and has grown steadily in importance. Its work
has been based on the principle that the successful prosecution of the
war demands the participation of all available workers regardless of
race, creed or color, and that the policy of the United States was to
encourage all such persons to full participation in the war effort.

The war is not over. In fact a bitter and deadly conflict lies ahead
of us. To abandon at this time the fundamental principle upon which
the Fair Employment Practice Committee was established is un-
thinkable.

Even if the war were over, or nearly over, the question of fair employment practices during the reconversion period and thereafter would
be of paramount importance. Discrimination in the matter of employment against properly qualified persons because of their race, creed,
or color is not only un-American in nature, but will lead eventually to
industrial strife and unrest. It has a tendency to create substandard
conditions of living for a large part of our population. The principle
and policy of fair employment practice should be established permanently as a part of our national law.

I understand that one reason assigned for omitting an appropriation
for the present Committee is that a proposal is now before the Congress

to establish a permanent and statutory Fair Employment Practice Commission.

The legislation providing for this Commission is now in the Rules Committee.

Unless it is sent to the floor, the Members of the House will have no opportunity to vote upon it. The result will be that on July 1st next the principle of fair employment practices will have been abandoned by the House of Representatives.

I therefore urge the Rules Committee to adopt a rule permitting this legislation to be voted upon by the Members of the House as quickly as possible.

Very sincerely yours,

HARRY S. TRUMAN

[The Honorable Adolph J. Sabath, Chairman, Rules Committee, House of Representatives]

52 The President's News Conference of *June 7*, 1945

THE PRESIDENT. [1.] The first thing, I am exceedingly happy over the Bretton Woods—345 to 18. And the nonpartisan character of the support of that legislation makes me believe that the Congress really is for a peace treaty.

[2.] In connection with Justice Jackson's war crimes report, which was given to you this morning,[1] I have been reminded that next Sunday, the 10th, will be the third anniversary of the ruthless destruction of that Bohemian village of—I don't know how to say it—L-i-d-i——

Voices: Lidice.

THE PRESIDENT. This is one of the most barbarous of all the crimes on the Nazi calendar. June 10th will be remembered always as another day of infamy.

[3.] I want to say something to you about the transportation situa-

---

[1] The 8-page report in the form of a letter to the President from Mr. Justice Robert H. Jackson, Chief of Counsel for the United States in the prosecution of Axis war criminals, is published in the Department of State Bulletin (vol. 12, p. 1071).

tion that we are facing now, on account of the redeployment situation.

Colonel Johnson was in to see me yesterday, and told me very plainly that we were going to have to meet this transportation situation in 10 months. We have only a third smaller job to do than the one which has just been finished, and it took—that was over a period of 48 months. This will be over a period of 10 months; that is, to transfer all our armed forces across the United States and the deployment in the Pacific—redeployment in the Pacific. The first transportation job was considered a miracle, and this one ahead of us is even bigger.

And I want to impress it on our citizens that their best contribution in this case will be to stay at home.

I have written a letter to Colonel Johnson on the subject, and a statement will be available when you go out. But that is most important, that redeployment transportation situation. It is going to strain every facility we have, in order to get it done on time.

[4.] Mr. H. A. Millis, Chairman of the National Labor Relations Board, has resigned, and I have appointed Paul M. Herzog of New York to be his successor. Mr. Millis has been trying to——

Q. May we have that again?

THE PRESIDENT. H. A. Millis, Chairman of the National Labor Relations Board, has resigned. He has been trying to quit for some time. I appointed Paul M. Herzog. He is in the Navy now, but the Navy will let him out, if he gets confirmed. And I think he will be.

[5.] I want to announce the—Stuart Symington of St. Louis will be appointed to succeed Senator Gillette when Senator Gillette's expiration date expires July 15th; but I have asked Mr. Symington to come up and get familiar with the job by cooperating with Judge Vinson, and the other two members of the Board, and Senator Gillette, before he leaves.

Q. Mr. President, may I ask a question there? Do you plan any change in the three-man board to a single administrator for the——

THE PRESIDENT. That is a congressional matter that will have to be done by law. I can't change it.

Q. Will Mr. Symington be Chairman of the Board?

THE PRESIDENT. He will be Chairman when Senator Gillette's expiration time expires.

Q. Did you say something about conferring with Mr. Vinson—you mean——

THE PRESIDENT. With the other two members of the Board, and Mr. Vinson.

Q. Is his full name Stuart Symington? Didn't he have another name at the first——

THE PRESIDENT. W. Stuart Symington.

Q. S-y, isn't it?

THE PRESIDENT. S-y-m-i-n-g-t-o-n. And he spells that Stuart in the English King manner—S-t-u-a-r-t.

[6.] Q. Mr. President, is this NLRB term for a new term, or the unexpired term?

THE PRESIDENT. It's to fill out the unexpired term, and for a new term also. The present term expires, I think, sometime in August.

[7.] I want to announce the resignation of Grover B. Hill as Under Secretary of Agriculture, and the appointment of John B. Hutson——

Q. H-u-t?

THE PRESIDENT. H-u-t-s-o-n—he is assistant to Judge Vinson—as the Under Secretary of Agriculture.

Q. What is Mr. Hutson's home originally? Do you know what State?

THE PRESIDENT. Kentucky.

Q. Kentuckian.

THE PRESIDENT. Ken-tucky!

[8.] I want to announce the resignation of Brigadier General Frank T. Hines as Veterans Administrator, and of the other job he has, and the—General Omar Bradley will be appointed in his place. [*Low whistles and exclamations*]

And I want to remind you of—[*laughter*]—a statement that was made at the press conference here, on May 15th, in which I said the Veterans Administration will be modernized, and that should be done as soon as possible. But at that time I was not ready to do the job immedi-

ately, because I hadn't obtained the consent of the War Department for
General Bradley to serve.

Q. Mr. President, will General Bradley be retired before——

THE PRESIDENT. He will not. He will still be a four star General
while he is in charge of the Veterans Bureau.

Q. Will he have the other job, too—Reemployment and Retraining?

THE PRESIDENT. I don't think so. I think I am going to dispose of
that in another way at a little later date.

Q. Mr. President, when is General Hines' resignation effective?
Immediately?

THE PRESIDENT. No. General Hines' resignation is effective at my
pleasure, and that will be when General Bradley can wind up his duties
in Europe and take over. That will probably take 30 to 60 days to be
accomplished.

I wrote General Hines a letter, and here is the way I wind it up. You
will get copies of both these letters, my letter and his letter of resignation
too.

[*Reading*]: "I want you to know that I have always had, and shall
continue to have, complete confidence in you, and in your handling of
public matters. In fact, I shall ask you within the near future to take
another post of public importance, and I hope you will accept it."

And he told me personally that he would.

Q. Mr. President, on that point, can you say anything about—now—
about the construction of the medical divisions of the Veterans Bureau?
Any change contemplated there?

THE PRESIDENT. I would rather not discuss it now, because I will discuss it at a later date. When General Bradley takes over here, I will
give you the complete layout of it—what we propose to do.

Q. Mr. President, you mean there will be a reorganization?

THE PRESIDENT. It will be modernized, let's put it that way. It will
be a Veterans Administration for World War II. That was the setup
for World War I, and has been very adequately handled for World
War I. But as a World War I soldier, I wouldn't have been happy to
have had the Spanish-American War veterans running the Veterans
Administration, and I don't think—[*laughter*]—the new veterans

would. I think they would much rather have a general of their own war in the place.

And General Hines thought so, too—after we discussed it.

Are there any questions? [*Laughter*]

[9.] Q. Mr. President, are you in complete agreement with Justice Jackson's report?

THE PRESIDENT. I am in entire agreement with it. I think it's a good report, and I think it shows just exactly what we are attempting to accomplish.

Q. Mr. President, can you shed any light on one section of that report, where Justice Jackson said that it was the inescapable responsibility of this Government to prosecute these war criminals, even if this Government had to do it alone?

THE PRESIDENT. That's just—it means just exactly what it says. That is what we propose——

Q. Is there any prospect that we will have to do it alone?

THE PRESIDENT. No, no. That's just to make it emphatic.

Q. Any prospect of an early answer from the other countries on our suggestion for a military tribunal?

THE PRESIDENT. Yes, I think so. I don't think there will be any delay on that.

Q. Mr. President, can you tell us——

THE PRESIDENT. The British have already come in, and I am sure the Russians and the French will.

I beg your pardon?

[10.] Q. Can you tell us whether you plan any early action to curb rises in real estate and security prices?

THE PRESIDENT. I haven't gone into that. I have been discussing it with Judge Vinson, but have come to no conclusion on them.

[11.] Q. Mr. President, have you any comment on the Federal Corporation Control bill, so called—Byrd-Butler bill?

THE PRESIDENT. Well, as a Member of the Senate, I was always against that bill.

[12.] Q. Mr. President, in connection with your statement about transportation, if the situation should become critical, would you be prepared to recommend Federal control, or rationing? In other words, controlling the traveling public?

THE PRESIDENT. I hope that will not be necessary, but if it becomes necessary, I will certainly do it.

[13.] Q. Mr. President, did you give your approval to the suit filed—[*inaudible words*]—on those oil lands by Justice——

THE PRESIDENT. I told the Department of Justice to file the suit.

[14.] Q. Mr. President, would you care to comment—what is your feeling on the St. Lawrence Seaway?

THE PRESIDENT. I will discuss that at a little later date. You will find the record on that in the Senate, also.

[15.] Q. Mr. President, do you—would you favor a Big Five meeting to settle the Syrian dispute?

THE PRESIDENT. I would not.

Q. Mr. President, would you care to comment on the progress of Mr. Hopkins' talks in Moscow?

THE PRESIDENT. I will discuss that when Mr. Hopkins returns—discuss it fully. I don't want to discuss it now.

Q. Do you have any comment now on the position of the veto in San Francisco?

THE PRESIDENT. That will be discussed from San Francisco very shortly.

Q. Sir, have you received from Mr. Hopkins a message, saying that he made better than hoped for progress in Moscow?

THE PRESIDENT. I hope you won't force me to answer that, because I want to discuss that when Mr. Hopkins gets back. [*Laughter*]

Q. Mr. President, would you elaborate on that subject—that statement you made, about being discussed from San Francisco?

THE PRESIDENT. The announcement will be made from San Francisco.

Q. Shortly?

THE PRESIDENT. Yes, very shortly.

Q. Mr. President, could you amplify your views on the Big Five meeting with Syria?

THE PRESIDENT. Well, the meeting that was contemplated is a Big Three meeting to discuss world affairs. I think that the Near Eastern situation will be worked out without any Big Five meeting.

Q. Any news on the Big Three meeting, when it may be?

THE PRESIDENT. Well, I think it will be sometime within the next 40 days. That is as near as I can come to it.

[16.]   Q. Apparently, you have been taking up this matter of commercial aviation in the postwar period, in your series of talks in the past week. Is there anything you could tell us about the position we are in, with reference to that now, or——

THE PRESIDENT. No, I can't. I am not in a position to make a statement on that, but I will be, I think, next week.

[17.]   Q. Mr. President, the labor leaders saw you today, and they told us they asked you to—for an upward revision of the Little Steel formula.

THE PRESIDENT. They did.

Q. What do you think of that?

THE PRESIDENT. They always ask that, every time they come around. [*Laughter*]

Q. Do you think it should be revised upward?

THE PRESIDENT. I am not in any position to make a statement on that. We will work out a survey of the situation at a later date, and then come to a conclusion. At present, it stands.

[18.]   Q. Mr. President, did you discuss taxes with Senator George this morning?

THE PRESIDENT. No, I did not. I did not.

[19.]   Q. Can you give us your views on this bill passed by the House, giving Congressmen $2500 for expense accounts, sir?

THE PRESIDENT. Well, my views are that the Members of the House and the Senate are grossly underpaid. I think they should have a salary commensurate with the work they do, and I have always thought that. And I can say it now, for I am no longer a Member of the Senate. [*Laughter*]

I think the Senators ought—and the Members of the House—ought to be in the position so that their principal employer would be the United States of America, and that they ought to pass an adequate salary bill for themselves. I would certainly sign it if they did, because

I know that they need it. I don't think the Senate or House should be a rich man's club. I think the common, ordinary citizen ought to have a chance to serve.

Q. Do you think it is, at the moment?

THE PRESIDENT. Not now. It has been.

Q. Does that mean, Mr. President, that you don't think this is the method to do it with?

THE PRESIDENT. No, I don't. I think they ought to come straight out and raise their salaries and be done with it.

Q. Would you veto the bill then, sir?

THE PRESIDENT. No, I won't veto it. This is a legislative job and I will—if they want it that way, let them have it, because I know they need the money; but I say it would be much better for them if they would come out for a straight salary raise.

Q. Have you a suggestion for an adequate salary?

THE PRESIDENT. Anywhere from $15,000 to $25,000 a year.

Q. Mr. President, you didn't mean to suggest that their principal employers weren't the United States? [*Laughter*]

THE PRESIDENT. No, I did not, but I know in my own case, in order to meet my bills, I had to make my wife my secretary. She had to work all the time in the public interest, instead of keeping house. I didn't like it! [*Laughter*] And you made a campaign issue out of it in the last campaign, and the people liked it. But that shouldn't happen, there is no sense in that at all. This Government is rich enough to pay its employees an adequate salary, and they ought to do it.

Q. Mr. President, do you think diplomats' salaries should be increased?

THE PRESIDENT. I do that. I think it is absolutely necessary.

[20.] Mr. President, can you comment on the visit of Justice Black with you this morning?

THE PRESIDENT. It was a social call. Justice Black and I have been friends ever since I went to the Senate. This is the first chance——

Q. [*Interposing loudly*] Thank you, Mr. President.

THE PRESIDENT. ——time he has had a chance to call on me. [*Laughter*]

NOTE: President Truman's tenth news conference was held in his office at the White House at 4 p.m. on Thursday, June 7, 1945.

53 Letter to the Director, Office of Defense Transportation, Concerning Redeployment of the Armed Forces. *June 7, 1945*

Dear Colonel Johnson:

The transportation facilities of the nation are now called upon for the most gigantic task in all the history of transportation. The American armies must be moved from the victorious battlefields of Europe to meet and wipe out the tyranny of the East. In order to do this job most of our soldiers will be transported the full length of the American continent.

It required every transportation ingenuity to assemble our armies in Europe over a period of four years. This time the job is to be done in ten months. The contemplation of this task would overtax our faith if we had not found during the course of this war that the impossible has become our daily job.

I am asking you to extend my congratulations to all of our transportation agencies—and their millions of workers—on the results they have accomplished. At the same time express my confidence in them for the greater effort that lies ahead.

Sincerely yours,
HARRY S. TRUMAN

[The Honorable J. Monroe Johnson, Director, Office of Defense Transportation]

54 Statement by the President on the Transportation Problem. *June 7, 1945*

ALL TOO FEW realize the transportation difficulties which are now developing and which will continue well into 1946. It is important that the public understand the situation and at once lend full cooperation in order that the burden may be minimized.

The transportation performance in mobilizing our victorious armies in Europe over a period of four long, difficult years required the utmost effort. The plan of battle now requires that our armies be transferred to the far Pacific in the very short time of 10 months. We must now complete in 10 months a task that is only one-third less than the previous job which required nearly 48 months. The transportation job in the first phase of the war has often been called a "miracle." The job ahead of us is even bigger.

The facilities for civilian passenger transportation will be greatly reduced. In order to obtain passenger equipment for troop movements, it will probably be necessary to reduce the capacity of sleeping car equipment on regular trains by 50 percent. Men in uniform, other than on troop movements, now comprise about one-third of the passengers on a regular train. If the number of these travelers in uniform remained constant, a 50 percent reduction in sleeping car capacity on regular trains would mean that only one out of four of the civilians now using this equipment could do so in the future. But the number of travelers in uniform will be greatly increased.

In addition, war material moving to the Pacific will be more than twice as much as heretofore. This tremendous increase must move over the western railroads, which are already loaded to capacity.

Thus the various transportation restrictions will not only be retained but undoubtedly increased. Those asking for relaxation of the restrictions are asking for the impossible.

The situation requires the cooperation and self-denial of all users of transportation. The speed with which our men and munitions can be carried to within striking distance of Japan will largely determine how long the war must continue. I know that every American wants to add his effort to that of the millions of transportation workers on whom this grave responsibility rests.

Remember, the returning soldier is here for a few days on his way from one conflict to another.

55   Letter to General William S. Knudsen on His Retirement
      From Active Duty.   *June 7, 1945*

Dear General Knudsen:

As you return to civilian life I want to express appreciation for the distinguished service you have rendered to your country in the prosecution of the war. Your organizational genius in transforming our peace-time industry to a vast war machine is one of the greatest stories of the war and has earned the thanks not only of every American, but also the thanks of our allies who have depended on American supplies and equipment. That equipment which you helped to produce is speeding the day of victory.

First as a leader of the Advisory Commission to the Council for National Defense, then as Director General of the Office of Production Management, and for the past three and a half years in your military capacity as Director of Production in the Office of the Under Secretary of War, you have been in the forefront of our national industrial effort. Twice your work has won for you recognition by the award of the Distinguished Service Medal.

Almost insurmountable difficulties have been overcome by your courage and determination in working with private industry and by your forethought in anticipating and planning for future exigencies. Your resourcefulness and unswerving devotion to duty have saved the Nation vast sums of money while at the same time expediting production of materials of war, and preventing the loss of countless precious American lives.

I extend to you my own gratitude and that of a grateful people for the masterful way in which you have accomplished this monumental task.

Very sincerely yours,

Harry S. Truman

[Lieutenant General William S. Knudsen, Office of the Under Secretary of War]

56 Statement by the President on the Forthcoming Visit of President Ríos of Chile. *June 8, 1945*

IT IS A PLEASURE to announce that His Excellency Juan Antonio Ríos, President of Chile, will visit the United States in October of this year as an official guest of this Government.

President Ríos originally planned to visit the United States in 1942 by invitation of President Roosevelt. However, circumstances necessitated a postponement of the contemplated visit. It was my privilege to renew this invitation, and I am gratified that President Ríos has found it possible to accept at this time. I look forward not only to welcoming President Ríos to this country, but also to the pleasure of knowing him personally.

57 Citation Accompanying the Distinguished Service Medal Honoring General Edwin M. Watson. *June 8, 1945*

MAJOR GENERAL Edwin M. Watson, United States Army, served as Military Aide to the President for a period of nearly twelve years, from 1 June 1933 to 20 February 1945, the last six years of which he also served as Secretary to the President. During this time momentous decisions were required on the most critical problems that have ever confronted the Nation. While General Watson filled the post of Military Aide to the President, the greatest peacetime Army in history was organized; the country was thrown into war on a world-wide scale and was well on the road to victory at the time of General Watson's death.

General Watson's broad and thorough knowledge and his genial manner enabled him as Military Aide to be of the greatest assistance to the Commander-in-Chief. His familiarity with the problems pertaining to the Army enabled him to enhance greatly the confidence reposed in the Nation's military leaders by the President and other high officials in the Government. His devotion to duty and unfailing loyalty to the Commander-in-Chief and the Army kept General Watson at his post despite failing health and against medical advice. He served as Military Aide to the President with distinction, thereby contributing in no small part to the successful prosecution of the war.

NOTE: The presentation was made by the President to Mrs. Watson in a ceremony at the White House. General Watson died February 28, 1945, while returning from the Crimea Conference.

58   Statement by the President on Paper Conservation. *June* 9, 1945

BEFORE WE WERE forced to fight this war we took for granted our abundance in a land of plenty. Early in the conflict, however, we learned the importance of conservation and salvage of critical materials. Paper in its varied forms is essential to the business of supplying, feeding and clothing our armed forces. As our fighting might expanded the need for more paper grew. Accordingly, we took steps to insure a constant supply. We saved paper. We learned to think twice before we destroyed paper—and other things—which could be used again.

I hope that every community will cooperate fully with all salvage committees who are doing their part in saving waste paper, particularly the boys and girls who are rendering such a patriotic service in collecting the paper. They deserve all of the help we can give them as well as our warm gratitude.

59   Letter to the President of the Senate and to the Speaker of the House of Representatives on the Salaries of Members of Congress. *June* 12, 1945

Dear Mr. —————:

The salaries of the Members of the House of Representatives and of the Senate should be commensurate with the nature and volume of their work and with their responsibilities. Equality between their pay and their job may never be achieved, but certainly there should be less inequity than at present. Under any measuring rod, the members of the federal legislature are underpaid.

The members of Congress are called upon to exercise seasoned judgment in every field of national interest. They must establish the policies that will advance the welfare of our people. They must draft and weigh the statutes to carry out these policies. They must review the administration of the law in order to determine whether the policies and the statutes should be changed. Day in and day out this work must be done in countless fields. Proposals now before Congress exemplify the broad scope of work. Among pending proposals are the international monetary structure, foreign trade policy, economic stabilization, appropriations for war, tax policy, unemployment compensation and full employment.

No business concern or private organization would even attempt to hire top-flight executives or advisors at the level of salaries which presently prevails in the American Congress.

Therefore, the salaries of members of Congress should be increased to a level more in line with the job they are called upon to do. It will not be possible or wise to do this all at once. The adjustment of Congressional salaries at present should be in the full amount consistent with the Little Steel formula and other stabilization criteria by which the government controls salaries and wages in private industry. When these wage and salary controls are lifted, Congressional salaries should be increased to at least $15,000.

Sincerely yours,

HARRY S. TRUMAN

NOTE: This is the text of identical letters addressed to the Honorable Kenneth McKellar, President pro tempore of the Senate, and to the Honorable Sam Rayburn, Speaker of the House of Representatives.

60 The President's News Conference of *June* 13, 1945

THE PRESIDENT. [1.] Well, the first thing I want to tell you about is that I called Mr. Hull yesterday, and asked him to go to San Francisco with me for the closing of the conference, whenever that takes place.

And he said he would like very much to go, but he thought it would be too strenuous a trip to be the first thing he would do after he gets right out of the hospital.

I wish he could have come. I wish he could go.

[2.] I sent down the name of former Governor William H. Wills— W-i-l-l-s—of Vermont to be a member of the Federal Communications Commission. He will succeed Norman S. Case, whose term expires on June 30. It's just a case of one Republican taking the place of another. [*Laughter*] Vermont is surely a Republican State, so they couldn't accuse me of playing politics up there. [*Laughter*]

[3.] I have another announcement I think I ought to make—it has already been announced—but John Snyder put a draft on Ed McKim to get him away from me for a special job, and I guess I'll have to let him go for the time being.

Q. Will he go out of the city, sir? Wouldn't he leave the city on that job?

THE PRESIDENT. No. He is going over to the office over here. He will probably have to go out of the city for some special reason if Mr. Snyder wants him to, but his headquarters will be here.

[4.] I wanted to say a word about the Office of War Information.

"In my judgment, the things being done by the Office of War Information need to be done, in the interest of a nation still fighting a war which is far from over, and which the people need to know is far from over. OWI's work in both the domestic and the foreign field is now being performed by a trained, integrated, and experienced organization. To abolish some of its major functions, while the war is on, would be a mistake. It would be equally a mistake to attempt a hurried redistribution of those functions among other agencies which are not now trained or equipped to undertake them."

I am hoping that the Congress will restore the budget estimate for that organization.

[5.] For the parade on the day that we welcome General Eisenhower, I have indicated that the departments and agencies may, in their discretion, permit employees whose services can be spared to leave work without charge of annual leave for such period as may be necessary for the purpose of participating in the city's welcoming of General Eisenhower between the hours of 11 a.m. and 3 p.m.

I don't think we could do too much to show our appreciation of General Eisenhower. That's the reason for that arrangement.

[6.] Now, the thing that you are somewhat interested in, I think, is Mr. Hopkins and Mr. Davies. They both returned, and I just want to say a short word as to the background for that, and then you can ask me questions, and I will answer them if I am able to.

"In order to secure an interchange of views more satisfactorily and quickly than by cable, I sent Mr. Hopkins to Moscow and Mr. Davies to London. Their discussions covered the arrangements for the time and place of the meeting of Prime Minister Churchill"——

Q. Will you go a little slow, Mr. President?

THE PRESIDENT.——"of Prime Minister Churchill, Marshal Stalin, and myself, as to what would be most convenient for all three."

Ready for me?

Q. Yes, sir.

THE PRESIDENT. "Since their return, Mr. Hopkins and Mr. Davies have made their reports to me. The results have been completely satisfactory and gratifying.

"The all important thing which confronts us is that the unity, mutual confidence, and respect which resulted in the military victory should be continued to make secure a just and durable peace."

Q. Can we have that again, please, Mr. President?

THE PRESIDENT. The last paragraph?

Q. The all important thing.

THE PRESIDENT. "The all important thing which confronts us is that the unity, mutual confidence, and respect which resulted in the military victory should be continued to make secure a just and durable peace."

In other words, Mr. Churchill, Mr. Stalin, and the President of the United States must be able to meet and talk and trust each other, in that we want to believe that each of us wants a just and durable peace. That is one of the reasons for the preliminary visits of Mr. Hopkins and Mr. Davies with those two gentlemen.

Q. Mr. President, has—can you say that a definite time and place has been set for the Big Three meeting?

THE PRESIDENT. It has, but I can't announce it, and won't, until we arrive there.

Q. Mr. President, does the success of these missions extend to other things besides arrangements for the Big Three meeting?

THE PRESIDENT. Yes.

Q. The Polish situation?

THE PRESIDENT. The Polish situation, yes.

Q. Have you been advised, sir, that one of the London Poles already has rejected the invitation to Moscow? [1]

THE PRESIDENT. No. I hadn't heard that.

Q. Can you tell us anything about the release of the 16 Poles at that——

THE PRESIDENT. I will. That was one of the things that I sent Mr. Hopkins to Moscow for, and conversations were had on that subject. No conclusions have as yet been reached, but every effort is being made in behalf of those 16 Poles by both the American Government and the British Government.

Q. Mr. President, in San Francisco some weeks ago, when the arrest of the Polish leaders was first revealed, the Secretary of State said that negotiations for working on the new government could not proceed until the question of why they were arrested was cleared up. Has that position been changed?

THE PRESIDENT. That position has been modified, let us say, and I think that we are on a road to a complete settlement; but I want to make no statements that will in any way embarrass the Russian Government.

Q. Mr. President,——

THE PRESIDENT. At least, we are in a much better position now than

---

[1] On June 12 the White House released a statement listing the representatives of the Polish Provisional Government and Polish democratic leaders in Poland and abroad who had been invited to Moscow for consultations concerning the reorganization of the Provisional Government of Poland on a broader democratic basis. The statement, issued simultaneously in Washington, London, and Moscow, is published in the Department of State Bulletin (vol. 12, p. 1095).

we were before Mr. Hopkins went to Moscow, and Mr. Davies went to London.

Q. Mr. President, did Mr. Pauley's statement on reparations, indicating the very firm American stand of our Government, have any effect on the Russian's position?

THE PRESIDENT. That matter had not been discussed with the Russian Government.

Q. Mr. President, will Mr. Hopkins go to——

THE PRESIDENT. I don't know what effect it had.

Q. ——the Big Three meeting?

THE PRESIDENT. Mr. Pauley set out the position which he was instructed to take when he left here.

What was your question here?

Q. Will Mr. Hopkins be going to the Big Three meeting, Mr. President?

THE PRESIDENT. Yes, he will.

Q. Mr. Byrnes?

THE PRESIDENT. Yes.

Q. Mr. President, do you plan to take——

THE PRESIDENT. Admiral Leahy will, also.

Q. Mr. Davies?

THE PRESIDENT. So will Secretary Stettinius.

Q. Mr. Davies?

THE PRESIDENT. I hadn't talked to Mr. Davies about it until his health permits. I may ask him to go. He hasn't been well, nor Mr. Hopkins, so that is contingent on both their physical conditions.

Q. Do you plan to take any congressional leaders to the Big Three——

THE PRESIDENT. I do not.

Q. Who else will go, Mr. President?

THE PRESIDENT. I can't name the others. All the Combined Chiefs of Staff will be there, I can say that much.

Q. Did I understand you to say you won't announce the place until after the arrival there?

THE PRESIDENT. Yes, that is correct.

Q. There is a story this morning that the meeting would be secret, that no newspaper reporters would be permitted——

THE PRESIDENT. That is correct.

Q. ——to be there.

THE PRESIDENT. That is correct.

Q. The meeting will be secret?

THE PRESIDENT. Well, it will not be public, such as this one is. [*Laughter*] There will be no reporters or press conferences at that meeting.

Q. Will there be any reporters at the meeting?

THE PRESIDENT. No, there will not be.

Q. Did you say the Combined Chiefs of Staff will be there?

THE PRESIDENT. Yes. All our members will be there. I can't speak for the other countries, but I guess——

Q. Do you know what continent it will be held——

THE PRESIDENT. I don't want to answer any questions in regard to that trip.

Q. Mr. President, has there been any change in American policy which has caused the Russians to change their position on the Polish issue?

THE PRESIDENT. No. There has been no change in the American policy. There has been a very pleasant yielding on the part of the Russians to some of the things in which we are interested, and I think if we keep our heads and be patient, we will arrive at a conclusion; because the Russians are just as anxious to get along with us as we are with them. And I think they have showed it very conclusively in these last conversations.

Q. Mr. President, could you tell us what the Russian chief of staff——

THE PRESIDENT. Tony,[1] you had better ask Mr. Stalin about that. [*Laughter*]

Q. You said Combined——

THE PRESIDENT. That is up to him. If he wants it, he will be there.

Q. Mr. President, on this no reporters, you will recall that on previous occasions all these meetings have been announced to the world by some

---

[1] Ernest B. Vaccaro of the Associated Press.

sources other than American sources first. Have you given any thought to that?

THE PRESIDENT. That will not be done. I think the American reporters will be given an exactly equal chance with all the rest, but these conferences can't be held in the limelight because we are trying to get ready for a peace conference,——

Q. Yes, sir.

THE PRESIDENT. ——and that is my objective.

Q. On other occasions, the news has been diluted by getting out in advance before official——

THE PRESIDENT. With everything that I am capable of doing, I will see that that does not happen this time, if I can prevent it.

Q. Mr. President, will White House Press Secretary Mr. Ross go with you?

THE PRESIDENT. He will, that is certain.

Q. Mr. President, anything new this week regarding the status of Secretary Stettinius?

THE PRESIDENT. Nothing new. Status hasn't changed. [*Laughter*]

Q. You said he was going to the conference?

THE PRESIDENT. Just keep on asking. He is going to the conference. [*Laughter*]

Q. For how long, Mr. President? [*More laughter*]

Q. Mr. President, do we still recognize the London Polish Government?

THE PRESIDENT. We are still recognizing the London Polish Government.

[7.] Q. Mr. President, I would like to ask a question about General Eisenhower. There is a story from Paris this morning which says there's a flurry of rumors that Eisenhower may not return to Europe. Is there any truth in that, sir?

THE PRESIDENT. That didn't start here. [*Laughter*]

[8.] Q. Mr. President, what was the—what would be the position of the London Polish Government, after the provisional Polish Government is set up as a result of the Moscow conversations?

THE PRESIDENT. If the Government of Unity, I believe they call it, in

Poland is set up and agreed to by the British Government, and the United States Government, and the Russian Government, the London Government will go out of existence.

Q. Mr. President, does the date of the conference fall within the 40 days that you mentioned last week?

THE PRESIDENT. Yes, it does.

Q. Mr. President, you said that if the Polish Government is set up, that the Polish Government will be—the London Polish Government will go out?

THE PRESIDENT. Isn't that the purpose of the meeting that is being held on Friday—to set up this government? That's right. That's correct.

[9.] Q. Mr. President, Justice Jackson said in his report that he favored the trial of the German General Staff. What is your position on punishment of members of the General Staff?

THE PRESIDENT. What is my position on what?

Q. The punishment for the German General Staff?

THE PRESIDENT. Well, that matter of punishment will have to be assessed by the trial courts and the prosecutors. I am not in a position to say what their punishment should be. That would be judging them in advance, and they have not been tried.

[10.] Q. Mr. President, did Mr. Hopkins' work in Russia result directly in a change of the Russian position on the veto question at San Francisco?

THE PRESIDENT. Yes, I think it did. It did. Categorically, it did.

[11.] Q. Mr. President, have you any comment at all on the FEPC situation?

THE PRESIDENT. The only comment I have to make is that I am sincerely hopeful that the House will give the House itself a chance—the Rules Committee will give the House a chance to vote on this question. That is what we are asking.

[12.] Q. Mr. President, have you rebuked Mr. Hopkins for saying that Russian women were more beautiful than American? [*Laughter*]

THE PRESIDENT. I am going to let Mr. Hopkins speak for himself on that. I think he was misquoted. [*Laughter*]

[13.] Q. Can you comment on the Wherry amendment?

THE PRESIDENT. What?

Q. Can you comment on the Wherry amendment—on the OPA bill?

THE PRESIDENT. It's a bad amendment, and I hope the House will throw it out.

[14.] Q. What will happen if the London Poles, which were designated to join this Government of Unity, refuse to join it?

THE PRESIDENT. Well, this is not a government now, and they are being asked to join a conference in Moscow, to set up a government. Then, unless they agree, there won't be any government set up. So that, I think, answers your question?

Q. Mr. President, can we assume that the first act of the new Polish Government of Unity will be to hold a free, democratic election now—with the old formula?

THE PRESIDENT. I hope so. That is the reason for setting it up.

[15.] Q. Mr. President, on several occasions Mr. Grew has deplored the fact that the American newspapers don't get more information by direct reporting within the Russian spheres of influence and occupation. Did Mr. Hopkins ask that that situation be "broke" down a little more?

THE PRESIDENT. We are exploring—we are working on that now.

[16.] Q. Mr. President, you said that if the London people don't go to this conference, in order to help set up a new government, no new government would be set up——

THE PRESIDENT. No, no. I said if they did not agree after they got there. They're going. Don't you worry about that. They're going. [*Laughter*]

Q. Do you mean that they have veto power over—England——

THE PRESIDENT. No. Don't get this thing tangled up now. What we are trying to do is to get the situation worked out that has been causing us a lot of embarrassment. And for God's sake, don't you go muddying it all up so as to make it worse! We have made arrangements so that all these factions can get together, the present Polish Government, the people in Poland who are not in the Polish Government, and the people in London, to see if they can't sit down and work out a government that will be satisfactory to Poland. Now, that's what this conference is for. We have succeeded in getting that far. But don't upset the applecart. Say we have made some progress and that I believe that we can get results that will do what we want, which is a free Polish Government.

Q. Isn't it true that no member of the present exiled government in London has been invited to go to Moscow for these discussions?

THE PRESIDENT. That is true.

Voices from the back of the room: Thank you, Mr. President.

Reporter: Thank you, Mr. President. [*Laughter*]

THE PRESIDENT. You're entirely welcome.

NOTE: President Truman's twelfth news conference was held in his office at the White House at 10:35 a.m. on Wednesday, June 13, 1945. The White House Official Reporter noted that Senator Green of Rhode Island was a guest at this conference.

61   Citation Accompanying Medal for Merit Honoring Rudolph Forster. *June 16, 1945*

CITATION TO ACCOMPANY THE AWARD OF THE

MEDAL FOR MERIT

TO

MR. RUDOLPH FORSTER (DECEASED)

HE SERVED his Government faithfully, intelligently, and modestly for a period which spanned almost a third of our national existence, assisting eight Presidents through peace and war, through good times and bad, in the solution of the multitude of administrative problems, related to every branch of a great Government's activities, which find their way to the White House; he distinguished himself, from the beginning of the present emergency, by outstanding success in expediting critical decisions and actions when every minute gained was important in the over-all strategy of the war; and he thereby rendered a service of incalculable value to all of his fellow citizens.

FRANKLIN D. ROOSEVELT

NOTE: President Truman made the award at a ceremony attended by members of Mr. Forster's family. Mr. Forster served in the White House from

March 5, 1897, until his death on July 7, 1943, at which time he was Executive Clerk in charge of the White House staff. The release accompanying the citation stated that President Roosevelt signed the citation some time before his death, but that an opportunity to make the presentation did not arise before he left Washington for the last time.

62 Statement by the President on Driving Safety.
June 18, 1945

MOTORISTS throughout the Nation will get an increase in their gasoline rations this week. This means more traffic on our streets and highways and more danger of accidents with loss of life and destruction of property.

Upon every man and woman who drives an automobile rests the responsibility of helping to avert this danger. Each can do his part by driving safely and by keeping his car in good operating condition.

The average automobile in use today is nearly twice as old as the average car on the highways before the war. Its mechanical condition is likely to be poor. Its tires are worn and often weak. Its brakes may be faulty. The International Association of Chiefs of Police advises me that a recent check-up showed one of every seven cars inspected in the United States and Canada had brakes that failed to meet minimum safety requirements.

By keeping his car in safe operating condition and by driving it with the utmost care, every motorist can help in relieving our serious transportation problem and thereby aid further in the whole war effort.

I am confident, in urging law enforcement officers everywhere to continue and increase their efforts, that all our people will give their full cooperation and support.

63 Special Message to the Congress on the Succession to the Presidency. *June* 19, 1945

To the Congress of the United States:

I think that this is an appropriate time for the Congress to reexamine the question of the Presidential succession.

The question is of great importance now because there will be no elected Vice President for almost four years.

The existing statute governing the succession to the office of President was enacted in 1886.   Under it, in the event of the death of the elected President and Vice President, members of the Cabinet successively fill the office.

Each of these Cabinet members is appointed by the President with the advice and consent of the Senate.   In effect, therefore, by reason of the tragic death of the late President, it now lies within my power to nominate the person who would be my immediate successor in the event of my own death or inability to act.

I do not believe that in a democracy this power should rest with the Chief Executive.

In so far as possible, the office of the President should be filled by an elective officer.   There is no officer in our system of government, besides the President and Vice President, who has been elected by all the voters of the country.

The Speaker of the House of Representatives, who is elected in his own district, is also elected to be the presiding officer of the House by a vote of all the Representatives of all the people of the country.   As a result, I believe that the Speaker is the official in the Federal Government, whose selection next to that of the President and Vice President, can be most accurately said to stem from the people themselves.

Under the law of 1792, the President Pro Tempore of the Senate followed the Vice President in the order of succession.

The President Pro Tempore is elected as a Senator by his State and then as presiding officer by the Senate.   But the members of the Senate are not as closely tied in by the elective process to the people as are the members of the House of Representatives.   A completely new House is elected every two years, and always at the same time as the President and Vice President.   Usually it is in agreement politically with the Chief Executive.   Only one third of the Senate, however, is elected with the President and Vice President.   The Senate might, therefore, have a majority hostile to the policies of the President, and might conceivably fill the Presidential office with one not in sympathy with the will of the majority of the people.

Some of the events in the impeachment proceedings of President Johnson suggested the possibility of a hostile Congress in the future seeking to oust a Vice President who had become President, in order to have the President Pro Tempore of the Senate become the President. This was one of the considerations, among several others, which led to the change in 1886.

No matter who succeeds to the Presidency after the death of the elected President and Vice President, it is my opinion he should not serve any longer than until the next Congressional election or until a special election called for the purpose of electing a new President and Vice President. This period the Congress should fix. The individuals elected at such general or special election should then serve only to fill the unexpired term of the deceased President and Vice President. In this way there would be no interference with the normal four-year interval of general national elections.

I recommend, therefore, that the Congress enact legislation placing the Speaker of the House of Representatives first in order of succession in case of the removal, death, resignation or inability to act of the President and Vice President. Of course, the Speaker should resign as a Representative in the Congress as well as Speaker of the House before he assumes the office of President.

If there is no qualified Speaker, or if the Speaker fails to qualify, then I recommend that the succession pass to the President Pro Tempore of the Senate, who should hold office until a duly qualified Speaker is elected.

If there be neither Speaker nor President Pro Tempore qualified to succeed on the creation of the vacancy, then the succession might pass to the members of the Cabinet as now provided, until a duly qualified Speaker is elected.

If the Congress decides that a special election should be held, then I recommend that it provide for such election to be held as soon after the death or disqualification of the President and Vice President as practicable. The method and procedure for holding such special election should be provided now by law, so that the election can be held as expeditiously as possible should the contingency arise.

In the interest of orderly, democratic government, I urge the Congress to give its early consideration to this most important subject.

HARRY S. TRUMAN

NOTE: On July 18, 1947, the President approved Public Law 199, 80th Congress (61 Stat. 380), providing for the performance of the duties of the office of the President in case of the removal, resignation, death, or inability both of the President and the Vice President.

64   The President's News Conference at Olympia, Washington. *June* 21, 1945

THE PRESIDENT. Mr. Ross——

Mr. Ross: Ladies and gentlemen, the same rules will prevail here as prevail at the Washington press conferences; that is to say, if the President says anything that is off the record, that means it may not be used at all. Anything else may be used, but may not be directly quoted; it may be paraphrased. For example, "he said that," but it may not be put within quotation marks. If, however, he says that a particular thing may be quoted, then of course it may be. Generally speaking, what he says must be paraphrased, not put in quotation marks. That's all.

THE PRESIDENT. All right.

[1.] The first thing I want to announce to you is that since the time of the closing of the San Francisco Conference has been extended over to next Tuesday, as announced from San Francisco last night, we will stop for 3 hours in Portland. We will leave here at 10 o'clock Monday morning and arrive in Portland around 11, and try to leave there about 12:30 or 1 o'clock, so as to arrive in San Francisco at 4 o'clock on Monday afternoon. That is for the reason that we feel we should pay visits to all the three Western States, and we have been urged for sometime by the people in Portland, and by the Portland Oregonian, to stop there.

I have a telegram this morning from Lew Wallace, Chairman of the Democratic Committee of Oregon—I don't know whether he is any kin to the fellow that wrote Ben Hur or not, but he signs his name the same way—[*laughter*]—"I am very anxious about your 3-hour stopover in Oregon. As Democratic National Committeeman representing the Pacific senior State of this Northwest"—[*looking around at Governor Wallgren, and laughing*]—"it is my full duty to strenuously urge this stopover. Bring Mon along. We like him too." [*Laughter*]

The San Francisco Conference seems to have accomplished its purpose, and as I told you before, the reason for the delay has been technical, and the fact that so many translations have to be made on the treaty and the translations have to be agreed on by all the interpreters. That is taking more time for the details than was anticipated, and that is the reason for the 2-day delay; but I am very happy that the Conference has been a success, and all that we anticipated that it would be.

[2.]　I want to read you just a short statement, which I will read very slowly, on how I feel about the Senate approval of the renewal of the trade agreements.

Mr. Ross: Mr. President, may I interrupt? This may be quoted.

THE PRESIDENT. This may be quoted directly, that's right.

"The action of the Senate in approving the legislation to renew and strengthen the Trade Agreements Act——"

Q. Hold it a minute! [*Laughter*] "The action of the Senate in approving?"

THE PRESIDENT. "The action of the Senate in approving the legislation to renew and strengthen the Trade Agreements Act is indeed gratifying." [*Pause*] All ready?

Voices: Yes, sir.

THE PRESIDENT. "The revitalization"—here's a $40 word—"the revitalization of this act places the United States squarely behind the principles of internationl trade cooperation, which must prevail in the interests of world peace and economic well-being. Trade cooperation, however, must go hand in hand with monetary and financial cooperation. I am confident that the Senate will also take favorable action on the Bretton Woods legislation dealing with these closely related subjects."

I was informed last night that the final vote on passage of the bill was 54 to 21, which is very gratifying indeed. That is more than two-thirds, and a majority is all that was necessary.

[3.] I had an interview yesterday afternoon with the Governor of Alaska and Senator Magnuson, and discussed the completion of the Alaska highway up through the "Trench." It requires a connection of about 600 miles to make that road complete from here to Fairbanks.

Q. Six hundred miles?

THE PRESIDENT. Six hundred miles. It's a 600-mile gap to fill. It is, I think, absolutely essential that this construction be considered as a postwar project in which Canada, British Columbia, and the United States are all three interested. Senator Magnuson and Governor Gruening are very much interested in this program, and I think I will revitalize the Commission which has had that under consideration, and try to find a way to have that road constructed. It will require the cooperation of all three Governments to do it. Of course, the State of Washington and the Pacific Coast are vitally interested in that connection, and from the standpoint of the State of Missouri, so are we. [*Laughter*] Senator Magnuson was on that Commission before, and I think the Governor was, too. It's a good project, and I shall support it.

Now, gentlemen, if you have any questions you want to ask, I will try to answer.

[4.] Q. Mr. President, there are stories in the eastern papers this morning getting rid of Mr. Ickes again, saying that Cap Krug is his possible successor. Do you anticipate any change in the post?

THE PRESIDENT. No, I don't. That's the first I heard of it, and it's news to me. I haven't discussed it with Mr. Ickes at all.

[5.] Q. Mr. President, a lot of people out here are interested in CVA. Have you any comment on that?

THE PRESIDENT. In what?

Q. The Columbia Valley Authority.

THE PRESIDENT. Yes. I am interested in it. I think the junior Senator from Washington, Mr. Hugh Mitchell, has introduced a bill for the Columbia Valley Authority, and I am for it.

[6.] Q. Mr. President, are there any other Cabinet changes in prospect?

THE PRESIDENT. None immediately anticipated.

Q. You told us to keep asking about Stettinius. We will ask you again, sir?

THE PRESIDENT. That's all right. No change is contemplated immediately. I will let you know when that—anything of the kind takes place, with regard to any members of the Cabinet, I hope in plenty of time, so that you can get it in the paper.

[7.] Q. Mr. President, is there any contemplated change in the discharge system, the lowering of the draft, or discharge ages?

THE PRESIDENT. None that I know of. That is strictly a military affair, and will be handled by the War and Navy Departments without interference from me. I think they have handled it, so far, in good shape.

[8.] Q. Mr. President, could you tell us anything about your plans for General Eisenhower?

THE PRESIDENT. I have no plans except that General Eisenhower is going back to finish his job in Germany. General Eisenhower is entitled to most anything he wants, and I want to help him get it. [*Laughter*] He is a grand gentleman, and an able leader, and a diplomat as well. An unusual combination in a military man.

Q. Mr. President, how long do you suppose it will be required for General Eisenhower to remain in Germany?

THE PRESIDENT. Your guess is as good as mine. I don't know. That is one of the things that will be settled at the conference of the Big Three, I hope.

Q. Mr. President, at the future meeting of the Big Three, do you consider Olympia as a suitable meeting place?

THE PRESIDENT. It will be an ideal place. [*Laughter*]

Q. Is there anything new on any Big Three plans that you could tell us?

THE PRESIDENT. No. I don't know of a thing that I can announce on it now.

[9.] Q. Have you decided definitely whether it will be possible to make the Mackinac Governors' Conference?

THE PRESIDENT. Well, due to this extended stay out here, and the fact that the situation in Missouri is one in which I must take a part, the

Governors' Conference may be in some doubt at present, but I am going to still try to make it, if I can. That will depend altogether on the business situation from the Presidential standpoint in Washington, by the time I get through in Independence. Although I am in close touch with everything that is going on back in Washington, it may be necessary for me to be present personally in Washington to sign papers and things of that sort.

[10.] Q. Mr. President, Mr. Hoover issued a lengthy statement about the food situation last night. He said that he thought the controls on meat distribution and meat prices had broken down completely. What is your reaction to that, sir?

THE PRESIDENT. Well, I don't care to make any comment. When the Food Administrator takes charge, I think things will straighten out automatically.

[11.] Q. Is there any likelihood of your visiting Fort Lewis while you are here?

THE PRESIDENT. Only by proxy. My military aide probably will go over there. I have visited Fort Lewis and nearly every camp in the United States at one time or another within the last 3½ years, and while I would like to visit Fort Lewis, the Governor and I have other things in contemplation besides inspection trips. [*Laughter*]

Q. What about Seattle, Mr. President? Will you visit there?

[12.] THE PRESIDENT. Well, I looked at Seattle from the air, and as I say, I visited Seattle on a number of occasions, and I think I am entitled to just a few days' vacation, and I would like to spend a vacation in Seattle, so far as that is concerned, but Olympia is a lovely place. [*Laughter*]

[13.] Q. Mr. President, touching on the food situation again, do you think the food situation will improve a great deal when the new Administrator takes over?

THE PRESIDENT. There isn't any question about that. We are working on that constantly all the time. This is no reflection on the present Administrator, who would straighten it out under him just the same. We are working constantly on it, and I hope we will get it straightened out. Mr. Hoover was helpful in the conversations I had with him on the subject, and I appreciated what he had to say. I haven't read his statement; therefore, that is the reason I can't comment on it.

[14.] Q. Mr. President, will your visit to Portland be limited to the airport, or will you go into the city proper?

THE PRESIDENT. Just speaking as I anticipate the thing, we will probably land at Portland about 11 o'clock and if they want to take a drive through the streets for a half hour or an hour, whatever they think is necessary, I can probably do that, and then come back and get aboard the plane and go on to San Francisco. It's just a courtesy call on the part of the President, on account of the urgings we had from the various people in Oregon, due to the fact that they claim to be the senior State in the Northwest. [*Laughter*] How about that?

Governor Wallgren: Too many arguments taking care of Missouri.

Q. Going to pay respects?

THE PRESIDENT. That's right. That is the intention exactly.

Q. Reversing the process?

THE PRESIDENT. Reversing the process. [*Laughter*]

[15.] Q. Mr. President, could you give us some comment on Admiral Nimitz' statement this morning, that the Japs have finally been completely defeated at Okinawa?

THE PRESIDENT. That is all I know about it. That is only the—what the Admiral has said, and I of course am very happy that they are finally defeated. I understand that there are still some mopping-up operations that will be required, just as always is the case; but we are in complete possession of Okinawa, and it will be the base from which we will make it more "pleasant" for the Japanese in Japan.

[16.] Q. Mr. President, is there any possibility of a single control of food prices and food administration generally?

THE PRESIDENT. That is what we are trying to arrive at now. I hope so.

Reporter: Thank you, Mr. President. [*Some hurried exits*]

THE PRESIDENT. You're welcome. It's nice to be with you.

Q. Mr. President, may we have an afterthought? Did you mean to say that prices and food control would be under one head?

THE PRESIDENT. No, no. I meant——

136

Q. Misunderstanding?

THE PRESIDENT. I didn't mean to convey that thought at all. I intended to have them in balance. That is the objective all the way along.

NOTE: President Truman's fourteenth news conference was held in Governor Mon C. Wallgren's office in the Legis- lative Building at the State Capitol in Olympia at 10 a.m. on Thursday, June 21, 1945.

65 Statement by the President Upon Signing Bill Continuing Certain Subsidy Payments. *June 23, 1945*

I HAVE SIGNED S. 502, a bill "to permit the continuation of certain subsidy payments and certain purchase and sale operations by corporations created pursuant to section 5d(3) of the Reconstruction Finance Corporation Act, as amended, and for other purposes." This bill authorizes subsidy payments or purchases during the fiscal year 1946 in amounts necessary to meet obligations incurred in prior years and in addition sets maximum limits on subsidy payments and anticipated losses from 1946 operations.

I have signed this bill because continuance of these subsidy payments is essential to assure necessary war output and to provide support for the stabilization program.

I interpret it as the desire of Congress that these subsidies shall be paid only as long as, and to the extent necessary to secure needed war production under existing price ceilings. As opportunity permits, therefore, subsidy programs will be reduced or discontinued as rapidly as feasible within the limits of the present laws. Due consideration will be given, of course, to the legitimate needs of producers and to the desirability of maintaining balance in our national and international procurement programs.

Administrative action to curtail copper, lead and zinc subsidies under the premium price plan would be prevented, however, during the fiscal year 1946 by the provision which makes all classes of such premiums non-cancellable during that year. If it becomes clear that continuance of these payments at present levels is no longer necessary for war purposes, I shall request enactment of supplemental legislation which would permit a reduction of such unnecessary subsidies. We must make sure that subsidies contribute to the essential purposes for which Congress authorized them.

NOTE: As enacted, S. 502 is Public Law 88, 79th Congress (59 Stat. 260).

66   Address in San Francisco at the Closing Session of the United Nations Conference.   *June 26, 1945*

Mr. Chairman and Delegates to the United Nations Conference on International Organization:

I deeply regret that the press of circumstances when this Conference opened made it impossible for me to be here to greet you in person. I have asked for the privilege of coming today, to express on behalf of the people of the United States our thanks for what you have done here, and to wish you Godspeed on your journeys home.

Somewhere in this broad country, every one of you can find some of our citizens who are sons and daughters, or descendants in some degree, of your own native land. All our people are glad and proud that this historic meeting and its accomplishments have taken place in our country. And that includes the millions of loyal and patriotic Americans who stem from the countries not represented at this Conference.

We are grateful to you for coming. We hope you have enjoyed your stay, and that you will come again.

You assembled in San Francisco nine weeks ago with the high hope and confidence of peace-loving people the world over.

Their confidence in you has been justified.

Their hope for your success has been fulfilled.

The Charter of the United Nations which you have just signed is a solid structure upon which we can build a better world. History will honor you for it. Between the victory in Europe and the final victory in Japan, in this most destructive of all wars, you have won a victory against war itself.

It was the hope of such a Charter that helped sustain the courage of stricken peoples through the darkest days of the war. For it is a declaration of great faith by the nations of the earth—faith that war is not inevitable, faith that peace can be maintained.

If we had had this Charter a few years ago—and above all, the will to use it—millions now dead would be alive. If we should falter in the future in our will to use it, millions now living will surely die.

It has already been said by many that this is only a first step to a lasting peace. That is true. The important thing is that all our thinking and all our actions be based on the realization that it is in fact only a first step. Let us all have it firmly in mind that we start today from a good beginning and, with our eye always on the final objective, let us march forward.

The Constitution of my own country came from a Convention which—like this one—was made up of delegates with many different views. Like this Charter, our Constitution came from a free and sometimes bitter exchange of conflicting opinions. When it was adopted, no one regarded it as a perfect document. But it grew and developed and expanded. And upon it there was built a bigger, a better, a more perfect union.

This Charter, like our own Constitution, will be expanded and improved as time goes on. No one claims that it is now a final or a perfect instrument. It has not been poured into any fixed mold. Changing world conditions will require readjustments—but they will be the readjustments of peace and not of war.

That we now have this Charter at all is a great wonder. It is also a cause for profound thanksgiving to Almighty God, who has brought us so far in our search for peace through world organization.

There were many who doubted that agreement could ever be reached by these fifty countries differing so much in race and religion, in language and culture. But these differences were all forgotten in one unshakable unity of determination—to find a way to end wars.

Out of all the arguments and disputes, and different points of view, a way was found to agree. Here is the spotlight of full publicity, in the tradition of liberty-loving people, opinions were expressed openly and freely. The faith and the hope of fifty peaceful nations were laid before this world forum. Differences were overcome. This Charter was not the work of any single nation or group of nations, large or small. It was the result of a spirit of give-and-take, of tolerance for the views and interests of others.

It was proof that nations, like men, can state their differences, can face them, and then can find common ground on which to stand. That is the essence of democracy; that is the essence of keeping the peace in the future. By your agreement, the way was shown toward future agreement in the years to come.

This Conference owes its success largely to the fact that you have kept your minds firmly on the main objective. You had the single job of writing a constitution—a charter for peace. And you stayed on that job.

In spite of the many distractions which came to you in the form of daily problems and disputes about such matters as new boundaries, control of Germany, peace settlements, reparations, war criminals, the form of government of some of the European countries—in spite of all these, you continued in the task of framing this document.

Those problems and scores of others, which will arise, are all difficult. They are complicated. They are controversial and dangerous.

But with united spirit we met and solved even more difficult problems during the war. And with the same spirit, if we keep to our principles and never forsake our objectives, the problems we now face and those to come will also be solved.

We have tested the principle of cooperation in this war and have found that it works. Through the pooling of resources, through joint and combined military command, through constant staff meetings, we have shown what united strength can do in war. That united strength forced Germany to surrender. United strength will force Japan to surrender.

The United Nations have also had experience, even while the fighting was still going on, in reaching economic agreements for times of peace. What was done on the subject of relief at Atlantic City, food at Hot Springs, finance at Bretton Woods, aviation at Chicago, was a fair test of what can be done by nations determined to live cooperatively in a world where they cannot live peacefully any other way.

What you have accomplished in San Francisco shows how well these lessons of military and economic cooperation have been learned. You have created a great instrument for peace and security and human progress in the world.

The world must now use it!

If we fail to use it, we shall betray all those who have died in order that we might meet here in freedom and safety to create it.

If we seek to use it selfishly—for the advantage of any one nation or any small group of nations—we shall be equally guilty of that betrayal.

The successful use of this instrument will require the united will and firm determination of the free peoples who have created it. The job will tax the moral strength and fibre of us all.

We all have to recognize—no matter how great our strength—that we must deny ourselves the license to do always as we please. No one nation, no regional group, can or should expect, any special privilege which harms any other nation. If any nation would keep security for itself, it must be ready and willing to share security with all. That is the price which each nation will have to pay for world peace. Unless we are all willing to pay that price, no organization for world peace can accomplish its purpose.

And what a reasonable price that is!

Out of this conflict have come powerful military nations, now fully trained and equipped for war. But they have no right to dominate the world. It is rather the duty of these powerful nations to assume the responsibility for leadership toward a world of peace. That is why we have here resolved that power and strength shall be used not to wage war, but to keep the world at peace, and free from the fear of war.

By their own example the strong nations of the world should lead the way to international justice. That principle of justice is the foundation stone of this Charter. That principle is the guiding spirit by which it must be carried out—not by words alone but by continued concrete acts of good will.

There is a time for making plans—and there is a time for action. The time for action is now! Let us, therefore, each in his own nation and according to its own way, seek immediate approval of this Charter—and make it a living thing.

I shall send this Charter to the United States Senate at once. I am sure that the overwhelming sentiment of the people of my country and of their representatives in the Senate is in favor of immediate ratification.

A just and lasting peace cannot be attained by diplomatic agreement alone, or by military cooperation alone. Experience has shown how deeply the seeds of war are planted by economic rivalry and by social injustice. The Charter recognizes this fact for it has provided for economic and social cooperation as well. It has provided for this cooperation as part of the very heart of the entire compact.

It has set up machinery of international cooperation which men and nations of good will can use to help correct economic and social causes for conflict.

Artificial and uneconomic trade barriers should be removed—to the end that the standard of living of as many people as possible throughout the world may be raised. For Freedom from Want is one of the basic Four Freedoms toward which we all strive. The large and powerful nations of the world must assume leadership in this economic field as in all others.

Under this document we have good reason to expect the framing of an international bill of rights, acceptable to all the nations involved. That bill of rights will be as much a part of international life as our own Bill of Rights is a part of our Constitution. The Charter is dedicated to the achievement and observance of human rights and fundamental freedoms. Unless we can attain those objectives for all men and women everywhere—without regard to race, language or religion—we cannot have permanent peace and security.

With this Charter the world can begin to look forward to the time when all worthy human beings may be permitted to live decently as free people.

The world has learned again that nations, like individuals, must know the truth if they would be free—must read and hear the truth, learn and teach the truth.

We must set up an effective agency for constant and thorough interchange of thought and ideas. For there lies the road to a better and more tolerant understanding among nations and among peoples.

All Fascism did not die with Mussolini. Hitler is finished—but the seeds spread by his disordered mind have firm root in too many fanatical brains. It is easier to remove tyrants and destroy concentration camps than it is to kill the ideas which gave them birth and strength. Victory on the battlefield was essential, but it was not enough. For a good peace, a lasting peace, the decent peoples of the earth must remain determined to strike down the evil spirit which has hung over the world for the last decade.

The forces of reaction and tyranny all over the world will try to keep the United Nations from remaining united. Even while the military machine of the Axis was being destroyed in Europe—even down to its very end—they still tried to divide us.

They failed. But they will try again.

They are trying even now. To divide and conquer was—and still is—their plan. They still try to make one Ally suspect the other, hate the other, desert the other.

But I know I speak for every one of you when I say that the United Nations will remain united. They will not be divided by propaganda either before the Japanese surrender—or after.

This occasion shows again the continuity of history.

By this Charter, you have given reality to the ideal of that great statesman of a generation ago—Woodrow Wilson.

By this Charter, you have moved toward the goal for which that gallant leader in this second world struggle worked and fought and gave his life—Franklin D. Roosevelt.

By this Charter, you have realized the objectives of many men of vision in your own countries who have devoted their lives to the cause of world organization for peace.

Upon all of us, in all our countries, is now laid the duty of transforming into action these words which you have written. Upon our decisive action rests the hope of those who have fallen, those now living, those yet unborn—the hope for a world of free countries—with decent standards of living—which will work and cooperate in a friendly civilized community of nations.

This new structure of peace is rising upon strong foundations.

Let us not fail to grasp this supreme chance to establish a world-wide rule of reason—to create an enduring peace under the guidance of God.

NOTE: The President spoke at the Opera House in San Francisco. His opening words "Mr. Chairman" referred to Secretary of State Edward R. Stettinius, who served as president of the Conference and as chairman of the U.S. delegation.

67 The President's News Conference at Independence, Missouri. *June 27, 1945*

THE PRESIDENT. This statement I want to make to you, you will all receive mimeographed copies of it, so don't worry about copying it down.

[1.] This is dated today, at Independence, and it is addressed to the Honorable Edward R. Stettinius, Jr.

"Dear Ed: On the day after the death of President Roosevelt, you submitted to me your resignation as Secretary of State. I asked you to continue at your post and to carry out the vitally important assignment for which you were then completing the last preparations—to act as chairman of the United States delegation at the United Nations Conference.

"You accepted that responsibility. It was a very grave responsibility. Upon the success of the San Francisco Conference depended, first of all, the hope that from this war the United Nations could build a lasting peace.

"The San Francisco Conference has now fulfilled its purpose. The Charter of a permanent United Nations has been written. You have every reason to be proud of your part in this achievement from the beginning.

"At the request of Mr. Hull after the Moscow Conference in 1943 you, as Under Secretary of State, organized and directed the preparations for Dumbarton Oaks. You were the representative of the United States and acted as the chairman of the Dumbarton Oaks Conference, where the Proposals were written that became the basis of the Charter. You were at President Roosevelt's right hand at Yalta, where further decisions on the world organization were made and agreement to hold the United Nations Conference was reached.

144

"All the preparations for the San Francisco Conference were under your direction. During its deliberations you served not only as chairman of the United States delegation but as President of the Conference, charged with the conduct of its business. The task of guiding the work of this Conference of fifty different nations toward unanimous agreement upon the Charter was a difficult one. You accomplished it with skill, unfaltering courage, and success.

"But the task of fulfilling the promise of the San Francisco Conference has only just begun. The Charter must be ratified and the United Nations organization brought into being and put to work. It is necessary to the future of America and the world that the words of this Charter be built into the solid structure of peace for which the world is waiting and praying.

"I can think of no better way to express the confidence of the United States in the future of the United Nations than to choose as the American representative in that task a man who has held with distinction the highest appointive office in the Government and has been more closely associated with the creation of the Charter than any other.

"I have asked you if you would accept nomination as the Representative of the United States to the United Nations, when the organization is established. As such you would be the United States member of the Security Council and chairman of the United States delegation in the General Assembly. You have told me that you would accept this great responsibility.

"I therefore now accept your resignation as Secretary of State.[1]

"I intend to submit the United Nations Charter to the Senate on Monday and to ask for its prompt ratification. You have told me that you feel it is of the utmost importance for you, as Chairman of the United States delegation, to be immediately available to the Senate for whatever assistance and information it needs in connection with its consideration of the Charter.

"I wanted you to come with me to the meeting with Marshal Stalin and Prime Minister Churchill which will take place next month. But,

---

[1] Mr. Stettinius served from December 1, 1944, through June 27, 1945.

since I shall be away during the congressional hearings, I have reluctantly agreed to your suggestion that you remain in Washington while I am away. In that capacity you will represent me before the Senate in all matters relating to the Charter.

"I also ask you to supervise, as the personal representative of the President, the work of the United States members of the Preparatory Commission pending ratification of the Charter and your nomination as the Representative of the United States to the United Nations.

"I am confident that you will continue to fulfill with honor to yourself and with benefit to America and the cause of peace the high trust which your country reposes in you."

Signed by me.

Any questions you want to ask?

[2.] Q. Mr. President, have you nominated a successor?

THE PRESIDENT. That will be done when we get back to Washington.

Q. Can you tell us who it will be, sir?

THE PRESIDENT. I will not.

Q. Is it someone in the Government now, Mr. President?

THE PRESIDENT. It is not.

Q. Is it Mr. Byrnes, Mr. President? [*Laughter*]

THE PRESIDENT. That question I cannot answer.

Q. Will Mr. Stettinius subsequently be appointed Ambassador to the Court of St. James?

THE PRESIDENT. He will not.

Q. Has he accepted this new post?

THE PRESIDENT. He has accepted it. It's the highest post in the gift of the Government. I don't see why it shouldn't be an honor to accept it.

Q. When does that take effect, Mr. President, the resignation?

THE PRESIDENT. Immediately. It is accepted today.

Q. Will Mr. Grew continue to serve as Acting Secretary?

THE PRESIDENT. That will be up to the Secretary of State to say, when he takes over. He will be Acting Secretary just as he has been when Mr. Stettinius is gone.

Q. Mr. President, you said that you would send up this nomination for the new successor as soon as you get back to Washington. Does that mean Monday?

THE PRESIDENT. Yes. Monday or Tuesday, probably.

Q. That means you might be returning——

THE PRESIDENT. I am returning to Washington on Sunday morning, and will be home in the afternoon at 2 o'clock, provided the *Sacred Cow* stays in the air. [*Laughter*]

Q. Wouldn't you like to say a few words about your reactions to this homecoming?

THE PRESIDENT. I was overwhelmed with it, of course. All these people have seen me two or three times a day, for the last 30 or 40 years. I can't see what there is about me now that would make them turn out like they did today.

Q. Mr. President, can you say anything about your plans on presenting the Charter to the Senate on Monday?

THE PRESIDENT. I have nothing to say about that, yet.

Q. Mr. President, could you say who will direct the banking system in Germany—under what branch of the Government that would come?

THE PRESIDENT. That's what I am going to try to arrange—that's the reason I am going to Germany.

Q. Mr. President, following up the question on the presentation of the Charter, can you say whether you will do that in person?

THE PRESIDENT. I don't want to say that today. I haven't made up my mind on it definitely.

Q. Mr. President, did you say when you would name a successor to Mr. Stettinius?

THE PRESIDENT. I will make the announcement in Washington.

Q. Probably Tuesday, did you say, Mr. President?

THE PRESIDENT. Probably.

Q. Who will accompany you to Berlin, Mr. President?

THE PRESIDENT. Well, whoever is necessary to carry on negotiations for the Government of the United States.

Q. In that connection, sir, you had previously announced that Mr. Byrnes would go——

THE PRESIDENT. I had asked Mr. Byrnes and Mr. Stettinius, and Mr.

Davies, and Admiral Leahy, and Harry Hopkins; and I am going to try to take everybody I need to transact the business.

Q. You are going to remove Mr. Stettinius from this trip?

THE PRESIDENT. He removed himself.

Q. Well, Mr. Byrnes is still in the trip though, sir?

THE PRESIDENT. He is. He is. There has been no change except this one which I have announced.

Q. Mr. President, will Justice Jackson go with you, by any chance?

THE PRESIDENT. Mr. Jackson is in England now, attending to the job to which he was appointed.

Q. Will he meet you——

Q. Mr. President, is the new Secretary of State going to the Big Three meeting?

THE PRESIDENT. I hope so. [*Laughter*]

Q. Mr. President, will Mr. Byrnes——

Q. Do you have a definite date on the meeting yet?

THE PRESIDENT. No. I will give you a definite date when you get back to Washington.

Q. Will Mr. Byrnes go there in the capacity of a private citizen?

THE PRESIDENT. Mr. Byrnes is going at my invitation. [*Laughter*]

Q. Sir, what was the date that you said you would give us when you returned?

THE PRESIDENT. The date of the conference——

Q. Yes, the conference.

THE PRESIDENT. ——in Europe.

Q. Will you have to add to the list, Mr. President, in order to include the new Secretary? [*Laughter*]

THE PRESIDENT [*laughing*]. I can't answer that question. I will have to look over the list and see.

[3.] Q. Mr. President, there are still persistent reports in Washington that Secretary Morgenthau is about to resign. Is there anything to that, Mr. President?

THE PRESIDENT. As I have told you time and again, I have the resignation of everybody who *can* resign in the Government, and I can accept them when I get ready, if it's necessary. I hadn't thought about accepting Mr. Morgenthau's, however.

Q. The same go for Mr. Ickes, Mr. President?

THE PRESIDENT. Yes. Anybody who can resign has resigned to me as the new President, as they should. Those who want to stay, may, as I have said time and again. Mr. Stettinius is getting a better job.

[4.] Q. Mr. President, has anything been done with respect to the possible grant-in-aid to Great Britain, which has been discussed?

THE PRESIDENT. No. Nothing has been done.

Reporter: Thank you, Mr. President.

THE PRESIDENT. All right—all right. [*Laughter*]

NOTE: President Truman's fifteenth news conference was held in Memorial Hall at Independence at 4 p.m. on Wednesday, June 27, 1945. The White House Official Reporter noted that the galleries were filled with visitors, including many children. He also noted that the day was hot and sultry and that the newspapermen and women were seated in chairs around the President's makeshift desk and chair, in front of the platform.

Before the President began speaking, the Press Secretary stated the rules governing news conferences as he had done at the conference at Olympia, Item 64.

68 Remarks Upon Receiving an Honorary Degree From the University of Kansas City. *June 28, 1945*

Mr. President, members of the Faculty, and Board of Trustees of the University of Kansas City:

I can't tell you how very much I appreciate this first honorary degree that you have conferred. I appreciate it more than I can tell you. I have been overwhelmed, since I have been back in Jackson County, to find out just what kind of fellow I am. You have been exceedingly kind to me. You have absolutely disproved that maxim, that a prophet is not without honor save in his own country. You certainly have honored me with everything possible. I hope I can deserve it.

I have a tremendous—a tremendous task, one that I dare not look at too closely, for the simple reason that it is one that no man can do by himself. I must have the wholehearted—the unqualified support of the country, to win the Japanese war, and then to win a peace.

And there is one thing we must learn. It has been a most difficult task for us to learn it; and that is that it is absolutely necessary for the greatest Republic that the sun has ever shone upon to live with the world as a whole, and not by itself.

It is difficult for us to appreciate the age in which we live. It is an attempt at an adjustment in this age that has brought about this terrible disaster through which we have just passed in the European situation, and through which we are now passing in the Pacific.

The night before last, I arrived in Salt Lake City, Utah, at 10 p.m. from San Francisco, which I had left on the same time schedule at 8 p.m. I left Salt Lake City the next morning after breakfast—and oh, what a breakfast that was!—and arrived in Kansas City, Missouri, in exactly three hours and a half.

My grandfather made that trip time and again from 1846 to 1854, and again from 1864 to 1870, and when he made that trip it took him exactly 3 months to go, and 3 months to come back.

That is the age in which we live. The time is coming when that trip, in my opinion, will be made in one hour and a half, instead of three hours and a half. The time is coming when we will be transporting the freight of the world, and the express of the world, and the mail of the world on a schedule that will be almost up with the travel of the earth in its turn on its axis.

We must become adjusted to that situation. No further from here to Salt Lake City, or Salt Lake City to San Francisco, than it was from here to Lonejack in Eastern Jackson County, when we used to go to the picnics there on the sixteenth of August to celebrate the beginning of the Democratic campaign in the fall.

I am anxious to bring home to you that the world is no longer county-size, no longer state-size, no longer nation-size. It is one world, as Willkie said. It is a world in which we must all get along.

And it is my opinion that this great Republic ought to lead the way. My opinion is that this great Republic ought to carry out those ideals of Woodrow Wilson and Franklin D. Roosevelt.

It was my privilege to be present at the signing of the Charter in San Francisco, which is the first step toward the accomplishment of world peace. Back in 1787 and 1788, our forefathers wrote a Constitution for thirteen independent States. They considered that Constitution imperfect. They had to go out on a selling program to get enough States to ratify that Constitution to put it into effect. One of those thirteen States did not ratify that Constitution until it was actually put into effect.

We are going to have to ratify this Constitution of San Francisco, and I want to see the United States do it first.

I am standing here with the degree of Doctor of Laws. That means that we live, in this country at least, in an age of law and an age of reason, an age in which we can get along with our neighbors.

Now we must do that internationally. It will be just as easy for nations to get along in a republic of the world as it is for us to get along in the republic of the United States.

Now, if Kansas and Colorado have a quarrel over a watershed they don't call out the National Guard of each State and go to war over it. They bring suit in the Supreme Court and abide by its decision. There isn't a reason in the world why we can't do that internationally.

There were two documents signed at San Francisco. One of them was the Charter of the United Nations. The other was the World Court. It will require the ratification of both of those Charters, and the putting of them into effect, if we expect to have world peace for future generations.

That is one of the tasks which have been assigned to me. I am accepting the responsibility. I am going to try to carry it out.

First, we must win the war with Japan, and we are winning it.

Then, we must win the peace in the world. And unless we lead the way, there will be no peace in the world.

Again, I can't tell you how much I appreciate this privilege, how much I appreciate the honor. I went to the Kansas City School of Law for two years and a half. As I told the Alumni this afternoon, I might have been able to finish that course in another year and a half—I say I *might* have been—if it hadn't been for the fact that at that time I was a public servant here in Jackson County—Judge of the County Court for the Eastern District; and I had so many people interested in the welfare of the county who wanted to see me that I couldn't study law.

Now I have just about—oh, I was going to say maybe a thousand times that many people who are interested in the welfare of the United States, but they have a much more difficult time discussing that with me individually than they did when I was a County Judge.

So here I am—on a half-finished course—a Doctor of Laws! And I sure appreciate it. I just didn't know how easy it was going to be to get that degree. I come back here as President of the United States, and I get the first honorary degree of Kansas University; and that certainly is appreciated by me.

When I come to Jackson County, I can't realize that I am the President of the United States. I feel like I am just one of your fellow citizens. I see the same faces, and I try to talk to the same people. But, you know, there is one thing that I have found it impossible to do, and that is to shake hands with and talk to five hundred thousand people in 3 days. I just can't do it, much to my regret. I wish I could shake hands with everybody here tonight, and listen to your tales of woe, if you have one, as I used to do; but that is impossible. I just can't do it.

So I want you to consider that, because I have come here and have seen all of you face to face, that I have theoretically shaken hands with every one of you, and you can go home and say that you have done it.

You want me to be physically able to carry out this tremendous task that has devolved upon me. I must be physically able to do that; and I can't possibly see everybody and talk to everybody in Jackson County and go back to Washington and convince the Senate that they ought to ratify this treaty. I know the Senate, because I worked in the Senate for about 10 years.

Again I want to thank you. I can't thank you enough. I don't dare to stop and think about it, because I would just stand up here and shed tears; and that is not what you want to see me do. I do appreciate that more than I can tell you.

Thank you very much.

NOTE: The President spoke in the Municipal Auditorium at Kansas City, Mo. His opening words "Mr. President" referred to Clarence R. Decker, president of the University.

69 Address Before the Senate Urging Ratification of the Charter of the United Nations. *July 2, 1945*

Mr. President—it has been a long time since I have said "Mr. President" in this Chamber, and my how I miss it!—and Members of the Senate of the United States:

It is good of you to let me come back among you. You know, I am sure, how much that means to one who served so recently in this Chamber with you.

You also remember how I was tied down in the last three months I was here. I couldn't speak, except to rule on the parliamentary questions; and two or three times I was ruled out of order because I would make a speech on parliamentary questions.

I have just brought down from the White House, and have delivered to your Presiding Officer the Charter of the United Nations. It was signed in San Francisco on June 26, 1945—6 days ago—by the representatives of 50 nations. The Statute of the International Court of Justice is annexed to the Charter.

I am appearing to ask for the ratification of the Charter, and the Statute annexed thereto, in accordance with the Constitution.

The Charter which I bring you has been written in the name of "We, the peoples of the United Nations." Those peoples—stretching all over the face of the earth—will watch our action here with great concern and high hope. For they look to this body of elected representatives of the people of the United States to take the lead in approving the Charter and the Statute and pointing the way for the rest of the world.

This Charter and the principles upon which it is based are not new to the United States Senate or to the House of Representatives.

Over a year and a half ago the Senate, after thorough debate, adopted the Connally resolution, which contained the essence of this Charter. It called for—and I quote from the Connally Resolution, "a general international organization based on the principle of the sovereign equality of all peace-loving states, and open to membership by all such states, large and small, for the maintenance of international peace and

153

security." That is the end of the quotation from the Connally Resolution. What I am now presenting to the Senate carries out completely this expression of national and international necessity.

Shortly before that, the House of Representatives passed the Fulbright resolution, also favoring the creation of international machinery with participation by the United States.

You and the House of Representatives thus had a hand in shaping the Dumbarton Oaks Proposals, upon which the Charter has been based.

No international document has been drawn in a greater glare of publicity than has this one. It has been the subject of public comment for months. This widespread discussion has created the impression in some quarters that there were many points of disagreement among the United Nations in drafting this Charter. Naturally, much more public attention was given to the items of disagreement than to the items of agreement. You know, if you want to get a headline, you want to fall out with some of your friends, and you will always get it. The fact is that there were comparatively few points upon which there was not accord from the very beginning. Disagreement was reduced to a minimum—and related more to methods than to principle.

Whatever differences there were, were finally settled. They were settled by the traditional democratic method of free exchange of opinions and points of view.

I shall not attempt here to go into the various provisions of the Charter. They have been so thoroughly discussed that I am sure you are all familiar with them. And they will be so thoroughly discussed on this floor that you and the people of the nation will all have a complete expression of views. I am sure of that.

In your deliberations, I hope you will consider not only the words of the Charter but also the spirit which gives it meaning and life.

The objectives of this Charter are clear.

It seeks to prevent future wars.

It seeks to settle international disputes by peaceful means, in conformity with the principles of justice.

It seeks to promote worldwide progress and better standards of living.

It seeks to achieve universal respect for, and observance of, human rights and fundamental freedoms for all men and women—without distinction as to race, language, or religion.

It seeks to remove the economic and social causes of international conflict and unrest.

It is the product of many hands and many influences. It comes from the reality of experience in a world where one generation has failed twice to keep the peace. The lessons of that experience have been written into this document.

The choice before the Senate is now clear. The choice is not between this Charter and something else. It is between this Charter and no Charter at all.

Improvements will come in the future as the United Nations gain experience with the machinery and methods which they have set up. For this is not a static treaty. It can be improved—and, as the years go by, it will be—just as our own Constitution has been improved.

This Charter points down the only road to enduring peace. There is no other. Let us not hesitate to join hands with the peace-loving peoples of the earth and start down that road, with God's help, and with firm resolve that we can and will reach our goal.

I urge ratification. I urge prompt ratification.

Thank you.

NOTE: The President spoke at 1 p.m. in the Senate Chamber.

The Charter of the United Nations together with the Statute of the International Court of Justice is printed in the U.S. Statutes at Large (59 Stat. 1031). It was approved by the Senate on July 28, 1945, and after ratification entered into force on October 24, 1945.

70 Memorandum Reducing the Workweek of Federal Employees to 44 Hours. *July 3, 1945*

To the heads of Executive Departments and Agencies:

The Federal Government has been maintaining a work schedule of a six-day, 48-hour week for both the departmental and field service. I believe that the time has now come when we should make a change in this schedule.

It is my desire, therefore, that, with the exception of the War Department, the Navy Department, the Treasury Department, the Veterans Administration, the Tennessee Valley Authority, and the Panama Canal, the head of each department and agency establish, effective July 1, a 44-hour workweek. In the case of the departments above named, it is my desire that they examine their various operations very carefully and, wherever possible, put into effect a 44-hour workweek.

If the head of any department or agency other than the War Department, the Navy Department, the Treasury Department, the Veterans Administration, the Tennessee Valley Authority, and the Panama Canal feels that it is still necessary for him to maintain a 48-hour workweek, contrary to the general policy above outlined, he should apply to the Director of the Bureau of the Budget for an exception to this policy.

It should be clearly understood that reductions in hours of work are not to constitute a basis for requests for additional funds or personnel.

HARRY S. TRUMAN

71 Letter Accepting Resignation of Harry L. Hopkins as Special Assistant to the President. *July 3, 1945*

Dear Harry:

I am sorry that I cannot persuade you to remain in government any longer. I should have liked it not only because of the great service which you could continue to render to the nation, but also because it would have given me great pleasure to have you associated with my Administration.

However, I understand fully the reasons which prompted your decision—and I do not feel that I can justifiably ignore them.

There are few people in the United States who know more fully than I the substantial role which you have played in the prosecution of our war. I know how much President Roosevelt relied upon you as he started the nation on the hard task of preparation to meet aggression from abroad. I know how much your efforts counted toward the successful carrying out of the Lend-Lease program during the days immediately preceding and following our entry into the war. And I know how much your tireless energy had to do with the carrying on of the war in all parts of the globe.

During the earlier days when our nation was recovering from the depths of the depression, your participation in government affairs—first as administrator of relief activities, and later as Secretary of Commerce—left its beneficial and lasting imprint on the economy of our nation.

I am sure that you must feel much pride and a deep sense of accomplishment in all your great and patriotic service to our country during the last twelve years.

I know that I shall have to call upon you in the future—and I hope that you will soon be fully and completely recovered so that you can give me the benefit of your counsel.

Very sincerely yours,

HARRY S. TRUMAN

[Honorable Harry L. Hopkins, The White House]

NOTE: Mr. Hopkins was appointed Special Assistant to the President by President Roosevelt in 1941. His letter of resignation, dated July 2, 1945, was released with President Truman's reply.

72   Statement by the President: The Fourth of July.
July 4, 1945

AGAIN THIS YEAR we celebrate July 4 as the anniversary of the day one hundred and sixty-nine years ago on which we declared our independence as a sovereign people.

In this year of 1945, we have pride in the combined might of this nation which has contributed signally to the defeat of the enemy in Europe. We have confidence that, under Providence, we soon may crush the enemy in the Pacific. We have humility for the guidance that has been given us of God in serving His will as a leader of freedom for the world.

This year, the men and women of our armed forces, and many

civilians as well, are celebrating the anniversary of American Independence in other countries throughout the world. Citizens of these other lands will understand what we celebrate and why, for freedom is dear to the hearts of all men everywhere. In other lands, others will join us in honoring our declaration that all men are created equal and are endowed with certain inalienable rights—life, liberty and the pursuit of happiness.

Here at home, on this July 4, 1945, let us honor our Nation's creed of liberty, and the men and women of our armed forces who are carrying this creed with them throughout the world.

73 Statement by the President on the Death of John Curtin, Prime Minister of Australia. *July 4, 1945*

IT IS with deep sorrow that I have learned of the death today of the Right Honorable John Curtin, Prime Minister of Australia, who has brought to the public service of his country not only great ability and integrity but also a deep sense of loyalty to the principles which have guided the United Nations through this war so victoriously ended in Europe and so successfully being waged in the Far East. The Government and people of the United States mourn with the people of Australia the passing of this great leader.

74 Statement by the President Commending the Work of the United National Clothing Collection. *July 4, 1945*

THE 7,300 local committees of the United National Clothing Collection have rendered a service to world peace. By meeting and exceeding their goal of 150,000,000 pounds of clothing, the American people have accomplished the task assigned to them by Franklin D. Roosevelt in a cause that was close to his heart. It is good to know that the clothing is now on its way overseas to relieve the suffering of war victims in Europe and the Far East.

NOTE: The statement was made follow-
ing the receipt of a report by Henry J.
Kaiser, chairman of the United National
Clothing Collection. For letter to Mr.
Kaiser asking him to head the second
United National Clothing Collection
campaign, see Item 144.

75   Joint Statement Following Discussions With Foreign Minister Sofianopoulos of Greece.   *July 5, 1945*

THE PRESIDENT today had the opportunity of a friendly conversation with Mr. Sofianopoulos, Foreign Minister of Greece, who arrived
yesterday in Washington after the conclusion of the San Francisco Conference where he headed the Greek delegation. The President expressed appreciation to Mr. Sofianopoulos for his excellent work in
San Francisco as chairman of one of the most important Conference
committees.

Mr. Sofianopoulos discussed with the President the United Nations
Charter, and the President was pleased with Mr. Sofianopoulos' expression of confidence that the friendly atmosphere and the resulting
success of the Conference enabled Greece, as one of the smaller nations,
to look forward to a period of international understanding and security
within the framework of a united family of nations.

The President remarked with satisfaction upon the recent official
notification to Tokyo by the Greek Government that Greece has considered itself in a state of war with Japan since its severance of diplomatic relations on December 8, 1941, and welcomed this further evidence that the Greek people, who played such a brave role in resisting
Axis aggression on their own soil, are stanchly lined up with the Allies
in their determination to see through to a victorious close the war
against Japan. The President assured Mr. Sofianopoulos that the
American people would never forget the heroic attitude of the Greek
people or the great sacrifices made by Greece in the common interest.

In discussing the urgent problems of rehabilitation and reconstruction facing Greece at this time, the President expressed to Mr. Sofianopoulos the sincere interest of this Government in seeing normal economic conditions reestablished in Greece as soon as possible. In this

connection the President assured Mr. Sofianopoulos of this Government's desire not only to facilitate the relief and rehabilitation program of UNRRA in Greece, but also to assist in every feasible way in Greek reconstruction.

Mr. Sofianopoulos expressed to the President the heartfelt gratitude of the Greek nation for the sympathy constantly manifested by the American Government and people during the dark years of occupation, and his appreciation for the new words of encouragement and hope which the President gave him for the Greek people.

76 The President's News Conference of July 5, 1945

THE PRESIDENT. [1.] I am sending down Edward C. Moran, Jr., former Congressman from Maine, as Second Assistant Secretary of Labor, at the request of the Secretary of Labor.

I am sending down Jesse M. Donaldson to be First Assistant Postmaster General, at the request of the Postmaster General.

Q. Where is he from, Mr. President?

THE PRESIDENT. Donaldson has been—I don't know where he is from. He has been with the Department all his life.

Q. That is First Assistant Postmaster General?

THE PRESIDENT. First Assistant Postmaster General. I have his record out there, which I will read to you, if you like.

[2.] I have a letter from the Secretary of the Treasury [1] [*reading*]: "When Franklin D. Roosevelt came to Washington, he asked me to come with him, stating that when he was through we would go back to Dutchess County together. For 12 of the most eventful years in American history, I was associated with him, actively participating in meeting the important problems confronting the country both before and during the war.

"Immediately after President Roosevelt's death, I told you how I felt, and stated that I wanted you to know that your hands were untied

---

[1] Henry Morgenthau, Jr.

as far as I was concerned. You were good enough to say that you needed my help and urged me to remain.

"Since then, with your support, I have completed many of the most urgent tasks that were then pending. As I told you this morning, I feel the time has now come when I can appropriately be released from my responsibilities. Accordingly, I now tender my resignation as Secretary of the Treasury. My preference was to have this resignation effective immediately, but since you stated this morning that you wish me to remain until you return from Europe I will, of course, comply with your wishes.

"Permit me to express my appreciation of the fine support you have given me since you became President.

"I most fervently hope for the great success of your Administration in solving the difficult problems which lie ahead.

"If you wish to consult me at any time, I shall always be at your service."

[3.] And I wrote him [*reading*]: "Dear Henry: I am indeed sorry to learn that you have come to the conclusion that the time has arrived to be released from your responsibilities as Secretary of the Treasury. I am grateful, however, that you are willing to remain until I return from Europe so as to carry on the arduous work of the Treasury during my absence.

"Yours has been a very long and efficient service to our country—both in peace and in war; and your departure from the Treasury will be a distinct loss.

"Your service to the nation began in 1933 in the days when you supervised the merger of the farm credit agencies into the Farm Credit Administration which has done so much to help the farmers of the nation.

"Since you have been in the Treasury you have participated in formulating and administering a federal tax program which has raised unprecedented tax revenues with a minimum of disturbance to our economy. These tax laws have seen an impartial and efficient administration under your supervision.

"Under your supervision the Treasury through the sale of bonds has raised over two hundred billion dollars with which to finance our defense and war activities. Raising this money was in itself a great achievement; but, in addition, it was accompanied by a substantial reduction in the average rate of interest on the public debt.

"You have been a steady champion of international monetary stabilization ever since the early days of your administration as Secretary of the Treasury. Through many years of activity and accomplishment in this field, your efforts are now bearing final fruit in the Bretton Woods legislation now pending before the Congress of the United States. In this, and in other ways, you have helped bring about the close fiscal cooperation which this government has had with its Allies during this war. Besides, in the days before the Lend-Lease statute was enacted, many measures of cooperation with our Allies were formulated in your office.

"I am sure that you must feel a great sense of accomplishment in this outstanding record of service to our country. On behalf of our people I extend to you the thanks of the nation.

"I am appreciative of your offer of service in the future, and I am sure that there will be many occasions on which I shall seek your counsel."

Q. May I interrupt you just there? Have you a successor in mind, Mr. President?

THE PRESIDENT. I have a successor in mind, but he will not be announced until I get back from Europe.

[4.] Now here is another letter from Chester Springs, Pennsylvania, dated June 30, 1945, addressed to the President [*reading*]: "As I have served as a member of the Supreme Court for more than fifteen years, and have attained the age of seventy years, I desire to avail myself of the provisions of Section 260 of the Judicial Code, as amended, (28 U.S. Code § 375),—"

Nobody but a Justice would write that. [*Laughter*]

"—and to resign my office as Associate Justice.

"Accordingly, I tender you my resignation, to take effect July 31, 1945.

"I am, Sir, with great respect, Sincerely yours, Owen J. Roberts"

[5.] "Dear Mr. Justice: I am indeed sorry that you have decided to retire from the Bench after your long service.

"The Supreme Court, in the period during which you have served as a member, has been called upon to pass upon some of the most important economic and social problems in the history of our country.

"As I told you this afternoon when I saw you and finally agreed to accept your resignation as of July 31, 1945, I do so only on your promise to continue to give your country the benefit of your sound judgment and advice as occasion arises.

"I extend to you the gratitude of the nation for the service you have rendered."

Q. Mr. President, I notice he resigned. Is that something different from the retirement the other Justices have?

THE PRESIDENT. I think he intended to retire. I think that is the sense under the statute he cites. I think he intends to retire from the bench. At least, that's how I took it.

Q. Have you picked a successor to Justice Roberts yet, sir?

THE PRESIDENT. I have not. I haven't thought about a successor.

I am ready for questions now, if you have any.

[6.] Q. Mr. President, can you tell us anything about the reported mission of Mayor La Guardia to France, before the Big Three conference?

THE PRESIDENT. Well, Mayor La Guardia has been wanting to go to France for some time, and I gave him the necessary permission the other day to go to France.

Q. Can you tell us——

THE PRESIDENT. He is going on his—for his own welfare and benefit. He is not going on a mission for the Government.

Q. He is not going in uniform, Mr. President?

THE PRESIDENT. No. [*Laughter*]

[7.] Q. Mr. President, there has been some talk on the Hill that the Bretton Woods legislation would be postponed until after the Charter. Do you think this could be done?

THE PRESIDENT. I think you had best ask the leaders of the two Houses that question, because I don't think it's going to be delayed that way. At least, that is not my information.

Q. Mr. President, is there any truth to the report that the Secretary of the Treasury will be appointed to the United Nations Bank as—that is, the American section?

THE PRESIDENT. I am not ready to answer that question at this time.

[8.]   Q. Mr. President, do you plan to hold a Big Two meeting with Prime Minister Churchill before going to the Berlin meeting?

THE PRESIDENT. I do not.   There is going to be a Big Three meeting, and all three will be there,——

Q. Mr. President,——

THE PRESIDENT. ——if you want to call it that.

[9.]   Q. Out in Independence, we asked you about Secretary Morgenthau and Ickes, and at that time you said you did not have it in mind to accept their resignations.

THE PRESIDENT. That is true.

Q. I wondered whether—about Ickes now, Mr. President? [*Laughter*]

THE PRESIDENT. The same answer at Independence goes for Mr. Ickes, and went for Mr. Morgenthau until this morning when he came in and told me that he simply wanted to quit and would be willing to stay until I got back from Europe.   That was his own suggestion and not mine.

Q. You do not have in mind, now, accepting Mr. Ickes' resignation?

THE PRESIDENT. No, I do not, for I am going to send Mr. Ickes to England to negotiate an oil treaty.

Q. When is that, sir?

THE PRESIDENT. They are getting ready for it now.   I don't know just what the date will be.

Q. Is that in relation to the Anglo-American oil agreement?

THE PRESIDENT. Yes, that's the one.

Q. Renegotiate?

THE PRESIDENT. Renegotiate, that's the word.

Q. They will be leaving relatively soon?

THE PRESIDENT. Well, I don't think the date has been definitely set, but it will be some time in the near future.

Q. That's the Middle East oil arrangement, sir?

THE PRESIDENT. Yes.   That's what it is.

Q. Any other big Government changes? [*Laughter*]

THE PRESIDENT. I can't think of any, right at the present time, you would be interested to know. [*More laughter*]

Q. Mildly. Mildly interested.

Q. Mr. President, can you give us the date of the Big Three meeting?

THE PRESIDENT. Not definitely, no. It will be some time in the next 3 weeks, let us say that.

Q. Any appointments anticipated, Mr. President, to the State Department—Secretaries—have you any of those in mind yet——

THE PRESIDENT. No.

Q. ——Under Secretaries, Assistants?

THE PRESIDENT. You heard what Mr. Byrnes said yesterday in his statement, that he had no intention of making any changes immediately, and I think that will be a matter for discussion when we get back from overseas.

[10.] Q. Mr. President, have you received the report from Stabilization Director Davis on speculation—curbs on speculation?

THE PRESIDENT. No, I have not. I haven't received it yet.

[11.] Q. Mr. President, could you tell us if, when you come back from Germany, you would like to see the Eiffel Tower again?

THE PRESIDENT. Of course I would like to see it, but I don't think I will probably get a chance to see it. If that is what you want? [*Laughter*]

Q. Do you expect to see General de Gaulle?

THE PRESIDENT. Not on this trip.

Q. Do you contemplate making another trip, then, to Europe soon?

THE PRESIDENT. I can't tell. I can't answer that.

Q. Is there anything, Mr. President, you can tell us about your route on return?

THE PRESIDENT. No, I can't at the present time, because it hasn't been definitely set. As soon as I have the information, I will give it to you.

Reporter: Thank you, Mr. President.

THE PRESIDENT. You are entirely welcome.

NOTE: President Truman's sixteenth news conference was held in his office at the White House at 4:05 p.m. on Thursday, July 5, 1945. The White

House Official Reporter noted that a few members of the press remained after the conference and that the Presi-dent showed them Field Marshal Goering's jewelled baton.

77 Statement by the President Announcing Establishment of Diplomatic Relations With the New Polish Government. *July 5, 1945*

IT IS with great satisfaction that I announce that effective today as of 7 p.m. Eastern War Time the Government of the United States has established diplomatic relations with the newly formed Polish Provisional Government of National Unity now established at Warsaw. The establishment of this Government is an important and positive step in fulfilling the decisions regarding Poland reached at Yalta and signed on February 11, 1945.

The New Polish Provisional Government of National Unity has informed me in a written communication that it has recognized in their entirety the decisions of the Crimea Conference on the Polish question. The new government has thereby confirmed its intention to carry out the provisions of the Crimea decision with respect to the holding of elections.

Mr. Arthur Bliss Lane, whom I have chosen as United States Ambassador to Poland, will proceed to Warsaw as soon as possible, accompanied by his staff.

78 Exchange of Messages With the Prime Minister of the Polish Provisional Government of National Unity. *July 5, 1945*

I AM GRATIFIED to learn from your message to me transmitted through your Ambassador at Moscow that the Polish Provisional Government of National Unity was established on June 28, 1945 in conformity with the Crimea decision. I am pleased to note that Your Excellency's Government has recognized in their entirety the decisions of the Crimea Conference on the Polish question thereby confirming the intentions of Your Excellency's Government to proceed with the holding of elections in Poland in conformity with the provisions of the Crimea decisions. The Government of the United States of America therefore on the basis of its assurances given at the Crimea Conference hereby establishes diplomatic relations with the Polish Provisional Government of National Unity. I have chosen as Ambassador Extraordinary and Plenipotentiary to Poland Mr. Arthur Bliss Lane, whom I have instructed to proceed to Warsaw as soon as possible.

Accept, Excellency, the assurances of my highest consideration.

HARRY S. TRUMAN

[His Excellency, Edward Osobka-Morawski, Prime Minister of the Polish Provisional Government of National Unity, Warsaw, Poland.]

NOTE: Prime Minister Osobka-Morawski's message follows:

His Excellency, Mr. Truman, President of the United States of America:

I have the honor to notify you that as a result of the understanding reached in Moscow between Representatives of the Warsaw Provisional Government and Polish Democratic leaders invited from Poland and from abroad under the auspices of the Commission of three set up at the Crimea Conference the Polish Provisional Government of National Unity was formed on the 28th of June, 1945, in accordance with article 45 of the constitution of the Polish Republic of 1921.

The Provisional Government of National Unity has recognized in their entirety the decisions of the Crimea Conference on the Polish question.

At the same time I have the honor in the name of the Provisional Government of National Unity to approach the Government of the United States of America with a request for the establishment of diplomatic relations between our nations and for the exchange of representatives with the rank of Ambassador.

Please accept the assurance of my highest consideration.

OSOBKA-MORAWSKI

79 Memorandum to Federal Agencies on the Handling of Government Funds. *July 6, 1945*

To the Heads of all Executive Departments and Agencies:

Throughout the war period I have been concerned with the necessity of extreme care in the handling of government funds, especially when expenditures are at such unprecedented levels and so many officials are charged with disbursement of these funds. I am certain that you share my satisfaction that there has been so little evidence of abuse, and that you also share my strong desire that this good record shall be preserved.

Therefore, I am asking you and the other Department and Agency heads to express and underscore my determination to insure the most exacting review of expenditures in every instance where there is the slightest ground to suspect either misuse or careless handling of government funds. Any such instance should be investigated promptly and, where appropriate, a vigorous disciplinary action should be invoked. I trust that you will transmit this message to your staff and supplement it with appropriate instructions of your own.

HARRY S. TRUMAN

NOTE: On the following day the President went aboard the U.S.S. *Augusta* at Newport News, Va., en route to the Potsdam Conference which opened on July 17. He returned to Washington on August 7.

80   Veto of Bill Relating to Law Enforcement in the District of Columbia. *July* 9, 1945

[Released July 9, 1945. Dated July 6, 1945]

To the House of Representatives:

The enrolled bill H.R. 2856, "To provide for better enforcement of law within the District of Columbia, and for other purposes," is returned herewith without my approval.

The language of section 1 of the bill, although obscure and indefinite, is apparently intended to transfer jurisdiction over felonies committed within the park areas in the District of Columbia from the United States Park Police to the Metropolitan Police of the District of Columbia in situations where detective services are required. I am convinced that the effect of such legislation would be to impair rather than to improve law enforcement in these park areas. In the event that felonies are committed on park lands without the perpetrators being immediately apprehended, the provisions of section 1 would seem to place any members of the United States Park Police, functioning in connection with the solution of such felonies, under the control of the detective force of the Metropolitan Police. During this time the United States officers, regardless of rank, would be subject to the orders of the Detective Bureau and precinct detectives of the Metropolitan Police force. This would require the members of the United States Park Police force to serve two masters whose authority over them would be uncertainly divided, and would necessarily have a demoralizing effect on that organization.

The Federal Bureau of Investigation of the Department of Justice and the Metropolitan Police are now authorized to participate with the United States Park Police in solving felony cases wherever their services are necessary. Approval of the bill would unsettle the practical working arrangements already set up for this purpose, without adding to the means available for the detection and apprehension of offenders.

An additional objection to the provisions of section 1 is that they would remove full authority over the United States Park Police force from the Secretary of the Interior, who is charged by law with the exclusive charge and control of the National Capital Park System.

Section 2 of the bill declares that no appropriations from the revenues of the District of Columbia shall be used to pay the salaries or for equipment of the United States Park Police, and section 3 would make this requirement effective from July 1, 1945. Although the reports of the committees which considered the bill state that the practical effect of section 2 is merely to require that members of the Park Police force who perform truly Federal services and are under the control of Federal authorities be paid out of the funds of the Federal Government, nevertheless the fact of the matter is that the appropriation for this purpose contained in the District of Columbia Appropriation Act for the fiscal year beginning July 1, 1945, has not been made from Federal funds. Because of the terms of section 3, approval of the bill might well be construed as a repeal of so much of this appropriation as would otherwise be available for the salaries and equipment of the personnel involved.

Both the Department of the Interior Appropriation Act for the fiscal year beginning July 1, 1945, and the Second Deficiency Appropriation

Act have been passed by the Congress in a form which makes no provisions for the 70 members of the United States Park Police force—a majority of that organization—whose salaries and equipment are, under the terms of the District of Columbia Appropriation Act, payable from revenues of the District of Columbia rather than from Federal funds. Hence the effect of a repeal of the appropriation for this purpose contained in that Act would be to deprive the United States Park Police of the necessary means for the pay of its personnel, and to jeopardize the performance of its essential protective functions.

For these reasons, I feel that it is my duty to withhold my approval from H.R. 2856.

HARRY S. TRUMAN

81 Statement by the President: Bastille Day.
July 13, 1945

IN BASTILLE DAY the people of France have given the world an undying symbol of Freedom. Throughout the long history of our friendship with France the people of the United States have shared the principles for which it stands. Never have those principles had a greater significance than in this year of the final overthrow of one of the darkest tyrannies that has ever tried to enslave mankind.

82 Letter to Secretary Morgenthau Concerning the Appointment of Fred M. Vinson as His Successor.
July 14, 1945

Dear Henry:

I have given careful consideration to your letter of July thirteenth urging that I send to the Senate immediately the nomination of Judge Vinson as Secretary of the Treasury.

I am inclined to agree with you that for the reasons you mention it would be preferable to take this action now instead of waiting for my return from Europe.

I appreciate very much the fine spirit and keen sense of public responsibility in which you have approached this matter.

With personal regards,

Sincerely yours,

HARRY S. TRUMAN

[The Honorable Henry Morgenthau, Jr., The Secretary of the Treasury]

NOTE: Secretary Morgenthau's letter, also released, pointed out that such matters as the continuation of war financing, the tax enforcement drive, revenue legislation, and many other problems called for prompt decision; and that his successor should be given the opportunity to make the decisions since it would become his duty to carry them out.

Secretary Morgenthau also referred to the possibility of a recess in the Senate, which would delay Judge Vinson's confirmation.

The letters were exchanged by wireless while the President was aboard the U.S.S. *Augusta* en route to the Potsdam conference.

83   Statement by the President on the Manpower Needs of the Western Railroads. *July 16, 1945*

IF THE DEMANDS of the Japanese war are to be met, the railroads in the west must have additional manpower immediately. The manpower shortage is so serious that the War Department recently ordered 4,000 experienced railroad men to be furloughed from the Army to help ease the situation, but they are only a fraction of the number needed.

The western railroads today need 65,000 men and need them badly. We must keep men and materiel flowing into the ports as fast as our convoys can transport them to the battle zone.

The effects of the shortage already are being felt, with the peak load still months away. Our soldiers returning from the European Campaign are not getting the best accommodations because many cars are in the shops awaiting repairs and overhauling. Some troops are being delayed at the ports because trains cannot be supplied promptly. Overworked crews must be given time to rest before taking trains out on long, hard trips. Trains are often late because of short switching crews which cannot keep traffic moving at top efficiency. Unless additional manpower is found those delays will become serious as the load increases.

That is why I am bringing this situation to the attention of the American people. Any patriotic American who is not already engaged in essential war work can make a real contribution toward the defeat of Japan by applying for a job on a western railroad during this emergency period. Those who are now working on railroads can do a great service to their country by remaining on the job.

NOTE: The statement was released at No. 2 Kaiserstrasse in Babelsberg, Germany, which served as headquarters for the President and his staff during the Potsdam conference. The President arrived at Babelsberg on July 15.

84 Special Message to the Congress on Amending the Surplus Property Act To Provide for a Single Administrator. *July 17, 1945*

To the Congress of the United States:

On October 3, 1944, the Congress enacted the Surplus Property Act of 1944, a comprehensive scheme for the declaration, handling and disposal of all types of surplus property.

The operations of the 3-man Surplus Property Board created by that Act have been marked by substantial achievements. It has set in motion the disposal machinery which Congress authorized and it has begun to implement the standards which Congress laid down for the disposal of surplus property. Regulations already promulgated or in the process of adoption cover the most important types of property—consumer goods, plant equipment, industrial plants and farm lands. The emphasis in the Board's task will then shift from the promulgation of policy to the effectuation of basic policies already established.

The task of administration becomes increasingly difficult as the rate of surplus declarations rapidly rises. That rate is rising sharply now. To dispose of this growing volume of surplus property in a manner that will fully achieve the objectives declared by Congress will require the most efficient possible administrative machinery.

While the present Surplus Property Act was under consideration by the Congress the then Director of War Mobilization and Reconversion, Mr. Byrnes, recommended provision for a single Administrator. I think experience has proved him right.

In a field which calls for quick and decisive action, it is undesirable to dilute responsibility for the disposal of surplus property. Administration by a multimember Board has complicated day-to-day operations under the Act.

More recently the retiring Chairman of the Board has stated to the Congress that although he originally shared the view that a 3-man Board was appropriate, his experience also led him to the belief that the Act can best be administered by a single Administrator.

I am convinced that the effective performance of the vast administrative task remaining for the disposal of surplus property imperatively requires that authority to make decisions and responsibility for those decisions should be centralized in a single official. Such an official should operate, as do all other executive agencies, under the general authority conferred by the President and the Congress on the Office of War Mobilization and Reconversion. Accordingly I request the Congress to amend the Surplus Property Act of 1944 by substituting a single Administrator for the present Surplus Property Board.

NOTE: On September 18, 1945, the President approved Public Law 181 (59 Stat. 533) providing for the administration of the Surplus Property Act of 1944 by a Surplus Property Administrator.

85 Letter to the President of the Senate and to the Speaker of the House of Representatives Transmitting Reports on Foreign War Relief Activities. *July 17, 1945*

[Released July 17, 1945. Dated July 14, 1945]

Sir:

I have the honor to transmit herewith reports prepared by the American Red Cross and the War Refugee Board reflecting foreign war relief operations which have been conducted during the period July 1, 1940 through April 30, 1945, from appropriations for foreign war relief consolidated and extended by the Second Deficiency Appropriation

Act, 1942, the Urgent Deficiency Appropriation Act, 1943, and the Second Deficiency Appropriation Act, 1944.

These reports supplement those previously submitted as of April 30, 1941, April 30, 1942, April 30, 1943, and April 30, 1944 and are of necessity of an interim nature since the foreign war relief program is still in progress.

The Second Deficiency Appropriation Act, 1945 has extended the availability of $2,150,000 of this appropriation until December 31, 1945 in order to provide for the termination of the program and a final report will be submitted following that date.

There is also transmitted herewith a statement of allocations that have been made to government purchasing agencies from this appropriation together with unobligated balances remaining in each allocation as of April 30, 1945. It will be noted that obligations reflected in this statement have been based on orders placed with vendors as distinguished from the report of the American Red Cross which was prepared on the basis of requisitions submitted to government purchasing agencies.

Respectfully yours,

HARRY S. TRUMAN

NOTE: This is the text of identical letters addressed to the Honorable Kenneth McKellar, President pro tempore of the Senate, and to the Honorable Sam Rayburn, Speaker of the House of Representatives.

The reports of the American Red Cross and the War Refugee Board and the report on status of appropriation and allocations are printed in House Document 262 (79th Cong., 1st sess.).

86   Remarks at the Raising of the Flag Over the U.S. Group Control Council Headquarters in Berlin.   *July* 20, 1945

General Eisenhower, officers and men:

This is an historic occasion. We have conclusively proven that a free people can successfully look after the affairs of the world.

We are here today to raise the flag of victory over the capital of our greatest adversary. In doing that, we must remember that in raising that flag we are raising it in the name of the people of the United States, who are looking forward to a better world, a peaceful world, a world in which all the people will have an opportunity to enjoy the good things of life, and not just a few at the top.

Let us not forget that we are fighting for peace, and for the welfare of mankind. We are not fighting for conquest. There is not one piece of territory, or one thing of a monetary nature that we want out of this war. We want peace and prosperity for the world as a whole. We want to see the time come when we can do the things in peace that we have been able to do in war.

If we can put this tremendous machine of ours, which has made this victory possible, to work for peace we can look forward to the greatest age in the history of mankind. That is what we propose to do.

NOTE: The President spoke shortly before 4 p.m. in the courtyard at the headquarters buildings. The flag used was the same one that had flown over the Capitol in Washington when war was declared against Germany.

87   Letter to David K. Niles, Administrative Assistant to the President. *July* 20, 1945

[Released July 20, 1945. Dated July 17, 1945]

Dear Dave:

I am glad that at my request you are remaining on in your post as one of the Administrative Assistants to the President. I know that your long record in government will be helpful to me as it was to the late President Roosevelt.

For ten years you have taken an important part in the activities of our government in Washington. Beginning with the work of relieving the distress of unemployment, and later in the Department of Commerce, the Office of Production Management, and for the last several years, as an Administrative Assistant you have had a hand in many of the important events of the last decade. It will be of great service to have the benefit of your ability and conscientious service, and the experience and information you have acquired during these years will be most valuable.

With kindest regards,

Very sincerely yours,

HARRY S. TRUMAN

[Honorable David K. Niles, Administrative Assistant to the President, The White House]

88 Letter Read by Secretary Vinson at the Humanitarian Award Dinner of the Variety Clubs of America. July 25, 1945

[Released July 25, 1945. Dated July 21, 1945]

Dear Mr. O'Donnell:

I deeply regret that circumstances will not permit me to be with you and with other admirers of Sir Alexander Fleming next Wednesday evening, when the Variety Clubs of America honor that great humanitarian and benefactor of mankind.

For all that Sir Alexander has done to alleviate pain and suffering, through the great discovery which ever will bear his name, the world owes a debt of gratitude difficult to estimate. It is particularly fitting, therefore, that Variety should give him its award for 1944 in recognition of unusual and unselfish service in behalf of all humanity.

From afar I welcome him to the Capital of the Nation and hail him as one who in our day and generation is going forward in the noble tradition of Lord Lister, William Harvey, and that other grand old Briton, Sir Thomas Browne.

I could not close this note without adding a word of heartfelt appreciation to the Variety Clubs of America for their unwearied efforts in support of the war and in aiding all good causes both in peace and war.

Very sincerely yours,

HARRY S. TRUMAN

[R. J. O'Donnell, Esq., National Chief Barker, The Variety Clubs of America]

176

NOTE: The dinner was held at the May-
flower Hotel in Washington. The letter, dated Potsdam, July 21, 1945, was
released in Washington together with
Secretary Vinson's remarks.

89 Letter to Alben W. Barkley on the Eighth Anniversary
    of His Election as Majority Leader of the Senate.
    July 27, 1945

Dear Alben:

Today marks the eighth anniversary of your service as Majority
Leader of the Senate. I understand that this is twice as long as any of
your predecessors have served. These years have been eventful ones.
They have been years of great moment to the United States and to
the world.

In all of the recent events which have meant so much in shaping the
future of our civilization you have played an important and effective
role. Not only have you helped to fulfill the ideals and principles of
our party, but you have been willing and anxious to lay aside all sem-
blance of partisanship or desire for party advantage whenever the welfare of our nation required it.

I congratulate you on your past service as Majority Leader, and, also,
on your thirty-three years of service in the Congress. The nation is
grateful to you for your patriotic share in the accomplishments of these
years, and I know that the years to come will be equally fruitful.

With all best wishes for your continued health and success from your
old friend,

Very sincerely yours,

HARRY S. TRUMAN

[Honorable Alben W. Barkley, The United States Senate]

90   Veto of Bill Authorizing the Improvement of Certain Harbors.   *July 31, 1945*

[Released July 31, 1945. Dated July 28, 1945]

To the House of Representatives:

I return herewith, without my approval, H.R. 3477, a bill "Authorizing the improvement of certain harbors in the interest of commerce and navigation."

The bill authorizes the improvement, for navigation, of Savannah Harbor, Georgia, and Two Harbors, Minnesota, in accordance with the reports of the Chief of Engineers, House Document No. 227, Seventy-ninth Congress, and House Document No. 805, Seventy-eighth Congress, respectively. The estimated cost of the Savannah Harbor project is $2,738,000, and of the Two Harbors $1,876,000.

Since the entry of the United States into the present war, omnibus river and harbor and flood control acts have contained specific provisions restricting construction of the projects so authorized to the postwar period, unless required for the prosecution of the war. The most recent enactment (Public Law 14, approved March 2, 1945) adopted 291 river and harbor projects at an aggregate estimate of cost of $381,968,332, subject to the specific provision:

"That no project herein authorized shall be appropriated for or constructed until six months after the termination of the present wars in which the United States is engaged unless the construction of such project has been recommended by an authorized defense agency and approved by the President as being necessary or desirable in the interest of the national defense and security, and the President has notified the Congress to that effect."

The bill under consideration does not contain such a restrictive provision, and the Secretary of War, in submitting the reports of the Chief of Engineers on the above-mentioned projects, stated that:

"Inasmuch as the proposed work would involve the use of manpower, material and equipment and since the project is not essential to the war effort, the Department is of the opinion that, if the project is approved, work thereon should not be initiated until after the war."

Approval of the bill under consideration would permit, upon the availability of funds therefor, the immediate undertaking of these two projects and thus place them in a status preferential to the large number of projects that have been authorized by the Congress during the war period which are not essential to the prosecution of the war.

Moreover, it seems to me that piecemeal legislation of this nature is inappropriate since it does not take into account a well-considered and well-rounded plan for projects to be undertaken in a definite order of national preference and desirability.

I therefore find it necessary to withhold my approval of the bill.

HARRY S. TRUMAN

91 Joint Report With Allied Leaders on the Potsdam Conference. *August 2*, 1945

I. REPORT ON THE TRIPARTITE CONFERENCE OF BERLIN

ON JULY 17, 1945, the President of the United States of America, Harry S. Truman, the Chairman of the Council of People's Commissars of the Union of Soviet Socialist Republics, Generalissimo J. V. Stalin, and the Prime Minister of Great Britain, Winston S. Churchill, together with Mr. Clement R. Attlee, met in the Tripartite Conference of Berlin. They were accompanied by the foreign secretaries of the three governments, Mr. James F. Byrnes, Mr. V. M. Molotov, and Mr. Anthony Eden, the Chiefs of Staff, and other advisers.

There were nine meetings between July seventeenth and July twenty-fifth. The conference was then interrupted for two days while the results of the British general election were being declared.

On July twenty-eighth Mr. Attlee returned to the conference as Prime Minister, accompanied by the new Secretary of State for Foreign Affairs, Mr. Ernest Bevin. Four days of further discussion then took place. During the course of the conference there were regular meetings of the heads of the three governments accompanied by the foreign secretaries, and also of the foreign secretaries alone. Committees appointed by the foreign secretaries for preliminary consideration of questions before the conference also met daily.

The meetings of the conference were held at the Cecilienhof near Potsdam. The conference ended on August 2, 1945.

Important decisions and agreements were reached. Views were exchanged on a number of other questions and consideration of these matters will be continued by the council of foreign ministers established by the conference.

President Truman, Generalissimo Stalin and Prime Minister Attlee leave this conference, which has strengthened the ties between the three governments and extended the scope of their collaboration and understanding, with renewed confidence that their governments and peoples, together with the other United Nations, will ensure the creation of a just and enduring peace.

II. ESTABLISHMENT OF A COUNCIL OF FOREIGN MINISTERS

The conference reached an agreement for the establishment of a Council of Foreign Ministers representing the five principal powers to continue the necessary preparatory work for the peace settlements and to take up other matters which from time to time may be referred to the Council by agreement of the governments participating in the Council.

The text of the agreement for the establishment of the Council of Foreign Ministers is as follows:

1. There shall be established a Council composed of the foreign ministers of the United Kingdom, the Union of Soviet Socialist Republics, China, France and the United States.

2. (i) The Council shall normally meet in London, which shall be the permanent seat of the joint secretariat which the Council will form. Each of the foreign ministers will be accompanied by a high-ranking deputy, duly authorized to carry on the work of the Council in the absence of his foreign minister, and by a small staff of technical advisers.

(ii) The first meeting of the Council shall be held in London not later than September 1, 1945. Meetings may be held by common agreement in other capitals as may be agreed from time to time.

3. (i) As its immediate important task, the Council shall be author-

ized to draw up, with a view to their submission to the United Nations, treaties of peace with Italy, Rumania, Bulgaria, Hungary and Finland, and to propose settlements of territorial questions outstanding on the termination of the war in Europe. The Council shall be utilized for the preparation of a peace settlement for Germany to be accepted by the government of Germany when a government adequate for the purpose is established.

(ii) For the discharge of each of these tasks the Council will be composed of the members representing those states which were signatory to the terms of surrender imposed upon the enemy state concerned. For the purpose of the peace settlement for Italy, France shall be regarded as a signatory to the terms of surrender for Italy. Other members will be invited to participate when matters directly concerning them are under discussion.

(iii) Other matters may from time to time be referred to the Council by agreement between the member governments.

4. (i) Whenever the Council is considering a question of direct interest to a state not represented thereon, such state should be invited to send representatives to participate in the discussion and study of that question.

(ii) The Council may adapt its procedure to the particular problem under consideration. In some cases it may hold its own preliminary discussions prior to the participation of other interested states. In other cases, the Council may convoke a formal conference of the state chiefly interested in seeking a solution of the particular problem.

In accordance with the decision of the conference the three governments have each addressed an identical invitation to the governments of China and France to adopt this text and to join in establishing the Council.

The establishment of the Council of Foreign Ministers for the specific purposes named in the text will be without prejudice to the agreement of the Crimea Conference that there should be periodic consultation among the foreign secretaries of the United States, the Union of Soviet Socialist Republics and the United Kingdom.

The conference also considered the position of the European Advisory Commission in the light of the agreement to establish the Council of Foreign Ministers. It was noted with satisfaction that the Commission had ably discharged its principal tasks by the recommendations that it had furnished for the terms of Germany's unconditional surrender, for the zones of occupation in Germany and Austria, and for the inter-Allied control machinery in those countries. It was felt that further work of a detailed character for the coordination of allied policy for the control of Germany and Austria would in future fall within the competence of the Allied Control Council at Berlin and the Allied Commission at Vienna. Accordingly, it was agreed to recommend that the European Advisory Commission be dissolved.

III. GERMANY

The Allied Armies are in occupation of the whole of Germany and the German people have begun to atone for the terrible crimes committed under the leadership of those whom in the hour of their success, they openly approved and blindly obeyed.

Agreement has been reached at this conference on the political and economic principles of a coordinated Allied policy toward defeated Germany during the period of Allied control.

The purpose of this agreement is to carry out the Crimea Declaration on Germany. German militarism and Nazism will be extirpated and the Allies will take in agreement together, now and in the future, the other measures necessary to assure that Germany never again will threaten her neighbors or the peace of the world.

It is not the intention of the Allies to destroy or enslave the German people. It is the intention of the Allies that the German people be given the opportunity to prepare for the eventual reconstruction of their life on a democratic and peaceful basis. If their own efforts are steadily directed to this end, it will be possible for them in due course to take their place among the free and peaceful peoples of the world.

The text of the agreement is as follows:

The Political and Economic Principles to Govern the Treatment of Germany in the Initial Control Period.

A. Political Principles.

1. In accordance with the agreement on control machinery in Germany, supreme authority in Germany is exercised on instructions from their respective governments, by the Commanders-in-Chief of the armed forces of the United States of America, the United Kingdom, the Union of Soviet Socialist Republics, and the French Republic, each in his own zone of occupation, and also jointly, in matters affecting Germany as a whole, in their capacity as members of the Control Council.

2. So far as is practicable, there shall be uniformity of treatment of the German population throughout Germany.

3. The purposes of the occupation of Germany by which the Control Council shall be guided are:

(i) The complete disarmament and demilitarization of Germany and the elimination or control of all German industry that could be used for military production. To these ends:

(a) All German land, naval and air forces, the S.S., S.A., S.D., and Gestapo, with all their organizations, staffs and institutions, including the General Staff, the Officers' Corps, Reserve Corps, military schools, war veterans' organizations and all other military and quasi-military organization, together with all clubs and associations which serve to keep alive the military tradition in Germany, shall be completely and finally abolished in such manner as permanently to prevent the revival or reorganization of German militarism and Nazism.

(b) All arms, ammunition and implements of war and all specialized facilities for their production shall be held at the disposal of the Allies or destroyed. The maintenance and production of all aircraft and all arms, ammunition and implements of war shall be prevented.

(ii) To convince the German people that they have suffered a total military defeat and that they cannot escape responsibility for what they have brought upon themselves, since their own ruthless warfare and the fanatical Nazi resistance have destroyed German economy and made chaos and suffering inevitable.

(iii) To destroy the National Socialist Party and its affiliated and supervised organizations, to dissolve all Nazi institutions, to ensure that they are not revived in any form, and to prevent all Nazi and militarist activity or propaganda.

(iv) To prepare for the eventual reconstruction of German political life on a democratic basis and for eventual peaceful cooperation in international life by Germany.

4. All Nazi laws which provided the basis of the Hitler regime or established discrimination on grounds of race, creed, or political opinion shall be abolished. No such discriminations, whether legal, administrative or otherwise, shall be tolerated.

5. War criminals and those who have participated in planning or carrying out Nazi enterprises involving or resulting in atrocities or war crimes shall be arrested and brought to judgment. Nazi leaders, influential Nazi supporters and high officials of Nazi organizations and institutions and any other persons dangerous to the occupation or its objectives shall be arrested and interned.

6. All members of the Nazi party who have been more than nominal participants in its activities and all other persons hostile to allied purposes shall be removed from public and semipublic office, and from positions of responsibility in important private undertakings. Such persons shall be replaced by persons who, by their political and moral qualities, are deemed capable of assisting in developing genuine democratic institutions in Germany.

7. German education shall be so controlled as completely to eliminate Nazi and militarist doctrines and to make possible the successful development of democratic ideas.

8. The judicial system will be reorganized in accordance with the principles of democracy, of justice under law, and of equal rights for all citizens without distinction of race, nationality or religion.

9. The administration of affairs in Germany should be directed towards the decentralization of the political structure and the development of local responsibility. To this end:

(i) Local self-government shall be restored throughout Germany on democratic principles and in particular through elective councils as rapidly as is consistent with military security and the purposes of military occupation;

(ii) All democratic political parties with rights of assembly and of public discussion shall be allowed and encouraged throughout Germany;

(iii) Representative and elective principles shall be introduced into regional, provincial and state (land) administration as rapidly as may be justified by the successful application of these principles in local self-government;

(iv) For the time being no central German government shall be established. Notwithstanding this, however, certain essential central German administrative departments, headed by state secretaries, shall be established, particularly in the fields of finance, transport, communications, foreign trade and industry. Such departments will act under the direction of the Control Council.

10. Subject to the necessity for maintaining military security, freedom of speech, press and religion shall be permitted, and religious institutions shall be respected. Subject likewise to the maintenance of military security, the formation of free trade unions shall be permitted.

B. Economic Principles.

11. In order to eliminate Germany's war potential, the production of arms, ammunition and implements of war as well as all types of aircraft and sea-going ships shall be prohibited and prevented. Production of metals, chemicals, machinery and other items that are directly necessary to a war economy shall be rigidly controlled and restricted to Germany's approved post-war peacetime needs to meet the objectives stated in paragraph 15. Productive capacity not needed for permitted production shall be removed in accordance with the reparations plan recommended by the Allied Commission on reparations and approved by the governments concerned or if not removed shall be destroyed.

12. At the earliest practicable date, the German economy shall be decentralized for the purpose of eliminating the present excessive concentration of economic power as exemplified in particular by cartels, syndicates, trusts and other monopolistic arrangements.

13. In organizing the German economy, primary emphasis shall be given to the development of agriculture and peaceful domestic industries.

14. During the period of occupation Germany shall be treated as a single economic unit. To this end common policies shall be established in regard to:

(a) Mining and industrial production and allocations;

(b) Agriculture, forestry and fishing;

(c) Wages, prices and rationing;

(d) Import and export programs for Germany as a whole;

(e) Currency and banking, central taxation and customs;

(f) Reparation and removal of industrial war potential;

(g) Transportation and communications.

In applying these policies account shall be taken, where appropriate, of varying local conditions.

15. Allied controls shall be imposed upon the German economy but only to the extent necessary:

(a) To carry out programs of industrial disarmament and demilitarization, of reparations, and of approved exports and imports.

(b) To assure the production and maintenance of goods and services required to meet the needs of the occupying forces and displaced persons in Germany and essential to maintain in Germany average living standards not exceeding the average of the standards of living of European countries. (European countries means all European countries excluding the United Kingdom and the Union of Soviet Socialist Republics.)

(c) To ensure in the manner determined by the Control Council the equitable distribution of essential commodities between the several zones so as to produce a balanced economy throughout Germany and reduce the need for imports.

(d) To control German industry and all economic and financial international transactions, including exports and imports, with the aim of preventing Germany from developing a war potential and of achieving the other objectives named herein.

(e) To control all German public or private scientific bodies, research and experimental institutions, laboratories, et cetera, connected with economic activities.

16. In the imposition and maintenance of economic controls established by the Control Council, German administrative machinery shall be created and the German authorities shall be required to the fullest extent practicable to proclaim and assume administration of such controls. Thus it should be brought home to the German people that the responsibility for the administration of such controls and any breakdown in these controls will rest with themselves. Any German controls which may run counter to the objectives of occupation will be prohibited.

17. Measures shall be promptly taken:

(a) To effect essential repair of transport;

(b) To enlarge coal production;

(c) To maximize agricultural output; and

(d) To effect emergency repair of housing and essential utilities.

18. Appropriate steps shall be taken by the Control Council to exercise control and the power of disposition over German-owned external assets not already under the control of United Nations which have taken part in the war against Germany.

19. Payment of reparations should leave enough resources to enable the German people to subsist without external assistance. In working out the economic balance of Germany the necessary means must be provided to pay for imports approved by the Control Council in Germany. The proceeds of exports from current production and stocks shall be available in the first place for payment for such imports.

The above clause will not apply to the equipment and products referred to in paragraphs 4(A) and 4(B) of the Reparations Agreement.

IV. REPARATIONS FROM GERMANY

In accordance with the Crimea decision that Germany be compelled to compensate to the greatest possible extent for the loss and suffering that she has caused to the United Nations and for which the German people cannot escape responsibility, the following agreement on reparations was reached:

1. Reparation claims of the U.S.S.R. shall be met by removals from the zone of Germany occupied by the U.S.S.R. and from appropriate German external assets.

2. The U.S.S.R. undertakes to settle the reparation claims of Poland from its own share of reparations.

3. The reparation claims of the United States, the United Kingdom and other countries entitled to reparations shall be met from the western zones and from appropriate German external assets.

4. In addition to the reparations to be taken by the U.S.S.R. from its own zone of occupation, the U.S.S.R. shall receive additionally from the western zones:

(A) 15 percent of such usable and complete industrial capital equipment, in the first place from the metallurgical, chemical and machine manufacturing industries, as is unnecessary for the German peace economy and should be removed from the western zones of Germany, in exchange for an equivalent value of food, coal, potash, zinc, timber, clay products, petroleum products, and such other commodities as may be agreed upon.

(B) 10 percent of such industrial capital equipment as is unnecessary for the German peace economy and should be removed from the western zones, to be transferred to the Soviet Government on reparations account without payment or exchange of any kind in return.

Removals of equipment as provided in (A) and (B) above shall be made simultaneously.

5. The amount of equipment to be removed from the western zones on account of reparations must be determined within six months from now at the latest.

6. Removals of industrial capital equipment shall begin as soon as possible and shall be completed within two years from the determination specified in paragraph 5. The delivery of products covered by 4(A) above shall begin as soon as possible and shall be made by the U.S.S.R. in agreed installments within five years of the date hereof. The determination of the amount and character of the industrial capital equipment unnecessary for the German peace economy and therefore available for reparations shall be made by the control council under

188

policies fixed by the Allied Commission on Reparations, with the participation of France, subject to the final approval of the zone commander in the zone from which the equipment is to be removed.

7. Prior to the fixing of the total amount of equipment subject to removal, advance deliveries shall be made in respect of such equipment as will be determined to be eligible for delivery in accordance with the procedure set forth in the last sentence of paragraph 6.

8. The Soviet Government renounces all claims in respect of reparations to shares of German enterprises which are located in the western zones of occupation in Germany as well as to German foreign assets in all countries except those specified in paragraph 9 below.

9. The Governments of the United Kingdom and the United States of America renounce their claims in respect of reparations to shares of German enterprises which are located in the eastern zone of occupation in Germany, as well as to German foreign assets in Bulgaria, Finland, Hungary, Rumania and Eastern Austria.

10. The Soviet Government makes no claims to gold captured by the Allied troops in Germany.

V. DISPOSAL OF THE GERMAN NAVY AND MERCHANT MARINE

The conference agreed in principle upon arrangements for the use and disposal of the surrendered German fleet and merchant ships. It was decided that the three governments would appoint experts to work out together detailed plans to give effect to the agreed principles. A further joint statement will be published simultaneously by the three governments in due course.

VI. CITY OF KOENIGSBERG AND THE ADJACENT AREA

The conference examined a proposal by the Soviet Government that pending the final determination of territorial questions at the peace settlement the section of the western frontier of the Union of Soviet Socialist Republics which is adjacent to the Baltic Sea should pass from a point on the eastern shore of the Bay of Danzig to the east, north of Braunsberg-Goldap, to the meeting point of the frontiers of Lithuania, the Polish Republic and East Prussia.

The conference has agreed in principle to the proposal of the Soviet Government concerning the ultimate transfer to the Soviet Union of the City of Koenigsberg and the area adjacent to it as described above subject to expert examination of the actual frontier.

The President of the United States and the British Prime Minister have declared that they will support the proposal of the conference at the forthcoming peace settlement.

VII. WAR CRIMINALS

The three governments have taken note of the discussions which have been proceeding in recent weeks in London between British, United States, Soviet and French representatives with a view to reaching agreement on the methods of trial of those major war criminals whose crimes under the Moscow Declaration of October 1943 have no particular geographical localization. The three governments reaffirm their intention to bring those criminals to swift and sure justice. They hope that the negotiations in London will result in speedy agreement being reached for this purpose, and they regard it as a matter of great importance that the trial of those major criminals should begin at the earliest possible date. The first list of defendants will be published before September first.

VIII. AUSTRIA

The conference examined a proposal by the Soviet Government on the extension of the authority of the Austrian Provisional Government to all of Austria.

The three governments agreed that they were prepared to examine this question after the entry of the British and American forces into the City of Vienna.

IX. POLAND

The conference considered questions relating to the Polish Provisional Government and the western boundary of Poland.

On the Polish Provisional Government of National Unity they defined their attitude in the following statement:

A—We have taken note with pleasure of the agreement reached

among representative Poles from Poland and abroad which has made possible the formation, in accordance with the decisions reached at the Crimea Conference, of a Polish Provisional Government of National Unity recognized by the three powers. The establishment by the British and United States Governments of diplomatic relations with the Polish Provisional Government has resulted in the withdrawal of their recognition from the former Polish Government in London, which no longer exists.

The British and United States Governments have taken measures to protect the interest of the Polish Provisional Government as the recognized government of the Polish States in the property belonging to the Polish State located in their territories and under their control, whatever the form of this property may be. They have further taken measures to prevent alienation to third parties of such property. All proper facilities will be given to the Polish Provisional Government for the exercise of the ordinary legal remedies for the recovery of any property belonging to the Polish State which may have been wrongfully alienated.

The three powers are anxious to assist the Polish Provisional Government in facilitating the return to Poland as soon as practicable of all Poles abroad who wish to go, including members of the Polish armed forces and the Merchant Marine. They expect that those Poles who return home shall be accorded personal and property rights on the same basis as all Polish citizens.

The three powers note that the Polish Provisional Government in accordance with the decisions of the Crimea Conference has agreed to the holding of free and unfettered elections as soon as possible on the basis of universal suffrage and secret ballot in which all democratic and anti-Nazi parties shall have the right to take part and to put forward candidates, and that representatives of the Allied press shall enjoy full freedom to report to the world upon developments in Poland before and during the elections.

B—The following agreement was reached on the western frontier of Poland:

In conformity with the agreement on Poland reached at the Crimea

Conference the three heads of government have sought the opinion of the Polish Provisional Government of National Unity in regard to the accession of territory in the north and west which Poland should receive. The President of the National Council of Poland and members of the Polish Provisional Government of National Unity have been received at the conference and have fully presented their views. The three heads of government reaffirm their opinion that the final delimitation of the western frontier of Poland should await the peace settlement.

The three heads of government agree that, pending the final determination of Poland's western frontier, the former German territories east of a line running from the Baltic Sea immediately west of Swinemunde, and thence along the Oder River to the confluence of the western Neisse River and along the western Neisse to the Czechoslovak frontier, including that portion of East Prussia not placed under the administration of the Union of Soviet Socialist Republics in accordance with the understanding reached at this conference and including the area of the former free City of Danzig, shall be under the administration of the Polish State and for such purposes should not be considered as part of the Soviet zone of occupation in Germany.

X. CONCLUSION OF PEACE TREATIES AND ADMISSION TO THE UNITED NATIONS ORGANIZATION

The conference agreed upon the following statement of common policy for establishing, as soon as possible, the conditions of lasting peace after victory in Europe:

The three governments consider it desirable that the present anomalous position of Italy, Bulgaria, Finland, Hungary and Rumania should be terminated by the conclusion of peace treaties. They trust that the other interested Allied governments will share these views.

For their part the three governments have included the preparation of a peace treaty for Italy as the first among the immediate important tasks to be undertaken by the new Council of Foreign Ministers. Italy was the first of the Axis powers to break with Germany, to whose defeat she has made a material contribution, and has now joined with the Allies in the struggle against Japan. Italy has freed herself from the Fascist regime and is making good progress towards the reestablishment of a democratic government and institutions. The conclusion of such a peace treaty with a recognized and democratic Italian government will make it possible for the three governments to fulfill their desire to support an application from Italy for membership of the United Nations.

The three governments have also charged the Council of Foreign Ministers with the task of preparing peace treaties for Bulgaria, Finland, Hungary and Rumania. The conclusion of peace treaties with recognized democratic governments in these states will also enable the three governments to support applications from them for membership of the United Nations. The three governments agree to examine each separately in the near future, in the light of the conditions then prevailing, the establishment of diplomatic relations with Finland, Rumania, Bulgaria, and Hungary to the extent possible prior to the conclusion of peace treaties with those countries.

The three governments have no doubt that in view of the changed conditions resulting from the termination of the war in Europe, representatives of the Allied press will enjoy full freedom to report to the world upon developments in Rumania, Bulgaria, Hungary and Finland.

As regards the admission of other states into the United Nations Organization, Article 4 of the Charter of the United Nations declares that:

"1. Membership in the United Nations is open to all other peace-loving states who accept the obligations contained in the present Charter and, in the judgment of the Organization, are able and willing to carry out these obligations;

"2. The admission of any such state to membership in the United Nations will be effected by a decision of the General Assembly upon the recommendation of the Security Council."

The three governments, so far as they are concerned, will support applications for membership from those states which have remained neutral during the war and which fulfill the qualifications set out above.

The three governments feel bound however to make it clear that they for their part would not favor any application for membership put forward by the present Spanish Government, which, having been founded with the support of the Axis powers, does not, in view of its origins, its nature, its record and its close association with the aggressor states, possess the qualifications necessary to justify such membership.

XI. TERRITORIAL TRUSTEESHIPS

The conference examined a proposal by the Soviet Government concerning trusteeship territories as defined in the decision of the Crimea Conference and in the Charter of the United Nations Organization.

After an exchange of views on this question it was decided that the disposition of any former Italian territories was one to be decided in connection with the preparation of a peace treaty for Italy and that the question of Italian territory would be considered by the September Council of Ministers of Foreign Affairs.

XII. REVISED ALLIED CONTROL COMMISSION PROCEDURE IN RUMANIA, BULGARIA, AND HUNGARY

The three governments took note that the Soviet representatives on the Allied Control Commissions in Rumania, Bulgaria and Hungary, have communicated to their United Kingdom and United States colleagues proposals for improving the work of the Control Commission, now that hostilities in Europe have ceased.

The three governments agreed that the revision of the procedures of the Allied Control Commissions in these countries would now be undertaken, taking into account the interests and responsibilities of the three governments which together presented the terms of armistice to the respective countries, and accepting as a basis the agreed proposals.

XIII. ORDERLY TRANSFERS OF GERMAN POPULATIONS

The conference reached the following agreement on the removal of Germans from Poland, Czechoslovakia and Hungary:

The three governments having considered the question in all its aspects, recognize that the transfer to Germany of German populations, or elements thereof, remaining in Poland, Czechoslovakia and Hungary, will have to be undertaken. They agree that any transfers that take place should be effected in an orderly and humane manner.

Since the influx of a large number of Germans into Germany would increase the burden already resting on the occupying authorities, they consider that the Allied Control Council in Germany should in the first instance examine the problem with special regard to the question of the equitable distribution of these Germans among the several zones of occupation. They are accordingly instructing their respective representatives on the Control Council to report to their governments as soon as possible the extent to which such persons have already entered Germany from Poland, Czechoslovakia and Hungary, and to submit an estimate of the time and rate at which further transfers could be carried out, having regard to the present situation in Germany.

The Czechoslovak Government, the Polish Provisional Government and the Control Council in Hungary are at the same time being informed of the above, and are being requested meanwhile to suspend further expulsions pending the examination by the governments concerned of the report from their representatives on the Control Council.

XIV. MILITARY TALKS

During the conference there were meetings between the Chiefs of Staff of the three governments on military matters of common interest.

Approved:

> J. V. STALIN
> HARRY S. TRUMAN
> C. R. ATTLEE

NOTE: The Potsdam conference adjourned at 12:30 a.m. on August 2. Shortly thereafter the President left for the airport in Gatow from which he flew to England. After a luncheon with King George VI aboard the H.M.S. *Renown* in Plymouth Harbor, he embarked for Newport News on the U.S.S. *Augusta* in the afternoon of August 2. He reached Washington on August 7.

The foregoing report, signed at Potsdam, was released simultaneously in Washington, London, and Moscow at 5:30 p.m. Washington time. A list of the delegations of the participating countries, made public by the White House with the report, is published in the Department of State Bulletin (vol. 13, p. 160).

92 Veto of Bill Conveying Certain Property to Norwich University. *August 4, 1945*

[Released August 4, 1945. Dated July 31, 1945]

To the House of Representatives:

I return herewith, without my approval, H.R. 3549, "To provide for the conveyance of certain Weather Bureau property to Norwich University, Northfield, Vermont."

The bill authorizes the return to Norwich University, Northfield, Vermont, of land which the University heretofore conveyed to the United States for a nominal consideration, and provides for the donation to the University of a two-story building and the weather station equipment therein, which the Government erected on such land at a cost of approximately $13,000, and which is now surplus to the needs of the Department of Commerce after many years use as a Weather Bureau station.

By the adoption of the Surplus Property Act of 1944, the Federal Government provided, within the frame-work of a single enactment, for a coordinated system of disposal of its surplus properties under uniform policies and procedures. If the Government is to succeed in its efforts to maintain a fair and impartial program for the disposal of its surpluses in the days ahead, I think it is important that the operating principles and standards of action governing such disposals should be kept confined within a single instrument. If we should discover from experience with the statute that its present policies are too narrow or inadequate, any changes found desirable should be accomplished by amendment of the act itself, so that all properties similarly situated or in particular categories may be disposed of under general prescriptions of the law. Individual enactments to provide relief in specific situations, or to govern special cases, which in effect are exceptions or amendments to the present law, it seems to me should be discouraged as detrimental to a sound public policy in a Government program of this character.

For these reasons, I feel obliged to not lend my approval to this measure.

HARRY S. TRUMAN

93   Statement by the President Announcing the Use of the
     A-Bomb at Hiroshima.   *August 6, 1945*

SIXTEEN HOURS AGO an American airplane dropped one bomb on Hiroshima, an important Japanese Army base. That bomb had more power than 20,000 tons of T.N.T. It had more than two thousand times the blast power of the British "Grand Slam" which is the largest bomb ever yet used in the history of warfare.

The Japanese began the war from the air at Pearl Harbor. They have been repaid many fold. And the end is not yet. With this bomb we have now added a new and revolutionary increase in destruction to supplement the growing power of our armed forces. In their present form these bombs are now in production and even more powerful forms are in development.

It is an atomic bomb. It is a harnessing of the basic power of the universe. The force from which the sun draws its power has been loosed against those who brought war to the Far East.

Before 1939, it was the accepted belief of scientists that it was theoretically possible to release atomic energy. But no one knew any practical method of doing it. By 1942, however, we knew that the Germans were working feverishly to find a way to add atomic energy to the other engines of war with which they hoped to enslave the world. But they failed. We may be grateful to Providence that the Germans got the V–1's and V–2's late and in limited quantities and even more grateful that they did not get the atomic bomb at all.

The battle of the laboratories held fateful risks for us as well as the battles of the air, land and sea, and we have now won the battle of the laboratories as we have won the other battles.

Beginning in 1940, before Pearl Harbor, scientific knowledge useful in war was pooled between the United States and Great Britain, and many priceless helps to our victories have come from that arrangement. Under that general policy the research on the atomic bomb was begun. With American and British scientists working together we entered the race of discovery against the Germans.

The United States had available the large number of scientists of

197

distinction in the many needed areas of knowledge. It had the tremendous industrial and financial resources necessary for the project and they could be devoted to it without undue impairment of other vital war work. In the United States the laboratory work and the production plants, on which a substantial start had already been made, would be out of reach of enemy bombing, while at that time Britain was exposed to constant air attack and was still threatened with the possibility of invasion. For these reasons Prime Minister Churchill and President Roosevelt agreed that it was wise to carry on the project here. We now have two great plants and many lesser works devoted to the production of atomic power. Employment during peak construction numbered 125,000 and over 65,000 individuals are even now engaged in operating the plants. Many have worked there for two and a half years. Few know what they have been producing. They see great quantities of material going in and they see nothing coming out of these plants, for the physical size of the explosive charge is exceedingly small. We have spent two billion dollars on the greatest scientific gamble in history—and won.

But the greatest marvel is not the size of the enterprise, its secrecy, nor its cost, but the achievement of scientific brains in putting together infinitely complex pieces of knowledge held by many men in different fields of science into a workable plan. And hardly less marvelous has been the capacity of industry to design, and of labor to operate, the machines and methods to do things never done before so that the brain child of many minds came forth in physical shape and performed as it was supposed to do. Both science and industry worked under the direction of the United States Army, which achieved a unique success in managing so diverse a problem in the advancement of knowledge in an amazingly short time. It is doubtful if such another combination could be got together in the world. What has been done is the greatest achievement of organized science in history. It was done under high pressure and without failure.

We are now prepared to obliterate more rapidly and completely every productive enterprise the Japanese have above ground in any city. We shall destroy their docks, their factories, and their communications. Let there be no mistake; we shall completely destroy Japan's power to make war.

It was to spare the Japanese people from utter destruction that the ultimatum of July 26 was issued at Potsdam. Their leaders promptly rejected that ultimatum. If they do not now accept our terms they may expect a rain of ruin from the air, the like of which has never been seen on this earth. Behind this air attack will follow sea and land forces in such numbers and power as they have not yet seen and with the fighting skill of which they are already well aware.

The Secretary of War, who has kept in personal touch with all phases of the project, will immediately make public a statement giving further details.

His statement will give facts concerning the sites at Oak Ridge near Knoxville, Tennessee, and at Richland near Pasco, Washington, and an installation near Santa Fe, New Mexico. Although the workers at the sites have been making materials to be used in producing the greatest destructive force in history they have not themselves been in danger beyond that of many other occupations, for the utmost care has been taken of their safety.

The fact that we can release atomic energy ushers in a new era in man's understanding of nature's forces. Atomic energy may in the future supplement the power that now comes from coal, oil, and falling water, but at present it cannot be produced on a basis to compete with them commercially. Before that comes there must be a long period of intensive research.

It has never been the habit of the scientists of this country or the policy of this Government to withhold from the world scientific knowledge. Normally, therefore, everything about the work with atomic energy would be made public.

But under present circumstances it is not intended to divulge the technical processes of production or all the military applications, pending further examination of possible methods of protecting us and the rest of the world from the danger of sudden destruction.

I shall recommend that the Congress of the United States consider promptly the establishment of an appropriate commission to control the production and use of atomic power within the United States. I shall give further consideration and make further recommendations to the Congress as to how atomic power can become a powerful and forceful influence towards the maintenance of world peace.

NOTE: This statement was released in Washington. It was drafted before the President left Germany, and Secretary of War Stimson was authorized to release it when the bomb was delivered. On August 6, while returning from the Potsdam Conference aboard the U.S.S. *Augusta,* the President was handed a message from Secretary Stimson informing him that the bomb had been dropped at 7:15 p.m. on August 5.

94   The President's News Conference of *August 8,* 1945

THE PRESIDENT. I have only a simple announcement to make. I can't hold a regular press conference today; but this announcement is so important I thought I would call you in.

Russia has declared war on Japan! That is *all!*

[*Much applause and laughter, as the reporters raced out*]

NOTE: President Truman's seventeenth news conference was held in his office at the White House at 3 p.m. on Wednesday, August 8, 1945. The White House Official Reporter noted that Fleet Admiral William D. Leahy and Secretary of State James F. Byrnes were special guests at this conference.

95   Letter to the Chairman, War Production Board, on Measures To Speed Reconversion. *August 9,* 1945

Dear Chairman Krug:

I have consulted with the Director of War Mobilization and Reconversion regarding steps to be taken by this Government to speed reconversion.

Every opportunity must be given to private business to exercise its ingenuity and forcefulness in speeding the resumption of civilian production, subject to war needs. The Government has a major responsibility to assist in the achievement of an orderly transition from war production to civilian production. This is essential to the war production that continues and to the development of a healthy national economy.

You and I have agreed that the War Production Board can and should play an important role in reconversion. In order to help industry to obtain unprecedented civilian production it is necessary, as you have suggested, for the War Production Board to continue, for the present, some of the effective measures it adopted to achieve our unprecedented war production. These controls, however, should be lifted as soon as they are no longer needed.

Accordingly, I request you to continue the following program which you have been carrying out:

1. A vigorous drive to expand production of materials which are in short supply, not only because of military demands, but to meet civilian demands as well.

2. Limitation upon the manufacture of products for which materials can not yet be made available, so as to avoid excessive pressure on supply which would threaten our stabilization program.

3. A broad and effective control of inventories so as to avoid speculative hoarding and an unbalanced distribution which would curtail total production and endanger our stabilization program.

4. Granting priority assistance to break bottlenecks which may impede the reconversion process.

5. Allocation of scarce materials necessary for the production of low-priced items essential to the continued success of the stabilization program.

In carrying out this request, I know that you will give due regard to the demobilization and reconversion policies established by the Congress, as set forth in Sections 203 and 204 of the War Mobilization and Reconversion Act of 1944, and act under the guidance and direction of the Director of War Mobilization and Reconversion.

I am appreciative of the tremendous accomplishment of the War Production Board under your direction and that of your predecessors. I am equally confident of the great contribution which you and your Agency can make to the transition from our fully mobilized war economy to a sound and fully employed peacetime economy.

To carry out these responsibilities I hope that all the officials and staff of your Board whose services are needed will stay on the job. Their work is not yet done. The people of the United States expect them to be good soldiers and remain in service until the need has passed.

Very sincerely yours,

HARRY S. TRUMAN

[Honorable J. A. Krug, Chairman, War Production Board]

96   Letter to Edward R. Stettinius Appointing Him U.S. Representative on the Preparatory Commission of the United Nations. *August 9, 1945*

My dear Ed:

I take pleasure in appointing you as the United States Representative on the Preparatory Commission of the United Nations established by agreement signed in San Francisco on June 26, 1945. In carrying out this responsibility you will have the personal rank of Ambassador.

With all best wishes for your success in this vitally important undertaking.

Sincerely yours,

HARRY S. TRUMAN

[The Honorable Edward R. Stettinius, Jr., Personal Representative of the President, The White House]

NOTE: The agreement establishing the Preparatory Commission of the United Nations is published in the Statutes at Large (59 Stat. 1411).

The White House release of the letter stated that it was not expected that Mr. Stettinius would attend the initial routine meetings of the Executive Committee of the Commission, called for August 16, but that the United States would be represented by an officer of the State Department.

97 Radio Report to the American People on the Potsdam
Conference. *August 9, 1945*

[Delivered from the White House at 10 p.m.]

My fellow Americans:

I have just returned from Berlin, the city from which the Germans intended to rule the world. It is a ghost city. The buildings are in ruins, its economy and its people are in ruins.

Our party also visited what is left of Frankfurt and Darmstadt. We flew over the remains of Kassel, Magdeburg, and other devastated cities. German women and children and old men were wandering over the highways, returning to bombed-out homes or leaving bombed-out cities, searching for food and shelter.

War has indeed come home to Germany and to the German people. It has come home in all the frightfulness with which the German leaders started and waged it.

The German people are beginning to atone for the crimes of the gangsters whom they placed in power and whom they wholeheartedly approved and obediently followed.

We also saw some of the terrific destruction which the war had brought to the occupied countries of Western Europe and to England.

How glad I am to be home again! And how grateful to Almighty God that this land of ours has been spared!

We must do all we can to spare her from the ravages of any future breach of the peace. That is why, though the United States wants no territory or profit or selfish advantage out of this war, we are going to maintain the military bases necessary for the complete protection of our interests and of world peace. Bases which our military experts deem to be essential for our protection, and which are not now in our possession, we will acquire. We will acquire them by arrangements consistent with the United Nations Charter.

No one can foresee what another war would mean to our own cities and our own people. What we are doing to Japan now—even with the new atomic bomb—is only a small fraction of what would happen to the world in a third World War.

That is why the United Nations are determined that there shall be no next war.

That is why the United Nations are determined to remain united and strong. We can never permit any aggressor in the future to be clever enough to divide us or strong enough to defeat us.

That was the guiding spirit in the conference at San Francisco.

That was the guiding spirit in the conference of Berlin.

That will be the guiding spirit in the peace settlements to come.

In the conference of Berlin, it was easy for me to get along in mutual understanding and friendship with Generalissimo Stalin, with Prime Minister Churchill, and later with Prime Minister Attlee.

Strong foundations of good will and cooperation had been laid by President Roosevelt. And it was clear that those foundations rested upon much more than the personal friendships of three individuals. There was a fundamental accord and agreement upon the objectives ahead of us.

Two of the three conferees of Teheran and Yalta were missing by the end of this conference. Each of them was sorely missed. Each had done his work toward winning this war. Each had made a great contribution toward establishing and maintaining a lasting world peace. Each of them seems to have been ordained to lead his country in its hour of greatest need. And so thoroughly had they done their jobs that we were able to carry on and to reach many agreements essential to the future peace and security of the world.

The results of the Berlin conference have been published. There were no secret agreements or commitments—apart from current military arrangements.

And it was made perfectly plain to my colleagues at the conference that, under our Constitution, the President has no power to make any treaties without ratification by the Senate of the United States.

I want to express my thanks for the excellent services which were rendered at this conference by Secretary of State Byrnes, and which were highly commended by the leaders of the other two powers. I am thankful also to the other members of the American delegation—Admiral Leahy and Ambassadors Harriman, Davies, and Pauley—and to the entire American staff. Without their hard work and sound advice the conference would have been unable to accomplish as much as it did.

The conference was concerned with many political and economic questions. But there was one strictly military matter uppermost in the minds of the American delegates. It was the winning of the war against Japan. On our program, that was the most important item.

The military arrangements made at Berlin were of course secret. One of those secrets was revealed yesterday, when the Soviet Union declared war on Japan.

The Soviet Union, before she had been informed of our new weapon, agreed to enter the war in the Pacific. We gladly welcome into this struggle against the last of the Axis aggressors our gallant and victorious ally against the Nazis.

The Japs will soon learn some more of the other military secrets agreed upon at Berlin. They will learn them firsthand—and they will not like them.

Before we met at Berlin, the United States Government had sent to the Soviet and British Governments our ideas of what should be taken up at the conference. At the first meeting our delegation submitted these proposals for discussion. Subjects were added by the Soviet and British Governments, but in the main the conference was occupied with the American proposals.

Our first nonmilitary agreement in Berlin was the establishment of the Council of Foreign Ministers.

The Council is going to be the continuous meeting ground of the five principal governments, on which to reach common understanding regarding the peace settlements. This does not mean that the five governments are going to try to dictate to, or dominate, other nations. It will be their duty to apply, so far as possible, the fundamental principles of justice underlying the Charter adopted at San Francisco.

Just as the meeting at Dumbarton Oaks drew up the proposals to be placed before the conference at San Francisco, so this Council of Foreign Ministers will lay the groundwork for future peace settlements. This preparation by the Council will make possible speedier, more orderly, more efficient, and more cooperative peace settlements than could otherwise be obtained.

One of the first tasks of the Council of Foreign Ministers is to draft proposed treaties of peace with former enemy countries—Italy, Rumania, Bulgaria, Hungary, and Finland.

These treaties, of course, will have to be passed upon by all the nations concerned. In our own country the Senate will have to ratify them. But we shall begin at once the necessary preparatory work. Adequate study now may avoid the planting of the seeds of future wars.

I am sure that the American people will agree with me that this Council of Foreign Ministers will be effective in hastening the day of peace and reconstruction.

We are anxious to settle the future of Italy first among the former enemy countries. Italy was the first to break away from the Axis. She helped materially in the final defeat of Germany. She has now joined us in the war against Japan. She is making real progress toward democracy.

A peace treaty with a democratic Italian government will make it possible for us to receive Italy as a member of the United Nations.

The Council of Foreign Ministers will also have to start the preparatory work for a German peace settlement. But its final acceptance will have to wait until Germany has developed a government with which a peace treaty can be made. In the meantime, the conference of Berlin laid down the specific political and economic principles under which Germany will be governed by the occupying powers.

Those principles have been published. I hope that all of you will read them.[1]

They seek to rid Germany of the forces which have made her so long feared and hated, and which have now brought her to complete disaster. They are intended to eliminate Nazism, armaments, war industries, the German General Staff and all its military tradition. They seek to rebuild democracy by control of German education, by reorganizing local government and the judiciary, by encouraging free

---

[1] See Item 91.

speech, free press, freedom of religion, and the right of labor to
organize.

German industry is to be decentralized in order to do away with
concentration of economic power in cartels and monopolies. Chief
emphasis is to be on agriculture and peaceful industry. German economic power to make war is to be eliminated. The Germans are not
to have a higher standard of living than their former victims, the people
of the defeated and occupied countries of Europe.

We are going to do what we can to make Germany over into a decent
nation, so that it may eventually work its way from the economic
chaos it has brought upon itself, back into a place in the civilized world.

The economic action taken against Germany at the Berlin conference included another most important item—reparations.

We do not intend again to make the mistake of exacting reparations
in money and then lending Germany the money with which to pay.
Reparations this time are to be paid in physical assets from those
resources of Germany which are not required for her peacetime
subsistence.

The first purpose of reparations is to take out of Germany everything with which she can prepare for another war. Its second purpose
is to help the devastated countries to bring about their own recovery
by means of the equipment and material taken from Germany.

At the Crimea conference a basis for fixing reparations had been proposed for initial discussion and study by the Reparations Commission.
That basis was a total amount of reparations of twenty billions of
dollars. Of this sum, one half was to go to Russia, which had suffered more heavily in the loss of life and property than any other
country.

But at Berlin the idea of attempting to fix a dollar value on the property to be removed from Germany was dropped. To fix a dollar value
on the share of each nation would be a sort of guarantee of the amount
each nation would get—a guarantee which might not be fulfilled.

Therefore, it was decided to divide the property by percentages of
the total amount available. We still generally agreed that Russia
should get approximately half of the total for herself and Poland, and

that the remainder should be divided among all the other nations entitled to reparations.

Under our agreement at Berlin, the reparations claims of the Soviet Union and Poland are to be met from the property located in the zone of Germany occupied by the Soviet Union, and from the German assets in Bulgaria, Finland, Hungary, Rumania and East Austria. The reparations claims of all the other countries are to be met from property located in the western zones of occupation in Germany, and from the German assets in all other countries. The Soviet waives all claim to gold captured by the Allied troops in Germany.

This formula of taking reparations by zones will lead to less friction among the Allies than the tentative basis originally proposed for study at Yalta.

The difficulty with this formula, however, is that the industrial capital equipment not necessary for German peace economy is not evenly divided among the zones of occupation. The western zones have a much higher percentage than the eastern zone, which is mostly devoted to agriculture and to the production of raw materials. In order to equalize the distribution and to give Russia and Poland their fair share of approximately 50 percent, it was decided that they should receive, without any reimbursement, 10 percent of the capital equipment in the western zones available for reparations.

As you will note from the communique, a further 15 percent of the capital equipment in the western zones not necessary for Germany's peace economy is also to be turned over to Russia and Poland. But this is not free. For this property, Poland and Russia will give to the western zones an equal amount in value in food, coal, and other raw materials. This 15 percent, therefore, is not additional reparations for Russia and Poland. It is a means of maintaining a balanced economy in Germany and providing the usual exchange of goods between the eastern part and the western part.

It was agreed at Berlin that the payment of reparations, from whatever zones taken, should always leave enough resources to enable the German people to subsist without sustained support from other nations.

The question of Poland was a most difficult one. Certain compro-

mises about Poland had already been agreed upon at the Crimea conference. They obviously were binding upon us at Berlin.

By the time of the Berlin conference, the Polish Provisional Government of National Unity had already been formed; and it had been
recognized by all of us. The new Polish Government had agreed to
hold free and unfettered elections as soon as possible, on the basis of universal suffrage and the secret ballot.

In acceptance—in accordance with the Crimea agreement, we did
seek the opinion of the Polish Provisional Government of National
Unity with respect to its western and northern boundaries.

They agreed, as did we all, that the final determination of the borders
could not be accomplished at Berlin, but must await the peace settlement. However, a considerable portion of what was the Russian zone
of occupation in Germany was turned over to Poland at the Berlin
conference for administrative purposes until the final determination
of the peace settlement.

Nearly every international agreement has in it the element of compromise. The agreement on Poland is no exception. No one nation
can expect to get everything that it wants. It is a question of give and
take—of being willing to meet your neighbor half-way.

In this instance, there is much to justify the action taken. The agreement on some line—even provisionally—was necessary to enable the
new Poland to organize itself, and to permit the speedier withdrawal
of the armed forces which had liberated her from the Germans. In
the area east of the Curzon line there are over 3,000,000 Poles who are
to be returned to Poland. They need room, room to settle. The new
area in the West was formerly populated by Germans. But most of
them have already left in the face of the invading Soviet Army. We
were informed that there were only about a million and a half left.

The territory the Poles are to administer will enable Poland better
to support its population. It will provide a short and more easily de-
fensible frontier between Poland and Germany. Settled by Poles, it
will provide a more homogeneous nation.

The Three Powers also agreed to help bring about the earliest possible
return to Poland of all Poles who wish to return, including soldiers,

with the assurance that they would have all the rights of other Polish citizens.

The action taken at Berlin will help carry out the basic policy of the United Nations toward Poland—to create a strong, independent, and prosperous nation with a government to be selected by the people themselves.

It was agreed to recommend that in the peace settlement a portion of East Prussia should be turned over to Russia. That, too, was agreed upon at Yalta. It will provide the Soviet Union, which did so much to bring about victory in Europe, with an ice-free port at the expense of Germany.

At Yalta it was agreed, you will recall, that the three governments would assume a common responsibility in helping to reestablish in the liberated and satellite nations of Europe governments broadly representative of democratic elements in the population. That responsibility still stands. We all recognize it as a joint responsibility of the three governments.

It was reaffirmed in the Berlin Declarations on Rumania, Bulgaria, and Hungary. These nations are not to be spheres of influence of any one power. They are now governed by Allied control commissions composed of representatives of the three governments which met at Yalta and Berlin. These control commissions, it is true, have not been functioning completely to our satisfaction; but improved procedures were agreed upon at Berlin. Until these states are reestablished as members of the international family, they are the joint concern of all of us.

The American delegation was much disturbed over the inability of the representatives of a free press to get information out of the former German satellite nations. The three governments agreed at Berlin that the Allied press would enjoy full freedom from now on to report to the world upon all developments in Rumania, Bulgaria, Hungary, and Finland. The same agreement was reaffirmed also as to Poland.

One of the persistent causes for wars in Europe in the last two centuries has been the selfish control of the waterways of Europe. I mean the Danube, the Black Sea Straits, the Rhine, the Kiel Canal, and all the inland waterways of Europe which border upon two or more states.

The United States proposed at Berlin that there be free and unrestricted navigation of these inland waterways. We think this is important to the future peace and security of the world. We proposed that regulations for such navigation be provided by international authorities.

The function of the agencies would be to develop the use of the waterways and assure equal treatment on them for all nations. Membership on the agencies would include the United States, Great Britain, the Soviet Union, and France, plus those states which border on the waterways.

Our proposal was considered by the conference and was referred to the Council of Ministers. There, the United States intends to press for its adoption.

Any man who sees Europe now must realize that victory in a great war is not something you win once and for all, like victory in a ball game. Victory in a great war is something that must be won and kept won. It can be lost after you have won it—if you are careless or negligent or indifferent.

Europe today is hungry. I am not talking about Germans. I am talking about the people of the countries which were overrun and devastated by the Germans, and particularly about the people of Western Europe. Many of them lack clothes and fuel and tools and shelter and raw materials. They lack the means to restore their cities and their factories.

As the winter comes on, the distress will increase. Unless we do what we can to help, we may lose next winter what we won at such terrible cost last spring. Desperate men are liable to destroy the structure of their society to find in the wreckage some substitute for hope. If we let Europe go cold and hungry, we may lose some of the foundations of order on which the hope for worldwide peace must rest.

We must help to the limits of our strength. And we will.

Our meeting at Berlin was the first meeting of the great Allies since victory was won in Europe. Naturally our thoughts now turn to the day of victory in Japan.

The British, Chinese, and United States Governments have given the Japanese people adequate warning of what is in store for them. We have laid down the general terms on which they can surrender. Our warning went unheeded; our terms were rejected. Since then the Japanese have seen what our atomic bomb can do. They can foresee what it will do in the future.

The world will note that the first atomic bomb was dropped on Hiroshima, a military base. That was because we wished in this first attack to avoid, insofar as possible, the killing of civilians. But that attack is only a warning of things to come. If Japan does not surrender, bombs will have to be dropped on her war industries and, unfortunately, thousands of civilian lives will be lost. I urge Japanese civilians to leave industrial cities immediately, and save themselves from destruction.

I realize the tragic significance of the atomic bomb.

Its production and its use were not lightly undertaken by this Government. But we knew that our enemies were on the search for it. We know now how close they were to finding it. And we knew the disaster which would come to this Nation, and to all peace-loving nations, to all civilization, if they had found it first.

That is why we felt compelled to undertake the long and uncertain and costly labor of discovery and production.

We won the race of discovery against the Germans.

Having found the bomb we have used it. We have used it against those who attacked us without warning at Pearl Harbor, against those who have starved and beaten and executed American prisoners of war, against those who have abandoned all pretense of obeying international laws of warfare. We have used it in order to shorten the agony of war, in order to save the lives of thousands and thousands of young Americans.

We shall continue to use it until we completely destroy Japan's power to make war. Only a Japanese surrender will stop us.

The atomic bomb is too dangerous to be loose in a lawless world. That is why Great Britain, Canada, and the United States, who have the secret of its production, do not intend to reveal that secret until means have been found to control the bomb so as to protect ourselves and the rest of the world from the danger of total destruction.

As far back as last May, Secretary of War Stimson, at my suggestion, appointed a committee upon which Secretary of State Byrnes served as my personal representative, to prepare plans for the future control of this bomb. I shall ask the Congress to cooperate to the end that its production and use be controlled, and that its power be made an overwhelming influence towards world peace.

We must constitute ourselves trustees of this new force—to prevent its misuse, and to turn it into the channels of service to mankind.

It is an awful responsibility which has come to us.

We thank God that it has come to us, instead of to our enemies; and we pray that He may guide us to use it in His ways and for His purposes.

Our victory in Europe was more than a victory of arms.

It was a victory of one way of life over another. It was a victory of an ideal founded on the rights of the common man, on the dignity of the human being, on the conception of the State as the servant—and not the master—of its people.

A free people showed that it was able to defeat professional soldiers whose only moral arms were obedience and the worship of force.

We tell ourselves that we have emerged from this war the most powerful nation in the world—the most powerful nation, perhaps, in all history. That is true, but not in the sense some of us believe it to be true.

The war has shown us that we have tremendous resources to make all the materials for war. It has shown us that we have skillful workers and managers and able generals, and a brave people capable of bearing arms.

All these things we knew before.

The new thing—the thing which we had not known—the thing we have learned now and should never forget, is this: that a society of self-governing men is more powerful, more enduring, more creative than any other kind of society, however disciplined, however centralized.

We know now that the basic proposition of the worth and dignity of man is not a sentimental aspiration or a vain hope or a piece of rhetoric. It is the strongest, most creative force now present in this world.

Now let us use that force and all our resources and all our skills in the great cause of a just and lasting peace!

The Three Great Powers are now more closely than ever bound together in determination to achieve that kind of peace. From Teheran, and the Crimea, from San Francisco and Berlin—we shall continue to march together to a lasting peace and a happy world!

NOTE: The President returned to Washington on August 7. He was welcomed by members of the Cabinet on his arrival at the White House at 11 p.m., after traveling by special train from Newport News where he had disembarked that afternoon.

98   Citation Accompanying the Distinguished Service Medal Presented to James F. Byrnes. *August 13, 1945*

CITATION FOR DISTINGUISHED SERVICE MEDAL

MR. JAMES F. BYRNES, as Director of War Mobilization from October 1942 to March 1945, discharged duties of great responsibility with outstanding success. Faced with the problem of aiding the Chief Executive in girding the nation for a conflict of unprecedented proportions, he accomplished his task with exceptional skill. His sympathetic consideration of both military and civilian needs struck a delicate balance that insured the armed forces sufficient manpower and materiel for a maximum effort in a global war while maintaining civilian economy at the highest level of any belligerent in World War II. When necessary, he did not hesitate to support unpopular measures essential to the successful prosecution of the war. He continually gave ready hearing to all sides of momentous questions and rendered logical, sound decisions. He accompanied the Commander-in-Chief to vital conferences, applying his extensive knowledge of inter-Allied problems to their prompt and effective solution. With vast understanding, exceptional ability as an arbiter, unswerving devotion to the national interests and firm determination, Mr. Byrnes performed difficult services (of high importance), making a major contribution to the war effort.

HARRY S. TRUMAN

NOTE: The presentation was made by the President in a ceremony in the Rose Garden at the White House.

99   Statement by the President on the 10th Anniversary of the Social Security Act.   *August 13, 1945*

IN A WORLD still at war it is well that we pause to celebrate one of the great peacetime achievements of the American people, namely, the enactment of the Social Security Act. It is only ten years ago that this act became law. Yet in this brief period of time social security has become an essential part of the American way of life.

We have a right to be proud of the progress we have already made in this field. We have a national system of old-age and survivors insurance under which forty million workers are insured not only for old-age annuities but also for monthly benefits to their wives, children, and dependent parents in case of the worker's death. Already there are well over one million beneficiaries actually receiving monthly checks under this insurance system.

We have a nationwide unemployment insurance system brought about by Federal action but administered by the States, under which thirty-six million workers are provided some protection against wage loss due to involuntary unemployment.

We have provided Federal grants-in-aid to the States to enable them to pay cash assistance to the needy aged, the needy blind, and dependent children. Today two and three-quarter million men, women, and children are receiving this assistance. In addition, there are other provisions of the Social Security Act which promote child welfare and public health.

But while we have made progress we still have a long way to go before we can truthfully say that our social security system furnished the people of this country adequate protection. Therefore, we should

58026

lose no time in making of our Social Security Act a more perfect instrument for the maintenance of economic security throughout this country.

I expect to present to the Congress specific recommendations looking toward this objective.

A sound system of social security requires careful consideration and preparation. Social security worthy of the name is not a dole or a device for giving everybody something for nothing. True social security must consist of rights which are earned rights—guaranteed by the law of the land. Only that kind of social security is worthy of the men and women who have fought and are now fighting to preserve the heritage and the future of America.

100 The President's News Conference of
August 14, 1945

THE PRESIDENT [*reading*]: "I have received this afternoon a message from the Japanese Government—"

Before I go any further, this will be in the form of releases, so you don't have to copy it unless you want to. "—in reply to the message forwarded to that Government by the Secretary of State on August 11. I deem this reply a full acceptance of the Potsdam Declaration which specifies the unconditional surrender of Japan. In the reply there is no qualification.

"Arrangements are now being made for the signing of the surrender terms at the earliest possible moment.

"General Douglas MacArthur has been appointed the Supreme Allied Commander to receive the Japanese surrender. Great Britain, Russia, and China will be represented by high-ranking officers.

"Meantime, the Allied armed forces have been ordered to suspend offensive action.

"Proclamation of V-J Day must wait upon the formal signing of the surrender terms by Japan.

"The following is the Japanese Government's message accepting our terms."

But before I start to read that, there are three releases to come; one has to do with a 2-day holiday.[1] The reason we are making it 2 days is because we didn't get to celebrate for the other. [*Laughter*] Then there is one that has to do with the draft.[2]

This is the official Swiss communique handed to the Secretary of State:

"Sir: I have the honor to refer to your note of August 11, in which you requested me to transmit to my Government the reply of the Governments of the United States, the United Kingdom, the Union of Soviet Socialist Republics, and China to the message from the Japanese Government which was communicated in my note of August 10.

"At 20.10 today (Swiss Time) the Japanese Minister to Switzerland conveyed the following written statement to the Swiss Government for transmission to the four Allied governments:

" 'Communication of the Japanese Government of August 14, 1945, addressed to the Governments of the United States, Great Britain, the Soviet Union, and China:

" 'With reference to the Japanese Government's note of August 10 regarding their acceptance of the provisions of the Potsdam declaration and the reply of the Governments of the United States, Great Britain, the Soviet Union, and China sent by American Secretary of State Byrnes under the date of August 11, the Japanese Government have the honor to communicate to the Governments of the four powers as follows:

" '1. His Majesty the Emperor has issued an Imperial rescript regarding Japan's acceptance of the provisions of the Potsdam declaration.

" '2. His Majesty the Emperor is prepared to authorize and ensure the signature of his Government and the Imperial General Headquarters of the necessary terms for carrying out the provisions of the Potsdam declaration. His Majesty is also prepared to issue his commands to all the military, naval, and air authorities of Japan and all the forces under their control wherever located to cease active operations, to surrender arms and to issue such other orders as may be required by the Supreme

---

[1] See Item 102.   [2] See Item 101.

Commander of the Allied Forces for the execution of the above-mentioned terms.'

"Accept, Sir, the renewed assurances of my highest consideration.
*"Chargé d'Affaires of the Swiss Government
in the United States"*

Voice: I congratulate you!

THE PRESIDENT. That is all.

Joe Fox, Washington Star: Thank you, Mr. President.

[*Applause and further congratulations*]

NOTE: President Truman's eighteenth news conference was held in his office at the White House at 7 p.m. on Tuesday, August 14, 1945. The White House Official Reporter noted that members of the Cabinet were present; also the President's official family, his secretariat, and Administrative Assistants George Schoeneman and David K. Niles. He also noted that former Secretary of State Cordell Hull was invited, but did not arrive until the conference was over.

101 Statement by the President Announcing a Reduction in the Draft. *August 14, 1945*

THE WAR DEPARTMENT has recommended, and I have approved, a request to the Director of Selective Service to reduce inductions immediately from 80,000 to 50,000 per month. This figure will provide only sufficient men to support the forces required for occupational duty and to permit the relief of long-service men overseas to the maximum extent transportation makes possible.

In justice to the millions of men who have given long and faithful service under the difficult and hazardous conditions of the Pacific War and elsewhere overseas a constant flow of replacements to the occupational forces is thought to be imperative.

Mathematically and morally no other course of action appears acceptable.

Transportation by air and sea should make possible the release from the Army of five to five and a half million men during the next twelve to eighteen months. It is too early to propose definite figures for the occupation forces which will be required in the Pacific twelve months from now or what reduction it may be possible to make in the strength of the Army force now allotted to occupation duties in Europe. It is apparent, however, that we can release as many men as can be brought home by the means available during the next year.

The present problem, therefore, centers on the readjustment of personnel now in uniform and the induction of new men through Selective Service to permit the earliest possible release from the Army of those men who have long records of dangerous, arduous and faithful service.

Requirements for future induction into the Army will be limited to the lowest age groups which will provide the numbers of men required. Preliminary estimates indicate that the age groups under 26 will satisfy this requirement.

102   Statement by the President Commending Federal Employees. *August* 14, 1945

ONE OF THE hardest working groups of war workers during the past four years—and perhaps the least appreciated by the public—has been the Federal employes in Washington and throughout the country. They have carried on the day-to-day operations of the government which are essential to the support of our fighting men and to the carrying on of the war.

On behalf of the nation, I formally express thanks to them.

As a token of this feeling, I hereby request all the heads of the departments, agencies and bureaus throughout the government to excuse the employes thereof for tomorrow and Thursday.

This action is to be without charge against the annual leave of the employes. Only skeleton forces need be maintained.

I hope that all of the employes of the government will enjoy this well-deserved—though inadequate—holiday.

NOTE: The President also recognized the contribution of war workers in private industry through a White House release announcing that he had amended Executive Order 9240 to declare August 15 and 16 legal holidays for premium pay purposes. See also Item 115.

103 Statement by the President: The Jewish New Year.
August 15, 1945

I EXTEND to all my fellow Americans of Jewish faith my hearty congratulations and best wishes for New Year's Day.

The enemies of civilization who would have destroyed completely all freedom of religion have been defeated. All faiths unite in thanksgiving to Almighty God on our victory over the forces of evil.

Let us now all join to create the kind of peace settlement which will keep alive freedom of religious belief all over the world, and prevent the recurrence of all this misery and destruction. That is the most fitting memorial we can erect to those who have fought and suffered and labored and died in this struggle to preserve decency for mankind.

104 Statement by the President Proposing Measures To
Insure Industrial Peace in the Reconversion Period.
August 16, 1945

OUR NATIONAL WELFARE requires that during the reconversion period production of civilian goods and services go forward without interruption, and that labor and industry cooperate to keep strikes and lockouts at a minimum. We must work out means for the peaceful settlement of disputes that might adversely affect the transition to a peacetime economy.

We have had an exceptionally good record of industrial peace during the war. We must take the necessary steps now to insure a continuation of this record in the reconversion period before us. We must also, in this period, continue the stabilization program, modifying it to meet the changes in our economy which are now taking place. To these ends:

1. In the near future I shall call a conference of representatives of organized labor and industry, for the purpose of working out by agreement means to minimize the interruption of production by labor disputes in the reconversion period.

The foundation of our wartime industrial relations was an agreement between representatives of industry and labor, who met at the call of the President immediately after Pearl Harbor. This agreement provided that "for the duration of the war there shall be no strikes or lockouts," upon condition that a National War Labor Board be established for the peaceful adjustment of unsettled disputes. Pursuant to that agreement the President, by Executive Order 9017, created the War Labor Board, and Congress, in the War Labor Disputes Act, confirmed and strengthened its authority.

The Board is an emergency agency. Its effectiveness has been rooted in the wartime agreement which led to its establishment. As a result of that agreement industry and labor, with but very few exceptions, have voluntarily accepted the Board's decisions in the disputes which have been certified to it as affecting the war effort. A new industry-labor agreement to minimize interruption of production by labor disputes during the reconversion period ahead of us is imperatively needed.

2. Pending the completion of the conference and until some new plan is worked out and made effective, disputes which cannot be settled by collective bargaining and conciliation, including disputes which threaten a substantial interference with the transition to a peacetime economy, should be handled by the War Labor Board under existing procedures. For that interim period I call upon the representatives of organized labor and industry to renew their no-strike and no-lockout pledges, and I shall expect both industry and labor in that period to continue to comply voluntarily, as they have in the past, with the directive orders of the War Labor Board.

3. The Stabilization Act is effective until June 30, 1946. During its continuance wage adjustments which might affect prices must continue to be subject to stabilization controls. With the ending of war production, however, there is no longer any threat of an inflationary bidding up of wage rates by competition in a short labor market. I am therefore authorizing the War Labor Board to release proposed voluntary wage increases from the necessity of approval upon condition that they will not be used in whole or in part as the basis for seeking an

increase in price ceilings. Proposed wage increases requiring price relief must continue to be passed upon by the Board.

4. The reconversion from wartime to peacetime economy will undoubtedly give rise to maladjustments and inequities in wage rates which will tend to interfere with the effective transition to a peacetime economy. For the remaining period of its existence, the Board should be given authority to deal with these maladjustments and inequities, whose scope and nature cannot be clearly foreseen. I am therefore issuing a new Executive Order which will carry forward the criteria for passing upon wage increases as originally laid down in Executive Order 9250, and which will also vest in the Board authority to approve or direct increases which are necessary to aid in the effective transition to a peacetime economy. The new Executive Order will continue the previous requirement that any proposed wage increase affecting prices, if approved or directed by the Board, will become effective only if also approved by the Director of Economic Stabilization.

5. The War Labor Board should be terminated as soon after the conclusion of the forthcoming Industry-Labor conference as the orderly disposition of the work of the Board, and the provisions of the War Labor Disputes Act permit; and after facilities have been provided to take care of the wage stabilization functions under the Act of October 2, 1942.

6. Meanwhile, the strengthening of the Department of Labor, and the unification under it of functions properly belonging to it, are going forward under plans being formulated by the Secretary of Labor. In these plans particular stress is being laid on the upbuilding of the U.S. Conciliation Service. With the return to a peacetime economy and the elimination of the present temporary wartime agencies and procedures, we must look to collective bargaining, aided and supplemented by a truly effective system of conciliation and voluntary arbitration, as the best and most democratic method of maintaining sound industrial relations.

105   Proclamation 2660: Victory in the East—Day of Prayer.
   August 16, 1945

By the President of the United States of America a Proclamation:

The war lords of Japan and the Japanese armed forces have surrendered. They have surrendered unconditionally. Three months after victory in Europe victory has come in the East.

The cruel war of aggression which Japan started eight years ago to spread the forces of evil over the Pacific has resulted in her total defeat.

This is the end of the grandiose schemes of the dictators to enslave the peoples of the world, destroy their civilization, and institute a new era of darkness and degradation. This day is a new beginning in the history of freedom on this earth.

Our global victory has come from the courage and stamina and spirit of free men and women united in determination to fight.

It has come from the massive strength of arms and materials created by peace-loving peoples who knew that unless they won decency in the world would end.

It has come from millions of peaceful citizens all over the world— turned soldiers almost overnight—who showed a ruthless enemy that they were not afraid to fight and to die, and that they knew how to win.

It has come with the help of God, Who was with us in the early days of adversity and disaster, and Who has now brought us to this glorious day of triumph.

Let us give thanks to Him, and remember that we have now dedicated ourselves to follow in His ways to a lasting and just peace and to a better world.

Now, THEREFORE, I, HARRY S. TRUMAN, President of the United States of America, do hereby appoint Sunday, August 19, 1945, to be a day of prayer.

I call upon the people of the United States, of all faiths, to unite in offering their thanks to God for the victory we have won, and in praying that He will support and guide us into the paths of peace.

I also call upon my countrymen to dedicate this day of prayer to the memory of those who have given their lives to make possible our victory.

In Witness Whereof, I have hereunto set my hand and caused the seal of the United States of America to be affixed.

Done at the City of Washington this sixteenth day of August, in the year of our Lord nineteen hundred and forty-five, and of [seal] the Independence of the United States of America the one hundred and seventieth.

Harry S. Truman

By the President:
James F. Byrnes,
Secretary of State

106 The President's News Conference of
August 16, 1945

THE PRESIDENT. Well, I called this press conference at the suggestion of Mr. Ross, because I thought you hadn't all had a chance to look me in the face or ask me any impertinent questions. [*Laughter*] I haven't anything that you would break your arms to get out of the door for this morning. [*Laughter*] If you have questions to ask me—

[1.] I have issued a proclamation setting aside Sunday as a day of prayer. After the 2 days' celebration I think we will need the prayer. [*Laughter*]

I am ready for any questions you have to ask. I will answer them if I can.

[2.] Q. Mr. President, the question I have written down here is: What is to be done with those three huge plants in the Manhattan project?

THE PRESIDENT. That is going to be up to the Congress. That Manhattan project product, in the long run, will be used for the welfare and benefit of the world instead of its destruction; and if Congress is willing to go along, we will continue the experiments to show how we can use that for peace instead of war.

Q. Are the wheels now turning?—do you happen to know?

THE PRESIDENT. The wheels are turning. I hope the Congress will want to go along.

224

[3.] Q. Mr. President, did you notice that the Japanese radio speakers indicate they are looking for revenge in the future?

THE PRESIDENT. Nearly every defeated people does that. That is natural. But I don't think they will have any chance at it. I don't think they will be able to implement it at all; at least, I hope not.

Q. Mr. President, there still seems to be a little confusion as to the legal status of V-J Day, when it comes.

THE PRESIDENT. V-J will be declared by proclamation when the terms of surrender are signed and implemented. The surrender isn't complete. There are still two million Japs fully armed.

Q. Will that day, once it is proclaimed—do you envision it as a holiday? People will not be expected to work, will they?

THE PRESIDENT. I think they have had their holidays. There is too much to do to declare too many holidays.

[4.] Q. Mr. President, one of the new bills is the full employment bill?

THE PRESIDENT. That's right.

Q. In Mr. Snyder's report there was no mention of that. Is there any intention of——

THE PRESIDENT. Full employment is a "must."

[5.] Q. Mr. President, will you or General MacArthur announce the signing of the surrender terms?

THE PRESIDENT. It will be announced from General MacArthur's headquarters.

[6.] Q. Mr. President, have you time to get back to the Supreme Court vacancy?

THE PRESIDENT. No, I haven't had any chance to get to anything but what we have been going through; but politics is open and free now. [*Laughter*]

[7.] Q. Mr. President, anything you can tell us about the tax situation?

THE PRESIDENT. There is nothing now. Experts are working on it, and when they get the figures ready, I will give them to you.

[8.] Q. Anything about the Jewish national state discussed at Potsdam?

THE PRESIDENT. There was. I discussed the matter with Mr. Churchill and Mr. Attlee, and we are still discussing it.

Q. Not with Stalin?

THE PRESIDENT. No, there was nothing he could do about it.

Q. Mr. President, are you aware of any negotiations or conversations now with Korea?

THE PRESIDENT. No, I am not.

Q. You know the situation; the Koreans are asking——

THE PRESIDENT. Yes, the Korean situation was discussed at Berlin, and the Korean program, I think, will be carried through as we anticipated—that it will be a free country.

[9.] Q. Mr. President, is Manila definitely fixed as the surrender place now?

THE PRESIDENT. I can't answer that. That is in the hands of the Allied Commander in Chief.

[10.] Q. Mr. President, did you take up the status of Hong Kong?

THE PRESIDENT. No, it was not discussed.

Q. Mr. President, there was a report General Eisenhower was returning here; have you any information on that.

THE PRESIDENT. I have not.

Q. Mr. President, was there any term of years fixed on the occupation of Germany?

THE PRESIDENT. No.

Q. Some thought the 2-year reparations period indicates that we might get out in that time.

THE PRESIDENT. The occupation will depend entirely on how well the Germans rehabilitate themselves on the democratic way of life.

Q. Does that apply to the Japanese also?

THE PRESIDENT. It certainly will.

Q. Mr. President——

THE PRESIDENT. Let this lady speak.

Q. Vivian Lovell, French News Agency: Have the different zones of occupation of Japan been discussed?

THE PRESIDENT. They have not.

Q. Are you anticipating any trips in the near future?

THE PRESIDENT. No; it's like moving a circus to get me around the country, and I will stay at home. [*Laughter*]

[11.] Q. Is Dean Acheson resigning from the Department of State?

THE PRESIDENT. That is a matter for the Secretary of State.

[12.] Q. What is the status of the War Labor Board under the new program—will it continue to exist?

THE PRESIDENT. No, the War Labor Board will only continue as long as there is a necessity, which I think will be only a limited time.

[13.] Q. Will there be occupation zones in Japan?

THE PRESIDENT. Japan will be occupied under the Commander in Chief for the Allies. I don't think there will be any necessity for zones of occupation in Japan. Probably there will be troops from the Allies in the occupation areas.

[14.] Q. How long do you think the draft will have to continue, Mr. President?

THE PRESIDENT. That is a matter that Congress will have to decide. The draft is only temporarily continued for the need to get those soldiers who have been fighting discharged first. There is no reason why these young fellows who have nothing to do now should not replace the ones who have done the fighting so they can be discharged. The Congress will have to pass on that when they meet.

Q. Mr. President, are you going to make recommendations on what kind of peacetime military training we are to have?

THE PRESIDENT. I am going to make recommendations to Congress on a universal military training program which is not peacetime conscription.

Q. When?

THE PRESIDENT. When Congress meets.

[15.] Q. Any changes in the War Labor Board? Who will handle that?

THE PRESIDENT. The Department of Labor.

[16.] Q. Do you care to go any further with that peacetime military training now?

THE PRESIDENT. No, that will be a new story I will give you later. I don't want to talk about it today.

[17.] Q. Do you envisage the appointment of a political adviser to General MacArthur like Bob Murphy is to General Eisenhower?

THE PRESIDENT. If that is necessary, it will be done. The situation is entirely different in the Pacific.

[18.] Q. What was the American view on Palestine at Berlin?

THE PRESIDENT. The American view of Palestine is, we want to let as many of the Jews into Palestine as it is possible to let into that country. Then the matter will have to be worked out diplomatically with the British and the Arabs, so that if a state can be set up there they may be able to set it up on a peaceful basis. I have no desire to send 500,000 American soldiers there to make peace in Palestine.

Q. Was the meeting at Berlin the last of the Big Three meetings, Mr. President?

THE PRESIDENT. I cannot answer that question. It will have to be decided later.

[19.] Q. Mr. President, are you in a position to discuss what you want to do with the Army and Navy after the war? There was some talk of combining them.

THE PRESIDENT. No, I don't want to discuss that this morning. I will discuss it at a later date.

[20.] Q. Any decision made on the future home of the United Nations?

THE PRESIDENT. No, there has been no discussion of it.

[21.] Q. Mr. President, do you contemplate calling a conference of capital and labor in the near future?

THE PRESIDENT. Yes, sometime after Congress meets.

[22.] Q. Mr. President, in view of the rather sudden collapse of Japanese resistance, are plans in readiness now for the occupation?

THE PRESIDENT. Yes, they are—for the control of the civilian government. General MacArthur has been working on those plans right along with his military plans.

Joe Fox, Washington Star: Thank you, Mr. President.

THE PRESIDENT. Nice to have seen you all.

NOTE: President Truman's nineteenth news conference was held in his office at the White House at 10:03 a.m. on Thursday, August 16, 1945. The White

House Official Reporter noted that Guy Innes of the British Ministry of Infor- mation was the special guest at this conference.

107 The President's News Conference of
August 23, 1945

THE PRESIDENT. I have a couple of announcements I want to read to you; they are mimeographed and you can get copies of them when you get through.

[1.] This is to the heads of Executive departments and agencies:

"It is my desire that not later than the week beginning September 9, 1945, all departments and agencies reduce their administrative work-week to the basic 40 hours a week, unless such reduction in hours would result in a serious detriment to their essential operations. This will permit the establishment of a 5-day workweek wherever feasible. In those cases where you decide that it is absolutely necessary to tempo-rarily maintain a workweek in excess of 40 hours, please report to the Director of the Bureau of the Budget the reasons for your decision."

[2.] Then this notice went out also:

"Since there would appear to be no further necessity for continuing the present requirements for work on public holidays, such holidays, as enumerated below, should be observed as nonwork days:

"The 1st day of January, the 22d day of February, the 30th day of May, the 4th day of July, the 1st Monday of September, the 11th day of November, the 4th Thursday in November, and Christmas Day.

"In addition, the general restrictions placed on leaves of absence be-cause of war conditions are no longer necessary and the departments and agencies should return to their normal policies in granting leaves of absence for vacation purposes." [1]

If you have any questions that I can answer, I'll try to answer them.

[3.] Q. Mr. President, is Secretary Ickes continuing in the Cabinet?

THE PRESIDENT. *Secretary Ickes will continue in the Cabinet.* I had a

---

[1] The White House release of August 23 stated that at the direction of the President, George J. Schoeneman, Administrative Assistant, addressed this memorandum to the heads of executive departments and agencies.

session with him yesterday, and he is going to take a trip to London on the negotiation of the oil matter.

Q. Is his service as Secretary contingent on the completion of that London mission?

THE PRESIDENT. It is *not*. It is contingent only on as long as he wants to remain; and I think he is satisfied to remain.

[4.] Q. General Hershey, in a speech in Boston last night, said that unless the Draft Act is amended the right of employment of the veterans would expire on V-J Day. Would you favor legislation on that?

THE PRESIDENT. I think General Hershey is speaking about the provision in the Draft Act that is apart from the provisions in the GI bill of rights.

Q. He said there was no such provision in the GI bill of rights.

THE PRESIDENT. I think it can be interpreted that way, but we can have that amended. The Draft Act ends with the proclamation declaring that hostilities have ceased and the war is over—which has not happened yet and won't happen for some time to come.

Q. Do I understand you to mean that the original intention of the Draft Act giving the veterans their jobs back would remain even if you had to patch it up with further legislation?

THE PRESIDENT. That's what I intended to say.

Q. Providing a new bill?

THE PRESIDENT. The question was only in reference to the guarantee to veterans of their jobs.

Q. Would that mean a new piece of legislation?

THE PRESIDENT. It probably would require an amendment to the GI bill of rights, if that is not interpreted to mean what it says.

[5.] Q. Mr. President, please tell us a little about your visit with General de Gaulle.

THE PRESIDENT. I had a very pleasant visit with the General. We discussed questions that affect France and the United States, and instructed the Foreign Minister of France and the Secretary of State of the United States to discuss all the matters which are at issue between France and the United States, and then submit those matters to General de Gaulle and myself for final decision if they could not reach an agreement which was satisfactory to both of us.

Q. You expect to see him again?

THE PRESIDENT. I imagine so. He is going to pay visits around various places in the United States. I imagine I will see him again.

[6.] Q. Do you favor the immediate and public trial of the officers who were responsible for Pearl Harbor?

THE PRESIDENT. What was that?

Q. Do you favor immediate and public trials to fix the responsibility of the Army and Navy officers who were in command at Pearl Harbor?

THE PRESIDENT. I think I am about to receive a recommendation from the Secretaries of Navy and War on that. I will answer that when it comes.

Q. Do you expect it soon?

THE PRESIDENT. You will be informed when that comes.

[7.] Q. Has Mr. Justice Roberts received an assignment from you and Mr. Byrnes?

THE PRESIDENT. He refused one from Mr. Byrnes and me. I hope he will change his mind.

Q. Could you tell us the nature of the assignment?

THE PRESIDENT. I would rather not discuss it until I am sure he will not take it.

[8.] Q. Anything on the Supreme Court appointment yet, sir?

THE PRESIDENT. No, no announcement. I haven't had a chance to give it the necessary thought.

[9.] Q. Mr. President, can you tell us anything about the progress of the hospitalization and construction program?

THE PRESIDENT. No, I can't; I haven't had a chance to go into that either. As soon as possible I will go into it and then I will answer your questions.

[10.] Q. Mr. President, do you plan any subsidies on copper and zinc, since these metals are now in good supply—plentiful?

THE PRESIDENT. If they are in plentiful supply the subsidy will not be necessary.

[11.] Q. Can you tell us anything about your conferences with Dr. Soong?

THE PRESIDENT. No, not at the present time. I will be glad to inform you as soon as I am in a position to do so without embarrassment to the Chinese Government, the Government of the United States, and the Soviet Union. All the relations between those three governments were discussed, but I am not at liberty to discuss that until the final conclusions have been reached.

[12.] Q. Anything on lend-lease that you might report on, Mr. President?

THE PRESIDENT. No, I think that very plainly stated the case.[1]

[13.] Q. Mr. President, do you take the view of General Hershey with regard to the Draft Act?

THE PRESIDENT. I am not legally inclined, and I don't know the legal provisions in the Draft Act, because I haven't studied it; so I can't give you my views on that.

Q. The Hershey view is——

THE PRESIDENT. General Hershey ought to know what he is talking about; he has been enforcing the Draft Act for some time. I will not discuss it because I am not familiar enough with it.

[14.] Q. Mr. President, have your ideas on reorganization reached the point where you want to discuss them?

THE PRESIDENT. I am trying to persuade the Congress to give me the power to make the reorganization, and until that is done I don't want to talk about it.

[15.] Q. Can you tell us anything about your luncheon today?

---

[1] The President referred to the following White House release, dated August 21, 1945:

The President has directed the Foreign Economic Administrator to take steps immediately to discontinue all lend-lease operations and to notify foreign governments receiving lend-lease of this action.

The President also directs that all outstanding contracts for lend-lease be canceled, except where Allied governments are willing to agree to take them over, or where it is in the interest of the United States to complete them.

The Foreign Economic Administrator furthermore is instructed to negotiate with Allied governments for possible procurement by them of lend-lease inventories now in stockpile and in process of delivery.

If the military needs lend-lease supplies for the movement of troops or for occupation purposes, the military will be responsible for procurement.

It is estimated that uncompleted contracts for non-munitions and finished goods in this country not yet transferred to lend-lease countries amount to about $2 billion and that lend-lease supplies in stockpile abroad amount to between $1 and $1½ billion.

THE PRESIDENT. Oh, I got kind of lonely to see some of my friends and telephoned Mr. Biffle I would be down to see him. I didn't expect to have an elaborate luncheon, but there were a dozen or so Senators and others present, and we had a very pleasant time, as we always do.

[16.] Q. Mr. President, are the Big Three, as reported, planning joint action to avert civil war in China?

THE PRESIDENT. That is a matter you better discuss with the Secretary of State. I haven't heard anything about it.

[17.] Q. There has been some criticism of the demobilization program; have you talked with the Secretaries of War and Navy about that?

THE PRESIDENT. Yes, I have talked with the Secretaries of War and Navy, General Marshall, and Admiral King; and their armed services are doing everything in their power to expedite demobilization. It wouldn't make any difference what sort of plan they had, somebody wouldn't like it.

[18.] Q. Mr. President, the British Prime Minister has discussed Franco-Spain; do you care to go a little further on that?

THE PRESIDENT. There was an agreement on Franco-Spain; I think the Prime Minister of England very clearly stated the matter. None of us like Franco or his government.

[19.] Q. Is there any news regarding labor-management? Have the arrangements been made yet?

THE PRESIDENT. No, as soon as they are made I will announce it.

Q. Who is drawing up the agenda?

THE PRESIDENT. There is none yet. We're trying to get that crowd together, and as soon as we have things arranged I'll tell you the whole story. That meeting takes place tomorrow—to try to make the arrangements.

[20.] Q. Mr. President, will your V-J Day statement proclaim the end of hostilities or the end of the national emergency?

THE PRESIDENT. Neither one; it will merely state V-J Day. The matter will then be put in the lap of Congress to make whatever statement is necessary, with the recommendation that Congress not act precipitately in the matter but make an orderly reconversion.

233

Q. What would be the legal significance of declaration of V-J Day?

THE PRESIDENT. That depends altogether on how it is worded. [*Laughter*]

[21.] Q. Mr. President, there were some very strange reports in the Dutch press the last few days claiming that this country wants to control Iceland, Greenland, and some Italian colonies. Any comment on that?

THE PRESIDENT. That's news to me; I can't discuss it because I don't know anything about it.

Q. Mr. President, would you care to discuss the future of Indochina and Thailand?

THE PRESIDENT. No, I wouldn't; that's a matter that the Foreign Ministers probably will discuss, and I don't care to discuss it here today.

Q. Thank you.

THE PRESIDENT. That's all right.

[22.] Q. I think Mr. Crowley yesterday said lend-lease would be cut off except in those instances where it would be to the best interest of the country. Will you give us an illustration of that?

THE PRESIDENT. No, I can't; I can't give you an illustration of it. If I find one I'll be glad to give it to you.

Q. Mr. President, did you take up with Mr. Crowley the question of the "pipeline" to Great Britain?

THE PRESIDENT. No, I didn't; he had no instructions from me except what you saw in the release.[1]

Q. Can you tell us the reasons for termination of lend-lease? There

---

[1] The President referred to a White House release dated August 21. For text, see footnote to [12] of this news conference.

On August 29 the following statement was released simultaneously in Washington, Ottawa, and London:

"On January 19th, 1945, the President of the United States and the Prime Ministers of Great Britain and Canada announced their decision to maintain the Combined Production and Resources Board, Combined Raw Materials Board and Combined Food Board until the end of the Japanese War. The three governments have now decided that these three boards will continue, for the time being, to operate on the existing basis in order to ensure that there is no break in combined machinery, which is handling various critical supply questions of immediate importance. They will also arrange without delay for a review of the work of each Board with the object of determining the necessity for continuing its operation."

See also Item 209.

have been statements that it was a direct blow at the British Government.

THE PRESIDENT. That is not true at all. The reason is that the bill was passed by Congress defining lend-lease as a weapon of war, and after we cease to be at war it is no longer necessary. I happened to be Vice President at the time that law was extended and I made such a promise. I am merely living up to the promise I made as Vice President of the United States.

Q. We haven't yet ceased to be at war. We——

THE PRESIDENT. No, but hostilities have ceased. Hostilities are not going on. We are not conducting a war. I think, technically, we have come to the point where it is not necessary to continue lend-lease.

[23.] Q. Sir, do you anticipate making any recommendation about the advance time— war time?

THE PRESIDENT. That will be taken care of in the message to Congress the 5th of September. I think we will go back to standard time. The States can do whatever they choose.

Q. Sir, what else might be in that message? [*Laughter*]

THE PRESIDENT. I'll give you that message when I get it ready.

Voices: Thank you, Mr. President.

NOTE: President Truman's twentieth news conference was held in his office at the White House at 4 p.m. on Thursday, August 23, 1945.

108 Memorandum Concerning Veteran Preference in Federal Agencies. *August* 24, 1945

[Released August 24, 1945. Dated August 23, 1945]

To the Heads of Executive Departments and Agencies:

Section 14 of the Veterans' Preference Act of 1944 sets forth certain definite procedures to be followed by the heads of departments and agencies in connection with the proposed discharge, suspension for more than thirty days, furlough without pay, or reduction in rank or compensation of an employee of the Federal Government who is entitled to veteran preference.

This Section likewise grants to the veteran, or his designated representative, the right of an appeal to the Civil Service Commission. The law also provides that the Commission shall conduct an investigation, consider the evidence submitted, and then submit its findings and recommendations to the proper administrative officer.

It is my desire that the heads of all departments and agencies arrange to put into effect as promptly as possible the recommendations which the Civil Service Commission makes under Section 14 of the Veterans' Preference Act of 1944. This constitutes another way in which the Federal Government can demonstrate that it intends to live up to both the letter and the spirit of the Veterans' Preference Act.

HARRY S. TRUMAN

109 Citation Accompanying the Legion of Merit Presented to President de Gaulle of France. *August 24, 1945*

CITATION FOR THE LEGION OF MERIT

DEGREE OF CHIEF COMMANDER

GENERAL CHARLES DE GAULLE, President of the Provisional Government of the French Republic and Commander-in-Chief of France's armed forces, performed distinguished services by maintaining his nation's effort in the struggle against the common enemy in Europe. From the chaos which followed the unleashing of the aggressor states' military power he emerged to keep bright the flame of liberty among his countrymen, to rally them in the cause of freedom, to merge their revived strength with the growing might of the United Nations. In victory he returned to his native soil, there to rebuild on firm principles a nation rededicated to liberty, equality and fraternity.

HARRY S. TRUMAN

NOTE: The presentation was made by the President in a ceremony at the White House.

110 Citation Accompanying the Legion of Merit Presented
to Georges Bidault, Minister of Foreign Affairs of
France. *August 24, 1945*

CITATION FOR THE LEGION OF MERIT
DEGREE OF COMMANDER

GEORGES BIDAULT, Minister of Foreign Affairs of the Provisional
Government of the French Republic, was called to the colors in the
autumn of 1939 and devotedly served his country as a sergeant of
infantry until the spring of 1940 when he was taken prisoner by the
Germans. In July 1941, after more than a year of captivity, he re-
gained his freedom, whereupon without regard for his own safety or
well-being he immediately became extremely active in French underground affairs. Displaying at all times zealous determination to drive
the invader from France, he played a major part in organizing the
French Resistance Movement for effective cooperation with the Allied
armies, and became President of the National Council of Resistance,
which post he occupied on the Day of Liberation. Continuing as
Minister of Foreign Affairs to cooperate with the United Nations in
the pursuit of their ideals, M. Bidault fostered a spirit of friendship
and harmony between his republic and that of the United States.

HARRY S. TRUMAN

NOTE: The presentation was made by the President in a ceremony at the White
House.

111 Statement by the President on the 25th Anniversary of
the Women's Suffrage Amendment. *August 25, 1945*

AUGUST 26, 1945, will mark the twenty-fifth anniversary of the ratification by the states of the Amendment to the National Constitution
granting suffrage to women.

Less than a century ago women in the United States were denied the
right to vote and were classed as inferiors under the law. In 1920
there occurred one of the great events in our history—the Federal Con-

stitution was amended to extend suffrage to the women of our country. Since that time the movement to raise the status of women in all other fields has gone steadily forward.

In the total war through which we have just passed the home front has been no mere phrase, but truly a battlefront where women bore a major part of the struggle.

Women walked into the pages of today's history as good citizens and good soldiers.

To praise women for making intelligent use of the ballot, or for doing their share in winning the war, would be an act of condescension the very opposite of that equal respect symbolized by the suffrage amendment. But on the twenty-fifth anniversary of the Nineteenth Amendment, it is fitting that we, men and women alike, should give thanks for an America in which women can stand on the level footing of full citizenship in peace and in war.

112 Statement by the President Concerning Veterans Hospitals. *August 25, 1945*

A PROGRAM for the construction of new hospital beds for the treatment of veterans was recently recommended by the Veterans Administration.

When these recommendations reached my desk I had decided to accept the resignation of General Hines as Veterans Administrator and to appoint General Omar N. Bradley as his successor.

In all fairness to General Bradley I thought he should have an opportunity to make his own recommendations, as he would be held responsible for his administration. In order that he might have this opportunity, I approved the program for the construction of 29,000 beds but withheld approval of any locations.

I expect General Bradley will expedite the submission of a program recommending locations for the beds. This will be acted on as promptly as possible.

113   Joint Statement Following Discussions With President
de Gaulle of France. *August 25, 1945*

THE VISIT of General de Gaulle, President of the Provisional Government of the French Republic, to the President of the United States of America, has been marked by an important exchange of views between the two Chiefs of State, who, in the course of their first meeting, expressed their sentiments of mutual high esteem.

The conversations, which began immediately after General de Gaulle's arrival in Washington, have made possible a thorough discussion of a wide range of subjects, among them those of most immediate interest to the two governments.

Subsequent to the second conversation between President Truman and General de Gaulle, and at their request, the Secretary of State, Mr. Byrnes, and Foreign Minister, Monsieur Bidault, had during two days a full and frank discussion of political and economic questions in which the two countries are deeply interested.

Following those discussions, both the Chiefs of State, and the Secretary of State and the French Foreign Minister, have fully recognized, in the course of a further meeting, the fundamental harmony between French and American aims in the construction of the postwar world and have expressed their readiness to act in accordance with this mutual understanding by establishing an even closer cooperation between the two countries.

114   Letter to the Chairmen of the Senate and House
Committees on Military Affairs on Army Manpower
Requirements. *August 27, 1945*

Dear ————:

It occurs to me that it would be helpful to your committee in planning its legislative program to have my views on the matters which will be under your consideration. As you know, coincident with Japan's acceptance of our surrender terms, two important steps were taken to adjust Army manpower requirements: A world-wide campaign to obtain the maximum number of volunteers was initiated, and Selective Service calls were reduced from 80,000 to 50,000 men a month.

The first of these steps will require legislative assistance. Present laws place a ceiling of 280,000 on the number of enlistments which can be accepted; only men now in the service or those who have been discharged for less than 90 days can be enlisted directly; and there are some legal uncertainties regarding reenlistment bonuses, grades, mustering-out pay and other benefits under the G–I Bill of Rights. These matters should be clarified as rapidly as may be to the end that there will be no legal impediments to the maximum procurement of volunteers. In addition the Congress will wish to consider what more can be done in the way of furnishing inducements which will stimulate voluntary enlistments. The more men who can be secured by this means, the fewer it will be necessary to induct into or continue in the service.

The continuance of inductions through the medium of Selective Service will be one of your most critical problems. From many standpoints, I wish it were possible for me to recommend that the drafting of men be stopped altogether and at once. But, sharing the deep feeling of our people that those veterans who have given long and arduous service must be returned to their homes with all possible speed and with the certainty that world conditions will require us during the transition period to settled peace to maintain a real measure of our military strength, I cannot so recommend. The situation in the Pacific continues to have many elements of danger, and war-torn and disorganized Europe is facing a difficult winter season with scarcities of food, fuel and clothing. Our occupation forces in those areas must be held at safe levels, determined largely by General MacArthur and General Eisenhower who are on the ground and familiar with the situation. We cannot stop the *certain* in-flow of replacements into the armed forces, without necessitating prolonged service of veteran soldiers.

My great concern at the present moment is for those now in the armed forces whose war service has separated them from their homes and loved ones for extended periods. An unforgivable discrimination

240

would result, if we should favor those who have had no military service by suspending their induction at the cost of requiring further sacrifice from those who have already done their part.

Based on the present unsettled conditions in Europe, the uncertainties of the Pacific, and decent consideration for all the men in the service who have borne the burden of the past years, I have approved continuation of inductions until such time as the Congress shall establish the broad national policies to govern full demobilization, occupation and world security.

While the question of how to provide adequate military forces and at the same time to restore veterans to their homes is a matter for determination by the Congress, it appears clear to me that we dare not depend solely on volunteers. The continuation of inductions through Selective Service at a rate depending upon the rate of volunteering is the only safe and acceptable solution. However, it is my view that these inductions should be for a two year period unless sooner discharged and should consist of men in the age group 18 to 25 inclusive.

It is my firm conviction, which I believe is shared by the majority in this country, that war veterans who do not volunteer to remain in the service should be discharged as soon as it is practicable to do so. This means that we must start at once to obtain personnel exclusive of these veterans to carry the burden of the occupational period. Volunteers should be procured in maximum numbers and the remainder of whatever strength is required obtained by post V-J Day inductions through Selective Service.

The War Department is stressing the procurement of volunteers to the utmost. How many will be obtained is problematical but from past experience and the most recent studies 300,000 appears to be the maximum to be expected by July next. Inductions, if continued at the present reduced rate, for the same period would produce approximately 500,000 men. On this basis there will be not more than 800,000 non-veterans and volunteers in the army next July.

It is certain that 800,000 men will be insufficient to meet over-all requirements next July. General Eisenhower's and General MacArthur's estimates alone total 1,200,000, exclusive of the numbers required for supporting troops in the United States and other areas. The difference between the 800,000 non-veterans and volunteers and whatever total strength is required must be made up by holding additional numbers of veterans in the service. It is evident that any curtailment in the number of Selective Service replacements will only accentuate the number of veterans who must be retained in the service. While it will not be possible to discharge all of them even under the proposed system as soon as we would like, we will have the satisfaction of knowing that the program will give them the best opportunity we can provide for their early return to civil life.

One other matter which deserves the immediate consideration of your Committee is the question of when the "emergency" or "war" should be officially terminated. I must emphasize the danger that lies in a too early unqualified formal termination. Tragic conditions would result if we were to allow the period of military service to expire by operation of law while a substantial portion of our forces had not yet been returned from overseas. I am confident that the Congress will take no action which would place the armed forces in such a position.

HARRY S. TRUMAN

NOTE: This is the text of identical letters addressed to the Honorable Elbert D. Thomas and to the Honorable Andrew J. May, Chairmen of the Senate and House Committees on Military Affairs, respectively.

115 Memorandum Concerning Reimbursement of War Contractors for Wages Paid for Work on August 15 and 16. *August 28, 1945*

[Released August 28, 1945. Dated August 24, 1945]

Memorandum to the Director of Contract Settlement and the Contracting Agencies of the Government:

When the news was received on August 14, 1945, that the Japanese had accepted the Potsdam declaration, a statement was issued from the White House that the days of August 15 and 16, 1945, would be declared holidays for war workers under Executive Order 9240, which provides for holiday premium pay. An Executive Order effectuating this was subsequently issued; and the Secretary of Labor publicly expressed my hope that war workers who did not work on those two days would be paid by their employers at straight-time rates. There was widespread observance of these holidays, which represented an appropriate recognition of the magnificent contribution made by war workers to our victory.

In view of these actions, contractors who pay the war workers among their employees for time off taken during these two days should be reimbursed by the Government to the extent that the Government is compensating these contractors on a cost basis. This would include the holders of cost-plus-a-fixed-fee or other cost-type war contracts, because such pay for time off is a reasonable and proper cost of performing such contracts. It would also include the holders of war contracts terminated for the Government's convenience to the extent that the cost of pay for time off is applicable to terminated work.

It would be impracticable to attempt any reimbursement on this account to the holders of fixed-price war contracts that are completed and not terminated, for this would involve making many thousands of minor contract amendments. Such contractors, moreover, are continuing to receive the contract price for their product.

Please take all necessary steps to effectuate the foregoing.

HARRY S. TRUMAN

NOTE: The text of Office of Contract Settlement Regulation No. 20, giving effect to the President's memorandum, was also released. The regulation is published in the Federal Register (10 F.R. 10985).

116 The President's News Conference of *August 29, 1945*

THE PRESIDENT. I have a release for you this morning which is being handed to you in the form of three documents. The release date is 1 o'clock today.

[*Reading*] I have here reports on the Pearl Harbor disaster. One is from the Army and one is from the Navy. The Navy report gives a "Finding of Facts" by a Navy Court of Inquiry. Attached to this Finding of Facts are indorsements by the Judge Advocate General of the Navy, Rear Admiral T. L. Gatch; Admiral E. J. King, Chief of Naval Operations, and the Secretary of the Navy. You will find a summation of the findings in the final indorsement by the Secretary of the Navy at the end of the document.

From the Army we have the report of the Army Pearl Harbor Board and, bound separately, a statement by the Secretary of War. Certain criticisms of the Chief of Staff, General Marshall, appear in the report of the Army Pearl Harbor Board. You will notice in the Secretary's statement, beginning on page nineteen, that he takes sharp issue with this criticism of General Marshall, stating that the criticism "is entirely unjustified." The conclusion of the Secretary of War is that General Marshall acted throughout this matter with his usual "great skill, energy and efficiency." I associate myself wholeheartedly with this expression by the Secretary of War.

Indeed I have the fullest confidence in the skill, energy and efficiency of all our war leaders, both Army and Navy. [*Ends reading*]

Now, these documents will be given to you. There is a lot of reading matter in them, and you have 2 hours to look them over before the release date comes. Any questions?

Q. Yes; can you give us a 30-word lead? [*Laughter*]

THE PRESIDENT. I could give you a 300-word lead. [*Laughter*]

Q. Are your remarks quotable—on the record?

THE PRESIDENT. My remarks are on the record. We can have a copy of my statement prepared for you. It is on the record.

Q. We have until 1 o'clock to——

THE PRESIDENT. You have until 1 o'clock to study these documents, and you can consult Mr. Ross and anybody else you wish to consult.

Q. Is what you are trying to clear up, sir, also for 1 o'clock release?

THE PRESIDENT. They are all for 1 o'clock release; everything in connection with it is for 1 o'clock release. That is to give you time to look these things over so you won't have to go off halfcocked.

Q. I suppose the documents are pretty well self-explanatory?

THE PRESIDENT. They are.

Q. Do they present any action?

THE PRESIDENT. They state the facts so that there won't be any more argument about what the facts are.

Q. What is the status on the court-martial matter?

THE PRESIDENT. I have nothing to say on the court-martial, except that if a court-martial is necessary, the gentlemen will have a prompt and fair trial.

Q. Mr. President, can you tell us something about the circumstances surrounding the decision to make this public at this time?

THE PRESIDENT. Well, there has been a great deal of conversation in regard to Pearl Harbor and various boards have looked into the facts, and I just decided that the country is entitled to the facts. There is nothing there that needs to be covered up now that hostilities have ceased, and I think the sooner the press and the public know the facts the better off everybody will be.

Any other questions?

Q. We still have a press conference tomorrow?

THE PRESIDENT. We still have a press conference tomorrow, so you can cross-question me then on these documents if you care to. [*Laughter*]

NOTE: President Truman's twenty-first news conference was held in his office at 11:03 a.m. on Wednesday, August 29, 1945. The White House Official Reporter noted that the following special guests attended this conference: Secretary of State James F. Byrnes, Under Secretary of War Robert P. Patterson, Secretary of the Navy James V. Forrestal, Fleet Admiral Ernest J. King, Maj. M. F. Correa from the office of the Secretary of the Navy, Leo T. Crowley, Administrator of the Foreign Economic Administration, and George E. Allen, member, board of directors, War Damage Corporation.

117   Letter to George E. Allen Concerning the Liquidation of War Agencies. *August 30, 1945*

Dear Mr. Allen:

As the various war agencies are dissolved from time to time, it will become necessary to liquidate such of their functions as are not transferred to the permanent Departments. This will involve unexpended funds, surplus personnel, and surplus equipment.

Many suggestions have been made as to the most efficient and economical method of carrying on this liquidation.

I have designated you as my Personal Representative to study the whole problem, and to make recommendations to me as to the best means of accomplishing liquidation.

Very sincerely yours,

HARRY S. TRUMAN

[Mr. George E. Allen, 1522 K Street NW., Washington 5, D.C.]

118   The President's News Conference of *August 30, 1945*

THE PRESIDENT. . [1.]   Byron Price has agreed to go to Germany in an advisory capacity on public relations. He is going with the approval of General Eisenhower and General Clay, and I am very happy that he is going, because I think he can be a great deal of help to that situation over there.

[2.]   In yesterday's report which I handed to you I did not know at the time, because I hadn't had time to read it completely myself, that there had been some aspersions cast on Cordell Hull. I want to agree fully and completely with Secretary Stimson on what he said about Cordell Hull.

[3.]   Ambassador Pauley this afternoon will hold a press conference at 3 p.m. on the reparations situation. I think it will be right interesting and instructive to those of you who are interested in reparations.

Now if there are any questions——

[4.]   Q. Mr. President, do you plan to confer with General de Gaulle again before he returns to France?

THE PRESIDENT. I don't know; if General de Gaulle returns to Washington I may see him.

[5.]   Q. In a magazine article you wrote, or that appeared under your name, when you were a Senator——

THE PRESIDENT. Things come back to haunt you! [*Laughter*]

Q. ——you said Admiral Kimmel and General Short were not on speaking terms. Admiral Kimmel subsequently said that was a false statement.

THE PRESIDENT. Apparently, according to this report, it was not a statement of fact. I was speaking with the best information I had at the time.

Q. Mr. President, was there any reason for putting out the report on the day that we entered Tokyo?

THE PRESIDENT. No, no reason except that there was so much conversation about it; there was no ulterior motive to it.

Q. Mr. President, despite what you said yesterday, there are some very strong reports on the Hill and elsewhere that you are going to order the Army and Navy to institute a court-martial proceeding against certain people.

THE PRESIDENT. I am not. The matter has not been brought up to me. I don't think I have authority to order a court-martial. I think it has to go through a form of procedure set up by Congress.

Q. There is a lot of talk that indicates some of them think the gentlemen, mentioning General Short and Admiral Kimmel, should have a court-martial if for no other reason than to make their side public.

THE PRESIDENT. If they want it, I have no objection to it. I want everybody to be fairly treated.

Q. You would like to see those fellows make their statement?

THE PRESIDENT. Perfectly satisfactory to me.

Q. Is there any reason why they can't make it without a court-martial?

THE PRESIDENT. I will not put a muzzle on them.

Q. Representative May represented the reports as a "whitewash." Do you agree with that?

THE PRESIDENT. I don't. I don't think Representative May read the report. [*Laughter*] If you read them very carefully, they are not a "whitewash."

Q. In that same article you discussed your feeling for need of unity

247

of command. In the light of these new reports is there anything more you would like to say about that?

THE PRESIDENT. I am still in favor of unity of command, and always have been.

[6.] Q. Mr. President, can you tell us about Mme. Chiang's visit yesterday?

THE PRESIDENT. She was in to pay her respects before returning to China. We had a very pleasant visit on the situation in the Far East. She was very happy over the Russian-Chinese treaty, just as all of us are.

[7.] Q. Mr. President, did you happen to receive a petition from some people in Indiana, near Indianapolis, about a boy named Colby who has been sentenced to hang in Germany?

THE PRESIDENT. I don't remember receiving any such petition.

[8.] Q. Mr. President, is there anything you can tell us about the general plans on what we are going to do to feed Europe this winter, now that lend-lease is——

THE PRESIDENT. I can't give you the details on that. The plans are being studied and worked on. As soon as the British representatives come here from Great Britain I think we will work out a plan that will be satisfactory to all concerned.

Q. You mean there will be an interim period between now and the time when the Bretton Woods monetary agreement begins?

THE PRESIDENT. That's the present plan.

Q. How much will that involve.

THE PRESIDENT. I can't tell you, because I haven't the figures.

[9.] Q. Will Byron Price be your representative or the representative of one of the departments?

THE PRESIDENT. He is my representative.

[10.] Q. Have you any international assignment for Senator Maybank?

THE PRESIDENT. I hope Senator Maybank will stay in the Senate. He is a very excellent Senator.

Q. We have that inference.

Q. Did you know he wanted a diplomatic post?

248

THE PRESIDENT. No, I didn't. He has never discussed the matter with me.

[11.] Q. Has Justice Roberts changed his mind about that international appointment you wanted to give him?

THE PRESIDENT. He hasn't made up his mind, and I would rather not discuss it until he does.

[12.] Q. If we may return to the Pearl Harbor report for a moment, it seems to me that anyone who tries to make that clear to himself has a very tough time clarifying such things as why, when Stimson reported that they had told Hull that the Army and Navy wanted 3 months more time, they didn't know about it, and why, when Hull had broken with these people, that information was not relayed to Hawaii.

THE PRESIDENT. I wasn't here then.

Q. No, but I wondered if you were clear in your own mind.

THE PRESIDENT. I have read it very carefully, and I came to the conclusion that the whole thing is the result of the policy which the country itself pursued. The country was not ready for preparedness. Every time the President made an effort to get a preparedness program through Congress, it was stifled. Whenever the President made a statement about the necessity of preparedness, he was vilified for doing it. I think the country is as much to blame as any individual in this final situation that developed in Pearl Harbor.

Q. May we have that in quotations, sir, exactly what you said?

THE PRESIDENT. Yes.

[13.] Q. Can you tell us anything more about the nature of Mr. Price's duties?

THE PRESIDENT. Oh, they just wanted an expert's advice, and when Price's job ceased over here, they asked that Price give us the benefit of his experience and advice.

Q. Is that for the benefit of both radio and press?

THE PRESIDENT. Everything that has to do with public relations.

Q. Does that apply to Great Britain?

THE PRESIDENT. And to the United States also.

[14.] Q. Mr. President, there is one thing in the Army and Navy Board reports about Marshall and Stark telling President Roosevelt they were not ready for war in November, and the Army report says that was transmitted November 27.

THE PRESIDENT. I only know what I see in the report.

Q. Mr. President, that's what made me think a court-martial would help to lay the whole thing out.

THE PRESIDENT. It might—it might. I have no objection to a court-martial, but I don't intend to order one.

Q. Any reason now why the whole Roberts committee report [1] should not be released?

THE PRESIDENT. Only that there is still some information that should not be divulged that has nothing to do with the Pearl Harbor situation. It is the system by which we get information. We need that source of information now as we needed it then.

Q. Mr. President, in all the pages of the volumes there is not a word about the two privates who gave the warning.

THE PRESIDENT. They have been promoted; one is a lieutenant and the other a sergeant, I think.

Q. The lieutenant who said "Forget it" is a lieutenant colonel.

THE PRESIDENT. Is he? I didn't know that.

[15.] Q. Mr. President, do you plan any early recommendation on the St. Lawrence Seaway?

THE PRESIDENT. Yes, I do. I will let you know about it when I get it ready.

[16.] Q. Mr. President, can you tell us further about the interim plan you have in mind between lend-lease and—which departments are working on it?

THE PRESIDENT. State, FEA, and War Department.

[17.] Q. Mr. President, do you have any idea when the 52 pages deleted from the Army report will be made public? [2]

THE PRESIDENT. I don't think they ever will be.

---

[1] The report "Attack Upon Pearl Harbor by Japanese Armed Forces" of the Commission appointed by President Roosevelt and headed by Associate Justice Owen J. Roberts is printed in Senate Document 159 (77 Cong., 2d sess.).

[2] Chapter V of the report of the Army Pearl Harbor Board (released by the President to the press at his news conference of August 29) was omitted in accordance with the Secretary of War's statement of that date, which the President also released. The missing 52 pages were made public by Secretary of War Patterson on October 5, 1945.

Q. Why?

THE PRESIDENT. For the reason I just told you; there are sources of information to be protected.

[18.] Q. Did Mme. Chiang talk with you about the relations of China with America and a meeting between you and the Generalissimo?

THE PRESIDENT. The Generalissimo would like very much to see me, and I would like very much to see him, but no definite plans were made for a visit either way.

Reporter: Thank you, Mr. President.

NOTE: President Truman's twenty-second news conference was held in his office at the White House at 10 a.m. on Thursday, August 30, 1945. The White House Official Reporter noted that the following special guests attended this conference: Secretary of State James F. Byrnes, Fleet Admiral William D. Leahy, and Mrs. Alfred (Frances) Burns, a reporter on the Boston Globe who was writing a special story on the President.

119 Letter to Byron Price Requesting Him To Study
      Relations Between U.S. Forces of Occupation and the
      German People. *August* 30, 1945

Dear Mr. Price:

In accordance with our previous discussions, I am asking you to go to Germany as my personal representative to survey the general subject of relations between the American forces of occupation and the German people. You are hereby authorized to visit any place you deem necessary for this purpose.

I hope you will place yourself at the disposal of General Eisenhower and General Clay for such advice and help as they may want in this field.

At the end of your assignment, the duration of which you yourself will determine, I request you to submit to me your report and recommendations.

Very sincerely yours,

HARRY S. TRUMAN

[Honorable Byron Price, Washington, D.C.]

NOTE: Mr. Price's report, dated November 9, 1945, was released on November 28. See Item 201.

120 Statement by the President Upon Signing Order
Concerning Government Information Programs.
August 31, 1945

I HAVE today signed an Executive Order abolishing the Office of War Information.

This agency and its able personnel, under the leadership of Elmer Davis, have made an outstanding contribution to victory. Our military commanders have acclaimed its psychological warfare work as a powerful weapon against the enemy. Its other overseas activities have aided our whole effort in the foreign field.

In its domestic activities, OWI has performed an invaluable service in coordinating the Government's wartime information and in utilizing the generous contribution of private press, radio, motion pictures, advertising and other facilities to inform the American people about their Government's wartime programs.

Although it is possible to curtail wartime governmental information activities, some of our foreign information operations will continue to be necessary.

Along with the international information functions of the OWI, this order also transfers to the Department of State the foreign information functions of the Office of Inter-American Affairs. The nature of present day foreign relations makes it essential for the United States to maintain informational activities abroad as an integral part of the conduct of our foreign affairs.

I have asked the Secretary of State to study our foreign informational needs, and to formulate during the remainder of this calendar year, the program which he considers should be conducted on a continuing basis.

The Office of Inter-American Affairs has played a major role in strengthening the relationships between the United States and the other American republics. As distinct from the informational activities, the work which the OIAA has been carrying on cooperatively with the governments of Latin American countries in public health, agriculture, and other fields will be continued by that agency.

To the fullest possible extent, American private organizations and individuals in such fields as news, motion pictures and communications will, as in the past, be the primary means of informing foreign peoples about this country. The government's international information program will not compete with them.

Instead it will be designed to assist American private enterprises engaged in the dissemination of information abroad, and to supplement them in those specialized informational activities in which commercial or other limitations make it difficult for private concerns to carry on all necessary information work.

This Government will not attempt to outstrip the extensive and growing information programs of other nations. Rather, it will endeavor to see to it that other peoples receive a full and fair picture of American life and of the aims and policies of the United States government.

The domestic work of OWI, such as cooperation with the press, radio, motion pictures, and other informational media in explaining governmental programs is no longer as necessary as it was. This order discontinues these activities and provides for the liquidation of OWI itself.

Hereafter each government agency will deal directly with the various private informational facilities. Certain prewar information activities, placed in the OWI as a wartime measure, such as the publication of the United States Government Manual and answering inquiries from the public, are transferred by this order to the Bureau of the Budget.

121   Statement by the President: Labor Day.

September 1, 1945

SIX YEARS AGO the workers of the United States, and of the world, awoke to a Labor Day in a world at war. The democracies of Western Europe had just accepted the challenge of totalitarianism. We in the United States had two years of grace, but the issue was squarely joined at that hour, as we now know. There was to be no peace until tyranny had been outlawed.

Today we stand on the threshold of a new world. We must do our part in making this world what it should be—a world in which the bigotries of race and class and creed shall not be permitted to warp the souls of men.

We enter upon an era of great problems, but to live is to face problems. Our men and women did not falter in the task of saving freedom. They will not falter now in the task of making freedom secure. And high in the ranks of these men and women, as a grateful world will always remember, are the workers of all free nations who produced the vast equipment with which victory was won.

The tasks ahead are great, and the opportunities are equally great. Your Government is determined to meet those tasks and fulfill those opportunities.

We recognize the importance and dignity of labor, and we recognize the right of every American citizen to a wage which will permit him and his dependents to maintain a decent standard of living.

122 Radio Address to the American People After the Signing of the Terms of Unconditional Surrender by Japan. *September 1, 1945*

[Broadcast from the White House at 10 p.m.]

My fellow Americans, and the Supreme Allied Commander, General MacArthur, in Tokyo Bay:

The thoughts and hopes of all America—indeed of all the civilized world—are centered tonight on the battleship *Missouri*. There on that small piece of American soil anchored in Tokyo Harbor the Japanese have just officially laid down their arms. They have signed terms of unconditional surrender.

Four years ago, the thoughts and fears of the whole civilized world were centered on another piece of American soil—Pearl Harbor. The mighty threat to civilization which began there is now laid at rest. It was a long road to Tokyo—and a bloody one.

We shall not forget Pearl Harbor.

The Japanese militarists will not forget the U.S.S. *Missouri*.

The evil done by the Japanese war lords can never be repaired or forgotten. But their power to destroy and kill has been taken from them. Their armies and what is left of their Navy are now impotent.

To all of us there comes first a sense of gratitude to Almighty God who sustained us and our Allies in the dark days of grave danger, who made us to grow from weakness into the strongest fighting force in history, and who has now seen us overcome the forces of tyranny that sought to destroy His civilization.

God grant that in our pride of the hour, we may not forget the hard tasks that are still before us; that we may approach these with the same courage, zeal, and patience with which we faced the trials and problems of the past 4 years.

Our first thoughts, of course—thoughts of gratefulness and deep obligation—go out to those of our loved ones who have been killed or maimed in this terrible war. On land and sea and in the air, American men and women have given their lives so that this day of ultimate victory might come and assure the survival of a civilized world. No victory can make good their loss.

We think of those whom death in this war has hurt, taking from them fathers, husbands, sons, brothers, and sisters whom they loved. No victory can bring back the faces they longed to see.

Only the knowledge that the victory, which these sacrifices have made possible, will be wisely used, can give them any comfort. It is our responsibility—ours, the living—to see to it that this victory shall be a monument worthy of the dead who died to win it.

We think of all the millions of men and women in our armed forces and merchant marine all over the world who, after years of sacrifice and hardship and peril, have been spared by Providence from harm.

We think of all the men and women and children who during these years have carried on at home, in lonesomeness and anxiety and fear.

Our thoughts go out to the millions of American workers and businessmen, to our farmers and miners—to all those who have built up this country's fighting strength, and who have shipped to our Allies the means to resist and overcome the enemy.

Our thoughts go out to our civil servants and to the thousands of Americans who, at personal sacrifice, have come to serve in our Government during these trying years; to the members of the Selective Service boards and ration boards; to the civilian defense and Red Cross workers; to the men and women in the USO and in the entertainment world—to all those who have helped in this cooperative struggle to preserve liberty and decency in the world.

We think of our departed gallant leader, Franklin D. Roosevelt, defender of democracy, architect of world peace and cooperation.

And our thoughts go out to our gallant Allies in this war: to those who resisted the invaders; to those who were not strong enough to hold out, but who, nevertheless, kept the fires of resistance alive within the souls of their people; to those who stood up against great odds and held the line, until the United Nations together were able to supply the arms and the men with which to overcome the forces of evil.

This is a victory of more than arms alone. This is a victory of liberty over tyranny.

From our war plants rolled the tanks and planes which blasted their way to the heart of our enemies; from our shipyards sprang the ships which bridged all the oceans of the world for our weapons and supplies; from our farms came the food and fiber for our armies and navies and for our Allies in all the corners of the earth; from our mines and factories came the raw materials and the finished products which gave us the equipment to overcome our enemies.

But back of it all were the will and spirit and determination of a free people—who know what freedom is, and who know that it is worth whatever price they had to pay to preserve it.

It was the spirit of liberty which gave us our armed strength and which made our men invincible in battle. We now know that that spirit of liberty, the freedom of the individual, and the personal dignity of man, are the strongest and toughest and most enduring forces in all the world.

And so on V-J Day we take renewed faith and pride in our own way of life. We have had our day of rejoicing over this victory. We have had our day of prayer and devotion. Now let us set aside V-J

Day as one of renewed consecration to the principles which have made us the strongest nation on earth and which, in this war, we have striven so mightily to preserve.

Those principles provide the faith, the hope, and the opportunity which help men to improve themselves and their lot. Liberty does not make all men perfect nor all society secure. But it has provided more solid progress and happiness and decency for more people than any other philosophy of government in history. And this day has shown again that it provides the greatest strength and the greatest power which man has ever reached.

We know that under it we can meet the hard problems of peace which have come upon us. A free people with free Allies, who can develop an atomic bomb, can use the same skill and energy and determination to overcome all the difficulties ahead.

Victory always has its burdens and its responsibilities as well as its rejoicing.

But we face the future and all its dangers with great confidence and great hope. America can build for itself a future of employment and security. Together with the United Nations, it can build a world of peace founded on justice, fair dealing, and tolerance.

As President of the United States, I proclaim Sunday, September the second, 1945, to be V-J Day—the day of formal surrender by Japan. It is not yet the day for the formal proclamation of the end of the war nor of the cessation of hostilities. But it is a day which we Americans shall always remember as a day of retribution—as we remember that other day, the day of infamy.

From this day we move forward. We move toward a new era of security at home. With the other United Nations we move toward a new and better world of cooperation, of peace and international good will and cooperation.

God's help has brought us to this day of victory. With His help we will attain that peace and prosperity for ourselves and all the world in the years ahead.

NOTE: The President's address was part of the broadcast of the surrender ceremonies on board the U.S.S. *Missouri*.

123 Radio Address to the Members of the Armed Forces.
September 2, 1945

[Broadcast from the White House at 9:19 p.m.]

Men and women of the Armed Forces:

I am speaking to you, the Armed Forces of the United States, as I did after V-Day in Europe,[1] at a high moment of history. The war, to which we have devoted all the resources and all the energy of our country for more than three and a half years, has now produced total victory over all our enemies.

This is a time for great rejoicing and a time for solemn contemplation. With the destructive force of war removed from the world, we can turn now to the grave task of preserving the peace which you gallant men and women have won. It is a task which requires our most urgent attention. It is one in which we must collaborate with our Allies and the other nations of the world. They are as determined as we are that war must be abolished from the earth if the earth, as we know it, is to remain. Civilization cannot survive another total war.

I think you know what is in the hearts of your countrymen on this night. They are thousands of miles away from most of you. Yet they are close to you in deep gratitude and in a solemn sense of obligation. They remember—and I know they will never forget—those who have gone from among you, those who are maimed, those who, thank God, are still safe after years of fighting and suffering and danger.

And I know that in this hour of victory their thoughts—like yours—are with your departed Commander in Chief, Franklin D. Roosevelt. This is the hour for which he so gallantly fought and so bravely died.

I think I know the American soldier and sailor. He does not want gratitude or sympathy. He had a job to do. He did not like it. But he did it. And how he did it!

Now, he wants to come back home and start again the life he loves—a life of peace and quiet, the life of the civilian.

But he wants to know that he can come back to a good life. He wants

---

[1] There is no White House release of an address specifically directed to the Armed Forces after V-E Day. The President may have been referring to his May 8 address to the Nation announcing the surrender of Germany.

to know that his children will not have to go back to the life of the foxhole and the bomber, the battleship and the submarine.

I speak in behalf of all your countrymen when I pledge you that we shall do everything in our power to make those wishes come true.

For some of you, I am sorry to say, military service must continue for a time. We must keep an occupation force in the Pacific to clean out the militarism of Japan, just as we are cleaning out the militarism of Germany. The United Nations are determined that never again shall either of those countries be able to attack its peaceful neighbors.

But the great majority of you will be returned to civilian life as soon as the ships and planes can get you here. The task of moving so many men and women thousands of miles to their homes is a gigantic one. It will take months to accomplish. You have my pledge that we will do everything possible to speed it up. We want you back here with us to make your contribution to our country's welfare and to a new world of peace.

The high tide of victory will carry us forward to great achievements in the era which lies ahead. But we can perform them only in a world which is free from the threat of war. We depend upon you, who have known war in all its horror, to keep this nation aware that only through cooperation among all nations can any nation remain wholly secure.

On this night of total victory, we salute you of the Armed Forces of the United States—wherever you may be. What a job you have done!

We are all waiting for the day when you will be home with us again.

Good luck and God bless you!

124 Letter to the Speaker of the House of Representatives Transmitting Proposed Reductions in Appropriations for Civilian War Agencies. *September* 5, 1945

The Speaker of the House of Representatives:

Sir: I have the honor to transmit herewith for the consideration of Congress (1) proposed rescissions of portions of several war-related appropriations available for the fiscal year 1946, amounting to $2,755,981,394, (2) proposed rescissions of portions of several contract authorizations available for the fiscal year 1946, amounting to $794,-561,208, (3) proposed reductions in the 1946 limitations on the administrative expenses of several Government corporations and agencies, amounting to $9,318,307, (4) proposed provisions extending the availability of several "national defense" appropriations to June 30, 1946, (5) a proposed provision returning a portion of funds of certain corporations to the United States Treasury, amounting to $1,190,500, and (6) a proposed provision authorizing the transfer of appropriated funds for the liquidation expenses of agencies.

In making these recommendations for reductions in wartime appropriations, I am sensitive to the responsibility which lies on Congress and the President to make such reductions in a way that will best serve the national interest. We shall be impelled by a natural desire to reduce war appropriations quickly but in many cases the question of whether reductions should be made or to what extent they should be made will involve decisions on problems of major importance to the future well-being of the Nation which require time for careful consideration and resolution.

With these considerations in mind it seems to me that a sound course is to take action to reduce appropriations only to the extent such reduction can be entirely supported by conditions existing or clearly foreseeable at the time. Where further reductions must be based partially on judgment as to unknown future conditions, I believe it is the sounder course to delay them until their effect can be predicted with more reasonable assurance.

I thus view this proposal as one of many which I shall make under the procedure for orderly reductions in war appropriations which Congress has provided by enacting section 303 of the Second Deficiency Appropriation Act of 1944. In a few days I shall transmit recommendations with respect to appropriations for the War and Navy Departments. I also plan another full review of war and war-related appropriations and a report to Congress on January 3, 1946, containing recommendations for further adjustments. In the meantime, I shall proceed to take administrative action to the full extent of my authority to speed reduction in war and war-related activities.

The details of this proposal are set forth in the letter of the Director of the Bureau of the Budget, transmitted herewith, in whose comments and observations thereon I concur.

Respectfully yours,

HARRY S. TRUMAN

NOTE: A White House release describing the President's proposal pointed out that 28 agencies were involved, that the recommended rescissions in war-related appropriations constituted a reduction of approximately 37 percent of current available balances of appropriations of $7,439,000,000, and that the recissions in contract authorizations constituted a reduction of about 58 percent.

The details of the proposal, as set forth in the letter of the Director of the Bureau of the Budget transmitted with the President's letter, are printed in House Document 280 (79th Cong., 1st sess.).

125   Citation Accompanying the Distinguished Service Medal Presented to Harry L. Hopkins. *September 5, 1945*

CITATION FOR DISTINGUISHED SERVICE MEDAL

MR. HARRY L. HOPKINS performed services of outstanding value to the United States of America from December 1941 to July 1945. As Special Adviser to the President during critical months of World War II, he assumed tasks of utmost urgency and far-reaching consequence, lightening the burden of the Commander-in-Chief. He gave great assistance to the armed forces in their relationships with the Chief Executive, attacking with piercing understanding the tremendous problems incident to the vast military operations throughout the world. As Chairman of the Munitions Assignment Board, he channeled material to all Allied forces with a skill measurable in terms of the steady successes which have been achieved in crushing Germany and closing with Japan in the final struggle. As Chairman of the President's Soviet Protocol Committee, he determined supply quotas to be dispatched to Russia, accomplishing this mission with statesmanshiplike skill. At major conferences of world powers he threw his every effort toward the speedy solution of weighty problems. With deep appreciation of the armed forces' needs and broad knowledge of the Commander-in-Chief's over-all policy, with exceptional ability to weld our Allies to the common purpose of victory over aggression, Mr. Hopkins made a selfless, courageous and objective contribution to the war effort.

HARRY S. TRUMAN

NOTE: The presentation was made by the President in the Rose Garden at the White House at 12:30 p.m., in a joint ceremony also honoring Howard Bruce (see Item 126).

126 Citation Accompanying the Distinguished Service Medal Presented to Howard Bruce. *September* 5, 1945

CITATION FOR THE DISTINGUISHED SERVICE MEDAL

MR. HOWARD BRUCE rendered exceptionally meritorious and distinguished service to the War Department in the performance of duties of great responsibility from July 1942 to June 1945. As Director of Materiel, Army Service Forces, during one of the most critical periods of the war, and in other highly important positions on the staff of the Commanding General, Army Service Forces, he displayed exceptional initiative and resourcefulness, and greatly assisted in developing and managing the greatest military procurement program in history. His leadership in conceiving and bringing to peak efficiency the Supply Control System greatly improved Army procurement methods. His early endeavors to create an orderly program to conserve critical materials helped alleviate supply shortages. His efforts in removing obstacles to production resulted in immediate and lasting improvement in the Army procurement program. With unusual perseverance and devotion to duty, Mr. Bruce contributed his energy and ability to the prosecution of the war. His accomplishments reflect great credit upon himself and the military service.

HARRY S. TRUMAN

NOTE: The presentation was made by the President in the Rose Garden at the White House at 12:30 p.m., in a joint ceremony also honoring Harry Hopkins (see Item 125).

127   The President's News Conference of
       September 5, 1945

THE PRESIDENT. I just called you in to give you an announcement on the Roosevelt Memorial Association meeting over in the White House. It was well attended, and the various proposals for memorials were discussed, and it was finally agreed to appoint a committee to nominate officers for the Roosevelt Memorial Association into an enlarged executive committee and to study plans and call another meeting to report back to the Executive Committee again. And the committee appointed—I was authorized to appoint the committee—was Mr. Hopkins, chairman; Miss Perkins, Mr. Morgenthau, Mr. Walker, and Admiral Leahy. And that was the substance of the meeting. Now, I am going to have a press conference tomorrow, and I will let you ask me all the questions you want then.

Reporter: Mr. President, it is going to be very pleasant to have you at the Byron Price dinner tomorrow night, at the Press Club.

THE PRESIDENT. Isn't that Saturday?

Reporter: No, tomorrow, Thursday.

THE PRESIDENT. I'll be there; but you must be careful of me. [*Laughter*]

NOTE: President Truman's twenty-third news conference was held in his office at the White House at 4 p.m. on Wednesday, September 5, 1945.

128   Special Message to the Congress Presenting a 21-Point
       Program for the Reconversion Period.
       September 6, 1945

To the Congress of the United States:

I regret that you have been compelled to cut short your recess period. I know, however, that you have been just as eager as any of us to meet the problems which naturally have crowded down upon us with the surrender of the Japanese.

You have cut short a well-merited vacation in order to do so. I hope that the American people realize as fully as I do, that from the very first days of the emergency, the Congress has most energetically and patriotically devoted its time, energies, and capabilities to the immediate problems of war and to the long-range problems of peace. The legislative branch of the Government is entitled to its full share of credit and glory for the victory of the Allied armies. I wish to take this opportunity on behalf of the Nation to congratulate you on the great victory which has been won—in which you played so important a part.

The Congress reconvenes at a time of great emergency. It is an emergency about which, however, we need have no undue fear if we exercise the same energy, foresight, and wisdom as we did in carrying on the war and winning this victory.

The sudden surrender of the Japanese has not caught us unawares. President Roosevelt, as early as the Fall of 1943, began to set up machinery which he foresaw would become necessary to meet the reconversion period. The Congress in its wisdom has adopted some of that machinery by statute, and has improved and added to it. As a result, Government agencies, for some time, have been able to plan for the immediate and long-range steps which now have to be taken.

As the Congress has undoubtedly noticed, many steps were taken immediately after the surrender of the Japanese. Many more have been taken since.

The process of reconversion will be a complicated and difficult one. The general line of approach to the problem is to achieve as full peacetime production and employment as possible in the most efficient and speedy manner. The following policies have been laid down and will be followed:

(1) Demobilize as soon as possible the armed forces no longer needed.

(2) Cancel and settle war contracts as quickly as possible.

(3) Clear the war plants so as to permit contractors to proceed with peacetime production.

(4) Hold the line on prices and rents until fair competition can operate to prevent inflation and undue hardship on consumers.

(5) Hold wages in line where their increase would cause inflationary

price rises. Where price ceilings would not be endangered, collective bargaining should be restored.

(6) Remove all possible wartime government controls in order to speed and encourage reconversion and expansion.

(7) Keep only those controls which are necessary to help reconversion and expansion by preventing bottlenecks, shortages of material, and inflation.

(8) Prevent rapid decrease of wage incomes or purchasing power.

The major objective, of course, is to reestablish an expanded peacetime industry, trade, and agriculture, and to do it as quickly as possible.

Obviously during this process there will be a great deal of inevitable unemployment. What we must do is to assist industry to reconvert to peacetime production as quickly and effectively as possible so that the number of unemployed will be swiftly and substantially reduced as industry and business and agriculture get into high production.

The Government is now doing what it can to hurry this reconversion process.

Through contract termination procedures it is providing quick payment to contractors.

It has released controls on practically all materials which are necessary for peacetime production, reserving only those few in which there is still a critical shortage.

It has made arrangements for credit facilities for industry.

By plant and surplus property disposal, it is helping private enterprise to get started again.

In the consumer field the Government has released controls over articles which were needed for the war in such large quantities that civilians had to go without.

For the information of the Congress, I am submitting as an appendix to this message a report by the Director of War Mobilization and Reconversion showing what has already been done by the Federal Government in reconversion.[1]

There is much that the Congress can do to help this process and to

---

[1] Mr. Snyder's report, dated September 4, 1945, and entitled "The Transition: Phase One," is printed with the message in House Document 282 (79th Cong., 1st sess.).

tide over the period between now and the time when reconversion is completed and civilian jobs are plentiful in a stable economy that provides full production, full employment, and a high standard of living.

I. UNEMPLOYMENT COMPENSATION

The end of the war came more swiftly than most of us anticipated. Widespread cut-backs in war orders followed promptly. As a result, there has already been a considerable number of workers who are between jobs as war industries convert to peace. Other workers are returning to a 40-hour week and are faced with a corresponding reduction in take-home pay.

This has led to a natural feeling of uneasiness among the rank and file of our people. Let me emphasize that there will be no reason for undue timidity. A vast backlog of orders may soon make possible the greatest peacetime industrial activity that we have ever seen. But this can happen only if the Congress and the administration move vigorously and courageously to deal with the economic problems which peace has created. Then there need be no reason to fear either the immediate future or the years that lie ahead of us.

Determined action now will create the atmosphere of confidence which is so vital to a rapid reconversion with a minimum of unemployment and hardship.

No matter how rapidly reconversion proceeds, however, no amount of effort or planning will be able immediately to provide a job for everyone displaced from war work. Obviously, displaced war workers cannot find jobs until industry has been regeared and made ready to produce peacetime goods. During this lag the Government should provide help. The cost of this transition from war to peace is as much a part of the cost of war as the transition from peace to war—and we should so consider it.

This course is recommended not only as a matter of justice and humanity, but also as a matter of sound business. Nothing would be more harmful to our economy than to have every displaced war worker stop buying consumer goods. And nothing would be more conducive to a large-scale cessation of buying than the feeling on the part of displaced

266

war workers that all their income had stopped and that their remaining financial resources had to be hoarded.

For one group of those who may become unemployed in the near future—the demobilized veterans—the Congress has already made special provision. Any veteran who has satisfactorily completed 90 days of service is now entitled by law to a weekly unemployment allowance of $20 for as much as 52 weeks depending on the length of his service.

By contrast, there are more than 15,000,000 workers not protected under our present unemployment insurance laws. There are many millions more for whom protection is inadequate. Many of these have been unable to accumulate adequate savings.

On May 28, 1945, I recommended to the Congress that the Federal Government immediately supplement the unemployment insurance benefits now provided by the several States. That is the only feasible way to provide at least a subsistence payment in all parts of the United States during this coming unemployment period.

As I pointed out then, the existing State laws relative to unemployment insurance are inadequate in three respects:

(1) Only about 30,000,000 of our 43,000,000 nonagricultural workers are protected by unemployment insurance. Federal Government employees, for example, such as Federal shipyard and arsenal workers, are not covered. Nor are employees of small businesses and small industrial establishments. Nor are the officers and men of the merchant marine who have braved enemy torpedoes and bombs to deliver supplies and the implements of war to our armed services and our allies.

(2) The weekly benefit payments under many of the State laws are now far too low to provide subsistence and purchasing power for the workers and their families. Almost half of the States have the clearly inadequate maximum of $15 to $18 a week.

(3) Many of the States pay benefits for too short a period. In more than one-third of the States, for example, 18 weeks is the maximum.

I recommended then, and I urgently renew my recommendation now, that the Congress take immediate action to make good these deficiencies for the present emergency period of reconversion.

Specifically, coverage should be extended to include Federal employees, maritime workers, and other workers not now insured. This additional compensation during the present emergency will have to be financed entirely by the Federal Government, but the benefits should appropriately be administered by the States.

I also recommended, and I now repeat that recommendation, that the Congress provide, through supplementary Federal emergency benefit payments, additional unemployment benefits so as to bring them up to adequate standards in all the States. All payments, however, should be made through the existing unemployment compensation machinery of the several States.

During this emergency every eligible worker should be entitled to 26 weeks of unemployment benefits in any one year. The maximum weekly payment for those workers whose previous earnings were high enough, should be not less than $25 per week.

If the Congress decides to take this very necessary step, it will also wish to reconsider and increase the unemployment allowance provided for veterans.

There has been so much misrepresentation about this temporary proposal that I think I should categorically state what the bill does *not* do.

It does *not* give everyone $25 a week. Under it, an applicant must be ready, willing, and able to work and must have earned wages high enough so that the percentage rate will yield this maximum figure.

It does *not* federalize the unemployment compensation system. It leaves it with the States.

It is *not* intended to take the place of the permanent amendments to the unemployment compensation system which are now being studied by the Congress. It is an emergency measure designed to expand the present system without changing its principles. It is designed only to meet the immediate pressing human problems of reconversion.

This recommendation is *not* to be confused with the broader question of extending, expanding, and improving our entire social security program of which unemployment insurance is only a part. I expect to communicate with the Congress on this subject at a later date. But I sincerely urge that we do not wait for consideration of such a complex question before enacting this much needed emergency legislation.

2. FAIR LABOR STANDARDS ACT

In addition to those workers who will temporarily lose their jobs, there will be millions of others whose incomes will fall sharply with the end of war production. These will be added to the several million wage earners who even now have hourly earnings much below what is necessary for a decent standard of living.

The inadequacy of these wages, in many cases, has been temporarily concealed by wartime increases in take-home pay resulting from overtime work. As these props to income are removed, however, low-wage earners will be hard pressed to feed, clothe, and house their families. This flies in the face of a sound public policy. Failure to correct this situation will slow down, if it will not actually stop, our drive toward an expanding market for business and agriculture.

The foundations of a healthy national economy cannot be secure so long as any large section of our working people receive substandard wages. The existence of substandard wage levels sharply curtails the national purchasing power and narrows the market for the products of our farms and factories.

In the Fair Labor Standards Act of 1938, the Congress adopted a program intended to provide a minimum wage standard for a large number of American workers.

In that statute, the Congress declared it to be our national policy to eliminate, from interstate industry, wage levels detrimental to the maintenance of minimum standards of living. The establishment then of a minimum wage of 25 cents per hour represented a first step toward the realization of that policy. The goal of 40 cents per hour, which under the act was to be made effective by 1945, was actually made fully effective more than a year ago by the voluntary action of the industry committees.

I believed that the goal of a 40 cent minimum was inadequate when established. It has now become obsolete.

Increases in the cost of living since 1938 and changes in our national wage structure, require an immediate and substantial upward revision of this minimum. Only in that way can the objectives of the Fair Labor Standards Act be realized, the national purchasing power protected, and an economy of full production and abundance preserved and maintained for the American people.

The high prosperity which we seek in the postwar years will not be meaningful for all our people if any large proportion of our industrial wage earners receive wages as low as the minimum now sanctioned by the Fair Labor Standards Act.

I therefore recommend that the Congress amend the Fair Labor Standards Act by substantially increasing the minimum wage specified therein to a level which will eliminate substandards of living, and assure the maintenance of the health, efficiency, and general well-being of workers.

The scope of the Fair Labor Standards Act also should be clarified and extended. In view of changes which have occurred since 1938, I believe it is no longer necessary to exclude from the minimum wage program the large number of workers engaged in agricultural processing who are now excluded. There now exists a twilight zone in which some workers are covered, and others, doing similar work, are not. Extension of coverage would benefit both workers and employers by removing competitive inequities.

Our achievements in this field during the last seven years of establishing minimum wages have been gratifying; but we must continue to move forward, step by step.

I urge that the Congress act promptly. The wage structure on which businessmen may make future plans should be settled quickly.

3. WARTIME CONTROLS

One of the outstanding achievements of the war has been the success of the Government in holding the line against inflation. This is the first time in any major war that the United States has been able substantially to stabilize its economy.

That fact now permits us to enter into the difficult period of readjustment without the threat of a disastrous price collapse.

For this result much credit is due to the Congress, which in the face of great insistence from many interested pressure groups refused steadfastly to take the easy way.

Great credit is due to the Office of Economic Stabilization, the War Labor Board, the Office of Price Administration, the War Food Administration, the War Production Board, and the other stabilization agencies. Despite great pressure and often unjust abuse, they continued to hold the line for the benefit of the great mass of Americans.

And above all, great credit is due to the people of the United States, the great body of average citizens, who, for four difficult years and with only a few exceptions, subordinated their personal interest to the long-range interest of the Nation as a whole.

Many of the demands of the war for commodities have now decreased. They will decrease further during the initial period of unemployment which will come with the cancellation of war contracts. As a result, prices of some commodities are bound to soften. But if that happens in the next few months, we cannot allow ourselves to be misled. We must keep in mind the experience of the period immediately after the first World War. After a lull of a few months following the Armistice of 1918, prices turned upward, scrambling for inventories started, and prices soon got completely out of hand. We found ourselves in one of the worst inflations in our history, culminating in the crash of 1920 and the disastrous deflation of 1920 and 1921.

We must be sure this time not to repeat that bitter mistake. When reconversion really gets under way, and men go back to work, and payrolls increase, and the pent-up demands of the war years at home and abroad for peacetime products begin to make themselves felt, we shall face the same scramble for goods, the same speculative excesses that developed in 1919. We must be in a position to overcome that danger if we expect to achieve an orderly transition to peacetime levels of full production and full employment. However, we must not allow inflationary dangers to obscure our vision of the possibilities of lower incomes and widespread unemployment. Our policy must guard against both contingencies.

Immediately after the Japanese decision to surrender, the Office of Price Administration moved promptly to eliminate rationing on gasoline, fuel oil, stoves, and processed foods.

During the transition period the Price Administrator, of course, will eliminate rationing and price controls on one commodity after another just as soon as supply comes into balance with demand. At the same time he will make whatever price adjustments are required to facilitate rapid reconversion and reemployment.

However, it will be necessary for him to continue to resist unreasonable pressures for higher prices on some commodities, just as he has resisted them all through the war. In resisting these pressures and in carrying out his difficult responsibilities, I must state clearly that he has both my backing and my confidence.

It will similarly be necessary for the Government to resist pressures for increases in wage rates which would imperil price ceilings.

Without some general stabilization the consumer cannot be protected. Without stabilization, reconversion cannot proceed as rapidly as it should; for stability of cost is indispensable to sound business planning.

The price control and stabilization program has received the backing of the great majority of businessmen throughout the war period. With few exceptions, business groups have realized clearly their own personal stake and the stake of our basic economy in the success of the anti-inflation program.

During the months that lie ahead, however, some groups in business may be tempted to substitute for this long-range wartime thinking, a short-range policy designed to secure prices high enough to provide immediate profits over and above their temporarily high costs of production due to their initial low volume.

These pressures must be resisted. Prices must be held firmly on reconversion items as well as on cost of living items during the coming months.

The American people are entitled to a firm assurance not only on the part of the Administration, but from the Congress itself, that rents and the prices of clothing, food, and other essentials will be held in line. They are also entitled to buy washing machines, vacuum cleaners, automobiles and other products at prices based on our traditional system of high output and low unit costs.

The promise of good profits for businessmen must not be based on small initial volume. It must be based on the full all-out production which it is my belief that American industry will rapidly achieve.

Because of heavy wartime needs, it has been necessary to allocate available supplies of many foods among various claimants within this country, and among other countries. It has been necessary to set aside large blocks of specified commodities in order to make these commodities available for military and other essential needs. Rationing of food for consumers has been necessary in the interest of fair distribution.

Many of these controls have already been eliminated and all remaining allocations, set-asides, and rationing will be removed as rapidly as the supply situation will permit.

However, supplies of some of our principal foods will continue beyond the end of 1945 to be too small for the demand.

For example, the world will be short of requirements for fats and oils and sugar for some months, and allocations and rationing will probably have to be continued into 1946. We must not move so rapidly as to endanger the orderly distribution of goods on which we have based our living during the emergency.

Let me add that in no case should rationing controls be removed if by so doing we should jeopardize our relief shipments to Europe and other distressed war areas. We have a moral obligation to the people of these liberated areas. More than that, our own enlightened self-interest tells us that hungry people are rarely advocates of democracy. The rehabilitation of these countries, and indeed the removal of American occupational troops, may be unnecessarily delayed if we fail to meet these responsibilities during the next few months.

During the reconversion period and as long as shortages in certain materials other than food continue, the War Production Board will have to support the stabilization program as it has done during the past four years.

It must be in a position to take action where necessary, to increase scarce materials and facilities, break bottlenecks, channel production to meet essential needs, safeguard the opportunities for small business concerns, and, above all, to control inventories so as to prevent speculative hoarding and unbalanced distribution.

As the Congress knows, the War Production Board has already removed a great majority of the controls which were in force during the war, and many more will be removed during the next few months.

I trust that the Congress will agree, however, that the controls which still remain and which are still considered necessary by the agency charged with responsibility should not be removed until the need for them disappears. The need to control a few critical materials which the war has caused to be in short supply will continue for some time until adequate supplies are again available. Foremost among these materials are tin and crude rubber.

It will also be necessary for some period to prevent the hoarding of items now badly needed and in great demand for the civilian economy. Many critical shortages can be avoided by the extension of general inventory controls which would prevent the accumulation of unreasonably large stocks in the hands of a few. This will speed the reconversion program and will also greatly assist in avoiding inflation of the price structure.

The extension of one further type of control should have consideration at this time. In the national interest, this Government has made and should continue to make agreements for securing our fair share of materials from certain foreign sources and also agreements for supplying various materials and products abroad. The Government should have authority to assure the carrying out of such commitments.

These production and inventory controls, as well as the allocations of food, set-asides of commodities, and rationing among consumers have been set up under the Second War Powers Act.

Most of the provisions of this act expire on December 31, 1945.

I am convinced that an orderly transition to a peacetime economy will require the use of some of these controls after the first of the year.

I request the Congress, therefore, to extend the provisions of the Second War Powers Act, either in its present form or with appropriate limitations, preserving the powers necessary to achieve the objectives I have outlined.

The Congress has my definite assurance that none of these war powers will be exercised by the executive branch of the Government unless they are deemed essential to the attainment of the objective of an orderly stabilized reconversion. The Congress should, of course, if it extends the statute, reserve the right to terminate it by legislation at any time it deems necessary.

I hope that the Congress will not delay the extension of this authority. Delay would retard reconversion by creating uncertainty on the part of business as to whether necessary controls will be retained or not. Businessmen, in planning for next year's activities, will be assisted greatly by knowing in advance whether or not the Government is going to keep a firm hand at the brakes to prevent inflation.

The termination of the wartime food subsidies, for which a total of $1,798,000,000 has been authorized for the current year, is one of the important problems in reconversion. Agencies dealing directly with this problem are now meeting jointly to determine in what order and at what time these food subsidies may be eliminated without an undue disturbance to farm income or living costs.

Subsidies for purposes other than food are also being reviewed by the agencies concerned, who are collecting the necessary data for an orderly liquidation at the earliest date compatible with the stabilization program.

Those subsidies which were designed originally to stimulate increased production should not be removed at a time or in a manner to incite inflation and upset our economy.

I have directed that early reports be made on this important problem.

4. WAR POWERS AND EXECUTIVE AGENCIES REORGANIZATION

I should like to bring to the attention of the Congress the legal difficulties that will arise unless care is taken in the drafting of legislation terminating wartime controls and wartime agencies.

I have asked the Attorney General to prepare a report on the principal statutes that confer wartime powers and on the various wartime agencies, with particular reference to the circumstances under which each terminates.

A copy of this memorandum [1] is attached for the information of the

---

[1] The report of the Attorney General to the President, in the form of a letter dated September 1, 1945, is printed with the message in House Document 282 (79th Cong., 1st sess.).

Congress. It is an able and comprehensive summary of the applicable laws.

Your attention is particularly called to the statement in the opinion of the Attorney General to the effect that the broad basis of governmental power on which the existing emergency and wartime statutes rest has not been terminated by the unconditional surrender of our enemies.

Certain of the wartime statutes which have been made effective "in time of war," "during the present war," or "for the duration of the war" continue to be effective until a formal state of peace has been restored, or until some earlier termination date is made applicable by appropriate governmental action. Another group of statutes which by their provisions terminate "upon the cessation of hostilities" or "upon termination of the war," will in fact and in law terminate only by a formal proclamation to that effect by the President or by appropriate congressional action.

From time to time action will be taken with respect to these agencies, with the general objective of streamlining the Government into a peacetime organization as quickly as possible.

The time has *not* yet arrived, however, for the proclamation of the cessation of hostilities, much less the termination of the war. Needless to say, such proclamations will be made as soon as circumstances permit.

It has been necessary during the course of the war to make numerous important redistributions of functions among executive agencies.

This has been accomplished by the President under the authority of title I of the First War Powers Act. This act expires six months after the termination of the war, or at such earlier time as may be designated by appropriate governmental action.

If the Congress or the President were formally to declare the present war terminated, it would automatically cause all the steps taken under the First War Powers Act with respect to the war agencies to expire, and would have the Government revert automatically to its preexisting status six months after the declaration.

If this were to occur, it would cause great confusion and chaos in the Government.

It is the policy of this administration not to exercise wartime powers beyond the point at which it is necessary to exercise them.

Similarly, the wartime agencies of the Government will not be allowed to continue to perform functions not required by present conditions.

Those functions of the wartime agencies which must be retained during part or all of the period of reconversion should be transferred as promptly as practicable to the permanent departments and agencies of the Government. The remaining functions, appropriate only to the crisis through which we have passed, should be terminated in an orderly, systematic fashion as soon as possible.

A program of winding up wartime agencies and distributing their functions on a peacetime basis is now being pursued under the powers vested in the President by title I of the First War Powers Act.

Therefore, I urge that the Congress do not yet adopt a resolution proclaiming the termination of the war or the termination of the emergency or the cessation of hostilities. Such a resolution would automatically cause the death of many war powers and wartime agencies before we are ready.

At the same time I recognize that the Congress may wish to repeal certain specific wartime statutes. If this is to be done, the repeal should be on a selective basis, through the adoption of specific statutes dealing with each wartime power which the Congress decides should be terminated.

In my message dated May 24, 1945, it was recommended that permanent legislation be enacted which would authorize the President to submit to the Congress, from time to time, plans providing for the reorganization of executive agencies, each such plan to become effective unless the Congress should reject it by concurrent resolution.

This type of joint action by the Congress and the President has produced, and will produce, far better results than can be achieved by the usual legislative process in the field of executive reorganization. If proper progress is to be made, it is necessary to permit the President to lay out the machinery for carrying out his responsibility for the conduct of the executive branch, subject to rejection by the two Houses of Congress. Executive initiative, subject to congressional veto, is an effective approach to governmental reorganization.

The responsibility of conducting the executive branch rests upon the President. It is fair and efficient to permit him to lay out the machinery for carrying out that responsibility.

The means for doing this should be generally along the lines of the Reorganization Act of 1939, which gives the initiative to the President, but reserves power to the Congress by a majority vote to nullify any action of the President which does not meet with its approval.

Considerable progress was made in efficiency of government under this Reorganization Act of 1939. I recommend that such powers be made of permanent duration and that the legislation be sufficiently flexible to permit any kind of adjustment for which necessity may arise.

It is clear to all of us that the Government has a difficult and important task in the years which lie ahead. Our Government belongs to the people and the people have a right to expect from their Government the greatest possible efficiency in carrying out its task.

Our Government has never been as efficient as we should like to see it. To some degree this may be charged to the size of some of the tasks assigned to it. To some extent, it is also due to the lack of trained Government personnel and the low salaries paid to Government officials.

There is no question that the war has taught us a great deal about Government administration. There is still, however, much room for improvement.

I have undertaken directly through the members of the Cabinet and also through the Directors of the Office of War Mobilization and Reconversion and the Bureau of the Budget to emphasize the need for more efficient operation in all the executive branches of the Government. I have requested them to examine administrative procedures, and to speed up and simplify their operations to the maximum practical degree.

I have also requested the Bureau of the Budget to examine closely with each department and agency head, the actual needs of his office

278

following the surrender of Japan. They have been asked to reduce budgets promptly and fully wherever cuts are indicated. The Bureau of the Budget is now completing studies which will result in reductions of millions of dollars in the expense of operating our Government.

We must continue relentlessly this program for increased Government efficiency. The Congress can depend upon the Executive to push this program with the utmost vigor.

5. FULL EMPLOYMENT

I am confident that, with the cooperation of American industry, labor, and agriculture, we can bridge the gap between war and peace.

When we have reconverted our economy to a peacetime basis, however, we shall not be satisfied with merely our prewar economy. The American people have set high goals for their own future. They have set these goals high because they have seen how great can be the productive capacity of our country.

The levels of production and income reached during the war years have given our citizens an appreciation of what a full production peacetime economy can be.

They are not interested in boom prosperity—for that only too often leads to panic and depression. But they are interested in providing opportunity for work and for ultimate security.

Government must do its part and assist industry and labor to get over the line from war to peace.

That is why I have asked for unemployment compensation legislation.

That is why I now ask for full-employment legislation.

The objectives for our domestic economy which we seek in our long-range plans were summarized by the late President Franklin D. Roosevelt over a year and a half ago in the form of an economic bill of rights. Let us make the attainment of those rights the essence of postwar American economic life.

I repeat the statement of President Roosevelt:

In our day these economic truths have become accepted as self-evident. We have accepted, so to speak, a second bill of rights under which a new basis of security and prosperity can be established for all—regardless of station, race, or creed.

Among these are:

The right to a useful and remunerative job in the industries, or shops or farms or mines of the Nation.

The right to earn enough to provide adequate food and clothing and recreation.

The right of every farmer to raise and sell his products at a return which will give him and his family a decent living.

The right of every businessman, large and small, to trade in an atmosphere of freedom from unfair competition and domination by monopolies at home or abroad.

The right of every family to a decent home.

The right to adequate medical care and the opportunity to achieve and enjoy good health.

The right to adequate protection from the economic fears of old age, sickness, accident, and unemployment.

The right to a good education.

All of these rights spell security. And after this war is won we must be prepared to move forward, in the implementation of these rights, to new goals of human happiness and well-being.

America's own rightful place in the world depends in large part upon how fully these and similar rights have been carried into practice for our citizens. For unless there is security here at home there cannot be lasting peace in the world.

I shall from time to time communicate with the Congress on some of the subjects included in this enumeration of economic rights.

Most of them, in the last analysis, depend upon full production and full employment at decent wages.

There has been much discussion about the necessity of continuing full employment after the war if we hope to continue in substantial degree the prosperity which came with the war years. The time has come for action along these lines.

To provide jobs we must look first and foremost to private enterprise—to industry, agriculture, and labor. Government must inspire enterprise with confidence. That confidence must come mainly through deeds, not words.

But it is clear that confidence will be promoted by certain assurances given by the Government:

Assurance that all the facts about full employment and opportunity will be gathered periodically for the use of all.

Assurance of stability and consistency in public policy, so that

enterprise can plan better by knowing what the Government intends
to do.

Assurance that every governmental policy and program will be
pointed to promote maximum production and employment in private
enterprise.

Assurance that priority will be given to doing those things first
which stimulate normal employment most.

A national reassertion of the right to work for every American citizen
able and willing to work—a declaration of the ultimate duty of Government to use its own resources if all other methods should fail to
prevent prolonged unemployment—these will help to avert fear and
establish full employment. The prompt and firm acceptance of this
bedrock public responsibility will reduce the need for its exercise.

I ask that full employment legislation to provide these vital assurances be speedily enacted. Such legislation should also provide machinery for a continuous full-employment policy—to be developed and
pursued in cooperation among industry, agriculture, and labor, between
the Congress and the Chief Executive, between the people and their
Government.

Full employment means full opportunity for all under the American economic system—nothing more and nothing less.

In human terms, full employment means opportunity to get a good
peacetime job for every worker who is ready, able, and willing to take
one. It does not mean made work, or making people work.

In economic terms, full employment means full production and the
opportunity to sell goods—all the goods that industry and agriculture
can produce.

In Government terms, full employment means opportunity to reduce
the ratio of public spending to private investment without sacrificing
essential services.

In world-wide terms, full employment in America means greater
economic security and more opportunity for lasting peace throughout
the world.

These goals and the machinery to carry them out are set forth in legislation now pending before the Congress on which extensive public hearings have been held. The country justifiably expects early action along these lines.

6. FAIR EMPLOYMENT PRACTICE COMMITTEE

During the years of war production we made substantial progress in overcoming many of the prejudices which had resulted in discriminations against minority groups.

Many of the injustices based upon considerations of race, religion, and color were removed. Many were prevented. Perfection was not reached, of course, but substantial progress was made.

In the reconversion period and thereafter, we should make every effort to continue this American ideal. It is one of the fundamentals of our political philosophy, and it should be an integral part of our economy.

The Fair Employment Practice Committee is continuing during the transition period. I have already requested that legislation be enacted placing the Fair Employment Practice Committee on a permanent basis. I repeat that recommendation.

7. LABOR DISPUTES AND WAGE STABILIZATION

Our national welfare requires that during the reconversion period production of civilian goods and services—as full production as possible—go forward without interruption, and that labor and industry cooperate to keep strikes and lock-outs at a minimum.

Those who have the responsibility of labor relations must recognize that responsibility. This is not the time for short-sighted management to seize upon the chance to reduce wages and try to injure labor unions. Equally it is not the time for labor leaders to shirk their responsibility and permit widespread industrial strife.

With this objective in view, I shall shortly convene a conference of representatives of organized labor and industry for the purpose of working out by agreement means to minimize labor disputes.

In the interim period, pending the convening of the conference, I have called upon the representatives of organized labor and industry to continue their adherence to the no-strike, no-lock-out policy. During this interim period, labor disputes which threaten a substantial interference with the transition to a peacetime economy should be submitted to the War Labor Board. They would there be handled by the Board under existing procedures. The country will expect parties to any such disputes to comply voluntarily with the determinations of the War Labor Board.

The threat of inflationary bidding-up of wage rates by competition in a short labor market has disappeared. Therefore the War Labor Board has removed the necessity of approving proposed voluntary wage increases, so long as they will not be used to obtain an increase in price ceilings.

I have conferred upon the War Labor Board adequate authority to correct maladjustments and inequities in wage rates arising in the reconversion period which will tend to interfere with the effective transition to a peacetime economy.

The Board should be terminated as soon after the conclusion of the forthcoming industry-labor conference as the orderly disposition of the work of the Board and the provisions of the War Labor Disputes Act permit, and after facilities have been provided to take care of the wage stabilization functions under the act of October 2, 1942.

Meanwhile, plans for strengthening the Department of Labor, and bringing under it functions properly belonging to it, are going forward. With the return to a peacetime economy and the elimination of the present temporary wartime agencies and procedures, we must look to collective bargaining, aided and supplemented by a truly effective system of conciliation and voluntary arbitration, as the best and most democratic method of maintaining sound industrial relations.

8. UNITED STATES EMPLOYMENT SERVICE EXTENSION

Placing demobilized veterans and displaced war workers in new peacetime jobs is the major human problem of our country's reconversion to a peacetime economy. It is imperative that this work be done swiftly and efficiently, and that men and women lose a minimum amount of time between jobs.

The next few months are crucial. What we do now will affect our American way of life for decades to come.

The United States Employment Service has an important responsibility in the performance of this task.

At present, this agency operates as a national and centralized system with a free flow of information among its offices. Under the 1946 appropriation act, the offices are to be turned back to the 48 States within 90 days after the cessation of hostilities.

Shortly after the declaration of war, the Government realized that the manpower of the Nation could be mobilized more efficiently if the United States Employment Service were centralized under Federal control. Hundreds of thousands of workers had to be recruited from all parts of the country. Often, they were wanted in regions far from their homes. Certain areas had surpluses of labor; others were desperately in need of more workers. This situation could be met only through a centrally operated employment service that covered the entire Nation.

Now we are faced with this problem in reverse. Hundreds of thousands of men and women will want to seek jobs in towns and cities other than those in which they worked during the war. They may want to return home, or they may want to strike out in search of new opportunities in new surroundings. Millions of veterans also will be coming back in search of peacetime jobs. They will want to know where such jobs can be found, not only in their own areas, but also in other parts of the land.

The task of helping this vast army of job seekers to fit themselves into peacetime economy is fully as difficult as the mobilization of manpower for war. To make any decided change in the machinery to handle this problem now would cause unnecessary hardship to workers and veterans. It would slow down the entire process of reconversion.

I urgently recommend that the Congress do not yet return the Employment Service to the States. Ultimately it should be so returned. However, it should be continued under Federal control at least until the expiration of the War Mobilization Act—June 30, 1947.

I also recommend that its appropriation be increased by $10,000,000 for the current fiscal year. Prompt action on this matter is especially important since personnel and facilities must be quickly enlarged to handle the rising tide of veterans and war workers who will be seeking jobs.

9. AGRICULTURE

One of the most magnificent production jobs in the war has been done by the farmers of the United States. They have met the unprecedented demands of the war, and, at the same time, have provided our civilian population with more food per capita than during the 1935–39 prewar period.

No other group in America labored longer or harder to meet the war demands put upon them. Food production last year reached a peak more than a third above the prewar years despite the fact that farm population has declined by about five million since 1940.

Fortunately, farmers were aided by better-than-average weather conditions over the country. We cannot, however, count on continuance of better-than-average weather. Therefore, because of the great demands for food that exist in this country and for relief abroad, the Department of Agriculture is planning for another year of full production. This does not mean the same volume of production for each individual crop, because the surrender of Japan has brought changes in the demand pattern. But the total acreage needed for next year will not be greatly different from this year.

The Government now must be prepared to carry out the Nation's responsibility to aid farmers in making their necessary readjustments from a wartime to a peacetime basis. The Congress already has provided postwar supports against price collapse for many farm products. This was a provision of wisdom and foresight.

After the First World War farm prices dropped more than 50 percent from the spring of 1920 to the spring of 1921. We do not intend to permit a repetition of the disaster that followed the First World War. The Secretary of Agriculture has assured me that he will use all means now authorized by the Congress to carry out the price-support commitments.

But there is need for additional measures to strengthen the machinery for carrying out price-support commitments, and for laying the basis for broader peacetime markets for agricultural products.

The Congress already has provided for one such postwar measure that needs now to be adapted to our changed situation. Recognizing that the lend-lease program required greatly increased production and that this increase could not be suddenly discontinued when the program stopped, the Congress wisely set aside $500,000,000 of lend-lease funds for price support of farm commodities. This money is now available for the purpose for which it was intended, but in order that it may be used most effectively whenever the need arises, I recommend early legislation which would make those funds available to the Commodity Credit Corporation on a continuing basis. Such action would reaffirm the specific intent of the Congress as to the use of this money in safeguarding farm prices.

Strengthening the machinery for carrying out price-support commitments is the one measure necessary to safeguard farm prices. Stimulation of the export of farm commodities is another. More food is needed in the war-ravaged areas of the world. In the process of meeting relief requirements abroad, we have the opportunity of developing export markets for the future.

The farmer has always faced certain specific problems which are peculiar to his occupation. His crops are at the mercy of the weather.

The factory owner and the worker at the machine have available to them insurance programs which protect them from losses. Our farmers have the right to the same kind of protection. Strengthening and further development of crop insurance for farmers, organized and backed by the Federal Government, can give them this protection. A well-rounded crop-insurance program, together with the assurance of reasonable and stable farm prices, will go a long way toward meeting basic problems which have plagued farmers in the past.

Much that has been accomplished during the war was made possible by the wise national program in support of scientific research in agriculture and forestry, and by the program for the conservation and improvement of our soil and forest resources. These policies have paid

286

large dividends during the war. We ought to continue and strengthen them.

Within recent years the Congress has enacted various measures which have done much to improve the economic status of this country's farmers and to make rural living more attractive. In enacting individual pieces of legislation it has not been possible to make adjustments in existing measures in keeping with the changing pattern of needs. The Secretary of Agriculture is now reexamining existing agricultural programs in the light of peacetime needs in order that they make the fullest contribution to the welfare of farmers and the people as a whole. I hope that the Congress also, through its appropriate committees, will give careful consideration to this problem with a view to making such adjustments as are necessary to strengthen the effectiveness of these various measures.

10. SELECTIVE SERVICE

While the cruel lessons of war are fresh in every mind, it is fitting that we now undertake appropriate measures for the future security of the United States.

The times call for a broad and realistic appraisal of our military needs and obligations. This Nation, and the other members of the family of nations, are facing the hazardous transition to a peace economy in a world grown acutely sensitive to power.

We have charted the course to a stable world peace, but that course still remains to be sailed.

We must, of course, plan for the immediate needs of this year and the next. But we would break faith with those who won for us the victory, if we should fail at the same time to adopt an integrated and long-range program for the national security.

As a sovereign nation, we must continue to be ready to defend our national integrity by maintaining and manning adequate defense establishments within this continent, at the Panama Canal, and at all our bases overseas. As a member of the Security Council of the United Nations, we have an immediate obligation to bear a share, commensurate with our national standing, in safeguarding the future security of all peace-loving nations. As a victor in the greatest war of history, we are committed now to an armed occupation of the lands of our defeated enemies until it is assured that the principles for which we fought shall prevail in the reconstruction of those lands.

To meet these immediate obligations will require the maintenance for some time of a real measure of our present land, sea, and air power.

And in this first year after victory our people have another obligation, one which is felt in almost every American home. We owe it to those now in the armed forces that they be returned to civilian life with all possible speed.

To provide the personnel necessary to meet these immediate obligations we must obtain replacements for those veterans who have already rendered long and arduous service.

We shall make every effort to raise these replacements by recruiting volunteers. To that end I ask that the Congress consider ways and means to assure the maximum success of the recruiting campaigns which have already been authorized. I suggest that legislation be enacted to remove the present restriction on eligibility for voluntary enlistment and to allow the armed forces to enlist a larger number of volunteers than is now authorized. It is further recommended that, in order to enable the armed forces satisfactorily to compete in the procurement of personnel, the Congress provide suitable inducements for volunteer service in the Army and Navy.

However, in view of our extensive national commitments, I am certain, as are the War and Navy Departments, that we cannot rely on voluntary recruitment as the sole method of procuring the necessary replacements.

I, therefore, urge that the Congress continue inductions to assure replacements for these veterans, in such numbers as are not supplied by volunteers.

An unforgivable discrimination would result if, by suspending inductions now, we should favor those who have had no military service at the cost of requiring continued sacrifice from those who have already done their part.

Our first concern should be for those who have been in the armed forces for several years. They have been separated from their homes and from their loved ones. Many of them have been under constant fire and continuous danger for months and even years. We should try to avoid imposing further service upon them.

The only way that this can be done is to continue the induction of young men who as yet have not served a tour of active duty in the armed services. Only when we find that we are able to obtain a sufficient number of volunteers to fill the necessary quotas for our occupational needs, can we discontinue the Selective Service System.

Of course it is entirely up to the Congress to choose the means by which we will provide and maintain the necessary strength to meet our commitments. The alternatives presented are very simple. There are no others. Either we retain men now in the service for a further indefinite period, or we provide replacements by further inductions.

As you know, I have already directed the Selective Service to cut down the number of inductions from 80,000 to 50,000 per month, and to limit them to the age group of 18 through 25.

It would seem reasonable to limit inductions hereafter to men between the ages of 18 and 25, inclusive, and fix their maximum term of service at two years.

Under the existing statute, inductees can be legally retained only for the duration of the war and a period of six months thereafter. I trust that, in any event, the Congress will not pass a resolution to the effect that the war has terminated for the purposes of this statute. To do so would give to all inducted men and temporary officers of the Army now on active duty the right to civilian status, and would create an impossible demobilization situation.

These are the military steps which it is apparent must be taken at once to meet the needs of the transition from war to peace. First things necessarily come first.

But the full needs of our national security run far beyond this immediate period of transition. We should make timely preparations for the Nation's long-range security, while we are still mindful of what it has cost us in this war to have been unprepared.

It is, therefore, my intention to communicate with the Congress from time to time during the current session with respect to a comprehensive and continuous program of national security, including a universal training program, unification of the armed services, and the use and control of atomic energy.

11. HOUSING

The largest single opportunity for the rapid postwar expansion of private investment and employment lies in the field of housing, both urban and rural. The present shortage of decent homes and the enforced widespread use of substandard housing indicate vital unfulfilled needs of the Nation. These needs will become more marked as veterans begin to come back and look for places to live.

There is wide agreement that, over the next ten years, there should be built in the United States an average of from a million to a million and a half homes a year.

Such a program would provide an opportunity for private capital to invest from six to seven billion dollars annually. Private enterprise in this field could provide employment for several million workers each year. A housing program of this realistic size would, in turn, stimulate a vast amount of business and employment in industries which make house furnishings and equipment of every kind, and in the industries which supply the materials for them. It would provide an impetus for new products, and would develop new markets for a variety of manufactured articles to be made by private enterprise.

Housing is high on the list of matters calling for decisive Congressional action. This is reflected in recommendations contained in reports recently issued by the postwar committees of the Senate and of the House of Representatives. While differing opinions may be held as to detail, these proposals for action already developed in the Congress appear to me sound and essential.

I urgently recommend that the Congress, at an early date, enact broad and comprehensive housing legislation.

The cardinal principle underlying such legislation should be that house construction and financing for the overwhelming majority of our citizens should be done by private enterprise.

We should retain and improve upon the present excellent Government facilities which permit the savings of the people to be channeled voluntarily into private house construction on financing terms that will serve the needs of home owners of moderate income.

The present principles of insurance of housing investment—now tested by years of experience—should be retained and extended, so as to encourage direct investment in housing by private financing institutions.

The Government, in addition to providing these facilities to help private enterprise and private capital build homes, should take effective measures to stimulate research in methods and materials of housing construction. In this way, better and cheaper methods may be developed to build homes.

In addition to this type of research, the Government might well undertake to assist communities in making recurrent community studies in matters relating to housing and real estate generally. Such a program would contribute in great degree to the progress of private initiative and private capital investment in housing.

We must go on. We must widen our horizon even further. We must consider the redevelopment of large areas of the blighted and slum sections of our cities so that in the truly American way they may be remade to accommodate families not only of low-income groups as heretofore, but of every income group. We must make it possible for private enterprise to do the major part of this job. In most cases, it is now impossible for private enterprise to contemplate rebuilding slum areas without public assistance. The land cost generally is too high.

The time has come for the Government to begin to undertake a program of Federal aid to stimulate and promote the redevelopment of these deteriorating areas. Such Federal aid should be extended only to those communities which are willing to bear a fair part of the cost of clearing their blighted city areas and preparing them for redevelopment and rebuilding.

The rebuilding of these areas should conform to broad city plans, provide adequately for displaced families and make maximum use of private capital. Here lies another road toward establishing a better standard of city living, toward increasing business activity and providing jobs.

This Nation has recognized the need of using public funds to clear slums and to provide homes for those families who could not otherwise enjoy adequate housing because of the difference between their present earning power and the cost or rental of a decent home. We cannot, and we will not, recede from these purposes.

For those low-income groups, representing but a small portion of the total housing need, our prewar program of Federal aid to communities for low-rent housing should be resumed. Only in that way can we make progress toward our ultimate goal laid down in the economic bill of rights of a decent home for every American family.

I recommend, also, that we quicken our rate of progress in rural housing. As a general rule, housing conditions on farms and in rural areas are relatively worse than in our cities. In housing, as well as in other benefits of the American system, farm families should enjoy equality with city dwellers.

A decent standard of housing for all is one of the irreducible obligations of modern civilization. The housing challenge is now squarely before us. The people of the United States, so far ahead in wealth and productive capacity, deserve to be the best housed people in the world. We must begin to meet that challenge at once.

12. RESEARCH

Progress in scientific research and development is an indispensable condition to the future welfare and security of the Nation. The events of the past few years are both proof and prophecy of what science can do.

Science in this war has worked through thousands of men and women who labored selflessly and, for the most part, anonymously in the laboratories, pilot plants, and proving grounds of the Nation.

Through them, science, always pushing forward the frontiers of knowledge, forged the new weapons that shortened the war.

Progress in science cannot depend alone upon brilliant inspiration or sudden flights of genius. We have recently had a dramatic demonstration of this truth. In peace and in war, progress comes slowly in small new bits, from the unremitting day-by-day labors of thousands of men and women.

No nation can maintain a position of leadership in the world of today unless it develops to the full its scientific and technological resources. No government adequately meets its responsibilities unless it generously and intelligently supports and encourages the work of science in university, industry, and in its own laboratories.

During the war we have learned much about the methods of organizing science, and about the ways of encouraging and supporting its activities.

The development of atomic energy is a clear-cut indication of what can be accomplished by our universities, industry, and Government working together. Vast scientific fields remain to be conquered in the same way.

In order to derive the full profit in the future from what we have learned, I urge upon the Congress the early adoption of legislation for the establishment of a single Federal research agency which would discharge the following functions:

1. Promote and support fundamental research and development projects in all matters pertaining to the defense and security of the Nation.

2. Promote and support research in the basic sciences and in the social sciences.

3. Promote and support research in medicine, public health, and allied fields.

4. Provide financial assistance in the form of scholarships and grants for young men and women of proved scientific ability.

5. Coordinate and control diverse scientific activities now conducted by the several departments and agencies of the Federal Government.

6. Make fully, freely, and publicly available to commerce, industry, agriculture, and academic institutions, the fruits of research financed by Federal funds.

Scientific knowledge and scientific research are a complex and interrelated structure. Technological advances in one field may have great significance for another apparently unrelated. Accordingly, I urge upon the Congress the desirability of centralizing these functions in a single agency.

Although science can be coordinated and encouraged, it cannot be dictated to or regimented. Science cannot progress unless founded on the free intelligence of the scientist. I stress the fact that the Federal research agency here proposed should in no way impair that freedom.

Even if the Congress promptly adopts the legislation I have recommended, some months must elapse before the newly established agency could commence its operations. To fill what I hope will be only a temporary gap, I have asked the Office of Scientific Research and Development and the Research Board for National Security to continue their work.

Our economic and industrial strength, the physical well-being of our people, the achievement of full employment and full production, the future of our security, and the preservation of our principles will be determined by the extent to which we give full and sincere support to the works of science.

It is with these works that we can build the highroads to the future.

13. TRANSITION TAX REVISION

Taxes will play a vital role in attaining a prosperous peace.

I recommend that a transitional tax bill be enacted as soon as possible to provide limited tax reductions for the calendar year 1946. Like the Tax Adjustment Act of 1945, the new bill should aim principally at removing barriers to speedy reconversion and to the expansion of our peacetime economy.

This matter has been under study jointly by congressional and Treasury tax staffs. I am assured that a program will be ready for early consideration by the Congress.

We must reconcile ourselves to the fact that room for tax reduction at this time is limited. A total war effort cannot be liquidated overnight.

It is estimated that war expenditures in the current fiscal year will drop 40 billion dollars below last year, but that they will still amount to 50 billion dollars out of total expenditures of 66 billion dollars. With current receipts estimated at 36 billion dollars, we face an estimated deficit of 30 billion dollars in the current fiscal year. Expenditures, although further reduced, will necessarily continue at high levels in the fiscal year 1947.

In considering tax reductions for 1946 we must not lose sight of the budgetary situation and our obligations to 85,000,000 bondholders.

After passage of the transitional bill, I hope that the Congress will give careful consideration to the modernization of the Federal tax structure. A major objective of this modernization should be the encouragement of business incentives and expansion, and of consumer purchasing power. In this connection consideration of further tax reductions should have due regard to the level of governmental expenditures and the health and stability of our economy.

14. SURPLUS-PROPERTY DISPOSAL

On July 17 I recommended that the Congress enact legislation creating a single Surplus Property Administrator in place of the board of three which was provided in the statute enacted last year.

I realize that this recommendation came too late to be dealt with prior to your recess, but I strongly urge that you act on it now.

A single administrator can do much to obviate the confusion which still exists in this field, and will be able to expedite the disposal of the many billions of dollars of surplus property.

The disposition of plants and equipment is of particular urgency. They should be disposed of promptly by sale or lease on a basis that is fair to the Government and to industry. Our objectives should be to provide early and continuous employment, and through private production, to supply hungry markets and check inflationary tendencies. Leases may often enable the Government and the operator to determine actual value by actual experience. The sooner we can put plants and equipment to work, the sooner we can discard our wartime controls in the transition from war to peace.

15. SMALL BUSINESS

During the war special attention was paid to small business. The American small business is the backbone of our free-enterprise system. The efforts of the Congress in protecting small business during the war paid high dividends, not only in protecting small business enterprise, but also in speeding victory. In spite of the fact, however, that many businesses were helped and saved, it is true that many thousands of them were obliged to close up because of lack of materials or manpower or inability to get into war production.

It is very important to the economy of the United States that these small businesses and many more of them be given opportunity to become a part of American trade and industry. To do this, assistance should be given to small businesses to enable them to obtain adequate materials, private financing, technological improvements, and surplus property.

While some special facilities for small business are required, the greatest help to it will come from the maintenance of general prosperity and full employment. It is much more difficult for small business to survive the hazards which come from trade recessions and widespread unemployment. What small business needs chiefly is a steady supply of customers with stable purchasing power.

I am sure that the Congress will see to it that in its legislation adequate protection and encouragement will be given to the small business of the Nation.

16. VETERANS

It has been a fundamental objective of the Congress and of the administration to make generous provision for those who have served the Nation in its armed forces, and for the dependents of those who have died in their country's cause.

Although a full list of what has been done toward this objective would be entirely too long to enumerate here, it might be well to list some of the major steps already taken:

(1) Adoption of a National Service Life Insurance Act under which about 17½ million insurance applications have been approved, result-

ing in insurance coverage of more than $135,000,000,000.

(2) Provision of increased compensation or pension for disabled veterans.

(3) Extension and expansion of hospital benefits.

(4) Vocational education and training for veterans having a service-connected disability constituting a vocational handicap.

(5) Mustering-out pay ranging from $100 to $300 dependent upon length of service and rate of pay.

(6) Education or training for any veteran whose education or training was interrupted by entrance into the service.

(7) Guarantee of loans to veterans for the purchase of a home, a farm, or a business.

(8) Legislation to protect the veteran's right to reemployment in his preservice job, if desired.

(9) Provision of unemployment allowances for veterans who become unemployed at any time within two years after discharge, of $20 per week for not to exceed 52 weeks.

(10) Civil-service laws to insure preference to veterans in governmental service.

(11) There has also been instituted in each State pursuant to law an efficient system whereby the counseling and placement needs of veterans will be the responsibility of veterans appointed for that special work.

The transition of veterans from military to civilian activities cannot be accomplished satisfactorily by the Federal Government alone or the States alone, or, indeed, by both. Government can help chiefly through organization and over-all planning. But the real work must be done in each community, through cooperation of the industrial, labor, and civic organizations interested in the welfare of the community and of the veterans.

There have been established information centers in all the field activities of the Selective Service System, United States Employment Service, and Veterans Administration totaling more than 8,000. Veterans may there obtain information on any question of interest to them.

Also, the Retraining and Reemployment Administration in cooperation with the leadership of local communities has established approximately 1,450 community information centers. There are therefore 9,000 information centers of all types throughout the country available to veterans for information purposes. With respect to agricultural interests, use has been made of county committees.

Broad and generous as this legislation for veterans has been, there will be need of amendments and improvements. I recommend that the Congress give prompt consideration to the recommendations which have been made by the Veterans Administration for the purpose of clarifying and liberalizing the provisions relative to hospital and medical care, to vocational training under the Vocational Rehabilitation Act, and to education and training under the Servicemen's Readjustment Act. I also urge consideration of the suggestions made by the Veterans Administration with respect to the loan guarantee features of the latter Act, to amendments clarifying and liberalizing the National Service Life Insurance Act, and those which would increase the rates of compensation for specific injuries including multiple amputations.

I have recommended that the Selective Training and Service Act be continued; but if the Congress determines to the contrary, I urgently recommend that it clarify the provisions thereof which specifically deal with the right of reemployment.

Favorable consideration should be given by the Congress to Federal reclamation projects as outstanding opportunities for returning veterans. The great Columbia Basin project in the Northwest, the projects in the Missouri River Basin, and others of equal significance will bring into existence many thousands of new family-size farms upon which returning veterans can secure a livelihood for themselves and their families and create new wealth for the Nation. A number of farms can be made ready for veterans rapidly if legislation now pending is enacted without delay. This legislation would authorize necessary and proper assistance to veterans who seek to develop farm homes on irrigated lands in Federal reclamation project areas.

I also recommend that the Congress expedite legislation giving veterans social-security coverage credit for the period of their service in the armed services.

The latest available statistics in the Veterans' Administration shows that pension payments in varying amounts are now going forward each month to approximately 600,000 veterans of World War II and to the dependents of more than 100,000 deceased veterans of World War II.

Insurance claims under the National Service Life Insurance Act have been allowed in a total of 361,000 cases involving insurance of approximately 2½ billion dollars.

More than 200,000 World War II veterans have already been afforded hospital care in Veterans Administration facilities.

At the time of Pearl Harbor, the Veterans Administration and the Federal Board of Hospitalization had under way a hospital-building program which by 1949, the estimated peak of needs for World War I veterans, would have provided a total of 100,000 beds for hospital and domiciliary care. Since Pearl Harbor the hospital-building program has been expedited.

The Veterans Administration now has approximately 82,000 hospital and 14,000 domiciliary beds. Thirteen thousand beds are now under construction, and funds are available for 15,000 more.

The Servicemen's Readjustment Act authorizes appropriations to the extent of $500,000,000 for the construction of veterans' hospitals and also the transfer to the Veterans Administration of suitable facilities of the Army and Navy after the end of the war, when surplus to their needs. The program of the Veterans Administration and the Federal Board of Hospitalization contemplates keeping abreast of developing needs through such transfers and additional construction. To this end a plan has just been approved for construction of 29,000 additional beds.

Since World War I there have been more than 3,000,000 hospital admissions in veterans' facilities—and most of them since 1925. Considering that the total number of veterans of World War I and all living veterans of prior wars did not exceed one-third the number of the veterans of World War II, it can readily be seen how important it is to provide hospital privilege. The subject is one which should receive the most careful consideration from the point of view of the extent and quality of facilities to be provided and maintained.

In the last analysis, if we can insure the proper economic conditions, we may be sure that the genius and initiative of Americans who met successfully all demands of the greatest war in history, both on the fighting front and on the production front, will make certain the reintegration of veterans into an expanding civilian economy. Anything less would not meet the country's obligations to its veterans.

17. PUBLIC WORKS AND NATIONAL RESOURCES

During the war years we have expended our resources—both human and natural—without stint. We have thrown into the battle for freedom everything we had.

Thousands of our finest young men—our best human resources—have given their lives. Additional thousands have been injured so that they may not be able to realize their full promise. The education of millions of young men and young women has been disrupted. At best, the Nation will be deprived of the full benefit of their services as scientists, doctors, technicians, lawyers, and educators for 3 to 5 years, or even longer, while they complete the preparation which the necessities of war interrupted.

The depletion of our natural resources is even more startling. We have torn from the earth copper, petroleum, iron ore, tungsten, and every other mineral required to fight a war, without regard to our future supplies. We have taken what we needed. We were not able to, and we did not, take account of tomorrow.

At the same time, our splendid prewar program to build up our national resources was sharply halted. The diligent and constant search for additional deposits of minerals was almost abandoned in favor of a frantic effort to discover and make possible the production of the materials of war.

The long-range programs to conserve the precious inches of topsoil which, in many parts of the country, lie between plenty and poverty were necessarily interrupted. We had neither the manpower nor the materials to spare for projects to prevent the ravages of floods which constantly despoil our land. We had neither the men nor the facilities to continue a large-scale program of reclaiming land and of bringing new land into cultivation.

With a few exceptions, we were forced to suspend the program to which this Nation is committed of harnessing the waters of our great rivers so that they may become vehicles of commerce, beneficent producers of cheap electric power, and servants of the Nation instead of instruments of destruction.

In brief, although during this war this Nation has reached the apex of its power—a peak of greatness and might which the world had never seen—our national capital account has greatly suffered. We must proceed with all possible diligence not merely to restore these depleted resources to their prewar standards but to make them greater and richer than ever before.

We must make a diligent effort to discover new deposits of the precious and indispensable minerals upon which our national life is founded.

We must develop for the use of industry new technologies so that the vast deposits of low-grade ores that have not heretofore been considered usable may be put to work for the good of all of us.

We should build and improve our roads—the arteries of commerce; we must harness our streams for the general welfare; we must rebuild and reclaim our land; we must protect and restore our forests.

This is not only to provide men and women with work, it is to assure to the Nation the very basis of its life. It is to play the part of a good businessman who insists carefully on maintaining and rebuilding his plant and machinery.

We know that by the investment of Federal funds we can, within the limits of our own Nation, provide for our citizens new frontiers—new territories for the development of industry, agriculture, and commerce.

We have before us the example of the Tennessee Valley Authority, which has inspired regional resource development throughout the entire world.

We know that we have programs, carefully considered and extensively debated, for regional development of the Columbia River in the great Northwest, the Missouri River, the Central Valley of California, and the Arkansas River.

In the Columbia Valley the first major step has been completed for the reclamation of barren land and the production of enormous quantities of power. The waters of the Missouri and the Arkansas and the rivers of California can be put to work to serve the national interest in a similar fashion.

If these rivers remain scourges of our Nation, it is only because we do not have the prudence to harness them for the benefit of our people. If there are among us for any period of time farmers who do not farm because there is no suitable land available to them; workers who do not work because there is no labor for their hands, we have only ourselves to blame so long as we fail to make available to them the opportunities before our very eyes.

I hope that the Congress will proceed as rapidly as possible to authorize regional development of the natural resources of our great river valleys.

It should be unnecessary to say that the conservation and development of the national plant must proceed according to an intelligent and coordinated design. The watersheds of this Nation are not utterly independent, one of the other; our irreplaceable wealth of minerals, land, and timber is not composed of segments which can effectively be dealt with separately. Any program of public works must have as its unifying purpose the greatest possible contribution to the wealth of the Nation and to the wealth-producing capability of the Nation.

It is necessary that we proceed as speedily as possible to set up machinery to make an inventory of our national wealth and our basic resources, and to test the suitability of plans and proposals for public works in light of this purpose. An agency of this sort could provide us with consistent direction toward the goal of rehabilitation and improvement of our basic national resources.

Shortages of materials and manpower made it necessary in the interests of the war effort to suspend many public works which might otherwise have been undertaken. Now that materials and manpower will become more plentiful, we should be prepared to undertake a program of useful public works, not only to improve the physical plant of the United States but to provide employment to great masses of our citizens when private industry cannot do so. Only such public works should now be undertaken, however, as will not compete with the use of materials and manpower by private industry. Plans for other public works should be perfected and put in reserve.

In this connection I have several recommendations:

(1) During the war the construction of Federal public works has been restricted to those necessary for national defense and the prosecution of the war. Projects which normally would have been constructed were deferred, and a large backlog of needed construction has accumulated. Plans for some of these projects—specifically those relating to reclamation, rivers and harbors, flood control, and the conservation of our natural resources—are now ready, and their construction can go forward when funds are provided and materials and manpower are available without competing with private industry. Plans for other Federal projects are being prepared through the use of funds wisely appropriated by the Congress for advance preparation. Additional funds are needed for this purpose, and I urge that the Congress provide them.

(2) I recommend that the Congress enact legislation authorizing additional construction of certain Federal buildings. A portion of this program has already been authorized but has been held up by reason of cost limits imposed upon the buildings which cannot now be met because of increased needs and costs.

(3) I recommend that the Congress release the funds for the highway program authorized under the Federal Aid Highway Act of 1944 (Public Law 521, 78th Cong.). Under this act $500,000,000 has been authorized for the first year and $500,000,000 for each of the two succeeding years, making a total authorization of 1½ billion. With the States' share of the cost included, this would provide a total highway construction program of $3,000,000,000 for a 3-year period.

(4) I recommend that the Congress appropriate $25,000,000 to con-

tinue the construction of the Inter-American Highway through the Central American Republics to the Canal Zone.

(5) I recommend that the Congress enact legislation to provide the necessary airports and airport facilities to serve the great needs of an expanded postwar air transportation and commerce. A well-planned airport program would improve transportation, amplify the usefulness of the airplane, and contribute to a healthy aircraft manufacturing industry.

The Congress now has before it a survey of the present and future needs for airports in the United States prepared by the Secretary of Commerce. This report indicates the necessity for approximately 3,000 new airports and for improvements to more than half of the existing 3,000 airports. The report recommends that the program be spread over a period of 10 years and that the cost be shared equally between Federal and non-Federal governmental agencies. I recommend passage of appropriate legislation to implement this program.

(6) States and local governments should be encouraged to construct useful public works of the types that must necessarily supplement and go along with the private construction of homes and industrial facilities. If private construction is to move forward at a rapid rate, it is vitally important that local governments promptly proceed with the construction of such facilities as streets, sewers, water supply, hospitals, airports, schools, and other necessary public facilities. Such projects should be undertaken at this time where they supplement and encourage private construction, not where they compete with it for manpower and materials.

The Congress has already authorized under title V of the War Mobilization and Reconversion Act of 1944 appropriations for advances of Federal funds to State and local governments to assist them in the preparation of detailed drawings and specifications for their public works. The appropriation thus far made is entirely inadequate and I shall request additional funds in order to speed up this important activity during the reconversion period.

The majority of State and local governments are awaiting a decision concerning Federal assistance. In order to get needed public facilities started promptly which do not compete with private construction, I recommend that the Congress give early consideration to grants for such public works under conditions that will insure that each level of government, Federal, State, and local, shall make its appropriate contribution.

(7) The Congress has also been giving consideration to legislation with respect to the construction of hospitals and health centers throughout the country. During the war the Government, through the Federal Works Agency and the Public Health Service, has assisted State and local governments and nonprofit organizations in the construction of such facilities. The beneficial results of this program are well known. The Federal Government must continue to recognize its obligation to maintain and improve the health of the Nation by providing Federal grants where necessary for the construction of hospital and health centers.

Programs of internal improvements of a public character—Federal, State, and local—must preserve competitive bidding, guarantee collective bargaining and good wages for labor, utilize the skills of our returned veterans to the fullest extent, and effectively prevent discrimination because of race, creed, or color.

18. LEND-LEASE AND POSTWAR RECONSTRUCTION

With the arrival of VJ-day lend-lease aid has practically come to an end. It was always understood that it would come to an end at that time. Immediately after Japan accepted the terms of unconditional surrender, I instructed the Foreign Economic Administrator to advise promptly all governments that deliveries of supplies under lend-lease would cease on VJ-day.

I also directed the Administrator in advance of the actual termination of lend-lease deliveries on VJ-day to enter into immediate negotiations with the receiving governments for the purchase of all goods in the pipe line or in storage. These negotiations are proceeding satisfactorily.

In due time we must consider the settlement of the lend-lease obligations which have been incurred during the course of the war. We must recognize that it will not be possible for our Allies to pay us dollars for the overwhelming portion of the lend-lease obligations which they have incurred. But this does not mean that all lend-lease obligations are to be canceled. We shall seek under the procedure prescribed in the Lend-Lease Act and in subsequent agreements with other governments to achieve settlements of our wartime lend-lease relations which will permit generally a sound world-wide economy and will contribute to international peace and our own national security.

We must turn from economic cooperation in war to economic cooperation in peace. We have taken steps to carry out the Bretton Woods proposals for an international monetary fund and an International Bank. We are preparing to extend the operations of the Export-Import Bank. Our objective is to enable the peace-loving nations of the world to become self-supporting in a world of expanding freedom and rising standards of living.

Further legislation is also necessary. If we are to avoid the maintenance of governmental monopoly of international credit, the Johnson Act must be repealed. Private loans on a sane basis are an essential adjunct to the operations of the Export-Import and International Bank operations.

I am directing the executive agencies to give full weight to foreign requirements in determining the need for maintaining domestic and export controls and priorities.

We have already solemnly stated that we will do all that is reasonably possible to help war-torn countries to get back on their feet. I am sure that the Congress will wish the Government to live up to that pledge.

Further legislative action is needed in connection with the United Nations Relief and Rehabilitation Administration. I recommend that the Congress fulfill the commitment already made by appropriating the remaining $550,000,000 granted by the Congress for United States participation.

The Council Meeting of the United Nations Relief and Rehabilitation Administration has just been brought to a successful conclusion. At that meeting our delegate found the need for an additional contribution from all participating countries, to enable the United Nations

306

Relief and Rehabilitation Administration to complete its work in Europe and Asia. On his motion, the Council voted to recommend to member countries a further contribution. Our own share will amount to approximately $1,350,000,000. I am confident that you will find this request for an additional authorization and appropriation fully justified, and I ask for prompt examination and consideration of the request.

In meeting the needs of the United Nations Relief and Rehabilitation Administration, surplus military and lend-lease goods will be used to the fullest possible extent.

Finally, I foresee the need for additional interim lending power to insure a rapid and successful transition to peacetime world trade. Appropriate recommendations will be made to the Congress on this matter when we have completed the exploratory conversations already begun with our associates. We wish to maintain the flow of supplies without interruption. Accordingly, I have directed the executive agencies to complete their conversations and studies at the earliest possible moment. I ask the Congress for speedy consideration of the recommendations when they are made.

19. CONGRESSIONAL SALARIES

Now that restrictions on voluntary salary increases have been removed, I hope that the Congress will take action soon on the salaries of its Members.

My experience as a Member of the Senate has given me a very keen appreciation of the quantity and quality of the work of the Members of the Congress. They are called upon to carry great responsibility and make important decisions in a multitude of matters involving the welfare of the Nation and of the world. Their tasks continue day in and day out. They have increased in number and in importance year by year.

There is no doubt in the mind of any thinking American that Members of the Congress are grossly underpaid and have been for many years. I think that they are entitled—and have already so expressed myself—to a salary anywhere from fifteen to twenty-five thousand dollars a year. I recommend that the Congress enact legislation providing that the salaries of its Members be increased to twenty thousand dollars per year.

At the same time I recommend the repeal of the provision now applicable to the House of Representatives for an additional expense allowance. There should be a straight, out-and-out salary increase for all Members. We should make service in the Congress of the United States available without hardship to ordinary citizens who have to look to the salary for their sole support. I also recommend that an adequate retirement system should be provided for the Members of the Congress who have served for a long period of years.

This should be the first step in creating a decent salary scale for all Federal Government employees—executive, legislative, and judicial.

The most important impediment to obtaining efficient administrative officials in the Federal Government has been the pitiful wage scale. During the war many able and experienced men were obtained for Federal service on purely patriotic grounds. Some of these men who are unable to continue at the present salary scales would be willing to remain at adequate salaries.

In most of the various classifications of Federal employees, the wage scales, with few exceptions, are obsolete and inadequate. This is particularly true of the Federal judiciary.

I sincerely hope that the Congress will take early steps to provide decent wage scales for its Members and for the executive and judicial branches of the Government.

20. SALE OF SHIPS

Prompt resumption of the normal operation of our merchant marine to expedite the reestablishment of our foreign trade is a major part of general reconversion from a wartime to a peacetime economy. The Maritime Commission has already received numerous inquiries and applications from potential purchasers of ships at home and abroad for private ownership and operation.

It is recommended that suitable legislation to permit such sales be expedited so that the uncertainty about the disposal of our large surplus tonnage may be removed. In this way, American shipping companies may undertake commercial operation as rapidly as ships can be released from Government control, and the foreign market can also be used for selling those vessels which are in excess of the needs of our postwar American merchant marine and national defense.

21. STOCK PILING OF STRATEGIC MATERIAL

One of the costliest lessons of our unpreparedness for this war was the great danger involved in depending upon foreign sources for supplies of raw materials necessary in times of national emergency. The United States should never again permit itself to be placed in a position where its defense may be jeopardized by the fact that it has been cut off from the source of strategic raw materials.

I recommend that the Congress enact legislation to bring about the acquisition and retention of stock piles of materials in which we are naturally deficient but which are necessary to supply the needs of the Nation for its defense.

I shall shortly communicate with the Congress recommending a national health program to provide adequate medical care for all Americans and to protect them from financial loss and hardships resulting from illness and accident. I shall also communicate with the Congress with respect to expanding our social-security system, and improving our program of education for our citizens.

In this hour of victory over our enemies abroad, let us now resolve to use all our efforts and energies to build a better life here at home and a better world for generations to come.

The Congress has played its full part in shaping the domestic and foreign policies which have won this victory and started us on the road to lasting peace.

The Congress, I know, will continue to play its patriotic part in the difficult years ahead. We face the future together with confidence— that the job, the full job, can and will be done.

HARRY S. TRUMAN

129 The President's News Conference of
September 6, 1945

THE PRESIDENT. [1.] By memorandum on May 6 [1942] the President
prescribed a policy to effectuate the maximum utilization of the facilities of the domestic airline companies in the prosecution of the war.
It now seems desirable that the policy prescribed in the memorandum
be terminated. Accordingly, the War Department need no longer
follow the policy except with respect to paragraph 6 of the memorandum concerning priorities for air transportation which shall be
followed until October 15.

That means that all priorities in air travel will be removed by
October 15.

[2.] I want to announce the appointment of the Honorable Paul V.
McNutt as United States High Commissioner to the Philippines. Mr.
McNutt served as High Commissioner to the Philippines from 1937 to
1939. He was succeeded by Francis B. Sayre, who resigned in 1942.
The High Commissioner is the representative of the President of the
United States in the Philippines. Since September 16, after the withdrawal from Corregidor, the Secretary of the Interior has been handling
the affairs without the help of a High Commissioner. Now it is desirable and necessary to appoint a High Commissioner so that all the
activities of the United States Government in the rehabilitation of the
Philippines can be coordinated and handled for the best interests of
the Philippine Islands.

Q. When does he take over?

THE PRESIDENT. As soon as he can qualify. His name went up to the
Senate today.

Q. Is that for the Philippines only?

THE PRESIDENT. The Philippines only. That's the only place we have
a right to appoint a High Commissioner, and that is to expedite the
things that are necessary to be done to help the Philippines to recover
their position so that they can have independence as quickly as possible.

That's all I have; if you have any questions——

Q. Mr. President, what about Mr. McNutt's report or survey on health and rehabilitation? Do you wish to comment upon that?

THE PRESIDENT. I didn't understand the question.

Q. Mr. McNutt was head of the conservation commission on Philippine health and rehabilitation.

THE PRESIDENT. Yes, he was, and that will be a part of his job to implement the findings of that commission and whatever else is necessary to be done to put the Philippines on its feet. There is certain legislation pending in the Congress which is necessary to be passed to have that object carried out, and we have to have a High Commissioner in the Philippines.

[3.] Q. Would you have anything to say on the Navy's proposal for the retention of bases in the far Pacific?

THE PRESIDENT. No, I am not familiar with what the Navy's proposal was. As I said in the speech after the Potsdam conference, we expect, by negotiation and otherwise, to occupy the necessary bases there for the peace of the world and for our own welfare in the Pacific Ocean and elsewhere.

Q. The Navy didn't mention Okinawa specifically. I wonder if you have anything to say about that?

THE PRESIDENT. I have not studied it, but if it is necessary to have one on Okinawa, I think we can negotiate so we can have it.

[4.] Q. It is reported that you have selected Bob Patterson of the War Department to be a member of the Supreme Court.

THE PRESIDENT. Somebody knows more than I do, then. [*Laughter*] I haven't yet made up my mind on an appointment for that vacancy.

Q. In that connection there are a lot of reports that you plan to appoint Bennett Clark to the Court of Appeals for the District of Columbia, and also E. Barrett Prettyman to——

THE PRESIDENT. I saw that in the paper, too; that is most interesting.

Q. Do you want to comment further on that?

THE PRESIDENT. I have no comment now. When I am ready to make those appointments I will announce them to you, but there'll be a lot more rumors before they are announced. [*Laughter*]

[5.] Q. Again back to Mr. McNutt's appointment as High Commissioner of the Philippines. The News has carried stories that it will be to the Western Pacific. Could you outline that a little more? Is it only to the Philippines?

THE PRESIDENT. That's what the law requires. It is for the Philippines only. He has nothing to do with the other parts of the Pacific Ocean. There are other things that will have to be done from the peace table.

[6.] Q. Can you say what Snyder, Symington, and Biffle are to do on their European trip?

THE PRESIDENT. Yes, I can; they are going there to investigate the surplus property proposition, to see how much can be turned over through UNRRA to the countries on a starvation basis.

[7.] Q. Mr. President, Mr. Barkley announced that you had announced your support of a possible congressional investigation of Pearl Harbor. Can you indicate to us some of the things you hope such an investigation will reveal?

THE PRESIDENT. The only thing I hope is that it will get at the truth, the whole truth, and nothing but the truth.

Q. Mr. President, may we infer from that that you do not think any of the reports so far have told the truth?

THE PRESIDENT. I took the reports as they were given. They satisfied me, but apparently they did not satisfy everybody.

[8.] Q. Has Justice Roberts indicated yet whether he is going to accept whatever international post you offered him?

THE PRESIDENT. He has decided not to accept it.

Q. Can you tell us now what the post was?

THE PRESIDENT. Yes, I wanted him to be judge of the court to try war criminals.

Q. Japanese?

THE PRESIDENT. No, the international military tribunal to try war criminals. He decided not to accept.

[9.] Q. Have you given any thought to releasing the transcript of the testimony of those saboteur trials back in 1943?

THE PRESIDENT. I haven't thought about it.

Q. Do you see any reason why they should not be released now?

THE PRESIDENT. No, I don't, but I would have to look into it.

[10.]   Q. Do you think the 52 pages of the Army and Navy initial report should be turned over to Congress?

THE PRESIDENT. Congress will have the right of access to all the testimony there is available.

[11.]   Q. Mr. President, I wonder if you have any guess as to what the total budget might be in this country the next few years if your program is put into effect?

THE PRESIDENT. I could tell you if I were going to submit a guess to Congress tomorrow, but it can't be submitted until we have the information about the military needs. I am not going to guess at it. When it comes time for the budget estimates I will have them ready.

[12.]   Q. Mr. President, you said the other day you had been considering the St. Lawrence Waterway.

THE PRESIDENT. I am considering it.

Q. The question at that time was brief, and your answer was brief. I was wondering if there is anything further you can tell us on that.

THE PRESIDENT. I can't tell you now, but I think I will be in a position in a few days to announce it. I will give you all the facts then.

Q. Is the program of the various watersheds tied together?

THE PRESIDENT. It is not.

[13.]   Q. There are reports that you might name Ellis Arnall as Solicitor General.

THE PRESIDENT. I have nothing to say about that at the present time.

Q. There is a report that General Kutz is to be relieved as Engineer Commissioner; have you anything to say about that?

THE PRESIDENT. I think he is probably reaching the retirement age; if he is, he will have a successor. That is a regular Army routing matter.

Q. Can you say anything about the Office of Contingent Services now?

THE PRESIDENT. No, I can't at the present time.

Reporter: Thank you, Mr. President.

THE PRESIDENT. You are entirely welcome.

NOTE: President Truman's twenty-fourth news conference was held in his office at the White House at 4 p.m. on Thursday, September 6, 1945.

130   Letter to the Surgeon General Concerning Termination
of the Nurses Training Program.   *September* 8, 1945

[Released September 8, 1945.   Dated September 6, 1945]

My dear Dr. Parran:

In view of recent developments in the course of the war, measures
should be taken to bring about an early termination of the program for
the training of nurses that was established by the act of June 15, 1943
(57 Stat. 153).

It appears that it will not be necessary or in the public interest to
continue to initiate training courses for this program after October 15,
1945, for the purpose of assuring a supply of nurses for the armed services, Governmental and civilian hospitals, health agencies and war
industries.   I therefore request you to terminate the recruitment of
student and graduate nurses immediately and to see to it that no
students are enrolled in courses under the Act which begin after
October 15, 1945.

Sincerely yours,

HARRY S. TRUMAN

[Dr. Thomas Parran, Surgeon General, Public Health Service]

NOTE: The White House release of the
letter noted that the President's action
would permit more than 1100 nurses
training schools to make necessary adjustments in their educational programs, budgets, and hospital nursing
services; furthermore, it would enable
some 30,000 young women enrolled under the U.S. Cadet Nurse Corps in
classes then starting to receive Federal
assistance toward their education.

131   Citation Accompanying the Congressional Medal of
Honor Presented to General Jonathan M. Wainwright.
September 10, 1945

CITATION FOR THE MEDAL OF HONOR

GENERAL JONATHAN M. WAINWRIGHT, Commanding
United States Army forces in the Philippines from 12 March to 7 May
1942, distinguished himself by intrepid and determined leadership

against greatly superior enemy forces. At the repeated risk of life above and beyond the call of duty in his position, he frequented the firing line of his troops where his presence provided the example and incentive that helped make the gallant efforts of these men possible. The final stand on beleaguered Corregidor, for which he was in an important measure personally responsible, commanded the admiration of the nation's allies. It reflected the high morale of American arms in the face of overwhelming odds. His courage and resolution were a vitally needed inspiration to the then sorely pressed freedom-loving peoples of the world.

HARRY S. TRUMAN

NOTE: The presentation was made by the President in the Rose Garden at the White House on the occasion of General Wainwright's return to Washington after his release from imprisonment by the Japanese.

132   The President's News Conference of
September 12, 1945

THE PRESIDENT. [1.] I want to announce the appointment of Francis Biddle to represent the United States on the International Court to try war criminals. Federal Judge John J. Parker is his alternate.

I announce the appointment of E. Barrett Prettyman of Washington, D.C., to succeed Justin Miller as Associate Justice of the United States Court of Appeals for the District of Columbia.

Q. Justin what?

THE PRESIDENT. Justin Miller. Mr. Ross will have you a release on their lives and who they are succeeding, and everything, after this is over.

I announce the appointment of former Senator Bennett Champ Clark to be Associate Justice of the United States Court of Appeals for the District of Columbia, succeeding Thurman Arnold, resigned.

I announce the appointment of Wilbur K. Miller to be an Associate Justice of the United States Court of Appeals for the District of Columbia to succeed Fred M. Vinson.

Q. Miller—where from?

THE PRESIDENT. Owensboro, Kentucky.

Q. Wilbur K., sir?

THE PRESIDENT. Wilbur K., W-i-l-b-u-r.

Q. What's that court again?

THE PRESIDENT. United States Court of Appeals.

I am appointing Alexander Holtzoff of Chicago to be Associate Justice of the District Court of the United States for the District of Columbia.

Q. H-e-r-t——

THE PRESIDENT. Holtzoff, H-o-l-t-z-o-f-f.

Q. Where does he live?

THE PRESIDENT. He lives here in Washington. Biographical sketches will be given out by the press office.

I'm appointing John J. O'Connell of Pittsburgh to be Judge of the United States Circuit Court of Appeals for the Third Circuit, a new position created by the Congress. He lives at Pittsburgh, Pennsylvania.

I announce the appointment of Harrington Wimberly of Oklahoma to be a member of the Federal Power Commission, succeeding——

Q. Wimberly?

THE PRESIDENT. W-i-m-b-e-r-l-y.

Q. Where from?

THE PRESIDENT. Altus, Oklahoma—A-l-t-u-s.

Q. To be a member of the Federal Power Commission?

THE PRESIDENT. Yes, succeeding Basil Manly, and you will be furnished details on that by Mr. Ross.

Q. Succeeding Basil Manly?

THE PRESIDENT. Yes. Manly's resignation takes place—is effective the 1st of October.

Q. Does the Commission elect its own chairman?

THE PRESIDENT. Yes.

I announce the appointment of Richard Sachse to be a member of the Federal Power Commission, succeeding John W. Scott.

Q. Spelled how, sir?

THE PRESIDENT [*after a pause*]. S-a-c-h-s-e. I had to look that up.

Q. Succeeding John W.——

THE PRESIDENT. Succeeding John W. Scott. Sachse is from California; I don't know what town. He's on the Railroad Commission of the State of California. I don't know what his home town is; I think he lives in southern California, though.

I announce the resignation of Elmer Davis. Neil Dalton has been appointed to carry out the liquidation of the Office of War Information. You will find an exchange of letters on that.

Q. Do you know where Mr. Dalton is from?

THE PRESIDENT. No, I don't.

Voice: Louisville.

Q. D-a-l-t-o-n?

THE PRESIDENT. D-a-l-t-o-n.

Q. N-e-i-l?

THE PRESIDENT. Yes, Neil Dalton.

Gael E. Sullivan to be Second Assistant Postmaster General in the place of Smith Purdum, effective October 1st. Don't seem to have anything on him. He takes the place of Smith Purdum.

Q. How do you spell that last name?

THE PRESIDENT. Gael Sullivan, G-a-e-l S-u-l-l-i-v-a-n. He takes the place of Purdum, P-u-r-d-u-m.

Q. Where is Mr. Sullivan from, Mr. President?

THE PRESIDENT. Chicago.

[2.] Q. Mr. President, can you tell us the reason why Justice Roberts turned down the job on the International Court?

THE PRESIDENT. To quote Justice Roberts himself, he wanted to take it, but he said he had been working so long and so continuously that he thought he was entitled to a rest and he would rather not take it, so we had to let him off.

[3.] Q. Would you tell us what you think of the Senate attitude on the unemployment compensation bill?

THE PRESIDENT. My statement is in the message. When the bill comes to me I will comment on it.

[4.] Q. The view was expressed in some quarters that the United States ought not to extend financial assistance to Britain because it would be underwriting a Socialist government. What is your thought on that?

THE PRESIDENT. I think it is a perfectly silly conclusion. [*Laughter*]

Q. Mr. President, may we quote you on that?

THE PRESIDENT. Yes. That is just what I think. Great Britain is entitled to the sort of government Great Britain wants, and I think it is none of our affair so long as we are friendly with Great Britain.

[5.] Q. Mr. President, there's a feeling in Australia that the Japanese are getting rather kid-glove treatment. In view of the fact that Australia is very near Japan, they are very much worried. Would you like to comment on that?

THE PRESIDENT. I think the government will be worked out in the manner that it should be worked out, and I think if Australia will be just a little patient she will be satisfied with what is done.

[6.] Q. There seems to be some question about Korea, the use of Japanese overlords there to administer their government; is that a theater decision or a Washington decision?

THE PRESIDENT. It is a theater decision and it is a practical matter. As soon as it is possible to remove the Japanese, they will be removed. The policy toward Korea will be announced later.

Q. Would you have any comment, sir, on that announcement that the Japanese will be removed in due time? That might mean a day, a month, or a year. Would you like to put a limitation on the time?

THE PRESIDENT. What do you mean?

Q. Would you like to put a limitation on it to a month or a year?

THE PRESIDENT. I would suggest that you ask General MacArthur what the conditions are. He can tell you better than anyone else.

[7.] Q. Mr. President, this morning's Post has an editorial saying it thinks you ought to appoint a lot of Republicans. Would you——

THE PRESIDENT. I'm a Democrat. [*Laughter*]

Q. Would you tell us, sir—perhaps—do you have an analysis in your own mind as to the appointments you made this morning?

THE PRESIDENT. I have not. I didn't appoint them from a political point of view but for their fitness for the place.

Q. Are you a Democrat, Mr. President, who is going to the left, or to the right?

THE PRESIDENT. You'll have to work that out by the acts as they come forward. I'll give you no leads on that.

[8.] Q. Mr. President, is there anything to add on your trip south in November to North Carolina and Georgia?

THE PRESIDENT. I'm going down there to pay a visit to the district of Mr. Doughton—a promise which I made while I was Vice President. It has no connection with his place with the Ways and Means Committee of the House. He and I have been friends for a long time.

[9.] Q. Do you expect to attend the Annapolis centennial on October 10?

THE PRESIDENT. I have been trying to make arrangements to attend; I don't want to say definitely that I will go.

[10.] Q. Dispatches out of Turkey this morning claim you had sent a communication on the Dardanelles.

THE PRESIDENT. I read that communication at Potsdam. It is a communication for the foreign ministers conference in London.

Q. In the meantime you have informed Turkey of your position?

THE PRESIDENT. Not that I know of. I have had no direct communication with Turkey.

[11.] Q. Have you decided on the labor delegate to the International Labor Organization?

THE PRESIDENT. That is a matter that the Labor Department will decide.

Q. Mr. President, is there anything you can tell us about the Solicitor General appointment?

THE PRESIDENT. Not yet. I will be able to make an announcement on that in a few days.

Q. And the Supreme Court?

THE PRESIDENT. I am still considering men for the Supreme Court. I have reached no decision.

Q. Is Judge Clark under consideration for that?

THE PRESIDENT. I don't want to answer that question.

Q. There are reports that Mr. Stimson is retiring.

THE PRESIDENT. That is a matter for Mr. Stimson to announce at the proper time. I have no comment to make on that now.

Voice: Thank you, Mr. President.

THE PRESIDENT. You're welcome.

NOTE: President Truman's twenty-fifth news conference was held in his office in the White House at 10:32 a.m. on Wednesday, September 12, 1945.

133 Message to General Pershing on His 85th Birthday.
September 13, 1945

Dear General Pershing:

This should be one of the happiest of your many birthdays as you remember that this time we went all the way through to Berlin, as you counseled in 1918. I hail a great soldier who happily exemplified also the vision of the statesman.

With every good wish.

Very sincerely yours,

HARRY S. TRUMAN

[General John J. Pershing, Walter Reed Hospital]

134 Letter to the Speaker of the House of Representatives Transmitting Proposed Reductions in Appropriations for the Navy. *September* 14, 1945

[Released September 14, 1945. Dated September 13, 1945]

The Speaker of the House of Representatives:

Sir: With reference to appropriations and contract authorizations for the Navy Department and naval service, I have the honor to transmit for the consideration of Congress (1) proposed rescissions of several appropriations available in the fiscal year 1946, amounting to $8,305,-859,122, (2) proposed rescissions of several contract authorizations available in the fiscal year 1946, amounting to $3,212,442,131, (3) proposed rescissions of the unrequired balances of prior year appropriations, amounting to $5,306,252,674, and (4) proposed decreases in the amounts

which may be transferred from various naval appropriations to the
appropriations for printing and binding, and contingent expenses, for
the fiscal year 1946.

In making these recommendations for reductions, consideration has
been given to the tremendous problem of demobilization and the yet
undetermined requirements for a peacetime Navy.

As indicated in my letter of September 5, 1945, I plan a continuing
review of naval appropriations with the view to recommending further
adjustments as conditions warrant. It is also suggested that the appropriate committees of Congress give consideration to a complete review
of existing legislation authorizing the construction of naval vessels.

The details of these proposed rescissions are set forth in the letter of
the Director of the Bureau of the Budget, transmitted herewith, in
whose comments and observations thereon I concur.

Respectfully yours,

HARRY S. TRUMAN

NOTE: A White House release announcing the President's action pointed out
that proposed rescissions (1) and (2)
referred to in the first paragraph of the
letter and totaling $11.5 billion included
$3,212,442,131 of contract authoriza-
tions available in fiscal year 1946, and
appropriations for the following major
items:

Savings because of demobilization in
enlisted personnel from a strength of
3,300,000 at the rate of approximately
250,000 per month; cutbacks in ship
construction which permitted withdrawal of $1,047,366,607 in cash which
would not be expended during fiscal
year 1946; maintenance and operation
of ships and Navy yards, including fuel,
$1,372,183,000; aviation program, $1,-
404,300,000; ordnance, $2,550,451,000.

The details of the proposed rescissions as set forth in the letter of the Director of the Bureau of the Budget
transmitted with the President's letter,
are printed in House Document 286
(79th Cong., 1st sess.).

135 Statement by the President on the European Relief and
Rehabilitation Program. *September 17, 1945*

THE UNITED STATES GOVERNMENT is now in a position to
fulfill the main requests of Europe—with the exception of sugar, fats
and oils—from this date until January 1 as these requests have been
stated to it by the governments of the liberated countries and by
UNRRA.

Provision of the supplies thus requested does not, however, mean that the civilian populations of Europe will reach even a minimum level of subsistence, and much suffering may be expected during the coming winter in certain areas of the continent.

The limiting factor in meeting the minimum needs of the liberated peoples is no longer one of shipping. For the moment, in the case of most commodities, it is no longer a problem of supply. Today it is primarily a twofold financial problem; first, to work out credits or other financial arrangements with the European governments; second, to make additional funds available to UNRRA for emergency relief.

This Government is bending every effort to find solutions to this problem, in cooperation with the respective claimants, with a view to increasing the flow of urgently needed supplies. Pending such settlements this government is taking necessary measures in relation to production, distribution and shipping of supplies to insure a broad, equitable and continuous flow of current stocks and new production of relief and rehabilitation supplies for liberated areas, which it is anticipated will be required, in addition to those quantities which they have already requisitioned. One purpose of such measures is to prevent the dissipation of available supplies in domestic channels where they are not essential.

When I returned from Potsdam I said, "If we let Europe go cold and hungry, we may lose some of the foundations of order on which the hoped for world-wide peace must rest. We must help to the limits of our strength. And we will." That pledge, made not only to our Allies, but to the American people, must be kept. It should be made perfectly clear that, contrary to the belief of many, relaxation of rationing on the home front is not a factor in the allocation of relief supplies to Europe. The Department of Agriculture reports that, despite the release of cheese from rationing controls, and the possible relaxation of domestic meat rationing, we have sufficient quantities of meat and dairy products to fulfill the requirements placed upon us by UNRRA and the paying governments for the last quarter of the year. Furthermore, should UNRRA secure the additional financial resources it so urgently needs, and the paying governments conclude more satisfactory financial arrangements, again raising the problem of supply, both the Department of Agriculture and the War Production Board have the authority to issue set-aside orders on specific quantities of commodities purchased, regardless of whether they are rationed, to insure deliveries abroad. This does not mean that it may not become necessary to resume ration controls of certain items if they become so short in supply that such controls are required to insure more equitable distribution.

RELIEF NEEDS SUMMARIZED

The most desperate needs of the liberated people are for coal, transportation and food, in that order of priority. Other commodities urgently required include hides and leather, cotton, wool, textiles, soap, farm equipment, including fertilizer and seeds, repair parts and machinery, medical supplies, and a general list of raw materials. The items which are causing major concern because of worldwide shortages are coal, sugar and fats, hides and leather, textiles, and a few of the raw materials, in minor quantities. Locomotives constitute a special and acute problem because of the time factor involved in their manufacture.

Coal presents not only the most serious but the most complicated problem. Once self-sufficient in this commodity, Europe is now without the labor, the food, the transportation, the housing and the machinery needed to restore production quickly to its pre-war level. The Allied Control Commission is making every effort to speed the resumption of German production in order to supply the liberated areas, but despite considerable progress, the people of these areas face a winter of extreme hardship.

WHAT IS BEING DONE

The United States is now shipping approximately 1,400,000 tons of coal to Europe a month. For the period ending January 1 the goal is 8,000,000 tons, or slightly more than one percent of our domestic production. The limiting factor is not primarily one of supply, but of inland transportation facilities both here and abroad.

The Department of Agriculture reports that shipments of food to the

323

paying governments and UNRRA during the last quarter of this year will include approximately these quantities:

150 million pounds of meat and meat products;
70 million bushels of wheat;
28 thousand short tons of raw sugar;
90 million pounds of dried peas and beans;
13 million pounds of lard.

In addition, the Department of Agriculture is prepared to ship the following supplies of dairy products, in at least these quantities, as soon as financial arrangements have been satisfactorily completed:

60 million pounds of cheese;
200 million pounds of evaporated milk;
25 million pounds of dry whole milk powder;
80 million pounds of dry skim milk powder;
15 million pounds of condensed milk.

It should be remembered that these supplies will serve not to improve, but only to sustain the diet of the liberated peoples, which remains below the minimum level of subsistence. In some cases the doubling of these food shipments waits only upon the conclusion of satisfactory financial arrangements.

This Government has abundant evidence that the American people are aware of the suffering among our allies. They have also made plain their determination that this country shall do its full part, along with other supplying nations, in helping to restore health and strength to those who fought at our side both in Europe and in the Far East. It is an American responsibility not only to our friends, but to ourselves, to see that this job is done and done quickly.

136 Statement by the President on the Liberation of Korea.
September 18, 1945

THE SURRENDER of the Japanese forces in Seoul, ancient Korean capital, heralds the liberation of a freedom-loving and heroic people.

Despite their long and cruel subjection under the warlords of Japan, the Koreans have kept alive their devotion to national liberty and to their proud cultural heritage. This subjection has now ended. The Japanese warlords are being removed. Such Japanese as may be temporarily retained are being utilized as servants of the Korean people and of our occupying forces only because they are deemed essential by reason of their technical qualifications.

In this moment of liberation we are mindful of the difficult tasks which lie ahead. The building of a great nation has now begun with the assistance of the United States, China, Great Britain and the Soviet Union, who are agreed that Korea shall become free and independent.

The assumption by the Koreans themselves of the responsibilities and functions of a free and independent nation and the elimination of all vestiges of Japanese control over Korean economic and political life will of necessity require time and patience. The goal is in view but its speedy attainment will require the joint efforts of the Korean people and of the allies.

The American people rejoice in the liberation of Korea as the Tae-gook-kee, the ancient flag of Korea, waves again in the Land of the Morning Calm.

137 The President's News Conference of *September* 18, 1945

THE PRESIDENT. [1.]   I am reorganizing the Labor Department, putting all the functions of the War Labor Board, the War Manpower Commission, and the USES into the Labor Department, and transferring their functions to the Secretary of Labor, giving him all their powers and appropriations and everything else that goes with them; and eventually we will centralize every labor function in the Labor Department, so far as possible.

[2.]   I am transferring OES, Office of Economic Stabilization, to War Mobilization and Reconversion; that is, to Mr. Snyder.

[3.]   I signed the act providing for a single Surplus Property Administrator this morning. I appointed Stuart Symington to that job.

[4.] I received an acceptance from Judge Owen Roberts today to act as chairman of the committee to award Medals of Merit to civilians.

[5.] Now I have accepted the resignation of Mr. Stimson today as Secretary of War and appointed Robert P. Patterson to be Secretary of War. I accepted Mr. Stimson's resignation very reluctantly. I think he is one of our great public servants. I want to announce also that the Assistant Secretaries, John J. McCloy and Robert Lovett, sent me their resignations at the same time Mr. Stimson did, but I am not accepting them immediately.

[6.] I am appointing Senator Harold H. Burton of Ohio to be Associate Justice of the United States Supreme Court. [*Subdued laughter and a surprised low whistle*]

Q. Anything *else*, Mr. President?

[7.] Q. We do have a question, Mr. President. I wonder if you can tell us what action the reorganized Labor Department might be taking in the Detroit situation.

THE PRESIDENT. That will be entirely in the hands of the Secretary of Labor, and he will take whatever action is necessary, whatever action he can, under the law.

Q. Do you plan to put the FEPC under the Labor Department, too?

THE PRESIDENT. If it belongs to the War Manpower Commission, that's where it will go.

[8.] Q. What happens to the Chairman of OES?[1]

THE PRESIDENT. The Chairman of the OES? Well, he won't have anything to do. John Snyder will take his job.

[9.] Q. Mr. President, did you have any advance information, or know what General MacArthur said about the number of troops needed in Japan?

THE PRESIDENT. No, I didn't. I'm glad to see that the General won't need as many as he thought. He said first 500,000, later 400,000 and now 200,000. It helps to get as many more men out of the Army as possible.

---

[1] William H. Davis, Director, Office of Economic Stabilization.

[10.] Q. Mr. President, is there going to be any change in the Executive order of August 18 on the loan policy?

THE PRESIDENT. No.

[11.] Q. May I follow that with another question, sir? Mr. Davis, who was Economic Stabilizer, some few days ago said it was planned to increase wages 50 percent in 5 years without increasing prices.

THE PRESIDENT. He wasn't speaking for the administration when he made *that* statement.

[12.] Q. With this cut in occupation troops in Japan, do you see an earlier end to the draft than previously?

THE PRESIDENT. I can't answer that until I know the policy of the War Department and know how many troops of occupation are needed. The draft will not be continued any longer than is absolutely necessary.

Q. Is there any indication General Eisenhower's request for troops may be reduced?

THE PRESIDENT. There has been some indication of that—yes.

Reporter: Thank you, Mr. President.

NOTE: President Truman's twenty-sixth news conference was held in his office at the White House at 4 p.m. on Tuesday, September 18, 1945. The White House Official Reporter noted that the following special guests attended this conference: Lewis B. Schwellenbach, Secretary of Labor; John W. Snyder, Director, Office of War Mobilization and Reconversion; and David R. Calhoun of St. Louis.

138 Statement by the President Concerning Demobilization of the Armed Forces. *September* 19, 1945

EVERY AMERICAN has an interest in when our soldiers and sailors will return to civilian life. With many of us, this is a personal interest. We all want to feel sure that no one is going to be held in the service a day longer than is necessary to see the job through.

I think we should all be very clear about one thing. An impression has spread that the speed of demobilization is governed by our future needs for occupation and other forces. That is, of course, not true.

No one now can accurately forecast what those needs are going to be.

Our earlier estimates are being constantly revised. For example, General MacArthur this week stated that he would be able to handle the occupation of Japan and Korea with half the troops that only a month ago he estimated he would need for that purpose.

Carrying on our demobilization as rapidly as we can—which we are now doing—we shall not really face the problem of the size or makeup of the occupation forces until next Spring. By that time, we ought to know how many men we shall need for occupation and to what extent that need can be met through volunteers.

I think the Army has given all of us good reason for the same confidence in its ability to win the battle of demobilization which we had in its ability to win the war. The day Japan surrendered the Army had to scrap all its plans for an all-out assault and do a right-about face. That was August 14th. In less than one month since then the number of men discharged from the Army each day has risen from 4,200 to more than 15,200. Our soldiers are now being returned to civilian life at a rate in excess of 650 per hour, 24 hours per day. This represents a speedup of better than 375 percent in 30 days. Such a performance justifies full confidence.

The Army's plans call for the return to their homes of more than 2,000,000 soldiers between V–J Day and Christmas, 1945. Between now and Christmas the discharge rate will steadily rise from the present daily figure of 15,200 to not less than 22,000 per day and by January, 1946, to more than 25,000 per day.

The Army and Navy mean to do the task set for them with the minimum number of men. There will be no padding in our armed forces. America is going to keep the full strength she needs for her national commitments. But the rest of the men are coming back home, and coming as fast as the Services can get them out.

139 Letter Accepting Resignation of Henry L. Stimson as
Secretary of War. *September 20, 1945*

[Released September 20, 1945. Dated September 19, 1945]

Dear Mr. Secretary:

The time has come when a grateful Nation must recognize your right to enter into the retirement which you have earned through forty years of outstanding public service. I therefore accept, effective as of the close of business on Friday, September twenty-first, your resignation as Secretary of War. By a happy coincidence you will lay down the burden of office on your seventy-eighth birthday.

I trust that the day may be as happy to you personally as it will be memorable in the national history. My warmest greetings to a hale veteran young in all save years. You richly merit the leisure which is now yours to enjoy.

It is difficult to estimate the value of the long public service in which you have attained high eminence in such diverse fields of activity. You have held three Cabinet posts under four Presidents. To the discharge of the duties of each of these posts you have brought wisdom, vision and true statesmanship. No one saw more clearly than you how the shape of things to come was foreshadowed in the Japanese aggression in Manchuria. Historians will speculate whether the holocaust which spread over the whole world within a decade could not have been prevented had your advice as Secretary of State been followed.

The Nation and the world are familiar with the inadequacy of our Army when you went back to the Department of War, a little more than five years ago. Under your administration it reached the greatest strength in our history and became the best trained and best equipped army in the world.

These are but two phases of your public service. As I tender to you the thanks of the Nation, I cherish the hope that we may continue to rely on the counsel which you can give out of so rich an experience.

Very sincerely yours,

HARRY S. TRUMAN

[Honorable Henry L. Stimson, Secretary of War]

NOTE: Secretary Stimson served from July 10, 1940, through September 21, 1945.

140 Letter to General William J. Donovan on the Termination of the Office of Strategic Services.
September 20, 1945

My dear General Donovan:

I appreciate very much the work which you and your staff undertook, beginning prior to the Japanese surrender, to liquidate those wartime activities of the Office of Strategic Services which will not be needed in time of peace.

Timely steps should also be taken to conserve those resources and skills developed within your organization which are vital to our peacetime purposes.

Accordingly, I have today directed, by Executive order, that the activities of the Research and Analysis Branch and the Presentation Branch of the Office of Strategic Services be transferred to the State Department. This transfer, which is effective as of October 1, 1945, represents the beginning of the development of a coordinated system of foreign intelligence within the permanent framework of the Government.

Consistent with the foregoing, the Executive order provides for the transfer of the remaining activities of the Office of Strategic Services to the War Department; for the abolition of the Office of Strategic Services; and for the continued orderly liquidation of some of the activities of the Office without interrupting other services of a military nature the need for which will continue for some time.

I want to take this occasion to thank you for the capable leadership you have brought to a vital wartime activity in your capacity as Director of Strategic Services. You may well find satisfaction in the achievements of the Office and take pride in your own contribution to them. These are in themselves large rewards. Great additional reward for your efforts should lie in the knowledge that the peacetime intelligence services of the Government are being erected on the foundation of the facilities and resources mobilized through the Office of Strategic Services during the war.

Sincerely yours,

HARRY S. TRUMAN

[Major General William J. Donovan, Director of Strategic Services]

141 Letter to Secretary Byrnes Concerning the Development
     of a Foreign Intelligence Program. *September* 20, 1945

My dear Mr. Secretary:

I have today signed an Executive order which provides for the transfer to the State Department of the functions, personnel, and other resources of the Research and Analysis Branch and the Presentation
Branch of the Office of Strategic Services. The order also transfers the
remaining activities of the Office of Strategic Services to the War Department and abolishes that Office. These changes become effective
October 1, 1945.

The above transfer to the State Department will provide you with
resources which we have agreed you will need to aid in the development
of our foreign policy, and will assure that pertinent experience accumulated during the war will be preserved and used in meeting the problems of the peace. Those readjustments and reductions which are
required in order to gear the transferred activities and resources into
State Department operations should be made as soon as practicable.

I particularly desire that you take the lead in developing a comprehensive and coordinated foreign intelligence program for all Federal
agencies concerned with that type of activity. This should be done
through the creation of an interdepartmental group, heading up under
the State Department, which would formulate plans for my approval.
This procedure will permit the planning of complete coverage of the
foreign intelligence field and the assigning and controlling of operations in such manner that the needs of both the individual agencies and
the Government as a whole will be met with maximum effectiveness.

Sincerely yours,

HARRY S. TRUMAN

[The Honorable, The Secretary of State]

142 Citation Accompanying the Distinguished Service Medal Presented to Henry L. Stimson. *September* 21, 1945

CITATION FOR DISTINGUISHED SERVICE MEDAL

AS SECRETARY OF WAR from the beginning of the actual mobilization of the Army to the final victory over Japan, HENRY LEWIS STIMSON gave the United States of America a measure of distinguished service exceptional in the history of the nation.

Following 40 years of conspicuous public service in which he fought as a combat officer in one war and twice served in the cabinets of Presidents, Mr. Stimson unhesitatingly accepted the vast responsibility for the development of the American armies to play a determining part in the desperate human conflict now victoriously terminated.

His fearlessness, his integrity, his rich experience, his wisdom and his statesmanship were largely contributory to the successful mobilization, deployment and operations of an Army in which his countrymen may take everlasting pride. His steadfast purpose and unselfish devotion were an inspiration to men-at-arms in American forces throughout the world in their bitter fight to maintain moral right, freedom, justice and civilization itself.

HARRY S. TRUMAN

NOTE: The presentation was made by the President in a ceremony in the Rose Garden at the White House on the last day of Mr. Stimson's term of service as Secretary of War.

143 Statement of Policy, Approved by the President, Relating to Post-War Japan. *September* 22, 1945

[Released September 22, 1945. Dated September 6, 1945]

U.S. INITIAL POST-SURRENDER POLICY FOR JAPAN

Purpose of this Document

This document is a statement of general initial policy relating to Japan after surrender. It has been approved by the President and distributed to the Supreme Commander for the Allied Powers and to appropriate U.S. departments and agencies for their guidance. It does not deal with all matters relating to the occupation of Japan requiring policy determinations. Such matters as are not included or are not fully covered herein have been or will be dealt with separately.

PART I—*Ultimate Objectives*

The ultimate objectives of the United States in regard to Japan, to which policies in the initial period must conform, are:

(a) To insure that Japan will not again become a menace to the United States or to the peace and security of the world.

(b) To bring about the eventual establishment of a peaceful and responsible government which will respect the rights of other states and will support the objectives of the United States as reflected in the ideals and principles of the Charter of the United Nations. The United States desires that this government should conform as closely as may be to principles of democratic self-government but it is not the responsibility of the Allied Powers to impose upon Japan any form of government not supported by the freely expressed will of the people.

These objectives will be achieved by the following principal means:

(a) Japan's sovereignty will be limited to the islands of Honshu, Hokkaido, Kyushu, Shikoku and such minor outlying islands as may be determined, in accordance with the Cairo Declaration and other agreements to which the United States is or may be a party.

(b) Japan will be completely disarmed and demilitarized. The authority of the militarists and the influence of militarism will be totally eliminated from her political, economic, and social life. Institutions expressive of the spirit of militarism and aggression will be vigorously suppressed.

(c) The Japanese people shall be encouraged to develop a desire for individual liberties and respect for fundamental human rights, particularly the freedoms of religion, assembly, speech, and the press. They shall also be encouraged to form democratic and representative organizations.

(d) The Japanese people shall be afforded opportunity to develop for themselves an economy which will permit the peacetime requirements of the population to be met.

PART II—*Allied Authority*

1. *Military Occupation.*

There will be a military occupation of the Japanese home islands to carry into effect the surrender terms and further the achievement of the ultimate objectives stated above. The occupation shall have the character of an operation in behalf of the principal allied powers acting in the interests of the United Nations at war with Japan. For that reason, participation of the forces of other nations that have taken a leading part in the war against Japan will be welcomed and expected. The occupation forces will be under the command of a Supreme Commander designated by the United States.

Although every effort will be made, by consultation and by constitution of appropriate advisory bodies, to establish policies for the conduct of the occupation and the control of Japan which will satisfy the principal Allied powers, in the event of any differences of opinion among them, the policies of the United States will govern.

2. *Relationship to Japanese Government.*

The authority of the Emperor and the Japanese Government will be subject to the Supreme Commander, who will possess all powers necessary to effectuate the surrender terms and to carry out the policies established for the conduct of the occupation and the control of Japan.

In view of the present character of Japanese society and the desire of the United States to attain its objectives with a minimum commitment of its forces and resources, the Supreme Commander will exercise his authority through Japanese governmental machinery and agencies, including the Emperor, to the extent that this satisfactorily furthers United States objectives. The Japanese Government will be permitted, under his instructions, to exercise the normal powers of government in matters of domestic administration. This policy, however, will be subject to the right and duty of the Supreme Commander to require changes in governmental machinery or personnel or to act directly if the Emperor or other Japanese authority does not satisfactorily meet the requirements of the Supreme Commander in effectuating the surrender terms. This policy, moreover, does not commit the Supreme Commander to support the Emperor or any other Japanese governmental authority in opposition to evolutionary changes looking toward the attainment of United States objectives. The policy is to use the existing form of Government in Japan, not to support it. Changes in the form of Government initiated by the Japanese people or government in the direction of modifying its feudal and authoritarian tendencies are to be permitted and favored. In the event that the effectuation of such changes involves the use of force by the Japanese people or government against persons opposed thereto, the Supreme Commander should intervene only where necessary to ensure the security of his forces and the attainment of all other objectives of the occupation.

3. *Publicity as to Policies.*

The Japanese people, and the world at large, shall be kept fully informed of the objectives and policies of the occupation, and of progress made in their fulfilment.

PART III—*Political*

1. *Disarmament and Demilitarization.*

Disarmament and demilitarization are the primary tasks of the military occupation and shall be carried out promptly and with determination. Every effort shall be made to bring home to the Japanese people the part played by the military and naval leaders, and those who collaborated with them, in bringing about the existing and future distress of the people.

Japan is not to have an army, navy, airforce, secret police organization, or any civil aviation. Japan's ground, air and naval forces shall be disarmed and disbanded and the Japanese Imperial General Headquarters, the General Staff and all secret police organizations shall be dissolved. Military and naval materiel, military and naval vessels and military and naval installations, and military, naval and civilian aircraft shall be surrendered and shall be disposed of as required by the Supreme Commander.

High officials of the Japanese Imperial General Headquarters, and

335

General Staff, other high military and naval officials of the Japanese Government, leaders of ultra-nationalist and militarist organizations and other important exponents of militarism and aggression will be taken into custody and held for future disposition. Persons who have been active exponents of militarism and militant nationalism will be removed and excluded from public office and from any other position of public or substantial private responsibility. Ultra-nationalistic or militaristic social, political, professional and commercial societies and institutions will be dissolved and prohibited.

Militarism and ultra-nationalism, in doctrine and practice, including para-military training, shall be eliminated from the educational system. Former career military and naval officers, both commissioned and non-commissioned, and all other exponents of militarism and ultra-nationalism shall be excluded from supervisory and teaching positions.

2. *War Criminals.*

Persons charged by the Supreme Commander or appropriate United Nations Agencies with being war criminals, including those charged with having visited cruelties upon United Nations prisoners or other nationals, shall be arrested, tried and, if convicted, punished. Those wanted by another of the United Nations for offenses against its nationals, shall, if not wanted for trial or as witnesses or otherwise by the Supreme Commander, be turned over to the custody of such other nation.

3. *Encouragement of Desire for Individual Liberties and Democratic Processes.*

Freedom of religious worship shall be proclaimed promptly on occupation. At the same time it should be made plain to the Japanese that ultra-nationalistic and militaristic organizations and movements will not be permitted to hide behind the cloak of religion.

The Japanese people shall be afforded opportunity and encouraged to become familiar with the history, institutions, culture, and the accomplishments of the United States and the other democracies. Association of personnel of the occupation forces with the Japanese population should be controlled, only to the extent necessary, to further the policies and objectives of the occupation.

Democratic political parties, with rights of assembly and public discussion, shall be encouraged, subject to the necessity for maintaining the security of the occupying forces.

Laws, decrees and regulations which establish discriminations on grounds of race, nationality, creed or political opinion shall be abrogated; those which conflict with the objectives and policies outlined in this document shall be repealed, suspended or amended as required; and agencies charged specifically with their enforcement shall be abolished or appropriately modified. Persons unjustly confined by Japanese authority on political grounds shall be released. The judicial, legal and police systems shall be reformed as soon as practicable to conform to the policies set forth in Articles 1 and 3 of this Part III and thereafter shall be progressively influenced, to protect individual liberties and civil rights.

PART IV—*Economic*

1. *Economic Demilitarization.*

The existing economic basis of Japanese military strength must be destroyed and not be permitted to revive.

Therefore, a program will be enforced containing the following elements, among others; the immediate cessation and future prohibition of production of all goods designed for the equipment, maintenance, or use of any military force or establishment; the imposition of a ban upon any specialized facilities for the production or repair of implements of war, including naval vessels and all forms of aircraft; the institution of a system of inspection and control over selected elements in Japanese economic activity to prevent concealed or disguised military preparation; the elimination in Japan of those selected industries or branches of production whose chief value to Japan is in preparing for war; the prohibition of specialized research and instruction directed to the development of war-making power; and the limitation of the size and character of Japan's heavy industries to its future peaceful requirements, and restriction of Japanese merchant shipping to the extent required to accomplish the objectives of demilitarization.

The eventual disposition of those existing production facilities within Japan which are to be eliminated in accord with this program, as between conversion to other uses, transfer abroad, and scrapping will be determined after inventory. Pending decision, facilities readily convertible for civilian production should not be destroyed, except in emergency situations.

2. *Promotion of Democratic Forces.*

Encouragement shall be given and favor shown to the development of organizations in labor, industry, and agriculture, organized on a democratic basis. Policies shall be favored which permit a wide distribution of income and of the ownership of the means of production and trade.

Those forms of economic activity, organization and leadership shall be favored that are deemed likely to strengthen the peaceful disposition of the Japanese people, and to make it difficult to command or direct economic activity in support of military ends.

To this end it shall be the policy of the Supreme Commander:

(a) To prohibit the retention in or selection for places of importance in the economic field of individuals who do not direct future Japanese economic effort solely towards peaceful ends; and

(b) To favor a program for the dissolution of the large industrial and banking combinations which have exercised control of a great part of Japan's trade and industry.

3. *Resumption of Peaceful Economic Activity.*

The policies of Japan have brought down upon the people great economic destruction and confronted them with the prospect of economic difficulty and suffering. The plight of Japan is the direct outcome of its own behavior, and the Allies will not undertake the burden of repairing the damage. It can be repaired only if the Japanese people renounce all military aims and apply themselves diligently and with single purpose to the ways of peaceful living. It will be necessary for them to undertake physical reconstruction, deeply to reform the nature and direction of their economic activities and institutions, and to find useful employment for their people along lines adapted to and devoted to peace. The Allies have no intention of imposing conditions which would prevent the accomplishment of these tasks in due time.

Japan will be expected to provide goods and services to meet the needs of the occupying forces to the extent that this can be effected without causing starvation, widespread disease and acute physical distress.

The Japanese authorities will be expected, and if necessary directed, to maintain, develop and enforce programs that serve the following purposes:

(a) To avoid acute economic distress.

(b) To assure just and impartial distribution of available supplies.

(c) To meet the requirements for reparations deliveries agreed upon by the Allied Governments.

(d) To facilitate the restoration of Japanese economy so that the reasonable peaceful requirements of the population can be satisfied.

In this connection, the Japanese authorities on their own responsibility shall be permitted to establish and administer controls over economic activities, including essential national public services, finance, banking, and production and distribution of essential commodities, subject to the approval and review of the Supreme Commander in order to assure their conformity with the objectives of the occupation.

4. *Reparations and Restitution.*

Reparations. Reparations for Japanese aggression shall be made:

(a) Through the transfer—as may be determined by the appropriate Allied authorities—of Japanese property located outside of the territories to be retained by Japan.

(b) Through the transfer of such goods or existing capital equipment and facilities as are not necessary for a peaceful Japanese economy or the supplying of the occupying forces. Exports other than those directed to be shipped on reparation account or as restitution may be made only to those recipients who agree to provide necessary imports in exchange or agree to pay for such exports in foreign exchange. No form of reparation shall be exacted which will interfere with or prejudice the program for Japan's demilitarization.

Restitution. Full and prompt restitution will be required of all identifiable looted property.

5. *Fiscal, Monetary, and Banking Policies.*

The Japanese authorities will remain responsible for the management and direction of the domestic fiscal, monetary, and credit policies subject to the approval and review of the Supreme Commander.

6. *International Trade and Financial Relations.*

Japan shall be permitted eventually to resume normal trade relations with the rest of the world. During occupation and under suitable controls, Japan will be permitted to purchase from foreign countries raw materials and other goods that it may need for peaceful purposes, and to export goods to pay for approved imports.

Control is to be maintained over all imports and exports of goods, and foreign exchange and financial transactions. Both the policies followed in the exercise of these controls and their actual administration shall be subject to the approval and supervision of the Supreme Commander in order to make sure that they are not contrary to the policies of the occupying authorities, and in particular that all foreign purchasing power that Japan may acquire is utilized only for essential needs.

7. *Japanese Property Located Abroad.*

Existing Japanese external assets and existing Japanese assets located in territories detached from Japan under the terms of surrender, including assets owned in whole or part by the Imperial Household and Government, shall be revealed to the occupying authorities and held for disposition according to the decision of the Allied authorities.

8. *Equality of Opportunity for Foreign Enterprise within Japan.*

The Japanese authorities shall not give, or permit any Japanese business organization to give, exclusive or preferential opportunity or terms to the enterprise of any foreign country, or cede to such enterprise control of any important branch of economic activity.

9. *Imperial Household Property.*

Imperial Household property shall not be exempted from any action necessary to carry out the objectives of the occupation.

NOTE: The White House release of the text of this document stated that it was prepared jointly by the Department of State, the War Department, and the Navy Department, and that it was approved by the President on September 6. The release further stated that "the document in substance was sent to General MacArthur by radio on August 29 and after approval by the President by messenger on September 6."

144   Letter to Henry J. Kaiser Calling Upon Him To Head the Second United National Clothing Collection Campaign. *September 23, 1945*

[Released September 23, 1945. Dated August 21, 1945]

Dear Henry:

Again the need for used clothing for war sufferers all over the world is urgent. It is imperative that we act at once to provide clothing for the relief of men, women and children in war ravaged lands.

I am, therefore, calling upon you again to lead the Nation in this campaign to alleviate incalculable hardships which will be endured next winter unless we act without delay. The results achieved under your leadership earlier this year were magnificent.

Splendid as were the results of that effort, however, it is plainly evident that additional quantities of clothing must be secured to meet the tremendous war relief needs which the world now faces, not only in Europe but also in liberated areas in the Pacific. Other countries—Canada, Australia, New Zealand—will conduct collections to help meet this urgent situation, but the dire need justified another appeal to the people in the United States.

Without adequate clothing and other necessities of life to sustain victims of war on the long road to rehabilitation there can be no peace. I, therefore, ask you and the more than seven thousand local chairmen of the United National Clothing Collection to lead the Nation in another clothing collection drive for the relief of victims of war.

The universal response last spring, when all groups concerned with problems of war relief joined with United Nations Relief and Rehabilitation Administration in one great national appeal, has proven beyond any doubt the value and efficiency of the united endeavor which I now request you to carry on again.

Very sincerely yours,

HARRY S. TRUMAN

[Honorable Henry J. Kaiser, 1522 Latham Square Building, Oakland, California]

NOTE: Mr. Kaiser's letter of acceptance, dated August 24, 1945, was also released.

145 Message Approved by the President Concerning the Extent of General MacArthur's Authority in Japan. *September 24, 1945*

[Released September 24, 1945. Dated September 6, 1945]

1. THE AUTHORITY of the Emperor and the Japanese Government to rule the State is subordinate to you as Supreme Commander for the Allied powers. You will exercise your authority as you deem proper to carry out your mission. Our relations with Japan do not rest on a contractual basis, but on an unconditional surrender. Since your authority is supreme, you will not entertain any question on the part of the Japanese as to its scope.

2. Control of Japan shall be exercised through the Japanese Government to the extent that such an arrangement produces satisfactory results. This does not prejudice your right to act directly if required. You may enforce the orders issued by you by the employment of such measures as you deem necessary, including the use of force.

3. The statement of intentions contained in the Potsdam Declaration will be given full effect. It will not be given effect, however, because we consider ourselves bound in a contractual relationship with Japan as a result of that document. It will be respected and given effect because the Potsdam Declaration forms a part of our policy stated in good faith with relation to Japan and with relation to peace and security in the Far East.

NOTE: The White House release of the message stated that it was approved by the President on September 6 and was transmitted the same day to General MacArthur through the Joint Chiefs of Staff. It further stated that the message was prepared jointly by the Department of State, the War Department, and the Navy Department.

146   Letter to the Speaker of the House of Representatives Transmitting Proposed Reductions in Appropriations for the War Department.   *September 25, 1945*

The Speaker of the House of Representatives:

Sir: I have the honor to transmit herewith for the consideration of the Congress (1) proposed rescissions of portions of appropriations for the Military Establishment available for the fiscal year 1946, amounting to $28,692,772,000, and (2) a proposed provision authorizing certain transfers of appropriated funds.

I plan a continuing review of appropriations for the Military Establishment and will recommend such further adjustments as conditions warrant.

The details of these proposed rescissions and the proposed provision pertaining to existing appropriations are set forth in the letter of the Director of the Bureau of the Budget, transmitted herewith, in whose comments and observations thereon I concur.

Respectfully yours,

HARRY S. TRUMAN

NOTE: A White House release describing the President's proposal pointed out that, in addition to the recommended rescissions amounting to $28.7 billion, another half billion dollars would be returned to the Treasury by the War Department from funds available in special replacing accounts. The release also stated that the recommended reductions reflected savings due to the decrease in the strength of the Army and reduced requirements for supplies and equipment made possible by the surrender of Japan. The release further stated that it was contemplated that the Army would be reduced to a strength of 1,950,000 by June 30, 1946. It added that allowances had been made for an adequate research program, limited procurement of newly developed weapons of warfare, and for continued production on a reduced scale of advanced types of aircraft.

The details of the proposal as set

343

forth in the letter of the Director of the Bureau of the Budget, transmitted with the President's letter, are printed in House Document 290 (79th Cong., 1st sess.).

147 The President's News Conference of
September 26, 1945

THE PRESIDENT. Well, I've no particular announcements to make to you this morning; I just thought maybe it was time to have a press conference, and if you——

[1.] Q. Mr. President, what is your reaction to proposals from abroad for the establishment of an Allied Control Commission for Japan?

THE PRESIDENT. Well, the establishment of the Japanese Government was agreed to by all the Allied nations interested, and it is satisfactory to them. I hadn't received any notice there would be a discussion of that sort.

[2.] Q. Getting a little closer home, some weeks ago I asked you about the St. Lawrence Seaway, and you said you expected to have something for us soon.

THE PRESIDENT. I'm still expecting it; I haven't it ready yet.

Q. In view of the fact that Governor Dewey has sent in his protest about New York State being excluded from that proposed bill, can you tell us when you are going to reply to Governor Dewey?

THE PRESIDENT. Probably tomorrow. I'll give it to you when it's ready.

[3.] Q. There has been a lot of curiosity about the gift of that C–54 to General de Gaulle. The Treasury, the State Department, the White House, and the Attorney General don't seem to know under what statute or Executive order a President is authorized to make such a gift. I wonder if you could make some comment on that?

THE PRESIDENT. The gift was made to General de Gaulle the same as the gift to former Prime Minister Churchill, General Chiang Kai-shek, and the King of Saudi Arabia under the War Powers Act, and was done as a matter of good will, because we had more C–54's than we could use and General de Gaulle needed one. It was the Government of the United States in a gesture of friendship to the Government of France.

[4.] Q. May I return to the first question? I believe the statement from the White House the other day said that when the other countries are not in agreement on occupation policy, that the policy of the United States will prevail.

THE PRESIDENT. That is correct.

Q. The question I wanted to ask is, is there a mechanism to bring about a concerted policy on Japan? Is there a periodical opportunity to see that others agree?

THE PRESIDENT. The appointment of General MacArthur as Allied Commander in Chief was concurred in by all the interested powers, and he is designated to act for all the interested powers.

Q. Do the other interested powers have the opportunity to express views on evolving occupation policies?

THE PRESIDENT. Yes, they do, through the Joint Chiefs of Staff.

Q. What if the Russians desire to get in touch with General Mac-Arthur and they are not members of the Joint Chiefs of Staff?

THE PRESIDENT. They have a representative with General MacArthur through whom they can get in touch with him, or through me if they desire.

Q. Mr. President, do you have any comments to make on reports from London yesterday saying, I believe, that the Russians might want more part in the control of Japan?

THE PRESIDENT. No, I have no comment, because all I know is what I have seen in the papers.

Q. When do they expect Mr. Byrnes back, Mr. President?

THE PRESIDENT. I think sometime within the next 10 days. I don't know exactly.

Q. Mr. President, do you think General MacArthur may come or send someone to the United States for consultation?

THE PRESIDENT. No, I don't look for him to do that; unless he feels it is necessary, I have no reason to ask him to come.

[5.] Q. Any plans in the works for another Big Three conference?

THE PRESIDENT. Any what?

Q. Any plans for another Big Three meeting?

THE PRESIDENT. No.

[6.] Q. Anything to say on the reports of the failure of the Big Five foreign ministers' conference in London?

THE PRESIDENT. They're all surmises. You don't know a thing about the meeting until it's over. Let's wait until we hear the official report of the Big Five and see whether it's a failure or not.

[7.] Q. Mr. President, do you propose to send up a message this week on the atomic bomb and its disposition?

THE PRESIDENT. Sometime soon.

[8.] Q. Mr. President, do you care to comment on the Ways and Means Committee's killing the unemployment compensation bill?

THE PRESIDENT. I didn't know they had killed it. If they have, I'm sorry, and they'll hear from me later.[1]

[9.] Q. Mr. President, the papers in Arkansas say you are to be there October 5 and 6 for the cotton-picking championship. Is that so?

THE PRESIDENT. I was expecting to go to Caruthersville to the fair on the 6th, and I had said to the Governor of Arkansas that if I could manage it I would stop there, but it looks now as if I am not going to get to either one.

[10.] Q. May I ask you another question about the St. Lawrence Waterway: will there be a bill on that?

THE PRESIDENT. That's up to the Congress whether there'll be a bill. I have voted for that twice.

Q. You are expecting to send a message soon?

THE PRESIDENT. Yes.

[11.] Q. To go back from the St. Lawrence to Japan: what is the disposition of the fleet units that have been seized? Do we fall heir to the title to these, or are we going to split them up with the other——

THE PRESIDENT. They will probably be worked out as a reparations

---

[1] A White House release of September 30, 1945, stated that some of the comment on the President's supplementary unemployment compensation proposal had indicated a complete misunderstanding of the significance of the $25 a week maximum. As the President sought to make clear in his message to Congress on September 6th, the release continued, the $25 was a ceiling and not a guarantee that everyone would get $25 a week. All existing State laws which calculated weekly benefits as a percentage of wage loss would remain in effect, the release added.

question, just the same way the German and Italian fleets were worked out.

[12.] Q. Mr. President, do you think we are in more of an isolationist mood in this country now? David Lawrence wrote an article in the Star last night saying we are in more of an isolationist mood than in the past.

THE PRESIDENT. I don't agree with him. If we ever get to that point, we are on the road to ruin just as in 1920.

[13.] Q. Mr. President, did Mr. Roosevelt, in his past conferences, make a commitment to the King of Arabia that the United States would not make an issue out of the Palestine question?

THE PRESIDENT. No, there is no record of any conference between the King of Arabia and the President in which any such statement was made. I have looked for it very carefully.

[14.] Q. Is Leo Crowley planning to get out of Government?

THE PRESIDENT. Leo—Mr. Crowley—has been trying to resign for some time, and I have persuaded him to stay so far. He may want to do it again, and I will probably talk with him some more.[1]

[15.] Q. Mr. President, have you taken up with Senator Downey anything about his proposed bill—that 20 percent wage increase bill?

THE PRESIDENT. He was in and talked with me, but no conclusion was reached on it. He has a perfect right to introduce it if he wants to.

Q. Mr. President,——

Q. Mr. President, do you have a nomination on the Solicitor General?

THE PRESIDENT. Let the lady ask a question; you had one before.

[16.] Q. [*Lady reporter*] The strike situation was apparently a factor in the House Ways and Means Committee's shelving of the jobless bill; I wonder if you have anything to say on the strike situation?

THE PRESIDENT. No, the Secretary of Labor is working on the situation and I think he will bring it to a successful conclusion.

Q. Can you tell us anything on the increase of wages at all?

THE PRESIDENT. I would rather not make a comment on it now.

---

[1] A White House release dated September 27 announced that the President had that day accepted Mr. Crowley's resignation as Administrator of the Foreign Economic Administration and as a member of the board of directors of the Federal Deposit Insurance Corporation, effective at the close of business October 15. The release also included the text of the letters exchanged between the President and Mr. Crowley.

[17.] Q. Mr. President, what are the chances of the United Nations headquarters being in the United States?

THE PRESIDENT. That is a matter that will be up to the United Nations to be settled by vote. They're welcome to come to the United States if they so desire.

[18.] Q. I may have misunderstood you, but do you, by your Downey reference, do you mean to say that you have no views on the subject of the Downey bill?

THE PRESIDENT. No, I have no comment to make on the Downey bill.

[19.] Q. Mr. President, has this disposition of the remainder of the German fleet been worked out?

THE PRESIDENT. The disposition was worked out at Berlin. It was to be divided into three sections, one to go to Russia, one to Great Britain, and one to the United States.

Q. Will that same split likely be made with the Japanese fleet?

THE PRESIDENT. I can't answer that until I have more information.

[20.] Q. What about General Eisenhower's new directive on Germany?

THE PRESIDENT. He is following out the directive he received from the Potsdam conference—I like to call it the Berlin conference.

[21.] Q. Mr. President, do you favor sharing the atomic bomb with other nations?

THE PRESIDENT. I will answer that question in my message to Congress.

[22.] Q. Anything on the Labor conference agenda?

THE PRESIDENT. You better speak to the Secretary on that.

[23.] Q. How do you feel about the Alaska statehood question?

THE PRESIDENT. Of course when Alaska is ready for statehood, it will be given to her.

Reporter: Thank you, Mr. President.

NOTE: President Truman's twenty-seventh news conference was held in his office at the White House at 10:05 a.m. on Wednesday, September 26, 1945. The White House Official Reporter noted that the following special guests attended this conference: "Governor [Ransome J.] Williams of South Carolina; Mayor Edwin Wehman of Charleston; Mayor H. L. Smith, Georgetown, S.C.; Mr. Julian Mitchell, Chairman of the Board, National Banks, S.C.; Mr. B. M. Edwards, President of all National Banks, S.C.; Mr.

Arthur Simmons, Chairman of the Board, Ports Authority; Mr. James Smith, State Auditor; Mr. Morrison Tuten, Chairman, Ways and Means Committee; Mr. Thaddeus Street; Mr. Milton Pearlstine, on Ports Authority; Mr. Robert Figg, Solicitor of S.C.; Mr. Coatsworth Means, Director, Ports Authority; Mr. Howard Danna, Ports Authority; Hon. J. D. Parler, State Senator, S.C.; Hon. Solomon Blatt, Speaker of House of Representatives."

148 Telegram to the Governor of New York Concerning the St. Lawrence Seaway and Power Projects.
September 27, 1945

[Released September 27, 1945. Dated September 26, 1945]

Honorable Thomas E. Dewey
The Governor of the State of New York
Albany, New York

This is to acknowledge receipt of your telegram of September nineteenth with reference to the Great Lakes-St. Lawrence Seaway and Power Projects.

I am sure that you are aware of the fact that I have been and still am in favor of constructing both the Seaway and the Power projects; and was happy and proud to vote for them on December 12, 1944 when I was Vice President-elect but still a member of the United States Senate.

I continue to be enthusiastically in favor not only of the development of the St. Lawrence Waterway but also of the water power on the river. I also continue to believe very strongly that the necessary power facilities should be built by the Federal Government and turned over to the appropriate New York State agency in accordance with the agreement recommended by the Corps of Engineers of the United States Army and the Power Authority of the State of New York dated February 7, 1933. This was the program of President Roosevelt, and I have always been in favor of it.

A group of Senators interested in these same objectives, composed of Republicans and Democrats, have been holding meetings to discuss the best means of obtaining these results. I am informed that you have been kept fully advised about these conferences as they have progressed.

349

The conferees have been advising with my representatives as to the best manner to bring the proposals to a successful conclusion in the Congress of the United States.

Inasmuch as it is a legislative matter, I am inclined to follow their ultimate conclusions on the best means of avoiding continued fruitless discussion and of getting some early, definite action toward accomplishing both of these objectives. It is the early construction of the project— both power and seaway—which will benefit the people of New York and the Great Lakes area, and not the form of any particular bill.

As you know, I have always been, and still am, ready to cooperate in any way I can to have the Congress of the United States ratify as soon as possible the Canadian-American agreement of March 19, 1941 for the development of the Great Lakes-St. Lawrence Basin, and also take the appropriate steps to transfer to the State of New York the ownership and management of the St. Lawrence power facilities at the International Rapids.

I am not so much interested in the details of legislative procedure; nor do I feel that it is proper for me to interfere with the sponsors of the legislation as to the legislative procedure to be followed. I am, however, most interested in the ultimate objectives which I am sure you wish to attain just as I do.

Copies of this telegram are being sent to the interested Senators and to the members of the New York State Power Authority.

HARRY S. TRUMAN

NOTE: Governor Dewey's telegram, released with the President's reply, stated that he had been informed that the President intended to sponsor a bill which would merely ratify the international agreement for the development of the St. Lawrence and completely omit the accord between the Federal Government and the State of New York for the development of its power resources. The telegram further stated that it had been suggested that the President would urge an amendment to the bill, after introduction, to permit the inclusion of the Federal-State accord.

Governor Dewey stated that he was opposed to this procedure. "If the Federal-State accord is ultimately to be part of the bill," he added, "in fairness to the committee members considering it and to the vital interests of the people of the State of New York the accord should be a part of the bill from the very beginning."

The telegram concluded with a statement that copies were being sent to interested Senators and members of the New York State Power Authority.

149 Veto of Bill for the Relief of the City of Council Bluffs,
     Iowa. *September 27, 1945*

To the House of Representatives:

I return herewith, without my approval, H.R. 1634, 79th Congress,
1st Session, a bill for the relief of the City of Council Bluffs, Iowa.

The purpose of the measure is to authorize and direct payment of the
sum of $8,750.13 to the City of Council Bluffs, Iowa, in full settlement
of all claims against the United States for 50,144 sacks purchased by
the city which were used together with other sacks furnished by the
Engineer Corps, United States Army, to strengthen embankments
along the Missouri River in order to avert the flood which threatened
the city in the spring of 1943. The sacks for which payment is sought
were purchased directly by the City of Council Bluffs from a private
concern in advance of the threatened high waters.

It appears that during the high water conditions encountered, the
U.S. District Engineer at Omaha, Nebraska, rendered all possible assistance to local interests in the protection of private and public property
at Council Bluffs and in strengthening all flood protection systems.
This assistance also included rescue work.

As indicated in the report on the measure, it has been the policy of
the Engineer Department over a period of years to furnish Government property such as boats, barges and other equipment to stricken
communities for emergency use in protection of life and property when
no suitable private equipment was on hand. The cost of this assistance
has been borne by the War Department. It has never been the practice of the Engineer Department to make monetary restitution for
efforts or materials expended by local authorities in flood fighting.
The emergency flood protection measures taken by the City of Council
Bluffs do not appear to differ from those taken by other cities and
municipalities similarly affected by flood conditions.

Because the enactment of the bill would have the effect of establishing a precedent for the payment of similar expenditures made by local
interests during the 1943 flood emergency, as well as other emergencies
which might arise on all navigable waters and their tributaries which

have been improved in the aid of navigation, and for flood control purposes, I feel obliged to withhold my approval of the legislation.

HARRY S. TRUMAN

150 Proclamation 2667: Policy of the United States With Respect to the Natural Resources of the Subsoil and Sea Bed of the Continental Shelf. *September 28, 1945*

By the President of the United States of America a Proclamation:

WHEREAS the Government of the United States of America, aware of the long range world-wide need for new sources of petroleum and other minerals, holds the view that efforts to discover and make available new supplies of these resources should be encouraged; and

WHEREAS its competent experts are of the opinion that such resources underlie many parts of the continental shelf off the coasts of the United States of America, and that with modern technological progress their utilization is already practicable or will become so at an early date; and

WHEREAS recognized jurisdiction over these resources is required in the interest of their conservation and prudent utilization when and as development is undertaken; and

WHEREAS it is the view of the Government of the United States that the exercise of jurisdiction over the natural resources of the subsoil and sea bed of the continental shelf by the contiguous nation is reasonable and just, since the effectiveness of measures to utilize or conserve these resources would be contingent upon cooperation and protection from the shore, since the continental shelf may be regarded as an extension of the land-mass of the coastal nation and thus naturally appurtenant to it, since these resources frequently form a seaward extension of a pool or deposit lying within the territory, and since self-protection compels the coastal nation to keep close watch over activities off its shores which are of the nature necessary for utilization of these resources;

Now, THEREFORE, I, HARRY S. TRUMAN, President of the United States of America, do hereby proclaim the following policy of the United

States of America with respect to the natural resources of the subsoil and sea bed of the continental shelf.

Having concern for the urgency of conserving and prudently utilizing its natural resources, the Government of the United States regards the natural resources of the subsoil and sea bed of the continental shelf beneath the high seas but contiguous to the coasts of the United States as appertaining to the United States, subject to its jurisdiction and control. In cases where the continental shelf extends to the shores of another State, or is shared with an adjacent State, the boundary shall be determined by the United States and the State concerned in accordance with equitable principles. The character as high seas of the waters above the continental shelf and the right to their free and unimpeded navigation are in no way thus affected.

In Witness Whereof, I have hereunto set my hand and caused the seal of the United States of America to be affixed.

Done at the City of Washington this twenty-eighth day of September, in the year of our Lord nineteen hundred and forty-five, and [SEAL] of the Independence of the United States of America the one hundred and seventieth.

Harry S. Truman

By the President:

Dean Acheson

Acting Secretary of State

NOTE: The White House press release issued with this proclamation reads in part as follows:

"The policy proclaimed by the President in regard to the jurisdiction over the continental shelf does not touch upon the question of Federal versus State control. It is concerned solely with establishing the jurisdiction of the United States from an international standpoint. It will, however, make possible the orderly development of an underwater area 750,000 square miles in extent. Generally, submerged land which is contiguous to the continent and which is covered by no more than 100 fathoms (600 feet) of water is considered as the continental shelf.

"Petroleum geologists believe that portions of the continental shelf beyond the 3-mile limit contain valuable oil deposits. The study of subsurface structures associated with oil deposits which have been discovered along the gulf coast of Texas, for instance, indicates that corresponding deposits may underlie the offshore or submerged land. The trend of oil-productive salt domes extends directly into the Gulf of Mexico off the Texas coast. Oil is also being taken at present from wells within the 3-mile limit off the coast of California. It is quite possible, geologists say, that the oil deposits extend beyond this traditional limit of national jurisdiction.

"Valuable deposits of minerals other than oil may also be expected to be found in these submerged areas. Ore mines now extend under the sea from the coasts of England, Chile, and other countries.

"While asserting jurisdiction and control of the United States over the mineral resources of the continental shelf, the proclamation in no wise abridges the right of free and unimpeded navigation of waters of the character of high seas above the shelf, nor does it extend the present limits of the Territorial waters of the United States.

"The advance of technology prior to the present war had already made possible the exploitation of a limited amount of minerals from submerged lands within the 3-mile limit. The rapid development of technical knowledge and equipment occasioned by the war now makes possible the determination of the resources of the submerged lands outside of the 3-mile limit. With the need for the discovery of additional resources of petroleum and other minerals, it became advisable for the United States to make possible orderly development of these resources. The proclamation of the President is designed to serve this purpose."

Executive Order 9633, reserving and setting aside the resources of the continental shelf and placing them for administrative purposes, pending legislative action, under the jurisdiction and control of the Secretary of the Interior, was released with the foregoing proclamation. For text see 3 CFR, 1943–1948 Comp., p. 437.

151 Statement by the President on Announcing the Termination of the American Production Mission in China. *September 29, 1945*

WHILE concluding this war mission, the American Government desires to continue its close cooperation with China. The American Production Mission is tangible evidence of the enduring friendship of our two nations. Out of our work together on problems of war production have come practical experience and mutual high regard which will be of great value to the future economic relations of our two countries and the world.

NOTE: This statement is part of a White House release announcing that the President was sending his Personal Representative, Edwin A. Locke, Jr., to China to discuss with Generalissimo Chiang Kai-shek and key Chinese officials ways in which the industrial experience of the United States could best be utilized to aid sound peacetime economic reconstruction and development of China. The release stated that Mr. Locke would give particular attention to the situation confronting the Chinese as a result of China's acquisition of large industries in Manchuria and other liberated provinces. The release further stated that Mr. Locke would be accompanied by his Economic Adviser, Albert Z. Carr.

In announcing that Mr. Locke would make arrangements for terminating the work of the American Production Mission, established late in 1944 to aid China's war effort, the release stated that the Mission had maintained a staff of about 20 American industrial specialists in Chungking. The release continued: "Their close collaboration with the Chinese Government has been instrumental in obtaining increased production of munitions and basic raw materials from Free China's industrial facilities. Since the Japanese surrender the Mission has been aiding the Chinese Government in dealing with the initial problems of reconversion and industrial revival."

152 Letter to General Eisenhower Concerning Conditions Facing Displaced Persons in Germany.
September 29, 1945

[Released September 29, 1945. Dated August 31, 1945]

My dear General Eisenhower:

I have received and considered the report of Mr. Earl G. Harrison, our representative on the Intergovernmental Committee on Refugees, upon his mission to inquire into the condition and needs of displaced persons in Germany who may be stateless or non-repatriable, particularly Jews. I am sending you a copy of that report. I have also had a long conference with him on the same subject matter.

While Mr. Harrison makes due allowance for the fact that during the early days of liberation the huge task of mass repatriation required main attention, he reports conditions which now exist and which require prompt remedy. These conditions, I know, are not in conformity with policies promulgated by SHAEF, now Combined Displaced Persons Executive. But they are what actually exists in the field. In other words, the policies are not being carried out by some of your subordinate officers.

For example, military government officers have been authorized and even directed to requisition billeting facilities from the German popula-

355

tion for the benefit of displaced persons. Yet, from this report, this has not been done on any wide scale. Apparently it is being taken for granted that all displaced persons, irrespective of their former persecution or the likelihood that their repatriation or resettlement will be delayed, must remain in camps—many of which are overcrowded and heavily guarded. Some of these camps are the very ones where these people were herded together, starved, tortured and made to witness the death of their fellow-inmates and friends and relatives. The announced policy has been to give such persons preference over the German civilian population in housing. But the practice seems to be quite another thing.

We must intensify our efforts to get these people out of camps and into decent houses until they can be repatriated or evacuated. These houses should be requisitioned from the German civilian population. That is one way to implement the Potsdam policy that the German people "cannot escape responsibility for what they have brought upon themselves."

I quote this paragraph with particular reference to the Jews among the displaced persons:

"As matters now stand, we appear to be treating the Jews as the Nazis treated them except that we do not exterminate them. They are in concentration camps in large numbers under our military guard instead of S.S. troops. One is led to wonder whether the German people, seeing this, are not supposing that we are following or at least condoning Nazi policy."

You will find in the report other illustrations of what I mean.

I hope you will adopt the suggestion that a more extensive plan of field visitation by appropriate Army Group Headquarters be instituted, so that the humane policies which have been enunciated are not permitted to be ignored in the field. Most of the conditions now existing in displaced persons camps would quickly be remedied if through inspection tours they came to your attention or to the attention of your supervisory officers.

I know you will agree with me that we have a particular responsibility toward these victims of persecution and tyranny who are in our zone.

We must make clear to the German people that we thoroughly abhor the Nazi policies of hatred and persecution. We have no better opportunity to demonstrate this than by the manner in which we ourselves actually treat the survivors remaining in Germany.

I hope you will report to me as soon as possible the steps you have been able to take to clean up the conditions mentioned in the report.

I am communicating directly with the British Government in an effort to have the doors of Palestine opened to such of these displaced persons as wish to go there.

Very sincerely yours,

HARRY S. TRUMAN

[General of the Army D. D. Eisenhower, G. Hq. USFET]

NOTE: Mr. Harrison's report, in the form of a letter to the President, was also released. It is published in the Department of State Bulletin (vol. 13, p. 456).

On October 16, the White House made public General Eisenhower's reply, dated October 8, 1945. The letter is published in the Department of State Bulletin (vol. 13, p. 607).

See also Items 187 and 188.

153 Letter to Harry L. Hopkins Concerning the Roosevelt National Memorial Committee. *October 1, 1945*

Dear Mr. Hopkins:

I have your letter of September twenty-ninth and approve the action taken by the committee appointed by me at the meeting of September fifth.

Now that your recommendations have been made, we can all proceed to take speedy action to set up a national memorial worthy of the historic achievements in war and peace of the late illustrious President.

Very sincerely,

HARRY S. TRUMAN

NOTE: Mr. Hopkins' letter, released with the President's reply, dealt with plans for designating permanent officers and enlarging the membership of the memorial committee.

154 Radio Address Opening the 1945 National War Fund
Campaign. *October 2, 1945*

[Broadcast from the White House at 10:30 p.m.]

My fellow citizens of the United States:

This is the month when in cities and towns throughout the country
the community war fund is making its annual appeal. Perhaps you
wonder why I am coming to you in behalf of a war fund drive, now
that all our enemies have surrendered. I shall tell you why.

First let me explain that your community war fund joins in one combined appeal the agencies of the National War Fund serving our own
armed forces and merchant marine and those agencies helping to relieve
the suffering and want of war victims among our Allies. The same
federated fund also unites—in Community Chest cities—with the appeal for local agencies guarding the health and welfare of our own
American homes and families.

We must support these war fund agencies because of their support
of our armed forces. Of course we gave our armed forces in the field
the best equipment and supplies that we could provide. We gave our
men the best training and leadership we could secure. We gave them
everything we could. But there was one thing that we had to depend
on the member agencies of the National War Fund to supply. That
was the plain, human friendship, the good-neighborliness, the little bit
of home, that they provided our service men and women through every
USO club and unit.

I am speaking to you tonight because it is important, because it is
imperative, that these War Fund agencies finish the job they were set
up to do. War service has not ended. I don't need to tell that to anyone whose son is still serving with the occupation forces or with the
service troops in this country. For them, the war is still going on.
That's why USO and USO-Camp Shows must go on with the fine
work they've been doing—until all our service men and women are
back home with us again.

Our returning veterans are looking forward to happy homes in which
their children can grow up the way they should. They are looking

358

forward to living in a community which is concerned with the welfare of its citizens. They may not think of this in terms of a child welfare program, a family service society, a scout troop, a recreation program, a visiting nurse or a clinic. But these services, which in most of our cities are performed by agencies of the local Community Chest, help to determine the quality of living in their community. These are the services from which everyone in the community benefits.

The appeal of the National War Fund and your local Community War Fund is a human appeal for three causes—for continued friendly services for the men and women who still have a job to do in the armed forces; for health and welfare services for our own people at home; and for relief and assistance for the war stricken people of liberated countries—our Allies who fought by our side.

We have won the victory of arms; now let us push on to greater conquests—to the total victory of human justice and decency and faith in mankind.

Let us be generous, and let us give abundant thanks to God in victory through our generosity.

155 Special Message to the Congress on the St. Lawrence
     Seaway. *October 3, 1945*

To the Congress of the United States:

As a part of our program of international cooperation, expanding foreign trade, and domestic progress in commerce and industry, I recommend the speedy approval by the Congress of the Agreement of March 19, 1941 between the United States and Canada for the development of the Great Lakes-St. Lawrence Basin. When approved, the two countries will be able to harness for the public benefit one of the greatest natural resources of North America, opening the Great Lakes to ocean navigation, and creating 2,200,000 horsepower of hydroelectric capacity to be divided equally between the people of the United States and Canada.

The development, utilization and conservation of our natural resources are among those fields of endeavor where the government's responsibility has been well recognized for many generations.

During the war we were forced to suspend many of the projects designed to harness the waters of our great rivers for the promotion of commerce and industry and for the production of cheap electric power. We must now resume these projects and embark upon others.

The Congress and the people of our country can take just pride and satisfaction in the foresight they showed by developing the Tennessee and Columbia Rivers and the rivers in the Central Valley of California. Without the power from these rivers the goal of 50,000 airplanes a year—considered fantastic only five short years ago, but actually surpassed twice over—would have been impossible. Nor could we have developed the atomic bomb as early as we did without the large blocks of power we used from the Tennessee and Columbia Rivers.

The timely development of these rivers shortened the war by many years, and saved countless American lives. We must ever be grateful for the vision of the late President Franklin D. Roosevelt and the wisdom of the Congress in urging and approving the harnessing of these priceless natural resources.

One of the great constructive projects of the North American continent, in fact, one of the great projects of the world, which was delayed by the exigencies of war, is the St. Lawrence Seaway and Power project.

For fifty years the United States and Canada under both Republican and Democratic administrations, under Liberal and Conservative governments, have envisioned the development of the project together, as a joint enterprise.

Upon the expectation that we would join with them in completing this great engineering project, Canada has already built more than half its share of the undertaking.

We, however, still have our major contribution to make.

Every engineering investigation during the past fifty years, every economic study in the past twenty-five years has found the project feasible and economically desirable. The case has been proved; the plans are ready.

The St. Lawrence Seaway will make it possible to utilize our war expanded factories and shipping facilities in the development of international economic cooperation and enlarging world commerce. New and increasing opportunities for production and employment by private enterprise can be expected from this cheap water transportation.

It is the kind of useful construction which will furnish lucrative employment to many thousands of our people.

The completion of the Seaway will bring many benefits to our great neighbor and ally on the North. The experience of two wars and of many years of peace has shown beyond question that the prosperity and defense of Canada and of the United States are closely linked together.

By development of our natural water power resources, we can look forward with certainty to greater use of electricity in the home, in the factory and on the farm. The national average annual consumption of electricity by domestic consumers has almost doubled in the past ten years. Even with that increase, the national average is only 65 per cent as high as in the Tennessee Valley where electric rates are lower. Increase in the consumption of electricity will mean more comforts on the farms and in city homes. It will mean more jobs, more income and a higher standard of living. We are only on the threshold of an era of electrified homes and mechanical aids to better living. We can encourage this trend by using the bounty of nature in the water power of our rivers.

If we develop the water power of the St. Lawrence River, the United States' share of that power will be available for distribution within a radius of 300 miles. This will include most of New York State and its neighbor states to the East. Public and private agencies will be able to pass on to the consumers in that area all the advantages of this cheap power.

Under the leadership of Governor and later President Roosevelt, the State of New York created the framework of a state power program. I have always been, and still am, in favor of that program.

Under it, the power facilities are to be constructed by the Federal Government and turned over by it to the State of New York. The terms of allocation of costs to the State of New York have been agreed upon in a memorandum of agreement dated February 7, 1933, recommended for execution by the United States Army Corps of Engineers and the Power Authority of the State of New York. This basis of allocation is fair and acceptable.

It has always been understood by the responsible proponents of this development that the water power project should become the property of the State of New York, and that the electric power should be developed and handled by the State. That should continue to be the policy, and I recommend that it be so declared by the Congress.

Any agreement with the State of New York to this end must protect the interests of the United States as well as the interests of neighboring states; and will, of course, have to be submitted for approval by the Congress before it can become effective.

I urge upon the Congress speedy enactment of legislation to accomplish these objectives so that work may start on this great undertaking at the earliest possible time.

HARRY S. TRUMAN

156   Special Message to the Congress on Atomic Energy.
        October 3, 1945

To the Congress of the United States:

Almost two months have passed since the atomic bomb was used against Japan. That bomb did not win the war, but it certainly shortened the war. We know that it saved the lives of untold thousands of American and Allied soldiers who would otherwise have been killed in battle.

The discovery of the means of releasing atomic energy began a new era in the history of civilization. The scientific and industrial knowledge on which this discovery rests does not relate merely to another weapon. It may some day prove to be more revolutionary in the development of human society than the invention of the wheel, the use of metals, or the steam or internal combustion engine.

Never in history has society been confronted with a power so full of potential danger and at the same time so full of promise for the future of man and for the peace of the world.   I think I can express the faith of the American people when I say that we can use the knowledge we have won, not for the devastation of war, but for the future welfare of humanity.

To accomplish that objective we must proceed along two fronts—the domestic and the international.

The first and most urgent step is the determination of our domestic policy for the control, use and development of atomic energy within the United States.

We cannot postpone decisions in this field.   The enormous investment which we made to produce the bomb has given us the two vast industrial plants in Washington and Tennessee, and the many associated works throughout the country.   It has brought together a vast organization of scientists, executives, industrial engineers and skilled workers—a national asset of inestimable value.

The powers which the Congress wisely gave to the Government to wage war were adequate to permit the creation and development of this enterprise as a war project.   Now that our enemies have surrendered, we should take immediate action to provide for the future use of this huge investment in brains and plant.   I am informed that many of the people on whom depend the continued successful operation of the plants and the further development of atomic knowledge, are getting ready to return to their normal pursuits.   In many cases these people are considering leaving the project largely because of uncertainty concerning future national policy in this field.   Prompt action to establish national policy will go a long way towards keeping a strong organization intact.

It is equally necessary to direct future research and to establish control of the basic raw materials essential to the development of this power whether it is to be used for purposes of peace or war.   Atomic force in ignorant or evil hands could inflict untold disaster upon the nation and the world.   Society cannot hope even to protect itself—much less to realize the benefits of the discovery—unless prompt action is taken to guard against the hazards of misuse.

I therefore urge, as a first measure in a program of utilizing our knowledge for the benefit of society, that the Congress enact legislation to fix a policy with respect to our existing plants, and to control all sources of atomic energy and all activities connected with its development and use in the United States.

The legislation should give jurisdiction for these purposes to an Atomic Energy Commission with members appointed by the President with the advice and consent of the Senate.

The Congress should lay down the basic principles for all the activities of the Commission, the objectives of which should be the promotion of the national welfare, securing the national defense, safeguarding world peace and the acquisition of further knowledge concerning atomic energy.

The people of the United States know that the overwhelming power we have developed in this war is due in large measure to American science and American industry, consisting of management and labor. We believe that our science and industry owe their strength to the spirit of free inquiry and the spirit of free enterprise that characterize our country. The Commission, therefore, in carrying out its functions should interfere as little as possible with private research and private enterprise, and should use as much as possible existing institutions and agencies. The observance of this policy is our best guarantee of maintaining the pre-eminence in science and industry upon which our national well-being depends.

All land and mineral deposits owned by the United States which constitute sources of atomic energy, and all stock piles of materials from which such energy may be derived, and all plants or other property of the United States connected with its development and use should be transferred to the supervision and control of the Commission.

The Commission should be authorized to acquire at a fair price, by purchase or by condemnation, any minerals or other materials from which the sources of atomic energy can be derived, and also any land containing such minerals or materials, which are not already owned by the United States.

The power to purchase should include real and personal property outside the limits of the United States.

The Commission should also be authorized to conduct all necessary research, experimentation, and operations for the further development and use of atomic energy for military, industrial, scientific, or medical purposes. In these activities it should, of course, use existing private and public institutions and agencies to the fullest practicable extent.

Under appropriate safeguards, the Commission should also be permitted to license any property available to the Commission for research, development and exploitation in the field of atomic energy. Among other things such licensing should be conditioned of course upon a policy of widespread distribution of peacetime products on equitable terms which will prevent monopoly.

In order to establish effective control and security, it should be declared unlawful to produce or use the substances comprising the sources of atomic energy or to import or export them except under conditions prescribed by the Commission.

Finally, the Commission should be authorized to establish security regulations governing the handling of all information, material and equipment under its jurisdiction. Suitable penalties should be prescribed for violating the security regulations of the Commission or any of the other terms of the Act.

The measures which I have suggested may seem drastic and far-reaching. But the discovery with which we are dealing involves forces of nature too dangerous to fit into any of our usual concepts.

The other phase of the problem is the question of the international control and development of this newly discovered energy.

In international relations as in domestic affairs, the release of atomic energy constitutes a new force too revolutionary to consider in the framework of old ideas. We can no longer rely on the slow progress of time to develop a program of control among nations. Civilization demands that we shall reach at the earliest possible date a satisfactory arrangement for the control of this discovery in order that it may become a powerful and forceful influence towards the maintenance of world peace instead of an instrument of destruction.

Scientific opinion appears to be practically unanimous that the essential theoretical knowledge upon which the discovery is based is already widely known. There is also substantial agreement that foreign research can come abreast of our present theoretical knowledge in time.

The hope of civilization lies in international arrangements looking, if possible, to the renunciation of the use and development of the atomic bomb, and directing and encouraging the use of atomic energy and all future scientific information toward peaceful and humanitarian ends. The difficulties in working out such arrangements are great. The alternative to overcoming these difficulties, however, may be a desperate armament race which might well end in disaster. Discussion of the international problem cannot be safely delayed until the United Nations Organization is functioning and in a position adequately to deal with it.

I therefore propose to initiate discussions, first with our associates in this discovery, Great Britain and Canada, and then with other nations, in an effort to effect agreement on the conditions under which cooperation might replace rivalry in the field of atomic power.

I desire to emphasize that these discussions will not be concerned with disclosures relating to the manufacturing processes leading to the production of the atomic bomb itself. They will constitute an effort to work out arrangements covering the terms under which international collaboration and exchange of scientific information might safely proceed.

The outcome of the discussions will be reported to the Congress as soon as possible, and any resulting agreements requiring Congressional action will be submitted to the Congress.

But regardless of the course of discussions in the international field, I believe it is essential that legislation along the lines I have indicated be adopted as promptly as possible to insure the necessary research in, and development and control of, the production and use of atomic energy.

HARRY S. TRUMAN

NOTE: The Atomic Energy Commission was established by the Atomic Energy Act of 1946 (60 Stat. 755).

157   The President's News Conference of
      October 3, 1945

THE PRESIDENT. [1.]   I want to announce some appointments first:

Watson B. Miller, of Maryland, to be Federal Security Administrator.

Lowell B. Mason, of Illinois, to be on the Federal Trade Commission for an unexpired term from September 25, 1942, succeeding Commissioner March, deceased.

Q. Do you know Commissioner March's full name?

THE PRESIDENT. No, I don't; I can get it for you, Tony.[1]

John F. Sonnett—S-o-n-n-e-t-t—to be Assistant Attorney General, succeeding Francis M. Shea, whose resignation was announced today; he's gone to work for Mr. Jackson over in Europe.

Q. Francis M. Shea?

THE PRESIDENT. Yes; he's the one that resigned, and John F. Sonnett is taking his place.

[2.]   I have a statement here on the Philippines I'm going to read:

"As you know, President Osmeña of the Philippines is in Washington. On Monday, I conferred with him and with the High Commissioner to the Philippines, Mr. McNutt, and the Acting Secretary of the Interior, Mr. Fortas. I propose to confer again with President Osmeña and to formulate a broad program for this government with respect to the Philippines. This program will, of course, reflect the traditional friendship of the people of the United States and of the Philippines, and it will take account of the heroic and loyal conduct of the Filipinos during the war. In preparation for my further conferences with President Osmeña, I have asked Mr. McNutt and Mr. Fortas to consult with the President of the Philippines with respect to all matters of mutual interest.

"At the moment, I want to clarify the question of the date upon which Philippine independence may be expected. Under the statutes now in force, independence is scheduled for July 4, 1946, or sooner if the President of the United States shall so proclaim. There has been wide speculation as to whether a date prior to July 4, 1946, will be fixed.

---

[1] Ernest B. Vaccaro, Associated Press.

367

This speculation has introduced a high degree of uncertainty at a very critical time in Philippine affairs, and has resulted in some confusion in the programs of both the Commonwealth government and United States agencies.

"It would be neither just nor fair to the loyal people of the Philippines who have been our brothers in war as well as in peace, to proclaim their independence until the necessary program for rehabilitation has been worked out and until there has been a determination of the fundamental problems involved in our mutual relationship after independence. Additional time is also required to enable the Philippine government to set its own house in order and to hold a free democratic election.

"To assist in the orderly working out of these problems, I am taking this opportunity to state that I do not intend to consider advancing the proclamation of Philippine independence to a date earlier than July 4, 1946, until the necessary measures which I have outlined have been taken."

I want to be sure that the Filipinos have been properly reconditioned so that when they do become a free and independent nation they can *stand* as a free and independent nation; and we owe that to the Filipinos because they have been our friends in this war.

[3.] I've got a new board—issued an Executive order setting up a new board to replace the existing board to make recommendations on the awarding of medals of merit to civilians who have performed meritorious service in the war. I appointed Judge Owen J. Roberts to be the chairman and Lt. Gen. William Knudsen and Stephen T. Early to be members of that board.

[4.] I sent down to Congress a few minutes ago a message on the atomic bomb, a copy of which will be available to you when you go out. It suggests to Congress that they set up a commission to control the atomic energy development so that it may not become a monopoly, and that the plants which we now have for the creation of atomic energy be maintained and kept in operation, and that further research and development be pursued for the welfare of humanity; and I also informed the Congress that I will send them at a later date a message with regard to the atomic bomb. On this first message the first part has to do with the control of atomic energy for peacetime purposes, and the control of it for wartime use is a matter that will be taken up at a later date.

I am ready for cross-examination.

[5.]   Q. Mr. President, is there anything you can say on the lack of policy on wages?

THE PRESIDENT. I think the only thing I can say—I thought somebody might ask me a question like that—will be to read an extract from an Executive order issued on August 18, 1945, which establishes wage policy. This is part IV; there are three paragraphs of it, and if you will bear with me I will read them to you. It's rather dry:

"1. The National War Labor Board, and such other agencies as may be designated"—

It has been said by a lot of people that there is no wage policy, nationally.

—"by the Director of Economic Stabilization with the approval of the Director of War Mobilization and Reconversion, are authorized to provide that employers may, through collective bargaining with duly certified or recognized representatives of the employees involved or, if there is no such representative, by voluntary action, make wage or salary increases without the necessity of obtaining approval therefor, upon the condition that such increases will not be used in whole or in part as the basis for seeking an increase in price ceilings, or for resisting otherwise justifiable reductions in price ceilings, or, in the case of products or services being furnished under contract with a federal procurement agency, will not increase the costs to the United States.

"2. In addition to the authority to approve increases to correct gross inequities and for other specified purposes, conferred by Section 2 of Title II of Executive Order 9250, the National War Labor Board or other designated agency is hereby authorized to approve, without regard to the limitations contained in any other orders or directives, such increases as may be necessary to correct maladjustments or inequities which would interfere with the effective transition to a peacetime economy; provided, however, that in dispute cases this additional authority shall not be used to direct increases to be effective as of a date prior to the date of this order.

"Where the National War Labor Board or other designated agency, or the Price Administrator, shall have reason to believe that a proposed wage or salary increase will require a change in the price ceiling of the commodity or services involved, such proposed increase, if approved by the National War Labor Board or such other designated agency under the authority of this section shall become effective only if also approved by the Director of Economic Stabilization.

"3. Officials charged with the settlement of labor disputes in accordance with the terms of Executive Order 9017 and Section 7 of the War Labor Disputes Act shall consider that labor disputes which would interrupt work contributing to the production of military supplies or interfere with effective transition to a peacetime economy are disputes which interrupt work contributing to the effective prosecution of the war."

That has been in effect ever since August 18, and I think is a definite labor policy—wage policy, I mean.

Q. Mr. President, that's a wage policy put into effect during the war, and——

THE PRESIDENT. No, August 18.

Q. What date did you say?

THE PRESIDENT. August 18, 1945. And that was set up with the approval of the Secretary of Labor, the labor organizations, and of industry. They all sat right here and approved that.

Q. You call attention to it because it's still——

THE PRESIDENT. It's still the policy of the Government; that's sure.

[6.] Q. Mr. President, anything to say about the London conference?

THE PRESIDENT. No, I haven't; Mr. Byrnes will be here in a short time, and we'll let him make the necessary report.

[7.] Q. What do you think of the Russian renewal of their demand for a four-power control commission for Japan?

THE PRESIDENT. I only know what I've seen in the papers; I've had no official notice, and I'll have to discuss it with Mr. Byrnes.

[8.] Q. Do you have any comment on the situation in Argentina?

THE PRESIDENT. No, I haven't.

[9.] Q. Mr. President, have you received any request from the British to send troops to Palestine?

THE PRESIDENT. No. I haven't.

[10.] Q. Mr. President, there seems to be a dispute about the use of funds for child-care centers; have you taken notice of that?

THE PRESIDENT. Yes, I have extended it to October 31, and I am considering seriously sending up a request to Congress that they extend it to March 31.[1] But that will require several million dollars.

[11.] Q. Has there been any request for this Government to assume joint responsibility with the people of Great Britain in the Palestine situation?

THE PRESIDENT. No.

[12.] Q. Have you talked with Ed Pauley about his future activities?

THE PRESIDENT. No, I haven't; I haven't seen Mr. Pauley for some time. He said he would come to see me.

[13.] Q. We hear from London that the United Nations has decided to locate within the United States; have you any particular sites in mind?

THE PRESIDENT. No, I haven't. I do have a message from Mr. Stettinius that they did vote to locate the headquarters in the United States, and that China and Australia favor San Francisco. He pointed out there were other available locations in the United States. The specific message will be discussed later. I just got it before this conference.

[14.] Q. Is it your intention to keep the Coast Guard under the Navy?

THE PRESIDENT. It will be returned to the Treasury at the proper time.

[15.] Q. Can you tell us anything about your conference with Mr. Mollison?

THE PRESIDENT. I appointed him to be judge of the Court of Customs.

Q. The nomination gone up?

THE PRESIDENT. Yes, it went up at noon.

Q. We didn't get it.

---

[1] See Item 159.

THE PRESIDENT. It was supposed to be in your hands. I thought I would be repeating it.

[16.] Q. It has been about a week since your conference with the Democratic Ways and Means Committee, and nothing has happened on the compensation bill. Are you thinking of——

THE PRESIDENT. I think if you give the Ways and Means Committee time, they'll do something about it.

[17.] Q. During Mr. Mackenzie King's call Sunday was there any consideration of the atomic bomb?

THE PRESIDENT. We discussed every subject in which Canada and the United States are interested, but I am not at liberty to make any statement.

[18.] Q. Mr. President, in your message about the atomic bomb do you have any recommendation about mineral lands not owned by the Government?

THE PRESIDENT. There's a recommendation that a commission be given power to purchase all such land.

Reporter: Thank you, Mr. President.

THE PRESIDENT. You are entirely welcome.

NOTE: President Truman's twenty-eighth news conference was held in his office at the White House at 4:05 p.m. on Wednesday, October 3, 1945.

158 Statement by the President Concerning Government Operation of Petroleum Refineries Closed by Strikes. *October 4, 1945*

I REGRET that it has become necessary for the Government to take over the plants of twenty-six oil producing and refining companies which have been shut down by strikes. It has become necessary to take this action in order to maintain adequate oil reserves for the needs of our armed forces.

During the past two weeks some fifty petroleum refineries, together with a number of related transportation and distribution facilities, have been shut down due to work stoppages. The shut down daily capacity amounts to 1,675,000 barrels, representing about one-third of the total refinery capacity of the Nation.

The plants remaining in operation are insufficient to produce enough petroleum to supply both the direct military requirements and the minimum essential war supporting activities on the home front. So critical has the supply situation become that essential military operations are already jeopardized. Throughout the Nation, serious shortages are developing which would, if not corrected immediately, impair essential industrial and agricultural production, and all forms of transportation.

Oil is so vital to the continuing military operation, and so essential to production for the armed services and national security at home, that we must move without further delay to protect our petroleum supply positions. The public interest, in an emergency of this character, transcends the interests of any group.

There is no other way, except by the action taken today, to prevent our armed forces from suffering through lack of necessary oil.

Nothing will be permitted to stand in the way of the adequate supplies of *any* kind for our armed forces and for their proper redeployment and demobilization.

NOTE: The text of Executive Order 9639 "Authorizing the Secretary of the Navy To Take Possession of and Operate Certain Plants and Facilities Used in the Transportation, Refining and Processing of Petroleum and Petroleum Products" (3 CFR, 1943–1948 Comp., p. 440) was released with the President's statement.

159 Letter to the President of the Senate and to the Speaker of the House of Representatives Concerning Federal Assistance for Child Care Centers. *October 4, 1945*

Dear Mr. ————:

In my communication of September 5, 1945, I transmitted for the consideration of the Congress proposed rescissions of portions of several war-related appropriations, including appropriations available to the Federal Works Agency under the heading "Office of the Administrator: War public works (community facilities)" to the extent of $19,115,000.

This item included funds that had been appropriated by the Congress for war-time child care centers on the understanding with the Federal Works Agency that when the need for women in war production and essential supporting services ended, Federal funds would be withdrawn. Therefore, my communication of September fifth was based upon that understanding.

On August twenty-seventh I requested the Federal Works Administrator to present to the Congress the problem which had arisen where local communities were not able to continue needed child care centers for children whose mothers are the wives or widows of servicemen. The Federal Works Administrator now advises me that the appropriate Committees of the Congress do not believe it feasible to enact special legislation to take care of this problem for this particular group of mothers.

Although some communities have already arranged with local funds to operate centers for children of working mothers, the majority of them have not yet completed such arrangements. In some communities, State or local laws or other limitations make it impossible for them to assume this responsibility by October thirty-first, the presently scheduled date for the termination of Federal assistance.

The reconversion of the war-time child care program to peacetime operations under which the local communities would assume the financial responsibility requires Federal assistance for a few more months. This extension of time would give working mothers more time to make other arrangements for the care of their children and would give local communities additional time to provide the necessary State or local funds.

Included in the amount which I have heretofore recommended for rescission is an item of $7,000,000 for service projects. If this amount is not repealed, the Federal Works Agency would be able to make Federal funds available for the operation of needed child care centers until March 1, 1946. I therefore now recommend that the amount of the proposed rescission for "War public works (community facilities)" be reduced to $12,115,000.

Yours very truly,

HARRY S. TRUMAN

NOTE: This is the text of identical letters addressed to the Honorable Kenneth McKellar, President pro tempore of the Senate, and to the Honorable Sam Rayburn, Speaker of the House of Representatives.

160 Remarks at the Presentation of the Congressional Medal of Honor to Fourteen Members of the Navy and Marine Corps. *October 5, 1945*

THIS IS ONE of the pleasant duties of the President of the United States. These are the young men who represent us in our fighting forces.

They said we were soft, that we would not fight, that we could not win. We are not a warlike nation. We do not go to war for gain or for territory; we go to war for principles, and we produce young men like these. I think I told every one of them that I would rather have that medal, the Congressional Medal of Honor, than to be President of the United States.

We fought a good fight. We've won two great victories. We're facing another fight, and we must win the victory in that. That is a fight for a peaceful world, a fight so we won't have to do this again, so we won't have to maim the flower of our young men, and bury them. Now let us go forward and win that fight, as we have won these other two victories, and this war will not have been in vain.

Thank you.

NOTE: The President presented the medals in a ceremony held at 10:30 a.m. on the South Lawn at the White House. The citations were read by Vice Adm. L. E. Denfeld.

A list of the recipients, in order of presentation, follows: Lt. Col. Gregory Boyington, USMCR; Lt. Comdr. George L. Street, USN; Maj. Louis H. Wilson, USMC; Capt. Joseph J. McCarthy, USMCR; 2nd Lt. Arthur J. Jackson, USMC; Sgt. William G. Harrell, USMCR; Pharmacist's Mate George E. Wahlen, USNR; Cpl. Richard E. Bush, USMCR; Cpl. Douglas T. Jacobson, USMCR; Cpl. Hershel W. Williams, USMCR; Hospital Apprentice First Class Robert Eugene Bush, USNR; Pfc. Jacklyn H. Lucas, USMCR; Pvt. Franklin E. Sigler, USMCR; and Pvt. Wilson D. Watson, USMCR.

161   Citation Accompanying the Distinguished Service Medal Presented to Admiral Chester W. Nimitz.
October 5, 1945

THE PRESIDENT of the United States takes pleasure in presenting the Gold Star in lieu of the Third Distinguished Service Medal to

FLEET ADMIRAL CHESTER WILLIAM NIMITZ, UNITED STATES NAVY

for service as set forth in the following

CITATION

For exceptionally meritorious service to the Government of the United States as Commander in Chief, United States Pacific Fleet and Pacific Ocean Areas, from June 1944, to August 1945. Initiating the final phase in the battle for victory in the Pacific, Fleet Admiral Nimitz attacked the Marianas, invading Saipan, inflicting a decisive defeat in the Japanese Fleet in the First Battle of the Philippines and capturing Guam and Tinian. In vital continuing operations, his Fleet Forces isolated the enemy-held bastions of the Central and Eastern Carolines and secured in quick succession Peleliu, Angaur and Ulithi. With reconnaissance of the main beaches on Leyte effected, approach channels cleared and opposition neutralized in joint operations to reoccupy the Philippines, the challenge by powerful task forces of the Japanese Fleet resulted in a historic victory in the three-phased Battle for Leyte Gulf, October 24 to 26, 1944. Accelerating the intensity of aerial offensive by pressure exerted at every hostile strong point, Fleet Admiral Nimitz culminated long-range strategy by successful amphibious assault on Iwo Jima and Okinawa. A wise, steadfast and indomitable leader, Fleet Admiral Nimitz, by his daring strategy and his faith in the courage and skill of the officers and men under his command, finally placed representative forces of the United States Navy in the harbor of Tokyo for the formal capitulation of the Japanese Empire. Through his mastery of naval warfare, his strategical skill, his sound judgment and his inspiring leadership, he demonstrated the highest qualities of a naval officer and rendered services of the greatest distinction to his country.

HARRY S. TRUMAN

NOTE: The President read the citation to Admiral Nimitz and presented him with the award in a ceremony held in the Rose Garden at the White House. Although the ceremony called for the Gold Star, the President also pinned the Distinguished Service Medal on Admiral Nimitz.

162   Letter Accepting Resignation of J. A. Krug as Chairman of the War Production Board.   *October* 5, 1945

[Released October 5, 1945. Dated October 4, 1945]

My dear Cap:

I have your letter in which you request to be relieved of your responsibilities as Chairman of the War Production Board. It is with regret that I accede to your wishes and accept your resignation as Chairman, effective at the close of business on November 3, 1945.

You have earned the thanks of the Nation—indeed of the United Nations—for an epic achievement in industrial production. During the critical months which have ensued since you assumed duties, first as Acting Chairman, and now for more than a year as Chairman, the results have been little short of miraculous. The prodigious tasks which have been performed by American industry under your leadership are reflected in the capitulation of our enemies in unconditional surrender.

For the magnificent work that you have done I desire to express the Nation's gratitude. As we go into the reconversion period, we shall like to think that we can call upon you from time to time for the counsel which you can give us out of your great experience.

Very sincerely yours,

HARRY S. TRUMAN

NOTE: Mr. Krug served as Acting Chairman of the War Production Board from August 27, 1944, to October 1, 1944, and then as Chairman through November 3, 1945. His letter of resignation, dated September 25, 1945, was released with the President's reply.

163   Remarks at the Pemiscot County Fair, Caruthersville,
Missouri. *October 7, 1945*

*Jim Ahern, my friends of Southeast Missouri, Northeast Arkansas,
Tennessee, Kentucky, and Illinois:*

It is a pleasure to be here today. Once again I am your guest at the
American Legion Fair. It is a customary procedure for me. This is
number twelve. I came down here the first time, if I remember correctly, in 1934. At that time I was the Presiding Judge of the County
Court of Jackson County, and a candidate for United States Senator.
The next time I came I was the United States Senator from Missouri,
and for nine times I came down here as the Senator from Missouri—
because I liked to come. I have almost as many friends in this part of
the great State of Missouri as I have in Jackson County, and that is
really saying something.

Last year I came as the candidate for Vice President of the United
States. Mr. Roosevelt and myself were the candidates on the Democratic ticket. We won that election, as you know, and I settled down
as President of the Senate and its Presiding Officer to happily enjoy a
4-year term.

Then suddenly, like a bolt out of the blue, Mr. Roosevelt passed
away—a great leader, a great humanitarian, the greatest of our war
Presidents. And the greatest responsibility that ever has fallen to a
human being in the history of the world fell to me.

In my first address to the Congress, after that happened, I explained
to them that I had not sought that responsibility, nor had I sought the
honor which goes with that responsibility. But I have been a public
servant in one phase or another for the past 30 years, and I have never
shirked a job. I shall not shirk this one.

I told the Members of Congress and the Nation that if we were to
be successful—and we will be, undoubtedly—it would require the
cooperation not only of the Congress but of the country as a whole, for
us to accomplish the things which Almighty God intended this great
Nation to accomplish.

Just to rehearse for your benefit a few of the things that have happened since April 12, 1945—just about 6 months ago. The San Francisco Conference was convened on the 25th day of April—just 13 days after I was sworn in as President of the United States. That conference was successful, and just about 4 months after it was convened, the United States Senate approved the Charter of the United Nations by an overwhelming majority. There were only two Senators against it, and I never did understand why they were against it. At any rate, the United States entered on an entirely new development of its foreign policy.

Some 3 months after that I went to Berlin to meet with the heads of the Governments of Russia, Great Britain, and the United States, in order to discuss the world outlook for the coming peace. The deliberations of that conference will be felt for generations in the final peace.

Just a little less than a month after I became President, that is, 26 days after I was inaugurated, the Axis powers in Europe folded up. On the 12th day of August, Japan folded up. In the meantime, one of the most earth-shaking discoveries in the history of the world was made—the development of atomic energy was discovered. That discovery was used in the last war effort against Japan, and the effect of that atomic bomb is too terrible for contemplation. But we have only begun on the atomic energy program. That great force, if properly used by this country of ours, and by the world at large, can become the greatest boon that humanity has ever had. It can create a world which, in my opinion, will be the happiest world that the sun has ever shone upon.

Now I am reminding you of all these things which have taken place in the last short 6 months to impress upon you the terrible responsibilities of the President of the United States. The President of the United States is your President. I am telling you just what his responsibilities are, because you are my friends and I think you understand the difficulties which I face.

Now it is just as necessary to have the cooperation of every branch, and every member of every part of the Government of the United States, from the constable in this township to the President of the Senate. We must have that cooperation. We must go forward—we are going forward.

We understand that the road to peace is just as difficult and maybe more difficult than was the road to victory during the war. And the reason for that difficulty is that we all distinctly understand that after every war there is bound to be a letdown, there is bound to be a change of attitude, there are bound to be a great many of us who say, "Oh well, I don't have to work any more. I don't have to take any interest in the welfare of my Government any more." We can't have that attitude. We must cooperate now as we never have before in the history of this country. We have the greatest production machine that the world has ever seen. We conclusively proved that free government is the most efficient government in every emergency. We conclusively proved that, by our victories over Germany and Italy and Japan and their allies. In order to prove to the world that our reconversion program can be handled just as efficiently, and that our tremendous production machine can be operated for peace as well as for war, we must all get in and push.

That doesn't require anything in the world but plain understanding among ourselves. That requires the cooperation of management and labor and the farmers, and every storekeeper, and every man who has an interest in the Government of the United States. And by showing that we ourselves know where we are going and why, we can show the rest of the world the road to liberty and to peace. We are not anywhere near stalled on that road. We are only beginning to travel it.

We are going to have difficulties. You can't do anything worthwhile without difficulties. No man who ever accomplishes anything can expect to do it without making mistakes. The man who never does anything never makes any mistakes. We may make mistakes. We may have difficulties, but I am asking you to exercise that admonition which you will find in the Gospels, and which Christ told us was the way to get along in the world: Do by your neighbor as you would be done by.

And that applies to you, and you, just as it applies to Great Britain and France and China and Russia and Czechoslovakia, and Poland and Brazil. When the nations decide that the welfare of the world is much more important than any individual gain which they themselves can make at the expense of another nation, then we can take this discovery which we have made and make this world the greatest place the sun has ever shone upon.

Now, in 1938, I stood on this platform right here and explained to you that our then isolationism would eventually lead to war. I made that speech after President Roosevelt made his speech at Chicago in 1937, in which he warned the world that we were approaching another world war.

We can't stand another global war. We can't ever have another war, unless it is total war, and that means the end of our civilization as we know it. We are not going to do that. We are going to accept that Golden Rule, and we are going forward to meet our destiny which I think Almighty God intended us to have.

And we are going to be the leaders.

Thank you very much.

NOTE: The President spoke at 4:30 p.m. at the Fair grounds. His opening words "Jim Ahern" referred to James T. Ahern, president of the American Legion Fair Association.

164 The President's News Conference at Tiptonville, Tennessee. *October 8, 1945*

[1.] Q. Mr. President, you made a statement, as near as I can remember, in your speech at the fair, that when the nations of the world learn to put total world progress ahead of individual gain at the expense of other states, then we could put this great discovery of the release of atomic energy to work, to make the world a better place to live in. Would it be too long a "bone" as to interpret your remark there as meaning that the atomic secret would not be shared, unless and until we had positive assurance that the world had progressed to that point?

THE PRESIDENT. No, that would not be true, for this reason. The scientific knowledge that resulted in the atomic bomb is worldwide knowledge already. It is only the know-how of putting that knowledge practically to work that is our secret; just the same as know-how in the construction of the B–29, and the plane that is following the B–29, the greatest long-distance bomber in the world, and the know-how to make automobiles by mass production, and anything else. So far as the scientific knowledge is concerned, all the scientists know the answer, but how to put it to work practically is our secret.

Q. What I am getting at is, would it apply to letting them in on the know-how?

THE PRESIDENT. Well, I don't think it would do any good to let them in on the know-how, because I don't think they could do it, anyway. You would have to have the industrial plant and our engineering ability to do the job, as well as the scientific knowledge, and there isn't any reason for trying to keep the scientific knowledge covered up, because all the great scientists know it in every country; but the practical know-how is our ability to do the job.

Q. Mr. President, what you mean——

THE PRESIDENT. That is our job. If they catch up with us on that, they will have to do it on their own hook, just as we did.

Q. You mean, then, that we will not share that knowledge with our allies?

THE PRESIDENT. Just the same as we haven't shared our engineering knowledge, or any of our engineering secrets. But so far as the scientific knowledge is concerned, they all know that, anyway.

Q. But so far as the bomb secret is concerned, we will not share that?

THE PRESIDENT. Not the know-how of putting it together, let's put it that way.

Mr. Ross: Are you talking on or off the record, Mr. President?

THE PRESIDENT. I am talking *on* the record, Charlie.

Mr. Ross: You understand that the President is not to be directly quoted, all you men who are not familiar with the rules.

Q. Mr. President, isn't Great Britain also in on that know-how?

THE PRESIDENT. Great Britain and Canada.

Q. Have they——

THE PRESIDENT. They are our partners.

Q. ——have they also agreed not to let the information out?

THE PRESIDENT. It hasn't been discussed with them, because we have all the information so far as the practical know-how is concerned, but I

am sure they would agree. You see, Great Britain started the program
by the expenditure of about $100 million in the beginning; and when
we got into the war, it was decided that it was such a great program
and required the expenditure of so much money that nobody could do
it but us, and that was true. We spent more than $2 billion in creating
it.

Q. Isn't it true that they couldn't do it themselves, and neither could
Canada?

THE PRESIDENT. No, they couldn't.

Q. Who are you going to name to conduct conversations with
Britain and Canada?

THE PRESIDENT. The Secretary of State.

Q. Will you name any special advisers for him?

THE PRESIDENT. No. That's what I have the Secretary of State for.

[2.] Q. Mr. President, on the general foreign situation, are you
disturbed at all, or how do you feel about the apparent failure of the
London conference to produce——

THE PRESIDENT. I don't think it's a failure. I think it was one step
in arriving at a final conclusion. I am not in the slightest alarmed at
the world situation. It will work out. Just as much as the domestic
situation will work out in the long run.

Mr. Ross: Mr. President, you might want to say a word, in addition
to what you said yesterday, about world leadership in the application
of the Golden Rule.

THE PRESIDENT. Well, the world leadership I was referring to was
leadership in the application of the Golden Rule. I did not want to
assume that we would automatically take leadership in every field, but
I think we can take leadership in that thing, that we would treat the
other nations as we would like to be treated.

[3.] Q. What do you think accounts for this wave of work stoppages and general labor unrest?

THE PRESIDENT. Reaction. Reaction of the—from the tremendous
war effort. Everybody feels like letting down, and that has been the
case after every war we have ever fought, the Revolution, the War of
1812, the Mexican War, War Between the States, Spanish-American

War, the First World War, and this one. And this one, of course, is much greater than any of the rest of them, and we are going to have comparatively greater difficulty in getting people to realize that the readjustment job is their job. And they will finally realize it. I am not worried about it at all.

Q. Mr. President, there has been a reduction in take-home pay in most—in many cases. Isn't that a part of it?

THE PRESIDENT. To some extent. Doesn't make any difference, because it would be about the same whether there was a reduction in pay or not. Well, that is one of the contributing causes.

[4.] Q. Mr. President, if we can return to the atomic bomb subject for just a minute, sir——

THE PRESIDENT. Sure.

Q. ——have any of these other countries that are our allies asked for the secret of the know-how?

THE PRESIDENT. No.

Q. They have not?

THE PRESIDENT. No.

Q. Mr. President, in that connection, I have read that one of the causes for the lack of accord between this country and Russia—or on Russia's part, at least—grows out of the fact that we have the atomic bomb, and Russia doesn't.

THE PRESIDENT. It isn't true—it isn't true at all. The difficulty, I think, is a matter of understanding between us and Russia. There has always been a difficulty, principally because we don't speak the same language. It is a most difficult matter to translate the meaning of what I am saying right now into Russian, so it will mean the same thing in Russian as it means in English. The same thing is true when you translate Russian into English. When I was at the conference with Stalin at Berlin, he had an interpreter and I had one, and it took the four of us to be sure that we each understood the meaning of the other; and when we did, there was no difficulty in arriving at an agreement.

Q. Mr. President, in connection with that last question on the atomic bomb subject again, when will you send your message down to Congress?

THE PRESIDENT. On the foreign situation?

Q. On the atomic bomb. You remember you said at your last conference you were going to send one on the international phase of the bomb——

THE PRESIDENT. That's right, but I am not ready to do that yet, so I can't make any specific statement on the subject. I will do it when I get ready. I will tell you about it.

[5.] Q. Mr. President, there has been a lot written about your making some sort of direct appeal to management and labor to get together, along the lines of the cooperation you spoke about at the fair?

THE PRESIDENT. I made it yesterday.

Q. Is that all? I see.

THE PRESIDENT. That's all. I wouldn't say that's all, but I don't want to answer the question.

Q. Thank you, sir.

[6.] Q. Mr. President, not for use now, but when you do make your speech at Gilbertsville—we have been reading the text of the speech today, preparing for our advance stories—are you retreating at all from your idea of the big basic regional power authorities——

THE PRESIDENT. No, I am not.

Q. ——directed by the Federal Government?

THE PRESIDENT. I am not retreating at all. I think if you read the speech carefully, it is consistent and stays with the program as outlined in my New Orleans speech in 1944. You were there, Eddie.[1]

Q. Yes, sir.

[7.] Q. You described this reaction from the war as a letdown, and you said you are not terribly worried about it. Can you elaborate on that, and tell us what you foresee in the working out of this thing? There is tremendous interest in it.

THE PRESIDENT. Well, I think we are facing the greatest era in the history of the world, and I don't think we need be alarmed at the difficulties that will be in the way of arriving at the consummation of that era. It doesn't worry me, because there hasn't been a war in which we fought that we finally haven't come out in much better shape than

---

[1] Edward B. Lockett, Time Magazine.

we were previous to the period, and I don't think there is going to be any change from that.

[8.] Q. Mr. President, if you don't mind my going back to the speech——

THE PRESIDENT. Shoot.

Q. ——when you said that in each case you think the local people—in your speech I am speaking about the next one—should make the final decision, I didn't know whether you were speaking of the decision as to whether greater emphasis should be put on flood control, or power, or other things, or on the decision of who would have responsibility for the operation——

THE PRESIDENT. Well, being from Missouri, I think always of the Missouri River as a common example. That river has four different projects, each one of which is important in a certain section of that river. The river from Sioux City, Iowa, to St. Louis—or from Omaha to St. Louis, if you want to make it easier—is interested in flood control first, and then in navigation. From the mouth of the Platte River in Nebraska up to Montana, they are interested in irrigation, and when you get to the "clear" sections of the river, in power. Those four things will have to be coordinated, and each section of the river developed for the benefit of the people of the river in those various sections, but there isn't any reason why an authority couldn't do that.

Q. Including TVA?

THE PRESIDENT. That's right.

Q. Just a question of emphasis?

THE PRESIDENT. That's right.

Q. Your idea is that these other developments in the country should be patterned along the lines of the TVA?

THE PRESIDENT. I think so. I think it has been very successful. The Columbia River, I think, can easily be developed along the lines of the TVA, because it's the same sort of river—it's a "clear" river, if you know what I mean. It doesn't carry a lot of silt.

Q. In other words, there were seven other regional authorities, which I believe Mr. Roosevelt proposed;——

THE PRESIDENT. I think so, yes.

Q. ——and you were pretty much in accord with that at the time, as I remember?

THE PRESIDENT. That's right.

[9.] Q. Mr. President, to return to the original question, as I get your reply, there is nothing on the horizon, or foreseeable in the immediate future that would influence your administration to give away the engineering know-how to any country?

THE PRESIDENT. We never have done that.

Q. That is what I understand.

Q. Is anybody in position to use that know-how, if we offered it to them?

THE PRESIDENT. No. That is the best answer.

Q. At some future time, Mr. President, wouldn't Russia be able to use it?

THE PRESIDENT. Your guess is as good as mine on that. I can't answer that. You will have to go there and take a look around. I have never been there.

Q. Are you going there? [*Laughter*]

THE PRESIDENT. No, Smitty,[1] I am not.

Q. Said he, hopefully! [*More laughter*]

THE PRESIDENT. I would like very much to go, and to see Russia as it is, for my own information; but, of course, there isn't a chance of my getting to do that. I think Russia has been badly misrepresented in this country, as we have been badly misrepresented in Russia. If there is complete understanding, there wouldn't be very many difficulties between us, because Russia's interests and ours do not clash, and never have. We have always been friends, and I hope we always will be.

Q. Are there more difficulties, Mr. President, than merely a question of expenditure of the large sums of money in the development of the know-how of the atomic bomb?

THE PRESIDENT. Well, it's the engineering know-how, and it's the scientific knowledge, the practical use. That is the only difficulty there is.

---

[1] Merriman Smith, United Press Associations.

Q. Is it a matter of resources also?

THE PRESIDENT. Yes.

Q. Mineral resources?

THE PRESIDENT. Resources and industrial plant, principally.

[10.] Q. Mr. President, you were asked at a White House press conference one day if the meeting in Berlin was the last of the Big Three meetings, as I remember; and you said you didn't know at that time.

THE PRESIDENT. I don't know yet.

Q. You don't know? That story keeps popping up, particularly from London, saying that there is another Big Three meeting in the wind.

THE PRESIDENT. I don't know. Your guess is as good as mine. I am not in on the inside. [*Laughter*]

Q. You can't write all the copy.

THE PRESIDENT. No, I can't. That's the truth. I am telling you the truth.

Q. Mr. President, how far would you go into the future on that phase of it—not having a meeting now, or in the near future?

THE PRESIDENT. Well, I can't go into it because I don't know what the developments will be. If a Big Three meeting would be necessary to clarify the program, I would not stand in the way of a Big Three meeting. In fact, we had a very successful one in Berlin. At least, *I* thought it was a successful one.

Q. In other words, if things—a Big Three meeting would help understanding, we would have it?

THE PRESIDENT. Certainly we would have it. That's the best answer. But I see no reason for one in the immediate future.

Reporter: Well, thank you, Mr. President.

NOTE: President Truman's twenty-ninth news conference was held on the porch of Linda Lodge on Reelfoot Lake, near Tiptonville, Tenn., at 8:15 p.m. on Monday, October 8, 1945.

165   Address and Remarks at the Dedication of the Kentucky
      Dam at Gilbertsville, Kentucky.   *October* 10, 1945

Ladies and gentlemen:

Nine years ago the first dam of the Tennessee Valley Authority—
the Norris Dam on the Clinch River—was dedicated by my illustrious
predecessor—Franklin D. Roosevelt.   At the very start of his Presidency,
he had the great vision and foresight to recommend and encourage the
comprehensive development of this entire great Valley.

It is now a matter of great pride to me to dedicate the sixteenth great
structure built by the TVA—the Kentucky Dam.   The system of dams
across the Tennessee now puts under the control of man a whole vast
river—and harnesses it to do his work.   This has not yet happened on
any other river.   The completion of this dam marks a new high point
in modern pioneering in America.

Nine years ago TVA was a highly controversial subject.   Today it is
no longer an experiment, but a demonstration.   By all except a small
minority it is now regarded as a great American accomplishment, of
which all of us are proud.

Here in this great valley American enterprise and courage and skill
have come through again with a genuine achievement.   The TVA does
not belong to the people of the Tennessee Valley alone.   It belongs to
all the United States.   And indeed, it has inspired regional resource
development all over the world.   Distinguished observers from more
than fifty countries have come to this historic American Valley.   They
came here to study what has been done.   They went away to try to
adapt to their own regions the lessons that have been learned here from
actual experience.

As a Senator I was always a strong supporter of the TVA.   And I can
say to you that I have never had occasion to regret my support of the
TVA and of the idea it represents.   Its record has fully justified the
hopes and the confidence of its old friends.

But it is more than dams and locks and chemical plants and power
lines.   It is an important experiment in democracy.   In it, administrative methods have been devised which bring the people and their Fed-

389

eral Government closer together—not in Washington, but right where the people live. Here in this Valley there has been firmly established the basic principle of development of resources on an autonomous regional basis.

Why has TVA succeeded so well? Why does it have the esteem of the people of this Valley, and attract the attention of other regions of America, and of the entire world? To me the answer is clear—TVA is just plain commonsense. It is commonsense hitched up to modern science and good management. And that's about all there is to it.

Instead of going at the river piecemeal with a dam here and a dam there, the river was treated as a whole. The dams were all designed so that they would fit together as a unit and in that way get the most service out of the river for mankind.

Consider Kentucky Dam itself. This dam will hold back four million acre feet of flood water from the lower Ohio and Mississippi Rivers. The people behind the levees on those rivers know how much that will mean to them in protection from disaster. When the danger of flood is past, those flood waters are not to be wasted. They will be put through the water wheels here at the dam to produce great quantities of electricity. That electricity will rush to serve the people of the Valley, their homes and farms and industries.

Kentucky Dam also provides a deep-water, navigable channel 183 miles long. The other TVA dams carry that reliable deep water channel all the way to Knoxville in east Tennessee, 650 miles away. As a result, the South and the Middle West of this Nation are now connected by water transportation. The benefits of this dam go not only to the Tennessee Valley; they go to Saint Paul and Minneapolis, to New Orleans and Memphis, to Saint Louis and Kansas City, to Omaha and Sioux City—to all the communities in the great Mississippi Valley that are served by our inland waterways.

In addition to power and flood control and navigation, there is recreation. TVA has joined with the various States and local communities in the development of great lakes here in the South. Here we have boating, fishing, and hunting where thousands upon thousands of people in the Tennessee Valley and the Middle West may enjoy themselves.

As President Roosevelt said when he first recommended the creation of the Tennessee Valley Authority in April of 1933:

". . . The usefulness of the entire Tennessee River . . . transcends mere power development; it enters the wide fields of flood control, soil erosion, afforestation, elimination from agricultural use of marginal lands, and distribution and diversification of industry."

His prophecy has been fulfilled, for in the TVA the Congress has provided for a tying together of all the things that go to make up a well rounded economic development.

It is easy to see that most of these commonsense principles can be applied to other valleys, and I have already recommended to the Congress that a start be made in that direction. Careful planning and commonsense development can convert the idle and wasting resources of other valleys into jobs and better living.

No two valleys are exactly alike, of course. For that reason, the details of just how this region or that region should be developed are matters that require study and judgment in each particular case. The procedure in each valley may have to be a little different. The details of administration and control may have to be different. But the underlying commonsense principles of this development here in the Tennessee Valley can provide guidance and counsel to the people in other regions who likewise aspire to put their resources to the greatest use.

Let me emphasize that in the last analysis such development is a matter for the people themselves to decide. Here in this Valley, State and local agencies, public and private, have joined with TVA in a two-way partnership. This was a natural result of the policy of regional decentralization. That same policy ought to be followed in the other river valleys as regional agencies are created by the Congress and set to work.

We must continue all over the United States to wage war against flood and drought. Our vast store of natural resources can be made to serve us in peace with the same efficiency as they did in war. We should exercise our commonsense, go ahead, and continue to get the job done.

Much has already been done in the past 12 years on river development in other parts of the country—on the Columbia and Colorado, on the Missouri, on the rivers of the Central Valley of California. They are all designed to make the rivers and their generous bounty serve instead of injuring mankind.

Waters are now being harnessed and changed into electricity—electricity which has helped supply the weapons of victory in war—electricity which can be used to improve the standards of living and comfort and efficiency in the farms and homes of thousands of American families. Waters are now making crops grow on land where recently there was only desert dust.

The valleys of America await their full development. The time has come—now that materials and manpower are more plentiful—to press forward. The days of the pioneer are not dead. The development of our natural resources calls for men of courage, of vision, of endurance, just as in the pioneering days of old.

The Nation, I am sure, is determined to march forward. We will not listen to the whispers of the timid, that dreams like those of the Tennessee Valley are impossible to accomplish. In the great valleys of America there is a challenge to all that is best in our tradition. Ahead of us lies a great adventure in building even stronger the foundations of our beloved country. America will not hesitate to meet that challenge.

[*Informal remarks at the conclusion of the address*]

Now I want to say to you how very happy and how glad I am to be your guest here today. I am particularly glad because Senator Barkley and Congressman Gregory informed me that people always turn out like this for them when they come home. Barkley whispered to me coming over here that if people keep treating him like this, there is no possible way for him to retire from public life. I hope that time will never come, because Barkley is a good public servant.

As for Congressman Gregory, I had the pleasure of giving him his first plane ride the other day. He said he didn't like riding in a plane. A lot of people are averse to riding in a plane, even my wife hates to ride in a plane; but after I got Gregory aboard, he confessed that if he was going to get his neck broken, he would just as soon break his neck with Barkley and me as anybody he knew.

I hope that the development of this great Valley here will result in the development of our other river valleys along the same line. You know, our resources have barely been touched. Some of our natural resources—lumber, for instance—have been exhausted by senseless deforestation. We are trying to remedy that situation now by reforestation.

This great development has proven conclusively that a free people can do anything that is necessary for the welfare of the human race as a whole. We created the greatest production machine in the history of the world. We made that machine operate, to the disaster of the dictators. Now then, we want to keep that machine operating. We must keep that machine operating. We have just discovered the source of the sun's power—atomic energy; that is, we have found out how to turn it loose. We had to turn it loose in the beginning for destruction. We are not going to use it for destruction any more, I hope. But that tremendous source of energy can create for us the greatest age in the history of the world if we are sensible enough to put it to that use and to no other. I think we are going to do just that. I think our Allies are going to cooperate with us in peace, just as we cooperated with them in war.

I think we can look forward to the greatest age in history, and I have said that every time I have had an opportunity to address anybody. The greatest age in history is upon us. We must assume that responsibility. We are going to assume it, and every one of you, and all of us, are going to get in and work for the welfare of the world in peace, just as we worked for the welfare of the world in war. That is absolutely essential and necessary.

We are having our little troubles now—a few of them. They are not serious—just a blowup after the letdown from war. You remember what a terrible time we had the first two days after the Japanese folded up. Everybody had to blow off steam. Well, there is still some of that steam that wants to be blown off, and we still have a few selfish men who think more of their own personal interests than they do of the public welfare.

But they are not going to prevail. You are not going to let them prevail. You are going to force everybody to get into this harness, and push and pull until that great age I am prophesying comes about.

We can't do it tomorrow. We can't do it next month. We probably can't do it all next year. It is going to take some time for us to realize just exactly what we have and what we will do with it.

Now, let's all go home and go to work. Cut out the foolishness and make this country what it ought to be—the greatest nation the sun has ever shone upon.

Thank you very much.

166 Statement by the President on the 34th Anniversary of the Chinese Republic. *October 10, 1945*

THE AMERICAN PEOPLE today join the people of all free nations in saluting the people of China upon this thirty-fourth anniversary of China's national revolution. For the first time in fourteen years China is able to celebrate the Double Tenth without fear of aggression. The tremendous sacrifices which the Chinese people made for so long in their stirring and effective resistance to the Japanese invader have finally been rewarded in complete victory over the enemy, and the American people take pride in the decisive role played by our gallant ally in this titanic struggle for world freedom.

With final victory in the war achieved, China now faces the urgent problems of reconstruction of her devastated nation—a task which will require all of the inspired leadership and full cooperation of the Chinese people which have been so evident during these years of desperate struggle for survival and without which Japan's savage aims of aggression might have succeeded.

On behalf of the American people I take pleasure in reaffirming our abiding faith in the ability of the Chinese nation to accomplish the democratic objectives established for it by Dr. Sun Yat-sen and in pledging our assistance and support to the attainment of this end.

167 Remarks on Presenting the Congressional Medal of
     Honor to Fifteen Members of the Armed Forces.
     October 12, 1945

WELL, once again I have had a very great privilege. I would rather do what I have been doing this morning than any other one of my arduous duties. This one is a pleasure.

When you look at these young men, you see the United States of America, the greatest republic on earth, the country that can meet any situation when it becomes necessary.

These young men were doing their duty. They didn't think they were being heroes. They didn't think they were doing anything unusual. They were just doing what the situation called for.

As I have told the rest of these young men who have been here before me, I would much rather have that Medal around my neck than to be President of the United States. It is the greatest honor that can come to a man. It is an honor that all of us strive for, but very few of us ever achieve.

Now these young men will go back and become citizens of this great country, and they will make good citizens; and you won't find any of them bragging about what they have done or what they propose to do. They are just going to be good citizens of the United States, and they are going to help us take this Republic to its leadership in the world, where it belongs, and where it has belonged for the past 25 years.

Thank you very much for giving me this pleasure and this privilege.

NOTE: The presentation was made by the President in a ceremony on the South Lawn at the White House. The Congressional Medal of Honor was awarded to the following members of the Armed Forces from the European and Pacific theaters: Cpl. T. A. Atkins, Cpl. Edward A. Bennett, Cpl. M. E. Biddle, Capt. J. M. Burt, Cpl. C. B. Craft, Cpl. Desmond T. Doss, T. Sgt. F. V. Horner, T. Sgt. C. H. Karaberis, Sgt. T. J. Kelly, Sgt. D. J. Kerstetter, Sgt. N. Oresko, T. Sgt. C. Rodriguez, 1st Lt. E. A. Silk, 2d Lt. J. C. Sjogren, and Pfc. W. A. Soderman.

168   Letter to Representative Powell of New York Regarding
the Refusal of Permission to His Wife for a Concert in
Constitution Hall.   *October 12, 1945*

Dear Congressman Powell:

I have your telegram in which you inform me that your wife, Miss
Hazel Scott, has been refused the use of Constitution Hall for a concert
on October twentieth.

Artistic talent is not the exclusive property of any one race or group.
One of the marks of a democracy is its willingness to respect and reward talent without regard to race or origin.

We have just brought to a successful conclusion a war against totali-
tarian countries which made racial discrimination their state policy.
One of the first steps taken by the Nazis when they came to power
was to forbid the public appearance of artists and musicians whose
religion or origin was unsatisfactory to the "Master-race."

I am sure that you will realize however the impossibility of any interference by me in the management or policy of a private enterprise
such as the one in question.

Very sincerely,

HARRY S. TRUMAN

NOTE: The White House also released
a telegram from Mrs. Truman to Representative Powell, acknowledging his
telegram of October 11 concerning the
invitation she had accepted to attend a
tea given by the Daughters of the
American Revolution, who had refused
permission to Miss Scott to give a concert in Constitution Hall. In her telegram Mrs. Truman called attention to
the fact that the invitation was extended
and accepted prior to the controversy
over the use of Constitution Hall by
Miss Scott.

169   Special Message to the Congress on Puerto Rico.
October 16, 1945

To the Congress of the United States:

It is the settled policy of this Government to promote the political,
social and economic development of people who have not yet attained

full self-government, and eventually to make it possible for them to determine their own form of government.

It is our pride that this policy was faithfully pursued in the case of the Philippines. The people of the Philippines determined that they desired political independence, and the Government of the United States made provision to this effect.

It is now time, in my opinion, to ascertain from the people of Puerto Rico their wishes as to the ultimate status which they prefer, and, within such limits as may be determined by the Congress, to grant to them the kind of government which they desire.

The present form of government in the Island appears to be unsatisfactory to a large number of its inhabitants. Different groups of people in Puerto Rico are advocating various changes in the present form of government.

These advocated changes include different possibilities: (1) the right of the Puerto Ricans to elect their own Governor with a wider measure of local self-government; (2) Statehood for Puerto Rico; (3) complete independence; and (4) a Dominion form of government.

Each of these propositions is being urged in the Island, and each has its own advocates. Uncertainty has been created among the people as to just what the future of Puerto Rico is to be. These uncertainties should be cleared away at an early date.

To this end, I recommend that the Congress consider each of the proposals, and that legislation be enacted submitting various alternatives to the people of Puerto Rico. In that way, the Congress can ascertain what the people of Puerto Rico themselves most desire for their political future.

However, in the interest of good faith and comity between the people of Puerto Rico and those of us who live on the mainland, Congress should not submit any proposals to the Puerto Ricans which the Congress is not prepared to enact finally into law. We should be prepared to carry into effect whatever options are placed before the people of Puerto Rico, once the Puerto Ricans have expressed their preference.

I hope that this problem can be considered by the Congress at an early date, and that appropriate legislation be enacted designed to make definite the future status of Puerto Rico.

Harry S. Truman

NOTE: A bill providing for the organization of a constitutional government by
the people of Puerto Rico (S. 3336),
as enacted July 3, 1950, is Public Law
600, 81st Congress (64 Stat. 319). H.J.

Res. 430 approving the constitution of
the Commonwealth of Puerto Rico, as
enacted July 3, 1952, is Public Law 447,
82d Congress (66 Stat. 327), which became effective on July 25, 1952.

170 Statement by the President Following the Visit of President Ríos of Chile. *October 16, 1945*

PRESIDENT RÍOS of Chile left Washington yesterday after an official visit, during which it was my privilege to have him as a guest at the White House. It was a great pleasure to meet him, not only as a friend and statesman, but also as the representative of a democratic people and a functioning democracy.

We discussed the mutual desire to strengthen the solidarity of the republics of the Western Hemisphere on the basis of the ideals for which the war was fought and won.

171 Memorandum on the Community War Fund Campaign in the National Capital Area. *October 17, 1945*

To the Heads of the Executive Departments and Agencies:

Analysis of the present situation in the Community War Fund drive in the government service shows that to date only $900,625 has been pledged, or 41.6 percent of the Government's quota. There are only 13 days left in which to complete the quota, and clear the way for the Victory Bond drive.

I ask the members of the Cabinet and heads of independent establish-ments of the Federal and District Governments in this metropolitan area to do their utmost personally to hasten the coverage of their depart-ments and agencies and to explain to the officials and employees under them the real necessity for obtaining the funds necessary to keep the various welfare and service organizations supported by the Fund going successfully for another year.

I believe that a generous response may be expected if it can be made clear to everyone that these services are still needed, in spite of the cessation of hostilities, to aid and comfort our Armed Forces at home and abroad, to give assistance to our allies in lands devastated by the war, and to maintain in our own locality the Community Chest activities which are so essential to the health and welfare of our National Capital. The fact that more than half of these latter services during the past year were rendered to government employees makes me feel certain that all will wish to contribute.

Twelve government agencies have already exceeded their quota. I ask the others to push the campaign so that the quota may be reached in time to avoid overlapping the Victory Bond Drive. This will call for immediate measures on the part of department heads to speed up the campaign. It will also require special devotion and effort on the part of all the volunteer workers, as well as sympathetic understanding and response on the part of those asked to contribute.

HARRY S. TRUMAN

172   The President's News Conference of
      October 18, 1945

THE PRESIDENT. I have no particular announcements to make today, but I thought maybe you might like to ask me some questions and would rather come in and do it.

[1.] Q. Mr. President, do you think the passage of the Hatch-Ball-Burton bill at this time might be helpful?

THE PRESIDENT. I am not familiar enough with the provisions of the Hatch-Ball-Burton bill, because it was introduced just a short time before I left the Senate, and I can't answer the question.

[2.] Q. Mr. President, Generalissimo Chiang Kai-shek says in an interview today with the U.P. that he had told the late President Roosevelt that the fate of the Emperor of Japan should be decided by the

Japanese people themselves, through free elections. Is there any such plan?

THE PRESIDENT. Not that I know of. I think it's a good plan, however.

[3.] Q. Mr. President, Mr. Snyder in a series of speeches indicated that it is his purpose to hold the line firmly on price stabilization, while letting management and labor bargain it out collectively within the present price structure. Does that represent the settled policy of the administration?

THE PRESIDENT. That is in accordance with the Executive order of August 18 which I read to you, I think, at another press conference.[1]

Q. Mr. President, in that connection, after a talk with you the other day, Mr. Garrison said that you had asked or suggested some machinery outside the War Labor Board for wage and price settlements. Could you tell us anything about your ideas on that point?

THE PRESIDENT. We are discussing that tomorrow at a Cabinet meeting. I will have an announcement to make on it, I think, after the Cabinet meeting.

Q. Is there anything you might say at this point about the type of machinery?

THE PRESIDENT. No, there isn't.

[4.] Q. Mr. President, have you received any message from Mr. Stalin lately?

THE PRESIDENT. No—yes, I have received one message, but it was merely a formal message in answer to some former correspondence. It had nothing to do with the present situation.

Q. Thank you, sir.

[5.] Q. Have there been any developments looking toward resumption or possible elevation to the executive level of the London Council——

THE PRESIDENT. I couldn't hear you.

Q. Have there been any developments looking toward carrying through to the Truman-Stalin level the difficulties that developed in London?

---

[1] See Item 157 [5].

THE PRESIDENT. No.

Q. In other words, there is no Big Three meeting now planned?

THE PRESIDENT. Not in contemplation.

Q. Do you know why the Russian Ambassador came back here?

THE PRESIDENT. I wish I did. [*Laughter*] It seems to be interesting to most everybody. I suppose he was on his own personal business.

Q. Mr. President, is the State Department—or you—taking any initiative in any way to attempt to break the stalemate that developed in London, and has now developed here, on the Far East?

THE PRESIDENT. In correspondence with the other governments. I hope it will eventually be worked out. I am sure it will.

Q. Does that correspondence, sir, I presume, include Mr. Stalin as well as——

THE PRESIDENT. Naturally. It includes all the interested governments.

Q. Is that more than the Big Five, or just the Big Five?

THE PRESIDENT. All the interested governments in the Far East. There are 10 or 12.

[6.] Q. Mr. President, would you favor repeal of the Smith-Connally Act—the labor disputes act?

THE PRESIDENT. That matter is to be considered by the Congress. It is up to them to decide what ought to be done with that. When it comes up for consideration, I shall express an opinion on it.

Q. Mr. President, could you cast any light on the sudden determination of John L. Lewis to call off the coal strike? Were there any conferences——

THE PRESIDENT. Mr. Lewis stated that he did it in the public interest, which made me very happy. If all these gentlemen will work in the public interest, you will have very little trouble.

[7.] Q. Mr. President, what is the administration's policy on the aluminum plants owned by the Government?

THE PRESIDENT. The policy has not been established as yet, but we hope as many of them as possible will be kept in operation.

Q. By the Government?

THE PRESIDENT. No. By private industry.

Q. Would you favor Government subsidies to run these plants?

THE PRESIDENT. I don't think it will be necessary.

[8.]   Q. Mr. President, is there anything you can tell us as to the length or content of your message to Congress Tuesday?

THE PRESIDENT. No. I will furnish you that message in plenty of time so you can study it before I deliver it.

[9.]   Q. Mr. President, I was wondering if Attorney General Clark has made any recommendation on that district judgeship vacancy out in Kansas?

THE PRESIDENT. No, he hasn't.

Q. You haven't made up your mind?

THE PRESIDENT. No. I haven't considered it at all. I just signed the bill yesterday.

[10.]   Q. Mr. President, have you had any further correspondence with Mr. Attlee relative to the Palestine question?

THE PRESIDENT. Not right recently. I had quite a voluminous correspondence with him at one time, and made some suggestions to him, which are still being considered.

Q. The time ripe yet for disclosure of his reply, or of your original note?

THE PRESIDENT. No, because the matter is still under consideration by the British Government, and I don't want to appear to be pushing them unduly. I think that request which I made of Mr. Attlee was a reasonable one, and I am hoping that he will comply with it. I asked him to admit a hundred thousand Jews into Palestine.[1]

Q. That would seem to indicate that his reply that has been received here was not conclusive?

THE PRESIDENT. He didn't want to admit as many as I asked him to.

Q. Was the figure quoted in Congress as 1,800 a month approximately correct?

THE PRESIDENT. No—well, it is approximately correct, but it is more than that. He would agree to more than that.

[11.]   Q. Mr. President, is there anything you can tell us on the selection for Chairman of the Federal Deposit Insurance?

THE PRESIDENT. No. No decision has been reached on it.

---

[1] See Item 188.

[12.] Q. Mr. President, there has been some talk on the Hill that you have urged prompt action on the atomic bomb bill, which is in your message. Do you object to the resumption of hearings, and to a delay of 2 or 3 weeks on that legislation?

THE PRESIDENT. I want the Congress to have all the information that it feels it needs, so that it can legislate intelligently, but I don't think there ought to be any undue delay.

[13.] Q. Mr. President, have your plans crystallized for the period between your Georgia trip and your next Missouri trip in about 10 days?

THE PRESIDENT. I will be right here at this desk.

Q. You are not going to Florida?

THE PRESIDENT. No.

Q. In other words, you are coming back from Warm Springs to Washington?

THE PRESIDENT. That's right. I will be right here at this desk.

[14.] Q. Mr. President, Members of Congress returning from overseas criticize UNRRA very severely. Do you have any other plan in mind for relief, other than UNRRA?

THE PRESIDENT. No. That is an implemented and agreed on plan between the interested governments, and unless we want to assume the whole burden ourselves, we will have to go through UNRRA.

Q. Would you consider the latter?

THE PRESIDENT. No, I would not. I think every nation ought to assume its part of the burden.

[15.] Q. Mr. President, returning to the atomic bomb question, does the May-Johnson bill seem satisfactory to you?

THE PRESIDENT. I think it is satisfactory. I don't know, because I haven't studied it carefully. When it comes up here for me to sign it, I will make up my mind on what I shall do with it. It is substantially in line with the suggestion in the message, I think.

Reporters: Thank you, Mr. President.

NOTE: President Truman's thirtieth news conference was held in his office at the White House at 10:05 a.m. on Thursday, October 18, 1945.

173 Statement by the President on the Anniversary of the
Founding of the Czechoslovak Republic.
October 22, 1945

ON THE anniversary of Czechoslovak independence I wish to extend
my own personal greetings and the wholehearted congratulations of
the American people to President Beneš and the people of Czechoslovakia. This commemoration of the founding of the Czechoslovak
Republic is of particular significance in marking the first time since the
German occupation that the Czechoslovak people have been able to
celebrate their independence in their own homeland as a free people.

The realization that the principles of democracy and freedom, out of
which the Republic was born twenty-seven years ago, have been victorious in two world wars, will inspire the Czechoslovak people to
make once more their contribution to world peace.

The American people watch with sympathetic interest the diligent
efforts now being made by the Czechoslovak people to erase the effects
of the Nazi rule and to restore their independent national life on the
traditions which have always been identified with the Czechoslovak
Republic. I am confident that the American people will aid the
Czechoslovak people in every way possible to achieve this goal.

174 Address Before a Joint Session of the Congress on
Universal Military Training. *October 23, 1945*

*Mr. Speaker, Mr. President, and Members of the Congress of the
United States:*

In my message to the Congress of September 6, 1945, I stated that I
would communicate further with respect to a long range program of
national military security for the United States. I now present to the
Congress my recommendations with respect to one essential part of
this program—universal training.

The United States now has a fighting strength greater than at any
other time in our history. It is greater than that of any other nation in
the world.

404

We are strong because of many things: our natural resources which we have so diligently developed; our great farms and mines, our factories, shipyards and industries which we have so energetically created and operated. But above all else, we are strong because of the courage and vigor and skill of a liberty loving people who are determined that this nation shall remain forever free.

With our strength comes grave responsibility. With it must also come a continuing sense of leadership in the world for justice and peace.

For years to come the success of our efforts for a just and lasting peace will depend upon the strength of those who are determined to maintain that peace. We intend to use all our moral influence and all our physical strength to work for that kind of peace. We can ensure such a peace only so long as we remain strong. We must face the fact that peace must be built upon power, as well as upon good will and good deeds.

Our determination to remain powerful denotes no lack of faith in the United Nations Organization. On the contrary, with all the might we have, we intend to back our obligations and commitments under the United Nations Charter. Indeed, the sincerity of our intention to support the Organization will be judged partly by our willingness to maintain the power with which to assist other peace-loving nations to enforce its authority. It is only by strength that we can impress the fact upon possible future aggressors that we will tolerate no threat to peace or liberty.

To maintain that power we must act now. The latent strength of our untrained citizenry is no longer sufficient protection. If attack should come again, there would be no time under conditions of modern war to develop that latent strength into the necessary fighting force.

Never again can we count on the luxury of time with which to arm ourselves. In any future war, the heart of the United States would be the enemy's first target. Our geographical security is now gone—gone with the advent of the robot bomb, the rocket, aircraft carriers and modern airborne armies.

The surest guaranty that no nation will dare again to attack us is to remain strong in the only kind of strength an aggressor under-stands—military power.

To preserve the strength of our nation, the alternative before us is clear. We can maintain a large standing Army, Navy, and Air Force. Or we can rely upon a comparatively small regular Army, Navy and Air Force, supported by well trained citizens, who in time of emergency could be quickly mobilized.

I recommend the second course—that we depend for our security upon a comparatively small professional armed force, reinforced by a well trained and effectively organized citizen reserve. The backbone of our military force should be the trained citizen who is first and fore-most a civilian, and who becomes a soldier or a sailor only in time of danger—and only when Congress considers it necessary. This plan is obviously more practical and economical. It conforms more closely to long-standing American tradition.

In such a system, however, the citizen reserve must be a trained re-serve. We can meet the need for a trained reserve in only one way—by universal training.

Modern war is fought by experts—from the atomic scientist in his laboratory to the fighting man with his intricate modern weapons. The day of the minute man who sprang to the flintlock hanging on his wall is over. Now it takes many months for men to become skilled in electronics, aeronautics, ballistics, meteorology, and all the other sci-ences of modern war. If another national emergency should come, there would be no time for this complicated training. Men must be trained in advance.

The sooner we can bring the maximum number of trained men into service, the sooner will be the victory and the less tragic the cost. Uni-versal training is the only means by which we can be prepared right at the start to throw our great energy and our tremendous force into the battle. After two terrible experiences in one generation, we have learned that this is the way—the only way—to save human lives and material resources.

The importance of universal training has already been recognized by the Congress, and the Congress has wisely taken the initiative in this program.

The Select Committee of the House of Representatives on Postwar Military Policy has organized hearings and has heard extended testimony from representatives of churches and schools, labor unions, veterans organizations, the armed services, and many other groups. After careful consideration the Committee has approved the broad policy of universal military training for the critical years ahead. I concur in that conclusion, and strongly urge the Congress to adopt it.

In the present hour of triumph, we must not forget our anguish during the days of Bataan. We must not forget the anxiety of the days of Guadalcanal. In our desire to leave the tragedy of war behind us, we must not make the same mistake that we made after the first World War when we sank back into helplessness.

I recommend that we create a postwar military organization which will contain the following basic elements:

First—A comparatively small regular Army, Navy and Marine Corps;

Second—A greatly strengthened National Guard and Organized Reserve for the Army, Navy and Marine Corps;

Third—A General Reserve composed of all the male citizens of the United States who have received training.

The General Reserve would be available for rapid mobilization in time of emergency, but it would have no obligation to serve, either in this country or abroad, unless and until called to the service by an Act of the Congress.

In order to provide this General Reserve, I recommend to the Congress the adoption of a plan for Universal Military Training.

Universal Military Training is not conscription. The opponents of training have labeled it conscription, and by so doing, have confused the minds of some of our citizens. "Conscription" is compulsory service in the Army or Navy in time of peace or war. Trainees under this proposed legislation, however, would not be enrolled in any of the armed services. They would be civilians in training. They would be no closer to membership in the armed forces than if they had no training. Special rules and regulations would have to be adopted for their organization, discipline and welfare.

Universal training is not intended to take the place of the present Selective Service System. The Selective Service System is now being used to furnish replacements in the armed forces for the veterans of this war who are being discharged.

Only the Congress could ever draw trainees under a Universal Training Program into the Army or the Navy. And if that time ever came, these trainees could be inducted only by a selective process, as they were inducted for World War I and World War II. The great difference between having universal training and no training, however, is that, in time of emergency, those who would be selected for actual military service would already have been basically trained.

That difference may be as much as a year's time. That difference may be the margin between the survival and the destruction of this great nation.

The emphasis in the training of our young men will not be on mere drilling. It will be on the use of all the instruments and weapons of modern war. The training will offer every qualified young man a chance to perfect himself for the service of his country in some military specialty.

Under the plan which I propose, provisions should be made within the armed services to help trainees improve their educational status. The year of universal training should provide ample opportunity for self-improvement. Some part of the training could be used to develop skills which would be useful in future civilian life just as such skills have been developed during the present war.

The period of training could well be used to raise the physical standards of the nation's manpower, to lower its illiteracy rate, and to develop in our young men the ideals of responsible American citizenship.

Medical examinations of the young trainees would do much toward removing some of the minor disabilities which caused the rejection of so many men during this war by the Selective Service System.

The moral and spiritual welfare of our young people should be a consideration of prime importance, and, of course, facilities for worship in every faith should be available.

But the basic reason for universal training is a very simple one—to guarantee the safety and freedom of the United States against any potential aggressor. The other benefits are all by-products—useful indeed, but still by-products. The fundamental need is, and always will be, the national security of the United States, and the safety of our homes and our loved ones.

Since training alone is involved, and not actual military service, no exemptions should be allowed for occupation, dependency, or for any other reason except total physical disqualification.

All men should be included in the training, whether physically qualified for actual combat service or not. There should be a place into which every young American can fit in the service of our country. Some would be trained for combat, others would be trained for whatever war service they are physically and mentally qualified to perform.

I recommend that the training should be for one year. Each young man should enter training either at the age of eighteen or upon his graduation from high school—whichever is later; but in any event before his twentieth birthday. A trainee who completes his high school education in his seventeenth year should be eligible, with parental consent, to enter the course of training.

After the first few months of training, selected trainees who are not physically qualified for military service could be trained in certain skills so that if war came, they could take their places in shipyards, munitions factories and similar industrial plants.

Upon completion of a full year's training, the trainee would become a member of the General Reserve for a period of six years. After that he should be placed in a secondary reserve status.

Present personnel in the Army and Navy Reserves would, of course, be retained, and the new trainees would provide the source from which Reserves of the future would draw their personnel.

Commissions would be granted to qualified men who complete the course of training and who then take additional instruction in Officer Candidate Schools, in the Reserve Officers Training Corps or Naval Reserve Officers Training Corps. Outstanding trainees could be selected after an adequate period of training, and sent to college with Government financial aid, on condition that they return, after graduation and with ROTC training, as junior officers for a year or more of additional training or service.

Such a system as I have outlined would provide a democratic and efficient military force. It would be a constant bulwark in support of our ideals of government. It would constitute the backbone of defense against any possible future act of aggression.

It has been suggested in some quarters that there should be no universal training until the shape of the peace is better known, and until the military needs of this country can be estimated and our commitments under the United Nations Organization can be determined. But it is impossible today to foresee the future. It is difficult at any time to know exactly what our responsibilities will require in the way of force. We do know that if we are to have available a force when needed, the time to begin preparing is right now.

The need exists today—and must be met today.

If, at some later time, conditions change, then the program can be reexamined and revalued. At the present time we have the necessary organization, the required camp installations, and the essential equipment and training grounds immediately available for use in a training program. Once we disband and scatter this set-up, it will be much harder and more expensive to reestablish the necessary facilities.

The argument has been made that compulsory training violates traditional American concepts of liberty and democracy, and even that it would endanger our system of government by creating a powerful military caste. The purpose of the program, however, is just the contrary. And it will have just the contrary result. The objective is not to train professional soldiers. It is to train citizens, so that if and when the Congress should declare it necessary for them to become soldiers, they could do so more quickly and more efficiently. A large trained reserve of peace-loving citizens would never go to war or encourage war, if it could be avoided.

It is no valid argument against adopting universal training at this time that there are now millions of trained veterans of this war. No fair minded person would suggest that we continue to rely indefinitely upon those veterans. They have earned the heartfelt gratitude of us all—and they have also earned the right to return promptly to civilian life. We must now look to our younger men to constitute the new reserve military strength of our nation.

There are some who urge that the development of rocket weapons and atomic bombs and other new weapons indicates that scientific research, rather than universal training, is the best way to safeguard our security. It is true that, if we are to keep ahead in military preparedness, continuous research in science and new weapons is essential. That is why in my message to the Congress of September sixth I urged that there be created a national research agency, one of whose major functions would be to carry on fundamental military research.

It is true that there must be continuous exploration into new fields of science in order to keep ahead in the discovery and manufacture of new weapons. No matter what the cost, we cannot afford to fall behind in any of the new techniques of war or in the development of new weapons of destruction.

Until we are sure that our peace machinery is functioning adequately, we must relentlessly preserve our superiority on land and sea and in the air. Until that time, we must also make sure that by planning—and by actual production—we have on hand at all times sufficient weapons of the latest nature and design with which to repel any sudden attack, and with which to launch an effective counter-attack.

That *is* the only way we can be sure—until we are sure that there is another way.

But research, new materials, and new weapons will never, by themselves, be sufficient to withstand a powerful enemy. We must have men trained to use these weapons. As our armed forces become more and more mechanized, and as they use more and more complicated weapons, we must have an ever-increasing number of trained men. Technological advances do not eliminate the need for men. They increase that need.

General of the Army George C. Marshall, in his recent report to the Secretary of War, has made this very clear. I quote from his report:

"The number of men that were involved in the delivery of the atomic bomb on Hiroshima was tremendous. First we had to have the base in the Marianas from which the plane took off. This first required preliminary operations across the vast Pacific, thousands of ships, millions of tons of supply, the heroic efforts of hundreds of thousands of men. Further, we needed the B–29's and their fighter escort which gave us control of the air over Japan. This was the result of thousands of hours of training and preparation in the United States and the energies of hundreds of thousands of men.

"The effect of technology on the military structure is identical to its effect on national economy. Just as the automobile replaced the horse and made work for millions of Americans, the atomic explosives will require the services of millions of men if we are compelled to employ them in fighting our battles.

"This war has made it clear that the security of the Nation, when challenged by an armed enemy, requires the services of virtually all able-bodied male citizens within the effective military age group."

That is the end of General Marshall's quotation.

The atomic bomb would have been useless to us unless we had developed a strong Army, Navy and Air Force with which to beat off the attacks of our foe, and then fight our way to points within striking distance of the heart of the enemy.

Assume that on December 7, 1941, the United States had had a supply of atomic bombs in New Mexico or Tennessee. What could we have done with them?

Assume that the United States and Japan both had had a supply of the bombs on December 7, 1941. Which would have survived?

Suppose that both England and Germany had had the atomic bomb in September of 1940 during the "Blitz" over England. Which country would have been destroyed?

The answer is clear that the atomic bomb is of little value without an adequate Army, Air and Naval Force. For that kind of force is necessary to protect our shores, to overcome any attack and to enable us to move forward and direct the bomb against the enemy's own territory. Every new weapon will eventually bring some counter-defense against it. Our ability to use either a new weapon or a counter-weapon will ultimately depend upon a strong Army, Navy and Air

Force, with all the millions of men needed to supply them—all quickly mobilized and adequately equipped.

Any system which is intended to guarantee our national defense will, of course, cause some inconvenience—and perhaps even some hardship—to our people. But we must balance that against the danger which we face unless we are realistic and hard-headed enough to be prepared. Today universal training is the only adequate answer we have to our problem in this troubled world.

There will be better answers, we hope, in the days to come. The United States will always strive for those better answers—for the kind of tried and tested world cooperation which will make for peace and harmony among all nations. It will continue to strive to reach that period quickly. But that time has not yet arrived.

Even from those who are loudest in their opposition to universal training, there has come no other suggestion to furnish the protection and security which we must have—nothing but pious hope and dangerous wishful thinking.

I urge that the Congress pass this legislation promptly—while the danger is still fresh in our minds—while we still remember how close we came to destruction four years ago—while we can vividly recall the horrors of invasion which our Allies suffered—and while we can still see all the ravages and ruin of war.

Let us not by a short-sighted neglect of our national security betray those who come after us.

It is our solemn duty in this hour of victory to make sure that in the years to come no possible aggressor or group of aggressors can endanger the national security of the United States of America.

NOTE: The President spoke at 12:31 p.m. in the chamber of the House of Representatives.

On June 24, 1948, the President approved the Selective Service Act of 1948 (62 Stat. 604), redesignated as the Universal Military Training and Service Act by amendment of June 19, 1951 (65 Stat. 75).

175   The President's News Conference of
       October 25, 1945

THE PRESIDENT. [1.] The first announcement is the appointment of
John R. Steelman as Special Assistant to the President.

Q. S-t-e-e——

THE PRESIDENT. John R. S-t-e-e-l-m-a-n.

Q. Executive Assistant?

THE PRESIDENT. No. Special Assistant.

Q. What field is he going to operate in, labor?

THE PRESIDENT. He is going to be a Special Assistant to the President,
to act in any field in which I want to use him.

Q. Is that a temporary appointment or a permanent one, Mr.
President?

THE PRESIDENT. Temporary.

Q. Dealing with labor relations, sir?

THE PRESIDENT. He will act in any capacity in which I want to use
him.

Q. His background has been mostly labor conciliation though, hasn't
it, Mr. President?

THE PRESIDENT. He is a labor expert.

[2.] I want to make a short statement about the Philippines, and
tomorrow morning some letters will be released to you on that subject.[1]

[*Reading*] "Since President Osmeña's arrival in Washington early
this month, I have had several conferences with him, Secretary Ickes,
and High Commissioner McNutt.

"All Americans feel a very warm friendship for the Filipino people,
who stood by us so heroically throughout the war and who now are in
dire need of help. I consider a program of assistance to the Philippines
essential to our relationship with the people there.

"We have made some progress and further conferences will be held
before President Osmeña and High Commissioner McNutt return to
Manila."

[3.] I have a letter from William Green, Philip Murray, Ira Mosher,

---

[1] For letters, see Item 176.

and Eric Johnston on the labor-management conference, and also the agenda for the conference, which will be furnished you in mimeographed form. There are copies for everybody.[1]

[4.] I am going to speak over the radio at 10 o'clock on Tuesday night, and discuss the wage-price program.

Q. Next Tuesday, sir?

THE PRESIDENT. Next Tuesday night, at 10 o'clock.

Q. All networks, sir?

THE PRESIDENT. All networks.

Q. What time, sir?

THE PRESIDENT. Ten o'clock.

Q. Half-hour speech, Mr. President?

THE PRESIDENT. Yes.

Q. Is the policy yet decided, Mr. President?

THE PRESIDENT. The policy is in the stage of being decided. It will be decided before I make the announcement on Tuesday night.

[5.] I have a new Presidential flag, Executive order for which will be issued. President Roosevelt had ordered the Navy Department to go to work on a new flag just before he died, and I thought maybe you might be interested in the history of the Presidential flag and the Presidential seal; and I have got a release for you in mimeographed form on that.

[*To General Vaughan*] Now raise that flag up, there. This flag here—in President Wilson's time there were two flags for the President, an Army flag for the President with a red star and a Navy flag for the President with a blue star.

---

[1] The letter (from William Green, President, American Federation of Labor; Ira Mosher, President, National Association of Manufacturers; Philip Murray, President, Congress of Industrial Organizations; and Eric Johnston, President, United States Chamber of Commerce), released October 25, was in response to a request by President Truman that the writers nominate delegates and plan the agenda for the National Labor-Management Conference scheduled to begin November 5. The letter stated that 36 delegates had been chosen, representing a wide diversity of interests in both management and labor. The agenda, it stated, was agreed upon unanimously by a subcommittee "chosen by ourselves and the Secretaries of Labor and Commerce." While stating that "no conference can possibly . . . clean the slate of all present and potential sources of friction in the highly-complicated American economy," the writers added that "it is equally obvious . . . that the establishment of long-range and agreed-upon policies designed to reduce industrial disagreement, and the provision of predetermined means of dealing with unavoidable disagreements will go far toward bringing about a new era of industrial harmony and progress."

President Wilson ordered a single flag for the President, and this was the result of that—[*General Vaughan displays flag*]—with the white eagle facing toward the arrows, which is the sinister side of the heraldic form, and no color.

This new flag—[*to General Vaughan*]—if you will raise that one up, now you will see—you can see the difference.   It will all be explained in the release which you will get.   This new flag faces the eagle toward the staff which is looking to the front all the time when you are on the march, and also has him looking at the olive branches for peace, instead of the arrows for war; and taking the 4 stars out of the corner and putting 48 stars around the Presidential seal.   You will get a release that will tell you all about it, and the why and the wherefore.[1]

---

[1] The release contained the text of Executive Order 9646 "Coat of Arms, Seal, and Flag of the President of the United States" (October 25, 1945, 3 CFR, 1943–1948 Comp., p. 445), together with background material reading in part as follows:

The Executive order establishes for the first time a legal definition of the President's coat of arms and his seal.   The design of the coat of arms and the seal has been changed slightly from the former design, and the Presidential flag has also been changed.   The flag will consist of the coat of arms in full color, surrounded by 48 white stars on a blue field.

The former Presidential flag was adopted in 1916 by President Wilson.   Prior to that time, the Army and the Navy had had separate flags for the Commander in Chief.   President Wilson instructed his Assistant Secretary of the Navy, Franklin D. Roosevelt, and the Aide to the Secretary of the Navy, Commander Byron McCandless, USN, to design a Presidential flag which would be suitable for use by both the Army and the Navy.   On May 29, 1916, President Wilson signed an Executive order adopting the flag suggested by Assistant Secretary Roosevelt and Commander McCandless.   The flag consisted of the Presidential coat of arms on a blue field with a white star in each of the corners.   That flag was in use from 1916 until today.

In March of this year, President Roosevelt discussed with his Naval Aide, Vice Admiral Wilson Brown, the advisability of changing the President's flag.   It seemed inappropriate to President Roosevelt for the flag of the Commander in Chief to have only four stars when there were five stars in the flags of Fleet Admirals and Generals of the Army, grades which had been created in December 1944.

It was natural that President Roosevelt should turn at this time to the officer who had worked with him in 1916, and who now holds the rank of Commodore, Byron McCandless.

For many years Commodore McCandless, who now commands the U.S. Naval Repair Base at San Diego, Calif., has studied the histories of the various flags of the United States.   When Vice Admiral Brown wrote to him, at President Roosevelt's request, late in March for suggestions for a new design for the President's flag, Commodore McCandless prepared several designs based upon early American flags.   His proposed designs arrived in Washington after the death of President Roosevelt and the President did not have the opportunity of seeing them until early in June.

The President and members of his staff examined them carefully and, preferring one design to the others, the President made several suggestions to Commodore McCandless concerning it.   The President believed that all of the States in the Union should be represented on the Commander in Chief's flag, and he asked Commodore McCandless to submit a new design with a circle of 48 stars around the coat of arms.

Commodore McCandless sent a painting of the proposed flag, with the circle of 48 stars, to the White House in July and when the President returned from Berlin in August, he tentatively approved that design.

It was then sent to the War and Navy Departments for comment and suggestions.   The

Now I am ready for questions.

[6.] Q. Mr. President, can we clear up a little bit about the November trips? Is the southern trip still on?

THE PRESIDENT. It is; unless conditions here are such that require my presence here. All Presidential trips are tentative.

Q. Mr. President, will you go to Waco, Texas, December 5? Is that decided?

THE PRESIDENT. That is another tentative appointment. They have asked me to come down and get a degree of Doctor of Laws from the great Baptist school down there, and I am inclined to go.

[7.] Q. Mr. President, have you decided as yet to accept the resignation of John Snyder?

THE PRESIDENT. John Snyder's resignation has never been under contemplation. John Snyder will stay with me as long as I want him, and until his job is finished.

Q. He hasn't resigned to you in a letter, sir?

THE PRESIDENT. No, sir. He never made any attempt to.

Q. Thank you very much.

THE PRESIDENT. He is a patriotic citizen, and he will stay here as long as I need him, although he is doing it at a very great sacrifice.

Chief of the Heraldic Section of the Office of the Quartermaster General of the Army, Mr. Arthur E. DuBois, like Commodore McCandless, has studied the history of flags and heraldic emblems for many years. Mr. DuBois made several suggestions to the President. He pointed out that there was no known basis in law for the coat of arms and the seal which has been used by Presidents since 1880 and which was reproduced on the flag. The seal had originated during the administration of President Hayes, apparently as an erroneous rendering of the Great Seal of the United States.

It is a curious fact that the eagle on the Great Seal faces to its own right, whereas the eagle on the seal in use by Presidents since 1880 faces to its own left. According to heraldic custom, the eagle on a coat of arms, unless otherwise specified in the heraldic description, is always made to face to its own right. There is no explanation for the eagle facing to its own left in the case of the President's coat of arms. To conform to heraldic custom, and since there was no authority other than usage for the former Presidential coat of arms, the President had Mr. DuBois redesign the coat of arms in accordance with the latter's suggestions.

In the new coat of arms, seal and flag, the eagle not only faces to its right—the direction of honor—but also toward the olive branches of peace which it holds in its right talon. Formerly the eagle faced toward the arrows in its left talon—arrows, symbolic of war.

The President also decided that the eagle on his seal and his flag should appear in the full color of the natural bird as is customary in most flags, rather than in white as it had been on the former flag.

The 48 stars in the circle represent the States collectively; no single star represents any particular State.

[8.] Q. Mr. President, the Washington Post this morning suggested that General Marshall be placed in charge of the program for universal military training. Granted that he needs a rest, but that he ought to add his prestige to that.

THE PRESIDENT. I think General Marshall will add his prestige to that universal training program, but General Marshall is still the Chief of Staff, and I need him as Chief of Staff.

[9.] Q. Mr. President, what would be the betting odds on whether you go to Georgia or not? [*Laughter*] Those people are worrying us to death.

THE PRESIDENT. Tony,[1] I'll let you make your own book. [*Laughter*]

Q. Mr. President, we are getting an awful lot of messages from down there, saying they have been told you are not coming down there?

THE PRESIDENT. Rumors are always circulating in Washington. It wouldn't be a good town if it weren't for the rumors.

[10.] Q. Did Henry Ford 2d call on you this week?

THE PRESIDENT. No, he hasn't. He came here to see the Secretary of Labor.

[11.] Q. Mr. President, after Mr. Wilson of General Motors visit here, he announced the 45-hour week idea. Did he get any encouragement here on that?

THE PRESIDENT. He did not.

[12.] Q. Mr. President, did you discuss the Alaska Highway with Governor Wallgren here?

THE PRESIDENT. Yes, and with Senator Magnuson, and with the Secretary of State.

Q. Making any progress?

THE PRESIDENT. Yes, we are making some progress.

[13.] Q. Mr. President, there have been a lot of stories that Leo Crowley might be appointed to the Export-Import Bank. Do you have any such intention?

THE PRESIDENT. I haven't made up my mind on the directors for the Export-Import Bank. I have been considering Mr. Crowley for a member of that Board.

---

[1] Ernest B. Vaccaro, Associated Press.

Q. Mr. President, on that point, there still seems to be some mystery about Mr. Crowley's departure from both the FDIC and the FEA. He wrote a letter specifically resigning from the FDIC. You accepted both resignations. Two Congressmen have told me that he testified that there was an additional letter dealing with his reasons for wanting to get out of FEA, and that it was up to the White House to release that. Would you release that letter now?

THE PRESIDENT. The letter is around here somewhere, but our conversations were verbal—sitting here in that chair; and the only reason I accepted Mr. Crowley's release was because he insisted on giving it to me, and said that he had been in public service for a long time, and he would like to be in a position to attend to his own business a little while. I didn't urge him in any way.

Q. But is there any reason why that letter should not be public knowledge?

THE PRESIDENT. No, there is no reason at all. It can be made public.[1]

[14.] Q. Mr. President, upon whose advice—if you were, sir—were you relying upon, in the decision to keep the know-how of the atomic bomb a secret in the United States? Did Mr. Vannevar Bush——

THE PRESIDENT. I was relying on my own judgment——

Q. It was published that you were relying on Bush's.

THE PRESIDENT. ——if that's worth anything to you.

Q. Mr. President, there has been some concern on the Hill regarding reported German scientists in Spain. Do you contemplate any inquiry or action?

THE PRESIDENT. That's the first I've heard of it.

Q. Mr. President, when do you expect to begin discussions for the control of the atomic bomb?

THE PRESIDENT. I will make an announcement on that at a later date which will clarify the whole situation. I am not ready to make it now.

[15.] Q. Mr. President, have you received any word now, whether Russia will attend this Far Eastern Advisory Commission meeting next week?

THE PRESIDENT. That is a matter that has been handled by the Secretary of State; and I have not been in touch with him on the subject.

---

[1] See footnote on page 347.

Q. Mr. President, the Secretary of State yesterday referred us to you on the question as to whether there had been any response to the correspondence that may have gone to Mr. Stalin. Has there been any response on the subject?

THE PRESIDENT. Not to me personally, no.

[16.] Q. In that same press conference, Mr. President, Mr. Byrnes said that he had not seen or read the Italian armistice. Have you studied the Italian armistice?

THE PRESIDENT. I have not.

[17.] Q. Mr. President, have you made a selection for the chairmanship of the Federal Deposit Insurance?

THE PRESIDENT. No, I haven't.

Q. You are considering a Congressman on the Hill, are you?

THE PRESIDENT. No, I am not considering anybody at the present time.

[18.] Q. Mr. President, have you made a request of the Congressman in charge of the full employment bill to speed action on it in the House?

THE PRESIDENT. Yes, I have. I am very anxious for that full employment bill to be reported out and passed. I am for it with everything that I have.

Q. Mr. President, do you expect to talk to the president of the United Rubber Workers Union this week?

THE PRESIDENT. I expect to talk to all the people who are on that— who have been invited to the Conference during the week. If he is on that list, he will be talked to.

Q. Does that include John L. Lewis, Mr. President?

THE PRESIDENT. Yes.

Q. When will you see him?

THE PRESIDENT. The program hasn't been made up. I will see him along with the other labor leaders.

Q. Mr. President, did Congressman Manasco tell you this morning— as he did to us outside—that that bill would not be passed or reported out without very great amendments?

THE PRESIDENT. He said there would be some difficulty about reporting the bill out. He didn't say anything about great amendments, or anything else; but I told him I wanted the bill reported out, to give the House a chance to vote on it.

[19.] Q. Mr. President, coming back to John Snyder, has Mr. Snyder—if I may ask—expressed a desire to you to resign?

THE PRESIDENT. No, he hasn't.

Reporter: Thank you, Mr. President.

NOTE: President Truman's thirty-first news conference was held in his office at the White House at 4 p.m. on Thursday, October 25, 1945.

176 Letters to the High Commissioner to the Philippines and to the Heads of Federal Agencies Recommending Measures for the Assistance of the Philippines.
October 26, 1945

[Released October 26, 1945.   Dated October 25, 1945]

To the High Commissioner to the Philippines:

My dear Mr. High Commissioner:

In the provinces near Manila thousands of share croppers organized some years ago to demand a more equitable division of the product of their labor. For several years there was no effective solution of the problem. During the war the tenants organized a guerrilla army which reportedly did good work against the enemy. After the enemy was defeated in their localities, they did not disband and today they constitute a special problem which threatens the stability of government. On the other hand, their legitimate claim to fair treatment and the assistance they rendered in resistance to the enemy require that they be not dealt with in a ruthless manner.

I therefore request you to order a prompt investigation of agrarian unrest in the Philippines with the cooperation of the Commonwealth Government, and to recommend the remedies or reforms which ought to be taken by the Commonwealth government and by the United States Government.

Sincerely,

HARRY S. TRUMAN

[The Honorable, The High Commissioner to the Philippines, Washington, D.C.]

To the Alien Property Custodian:

My dear Mr. Markham:

The United States Army has found and taken custody of considerable valuable property belonging to enemy nationals in the Philippines. Enemy property includes agricultural leaseholds held through "dummies". It is desirable that all property in which the enemy has or had interest should pass under the civil control of the United States government which is responsible for its custody under the usually accepted terms of international law.

I therefore direct that the Alien Property Custodian vest title in all enemy property in the Philippines and make lawful disposition of it. Should these operations extend beyond the date of independence, I shall endeavor to arrange by treaty, or otherwise, for the completion of the processes of vesting and liquidation.

Sincerely,

Harry S. Truman

[Honorable James E. Markham, Alien Property Custodian, Washington, D.C.]

To the Attorney General:

My dear Mr. Attorney General:

While the mass of the Filipino people and many of their leaders remained staunchly loyal during invasion and rendered invaluable assistance to our arms, it is necessary to admit that many persons served under the puppet governments sponsored by the enemy. Some of these, especially those engaged in health and educational work, remained at their posts of duty with an evident intention to sustain the physical and cultural welfare of their people. Others of the clerical and custodial services continued in office in order to earn their accustomed livelihood and participated in no way in enemy policy. But, regretably, a number of persons prominent in the political life of the country assisted the enemy in the formulation and enforcement of his political policies and the spread of his propaganda. Others in the field of trade and finance seized upon the occasion to enrich themselves in property and money at the expense of their countrymen.

Reports have appeared in the press which indicate that a number of persons who gave aid and comfort to the enemy are now holding important offices in the Commonwealth government. Reports further indicate that the Commonwealth government is only beginning to investigate, charge, and try the offenders. It is essential that this task be completed before the holding of the next Commonwealth general election.

Considering that disloyalty to the Commonwealth is equally disloyalty to the United States, I request that you send experienced personnel to the Philippines to discover the status and to recommend such action as may be appropriately taken by the United States. Such recommendations should be made through the United States High Commissioner to the Philippine Islands. I am further requesting that the Secretaries of War and Navy direct the staffs of their intelligence sections to cooperate with you and make available to you all records and evidence bearing on this important problem.

Representatives of the Federal Bureau of Investigation assigned to the Philippines should be directed to report through the United States High Commissioner in connection with this and other operations in the Philippine Islands.

Sincerely,

HARRY S. TRUMAN

[The Honorable, The Attorney General, Washington, D.C.]

To the Secretary of War:

My dear Mr. Secretary:

As a result of prolonged enemy occupation of the Philippines the law enforcement agencies of the Commonwealth Government were seriously disorganized. Bearing in mind the fact that the War Department was responsible originally for the organization of the Philippine Constabulary, which had such an excellent record prior to the war, I believe that the War Department should assist in every possible way by the assignment of officers and men and the transfer of necessary equipment in reorganizing the Constabulary on a non-military basis.

President Osmeña has advised me that the War Department has already been of assistance in this task and that considerable progress has been made by the Commonwealth Government. Both he and I feel, however, that continued assistance until the reorganization is completed would be helpful.

I ask that this continued assistance be extended to the Commonwealth Government so that law and order may be fully restored in the shortest possible time, and that you submit a report to me as soon as a program has been formulated.

Sincerely yours,

HARRY S. TRUMAN

[Honorable Robert P. Patterson, Secretary of War]

Memorandum for the Secretary of the Treasury, the Secretary of War:

It is my understanding that due to a shortage of legal currency in certain areas in the Philippine Islands early in the war and continually thereafter until the reoccupation of the islands by our forces, a considerable quantity of emergency currency was issued, some by properly authorized officers of the United States Government and some by representatives of the Philippine government. It would appear that to the extent that this currency was used either directly or indirectly for the prosecution of the war, its redemption is a responsibility of the United States Government.

I request that the War and Treasury Departments make a careful analysis of this situation and submit recommendations as to the necessary steps which should be taken to discharge the obligations that are properly responsibilities of the United States Government. Any arrangement proposed for the redemption of this currency should include provisions designed so far as possible to avoid any windfall to speculators.

HARRY S. TRUMAN

To the Secretary of the Treasury:

My dear Mr. Secretary:

During the period of their military invasion of the Philippine Islands, the Japanese issued an unbacked fiat peso and tried unsuccessfully to force its parity with the legitimate Philippine peso. The issue was so unlimited that it came to be worthless, and upon our landing in Leyte it was officially and quite properly declared not to be legal tender. However, during the invasion period it had a rapidly declining value as a medium for local trade, and numerous contracts which involved the enemy currency were settled or entered into. While it would be against the public interest to validate completely these contracts and settlements, a measure is needed to serve as a standard for judgments between debtors and creditors.

Since you have representation in the Philippines through a mission of the Foreign Funds Division, I request that you cooperate with the High Commissioner and the Commonwealth Government in drawing up a schedule showing the relative trend of the purchasing power and exchange rates of the Japanese Philippine peso during the period of invasion.

Sincerely yours,
HARRY S. TRUMAN

[The Honorable, The Secretary of the Treasury, Washington, D.C.]

To the Surplus Property Administrator:

My dear Mr. Administrator:

Prolonged enemy occupation and active warfare in the Philippine Islands have left in their wake a tremendous problem of relief and rehabilitation. It seems apparent that there must be large supplies of surplus government property now available which could be used to great advantage in the Philippines in the program which must be undertaken there by the Philippine Government. Such items as construction equipment, medical supplies and hospital equipment are badly needed.

Where such supplies can be used directly by the government of the Philippine Commonwealth, I believe this Government should make the supplies available without cost to the Commonwealth. It might perhaps be desirable to arrange the transfer on such terms as would prevent the property from being later offered for sale to the general public.

Since there is at present no legal authority to effect such transfers, I believe we should seek such authority.

Sincerely,

HARRY S. TRUMAN

[Honorable W. Stuart Symington, Surplus Property Administration, Washington, D.C.]

To the Administrator of Veterans' Affairs:

My dear General Bradley:

In connection with a general program of reestablishment of orderly government in the Philippine Islands and the discharge of just obligations of the United States Government therein, I request that the Veterans' Administration make a careful analysis of all phases of past and current benefits payable in the Philippine Islands to American and Filipino veterans, and submit to me at the earliest possible date a report which should be accompanied by recommendations for any new legislation which may be required.

Sincerely yours,

HARRY S. TRUMAN

[Gen. Omar N. Bradley, Administrator of Veterans' Affairs]

To the President of the Export-Import Bank:

My dear Mr. Taylor:

In connection with the rehabilitation of the Philippine Islands and the restoration of the normal economic life of the Islands, I believe that the Export-Import Bank should participate in this program. It should, it seems to me, be possible to work out a program to operate in the Islands on a purely business basis which would be of great assistance in restoring normal economic conditions.

May I have your comment on this suggestion, and in the event that you feel that the bank is at present without legal authority to function in the Philippines, your suggestions as to steps that might be necessary to permit it to do so?

Sincerely yours,

HARRY S. TRUMAN

[Honorable Wayne C. Taylor, President, Export-Import Bank of Washington]

426

To the Administrator of the War Shipping Administration:

My dear Admiral Land:

In connection with the rehabilitation of the Philippines and the restoration of normal economic life of the Islands, I am very anxious that all possible steps, consistent with our obligations elsewhere, be taken to supply adequate shipping to the Philippine Islands.

I would be glad to have a statement from you as to the plans of the War Shipping Administration and the amount of tonnage which is expected to be available for Philippine trade, particularly in the near future.

Sincerely yours,

HARRY S. TRUMAN

[Vice Admiral Emory S. Land, Administrator, War Shipping Administration]

To the Chairman of the Reconstruction Finance Corporation:

My dear Mr. Chairman:

The almost complete lack of consumers goods in the Philippines— goods ordinarily imported from the United States—has brought about serious price inflation and black markets which cause great distress among the people. An excellent start has been made by the Foreign Economic Administration in cooperation with the War Shipping Administration to eliminate inflation by facilitating normal import trade.

You are, therefore, requested to direct the United States Commercial Company to use resources and personnel within its jurisdiction to continue and to advance the Philippine program which it has undertaken, and, where necessary, to sell goods on credit terms not exceeding two years in duration.

Sincerely,

HARRY S. TRUMAN

[Honorable Charles B. Henderson, Chairman, Reconstruction Finance Corporation, Washington, D.C.]

427

177 Address in New York City at the Commissioning of the
U.S.S. Franklin D. Roosevelt.   *October 27*, 1945

Admiral Daubin, Captain Soucek, Mrs. Roosevelt, ladies and gentlemen:

One of the pleasant duties in the exacting life of a President is to award honors to our fighting men for courage and valor in war. In the commissioning of this ship, the American people are honoring a stalwart hero of this war who gave his life in the service of his country. His name is engraved on this great carrier, as it is in the hearts of men and women of good will the world over—Franklin D. Roosevelt.

If anyone can be called the father of the new American Navy which is typified by this magnificent vessel, it is he. From his first day as President he started to build that Navy.

Even as he started to build the Navy, he began to work for world peace. By his realistic good-neighbor policy, by reciprocal trade agreements, by constant appeal to international arbitration instead of force, he worked valiantly in the cause of peace. By his constant battle for the forgotten man he sought to remove the social and economic inequalities which have so often been at the root of conflict at home and abroad. And when he saw the clouds of aggression forming across the seas to the East and to the West, he issued warning after warning which, had they been heeded in time, might have staved off this tragic conflict.

But through it all, he never faltered in his work to build up the American Navy. For he understood, as few men did, the importance to the survival of this country of the mission of its Navy—the control of the sea. The Axis powers understood. That is why Germany sought to drive us from the sea by her submarines. That is why Japan tried to destroy our Navy. They knew that if they succeeded, they might conquer all the nations of the earth one by one, while the Allies were helpless to reach each other across the oceans of the world.

We won the Battle of the Oceans. By that victory the United Nations were knitted into a fighting whole, and the Axis powers were doomed to defeat everywhere.

That victory we owe to the men and women in the shipyards of the

428

Nation who in the last five and one-half years built carriers like this one, and over a hundred thousand other ships. We owe it to the workers in our factories who built 85,000 naval planes such as those which will soon take their places on the flight deck of this ship. We owe that victory to the fighting men who took those ships across the seas, running them right up to the home shores of the enemy; to the men who flew those planes against the enemy and dropped destruction on his fleet and aircraft and war industries.

We owe it to that great leader whose name this mighty carrier bears, who understood the importance of overwhelming naval power, and who rolled up his sleeves and got it.

Building this Navy was only a part of a still larger program of war production with which the workers and industries of this Nation amazed the whole world, friend and foe alike. It showed the abundant richness of our Nation in natural resources. But it also showed the skill and energy and power and devotion of our free American people.

Having done all this for war, can we do any less for peace? Certainly we *should* not. The same riches, the same skill and energy of America must now be used so that all our people are better fed, better clothed, better housed; so that they can get work at good wages, adequate care for their health, decent homes for their families, security for their old age, and more of the good things of life.

When we set these goals before ourselves we know that we are carrying on the work and vision, and the aims of the man whose name is on this ship. And no man in our generation, or in any generation, has done more to enable this Nation to move forward toward those objectives.

Commissioning this ship symbolizes another objective toward which Franklin D. Roosevelt started this Nation and the other nations of the world—the objective of world cooperation and peace. He who helped to formulate the Atlantic Charter, to organize the United Nations, he who pointed the way in cooperation among nations at Casablanca, Cairo, Quebec, Teheran, Dumbarton Oaks, and Yalta, and who planned the Conference at San Francisco—he knows as he looks down upon us today that the power of America as expressed in this mighty mass of steel is a power dedicated to the cause of peace.

For fourteen years, ever since Japan first invaded Manchuria, men and women have lived in a world ruled or threatened by force intended for aggression and conquest. Until El Alamein, Stalingrad, and Midway, the powers of evil were stronger than the powers of good—threatening to spread their rule across the world. We will not run that risk again.

This ship is a symbol of our commitment to the United Nations Organization to reach out anywhere in the world and to help the peace-loving nations of the world stop any international gangster. A hundred hours after leaving New York this ship could be off the coast of Africa. In five days she could cross the western Pacific from Pearl Harbor to the Philippines. This vessel alone could put more than one hundred fighting planes over a target.

We all look forward to the day when law rather than force will be the arbiter of international relations. We shall strive to make that day come soon. Until it does come, let us make sure that no possible aggressor is going to be tempted by any weakness on the part of the United States.

These, then, are the two huge tasks before us: realizing for our own people the full life which our resources make possible; and helping to achieve for people everywhere an era of peace. Franklin D. Roosevelt gave his life in search for the fulfillment of these tasks. And now, the American people are determined to carry on after him.

He did not find either of these tasks easy. Neither shall we. But we approach them in the spirit of Franklin D. Roosevelt whose words are inscribed in bronze on this vessel: "We can, we will, we must!"

NOTE: The President spoke shortly after 11 a.m. at the New York Navy Yard from a platform erected on the island of the U.S.S. *Franklin D. Roosevelt*. His opening words referred to Rear Adm. Freeland A. Daubin, commandant of the New York Navy Yard, Capt. Apollo Soucek, captain of the carrier, and Mrs. Franklin D. Roosevelt.

178   Address on Foreign Policy at the Navy Day Celebration
      in New York City.   *October 27, 1945*

Mayor La Guardia, ladies and gentlemen:

I am grateful for the magnificent reception which you have given me
today in this great city of New York. I know that it is given me only
as the representative of the gallant men and women of our naval forces,
and on their behalf, as well as my own, I thank you.

New York joins the rest of the Nation in paying honor and tribute
to the four million fighting Americans of the Navy, Marine Corps,
and Coast Guard—and to the ships which carried them to victory.

On opposite sides of the world, across two oceans, our Navy opened
a highway for the armies and air forces of the United States. They
landed our gallant men, millions of them, on the beachheads of final
triumph. Fighting from Murmansk, the English Channel and the
Tyrrhenian Sea, to Midway, Guadalcanal, Leyte Gulf and Okinawa—
they won the greatest naval victories in history. Together with their
brothers in arms in the Army and Air Force, and with the men of the
Merchant Marine, they have helped to win for mankind all over the
world a new opportunity to live in peace and dignity—and we hope,
in security.

In the harbor and rivers of New York City and in other ports along
the coasts and rivers of the country, ships of that mighty United States
Navy are at anchor. I hope that you and the people everywhere will
visit them and their crews, seeing for yourselves what your sons and
daughters, your labor and your money, have fashioned into an invincible weapon of liberty.

The fleet, on V-J Day, consisted of 1200 warships, more than 50,000
supporting and landing craft, and over 40,000 navy planes. By that day,
ours was a seapower never before equalled in the history of the world.
There were great carrier task forces capable of tracking down and
sinking the enemy's fleets, beating down his airpower, and pouring
destruction on his war-making industries. There were submarines
which roamed the seas, invading the enemy's own ports, and destroying
his shipping in all the oceans. There were amphibious forces capable

431

of landing soldiers on beaches from Normandy to the Philippines. There were great battleships and cruisers which swept the enemy ships from the seas and bombarded his shore defense almost at will.

And history will never forget that great leader who, from his first day in office, fought to reestablish a strong American Navy—who watched that Navy and all the other might of this Nation grow into an invincible force for victory—who sought to make that force an instrument for a just and lasting peace—and who gave his life in the effort—Franklin D. Roosevelt.

The roll call of the battles of this fleet reads like a sign post around the globe—on the road to final victory: North Africa, Sicily, Italy, Normandy, and Southern France; the Coral Sea, Midway, Guadalcanal, and the Solomons; Tarawa, Saipan, Guam, the Philippine Sea, Leyte Gulf; Iwo Jima and Okinawa. Nothing which the enemy held on any coast was safe from its attack.

Now we are in the process of demobilizing our naval force. We are laying up ships. We are breaking up aircraft squadrons. We are rolling up bases, and releasing officers and men. But when our demobilization is all finished as planned, the United States will still be the greatest naval power on earth.

In addition to that naval power, we shall still have one of the most powerful air forces in the world. And just the other day, so that on short notice we could mobilize a powerful and well-equipped land, sea, and air force, I asked the Congress to adopt universal training.

Why do we seek to preserve this powerful Naval and Air Force, and establish this strong Army reserve? Why do we need to do that?

We have assured the world time and again—and I repeat it now—that we do not seek for ourselves one inch of territory in any place in the world. Outside of the right to establish necessary bases for our own protection, we look for nothing which belongs to any other power.

We do need this kind of armed might, however, for four principal tasks:

First, our Army, Navy, and Air Force, in collaboration with our allies, must enforce the terms of peace imposed upon our defeated enemies.

432

Second, we must fulfill the military obligations which we are under-taking as a member of the United Nations Organization—to support a lasting peace, by force if necessary.

Third, we must cooperate with other American nations to preserve the territorial integrity and the political independence of the nations of the Western Hemisphere.

Fourth, in this troubled and uncertain world, our military forces must be adequate to discharge the fundamental mission laid upon them by the Constitution of the United States—to "provide for the common defense" of the United States.

These four military tasks are directed not toward war—not toward conquest—but toward peace.

We seek to use our military strength solely to preserve the peace of the world. For we now know that this is the only sure way to make our own freedom secure.

That is the basis of the foreign policy of the people of the United States.

The foreign policy of the United States is based firmly on funda-mental principles of righteousness and justice. In carrying out those principles we shall firmly adhere to what we believe to be right; and we shall not give our approval to any compromise with evil.

But we know that we cannot attain perfection in this world over-night. We shall not let our search for perfection obstruct our steady progress toward international cooperation. We must be prepared to fulfill our responsibilities as best we can, within the framework of our fundamental principles, even though we recognize that we have to operate in an imperfect world.

Let me restate the fundamentals of that foreign policy of the United States:

1. We seek no territorial expansion or selfish advantage. We have no plans for aggression against any other state, large or small. We have no objective which need clash with the peaceful aims of any other nation.

2. We believe in the eventual return of sovereign rights and self-government to all peoples who have been deprived of them by force.

433

3. We shall approve no territorial changes in any friendly part of the world unless they accord with the freely expressed wishes of the people concerned.

4. We believe that all peoples who are prepared for self-government should be permitted to choose their own form of government by their own freely expressed choice, without interference from any foreign source. That is true in Europe, in Asia, in Africa, as well as in the Western Hemisphere.

5. By the combined and cooperative action of our war allies, we shall help the defeated enemy states establish peaceful democratic governments of their own free choice. And we shall try to attain a world in which Nazism, Fascism, and military aggression cannot exist.

6. We shall refuse to recognize any government imposed upon any nation by the force of any foreign power. In some cases it may be impossible to prevent forceful imposition of such a government. But the United States will not recognize any such government.

7. We believe that all nations should have the freedom of the seas and equal rights to the navigation of boundary rivers and waterways and of rivers and waterways which pass through more than one country.

8. We believe that all states which are accepted in the society of nations should have access on equal terms to the trade and the raw materials of the world.

9. We believe that the sovereign states of the Western Hemisphere, without interference from outside the Western Hemisphere, must work together as good neighbors in the solution of their common problems.

10. We believe that full economic collaboration between all nations, great and small, is essential to the improvement of living conditions all over the world, and to the establishment of freedom from fear and freedom from want.

11. We shall continue to strive to promote freedom of expression and freedom of religion throughout the peace-loving areas of the world.

12. We are convinced that the preservation of peace between nations requires a United Nations Organization composed of all the peace-loving nations of the world who are willing jointly to use force if necessary to insure peace.

434

Now, that is the foreign policy which guides the United States. That is the foreign policy with which it confidently faces the future.

It may not be put into effect tomorrow or the next day. But nonetheless, it is our policy; and we shall seek to achieve it. It may take a long time, but it is worth waiting for, and it is worth striving to attain.

The Ten Commandments themselves have not yet been universally achieved over these thousands of years. Yet we struggle constantly to achieve them, and in many ways we come closer to them each year. Though we may meet setbacks from time to time, we shall not relent in our efforts to bring the Golden Rule into the international affairs of the world.

We are now passing through a difficult phase of international relations. Unfortunately it has always been true after past wars, that the unity among allies, forged by their common peril, has tended to wear out as the danger passed.

The world cannot afford any letdown in the united determination of the allies in this war to accomplish a lasting peace. The world cannot afford to let the cooperative spirit of the allies in this war disintegrate. The world simply cannot allow this to happen. The people in the United States, in Russia, and Britain, in France and China, in collaboration with all the other peace-loving people, must take the course of current history into their own hands and mold it in a new direction—the direction of continued cooperation. It was a common danger which united us before victory. Let it be a common hope which continues to draw us together in the years to come.

The atomic bombs which fell on Hiroshima and Nagasaki must be made a signal, not for the old process of falling apart but for a new era—an era of ever-closer unity and ever-closer friendship among peaceful nations.

Building a peace requires as much moral stamina as waging a war. Perhaps it requires even more, because it is so laborious and painstaking and undramatic. It requires undying patience and continuous application. But it can give us, if we stay with it, the greatest reward that there is in the whole field of human effort.

435

Differences of the kind that exist today among nations that fought together so long and so valiantly for victory are not hopeless or irreconcilable. There are no conflicts of interest among the victorious powers so deeply rooted that they cannot be resolved. But their solution will require a combination of forbearance and firmness. It will require a steadfast adherence to the high principles which we have enunciated. It will also require a willingness to find a common ground as to the methods of applying those principles.

Our American policy is a policy of friendly partnership with all peaceful nations, and of full support for the United Nations Organization. It is a policy that has the strong backing of the American people. It is a policy around which we can rally without fear or misgiving.

The more widely and clearly that policy is understood abroad, the better and surer will be the peace. For our own part we must seek to understand the special problems of other nations. We must seek to understand their own legitimate urge toward security as they see it.

The immediate, the greatest threat to us is the threat of disillusionment, the danger of insidious skepticism—a loss of faith in the effectiveness of international cooperation. Such a loss of faith would be dangerous at any time. In an atomic age it would be nothing short of disastrous.

There has been talk about the atomic bomb scrapping all navies, armies, and air forces. For the present, I think that such talk is 100 percent wrong. Today, control of the seas rests in the fleets of the United States and her allies. There is no substitute for them. We have learned the bitter lesson that the weakness of this great Republic invites men of ill-will to shake the very foundations of civilization all over the world. And we had two concrete lessons in that.

What the distant future of the atomic research will bring to the fleet which we honor today, no one can foretell. But the fundamental mission of the Navy has not changed. Control of our sea approaches and of the skies above them is still the key to our freedom and to our ability to help enforce the peace of the world. No enemy will ever strike us directly except across the sea. We cannot reach out to help stop and defeat an aggressor without crossing the sea. Therefore, the

436

Navy, armed with whatever weapons science brings forth, is still dedicated to its historic task: control of the ocean approaches to our country and of the skies above them.

The atomic bomb does not alter the basic foreign policy of the United States. It makes the development and application of our policy more urgent than we could have dreamed 6 months ago. It means that we must be prepared to approach international problems with greater speed, with greater determination, with greater ingenuity, in order to meet a situation for which there is no precedent.

We must find the answer to the problems created by the release of atomic energy—we must find the answers to the many other problems of peace—in partnership with all the peoples of the United Nations. For their stake in world peace is as great as our own.

As I said in my message to the Congress, discussion of the atomic bomb with Great Britain and Canada and later with other nations cannot wait upon the formal organization of the United Nations. These discussions, looking toward a free exchange of fundamental scientific information, will be begun in the near future. But I emphasize again, as I have before, that these discussions will not be concerned with the processes of manufacturing the atomic bomb or any other instruments of war.

In our possession of this weapon, as in our possession of other new weapons, there is no threat to any nation. The world, which has seen the United States in two great recent wars, knows that full well. The possession in our hands of this new power of destruction we regard as a sacred trust. Because of our love of peace, the thoughtful people of the world know that that trust will not be violated, that it will be faithfully executed.

Indeed, the highest hope of the American people is that world cooperation for peace will soon reach such a state of perfection that atomic methods of destruction can be definitely and effectively outlawed forever.

We have sought, and we will continue to seek, the attainment of that objective. We shall pursue that course with all the wisdom, patience, and determination that the God of Peace can bestow upon a people who are trying to follow in His path.

NOTE: The President spoke at 1:43 p.m. from a stand at the south end of the Sheep Meadow in Central Park, New York City. His opening words referred to Mayor Fiorello H. La Guardia. The address was carried over all radio networks.

179 Letter to Dr. Lyman J. Briggs on His Retirement as Director of the National Bureau of Standards. *October 29, 1945*

Dear Dr. Briggs:

Your retirement as the Director of the National Bureau of Standards will deprive the nation of the services of an eminent scientist and government administrator. You have well merited the wide recognition which has come to you by virtue of your personal achievements in the field of scientific research and by your competent direction of the Bureau's diversified operations.

I should like to take this occasion to comment on your long and unique record of public service. In World War I, military and naval developments which you sponsored and actively developed were a potent factor in our victory. In the decades of peace thereafter, you guided the Bureau's activities into fruitful channels and added to your own accomplishments, particularly in the then undeveloped field of aerodynamics. As World War II approached, President Roosevelt expressed his confidence in your capabilities by designating you as Chairman of the First Committee on the Investigation of Atomic Energy. The findings and recommendations of that Committee were an important factor in the decision to initiate the vast national effort for developing atomic weapons, and the subsequent discoveries of the National Bureau of Standards contributed greatly to the success of that effort.

Your record has been one of ever-increasing achievement, and you represent an outstanding example of the integrity and competence of government-sponsored science and research. I hope that you will fully enjoy your well-earned retirement, but that your rich fund of knowledge and experience will remain available for the guidance and counsel of those who continue the work of expanding the boundaries of scientific knowledge.

Sincerely yours,

HARRY S. TRUMAN

[Dr. Lyman J. Briggs, Director, National Bureau of Standards, Washington, D.C.]

180   Radio Address to the American People on Wages and Prices in the Reconversion Period.   *October 30, 1945*

[Broadcast from the White House at 10 p.m.]

Fellow citizens:

On August 18, 1945, four days after the surrender of Japan, I issued Executive Order 9599 which laid down the guiding policies of your Government during the transition from war to peace.

Briefly stated these policies are:

First, to assist in the maximum production of civilian goods.

Second, as rapidly as possible to remove Government controls and restore collective bargaining and free markets.

Third, to avoid both inflation and deflation.

Those are still our policies.

One of the major factors determining whether or not we shall succeed in carrying out those policies is the question of wages and prices. If wages go down substantially, we face deflation.   If prices go up substantially, we face inflation.   We must be on our guard, and steer clear of both these dangers to our security.

What happens to wages is important to all of us—even to those of us who do not work for wages.

It is important to business, for example, not only because wages represent an essential item in the cost of producing goods, but because people cannot buy the products of industry unless they earn enough wages generally.

What happens to wages is also important to the farmer.   The income he earns depends a great deal on the wages and purchasing power of the workers in our factories and shops and stores. They are the customers of the farmer and cannot buy farm products unless they earn enough wages.

The fact is that all of us are deeply concerned with wages, because all of us are concerned with the well-being of all parts of our economic system.

That is a simple truth. But like all simple truths, it is too often forgotten. Management sometimes forgets that business cannot prosper without customers who make good wages and have money in their pockets; labor sometimes forgets that workers cannot find employment and that wages cannot rise unless business prospers and makes profits.

Like most of you, I have been disturbed by the labor difficulties of recent weeks. These difficulties stand in the way of reconversion; they postpone the day when our veterans and displaced war workers can get back into good peacetime jobs. We need more of the good sense, the reasonableness, the consideration for the position of the other fellow, the teamwork which we had during the war.

It has been my experience in public life that there are few problems which cannot be worked out, if we make a real effort to understand the other fellow's point of view, and if we try to find a solution on the basis of give-and-take, of fairness to both sides.

I want to discuss the wage problem in just that spirit, and I hope that all of us in the United States can start thinking about it that way.

Let me begin by putting labor's position before you. I do not think all of us understand how hard a blow our industrial workers have suffered in the shift from war production to peace production.

You do know that sudden total victory caused millions of war workers to be laid off with very short notice or none at all. While we hope to overcome that condition before too many months have passed, unemployment is hardly a suitable reward for the contribution which veterans and war workers have made to victory.

Several months ago, I urged the Congress to amend the unemployment compensation law so as to help workers through the difficult months of unemployment until reconversion could be effected. The Congress has not yet passed that legislation.

The responsibility for that is solely up to Congress—and specifically I mean the Ways and Means Committee of the House of Representatives. I hope that this Committee will fulfill its obligation to the people of the Nation, and will give the Members of the House an early chance to vote on this important legislation. We must all recognize that legislation which will help sustain the purchasing power of labor until reconversion is completed, benefits not labor alone but all of us—business, agriculture, white-collar workers, and every member of our economic society.

I am sure that the workers of the Nation, those who depend upon manual labor for a livelihood, also feel a deep concern about full employment legislation which is now pending in the Congress. It is essential that the Congress speedily adopt some effective legislation which embodies the principles underlying full employment.

The American people are entitled to know now that this Government stands for prosperity and jobs—not depression and relief. Passage of a full employment bill will give the American people this assurance.

The responsibility for the damaging delay in enacting this legislation is definitely at the door of the Committee on Expenditures in the Executive Departments of the House of Representatives.

I am also sure that the workers of the Nation feel the same way about what is now happening to the United States Employment Service in the Senate and in the House. During the next year, millions of workers will have to look to efficient and centralized employment offices to find jobs for them anywhere in the country. The United States Employment Service has done so much during the war, and can do so much during the months ahead if it can continue to operate as a nationwide and unified organization, that I hope the Congress, for the time being, will keep this great public service under Federal management.

But quite as important as these problems of unemployment is the fact that the end of the war has meant a deep cut in the pay envelopes of many millions of workers. I wonder how many of you know that many war workers have already had to take, or will soon have to take, a cut in their wartime pay by one quarter or more. Think of what such a decrease in your own income would mean to you and to your families.

How does it happen that pay envelopes are being cut so deeply? There are three reasons.

First, there is the present decrease in the number of hours of employment. During the past few years of war, millions of workers were asked to put in abnormally long hours of work. Now that the need is past, the forty-hour week is being restored.

The changeover from a forty-eight to a forty-hour week means a decrease in take-home pay, the amount in the pay envelope. That decrease is much more than just the loss of eight hours pay. Workers have been receiving time and a half for overtime—for all the hours they worked over forty. That overtime pay is now gone in the change to a forty-hour week. The result has been a decrease of almost one quarter in the workers' weekly pay.

Second, weekly pay is being cut because many jobs are being reclassified to lower paying grades. The individual worker will feel these particularly when he changes from one job to another, starting at the bottom of the grade.

Third, the pay envelopes of workers will be thinner because millions of workers who were employed in the highly paid war industries will now have to find jobs in lower-wage, peacetime employment.

These three factors added together mean a drastic cut in the take-home pay of millions of workers. If nothing is done to help the workers in this situation, millions of families will have to tighten their belts—and by several notches.

It has been estimated that, unless checked, the annual wage and salary bill in private industry will shrink by over twenty billions of dollars. That is not going to do anybody any good—labor, business, agriculture, or the general public.

The corner grocer is going to feel it, just as well as the department

442

store, the railroads, the theaters, and the gas stations—and all the farmers of the Nation.

It is a sure road to wide unemployment.

This is what is known as deflation, and it is just as dangerous as inflation.

However, we must understand that we cannot hope, with a reduced work week, to maintain now the same take-home pay for labor generally that it has had during the war. There will have to be a drop. But the Nation cannot afford to have that drop too drastic.

Wage increases are therefore imperative—to cushion the shock to our workers, to sustain adequate purchasing power and to raise the national income.

There are many people who have said to me that industry cannot afford to grant any wage increases, however, without obtaining a corresponding increase in the price of its products. And they have urged me to use the machinery of Government to raise both.

This proposal cannot be accepted under any circumstances. To accept it would mean but one thing—inflation. And that invites disaster. An increase in wages if it were accompanied by an increase in the cost of living would not help even the workers themselves. Every dollar that we put in their pay envelopes under those circumstances would be needed to meet the higher living expenses resulting from increased prices.

Obviously, such a juggling of wages and prices would not settle anything or satisfy anyone. A runaway inflation would be upon us.

When inflation comes and the cost of living begins to spiral, nearly everybody suffers. Wage increases, under those conditions, would defeat their own purpose and mean nothing to labor. White-collar workers would find that their fixed salaries buy less food and clothing than before. Farmers' incomes would shrink because they would have to pay so much more for what they buy. Increased earnings would mean nothing to business itself. War bonds, insurance policies, pensions, annuities, bonds of all kinds would shrink in value, and their incomes would dwindle in buying power.

Therefore, wherever price increases would have inflationary tendencies, we must above all else hold the line on prices. Let us hold vigorously to our defense against inflation. Let us continue to hold the price line as we have held it since the spring of 1943. If we depart from this program of vigorous and successful price control, if we now begin to let down the bars, there will be no stopping place.

After the last war this Nation was confronted by much the same problem. At that time we simply pulled off the few controls that had been established, and let nature take its course. The result should stand as a lesson to all of us. A dizzy upward spiral of wages and the cost of living ended in the crash of 1920—a crash that spread bankruptcy and foreclosure and unemployment throughout the Nation.

If these twin objectives of ours—stability of prices and higher wage rates—were irreconcilable, if one could not be achieved without sacrificing the other, the outlook for all of us—labor, management, the farmer, and the consumer—would be very black indeed.

Fortunately, this is not so. While the positions of different industries vary greatly, there is room in the existing price structure for business as a whole to grant increases in wage rates.

And if all of us would approach the problem in a spirit of reasonableness and give-and-take—if we would sit down together and try to determine how much increase particular companies or industries could allow at a particular time—I think most businessmen would agree that wage increases are possible. Many of them, in fact, have already negotiated substantial wage increases without asking for any increase of prices.

There are several reasons why I believe that industry as a whole can afford substantial wage increases without raising prices.

First, the elimination of the time and a half for overtime has reduced labor costs per hour.

Second, the increase in the number of people needing jobs is resulting in a downward reclassification of jobs in many industries and in many sections of the country.

There is a third reason for believing that business can afford to pay wage increases—namely, increased output per hour of work or what is

444

generally called increased productivity. While increased production rests ultimately with labor, the time will soon come when improvements in machinery and manufacturing know-how developed in the war can certainly result in more goods per hour and additional room for wage increases.

As a fourth reason, business is in a very favorable profit position today, with excellent prospects for the period that lies ahead. Again, that is not true of all companies. Nevertheless, throughout industry and in every branch of industry, profits have been and still are very good indeed.

Finally, the Congress at my suggestion is now considering the elimination of the excess profits tax. Provision has already been made in our tax laws to enable corporations whose earnings dropped below their normal peacetime level to recapture a high proportion of the excess profits taxes which they have paid during the preceding two years. These and other provisions of the tax laws were designed to reduce to a minimum the risks entailed in reconversion—and that is precisely what they accomplish. They also add to the ability of industry to increase wages.

There are, however, important limits upon the capacity of industry to raise wages without raising prices. Let me put industry's position before you.

Industry has many risks and problems ahead that labor must recognize. For many companies, wartime products which were very profitable will have to be replaced by civilian products which will not be so profitable.

There are also problems of reconverting plants, of developing new sources of supply, new products, and new markets, of training inexperienced workers, of meeting increased costs of raw materials and supplies. All these will mean, at the beginning, lower volume and higher unit costs.

These problems and difficulties are particularly true in the case of small business—which is the backbone of the American competitive system.

I have said that not all companies can afford these wage increases. I

445

want to make clear, further, that there are companies where wages and even overtime pay continue high, and where no suffering will be caused to the workers during reconversion.

Labor must recognize these differences and not demand more than an industry or a company can pay under existing prices and conditions. It has a stern responsibility to see that demands for wage increases are reasonable. Excessive demands would deny to industry reasonable profits to which it is entitled, and which are necessary to stimulate an expansion of production. We must not kill the goose which lays the golden egg.

Labor itself has a responsibility to aid industry in reaching this goal of higher production and more jobs. It must strive constantly for greater efficiency and greater productivity—good work done, for good wages earned. Only in that way can we reach the mass production that has brought this country to the front of the industrial countries of the world.

Labor must constantly find ways within its own ranks of cutting down on absenteeism, reducing turn-over, avoiding jurisdictional disputes and "wild-cat" strikes. Labor and management must adopt collective bargaining as the effective and mature way of doing business.

The extent to which industry can grant wage increases without price increases will vary from company to company and from industry to industry. What can be paid today when we are on the threshold of our postwar production will be different from what can be paid next year and the year after, when markets have been established and earnings have become apparent. Both management and labor must keep on exploring these developments and determine from time to time to what extent costs have been reduced and profits have been increased, and how far these can properly be passed on in the form of increased wages.

Let me now turn to the question of just how wages are to be increased. Many people have asked the Government to step in and decide who is to increase wages and by exactly how much. I have, indeed, been criticised because I have not stepped in to lay down the law to business and labor. My refusal to do so has been deliberate.

Curiously enough, the same people who urge me to use Government wartime machinery of control to determine wage adjustments have on other occasions been the first to point out that the continued intervention of Government must spell the end of our system of free enterprise.

I am convinced that we must get away as quickly as possible from Government controls, and that we must get back to the free operation of our competitive system. Where wages are concerned, this means that we must get back to free and fair collective bargaining.

As a free people, we must have the good sense to bargain peaceably and sincerely. We must be determined to reach decisions based upon our long-range interest.

Let me emphasize, however, that the decisions that are reached in collective bargaining must be kept within the limits laid down by the wage-price policy of the Government.

This policy was described in the order of last August which I have already mentioned.

Briefly, it allows management to make wage increases without Government approval, but requires Government approval before the wage increase can be reflected in higher price ceilings. That is still the policy of the United States.

To guide labor and management in their interpretation of this Executive order, I have today issued an amendment—which I hope every one of you will read carefully in your newspapers tomorrow—amplifying the order and setting forth three classes of cases in which wage increases may be granted even though price ceiling increases may result.

They are all situations where wage increases are necessary, irrespective of price consequences. They will not cause many price increases.

In addition, the amendment makes two points of importance which I wish to emphasize here.

The first point has been true all along, but it has not been generally understood. If management does grant a wage increase, it is not prevented from coming in thereafter and requesting Government approval to have the wage increase considered for purposes of increasing prices. Whether such approval is sought before or after the wage increase is given, it receives the same consideration.

The second point is new and is very important. It is something which I am sure will help industry get over this very difficult period of readjustment. In cases where no approval of the wage increase has been requested by management, or even where a request has been made and denied by the Government, industry will not be asked by the Government to take an unreasonable chance in absorbing such wage increases. After a reasonable test period which, save in exceptional cases, will be six months, if the industry has been unable to produce at a fair profit, the entire wage increase will be taken into account in passing upon applications for price ceiling increases.

The Office of Price Administration will have to give its prompt consideration to all applications for price increases.

This is your Government's wage-price policy. For the time being, the machinery that administers it will remain the same as during the war.

But, as you know, I have called a conference here in Washington of the representatives of management and labor. It will start next week. One of their jobs is to recommend machinery for mediating or arbitrating differences wherever collective bargaining fails to work.

I hope the American people recognize how vital this conference actually is. Out of it can come the means of achieving industrial harmony and a new approach to human relationships in industry.

Until that machinery can be worked out, I urge upon labor and upon management the necessity of getting together on their problems. Public opinion will not countenance a refusal on the part of either management or labor to proceed in a peaceful, free, and democratic manner to arrive at just conclusions.

This is a time for proving the lessons we have learned during the war, the lessons of fair play, of give-and-take on a democratic basis, of working together in unity for the future. We all have a common aim, which is prosperity and security, and a just share of the good things of life. We can help attain this aim if we sit down at the conference table and iron out our troubles together. There is no room in our economy for unfair dealing or for greedy individuals or groups on either side

448

who want their own way regardless of the cost to others. The people will not stand for it. Their Government will not stand for it.

The country is entitled to expect that industry and labor will bargain in good faith, with labor recognizing the right of industry to a fair profit, and industry recognizing labor's need to a decent and sustained standard of living—and with both of them realizing that we cannot have either deflation or inflation in our economy.

The country, on the other hand, should be patient and realize that many of the parties are out of practice in collective bargaining. The point at which the people of the country are entitled to become impatient, and to consider the need of Government action, is when one of the parties fails to bargain in good faith or refuses a reasonable offer of conciliation or arbitration.

I know that this is not an easy way to solve the wage problem, but it is the sound way. It is the American way. I am convinced that if labor and management will approach each other, with the realization that they have a common goal, and with the determination to compose their differences in their own long-range interest, it will not be long before we have put industrial strife behind us. Labor is the best customer management has; and management is the source of labor's livelihood. Both are wholly dependent on each other; and the country in turn is dependent upon both of them.

Americans have always responded well in times of national need. There are no easy answers, there is no simple formula, for solving our difficult problems.

I have boundless faith in the commonsense and ultimate fairness of the American people. Given unity of purpose and a determination to meet the challenge of the times, there is nothing too difficult for them to accomplish. They have performed miracles during the war. They can, they will, surmount the difficulties which face them now on their road to continued peace and well-being.

449

181 The President's News Conference of
October 31, 1945

THE PRESIDENT. [1.] I thought maybe—I didn't have much to tell you this morning, I said it all last night—but I thought maybe you might be interested in the Hooper rating of the radio situation last night. It was 43.8 percent—32 million listeners. And 98.4 percent of all the radios that were in use were listening to the conversation. I will give you a copy of this, here.

[2.] I have a letter here from General Eisenhower, which is a most interesting document; and I haven't had a chance to have it mimeographed, but will have it mimeographed for you immediately after the conference so you can all have copies. It is dated October 26, and is from the headquarters of the United States Forces in the European theater, and it is addressed to me through the Chief of Staff. I am going to read it to you because it is a very, very interesting document.

Q. Slowly, will you, Mr. President?

THE PRESIDENT. I will read it slowly, but I will have it mimeographed so you can all have copies, if you don't get the gist of it, but I think you will.

[*Reading*] "You will recall that when you were in Frankfurt, you and I agreed upon the desirability of so organizing the Army's current functions in Europe as to facilitate turning U.S. participation in the government of Germany over to civil authority at the earliest possible moment. It is my understanding that the War Department completely supports this view. Every organizational step we have taken has been accomplished in such a way as to facilitate eventual transfer. Nevertheless, I am quite sure that there is a very widespread lack of realization as to the governing intent along this line, basing this statement upon the frequency with which visitors express astonishment that this purpose exists as a guiding policy.

"Naturally, I am not in position to recommend an exact date on which such transfer should take place, since I have assumed that the four interested governments would first have to agree in principle, and thereafter to make arrangements for simultaneous change from military to civil representatives. Moreover, there may be considerations, important to our government, of which I am unaware. However, from our local viewpoint, other governments could well be asked to agree to the proposal at the earliest date that can be mutually agreed upon, in no event later than June 1, 1946. As quickly as the matter could be agreed in principle, but not before, then actual completion of the American civil organization should be undertaken by whatever civilian you might, at that time, designate as its eventual head. Such things as these require time, but I am confident that we should not allow this detail to obscure, in the mind of any interested person, the clarity of the objective toward which we are striving.

"The matter of civil government of Germany is entirely separate from the occupational duty of the Army, which responsibility will persist as long as our own Government deems necessary. The true function of the Army in this region is to provide for the United States that reserve of force and power that can insure within our zone the prompt enforcement of all laws and regulations prescribed by the Group Council, or in the absence of such law and regulation, the policies laid down by our own Government for the United States zone.

"As you pointed out when here, separation of occupational and governmental responsibility is sound just as soon as there is no longer any military or security reason for holding them together, if for no other reason than because of its conformity to the American principle of keeping the Army as such out of the civil government field. Respectfully, Dwight D. Eisenhower."

I am in agreement with what the General has said. We discussed it while he was in Frankfurt, and eventually it will be carried out.

Q. Mr. President, may I ask you, was that June 1st or June 30th—that date?

THE PRESIDENT. June 1st, 1946.

Q. Mr. President, in other words, he wants to turn over by June 1st, 1946, the——

THE PRESIDENT. The civil government, which in no way affects the occupational forces as occupational forces; but the civil government would be under a civilian.

451

Q. The American civilian has to be appointed?

THE PRESIDENT. That's right.

Q. Mr. President, have we had any expressions from the other governments on that?

THE PRESIDENT. No. This is since I had the conversation at Frankfurt. This is the first discussion that I have had on it. And the State Department and the War Department and the President are in agreement on this policy.

Q. Will the next step be to see if that can be worked out with the other governments?

THE PRESIDENT. It will.

Q. Mr. President, will the principle eventually be followed as well in Japan?

THE PRESIDENT. Yes.

Q. Mr. President, would that entail the establishment of a German police force under American command to handle the direct policing——

THE PRESIDENT. Well, that is already in effect.

Q. That would be the general principle of the——

THE PRESIDENT. That is already in effect, and the military forces would be kept there merely as occupational forces to enforce the law, in case the local police could not do it.

Q. Would that government be under the State Department, or would it be a separate organization?

THE PRESIDENT. It would be a direct organization under the President of the United States.

Q. Mr. President, is it in connection with that letter from General Eisenhower that General Clay has now returned to the United States—or is now returning?

THE PRESIDENT. No. It has no connection. General Clay—as I know—is not returning only maybe on leave, or on some business of his own, because General Clay is one of our ablest generals, and we are trying to keep him over there.

Q. He is the military government man, more or less, and I thought he might be working out——

452

THE PRESIDENT. No. He is still working on the details of the government that is now in force over there.

[3.] Q. Mr. President, it was said in the House of Commons yesterday that President Roosevelt and former Prime Minister Churchill reached a secret agreement at Quebec on the peacetime use of the atom bomb. Do you——

THE PRESIDENT. I don't think that is true. As nearly as I can find out on the atom energy release program, Great Britain, Canada, and the United States are in equal partnership on its development. And Mr. Attlee is coming over here to discuss that phase of the situation with the President of the United States.

Q. Well, Mr. President, are these three countries in equal possession of the knowledge of how we produced that bomb?

THE PRESIDENT. They are.

Q. Great Britain knows as much about how we produce that as we do?

THE PRESIDENT. They do.

Q. Is that going to be the only topic that you and Mr. Attlee are going to discuss?

THE PRESIDENT. That is the only topic that has been requested to be discussed.

Q. But that doesn't foreclose the——

THE PRESIDENT. Mr. Attlee can talk to me about anything he chooses, but he is coming over here to talk to me about the atom bomb.

Q. Mr. President, a London paper suggested that—I believe the London Herald, a labor paper—suggested that this might be the prelude of a new Big Three conference. Do you feel that way about it, or is there any possibility of that?

THE PRESIDENT. I don't think I can intelligently answer that question, because the next step, after the Governments of Great Britain, Canada, and the United States have agreed on an international policy, will be to discuss the matter with the other governments of the world.

[4.] Q. In connection with this Big Three, have you had any reply from Mr. Stalin from the material presented to him by Mr. Harriman?

THE PRESIDENT. Yes, I have.

Q. Is there anything you can tell us about that reply?

THE PRESIDENT. It was a satisfactory reply.

Q. Does that mean, Mr. President, that you expect Russia will be represented at this Far Eastern Advisory Commission meeting?

THE PRESIDENT. I do.

Q. Can you say when that reply was received, sir?

THE PRESIDENT. While I was in New York City making a speech on Navy Day.

Q. Mr. Truman, does that also mean that there would be an early convening or reconvening of the Council of Foreign Ministers, possibly?

THE PRESIDENT. I can't answer that question until further developments.

Q. Mr. President, when you say you expect Russia to take part in the meeting now going on here, does that mean that an agreement has been reached on the control council?

THE PRESIDENT. No. This meeting is for the purpose of discussing that program, for the other Allies to join us in the occupation of Japan.

Q. Has direct acceptance or direct indication of Russia's intention to participate been received?

THE PRESIDENT. No, it has not.

Q. But you expect it to come in?

THE PRESIDENT. I do.

Q. Soon?

THE PRESIDENT. Yes.

Q. Did the letter from—or the answer from Marshal Stalin postulate any specific steps?

THE PRESIDENT. No. It was just a friendly answer to my communication to him.

Q. Is there any reason why it couldn't be made public, Mr. President?

THE PRESIDENT. Yes, there is. When the time comes for it to be made public, that will be made public; but the reason has not yet appeared.

[5.]   Q. What do you think about the legislation reported out by the House Military Affairs Committee yesterday, on prescribing penalties for breaking no-strike contracts?

THE PRESIDENT. When that comes to me for consideration, I will give you my opinion of it.

Q. Mr. President——

Q. Mr. President, do you have any answer from Mr. Attlee on the Palestine question?

THE PRESIDENT. Let the lady ask her question, and then I will answer you.

[6.]   Q. Mr. President, would you assent to Congress recessing before it has dealt with the legislation you dealt with last night?

THE PRESIDENT. The Congress has a right to vote its own recess, but I hope the Congress will not recess until the program is finished.

Q. Doesn't the Congress usually ask the President if he has further business?

THE PRESIDENT. I haven't been here long enough to answer that question. [*Laughter*] I'm sorry, I didn't mean to be sarcastic.

[7.]   Q. Mr. President, last week you told us that the Crowley letter was "somewhere around the White House." Could you tell us whether——

THE PRESIDENT. It had been released. The one to which I had referred had been released.[1]

Q. There is no other letter?

THE PRESIDENT. No other letter for release. I have had several letters from Mr. Crowley. The conversation with Mr. Crowley on his resignation from his job was verbal, and took place right here in this office, and I let him go reluctantly.

[8.]   Q. Mr. President, I repeat that question, have you had any answer from Mr. Attlee on the Palestine question?

THE PRESIDENT. I have had two or three messages from Mr. Attlee with regard to the Palestine question.

Q. Would you care to give us any indication as to what our Government's policy is in regard to that?

---

[1] See footnote on page 347.

THE PRESIDENT. No, because it is still under discussion.[1]

[9.]   Q. Mr. President, pursuing this Crowley thing, have you decided on the question of the Export-Import Bank appointments that you said you were considering last week?

THE PRESIDENT. I am trying to make a decision today. I have several people under consideration.

Q. Is Mr. Crowley still on that list?

THE PRESIDENT. Yes.

[10.]   Q. Mr. President, have you named the Government delegate to the ILO meeting in Denmark next month?

THE PRESIDENT. I don't think I have. There have been so many things across my desk, I can't remember having made that. I will look it up here and find out.

[11.]   Q. Mr. President, on your wage-price policy announcement last night, could you tell us what the maximum percentage wage increase on an industrywide basis——

THE PRESIDENT. There is no such maximum thing on an industry-wide basis. Each case is an individual case, and that is the reason we have got to do it by collective bargaining.

[12.]   Q. Mr. President, you said recently that politics is in the air again. Would you be a candidate for re-election in 1948? [*Laughter*]

THE PRESIDENT. On my individual rights, I don't think I have to testify against myself at this time. [*Laughter*]

Q. That's pretty good.

THE PRESIDENT. That matter has not entered my thoughts. I am too busy with other things.

Q. Is Mr. Hannegan too busy?

THE PRESIDENT. Mr. Hannegan is the political representative of the Democratic Party in the Cabinet of the President, and that is his job to look after those things, but I don't think he is working on anything of that kind.

Q. He seems to think he is, Mr. President. [*Laughter*]

---

[1] On November 13 the White House released a statement by the President concerning the problem of immigration of Jews into Palestine, together with a letter to Prime Minister Attlee dated August 31. See Items 187 and 188.

THE PRESIDENT. You will have to question him on that. I don't answer for him.

Reporter: Thank you, Mr. President.

THE PRESIDENT. You're welcome.

NOTE: President Truman's thirty-second news conference was held in his office at the White House at 10 a.m. on Wednesday, October 31, 1945.

182   Statement by the President on Announcing the Mission to Japan of Ambassador Edwin W. Pauley, Personal Representative of the President on Reparations Matters. *November 1, 1945*

THE PROBLEM of what to do with Germany and Japan is one of the greatest challenges in the whole effort to achieve lasting peace.

The program for reparations from Germany which was developed by Ambassador Pauley and adopted at the Berlin Conference will go a long way toward helping us achieve complete victory over Germany, by depriving her of the means ever again to wage another war. The reparations program which Ambassador Pauley will develop for Japan will be directed toward the same fundamental goal—to put an end for all time to Japanese aggression.

In carrying out this mission for me Ambassador Pauley and his staff will work in close cooperation with General MacArthur and his staff and will make full use of the surveys which have already been made by the industrial experts now on General MacArthur's staff.

NOTE: The White House release making public the statement noted that the President also announced the members of Ambassador Pauley's staff. The list is published in the Department of State Bulletin (vol. 13, p. 729).

183   Letter to Edgar F. Puryear on Receiving Report of the
        Review Committee on Deferment of Government
        Employees.   *November 1, 1945*

[Released November 1, 1945.   Dated October 31, 1945]

Dear Mr. Puryear:

Thank you for sending me the report of the Review Committee on
Deferment of Government Employees under your chairmanship.

I think that a splendid job has been done in keeping down the number
of deferments of employees of the Federal Government. I know that
a great deal of this accomplishment is due to your own patience, energy
and patriotic determination to see that the Selective Service System operated fairly and efficiently among government employees without
disrupting the Federal service too much.

I take this opportunity of thanking you and congratulating you on
the results achieved.

Very sincerely,

Harry S. Truman

[Honorable Edgar F. Puryear, Chairman, Review Committee on Deferment
of Government Employees, Washington, D.C.]

NOTE: The 4-page report, which was
released with the letter, is printed in
the Congressional Record (vol. 91, p.
A4825).

The report stated that Committee activities had resulted in the approval of
a far smaller proportion of deferments
than had been secured for non-Federal
employees during the period covered by
the report (February 1944–August
1945). The report also noted that due
to Committee policies occupational deferments for Federal employees had
been constantly reduced over the preceding 18 months, and that as of August
15, 1945, 80 percent of all agencies of
the Executive Branch of the Government had no approved occupational
deferments.

184   Address at the Opening Session of the Labor-
        Management Conference.   *November 5, 1945*

Ladies and gentlemen of the Labor-Management Conference:

In a radio broadcast to the American people last Tuesday night, I
said:

"I am convinced that if labor and management will approach each other, with the realization that they have a common goal, and with the determination to compose their differences in their own long-range interest, it will not be long before we have put industrial strife behind us. Labor is the best customer that management has; and management is the source of labor's livelihood. Both are wholly dependent upon each other; and the country in turn is dependent upon both of them."

This conference has been called to provide a nationwide opportunity to fulfill that objective. Representatives of labor and management are meeting here at this conference table, to discuss their common problems, and to settle differences in the public interest. Here is the democratic process in action—in its very best form.

On this conference have been based many high hopes of the American people. Their eyes are turned here in the expectation that you will furnish a broad and permanent foundation for industrial peace and progress.

I want to make it clear that this is your conference—a management-labor conference—and not a Government conference. You have not been chosen by me or by any other Government official. You have been selected by the leading labor and industrial organizations in the United States. There has been no interference by their Government in that selection.

By the very nature of the task before you, you appear here not as representatives merely of the organizations which chose you; but as public spirited citizens, who during the deliberations will consider the interests of all groups of our people. Each of you is now a member of the team which the American people hope will recommend definite policy in the field of industrial relations. We must begin with the firm realization that every citizen in our Nation has an identity of interest and a great stake in the maintenance of industrial peace and in the development of mature and effective ways of achieving it.

The time has come for labor and management to handle their own affairs in the traditional, American, democratic way. I hope that I can give up the President's wartime powers as soon as possible, so that management and labor can again have the full and undivided responsibility for providing the production that we *must* have to safeguard our domestic economy and our leadership in international affairs.

Your Government, although it is acting as your host, has no hand in the direction or recommendations of this conference. It has no vote.

This is your opportunity to prove that you can come to understanding and agreement without political or Government pressure. The outcome of this conference rests with the representatives of management and labor. But—as in all other public affairs—the outcome also rests with the American public who, by their interest and concern, can be a constant reminder that arbitrary selfishness and a refusal to see the other fellow's point of view have no place in these meetings.

Our country is worried about our industrial relations. It has a right to be. That worry is reflected in the Halls of Congress in the form of all kinds of proposed legislation. You have it in your power to stop that worry. I have supreme confidence in your ability to find a democratic way to compose industrial difficulties.

Under the patriotic pressure of a desperate war crisis, management and labor have performed a miracle of production for four years—working together voluntarily but under a measure of Government control. Those controls must soon disappear. Many have already gone. And yet as soon as the first ones were taken off, industrial strife appeared. Some of it was expected by the American people in this period of adjustment. But I am sure that they never expected anything like the amount of strife which has been threatened. And I know that the American people do not like it—especially after the solemn promise by representatives of both management and labor that they would cooperate with their Government through the reconversion period.

I make no effort to fix the blame. I have tried to lay fairly before the people the position of labor and the position of industry. They both have problems—grave and worrisome problems. But they are not insoluble problems. Essentially they are problems of adjustment to the drastic changes brought about by three and a half years of war.

The important thing is to remember that those problems—and their solution—cannot be allowed to stop us in our struggle to reconvert from war to peace. For until we successfully reconvert our productive ca-

pacity, we cannot hope to proceed toward our goal of full employment
and an increased standard of living. If labor and management, in an
industry or in a company, find that they cannot come to agreement, a
way must be found of resolving their differences without stopping
production.

Finding the best way to accomplish that result without Government
directive to either labor or industry—that is your job.

There are many considerations involved. At the basis of them all,
is not only the right, but the duty, to bargain collectively. I do not mean
giving mere lip service to that abstract principle. I mean the willingness on both sides, yes, the determination, to approach the bargaining
table with an open mind, with an appreciation of what is on the other
side of the table—and with a firm resolve to reach an agreement fairly.

If that fails, if bargaining produces no results, then there must be a
willingness to use some impartial machinery for reaching decisions on
the basis of proven facts and realities, instead of rumor or propaganda
or partisan statements. That is the way to eliminate unnecessary friction. That is the way to prevent lockouts and strikes. That is the way
to keep production going.

We shall have to find methods not only of peaceful negotiation of
labor contracts, but also of insuring industrial peace for the lifetime of
such contracts. Contracts once made must be lived up to, and should
be changed only in the manner agreed upon by the parties. If we expect confidence in agreements made, there must be responsibility and
integrity on both sides in carrying them out.

Some substitute must be found for jurisdictional strikes. Business
simply cannot stop, life and property just cannot be endangered, merely
because of some internal disagreement between factions of labor, in
which management can rightfully have no part or interest. There can
be no moral or economic justification for stopping production while
rival organizations contend with each other. Labor has a particular
interest in this matter—for nothing is so destructive of public confidence
in the motives of trade unionism as a jurisdictional strike.

On the other hand, management too often has looked upon labor
relations as a stepchild of its business, to be disregarded until the con-

461

troversy has reached a point where real collective bargaining becomes very difficult—if not almost impossible. It happens all too frequently that in the actual process of collective bargaining, delaying tactics are practised with the result that there is no real bargaining. There can be no justification for such tactics at the present time, or in the future.

If this conference can recommend answers to the public demand for machinery to prevent or settle industrial disputes, it will have made vast progress toward industrial peace. It will have laid a foundation for an era of prosperity and security.

The whole world now needs the produce of our mills and factories—everything stands ready and primed for a great future. But situations and circumstances can change rapidly. Our unparalleled opportunity may not long remain open. We must have production—vast production. We must have it soon.

In order to have it, labor and management must work together to expand the economy of our Nation—as they worked together to protect the safety of our Nation during the war. If we get the production that we need—the production which our resources and industrial skill make possible, the present problem of wages and prices will be easier to solve. Production means employment. It means economic wealth. It means higher wages and lower prices. It means the difference between strength and prosperity on the one hand, and uncertainty and depression on the other.

The men in this room direct a cross section of American industry, and lead American labor of all opinions. But you will fully succeed only if labor and industry as a whole willingly accept your decisions, and will adopt the convictions developed out of this conference.

The American people know the enormous size of your task. But the stakes are enormous too. If the people do not find the answers here, they will find them some place else. For these answers must and will be found. The whole system of private enterprise and individual opportunity depends upon finding them.

When industrial strife becomes widespread, all of us lose the things we need—the wages that labor wants, the earnings and dividends that businessmen and investors want, and the products that the consumers want. No realist can expect the millennium of a perfect no-strike, no lock-out era at once. But continued production and an expanding industry—unhampered as far as humanly possible by stoppages of work—are absolutely essential to progress.

That is the road to security at home and to peace abroad. We cannot fail in our efforts to move forward on that road.

NOTE: The President spoke in the Departmental Auditorium at approximately 12:15 p.m.

185　Letter to the Chairman, House Appropriations Committee, Concerning the Need for Additional Funds for Advance Planning of Public Works.
November 7, 1945

[Released November 7, 1945. Dated November 6, 1945]

Dear Clarence:

I wish to bring particularly to your attention my communication to the Speaker under date of October 18, 1945, (House Document No. 343), regarding the supplemental estimate of appropriation to permit the Federal Works Agency to continue and expand the program of advance planning of State and local public works under the basic authority contained in Title V of the War Mobilization and Reconversion Act of 1944.

You may recall that in my message to the Congress on September 6, 1945 (House Document No. 282), I invited attention to the fact that the appropriation thus far made for this purpose was entirely inadequate and that I would therefore request additional funds in order to speed up this important activity during the reconversion period. It was pursuant to this that I submitted my request of October 18, 1945, for an additional appropriation and contract authorization.

The matter of advance planning is one in which I have always had a close, personal interest. To have available for immediate construction a well developed and completely planned shelf of worthy public works projects is the best insurance against the waste which results when a program of construction is undertaken without detailed drawings and specifications being available. The fact that the law requires the repayment to the Treasury of advances when construction is undertaken tends to insure that the public works planned by the use of such funds are needed public projects of worthwhile character as the local communities are thereby using their own credit to finance this work.

It is my earnest hope that your Committee will give prompt and favorable consideration to the recommendations made in the message referred to above.

Very sincerely yours,

HARRY S. TRUMAN

[Honorable Clarence Cannon, Chairman, Appropriations Committee, House of Representatives]

NOTE: The President's communication of October 18 (printed in House Doc. 343, 79th Cong., 1st sess.) requested an additional appropriation of $50 million for fiscal year 1946 and an additional $57.5 million in contract authority for the Federal Works Agency. The details of the proposal, as set forth in a letter of the Director of the Bureau of the Budget, are also printed in House Document 343.

For the President's message of September 6, see Item 128 above.

186 Special Message to the Congress on U.S. Participation in the United Nations Relief and Rehabilitation Administration. *November 13, 1945*

To the Congress of the United States of America:

This country has pledged itself to do all that is reasonably possible to alleviate the suffering of our war-torn allies and to help them begin the task of restoring their economic productivity. The United Nations Relief and Rehabilitation Administration is one of the most important instrumentalities for accomplishing this great task.

As I stated in my message to the Congress on September 6, 1945, the forty-seven nations of the Council of United Nations Relief and Rehabilitation Administration determined at their Third Meeting in London last August that contributions beyond those originally made would be necessary if we expect to complete the minimum tasks assigned to UNRRA. The Council recommended, on the motion of the United States Delegate, that each member country, whose territory had not been invaded by the enemy, should contribute an additional amount equal to one percent of its national income for the fiscal year 1943.

In accordance with this recommendation, the United States' share would be $1,350,000,000, matching our original contribution authorized by the Act of Congress of March 28, 1944.

The original contributions of all the member nations have been applied principally to the activities of UNRRA in providing relief and rehabilitation assistance to the countries of eastern and southeastern Europe, and to the care of United Nations displaced persons stranded in enemy territory. UNRRA, of course, does not undertake relief or rehabilitation responsibilities in either Germany or Japan.

The invaded countries of northwest Europe, comprising France, Belgium, Holland, Denmark and Norway, by and large, possess sufficient resources in foreign currency and credit to acquire their own essential imports from abroad. Direct assistance to northwest Europe is, therefore, not being furnished by UNRRA.

Poland, Czechoslovakia, Yugoslavia, Greece and Albania, on the other hand, not only have suffered greatly at the hands of the enemy in the course of the war but they are almost entirely without foreign exchange or credit resources. Consequently to date they have been the chief objects of UNRRA's activity.

UNRRA has undertaken a limited program of $50,000,000 in Italy to provide for the health and care of children, and expectant or nursing mothers.

Italy, since her participation in the war as a co-belligerent with the United Nations, has contributed substantially in both manpower and facilities to the Allied victory, becoming, at the same time, one of the most severely contested battlefields of the war. The destitution and needs there are appalling. Italy has virtually no foreign exchange resources and without the aid of UNRRA the country might well lapse into starvation.

UNRRA has also assisted in the care and repatriation of millions of allied victims of Axis aggression who were deported to and enslaved in Germany. It has initiated a preliminary program of assistance to China.

By the end of this year UNRRA anticipates that all the funds which will be made available to it from all sources in accordance with the original contributions will have been spent or encumbered. The flow of supplies purchased with these funds cannot last beyond the early spring.

The end of the war with Japan has made it possible to estimate the magnitude of the relief requirements of China and other Far Eastern areas. Reports on the European harvest of 1945 reveal a serious short-age of all types of foodstuffs.

China presents the largest of all the relief responsibilities which UNRRA now faces. With inadequate supplies and resources it has struggled bravely for eight years to combat the enemy as well as the ravages of famine, disease and inflation. Other programs are required for Korea and Formosa, two areas of the Far East which are now being restored to the peaceful ranks of the United Nations after decades of Japanese oppression and extortion.

UNRRA proposes the extension of aid to Austria. This proposal is in accordance with the Moscow and Potsdam Declarations by the major powers to the effect that Austria should be treated independently of Germany and encouraged to resume the free and peaceful role which it played before being invaded by Hitler's legions.

A limited program of aid is also intended for the Soviet Republics of White Russia and the Ukraine. These areas constituted the principal battlefields in the struggle between Russia and Germany. They were the scene of some of the worst German atrocities, devastation and pillage.

The recommended additional contributions will hardly suffice to permit UNRRA to meet the most urgent and immediate needs for relief and rehabilitation for which it is responsible. We hope to fulfill a substantial part of this contribution through the use of military and lend-lease supplies which have become surplus since the surrender of our enemies.

I know that America will not remain indifferent to the call of human suffering. This is particularly true when it is suffering on the part of those who by sacrifice and courage kept the enemy from realizing the fruits of his early victories and from bringing his military might to bear upon our own shores.

UNRRA is the chosen instrument of forty-seven United Nations to meet the immediate relief and rehabilitation needs of the invaded countries.

UNRRA is the first of the international organizations to operate in the post-war period, one which the United States originally sponsored and in which it has played a leading part. Apart from purely humanitarian considerations, its success will do much to prove the possibility of establishing order and cooperation in a world finally at peace.

I, therefore, request the Congress to authorize a new appropriation of $1,350,000,000 for participation in the activities of UNRRA.

HARRY S. TRUMAN

NOTE: On December 18, 1945, the President approved a bill enabling the United States to further participate in the work of UNRRA (Public Law 262, 79th Cong., 59 Stat. 612).

187 Statement by the President on the Problem of Jewish Refugees in Europe. *November 13, 1945*

FOLLOWING the receipt of information from various sources regarding the distressing situation of the Jewish victims of Nazi and Fascist persecution in Europe, I wrote to Mr. Attlee on August 31 bringing to his attention the suggestion in a report of Mr. Earl G. Harrison that the granting of an additional 100,000 certificates for the immigration of Jews into Palestine would alleviate the situation. A copy of my letter to Mr. Attlee is being made available to the press. I continue to adhere to the views expressed in that letter.

I was advised by the British Government that because of conditions in Palestine it was not in a position to adopt the policy recommended, but that it was deeply concerned with the situation of the Jews in

Europe. During the course of subsequent discussions between the two Governments, it suggested the establishment of a joint Anglo-American Committee of Inquiry, under a rotating chairmanship, to examine the whole question and to make a further review of the Palestine problem in the light of that examination and other relevant considerations.

In view of our intense interest in this matter and of our belief that such a committee will be of aid in finding a solution which will be both humane and just, we have acceded to the British suggestion.

The terms of reference of this committee as agreed upon between the two Governments are as follows:

1. To examine political, economic and social conditions in Palestine as they bear upon the problem of Jewish immigration and settlement therein and the well-being of the peoples now living therein.

2. To examine the position of the Jews in those countries in Europe where they have been the victims of Nazi and Fascist persecution, and the practical measures taken or contemplated to be taken in those countries to enable them to live free from discrimination and oppression and to make estimates of those who wish or will be impelled by their conditions to migrate to Palestine or other countries outside Europe.

3. To hear the views of competent witnesses and to consult representative Arabs and Jews on the problems of Palestine as such problems are affected by conditions subject to examination under paragraphs 1 and 2 above and by other relevant facts and circumstances, and to make recommendations to His Majesty's Government and the Government of the United States for ad interim handling of these problems as well as for their permanent solution.

4. To make such other recommendations to His Majesty's Government and the Government of the United States as may be necessary to meet the immediate needs arising from conditions subject to examination under paragraph 2 above, by remedial action in the European countries in question or by the provision of facilities for emigration to and settlement in countries outside Europe.

It will be observed that among the important duties of this committee will be the task of examining conditions in Palestine as they bear upon the problem of Jewish immigration. The establishment of this

Committee will make possible a prompt review of the unfortunate plight of the Jews in those countries in Europe where they have been subjected to persecution, and a prompt examination of questions related to the rate of current immigration into Palestine and the absorptive capacity of the country.

The situation faced by displaced Jews in Europe during the coming winter allows no delay in this matter. I hope the Committee will be able to accomplish its important task with the greatest speed.

NOTE: For the President's letter of August 31 to Prime Minister Attlee, see Item 188. The Harrison report, released September 29, 1945, is published in the Department of State Bulletin (vol. 13, p. 456). See also Item 210.

188   Letter to Prime Minister Attlee Concerning the Need for Resettlement of Jewish Refugees in Palestine.
November 13, 1945

[Released November 13, 1945.   Dated August 31, 1945]

My dear Mr. Prime Minister:

Because of the natural interest of this Government in the present condition and future fate of those displaced persons in Germany who may prove to be stateless or non-repatriable, we recently sent Mr. Earl G. Harrison to inquire into the situation.

Mr. Harrison was formerly the United States Commissioner of Immigration and Naturalization, and is now the Representative of this Government on the Intergovernmental Committee on Refugees. The United Kingdom and the United States, as you know, have taken an active interest in the work of this Committee.

Instructions were given to Mr. Harrison to inquire particularly into the problems and needs of the Jewish refugees among the displaced persons.

Mr. Harrison visited not only the American zone in Germany, but spent some time also in the British zone where he was extended every courtesy by the 21st Army Headquarters.

I have now received his report. In view of our conversations at Potsdam I am sure that you will find certain portions of the report interesting. I am, therefore, sending you a copy.

I should like to call your attention to the conclusions and recommendations appearing on page 8 and the following pages—especially the references to Palestine. It appears that the available certificates for immigration to Palestine will be exhausted in the near future. It is suggested that the granting of an additional one hundred thousand of such certificates would contribute greatly to a sound solution for the future of Jews still in Germany and Austria, and for other Jewish refugees who do not wish to remain where they are or who for understandable reasons do not desire to return to their countries of origin.

On the basis of this and other information which has come to me I concur in the belief that no other single matter is so important for those who have known the horrors of concentration camps for over a decade as is the future of immigration possibilities into Palestine. The number of such persons who wish immigration to Palestine or who would qualify for admission there is, unfortunately, no longer as large as it was before the Nazis began their extermination program. As I said to you in Potsdam, the American people, as a whole, firmly believe that immigration into Palestine should not be closed and that a reasonable number of Europe's persecuted Jews should, in accordance with their wishes, be permitted to resettle there.

I know you are in agreement on the proposition that future peace in Europe depends in large measure upon our finding sound solutions of problems confronting the displaced and formerly persecuted groups of people. No claim is more meritorious than that of the groups who for so many years have known persecution and enslavement.

The main solution appears to lie in the quick evacuation of as many as possible of the non-repatriable Jews, who wish it, to Palestine. If it is to be effective, such action should not be long delayed.

Very sincerely yours,

HARRY S. TRUMAN

NOTE: Mr. Harrison's report, to which the President referred, is published in the Department of State Bulletin (vol. 13, p. 456). See also Item 187.

189 Letter to President Osmeña of the Philippines Upon
     Approving a Bill of the Philippine Congress.
     November 14, 1945

My dear President Osmeña:

I have for some time delayed my approval of House Bill No. 176 of
the first Philippine Congress, which provides a reduction of the required gold coverage of Philippine currency. This delay has been due
to the fact that there have been persistent charges that a sizable fraction of the Members of the Philippine Congress had been guilty of
collaboration with the enemy, and I have not wanted my approval of
the act to be distorted into approval of collaboration.

I am informed, however, that the provisions of House Bill No. 176
are necessary to the effective conduct of the Philippine Government and
I accordingly have approved the act. At the same time, I should like
to emphasize that my signature is in no sense an approval of the presence in the Philippine Congress of any person who has given aid to
the enemy or his political policies.

Sincerely yours,

HARRY S. TRUMAN

[Honorable Sergio Osmeña, President of the Philippines, 1617 Massachusetts
Avenue NW., Washington 6, D.C.]

190 Statement by the President on the Tenth Anniversary of
     the Philippine Commonwealth. *November 15, 1945*

NOVEMBER 15, 1945, marks the tenth anniversary of the inauguration of the Philippine Commonwealth. Those ten years were set aside
by Congress, and approved by the Filipino people, as a period of preparation for independence. The Philippines and the Filipinos were to
have been given those ten years to prepare their national economy
and their national government to assume the full responsibilities of
nationhood.

Neither we nor they knew, in 1935, what a test the Philippines would be called upon to pass in 1941—the test of war. The Filipino people went through the ordeals of war and of Japanese occupation in a manner to their immortal credit. It was a credit to them, and to us, who led the Philippines along the 40-year road from serfdom under Spain to commonwealth status. But more than that it was a credit to those ideals of democracy and human dignity which America introduced into the Philippines in 1898, ideals which took root there so firmly as to survive every savage effort of the Japanese to uproot them.

The Filipino people are spiritually worthy of independence. They have won their spurs as a nation. We will honor our promise and our pledges to them. The United States stands ready to aid the heroes of the Philippines in every way we can.

The United States honors the Filipino people on this tenth anniversary of Commonwealth Day.

191 The President's News Conference Following the Signing of a Joint Declaration on Atomic Energy.
November 15, 1945

[With Prime Minister Attlee of Great Britain and Prime Minister King of Canada]

THE PRESIDENT. Will you please listen for just a moment. I am going to read to you the document which has been signed by the Prime Minister of Great Britain and the Prime Minister of Canada, and the President of the United States. Copies will be handed to you as you go out, as soon as I finish reading.

Questions on this document will have to come at a later time, when you are familiar with it.

This is headed "The President of the United States, the Prime Minister of the United Kingdom, and the Prime Minister of Canada, have issued the following statement.

"1. We recognize that the application of recent scientific discoveries to the methods and practice of war has placed at the disposal of mankind means of destruction hitherto unknown, against which there can be no adequate military defense, and in the employment of which no single nation can in fact have a monopoly.

"2. We desire to emphasize that the responsibility for devising means to ensure that the new discoveries shall be used for the benefit of mankind, instead of as a means of destruction, rests not on our nations alone, but upon the whole civilized world. Nevertheless, the progress that we have made in the development and use of atomic energy demands that we take an initiative in the matter, and we have accordingly met together to consider the possibility of international action:

"(a) To prevent the use of atomic energy for destructive purposes.

"(b) To promote the use of recent and future advances in scientific knowledge, particularly in the utilization of atomic energy, for peaceful and humanitarian ends.

"3. We are aware that the only complete protection for the civilized world from the destructive use of scientific knowledge lies in the prevention of war. No system of safeguards that can be devised will of itself provide an effective guarantee against production of atomic weapons by a nation bent on aggression. Nor can we ignore the possibility of the development of other weapons, or of new methods of warfare, which may constitute as great a threat to civilization as the military use of atomic energy.

"4. Representing, as we do, the three countries which possess the knowledge essential to the use of atomic energy, we declare at the outset our willingness, as a first contribution, to proceed with the exchange of fundamental scientific information and the interchange of scientists and scientific literature for peaceful ends with any nation that will fully reciprocate.

"5. We believe that the fruits of scientific research should be made available to all nations, and that freedom of investigation and free interchange of ideas are essential to the progress of knowledge. In pursuance of this policy, the basic scientific information essential to the development of atomic energy for peaceful purposes has already been made available to the world. It is our intention that all further information of this character that may become available from time to time shall be similarly treated. We trust that other nations will adopt the same policy, thereby creating an atmosphere of reciprocal confidence in which political agreement and cooperation will flourish.

"6. We have considered the question of the disclosure of detailed information concerning the practical industrial application of atomic energy. The military exploitation of atomic energy depends, in large part, upon the same methods and processes as would be required for industrial uses.

"We are not convinced that the spreading of the specialized information regarding the practical application of atomic energy, before it is possible to devise effective, reciprocal, and enforceable safeguards acceptable to all nations, would contribute to a constructive solution of the problem of the atomic bomb. On the contrary we think it might have the opposite effect. We are, however, prepared to share, on a reciprocal basis with others of the United Nations, detailed information concerning the practical industrial application of atomic energy just as soon as effective enforceable safeguards against its use for destructive purposes can be devised.

"7. In order to attain the most effective means of entirely eliminating the use of atomic energy for destructive purposes and promoting its widest use for industrial and humanitarian purposes, we are of the opinion that at the earliest practicable date a Commission should be set up under the United Nations Organization to prepare recommendations for submission to the Organization.

"The Commission should be instructed to proceed with the utmost dispatch and should be authorized to submit recommendations from time to time dealing with separate phases of its work.

"In particular, the Commission should make specific proposals:

"(a) For extending between all nations the exchange of basic scientific information for peaceful ends,

"(b) For control of atomic energy to the extent necessary to ensure its use only for peaceful purposes,

"(c) For the elimination from national armaments of atomic weapons and of all other major weapons adaptable to mass destruction,

"(d) For effective safeguards by way of inspection and other means to protect complying states against the hazards of violations and evasions.

"8. The work of the Commission should proceed by separate stages, the successful completion of each one of which will develop the necessary confidence of the world before the next stage is undertaken. Specifically, it is considered that the Commission might well devote its attention first to the wide exchange of scientists and scientific information, and as a second stage to the development of full knowledge concerning natural resources of raw materials.

"9. Faced with the terrible realities of the application of science to destruction, every nation will realize more urgently than before the overwhelming need to maintain the rule of law among nations and to banish the scourge of war from the earth. This can only be brought about by giving wholehearted support to the United Nations Organization, and by consolidating and extending its authority, thus creating conditions of mutual trust in which all peoples will be free to devote themselves to the arts of peace. It is our firm resolve to work without reservation to achieve these ends."

And this document is signed by the three of us.

That's all.

Reporter: Thank you, Mr. President.

NOTE: President Truman's thirty-third news conference was held in his office at the White House at 11:05 a.m. on Thursday, November 15, 1945. The White House Official Reporter noted that Congressional leaders and other guests were sitting or standing around the President's desk—the President in the center with Mr. Attlee on his right, Mr. King on his left.

192   Special Message to the Congress Recommending a Comprehensive Health Program. *November* 19, 1945

To the Congress of the United States:

In my message to the Congress of September 6, 1945, there were enumerated in a proposed Economic Bill of Rights certain rights which ought to be assured to every American citizen.

One of them was: "The right to adequate medical care and the opportunity to achieve and enjoy good health." Another was the "right to adequate protection from the economic fears of . . . sickness. . . ."

Millions of our citizens do not now have a full measure of opportunity to achieve and enjoy good health. Millions do not now have protection or security against the economic effects of sickness. The time has arrived for action to help them attain that opportunity and that protection.

The people of the United States received a shock when the medical examinations conducted by the Selective Service System revealed the widespread physical and mental incapacity among the young people of our nation. We had had prior warnings from eminent medical authorities and from investigating committees. The statistics of the last war had shown the same condition. But the Selective Service System has brought it forcibly to our attention recently—in terms which all of us can understand.

As of April 1, 1945, nearly 5,000,000 male registrants between the ages of 18 and 37 had been examined and classified as unfit for military service. The number of those rejected for military service was about 30 percent of all those examined. The percentage of rejection was lower in the younger age groups, and higher in the higher age groups, reaching as high as 49 percent for registrants between the ages of 34 and 37.

In addition, after actual induction, about a million and a half men had to be discharged from the Army and Navy for physical or mental disability, exclusive of wounds; and an equal number had to be treated in the Armed Forces for diseases or defects which existed before induction.

Among the young women who applied for admission to the Women's Army Corps there was similar disability. Over one-third of those examined were rejected for physical or mental reasons.

These men and women who were rejected for military service are not necessarily incapable of civilian work. It is plain, however, that they have illnesses and defects that handicap them, reduce their working capacity, or shorten their lives.

It is not so important to search the past in order to fix the blame for these conditions. It is more important to resolve now that no American child shall come to adult life with diseases or defects which can be prevented or corrected at an early age.

Medicine has made great strides in this generation—especially during the last four years. We owe much to the skill and devotion of the medical profession. In spite of great scientific progress, however, each year we lose many more persons from preventable and premature deaths than we lost in battle or from war injuries during the entire war.

We are proud of past reductions in our death rates. But these reductions have come principally from public health and other community services. We have been less effective in making available to all of our people the benefits of medical progress in the care and treatment of individuals.

In the past, the benefits of modern medical science have not been enjoyed by our citizens with any degree of equality. Nor are they today. Nor will they be in the future—unless government is bold enough to do something about it.

People with low or moderate incomes do not get the same medical attention as those with high incomes. The poor have more sickness, but they get less medical care. People who live in rural areas do not get the same amount or quality of medical attention as those who live in our cities.

Our new Economic Bill of Rights should mean health security for all, regardless of residence, station, or race—everywhere in the United States.

We should resolve now that the health of this Nation is a national concern; that financial barriers in the way of attaining health shall be removed; that the health of all its citizens deserves the help of all the Nation.

There are five basic problems which we must attack vigorously if we would reach the health objectives of our Economic Bill of Rights.

1. The first has to do with the number and distribution of doctors and hospitals. One of the most important requirements for adequate health service is professional personnel—doctors, dentists, public health

and hospital administrators, nurses and other experts.

The United States has been fortunate with respect to physicians. In proportion to population it has more than any large country in the world, and they are well trained for their calling. It is not enough, however, that we have them in sufficient numbers. They should be located where their services are needed. In this respect we are not so fortunate.

The distribution of physicians in the United States has been grossly uneven and unsatisfactory. Some communities have had enough or even too many; others have had too few. Year by year the number in our rural areas has been diminishing. Indeed, in 1940, there were 31 counties in the United States, each with more than a thousand inhabitants, in which there was not a single practicing physician. The situation with respect to dentists was even worse.

One important reason for this disparity is that in some communities there are no adequate facilities for the practice of medicine. Another reason—closely allied with the first—is that the earning capacity of the people in some communities makes it difficult if not impossible for doctors who practice there to make a living.

The demobilization of 60,000 doctors, and of the tens of thousands of other professional personnel in the Armed Forces is now proceeding on a large scale. Unfortunately, unless we act rapidly, we may expect to see them concentrate in the places with greater financial resources and avoid other places, making the inequalities even greater than before the war.

Demobilized doctors cannot be assigned. They must be attracted. In order to be attracted, they must be able to see ahead of them professional opportunities and economic assurances.

Inequalities in the distribution of medical personnel are matched by inequalities in hospitals and other health facilities. Moreover, there are just too few hospitals, clinics and health centers to take proper care of the people of the United States.

About 1,200 counties, 40 percent of the total in the country, with some 15,000,000 people, have either no local hospital, or none that meets even the minimum standards of national professional associations.

478

The deficiencies are especially severe in rural and semirural areas and in those cities where changes in population have placed great strains on community facilities.

I want to emphasize, however, that the basic problem in this field cannot be solved merely by building facilities. They have to be staffed; and the communities have to be able to pay for the services. Otherwise the new facilities will be little used.

2. The second basic problem is the need for development of public health services and maternal and child care. The Congress can be justifiably proud of its share in making recent accomplishments possible. Public health and maternal and child health programs already have made important contributions to national health. But large needs remain. Great areas of our country are still without these services. This is especially true among our rural areas; but it is true also in far too many urban communities.

Although local public health departments are now maintained by some 18,000 counties and other local units, many of these have only skeleton organizations, and approximately 40,000,000 citizens of the United States still live in communities lacking full-time local public health service. At the recent rate of progress in developing such service, it would take more than a hundred years to cover the whole Nation.

If we agree that the national health must be improved, our cities, towns and farming communities must be made healthful places in which to live through provision of safe water systems, sewage disposal plants and sanitary facilities. Our streams and rivers must be safeguarded against pollution. In addition to building a sanitary environment for ourselves and for our children, we must provide those services which prevent disease and promote health.

Services for expectant mothers and for infants, care of crippled or otherwise physically handicapped children and inoculation for the prevention of communicable diseases are accepted public health functions. So too are many kinds of personal services such as the diagnosis and treatment of widespread infections like tuberculosis and venereal disease. A large part of the population today lacks many or all of these services.

Our success in the traditional public health sphere is made plain by the conquest over many communicable diseases. Typhoid fever, small-pox, and diphtheria—diseases for which there are effective controls—have become comparatively rare. We must make the same gains in reducing our maternal and infant mortality, in controlling tuberculosis, venereal disease, malaria, and other major threats to life and health. We are only beginning to realize our potentialities in achieving physical well-being for all our people.

3. The third basic problem concerns medical research and professional education.

We have long recognized that we cannot be content with what is already known about health or disease. We must learn and understand more about health and how to prevent and cure disease.

Research—well directed and continuously supported—can do much to develop ways to reduce those diseases of body and mind which now cause most sickness, disability, and premature death—diseases of the heart, kidneys and arteries, rheumatism, cancer, diseases of childbirth, infancy and childhood, respiratory diseases and tuberculosis. And research can do much toward teaching us how to keep well and how to prolong healthy human life.

Cancer is among the leading causes of death. It is responsible for over 160,000 recorded deaths a year, and should receive special attention. Though we already have the National Cancer Institute of the Public Health Service, we need still more coordinated research on the cause, prevention and cure of this disease. We need more financial support for research and to establish special clinics and hospitals for diagnosis and treatment of the disease especially in its early stages. We need to train more physicians for the highly specialized services so essential for effective control of cancer.

There is also special need for research on mental diseases and abnormalities. We have done pitifully little about mental illnesses. Accurate statistics are lacking, but there is no doubt that there are at least two million persons in the United States who are mentally ill, and that as many as ten million will probably need hospitalization for mental illness for some period in the course of their lifetime. A great many of these persons would be helped by proper care. Mental cases occupy more than one-half of the hospital beds, at a cost of about 500 million dollars per year—practically all of it coming out of taxpayers' money. Each year there are 125,000 new mental cases admitted to institutions. We need more mental-disease hospitals, more out-patient clinics. We need more services for early diagnosis, and especially we need much more research to learn how to prevent mental breakdown. Also, we must have many more trained and qualified doctors in this field.

It is clear that we have not done enough in peace-time for medical research and education in view of our enormous resources and our national interest in health progress. The money invested in research pays enormous dividends. If any one doubts this, let him think of penicillin, plasma, DDT powder, and new rehabilitation techniques.

4. The fourth problem has to do with the high cost of individual medical care. The principal reason why people do not receive the care they need is that they cannot afford to pay for it on an individual basis at the time they need it. This is true not only for needy persons. It is also true for a large proportion of normally self-supporting persons.

In the aggregate, all health services—from public health agencies, physicians, hospitals, dentists, nurses and laboratories—absorb only about 4 percent of the national income. We can afford to spend more for health.

But four percent is only an average. It is cold comfort in individual cases. Individual families pay their individual costs, and not average costs. They may be hit by sickness that calls for many times the average cost—in extreme cases for more than their annual income. When this happens they may come face to face with economic disaster. Many families, fearful of expense, delay calling the doctor long beyond the time when medical care would do the most good.

For some persons with very low income or no income at all we now use taxpayers' money in the form of free services, free clinics, and public hospitals. Tax-supported, free medical care for needy persons, however, is insufficient in most of our cities and in nearly all of our rural areas. This deficiency cannot be met by private charity or the kindness of individual physicians.

481

Each of us knows doctors who work through endless days and nights, never expecting to be paid for their services because many of their patients are unable to pay. Often the physician spends not only his time and effort, but even part of the fees he has collected from patients able to pay, in order to buy medical supplies for those who cannot afford them. I am sure that there are thousands of such physicians throughout our country. They cannot, and should not, be expected to carry so heavy a load.

5. The fifth problem has to do with loss of earnings when sickness strikes. Sickness not only brings doctor bills; it also cuts off income.

On an average day, there are about 7 million persons so disabled by sickness or injury that they cannot go about their usual tasks. Of these, about 3¼ millions are persons who, if they were not disabled, would be working or seeking employment. More than one-half of these disabled workers have already been disabled for six months; many of them will continue to be disabled for years, and some for the remainder of their lives.

Every year, four or five hundred million working days are lost from productive employment because of illness and accident among those working or looking for work—about forty times the number of days lost because of strikes on the average during the ten years before the war. About nine-tenths of this enormous loss is due to illness and accident that is not directly connected with employment, and is therefore not covered by workmen's compensation laws.

These then are the five important problems which must be solved, if we hope to attain our objective of adequate medical care, good health, and protection from the economic fears of sickness and disability.

To meet these problems, I recommend that the Congress adopt a comprehensive and modern health program for the Nation, consisting of five major parts—each of which contributes to all the others.

FIRST: CONSTRUCTION OF HOSPITALS AND RELATED FACILITIES

The Federal Government should provide financial and other assistance for the construction of needed hospitals, health centers and other medical, health, and rehabilitation facilities. With the help of Federal funds, it should be possible to meet deficiencies in hospital and health facilities so that modern services—for both prevention and cure—can be accessible to all the people. Federal financial aid should be available not only to build new facilities where needed, but also to enlarge or modernize those we now have.

In carrying out this program, there should be a clear division of responsibilities between the States and the Federal Government. The States, localities and the Federal Government should share in the financial responsibilities. The Federal Government should not construct or operate these hospitals. It should, however, lay down minimum national standards for construction and operation, and should make sure that Federal funds are allocated to those areas and projects where Federal aid is needed most. In approving state plans and individual projects, and in fixing the national standards, the Federal agency should have the help of a strictly advisory body that includes both public and professional members.

Adequate emphasis should be given to facilities that are particularly useful for prevention of diseases—mental as well as physical—and to the coordination of various kinds of facilities. It should be possible to go a long way toward knitting together facilities for prevention with facilities for cure, the large hospitals of medical centers with the smaller institutions of surrounding areas, the facilities for the civilian population with the facilities for veterans.

The general policy of Federal-State partnership which has done so much to provide the magnificent highways of the United States can be adapted to the construction of hospitals in the communities which need them.

SECOND: EXPANSION OF PUBLIC HEALTH, MATERNAL AND CHILD HEALTH
SERVICES

Our programs for public health and related services should be enlarged and strengthened. The present Federal-State cooperative health programs deal with general public health work, tuberculosis and venereal disease control, maternal and child health services, and services for crippled children.

These programs were especially developed in the ten years before the war, and have been extended in some areas during the war. They have already made important contributions to national health, but they have not yet reached a large proportion of our rural areas, and, in many cities, they are only partially developed.

No area in the Nation should continue to be without the services of a full-time health officer and other essential personnel. No area should be without essential public health services or sanitation facilities. No area should be without community health services such as maternal and child health care.

Hospitals, clinics and health centers must be built to meet the needs of the total population, and must make adequate provision for the safe birth of every baby, and for the health protection of infants and children.

Present laws relating to general public health, and to maternal and child health, have built a solid foundation of Federal cooperation with the States in administering community health services. The emergency maternity and infant care program for the wives and infants of servicemen—a great wartime service authorized by the Congress—has materially increased the experience of every State health agency, and has provided much-needed care. So too have other wartime programs such as venereal disease control, industrial hygiene, malaria control, tuberculosis control and other services offered in war essential communities.

The Federal Government should cooperate by more generous grants to the States than are provided under present laws for public health services and for maternal and child health care. The program should continue to be partly financed by the States themselves, and should be administered by the States. Federal grants should be in proportion to State and local expenditures, and should also vary in accordance with the financial ability of the respective States.

The health of American children, like their education, should be recognized as a definite public responsibility.

In the conquest of many diseases prevention is even more important than cure. A well-rounded national health program should, therefore, include systematic and wide-spread health and physical education and examinations, beginning with the youngest children and extending into community organizations. Medical and dental examinations of school children are now inadequate. A preventive health program, to be successful, must discover defects as early as possible. We should, therefore, see to it that our health programs are pushed most vigorously with the youngest section of the population.

Of course, Federal aid for community health services—for general public health and for mothers and children—should complement and not duplicate prepaid medical services for individuals, proposed by the fourth recommendation of this message.

THIRD: MEDICAL EDUCATION AND RESEARCH

The Federal Government should undertake a broad program to strengthen professional education in medical and related fields, and to encourage and support medical research.

Professional education should be strengthened where necessary through Federal grants-in-aid to public and to non-profit private institutions. Medical research, also, should be encouraged and supported in the Federal agencies and by grants-in-aid to public and non-profit private agencies.

In my message to the Congress of September 6, 1945, I made various recommendations for a general Federal research program. Medical research—dealing with the broad fields of physical and mental illnesses—should be made effective in part through that general program and in part through specific provisions within the scope of a national health program.

Federal aid to promote and support research in medicine, public health and allied fields is an essential part of a general research program to be administered by a central Federal research agency. Federal aid for medical research and education is also an essential part of any national health program, if it is to meet its responsibilities for high grade medical services and for continuing progress. Coordination of the two programs is obviously necessary to assure efficient use of Federal funds. Legislation covering medical research in a national health program should provide for such coordination.

FOURTH: PREPAYMENT OF MEDICAL COSTS

Everyone should have ready access to all necessary medical, hospital and related services.

I recommend solving the basic problem by distributing the costs through expansion of our existing compulsory social insurance system. This is not socialized medicine.

Everyone who carries fire insurance knows how the law of averages is made to work so as to spread the risk, and to benefit the insured who actually suffers the loss. If instead of the costs of sickness being paid only by those who get sick, all the people—sick and well—were required to pay premiums into an insurance fund, the pool of funds thus created would enable all who do fall sick to be adequately served without overburdening anyone. That is the principle upon which all forms of insurance are based.

During the past fifteen years, hospital insurance plans have taught many Americans this magic of averages. Voluntary health insurance plans have been expanding during recent years; but their rate of growth does not justify the belief that they will meet more than a fraction of our people's needs. Only about 3% or 4% of our population now have insurance providing comprehensive medical care.

A system of required prepayment would not only spread the costs of medical care, it would also prevent much serious disease. Since medical bills would be paid by the insurance fund, doctors would more often be consulted when the first signs of disease occur instead of when the disease has become serious. Modern hospital, specialist and laboratory services, as needed, would also become available to all, and would improve the quality and adequacy of care. Prepayment of medical care would go a long way toward furnishing insurance against disease itself, as well as against medical bills.

Such a system of prepayment should cover medical, hospital, nursing and laboratory services. It should also cover dental care—as fully and for as many of the population as the available professional personnel and the financial resources of the system permit.

The ability of our people to pay for adequate medical care will be increased if, while they are well, they pay regularly into a common health fund, instead of paying sporadically and unevenly when they are sick. This health fund should be built up nationally, in order to establish the broadest and most stable basis for spreading the costs of illness, and to assure adequate financial support for doctors and hospitals everywhere. If we were to rely on state-by-state action only, many years would elapse before we had any general coverage. Meanwhile health service would continue to be grossly uneven, and disease would continue to cross state boundary lines.

Medical services are personal. Therefore the nation-wide system must be highly decentralized in administration. The local administrative unit must be the keystone of the system so as to provide for local services and adaptation to local needs and conditions. Locally as well as nationally, policy and administration should be guided by advisory committees in which the public and the medical professions are represented.

Subject to national standards, methods and rates of paying doctors and hospitals should be adjusted locally. All such rates for doctors should be adequate, and should be appropriately adjusted upward for those who are qualified specialists.

People should remain free to choose their own physicians and hospitals. The removal of financial barriers between patient and doctor would enlarge the present freedom of choice. The legal requirement on the population to contribute involves no compulsion over the doctor's freedom to decide what services his patient needs. People will remain free to obtain and pay for medical service outside of the health insurance system if they desire, even though they are members of the system; just as they are free to send their children to private instead of to public schools, although they must pay taxes for public schools.

Likewise physicians should remain free to accept or reject patients. They must be allowed to decide for themselves whether they wish to participate in the health insurance system full time, part time, or not at all. A physician may have some patients who are in the system and some who are not. Physicians must be permitted to be represented through organizations of their own choosing, and to decide whether to carry on in individual practice or to join with other doctors in group practice in hospitals or in clinics.

Our voluntary hospitals and our city, county and state general hospitals, in the same way, must be free to participate in the system to whatever extent they wish. In any case they must continue to retain their administrative independence.

Voluntary organizations which provide health services that meet reasonable standards of quality should be entitled to furnish services under the insurance system and to be reimbursed for them. Voluntary cooperative organizations concerned with paying doctors, hospitals or others for health services, but not providing services directly, should be entitled to participate if they can contribute to the efficiency and economy of the system.

None of this is really new. The American people are the most insurance-minded people in the world. They will not be frightened off from health insurance because some people have misnamed it "socialized medicine".

I repeat—what I am recommending is *not* socialized medicine.

Socialized medicine means that all doctors work as employees of government. The American people want no such system. No such system is here proposed.

Under the plan I suggest, our people would continue to get medical and hospital services just as they do now—on the basis of their own voluntary decisions and choices. Our doctors and hospitals would continue to deal with disease with the same professional freedom as now. There would, however, be this all-important difference: whether or not patients get the services they need would not depend on how much they can afford to pay at the time.

I am in favor of the broadest possible coverage for this insurance system. I believe that all persons who work for a living and their dependents should be covered under such an insurance plan. This would include wage and salary earners, those in business for themselves, professional persons, farmers, agricultural labor, domestic employees, government employees and employees of non-profit institutions and their families.

488

In addition, needy persons and other groups should be covered through appropriate premiums paid for them by public agencies. Increased Federal funds should also be made available by the Congress under the public assistance programs to reimburse the States for part of such premiums, as well as for direct expenditures made by the States in paying for medical services provided by doctors, hospitals and other agencies to needy persons.

Premiums for present social insurance benefits are calculated on the first $3,000 of earnings in a year. It might be well to have all such premiums, including those for health, calculated on a somewhat higher amount such as $3,600.

A broad program of prepayment for medical care would need total amounts approximately equal to 4% of such earnings. The people of the United States have been spending, on the average, nearly this percentage of their incomes for sickness care. How much of the total fund should come from the insurance premiums and how much from general revenues is a matter for the Congress to decide.

The plan which I have suggested would be sufficient to pay most doctors more than the best they have received in peacetime years. The payments of the doctors' bills would be guaranteed, and the doctors would be spared the annoyance and uncertainty of collecting fees from individual patients. The same assurance would apply to hospitals, dentists and nurses for the services they render.

Federal aid in the construction of hospitals will be futile unless there is current purchasing power so that people can use these hospitals. Doctors cannot be drawn to sections which need them without some assurance that they can make a living. Only a nation-wide spreading of sickness costs can supply such sections with sure and sufficient purchasing power to maintain enough physicians and hospitals.

We are a rich nation and can afford many things. But ill-health which can be prevented or cured is one thing we cannot afford.

FIFTH: PROTECTION AGAINST LOSS OF WAGES FROM SICKNESS AND DISABILITY

What I have discussed heretofore has been a program for improving and spreading the health services and facilities of the Nation, and providing an efficient and less burdensome system of paying for them.

But no matter what we do, sickness will of course come to many. Sickness brings with it loss of wages.

Therefore, as a fifth element of a comprehensive health program, the workers of the Nation and their families should be protected against loss of earnings because of illness. A comprehensive health program must include the payment of benefits to replace at least part of the earnings that are lost during the period of sickness and longterm disability. This protection can be readily and conveniently provided through expansion of our present social insurance system, with appropriate adjustment of premiums.

Insurance against loss of wages from sickness and disability deals with cash benefits, rather than with services. It has to be coordinated with the other cash benefits under existing social insurance systems. Such coordination should be effected when other social security measures are reexamined. I shall bring this subject again to the attention of the Congress in a separate message on social security.

I strongly urge that the Congress give careful consideration to this program of health legislation now.

Many millions of our veterans, accustomed in the armed forces to the best of medical and hospital care, will no longer be eligible for such care as a matter of right except for their service-connected disabilities. They deserve continued adequate and comprehensive health service. And their dependents deserve it too.

By preventing illness, by assuring access to needed community and personal health services, by promoting medical research, and by protecting our people against the loss caused by sickness, we shall strengthen our national health, our national defense, and our economic productivity. We shall increase the professional and economic opportunities of our physicians, dentists and nurses. We shall increase the effectiveness of our hospitals and public health agencies. We shall bring new security to our people.

We need to do this especially at this time because of the return to civilian life of many doctors, dentists and nurses, particularly young men and women.

Appreciation of modern achievements in medicine and public health has created widespread demand that they be fully applied and universally available. By meeting that demand we shall strengthen the Nation to meet future economic and social problems; and we shall make a most important contribution toward freedom from want in our land.

HARRY S. TRUMAN

193   The President's News Conference of
        November 20, 1945

THE PRESIDENT. [1.]   I want to announce some very important changes in the Army command.

[*Reading*] "Ever since Japan's surrender, General Marshall has been desirous of relinquishing his position as Chief of Staff. He feels that his primary duty of directing the mobilization, the training, and employment of our wartime armies has been completed, and that the military is entering a new and lengthy administration of an interim and postwar army. General Marshall is of the firm opinion that the decisions incident to that administration should be made by his successor in office, who will be charged with the responsibility of carrying out those decisions.

"I need not reiterate my reasons as to why I am loath to deprive myself of General Marshall's services as Chief of Staff of the Army."

I have said that I think he is the greatest military man that this country ever produced—or any other country, for that matter.

[*Continuing reading*] "Accordingly, I am relieving him of his duties as Chief of Staff of the Army, and will today send to the Senate the nomination of General of the Army Dwight D. Eisenhower as General Marshall's successor in that office. Pending the action of the Senate, I have designated General Eisenhower as acting Chief of Staff of the Army.

"I have also approved the selection of General Joseph T. McNarney to relieve General Eisenhower as Commanding General, United States Forces, European Theater, and Commander in Chief of the United States Forces of Occupation in Germany and the Representative of the United States of America on the Control Council of Germany." [*Ends reading*]

I am also appointing—sending down the name of Fleet Admiral Chester W. Nimitz to be Chief of Naval Operations in the Department of the Navy to succeed Admiral King. Admiral Nimitz will return to the Pacific, and Admiral Spruance will take over the Pacific command. Then Admiral Nimitz will come back here for a few weeks' rest, and then he and Admiral King will work out the taking over of the Chief of Naval Operations, after he has had his vacation.

Q. Didn't Admiral King have two jobs, Mr. President? Isn't he Commander in Chief of the Fleet and Chief of Naval Operations both?

THE PRESIDENT. He was Chief of Naval Operations, but Admiral Nimitz is in command of the Pacific Fleet. I don't think Admiral King had the job——

Q. He had a dual title, Mr. President. Commander of the United States Fleet——

THE PRESIDENT. That's right.

Q. ——and Chief——

THE PRESIDENT. And Chief of the whole Navy.

Q. He doesn't retain any status in the Navy?

THE PRESIDENT. No. Admiral King asked to be relieved at the same time General Marshall asked to be relieved, immediately after the close of the Japanese—after the Japanese surrender, and I didn't want either one of them to quit and have prevented it up to this time, but I think it has to be accepted.

Q. What are Spruance's initials?

THE PRESIDENT. I don't know what Admiral Spruance's initials are.

Q. Does Admiral Nimitz get both jobs? He is Commander in Chief of the Fleet——

THE PRESIDENT. He will have the same position as Admiral King has.

Q. That is more or less indefinite, then—I mean as to the time?

THE PRESIDENT. Yes. It will be after Christmas before Admiral Nimitz will relieve Admiral King.

Q. When will the Eisenhower-Marshall change take place, Mr. President?

THE PRESIDENT. Immediately.

Q. Immediately? Thank you.

[2.] Q. Mr. President, do you have any comment on the progress, or rather lack of progress, of the Labor-Management Conference?

THE PRESIDENT. I am still hopeful that they will come out with a concrete program for the settlement of disputes between labor and management, just as I suggested that they do when they started to work.

[3.] Q. Mr. President, do you have anything on the resignations of General Arnold and General Somervell, who wanted to quit at the same time General Marshall did?

THE PRESIDENT. They have both asked to be relieved, but their resignations have not yet been accepted.

[4.] Q. Mr. President, the Washington Post has started a public opinion poll among the voteless citizens here——

Q. Mr. President, what was that paper? [*The President reached for a copy of the Washington Post, and held it up to the newsmen*]

THE PRESIDENT. This is it. [*Laughter*] Of course I believe that every citizen of the United States ought to have the right to vote—including the citizens of Washington.

Q. What do you think of the poll? [*Laughter*]

THE PRESIDENT. Well, I suppose it is as accurate as the Gallup poll, isn't it? [*Continued laughter*]

Q. The idea behind it, Mr. President?

THE PRESIDENT. The idea behind it is all right. There are practical difficulties, however, which should be worked out for the benefit of the citizens of Washington and for the benefit of the Government of the United States; and I am sure that they will be properly worked out.

[5.] Q. Mr. President, are there any indications that your office might act in the Detroit strike?

THE PRESIDENT. What is that?

Q. Are there any indications your office might take a hand in the Detroit strike trouble?

THE PRESIDENT. No.

[6.] Q. Mr. President, are you ready as yet to name the members of the Anglo-American Commission on Palestine?

THE PRESIDENT. No, I am not. I am considering several people. I can't name them, however, until the government of the—Great Britain and our own Government agree on the size of the Commission and its number.

[7.] Q. Mr. President, this morning there was a résumé of the different troubles that we are in throughout the world in connection with war, with the idea that there is peace but it is still not peace. Is there anything that you could say to us, sir, that would—that would be a sort of a beacon for——[*here the questioner paused*]

THE PRESIDENT. Beacon for what? [*Laughter*]

Q. I thought you would finish it. [*Laughter*]

THE PRESIDENT. Finish your question and I will answer it—I will make an attempt to answer it.

Q. Have something for the people to shoot at? [*Loud and uproarious laughter*]

THE PRESIDENT. Well, it isn't a matter of being something for the people to shoot at. It is something for the establishment of world peace, and I think the conference which was held last week was a first step toward implementing the United Nations Organization which will be the fundamental organization through which we can get peace in the world. And it is necessary to establish confidence between the various governments in the world in order to have that peace. That takes a little time, a little exchange of—a little necessary exchange of viewpoints and ideas.

Every country is having exactly the same sort of troubles that we are, and I think every country is trying to meet its domestic troubles and not paying as much attention to the international situation as they will at a later date.

I am not at all pessimistic on the final outcome. We will have permanent peace in the world. It is necessary that we have permanent peace. We are on the threshold, I think, of the greatest age in the history of mankind. We must grasp that opportunity, else the other road is complete destruction.

[8.]   Q. Mr. President, may I ask if it is your intention to ask the United Nations session, which holds its first meeting in January, to set up the atomic bomb commission which has been proposed as a result of last week's conference?

THE PRESIDENT. That's the—that's the program.

Q. At the first meeting?

THE PRESIDENT. That's the program.

Q. Thank you.

Q. Mr. President, will that request go to the Assembly, or to the Security Council, or what are your ideas for its construction?

THE PRESIDENT. It will. We will have to work out that concrete practical program when the United Nations session takes place. I think every one of the countries ought to have a hand in it.

Q. Mr. President, have you had any official expressions of opinion from Russia, China, or France as to the Anglo-American-Canadian pronouncement on the atomic bomb?

THE PRESIDENT. No. We haven't had time to get the replies yet.

Q. Mr. President, to clear up that one point that every country ought to have a hand in it, are we to take it to mean that you mean the Assembly should construct it?

THE PRESIDENT. That's right.

Q. Mr. President, are we still manufacturing atomic bombs?

THE PRESIDENT. Yes, we are.

Q. What for, Mr. President?

THE PRESIDENT. Experimental purposes.

[9.]   Q. Mr. President, are you ready to announce anything about a new Farm Security Administrator?

THE PRESIDENT. No, I am not.

Q. Mr. Anderson is worrying about it.

[10.] Q. Mr. President, on that bomb question, there are some of us who thought that even after the industrial know-how was made available that there would be a missing link, so to speak, between the industrial production and manufacturing of the bomb, and we were not turning loose that secret. Is that correct, sir?

THE PRESIDENT. That is a question that I can't answer intelligently because it takes a scientist who is familiar with all the p's and q's and I don't claim to be a physicist; but it is the program as outlined in the agreement between Great Britain, Canada, and ourselves, to try to implement that tremendous discovery which we have made for peacetime purposes instead of for wartime purposes.

And one of the ways to do that would be to use the material which has been set aside for—which has been made into the bombs—for experimental purposes for peacetime use in industrial programs. That will take some time. It will take a lot of scientific research and information, but I think we will finally arrive at that stage. We *must* arrive at that stage, or else we will arrive at a stage of destruction.

[11.] Q. Mr. President, is there any reason why the Byron Price report on Germany can't be released for publication?

THE PRESIDENT. No, there isn't—we are not ready to release it. It will be released at the proper time.[1]

[12.] Q. Mr. President, the two new military leaders—Eisenhower and Nimitz—took conflicting sides on how they ought to reorganize the postwar defenses. Does the Commander in Chief have a point of view?

THE PRESIDENT. Yes, the Commander in Chief has a point of view, and he will express it at the proper time. [*Laughter*]

Q. In a message to the Congress?

THE PRESIDENT. Yes, and I think that they will all be in the boat when the Commander in Chief expresses his opinion.

[13.] Q. Mr. President, do you contemplate an early meeting of the Big Three?

---

[1] See Item 201.

THE PRESIDENT. I do not.

Reporter: Thank you, Mr. President.

NOTE: President Truman's thirty-fourth news conference was held in his office at the White House at 4 p.m. on Tuesday, November 20, 1945.

194   Letter to General Hans Kramer Appointing Him U.S. Representative in Negotiations Between Colorado and Kansas for Division of Waters of Arkansas River. *November* 21, 1945

[Released November 21, 1945.   Dated November 20, 1945]

My dear General Kramer:

By virtue of the authority placed in me by the act approved April 19, 1945, granting the consent of Congress to the States of Colorado and Kansas to negotiate and enter into a compact for the division of the waters of the Arkansas River, I am appointing you, effective January 1, 1946, representative of the United States to participate in the negotiations between the States and to make the necessary reports to Congress.

I am asking the Congress to provide funds to the Geological Survey of the Department of the Interior for the payment of your compensation, which I am setting at a per diem rate of $100 for the time, including time performed in travel, actually spent on the work involved, and for expenses incurred as a result of your undertaking this office.   You are authorized under this appointment to undertake in accordance with standard government travel regulations such travel as may be necessary between your home and such points as may be proper in the conduct of the work.

Prior to submitting to Congress any reports you are required to make under the law, I would like you to send them to me through the Director of the Bureau of the Budget.

Sincerely yours,

HARRY S. TRUMAN

[Brigadier General Hans Kramer, U.S.A., Retired, Office of the President, Mississippi River Commission, Vicksburg, Miss.]

195 Statement by the President Concerning Government Operation of Transit Facilities in the District of Columbia. *November* 21, 1945

I HAVE TODAY directed the Office of Defense Transportation to take over the control and operation of the buses, street cars and other facilities of the transportation system of the District of Columbia.

The strike now in effect by the members of Division 689 of the Amalgamated Association of Street, Electric, Railway and Motor Coach Employees of America has been called for the second time during this month in violation of a formal written agreement between the union and the employer.

The present agreement does not expire until June 30, 1946. It provides for arbitration of any disputes, and guarantees that service upon the transportation lines of the District shall not be interrupted or interfered with by either party during the life of the contract.

The agreement does provide for opening wage scale negotiations under certain conditions, but it is clear that arbitration instead of a strike is intended to be the means of settlement if agreement can not be voluntarily reached.

The present action of the union in walking out is therefore contrary to the agreement. It is also contrary to the orders of the officials of the local union and of the international union.

The effect of the strike is to tie up all transportation at the seat of government and thereby prevent efficient and normal operation of the agencies of government during this vital reconversion period. It is a blow at the sanctity of labor agreements. It strikes, too, at the very roots of orderly government. The action of this union brings discredit upon the whole body of organized labor, which naturally decries any violation of sacred covenant.

The Federal Government will not permit this kind of action to interfere with its processes either in the capital or any part of the nation.

NOTE: Executive Order 9658 (3 CFR, 1943–1948 Comp., p. 476) directing the Office of Defense Transportation to take possession, control, and operate the facilities of the Capital Transit Company in Washington, was released with the President's statement.

196   Citation Accompanying the Legion of Merit Awarded
to Crown Prince Olav of Norway.   *November 23, 1945*

CITATION FOR LEGION OF MERIT

DEGREE OF CHIEF COMMANDER

HIS ROYAL HIGHNESS, Crown Prince Olav of Norway, displayed exceptionally meritorious conduct in the performance of outstanding services from August 1944 to July 1945. His friendly cooperation, diligent effort and tireless energy greatly assisted United States forces fighting for the liberation of Norway. Through his loyal and thorough devotion to freedom and his sincere desire for the triumph of the Allied cause, he encouraged the Norwegian forces and people in their sustained effort against the enemy. His active participation in the solution of many problems arising in connection with the defeat of the German forces gained for Prince Olav the admiration and respect of the Allied nations.

HARRY S. TRUMAN

NOTE: The citation was released with the following letter from Crown Prince Olav, dated October 22, 1945:

My dear Mr. President:

On the occasion of your most generous presentation of the Cross of Chief Commander of the Legion of Merit, together with a most kind citation, I wish to express, in a more personal way, my sincerest thanks for the great honor you, Sir, have been kind enough to show me.

I feel very strongly that this honor has been given me, not so much for my small services to our great common cause, but as a recognition of the part played by the Norwegian Armed Forces and the Norwegian Merchant Marine in the great conflict which at last has been so triumphantly won by our combined efforts, and in which you, your

great predecessor President Roosevelt and the whole of the people of the United States have taken such a great part and which you have brought to such a sweeping conclusion.

Allow me, Sir, to say how closely we have followed the achievements of your Armed Forces on all battlefronts and the overwhelming battle of production on the Home Front. We have noted with admiration the victorious progress against Japan as the last of the Axis powers to fall to the combined might of the United Nations, of which the brunt was carried by the United States.

Let me once more tell you, Sir, how much I and my Family have appreciated all the kindness and friendship which has been shown us during our stay in the United States, and how strongly we have felt the understanding and goodwill towards our people during these years of oppression and plight.

Everyone here has, I believe, enjoyed having your soldiers amongst us. It is with great regret we have had to say goodbye to fine men and good friends, even if we are all pleased to know that their work, which was performed in such a fine and pleasing way, is done.

I am sure that the friendships which have been established here between the American soldiers and the Norwegians will strengthen and cement even more closely the feeling of comradeship and kinship which has always existed between our two peoples.

May the lesson of interdependence of all freedom-loving people be really and truly learnt and remembered, so that we may stand together, and together go in for an active Peace in such a manner that we will not tolerate anyone to break that peace, or allow aggression to raise its ugly and greedy head again.

I once more renew my most heartfelt thanks for all kindness shown to me and my Family.

With the Crown Princess's and my own best and warmest regards to yourself, Sir, and to Mrs. Truman, I remain,

Most gratefully and sincerely yours,

OLAV

197 Citation Accompanying the Distinguished Service Medal Awarded to Field Marshal Sir Henry M. Wilson. *November 27, 1945*

CITATION FOR DISTINGUISHED SERVICE MEDAL

FIELD MARSHAL Sir Henry Maitland Wilson, G.C.B., G.B.E., D.S.O., performed outstanding and distinguished services as head of the British Joint Staff Mission from January to September 1945. As the military representative of the Prime Minister, he was charged with the responsibility of presenting to the United States Government the views and policy of His Majesty's Government on military matters, and was a British member of the Combined Chiefs of Staff in Washington. He coordinated the activities of the Air Staff, the Army Staff and the British Admiralty Delegation. Drawing on his rich experience and thorough knowledge of military affairs and exercising profound diplomacy, he played an important role in the development and execution of the Allied strategy leading to victory. By his untiring energy and singleness of purpose in the conduct of a mission of highest importance, Field Marshal Wilson made a practical contribution of the greatest significance to the difficult task of coordinating the combined military effort on all levels.

HARRY S. TRUMAN

NOTE: The presentation was made by the President at the White House in a joint ceremony honoring British mem- bers of the Combined Chiefs of Staff. See also Items 198, 199, 200.

198   Citation Accompanying the Legion of Merit Awarded to Lieutenant General Sir Gordon N. Macready. *November 27, 1945*

CITATION FOR THE LEGION OF MERIT

DEGREE OF COMMANDER

LIEUTENANT GENERAL Sir Gordon N. Macready, K.B.E., C.B., C.M.G., D.S.O., M.C., performed exceptionally meritorious service as Commander, British Army Staff, Washington, from June 1942 to September 1945. He represented the British Army Council in North America and was responsible for all liaison between the British War Office and the United States War Department. During his tenure the Allied armies victoriously assaulted Fortress Europe from all sides and brought the war on that continent to a successful conclusion. To this combined achievement, he made a distinguished contribution by assuring close and complete liaison, thus aiding materially in the task of developing and delivering the full measure of our military might. As representative of the Chief of the Imperial General Staff on the Combined Chiefs of Staff, General Macready gave a full measure of his rich military experience and superior judgment to the making of important strategic decisions. As British military representative on the Munitions Assignment Board and the Combined Production and Resources Board, he rendered highly valuable services in the determination of policies related to the combined logistical effort. As a member of the Combined Civil Affairs Committee, he demonstrated his wisdom and keenness of insight in dealing with problems affecting the rehabilitation of a war-ravaged world. By his outstanding performance of duty, General Macready reflected great credit upon himself as a soldier and upon the British Army which he represented.

HARRY S. TRUMAN

NOTE: The presentation was made by the President at the White House in a joint ceremony honoring British members of the Combined Chiefs of Staff. See also Items 197, 199, 200.

199 Citation Accompanying the Legion of Merit Awarded to Air Marshal Douglas Colyer. *November* 27, 1945

CITATION FOR THE LEGION OF MERIT

DEGREE OF COMMANDER

AIR MARSHAL Douglas Colyer, C.B., D.F.C., performed exceptionally meritorious service as Head of the Royal Air Force Delegation to Washington from December 1944 to September 1945. His principal responsibility was with the allocation of aircraft, in connection with which he served as Royal Air Force representative on the Munitions Assignment Board. By his thorough knowledge of the special requirements confronting the Allied air forces and his broad understanding of the logistic problems of aircraft allocation, he materially advanced the work of the Munitions Assignment Board. The quality of his leadership set a high standard which was fulfilled throughout the Royal Air Force delegation. By his tireless devotion to duty and his practical cooperation in solving the many problems met in the combined war effort, Air Marshal Colyer rendered a service of highest importance. His outstanding conduct in the performance of his duties reflects great credit upon himself and upon the Royal Air Force.

HARRY S. TRUMAN

NOTE: The presentation was made by the President at the White House in a joint ceremony honoring British members of the Combined Chiefs of Staff. See also Items 197, 198, 200.

200   Citation Accompanying the Legion of Merit Awarded to
      Fleet Admiral Sir James F. Somerville.
      November 27, 1945

CITATION FOR THE LEGION OF MERIT
DEGREE OF COMMANDER

ADMIRAL OF THE FLEET Sir James Fownes Somerville, GCB,
KBE, DSO, Royal Navy, for exceptionally meritorious conduct in the
performance of outstanding services to the Government of the United
States as Head of the British Admiralty Delegation in Washington,
D.C., from October 28, 1944 to September 25, 1945. Throughout this
critical period of war, Admiral of the Fleet Somerville, by his astute
judgment and comprehensive knowledge of the grand global strategy
involved, rendered invaluable assistance in achieving close cooperation
between the United States and British Navies in vital naval operations
against the common enemy and his brilliant professional ability and tireless devotion to the fulfillment of his important task were vital factors
in the ultimate success of Allied forces over all enemy opposition.

HARRY S. TRUMAN

NOTE: The presentation was made by
the President at the White House in a
joint ceremony honoring British members of the Combined Chiefs of Staff.
See also Items 197, 198, 199.

201   Letter Transmitting Report on the Occupation of
      Germany to the Secretaries of State, War, and Navy.
      November 28, 1945

Dear Mr. Secretary:

   I am enclosing a copy of the report of Byron Price dated November 9.
I asked Mr. Price to go to Germany to study the relationship between
the American Forces of Occupation and the German people.

   Mr. Price, as you know, is an able and experienced observer, and I
believe that his report is worthy of the most careful consideration.

You will note that the Price report embodies eight specific suggestions.

It is requested that the Secretaries of State, War and Navy give careful consideration to this report, with a view to taking whatever joint action may be indicated.

Sincerely yours,

HARRY S. TRUMAN

NOTE: This is the text of identical letters addressed to Secretary of State James F. Byrnes, Secretary of War Robert P. Patterson, and Secretary of the Navy James Forrestal.

The Price report, submitted in response to the President's letter of August 30 (Item 119), was also released. In the form of a memorandum to the President the report offered eight suggestions for maintaining sound relations between the Military Government and the German people, as follows:

1. That the full force and prestige of American diplomatic power be used to break the deadlock, caused by French obstruction, in the Berlin Control Council, thereby permitting Germany to be dealt with as a single economic unit.

2. That the highest type of civilian administrators be assigned to ensure the success of the changeover of the Military Government from Army to civilian control.

3. That the detailed instructions issued to the Military Government from Washington, drafted at the Pentagon early in 1945, be revised in the light of experience, and that they be reduced to a few hundred words stating general principles only.

4. That the daily food ration—1550 calories—be increased to 2000.

5. That the Military Government be given greater leeway to decide locally when and how de-Nazification in essential services could best be effected.

6. That the Information Control Branch, which supervised publications, broadcasting, and theaters, be made an integral part of the Military Government.

7. That demobilization of American forces should not proceed at a pace which would interfere with the maintenance of order, particularly in view of the threat posed by the former Hitler Youth, "potentially the most dangerous single element of the population."

8. That the Nürnberg trials be held without delay so that the Military Government could begin dealing with the 80,000 lesser Nazis then in prison.

The full text of the Price report is published in the Department of State Bulletin (vol. 13, p. 885).

202 The President's News Conference of *November* 29, 1945

THE PRESIDENT. [1.] I have just signed an Executive order, seizing the facilities of the Great Lakes Towing Company of Cleveland, Ohio, because of a labor dispute.

Q. Great Lakes——

THE PRESIDENT. —— Towing Company of Cleveland, Ohio. The mimeographed order is available when you leave here.

Q. Who takes it over, Mr. President?

THE PRESIDENT. The ODT—Office of Defense Transportation.

[2.] I have named the following persons to the Interstate Commerce Commission as reappointments. William E. Lee of Idaho——

Q. William E.——

THE PRESIDENT. —— Lee.

Q. Is that L-e-e?

THE PRESIDENT. L-e-e. And William J. Patterson of North Dakota—both Republicans, and reappointments.

And I have named Lynn U. Stambaugh of North Dakota as a Republican Director on the Export-Import Bank.

All the appointments seem to be nonpartisan this morning. [*Laughter*]

Q. Lynn U. Stambaugh?

THE PRESIDENT. Lynn U. Stambaugh.

Q. Former National Commander, American Legion.

THE PRESIDENT. Lynn U. Stambaugh of the Legion, I believe, is the rest of it.

Q. Does that leave one more vacancy?

THE PRESIDENT. There is still one more Republican vacancy.

Q. One Democratic, isn't there? No?

THE PRESIDENT. No. The Democrats have all been filled. Martin, the other day, was just made Chairman of that Export-Import Bank; and it is, in my opinion, one of the most important organizations we have for the welfare of the country and the world.

Q. That means, Mr. President, that Mr. Crowley is definitely not coming back to Government service?

THE PRESIDENT. That's what it means. At least not in that capacity.

[3.] I have got a statement here that will be interesting to you. It will—you will be furnished with mimeographed copies as you go out.

[*Reading, not literally*] "The first 100 days of reconversion. We have made the following progress:

"On manpower. The great part of the layoffs from war plants has now been completed, except in the shipyards. And employment in non-war activities has increased since V-J Day. Total employment has now returned to the V-J Day level and is expected to continue to rise.

"Unemployment, so far, is less than had been expected. This means that the disruption of our economy has been less drastic than anticipated. However, we are still in a transition period. The rapid demobilization of the armed forces will undoubtedly increase the unemployment total over the next few months.

"During these first 100 days, 3,500,000 men and women have been demobilized. We have stepped up the rate to 50,000 a day, and expect to continue at this pace.

"Plant reconversion."—And this is exceedingly interesting, in view of some of the things that have been said.—"The job of reconverting our plants from war to peace is virtually completed. Ninety-three percent of all plants have been cleared in 60 days or less after request."

Q. Ninety-three percent?

THE PRESIDENT [*continuing reading, not literally*]. "Ninety-three percent have been cleared in 60 days or less after request. Two-thirds of these plants were cleared in 40 days or less. Twenty-seven billion dollars' worth of war contracts have been canceled since the surrender of Japan. Approximately one-third of the 122,000 war contracts canceled since V-J Day have been settled.

"Lifting of wartime controls. All war manpower controls were lifted the day after Japan surrendered. OPA has removed several hundred items from price control, removed all rationing except sugar and tires, and completed the pricing of reconversion goods almost 100 percent. OPA has reduced orders and regulations on its books to 55 from a wartime peak of 650. ODT has 14 orders standing, as compared with 3,050 during the war. About 85 percent of wartime export controls have been lifted, and 75 percent of wartime import controls.

"Production. Most peacetime products are already in production or ready to roll. The metal-working trades on which we depend for most of our consumer durable goods are in such shape that they expect by the middle of 1946 to ship goods at two and one-half times the 1939 rate.

"Business continues good. Here are some indications:

"Retail sales are up 10 percent now as compared with the same period last year; steel ingot production is back to 82 percent capacity today as compared with 60 percent capacity right after V-J Day; electric power production now is only 14 percent below the wartime peak."

Now I am going to read you some official—*official* Labor Department figures.

[*Continuing reading, not literally*] "There has been an upsurge of strikes since V-J Day. The increase has been due in part to the fact that all parties held their grievances in check during the war and observed the no-strike pledge. New strikes since August total approximately 1,500, involving about 1,500,000 workers. During the same time 924 strikes were averted, involving about 400,000 workers; and 868 strikes were settled through the Conciliation Service of the Labor Department, involving more than 525,000 workers. Labor dispute cases settled through November 24th numbered 2,821, involving about 1,150,000 workers. Time lost through work stoppages since August is estimated at 0.76 of 1 percent of the total working time available.

"The cost of living—according to the figures customarily used for that purpose—has declined 0.3 of 1 percent since the surrender of Japan, as compared with a rise of approximately 1.3 percent in a comparable period after the last war. Some of the decrease this time, however, is due to seasonable decrease in some food prices. Direct controls over wages and salaries have been removed in most fields, but increases have not been allowed to affect price ceilings or costs to the United States, except in some specific and narrowly defined cases to correct maladjustments or inequities.

"Inflationary pressures are still great, and danger signals pointing to a further building up through the winter and spring are the rise of real estate, wholesale, and raw materials prices. We must continue to hold the line. We cannot permit inflation."

Now, while this is a good report, we must be sure that we are still in the midst of reconversion, and we must do everything in our power to prevent this inflationary pressure from taking the advantage of us under these conditions.

I have read you these figures to indicate to you that the administration has not been asleep on the job, and we shall continue to do everything in our power to go forward with this reconversion program on the basis which we anticipated to begin with. We are way ahead of schedule. But bear in mind that the difficulties we are facing are just as great as they have ever been in the history of the country.

Now I am ready for questions.

Q. Mr. President, in connection with that statement itself, hasn't the Advisory Board of the War Mobilization expressed some trepidation about the possibility of deflation as well as inflation?

THE PRESIDENT. That's true.

Q. I suppose that is taken into consideration——

THE PRESIDENT. That is taken into consideration.

Q. ——in the general reconversion program?

THE PRESIDENT. That's right. We are trying to prevent deflation just as much as inflation.

Q. Do you regard that danger as anywhere near the danger of inflation?

THE PRESIDENT. No, I do not.

[4.] Q. Mr. President, Mr. Ross yesterday indicated we may expect those appointments to the Anglo-American Commission for investigation of the Palestine situation today.

THE PRESIDENT. They are not ready yet.

Q. Do you expect them today?

THE PRESIDENT. No, I do not.

Q. Mr. President, in that connection—if I may ask one more question—some people who have been interested in the Zionist movement said that you gave prior approval, or at least prior acquiescence, to the Wagner resolution on a Jewish commonwealth in Palestine. Did you have any conversation on that subject?

THE PRESIDENT. I had some conversation on that subject, and was not opposed to that situation. I was Vice President then.

Q. Do you still favor the resolution?

THE PRESIDENT. I do not. The conditions have changed. And if that resolution is passed, there isn't any use trying to have a factfinding commission finding facts and making recommendations.

[5.]   Q. Mr. President, the same OWMR Advisory Board suggested the other day it would be a good thing—in connection with strikes— it would be a good thing if General Motors sat down and talked things over with the strikers. Do you agree with that?

THE PRESIDENT. I do.

Q. Mr. President, the report does not say very specifically what cost-of-living figures those are.

THE PRESIDENT. The ones that are usually used—the Labor Department's index.

Q. That very controversial one?

THE PRESIDENT. The very controversial one. It's the only one we have.

Q. The same one.

THE PRESIDENT. The only official one we have.

Q. Mr. President, you said that you are anticipating, perhaps, a rise in real estate prices next winter. There were discussions of some controls to be placed on real estate, which I think Mr. Davis had under consideration when he was with the OES.

THE PRESIDENT. They are still under consideration.

Q. They are?

THE PRESIDENT. They are. It is the most difficult thing to try to get controls that will work. That is difficult.

[6.]   Q. Mr. President, I wonder if you could also discuss the problem of the first 100 days of reconversion on the international front? I mean specifically that in the squabbles of Hurley, and the debates on the United Nations Organization, and the discussions of UNRRA on the Hill, all through it there seems to be running a thread containing two fears: one, an unholy fear that Russia will not cooperate with the other nations, and second——

THE PRESIDENT. That's a fear—[*inaudible words*].

Q. ——second, a fear that noncooperation on the part of Russia will eventually lead to war. Do you share either of those fears, sir?

THE PRESIDENT. I do not, and I will discuss that situation at a later date, fully and completely.

Q. In a message to Congress, sir?

THE PRESIDENT. No, not necessarily. That may be at a press conference. When the turmoil gets hot enough, I will talk with you about it.

Q. Don't you think it's very hot now? [*Laughter*]

THE PRESIDENT. Well, it's stirred up. We should let it settle a little bit.

[7.] Q. Mr. President, what would be the effect of a great strike on this reconversion schedule?

THE PRESIDENT. It would hold it back, of course.

Q. What would the administration do to prevent such a strike?

THE PRESIDENT. I will handle that situation when it appears before me.

[8.] Q. Mr. President, on the Palestine question, has an agreement been reached, at least on how many members each government will have?

THE PRESIDENT. We will hope to reach that agreement today. I think maybe the Secretary of State will announce it.

[9.] Q. Byron Price in his report recommended a revision of the Potsdam Declaration. Would you approve of that?

THE PRESIDENT. I would. But that requires a four-power agreement in order to make that revision.

Q. Are any steps being taken——

THE PRESIDENT. Yes.

Q. ——in that direction to change it?

THE PRESIDENT. Yes. We will make an effort to approach the situation.

Q. You mean by "we"—you mean our Government alone?

THE PRESIDENT. Our Government alone? Well, I can't answer that, because it is still in the negotiating stage.

Q. Mr. President, do you mean revision of the entire Potsdam Declaration, or just certain phases?

THE PRESIDENT. Certain phases of it.

Q. Where they apply to the four-power control of Germany?

THE PRESIDENT. That's right. It's—it's a detail proposition that will have to be worked out on the ground by the four powers.

Q. Could you, at this time, throw any light on those efforts at revision?

THE PRESIDENT. No, I can't.

Q. Mr. President, are you doing anything to try and change that veto plan that is in the four-power control, where one member can veto——

THE PRESIDENT. That is one of the things that will be under discussion.

Q. Will that be done in another Big Three conference, sir?

THE PRESIDENT. No, sir, it will not. I am not in favor of special conferences, because I want to see the United Nations do its job. The League of Nations was ruined by a lot of special conferences. I am not in favor of special conferences, and never have been.

Q. The suggestion for elimination of the veto power is wholly American then, I take it?

THE PRESIDENT. No, not necessarily. I can't answer those questions intelligently, because it's a matter of negotiation, and I don't want to be specific because it might ruin the negotiations.

Q. Mr. President, is the United Nations Organization raising the point whether it can take over these——

THE PRESIDENT. It will, very shortly.

Q. How soon do you anticipate——

THE PRESIDENT. I think some time in the next 90 days—I hope.

Q. And that will obviate a three-power conference?

THE PRESIDENT. That's what that United Nations is for; and I want to see it work, and we are behind it wholeheartedly to see that it does work.

Q. Do you think other nations are equally behind it, Mr. President?

THE PRESIDENT. I think so. Most of them are, I think.

Q. Would you make any exceptions?

THE PRESIDENT. No, I wouldn't make any exceptions because I can't speak for the other nations. They must speak for themselves.

[10.] Q. Mr. President, has the Anglo-American financial conference concluded its work?

THE PRESIDENT. No, they have not.

Q. Are you—do you believe that it will be concluded successfully?

THE PRESIDENT. I do, of course.

[11.] Q. Mr. President, have you received the resignation of Danny
Bell as Under Secretary of the Treasury?

THE PRESIDENT. I don't think so. I have a drawer full of resignations
here—[*laughter*]—a lot of which I have refused to accept, and some of
which I have had to accept. I don't know whether his is in there or
not.

Q. Would you care to tell us about some of them?

THE PRESIDENT. No, I wouldn't. I will tell you about them as they
come up.

Q. Mr. President, are those on the top shelf, Mr. President?

THE PRESIDENT. No.

Q. Mr. President, when was the Hurley resignation put in the
drawer?

THE PRESIDENT. It was put in the drawer this morning. It just reached
me this morning only.

Q. Mr. President, what do you think of the various accusations Ambassador Hurley made as he quit?

THE PRESIDENT. I would rather not express an opinion on the matter.

[12.] Q. Can you tell us, sir, the instructions under which General
Marshall is going to China, as a result of your conversation yesterday?

THE PRESIDENT. No, I cannot, because they are still being worked out.
I will give them to you in toto whenever that is accomplished.

Q. Is that appointment a temporary——

THE PRESIDENT. He is Special Envoy to China for a special job, and
it is temporary.

Q. Mr. President, on the question of instructions to Marshall, does
that mean he will get a directive which will be published—on a new
statement of policy?

THE PRESIDENT. I can't answer that intelligently yet. He will go and carry out the policy which we have always had in China. We might state it more specifically than it has been stated.

Q. Could you state that policy briefly, Mr. President?

THE PRESIDENT. No, I will not. [*Laughter*]

[13.] Q. Do you anticipate that there will be any need for further Big Three conferences at any time?

THE PRESIDENT. If the United Nations Organization works as it should, there shouldn't be any reason for a Big Three conference or any other sort of conference outside the United Nations.

Q. Yes, sir.

[14.] Q. Mr. President, it seems to me Senator Fulbright said the awfullest thing about the administration when he said that your foreign policy was just "playing by ear."

THE PRESIDENT. Well, Senator Fulbright has a right to his opinion the same as I have a right to mine.

Q. But as a musician——

THE PRESIDENT. I think it's playing by music.

[15.] Q. Mr. President, have you any indication as to when Mr. Marshall will leave?

THE PRESIDENT. Very shortly, in 3 or 4 days.

Q. Will that give the Pearl Harbor investigating committee a chance——

THE PRESIDENT. That is up to them.

[16.] Q. Mr. President, who are you betting on, on Saturday—Army or Navy? [*Laughter*]

THE PRESIDENT. I am neutral. [*Laughter*]

Q. You have to be.

THE PRESIDENT. I have to be neutral. One half is Army, and the other half is Navy.

Q. Does that neutrality go for the Army and Navy fight on unification, Mr. President?

THE PRESIDENT. I will make an announcement on that very shortly.

Reporter: Thank you, Mr. President.

NOTE: President Truman's thirty-fifth news conference was held in his office at the White House at 10:05 a.m. on Thursday, November 29, 1945. The White House Official Reporter noted that Mrs. Truman and Margaret Truman attended this conference.

203   Letter to the President, Society for the Advancement of Management, Concerning Full Employment.
November 30, 1945

[Released November 30, 1945.   Dated November 26, 1945]

Dear Mr. Zimmerman:

I am happy to know that the theme of your annual conference this year is "Management Factors for Full Employment". Full employment in the United States is of the greatest importance to our country and to the world.

In my recent Message to Congress I said:

"Full employment means full opportunity for all under the American economic system—nothing more and nothing less.

"In human terms, full employment means opportunity to get a good peace-time job for every worker who is ready, able and willing to take one. It does not mean made work, or making people work.

"In economic terms, full employment means full production and the opportunity to sell goods—all the goods that industry and agriculture can produce.

"In government terms, full employment means opportunity to reduce the ratio of public spending to private investment without sacrificing essential services.

"In world-wide terms, full employment in America means greater economic security and more opportunity for lasting peace throughout the world.

"To provide jobs, we must look first and foremost to private enterprise—to industry, agriculture, and labor. Government must inspire enterprise with confidence. That confidence must come mainly through deeds, not words. But it is clear that confidence will be promoted by certain assurances given by the government:

"Assurance that all the facts about full employment and opportunity will be gathered periodically for the use of all. Assurance of stability and consistency in public policy, so that enterprise can plan better by knowing what the government intends to do. Assurance that every governmental policy and program will be pointed to promote maximum production and employment in private enterprise."

If as a nation we are to succeed in maintaining high production industry must do its job and gear itself with the public interest. This means that day-to-day management decisions must be sound. Every time you set a price or a wage or a specification for a job, every time you select a product design or a machine or a merchandising policy, every time you accept or reject a proposed extension or improvement, you are deciding just those practical matters which determine the outcome. If these separate private decisions are not well taken, they will not add up to the right score in high production.

That is why it is of the greatest importance that management people everywhere should fully discuss and understand the management factors for full employment. I am glad that the Society for the Advancement of Management is doing this as part of its concern for better management from one end of the country to the other. I congratulate the Society on the timeliness and significance of this meeting and wish you every success in carrying forward your important work.

Very sincerely yours,

HARRY S. TRUMAN

[Honorable R. R. Zimmerman, President, The Society for the Advancement of Management, 84 William Street, New York 7, N.Y.]

NOTE: The White House release accompanying the text of the letter stated that it was read by Mr. Zimmerman at the annual dinner meeting of the Society for the Advancement of Management, held on November 30 at the Waldorf-Astoria Hotel in New York City.

204   Special Message to the Congress on Labor-Management
         Relations.   *December 3, 1945*

To the Congress of the United States:

All who think seriously about the problem of reconversion—of
changing our economy from war to peace—realize that the transition
is a difficult and dangerous task. There are some who would have the
Government, during the reconversion period, continue telling our citizens what to do, as was so often necessary when the very life of our
nation was at stake during the period of world conflict.

That however is not the policy of the Government. The policy is to
remove wartime controls as rapidly as possible, and to return the free
management of business to those concerned with it.

It was for the express purpose of getting away as soon as possible
from some of the wartime powers and controls that the recent National
Labor-Management Conference was called in Washington. Instead of
retaining in the Federal Government the power over wages and labor
agreements and industrial relations which a global war had made necessary, the top leaders of management and labor were invited to recommend a program under which labor relations would be turned back into
the hands of those involved.

It was decided that full responsibility for reaching agreement on such
a program would be left with the representatives of labor and management. Accordingly the conference was made up of leaders of labor and
management only. Government representatives participated only as
observers, without vote. The agenda and the entire program were
worked out by the leaders themselves.

In opening the conference I said:

"I want to make it clear that this is your conference—a management-
labor conference—and not a Government conference. You have not
been chosen by me or by any Government official. You have been
selected by the leading labor and industrial organizations in the United
States. There has been no interference by Government in that
selection. . . .

"The time has come for labor and management to handle their own affairs in the traditional American, democratic way. I hope that I can give up the President's wartime powers as soon as possible, so that management and labor can again have the full and undivided responsibility for providing the production that we must have to safeguard our domestic economy and our leadership in international affairs."

I am sure that it was the hope of the American people that out of this conference would come some recommendation for insuring industrial peace where collective bargaining and conciliation have broken down.

The conference is now closed. The very fact that the top leaders of labor and management have met and worked together for more than three weeks is itself some progress.

Some agreements on a few general principles were also reached. For example, agreement on the principles of collective bargaining, and recommendations on the detailed procedure to be used; agreement on strengthening and enlarging governmental conciliation services; recognition of the necessity of eliminating discrimination in employment; agreement on settling by voluntary arbitration grievances under labor contracts and disputes concerning their interpretation—these are all valuable.

But on the all-important question of how to avoid work stoppages when these expedients have failed, the conference arrived at no accord. Failing in that, the conference was unable to attain the objective most necessary to successful reconversion.

If industrial strife continues, the quick reconversion which has been planned, and which is now proceeding on schedule or even ahead of schedule on many fronts, will fail. In that event, we shall face a period of low production, low consumption, and widespread unemployment— instead of the high production, high employment, good markets and good wages that are within our grasp.

The history of labor relations has proven that nearly all labor disputes can and should be settled by sincere and honest collective bargaining. The vast majority of those disputes which are not adjusted by collective bargaining are settled through Government conciliation. For example during the month of October last, 354 strikes were settled

517

by the Conciliation Service, and 1282 labor controversies were adjusted before any work stoppages occurred.

The American people commend the many instances where management and labor have settled their problems peacefully. Many of these were in critical industries where work stoppages would have gained great prominence in the newspapers and over our radios. But when industrial disputes were settled, little notice was taken of them by press or radio.

We know, however, that there are always some disputes that cannot be settled this way.

Industrial strife in some key industries means not only loss of a great amount of wages and purchasing power; but it may have ramifications throughout the country affecting the whole reconversion process. In such industries, when labor and management cannot compose their differences, the public through the Federal Government has a duty to speak and to act. In the last analysis, labor, management and the public have the same interest.

The reconversion effort is now going well. The people have a right to expect it to succeed. Specific obstacles that stand in its way must not be allowed to defeat that expectation.

Good labor relations are just as important now as they were during the war. They should be based on justice, and not on tests of strength. Any industrial dispute which depends for settlement upon the respective strength of the parties results in loss to everyone; it causes loss of wages to the worker and his family, loss of dividends to the stockholders and owners of the industry, loss of goods to the public.

I regret that labor and management have not been able to agree on machinery that would provide a solution for existing strikes in some of the major industries and for the strikes which are threatened. Strikes already in effect may possibly cripple our reconversion program. Negotiations have broken down in other industries, and stoppages are threatened.

The American people have been patient. They have waited long in the hope that those leaders in labor and management whose business it was to handle this problem would be able to do so in agreement. The

Federal Government declined time and again to make any suggestion to the conference as to proper machinery. All that the Government did was to point out the objective which the American people expected it to attain.

Now that the conference has adjourned without any recommendation on the subject, it becomes the duty of the Government to act on its own initiative. Therefore, I now suggest to the Congress that well-reasoned and workable legislation be passed at the earliest possible moment to provide adequate means for settling industrial disputes and avoiding industrial strife.

I recommend that for the settlement of industrial disputes in important nation-wide industries there be adopted the principles underlying the Railway Labor Act. The general pattern of that Act is not applicable to small industries or to small local disputes in large industries. But it would be effective, as well as fair, in such wide-spread industries, for example, as steel, automobile, aviation, mining, oil, utilities and communications. I do not intend to make this list exclusive. Nor do I think that local inconsequential strikes even within these industries should be included. The objective should be to cover by legislation only such stoppages of work as the Secretary of Labor would certify to the President as vitally affecting the national public interest.

In industrial disputes in such industries, where collective bargaining has broken down, and where the Conciliation Service of the Federal Government has been unable to bring the parties to agreement, and where the Secretary of Labor has been unable to induce the parties voluntarily to submit the controversy to arbitration, I recommend the following procedure:

Upon certification by the Secretary of Labor to the effect that a dispute continues despite his efforts, and that a stoppage of work in the affected industry would vitally affect the public interest, the President, or his duly authorized agent, should be empowered to appoint, within five days thereafter, a Fact-finding Board similar to the Emergency Board provided for under the Railway Labor Act.

I recommend that during these five days after the Secretary of Labor has made the above certificate, it be unlawful to call a strike or lockout, or to make any change in rates of pay, hours, or working conditions, or in the established practices in effect prior to the time the dispute arose.

The Board should be composed of three or more outstanding citizens, and should be directed to make a thorough investigation of all the facts which it deems relevant in the controversy. In its investigation it should have full power to subpoena individuals and records, and should be authorized to call upon any Government agency for information or assistance. It should make its report within twenty days, unless the date is extended by agreement of the parties with the approval of the President. The report should include a finding of the facts and such recommendations as the Board deems appropriate.

While the Fact-finding Board is deliberating and for five days thereafter it should be made unlawful to call a strike or lock-out, or to make any change in rates of pay, hours, working conditions or established practices, except by agreement.

The parties would not be legally bound to accept the findings or follow the recommendations of the Fact-finding Board, but the general public would know all the facts. The result, I am sure, would be that in most cases, both sides would accept the recommendations, as they have in most of the railway labor disputes.

I believe that the procedure should be used sparingly, and only when the national public interest requires it.

The legislation should pay particular attention to the needs of seasonal industries, so that the so-called "cooling-off period" can be arranged in those industries in a manner which will not subject labor to an undue disadvantage.

There are other subjects which were on the agenda of the Labor-Management Conference, on which no agreement was reached. The most immediate, the most pressing, however, is this one of machinery. I hope that the Congress will act upon this matter as quickly as possible—and certainly before its Christmas recess.

In order to avoid any delay in the settlement of the most important existing strikes, I am appointing such a Fact-finding Board for the present stoppage in the dispute between General Motors Corporation and the United Automobile Workers. While this Board will not have the statutory powers which I hope the Congress will soon authorize, I am sure that the American people will expect the employer and the employees to cooperate with the board as fully as if appropriate legislation had already been passed.

In the meantime, I am asking both parties to the dispute to display the same kind of patriotism as they displayed during the war. I am asking all the workers to return to work immediately, and I am asking the employers to proceed energetically with full production. I make this appeal on behalf of the American people to their fellow citizens who are now responsible for this major obstacle holding up our reconversion program.

In connection with the threatened strike involving the United States Steel Corporation and the United Steel Workers, I am appointing a similar board. The public will expect full co-operation with the board by both sides. I am making the same appeal to the United Steel Workers to remain at work pending the report of the board's findings and recommendations.

I hope that the Congress will approve the steps which I am now taking. They are being taken in the interest of accelerating our production, promoting our reconversion program, and pushing forward to a higher standard of living.

This is an immediate program which is fair to both sides. I hope that the Congress, naturally disappointed at the failure of labor and management to agree upon a solution for the prevention of industrial disputes, will not adopt repressive or coercive measures against either side. A free American Labor and a free American private enterprise are essential to our free democratic system. Legislation which would stifle full freedom of collective bargaining on either side would be a backward step which the American people would not tolerate.

I am sure that the Congress will give its calm and careful consideration to this matter so essential to the progress of American life.

HARRY S. TRUMAN

205 Veto of Bill Granting Benefits to Enlisted Men for
Foreign Service Between 1898 and 1912.
December 3, 1945

To the House of Representatives:

I return herewith, without my approval, H.R. 1512 providing that retired enlisted men who have been, or may be, retired with credit for thirty years' service in the Army, Navy, or Marine Corps and who served beyond the continental limits of the United States between 1898 and 1912, such service having been computed under previous laws as double time toward retirement, shall be entitled to receive the maximum retired pay now provided for the grade in which retired.

While enlisted men who performed certain foreign service between 1898 and 1912 may count such service double in computing length of service for retirement, they do not receive double credit for such service for longevity pay purposes. H.R. 1512 would, in effect, grant double credit in computing longevity pay for the foreign service which was counted double in determining their right to retirement.

Enlisted men who enlisted subsequent to August 24, 1912 may not count such foreign service as double for any purpose. Thus those who performed such service prior to 1912 and retired with less than thirty years of actual service have already received a substantial benefit. I am unable to see any reason for granting further benefits to those included within the particular group covered by this bill, who have already received more favorable treatment with respect to retirement benefits than other service personnel who could retire only after thirty years' actual service.

HARRY S. TRUMAN

206 Telegrams to Management and Labor Leaders
Concerning Industrial Disputes Involving the General
Motors Corporation and the U.S. Steel Corporation.
December 3, 1945

I HAVE TODAY sent a message to the Congress recommending legislation authorizing the President to appoint fact finding boards in industrial disputes involving nation-wide industries on the certification by the Secretary of Labor that collective bargaining and conciliation have failed to produce agreement and that stoppage of work would vitally affect the national public interest.

The following is an excerpt from that message:

"In order to avoid any delay in the settlement of the most important existing strikes, I am appointing such a Fact-finding Board for the present stoppage in the dispute between General Motors Corporation and the United Automobile Workers. While this board will not have the statutory powers which I hope the Congress will soon authorize, I am sure that the American people will expect the employer and the employees to cooperate with the board as fully as if appropriate legislation had already been passed.

"In the meantime, I am asking both parties to the dispute to display the same kind of patriotism as they displayed during the war. I am asking all the workers to return to work immediately, and I am asking the employers to proceed energetically with full production. I make this appeal on behalf of the American people to their fellow citizens who are now responsible for this major obstacle holding up our reconversion program.

"In connection with the threatened strike involving the United States Steel Corporation and the United Steel Workers, I am appointing a similar board. The public will expect full cooperation with the board by both sides. I am making the same appeal to the United Steel Workers to remain at work pending the report of the board's findings and recommendations."

I hope very much that it will be possible for you to comply with this request of the President of the United States.

HARRY S. TRUMAN

NOTE: This is the text of identical telegrams addressed to Mr. Charles E. Wilson, President, General Motors Corporation; Mr. Philip Murray, President, United Steel Workers of America; Mr. Benjamin F. Fairless, President, United States Steel Corporation; Mr. R. J. Thomas, President, and Mr. Walter Reuther, Vice President, United Automobile Workers of America.

207   Statement by the President Upon Signing the
Government Corporation Control Act.
December 6, 1945

I FOUND much satisfaction in signing today the Government Corporation Control Act, for I have long believed in the principle it embodies. In requiring these corporations to submit their budgetary programs to the Bureau of the Budget and their expenditures to an audit by General Accounting Office, the Congress has made a forward step in furthering the business-like management of Government. This Act increases the orderly control by the Executive and the Congress of the Government corporations without impairing their usefulness. Because of the time element, it will not be possible to include budget programs for the corporations in the budget I shall submit to the Congress in January. I shall, however, submit by next Spring these corporation budgets for the fiscal year beginning July 1, 1946.

NOTE: The Government Corporation Control Act is Public Law 248, 79th Congress (59 Stat. 597).

208   The President's News Conference of
December 7, 1945

THE PRESIDENT. I didn't have any special announcements to make to you today, but since you haven't had a press conference in the afternoon this week, I thought I had better let you come in and ask some questions. You might have something to say to me.

[1.] Q. Well, Mr. President, we have. The White House Correspondents' Association each year makes a small gift to the Warm Springs Foundation through the White House, and the President customarily receives it, and we would appreciate your accepting it.

THE PRESIDENT. Well, thank you—thank you.

Q. A thousand dollars.

THE PRESIDENT. A thousand dollars. From the White House Correspondents' Association to the National Foundation for Infantile Paralysis—a thousand dollars. Well, thank you. On behalf of the Foundation, I thank you. And I will see that that gets into the proper pocket. [*Laughter*]

[2.] Q. Mr. President, there are dispatches coming to us from London which indicate that Foreign Minister Bevin may announce some time today a five-power meeting of foreign ministers and perhaps a three-power atomic conference.

THE PRESIDENT. I am not familiar with it. I can't answer it. I don't know.

[3.] Q. Mr. President, could you make any comment on the northern Governors' suit to set aside the ICC freight rate decision?

THE PRESIDENT. Is that the one that breaks up the combination?

Q. Well, that is the suit that involves the class rate ruling of the ICC, rather than the antitrust act.

THE PRESIDENT. I am not familiar with it, but I want a freight rate structure in this country that is fair to every section of it. I don't like the structure that has been in effect in the country with different brands in different parts of the United States. I have spent most of my time in the Senate trying to break that.

[4.] Q. Mr. President, have you yet selected your American members of the Palestine commission?

THE PRESIDENT. No, but they will be announced. I think we will be in a position to announce it Monday.

[5.] Q. Mr. President, are you doing anything about the reinstitution of controls on building material?

THE PRESIDENT. Yes, we are. We are trying to make some arrangement to channel building materials for residence purposes. I thought I would have a special announcement to make to you this afternoon, but we didn't get it ready.

Q. Did any event hold that announcement up?

THE PRESIDENT. No. No. We just weren't ready.

Q. Could you explain that word "channel"?

THE PRESIDENT. Well, see that building materials are used principally for residence purposes. Might use priorities. Probably would be better than channeling.

[6.] Q. Mr. President, do you intend to act on the recommendation of the Democratic National Committee that Governor Tugwell of Puerto Rico be removed immediately?

THE PRESIDENT. The Democratic Committee has made no such recommendation to me. We didn't know here—neither did the Democratic Committee—until we saw his name in the paper.

[7.] Q. Mr. President, can you give us the names of the factfinding board you said you would appoint in the General Motors case?

THE PRESIDENT. I am not quite ready right now with them. I can announce it in a very short time, but I can't give them to you today.

[8.] Q. Mr. President, do you know of any instance where agencies of another power have got hold of any part of the atomic secret we have?

THE PRESIDENT. I am not familiar with any specific instance. I have heard rumors to that effect, but rumors you can't give as facts.

[9.] Q. Can you give us any comment, Mr. President, on Mr. Murray's observations regarding your labor program?

THE PRESIDENT. No comment.

[10.] Q. Mr. President, do you want to comment on the increasing rate of highway accidents? Is there anything the Government can do about it?

THE PRESIDENT. Well, let me see. I think in 1935 I succeeded in getting a bill through the Senate to regulate drivers on interstate highways. That bill was passed by the Senate and was killed three times in the House. It had to do with proper examinations for drivers, before they would be allowed to drive on highways in interstate traffic.

I still think some sort of regulation is going to have to be made of these drivers, either by State laws such as the ones they have in Massachusetts and I think in four other States in the Union—or five—or else the Federal Government is going to have to take a hand in stopping these accidents.

Up to 1935 there had been more highway deaths from accidents than we had lost men in all the wars we ever fought, beginning with the Revolution. There had been a property damage rate of about a billion dollars a year. That is a tremendous price to pay for crackpots to drive automobiles.

[11.] Q. Mr. President, what is the next step on the British loan?

THE PRESIDENT. It will be sent to the Congress in the form of a message, and then the Congress will have to act upon it.

Q. Will it be this week?

THE PRESIDENT. It will be some time in the near future. We can't set the date now.

[12.] Q. Mr. President, Ambassador Hurley in his testimony before the Foreign Relations Committee accused Under Secretary Acheson of destroying American foreign policy in Iran. Do you think that American foreign policy has been destroyed in the Near East?

THE PRESIDENT. No. The first I had heard of that view was when Mr. Hurley made the statement to the Senate committee.

[13.] Q. Mr. President, have you any plans for starting negotiations with Soviet Russia for a loan? They have asked for $6 billion, I believe.

THE PRESIDENT. If they have, it has never been officially given to me. They never asked me for a $6 billion loan, since I have been President.

Q. Have there been any moves by the Government, Mr. President, to survey what the total possible loans may have to be, along the lines of Mr. Baruch's statement in a letter to Representative Gore?

THE PRESIDENT. No.

[14.] Q. Mr. President, Congressman Manasco's committee reported a bill on the full employment idea, which pretty much emasculates your program. They have even stricken the words "full employment" and put in the idea of high-level employment. Do you have any comment on that committee's action?

THE PRESIDENT. No, I haven't; but I hope the House will pass some sort of bill so we can get the conference and probably work out a bill.

[15.] Q. Mr. President, do you contemplate any action in the near future in returning the Coast Guard to the Treasury?

THE PRESIDENT. Yes—yes. I don't know exactly when it will be done, but it will be done sometime soon, as soon as I can get the Secretary of the Treasury and the Secretary of the Navy to agree on a date.

[16.] Q. Mr. President, do you have any comment at this time on unification?

THE PRESIDENT. No. I will have something to say about that in the very near future.

Q. Does that mean a message next week, Mr. President?

THE PRESIDENT. I hope so.

[17.] Q. Can you tell us, Mr. President, anything about the instructions to General Eisen—Marshall at this time?

THE PRESIDENT. No. General Marshall has been so busy with other things that I haven't had a chance to discuss the program with him and the Secretary of State.

Q. Will General Marshall try getting the two factions in China together again, Mr. President?

THE PRESIDENT. I hope so. I will give you that when the instructions are published.

[18.] Q. Mr. President, have you got any comment on the resignation of Charles Houston from the FEPC?

THE PRESIDENT. I wrote a letter on that, which was published in to-day's papers, which covers the situation thoroughly.[1]

[19.] Q. Mr. President, in connection with housing, are you going to take any position on price ceilings on houses, as in the Patman bill?

THE PRESIDENT. We hope to.

Q. Do you advocate price ceilings?

THE PRESIDENT. Some sort of control on real estate prices, I think, is going to be necessary, unless we are going to have real estate inflation. I don't know whether we will be able to do it or not. That is a matter that will have to be worked out after much thought. I don't want to say right now that it will be done, but some sort of arrangement will have to be made to prevent inflation in real estate prices, especially the small residence section.

[20.] Q. Mr. President, the Red Cross central committee was supposed to meet December 4th, I think, to name a chairman or rather

---

[1] The letter accepting Mr. Houston's resignation, not published herein, was released by the White House on December 7. The letter referred to an apparent contradiction between the law—which required the Government to operate seized properties under the terms and conditions of employment which were in effect at the time of seizure—and a proposed FEPC order concerning the Capital Transit Company in the District of Columbia.

to get a recommendation from you. Could you tell us anything about your recommendation with regard to that?

THE PRESIDENT. They didn't meet, and I didn't make a recommendation.

Q. They were scheduled——

THE PRESIDENT. No, I don't think so.

Q. Is there any change there in prospect, so far as you know, sir?

THE PRESIDENT. I will announce that on the 12th of December.

Q. You mean you are announcing a change? [*Laughter*]

THE PRESIDENT. I will announce the chairman of the Red Cross on the 12th of December.

[21.] Q. Mr. President, can you tell us anything about the Pacific Northwest light metals plant situation, as a result of your conference with Senator Mitchell today?

THE PRESIDENT. Well, Senator Mitchell was here to discuss the continued operation of those light metals plants in the Northwest, and no conclusions were reached.

Reporter: Thank you, Mr. President.

THE PRESIDENT. You're welcome.

NOTE: President Truman's thirty-seventh news conference was held in his office at the White House at 4 p.m. on Friday, December 7, 1945.

209   Joint Statement With the Prime Ministers of Great Britain and Canada Concerning Removal of Wartime Trade Controls. *December* 10, 1945

THE PRESIDENT of the United States and the Prime Ministers of Great Britain and Canada issue the following statement:

We announced on August 29 that the Combined Production and Resources Board, the Combined Raw Materials Board and the Combined Food Board would continue to operate on their existing basis for the time being. As then proposed, however, the situation has been further examined with a view to the earliest possible removal of all wartime controls of international trade.

We take this opportunity of paying tribute to the outstanding achievements of the Boards in the full and equitable utilization of resources for the effective prosecution of the war. This novel experiment in economic collaboration unquestionably hastened the moment of victory.

It is however, our view that the work of the C.P.R.B. and C.R.M.B. on its existing basis should come to an end. It has accordingly been agreed that these two Boards terminate on December 31, 1945.

There remain, however, a few commodities which call for continued attention inasmuch as they are in global short supply in relation to the needs in consuming countries. For cotton textiles, tin, rubber and hides and leather it is proposed that the committees set up under the Boards which are concerned with these supplies should be continued during such period as the shortage of supply in relation to needs renders necessary. It is also proposed that in all cases representation on the committees should be on an appropriate international basis having regard to their independent status following the dissolution of the Boards. In most cases Committee membership already includes countries having a major interest in the problems involved. In the case of coal, there exists an organization in respect of Europe, but special considerations make it desirable that, for the time being, the coal committees in Washington and London now under the Boards continue in their present form. As regards some additional commodities in uncertain supply, the Boards may make suitable distribution arrangements before the end of the year to extend into 1946.

It has been concluded that conditions do not yet permit the dissolution of the Combined Food Board. Because many foodstuffs are still in world short supply and because of their close inter-relationship, it is believed desirable to retain the Board as a supervisory and coordinating mechanism. The commodity committees of the Board will be abandoned as soon as the foodstuffs with which they deal cease to require international allocation. It is anticipated that the Combined Food Board itself will be dissolved on June 30, 1946, or sooner if conditions permit. However, a few of the commodity committees may have to be retained beyond that date to recommend allocations of products which continue to be in serious short supply. Arrangements were made last summer to associate other major exporting and importing countries with the work of the commodity committees. These committees will continue to operate on this principle.

NOTE: The statement was released simultaneously in Washington, London, and Ottawa at 10 a.m., Washington time.

210 Statement by the President Concerning the Anglo-American Committee of Inquiry (Palestine Commission). *December* 10, 1945

THE COMPOSITION of the Anglo-American Committee of Inquiry which was announced in Washington and London on November 13, and which will operate under a rotating chairmanship will be as follows:

Joseph C. Hutcheson, Judge of the Fifth Circuit Court at Houston, Texas (American Chairman).

Sir John E. Singleton, Judge of the King's Bench Division of the High Court of Justice, London (British Chairman).

Frank Aydelotte, formerly President of Swarthmore College, now Director of the Institute of Advanced Study at Princeton, and American Secretary of the Rhodes Trust.

Frank W. Burton, Editor of the Boston Herald.

Wilfred P. Crick, Economic Adviser to the Midland Bank, London, formerly with Ministry of Food.

Richard H. S. Crossman, Member of Parliament (Labour); formerly Fellow and Tutor of New College, Oxford, assistant editor of New Statesman and Nation, and Deputy Director of Psychological Warfare, A.F.H.Q., Algiers.

O. Max Gardner, former Governor of North Carolina, now practicing law in Washington.

Sir Frederick Leggett, until recently Deputy Secretary of the Ministry of Labour and National Services.

Major Reginald E. Manningham-Buller, Member of Parliament (Conservative), a barrister.

531

James G. McDonald, formerly Chairman of the Board, Foreign Policy Association, High Commissioner for Refugees, and member of the editorial staff of the New York Times.

Lord Morrison (Robert Craigmyle, Baron Morrison), Member of Parliament (Labour).

William Phillips, formerly Under Secretary of State, Ambassador to Italy, personal representative of the President with the rank of Ambassador at New Delhi, and Delegate to the London Naval Conference, 1935.

As announced by the two Governments on November 13, 1945, the terms of reference of the Committee will be as follows:

1. To examine political, economic and social conditions in Palestine as they bear upon the problem of Jewish immigration and settlement therein and the well-being of the peoples now living therein.

2. To examine the position of the Jews in those countries in Europe where they have been the victims of Nazi and Fascist persecution, and the practical measures taken or contemplated to be taken in those countries to enable them to live free from discrimination and oppression and to make estimates of those who wish or will be impelled by their conditions to migrate to Palestine or other countries outside Europe.

3. To hear the views of competent witnesses and to consult representative Arabs and Jews on the problems of Palestine as such problems are affected by conditions subject to examination under paragraphs 1 and 2 above and by other relevant facts and circumstances, and to make recommendations to His Majesty's Government and the Government of the United States for ad interim handling of these problems as well as for their permanent solution.

4. To make such other recommendations to His Majesty's Government and the Government of the United States as may be necessary to meet the immediate needs arising from conditions subject to examination under paragraph 2 above, by remedial action in the European countries in question or by the provision of facilities for emigration to and settlement in countries outside Europe.

The Governments of the United States and Great Britain urge on the Committee the need for the utmost expedition in dealing with the subjects committed to it for investigation and request that they may be furnished with its report within 120 days of the inception of the inquiry.

The procedure of the Committee will be determined by the Committee itself, and it will be open to it, if it thinks fit, to deal simultaneously through the medium of sub-committees with its various terms of reference.

NOTE: A similar statement was released simultaneously in London at 10 a.m. Washington time.

211 The President's News Conference of
   December 12, 1945

THE PRESIDENT. [1.]   I have received a report from Mr. Snyder, head of OWMR, on the housing situation, which will be handed to you. It is a mimeographed sheet of three pages, and recommends the appointment of a Housing Expediter to carry out the suggestions which he makes to me and which I have approved.

And I am appointing the Honorable Wilson Wyatt, former Mayor of Louisville, Kentucky, to that position; and a copy of my letter to him, and Mr. Snyder's report, are available for you.

Q. Mr. President, does that reinstitute priority controls on building materials?

THE PRESIDENT. Eventually it will.

Q. Eventually it will?

THE PRESIDENT. Yes.   It is completely explained in there.

Q. Could you give us a brief résumé, in 20 well-chosen words, Mr. President?   [*Laughter*]

THE PRESIDENT. Well, if you are going to insist on having something read to you—well, I will do that.

[*Reading*] "The first step is a program for speeding up release of surplus housing units and building materials, held by the Government. It is ready to operate.

"This program makes immediately available to the States and local communities surplus Government property suitable for housing, including Army and Navy barracks and dormitories. Wherever possible these facilities, many of which are near crowded cities, will be utilized on their present sites to house veterans and their families."

That's the first one.

[*Continuing reading*] "The second step is a regulation which is now being prepared and which should be released before the middle of the month, establishing priorities on building materials.

"In general terms, this regulation will establish such priorities for single or multiple dwelling housing units costing $10,000 or less per unit. This will mean that about 50 percent of all building materials will be channeled into this type of building. The balance will be available for commercial, industrial, higher-priced dwelling, and all other construction—public and private.

"The third step relates to ceiling prices on old and new housing. Sharp increases in the price of housing already have occurred. The threat of inflation in this field is the most menacing in our economy, and we are using all the powers that have been granted the Administration to combat it."

It goes into further explanation on each one of those, with the preliminary statement of why it is done.

[*Continuing reading*] "First, to increase the supply of building materials; second, to strengthen inventory controls to prevent hoarding; third, to strengthen price controls over building materials; fourth, to discourage unsound lending practices and speculation; fifth, to enlist industry support in increasing production and fighting inflation; and sixth, to provide information and advisory service on home values to the public."

And you have all that entirely and completely set out in this memorandum.[1]

Q. Mr. President, are those price ceilings operative right away?

THE PRESIDENT. Just as soon as we can get the orders out.

Q. You don't have to have OPA come in on that at all?

---

[1] The full text of Mr. Snyder's memorandum was released by the White House.

THE PRESIDENT. It will be—yes, yes.

Q. Mr. President, no legislation will be necessary on it?

THE PRESIDENT. No, because this is under the War Powers Act—this is under the War Powers Act, although we are supporting certain legislation which is explained in here that will help implement that.[2]

[2.] Then, I am appointing the factfinding board for the General Motors strike: Judge Walter Parker Stacy; Lloyd K. Garrison, chairman of the War Labor Board; and Milton S. Eisenhower, president of the Kansas State College, in Manhattan.

Q. Just a minute—Milton S. Eisenhower, what's he president——

THE PRESIDENT. President of Kansas State College, in Manhattan—that's an agricultural college in Kansas. Lloyd Garrison, who heads the War Labor Board, and Judge Stacy was chairman of the——

Q. Mr. President, may I ask you a question?

THE PRESIDENT. Certainly.

Q. This General Motors thing—as you probably know, labor has put up an——

Q. Louder.

Q. ——argument that the factfinding——

THE PRESIDENT. Say that again.

Q. I say that I am asking—saying to the President that, as he probably knows, labor objects to the idea of factfinding boards, with their argument being that they could string out the time of the factfinding to an interminable degree. I thought possibly this might be a good time to ask you a question about that, what your comment is on it?

THE PRESIDENT. My comment is that it is specifically stated in the message that the factfinding period should be 20 days—5 days to get ready, and 5 days after the 20 days—making up 30 days altogether; so this factfinding program can't last more than 20 days.

---

[2] After the news conference the White House issued a release clarifying the President's reply as follows:

"The President made this reply under a misapprehension. Legislation *is* necessary to fix price ceilings. The memorandum issued today points that out on Page 3, Section 3.

"Legislation is not necessary for the establishment of priorities on building materials; and, as indicated in Section 2, on Page 3 of the memorandum, priorities are being set up under the War Powers Act without legislation.

"The President in answering the question was under the impression that the question referred to priorities rather than price ceilings."

Q. Is it somewhere in your proposal—do you not authorize them to have more time if they want it?

THE PRESIDENT. If it is absolutely essential.

Q. You know what I am talking about?

THE PRESIDENT. Yes.

Q. It has been brought up that it was a device for stopping all labor——

THE PRESIDENT. I don't think it is any such device. It is merely a program for the purpose of finding out exactly what the conditions are on labor's side and on management's side, and then making a recommendation that is fair to the public. That's the principle of the thing.

[3.] Q. Mr. President, in connection with the inflationary aspects of the real estate market, are you also looking into the very active stock market now?

THE PRESIDENT. I hadn't been looking into it. In fact, I have had so many things to think about that I hadn't looked at the stock market, because I have never been interested in the stock market personally.

[4.] Q. Mr. President, will this factfinding board have the right to go into the company's books?

THE PRESIDENT. Not without legislation. I am of the opinion that people will want to cooperate with the President of the United States in an effort to settle these strikes in the public interest.

Q. You expect the company to open its books?

THE PRESIDENT. I expect cooperation from both sides.

[5.] Q. Mr. President, will you appoint a factfinding board for steel?

THE PRESIDENT. Yes, I shall.

Q. When will you announce that?

THE PRESIDENT. Just as quickly as we can get it ready.

[6.] Q. Mr. President, in addition to criticism of the labor program, there have been some personal attacks on you. I wonder if you could say how you regarded those?

THE PRESIDENT. I didn't even read them. I am not interested in them.

I don't think there's any truth in them, so why worry about them. I have been attacked before.

[7.] Q. We have received some reports that Senator Maybank might be appointed to some diplomatic post, specifically Brazil—a possibility of a vacancy there?

THE PRESIDENT. News to me. That's the first I have heard of it.

[8.] Q. Mr. President, I have been asked to inquire when the Marines will be taken out of China?

THE PRESIDENT. The Marines will be taken out of China when our surrender terms with Japan have been carried out. At a later time, when General Marshall starts for China, I shall announce a complete policy for the guidance of General Marshall; and I will announce it here at a press conference.

[9.] Q. To get back to labor, Mr. President, I believe in your message you asked that the enabling legislation be passed before the Christmas recess.

THE PRESIDENT. I did.

Q. Indications on the Hill now are that action will not be completed by the time for the recess. Are you doing anything to expedite that?

THE PRESIDENT. My best information is that it will be completed.

Q. It will be before the recess?

THE PRESIDENT. Yes.

Q. Do you take into consideration the possibility of a great deal of conversation on the subject in the Senate?

THE PRESIDENT. The Senate is always entitled to conversation. That's one of the reasons for the existence of the Senate. [*Laughter*] That's the only legislative body left in the world with unlimited debate, and under no circumstances would I limit that debate. I have been a Senator, and I know what it means for a Senator not to be able to say what he pleases. [*Laughter*]

[10.] I have another appointment here that I think you will be interested in. I am appointing Michael W. Straus who was the First Assistant Secretary of the Interior, to succeed Harry W. Bashore, who has passed the retirement age and is retiring from the Reclamation Board. Mr. Straus will be Commissioner of the Bureau of Reclamation.

Q. Does that interfere with his present job at all, sir?

THE PRESIDENT. He is resigning as Assistant Secretary of the Interior to take this job.

Q. How does Mr. Bashore spell his name?

THE PRESIDENT. I will spell it for you. I have got it right here: B-a-s-h-o-r-e. His name is Harry W.

Q. Mr. President, Mike is a very close associate of Mr. Harold Ickes. Should we take that move as any indication of a move on Mr. Ickes' part in the future?

THE PRESIDENT. No, I don't think so. He is a very capable person and has done an excellent job as Assistant Secretary, and comes to me highly recommended by everybody in connection with the thing; and so I appointed him. That's a job that needs to be well done.

[11.] Q. Mr. President, can you give us any hint as to what you are going to do about this bill turning over the USES to the States?

THE PRESIDENT. I haven't seen the bill yet. It hasn't been presented to me. When it comes up to me I will make an announcement on it, as soon as I have had a chance to study it.

[12.] Q. Mr. President, do you have any comment on Secretary Byrnes' departure for Moscow today?

THE PRESIDENT. I don't think it's necessary for me to make any comment. That trip was planned a long time ago. It's a part of the program as set out at Yalta for the foreign ministers of Russia, Great Britain, and the United States to meet at least every 4 months. It was just due now to meet in Moscow; and the next meeting will be held in Washington—probably March or April.

[13.] Q. Mr. President, this is a frivolous question, but what are you going to do for Christmas?

THE PRESIDENT. What am I going to do at Christmas?

Q. We keep getting messages from our editors. Are you going to be here?

THE PRESIDENT. No, I am not going to be here. The family will leave for home about the 18th, and I shall fly home for Christmas dinner on Christmas Day, as I have done in the past.

Q. Are you going to eat your regular three turkey dinners on Christmas that you used to?

THE PRESIDENT. If they are available, I certainly am. [*Laughter*]

Q. Let's see, you usually eat one with your mother, and one with your wife's mother——

THE PRESIDENT. That's right. And one with my aunt, who is 96 years old.

Reporter: Thank you, Mr. President.

NOTE: President Truman's thirty-eighth news conference was held in his office at the White House at 10:05 a.m. on Wednesday, December 12, 1945.

212 Letter to Wilson Wyatt Appointing Him Housing Expediter. *December 12, 1945*

Dear Mr. Wyatt:

This country is faced by an acute shortage of housing. Veterans are returning to homeless communities. Former war workers have come back to their home towns, and have found no place in which to live.

It is urgent that every available temporary living quarter be used in over-crowded communities, that the production of building materials be expedited, that the production of homes be hurried, that the cost of housing be protected from further inflation.

I am asking you to assume the role of housing expediter in the Office of War Mobilization and Reconversion. I am asking you to search out all bottlenecks at whatever level of industry or of government—local, state or national—you may find them; to try to break those bottlenecks; and to make the machinery of housing production run as smoothly and speedily as possible, so that we may be able to make the peace production of homes equal to the task of housing our veterans and other civilians.

Very sincerely,

HARRY S. TRUMAN

[Honorable Wilson Wyatt, Louisville, Kentucky]

NOTE: This letter was made public together with a report on housing submitted to the President by John W. Snyder, Director of War Mobilization and

Reconversion. The report, in the form of a memorandum dated December 8, was read in part at the President's news

conference of December 12 (see Item 211).

213 Citation Accompanying the Medal for Merit Awarded to Henry Morgenthau. *December* 12, 1945

CITATION TO ACCOMPANY THE AWARD OF

THE MEDAL FOR MERIT

TO

HENRY MORGENTHAU, JR.

HENRY MORGENTHAU, JR., Secretary of the Treasury, 1934–1945, for exceptionally meritorious conduct in the performance of outstanding services in such office. Under his supervision, the Treasury Department, through the sales of bonds, raised two hundred billion dollars with which to finance our defense and war activities. This great achievement was accompanied by a substantial reduction in the average rate of interest on the public debt. He participated in formulating and administering a wartime Federal tax program which raised unprecedented tax revenues with a minimum disturbance to the domestic economy. He contributed immeasurably to the close fiscal cooperation which this Government has had with its allies during the war. His many years of activity and accomplishment in the field of international monetary stabilization bore fruit in the Bretton Woods Agreements for an International Monetary Fund and Bank, ratified by the Congress early this year. In the days prior to our entrance into the war, both before and after the enactment of the lend-lease legislation, he was in the forefront in facilitating and urging aid to our allies. His vision, skill, and determination in financing the war, in preserving the stability of our domestic economy during the difficult war period, and in fostering international fiscal cooperation are exemplary of the highest standards of civilian services to the United States.

HARRY S. TRUMAN

NOTE: The presentation was made by the President in a ceremony held in the White House.

214 Citation Accompanying the Medal for Merit Awarded to
Ralph K. Davies. *December 12, 1945*

CITATION TO ACCOMPANY THE AWARD OF
THE MEDAL FOR MERIT

TO

RALPH K. DAVIES

RALPH K. DAVIES, for exceptionally meritorious conduct in the performance of outstanding services to the United States. As Deputy Petroleum Administrator, Mr. Davies organized and directed the unique
government-industry combination that achieved one of the outstanding
victories of the war—the assurance of petroleum for every military and
essential civilian need of the United Nations. Under his guidance, this
unprecedented partnership furnished the United Nations with their
most vital and most used munition. As a member of the President's
Committee on Oil, Mr. Davies played a leading part in formulating
and negotiating an international oil agreement, executed by officials of
the United States and Great Britain. To these high duties Mr. Davies
brought profound oil knowledge, an incisive intellect, rare vision, the
quiet power of a gifted organizer and executive, the courageous devotion of a man characterized by unflinching determination, and a deep
sense of public service.

HARRY S. TRUMAN

NOTE: The presentation was made by the President in a ceremony held in the White
House.

215 Citation Accompanying the Distinguished Service Medal
Awarded to Admiral Ernest J. King. *December 14, 1945*

THE PRESIDENT of the United States takes pleasure in presenting
the Gold Star in lieu of the Third Distinguished Service Medal to

FLEET ADMIRAL ERNEST J. KING, UNITED STATES NAVY

for service as set forth in the following

CITATION:

For exceptionally meritorious service to the Government of the United States in a duty of great responsibility as Commander-in-Chief of the United States Fleet from December 20, 1941, and concurrently as Chief of Naval Operations from March 18, 1942, to October 10, 1945. During the above periods, Fleet Admiral King, in his dual capacity, exercised complete military control of the naval forces of the United States Navy, Marine Corps, and Coast Guard and directed all activities of these forces in conjunction with the U.S. Army and our Allies to bring victory to the United States. As the United States Naval Member of the Joint Chiefs of Staff and the Combined Chiefs of Staff, he coordinated the naval strength of this country with all agencies of the United States and of the Allied Nations, and with exceptional vision, driving energy, and uncompromising devotion to duty, he fulfilled his tremendous responsibility of command and direction of the greatest naval force the world has ever seen and the simultaneous expansion of all naval facilities in the prosecution of the war. With extraordinary foresight, sound judgment, and brilliant strategic genius, he exercised a guiding influence in the Allied strategy of victory.

Analyzing with astute military acumen the multiple complexity of large-scale combined operations and the paramount importance of amphibious warfare, Fleet Admiral King exercised a guiding influence in the formation of all operational and logistic plans and achieved complete coordination between the U.S. Navy and all Allied military and naval forces.

His outstanding qualities of leadership throughout the greatest period of crisis in the history of our country were an inspiration to the forces under his command and to all associated with him.

HARRY S. TRUMAN

NOTE: The presentation was made by the President in a ceremony in the East Room at the White House.

216 Statement by the President: United States Policy Toward
    China. *December 15, 1945*

THE GOVERNMENT of the United States holds that peace and prosperity of the world in this new and unexplored era ahead depend upon
the ability of the sovereign nations to combine for collective security in
the United Nations organization.

It is the firm belief of this Government that a strong, united and
democratic China is of the utmost importance to the success of this
United Nations organization and for world peace. A China disorganized and divided either by foreign aggression, such as that undertaken by the Japanese, or by violent internal strife, is an undermining
influence to world stability and peace, now and in the future. The
United States Government has long subscribed to the principle that the
management of internal affairs is the responsibility of the peoples of
the sovereign nations. Events of this century, however, would indicate
that a breach of peace anywhere in the world threatens the peace of
the entire world. It is thus in the most vital interest of the United
States and all the United Nations that the people of China overlook no
opportunity to adjust their internal differences promptly by methods of
peaceful negotiation.

The Government of the United States believes it essential:

(1) That a cessation of hostilities be arranged between the armies of
the National Government and the Chinese Communists and other dis-
sident Chinese armed forces for the purpose of completing the return
of all China to effective Chinese control, including the immediate
evacuation of the Japanese forces.

(2) That a national conference of representatives of major political
elements be arranged to develop an early solution to the present internal strife—a solution which will bring about the unification of
China.

The United States and the other United Nations have recognized the
present National Government of the Republic of China as the only legal
government in China. It is the proper instrument to achieve the objective of a unified China.

The United States and the United Kingdom by the Cairo Declaration in 1943 and the Union of Soviet Socialist Republics by adhering to the Potsdam Declaration of last July and by the Sino-Soviet Treaty and Agreements of August 1945, are all committed to the liberation of China, including the return of Manchuria to Chinese control. These agreements were made with the National Government of the Republic of China.

In continuation of the constant and close collaboration with the National Government of the Republic of China in the prosecution of this war, in consonance with the Potsdam Declaration, and to remove possibility of Japanese influence remaining in China, the United States has assumed a definite obligation in the disarmament and evacuation of the Japanese troops. Accordingly the United States has been assisting and will continue to assist the National Government of the Republic of China in effecting the disarmament and evacuation of Japanese troops in the liberated areas. The United States Marines are in north China for that purpose.

The United States recognizes and will continue to recognize the National Government of China and cooperate with it in international affairs and specifically in eliminating Japanese influence from China. The United States is convinced that a prompt arrangement for a cessation of hostilities is essential to the effective achievement of this end. United States support will not extend to United States military intervention to influence the course of any Chinese internal strife.

The United States has already been compelled to pay a great price to restore the peace which was first broken by Japanese aggression in Manchuria. The maintenance of peace in the Pacific may be jeopardized, if not frustrated, unless Japanese influence in China is wholly removed and unless China takes her place as a unified, democratic and peaceful nation. This is the purpose of the maintenance for the time being of United States military and naval forces in China.

The United States is cognizant that the present National Government of China is a "one-party government" and believes that peace, unity and democratic reform in China will be furthered if the basis of this Government is broadened to include other political elements in the country. Hence, the United States strongly advocates that the national conference of representatives of major political elements in the country agree upon arrangements which would give those elements a fair and effective representation in the Chinese National Government. It is recognized that this would require modification of the one-party "political tutelage" established as an interim arrangement in the progress of the nation toward democracy by the father of the Chinese Republic, Doctor Sun Yat-sen.

The existence of autonomous armies such as that of the Communist army is inconsistent with, and actually makes impossible, political unity in China. With the institution of a broadly representative government, autonomous armies should be eliminated as such and all armed forces in China integrated effectively into the Chinese National Army.

In line with its often expressed views regarding self-determination, the United States Government considers that the detailed steps necessary to the achievement of political unity in China must be worked out by the Chinese themselves and that intervention by any foreign government in these matters would be inappropriate. The United States Government feels, however, that China has a clear responsibility to the other United Nations to eliminate armed conflict within its territory as constituting a threat to world stability and peace—a responsibility which is shared by the National Government and all Chinese political and military groups.

As China moves toward peace and unity along the lines described above, the United States would be prepared to assist the National Government in every reasonable way to rehabilitate the country, improve the agrarian and industrial economy, and establish a military organization capable of discharging China's national and international responsibilities for the maintenance of peace and order. In furtherance of such assistance, it would be prepared to give favorable consideration to Chinese requests for credits and loans under reasonable conditions for projects which would contribute toward the development of a healthy economy throughout China and healthy trade relations between China and the United States.

217 Veto of Bill Raising the Rank of Chiefs and Assistant
     Chiefs of Naval Bureaus. *December 17, 1945*

The House of Representatives:

I return herewith, without my approval, H.R. 1862, the principal purpose of which would be to give to chiefs of naval bureaus the rank of vice admiral and to the assistant chiefs of naval bureaus the rank of rear admiral.

This enactment would extend preferential rank and retirement benefits to a particular group in one of the branches of our armed forces, and would not take into account the matter of rank and other benefits for personnel holding comparable assignments within other branches. This is piecemeal legislation. The time has arrived when we must consider all branches of our armed forces in the enactment of laws governing rank, promotion, and other privileges and benefits and conditions of service. The matter of increased permanent rank for chiefs of bureaus of the Navy Department and their assistants should await decision by the Congress on the matter of the organization and composition of our whole post-war military establishment and consideration of the problem of suitable rank for higher commands and staff assignments in the ground, sea, and air forces.

HARRY S. TRUMAN

218 Special Message to the Congress Recommending the
     Establishment of a Department of National Defense.
     December 19, 1945

To the Congress of the United States:

In my message of September 6, 1945, I stated that I would communicate with the Congress from time to time during the current session with respect to a comprehensive and continuous program of national security. I pointed out the necessity of making timely preparation for the Nation's long-range security now—while we are still mindful of what it has cost us in this war to have been unprepared.

On October 23, 1945, as part of that program, there was presented for your consideration a proposal for universal military training. It was based upon the necessities of maintaining a well-trained citizenry which could be quickly mobilized in time of need in support of a small professional military establishment. Long and extensive hearings have now been held by the Congress on this recommendation. I think that the proposal, in principle, has met with the overwhelming approval of the people of the United States.

We are discharging our armed forces now at the rate of 1,500,000 a month. We can with fairness no longer look to the veterans of this war for any future military service. It is essential therefore that universal training be instituted at the earliest possible moment to provide a reserve upon which we can draw if, unhappily, it should become necessary. A grave responsibility will rest upon the Congress if it continues to delay this most important and urgent measure.

Today, again in the interest of national security and world peace, I make this further recommendation to you. I recommend that the Congress adopt legislation combining the War and Navy Departments into one single Department of National Defense. Such unification is another essential step—along with universal training—in the development of a comprehensive and continuous program for our future safety and for the peace and security of the world.

One of the lessons which have most clearly come from the costly and dangerous experience of this war is that there must be unified direction of land, sea and air forces at home as well as in all other parts of the world where our Armed Forces are serving.

We did not have that kind of direction when we were attacked four years ago—and we certainly paid a high price for not having it.

In 1941, we had two completely independent organizations with no well-established habits of collaboration and cooperation between them. If disputes arose, if there was failure to agree on a question of planning or a question of action, only the President of the United States could make a decision effective on both. Besides, in 1941, the air power of the United States was not organized on a par with the ground and sea forces.

Our expedient for meeting these defects was the creation of the Joint

Chiefs of Staff. On this Committee sat the President's Chief of Staff and the chiefs of the land forces, the naval forces, and the air forces. Under the Joint Chiefs were organized a number of committees bringing together personnel of the three services for joint strategic planning and for coordination of operations. This kind of coordination was better than no coordination at all, but it was in no sense a unified command.

In the theaters of operation, meanwhile, we went further in the direction of unity by establishing unified commands. We came to the conclusion—soon confirmed by experience—that any extended military effort required over-all coordinated control in order to get the most out of the three armed forces. Had we not early in the war adopted this principle of a unified command for operations, our efforts, no matter how heroic, might have failed.

But we never had comparable unified direction or command in Washington. And even in the field, our unity of operations was greatly impaired by the differences in training, in doctrine, in communication systems, and in supply and distribution systems, that stemmed from the division of leadership in Washington.

It is true, we were able to win in spite of these handicaps. But it is now time to take stock, to discard obsolete organizational forms and to provide for the future the soundest, the most effective and the most economical kind of structure for our armed forces of which this most powerful Nation is capable.

I urge this as the best means of keeping the peace.

No nation now doubts the good will of the United States for the maintenance of a lasting peace in the world. Our purpose is shown by our efforts to establish an effective United Nations Organization. But all nations—and particularly those unfortunate nations which have felt the heel of the Nazis, the Fascists or the Japs—know that desire for peace is futile unless there is also enough strength ready and willing to enforce that desire in any emergency. Among the things that have encouraged aggression and the spread of war in the past have been the unwillingness of the United States realistically to face this fact, and

548

her refusal to fortify her aims of peace before the forces of aggression could gather in strength.

Now that our enemies have surrendered it has again become all too apparent that a portion of the American people are anxious to forget all about the war, and particularly to forget all the unpleasant factors which are required to prevent future wars.

Whether we like it or not, we must all recognize that the victory which we have won has placed upon the American people the continuing burden of responsibility for world leadership. The future peace of the world will depend in large part upon whether or not the United States shows that it is really determined to continue in its role as a leader among nations. It will depend upon whether or not the United States is willing to maintain the physical strength necessary to act as a safeguard against any future aggressor. Together with the other United Nations, we must be willing to make the sacrifices necessary to protect the world from future aggressive warfare. In short, we must be prepared to maintain in constant and immediate readiness sufficient military strength to convince any future potential aggressor that this Nation, in its determination for a lasting peace, means business.

We would be taking a grave risk with the national security if we did not move now to overcome permanently the present imperfections in our defense organization. However great was the need for coordination and unified command in World War II, it is sure to be greater if there is any future aggression against world peace. Technological developments have made the Armed Services much more dependent upon each other than ever before. The boundaries that once separated the Army's battlefield from the Navy's battlefield have been virtually erased. If there is ever going to be another global conflict, it is sure to take place simultaneously on land and sea and in the air, with weapons of ever greater speed and range. Our combat forces must work together in one team as they have never been required to work together in the past.

We must assume, further, that another war would strike much more suddenly than the last, and that it would strike directly at the United States. We cannot expect to be given the opportunity again to experiment in organization and in ways of teamwork while the fighting proceeds. True preparedness now means preparedness not alone in armaments and numbers of men, but preparedness in organization also. It means establishing in peacetime the kind of military organization which will be able to meet the test of sudden attack quickly and without having to improvise radical readjustment in structure and habits.

The basic question is what organization will provide the most effective employment of our military resources in time of war and the most effective means for maintaining peace. The manner in which we make this transition in the size, composition, and organization of the armed forces will determine the efficiency and cost of our national defense for many years to come.

Improvements have been made since 1941 by the President in the organization of the War and Navy Departments, under the War Powers Act. Unless the Congress acts before these powers lapse, these Departments will revert to their prewar organizational status. This would be a grievous mistake.

The Joint Chiefs of Staff are not a unified command. It is a committee which must depend for its success upon the voluntary cooperation of its member agencies. During the war period of extreme national danger, there was, of course, a high degree of cooperation. In peacetime the situation will be different. It must not be taken for granted that the Joint Chiefs of Staff as now constituted will be as effective in the apportionment of peacetime resources as they have been in the determination of war plans and in their execution. As national defense appropriations grow tighter, and as conflicting interests make themselves felt in major issues of policy and strategy, unanimous agreements will become more difficult to reach.

It was obviously impossible in the midst of conflict to reorganize the armed forces of the United States along the lines here suggested. Now that our enemies have surrendered, I urge the Congress to proceed to bring about a reorganization of the management of the Armed Forces.

Further studies of the general problem would serve no useful purpose. There is enough evidence now at hand to demonstrate beyond question the need for a unified department. A great many of the reasons for establishing a single department have been brought out already in public discussion and in Congressional committee hearings. To me the most important reasons for combining the two existing Departments are these:

1. *We should have integrated strategic plans and a unified military program and budget.*

With the coming of peace, it is clear that we must not only continue, but strengthen, our present facilities for integrated planning. We cannot have the sea, land, and air members of our defense team working at what may turn out to be cross purposes, planning their programs on different assumptions as to the nature of the military establishment we need, and engaging in an open competition for funds.

Strategy, program, and budget are all aspects of the same basic decisions. Using the advice of our scientists and our intelligence officers, we must make the wisest estimate as to the probable nature of any future attack upon us, determine accordingly how to organize and deploy our military forces, and allocate the available manpower, materiel, and financial resources in a manner consistent with the over-all plan.

Up to the present time, the makeup and balance of our Armed Forces have not been planned as a whole. Programs and budget requests from the Army and Navy have been formulated separately, on the basis of independent concepts of mission and function. These separate programs and budgets have not been considered together until after they have passed out of military hands and even out of the hands of the Secretaries of War and the Navy. The whole job of reconciling the divergent claims of the Departments has been thrust upon the President and the Congress.

This war has demonstrated completely that the resources of this nation in manpower and in raw materials are not unlimited. To realize this is to comprehend the urgent need for finding a way to allocate these resources intelligently among the competing services. This means designing a balanced military structure reflecting a considered apportionment of responsibility among the services for the performance of a joint mission.

From experience as a member of the Congress, I know the great difficulty of appraising properly the over-all security needs of the nation from piecemeal presentations by separate departments appearing before separate congressional committees at different times. It is only by combining the armed forces into a single department that the Congress can have the advantage of considering a single coordinated and comprehensive security program.

2. *We should realize the economies that can be achieved through unified control of supply and service functions.*

Instances of duplication among Army and Navy activities and facilities have been brought to the attention of the Congress on many occasions. The degree of unity that was accomplished during the war in strategic planning and in theater command is in striking contrast with the separatism that prevailed in the whole range of supply and service functions.

It will never be possible to achieve absolute coordination of the supply and service functions of all services. Neither the War Department nor the Navy Department has been able to eliminate all duplication even within its own organization. But there is no question that the extent of waste through lack of coordination between the two Departments is very much greater than the waste resulting from faulty coordination within each. If we can attain as much coordination among all the services as now exists within each department, we shall realize extensive savings.

Consolidation of the Departments will, for example, reduce the volume of supplies that need to be procured. Supply requirements, for example, begin with a calculation of so many items per man to be supplied. But to this basic figure must be added margins of safety, to account for items in storage, transportation lags, breakdowns in delivery, emergency demands, and so forth. In these margins, savings can be made through unified systems of supply. As the volume handled in any supply system grows, the percentage factor which has to be added for reserves is reduced.

In the same way, both the Army and the Navy must add a margin of safety to their requirements for production plants, depots, hospitals, air training fields, and other types of construction common to both services. When the requirements are pooled, the total amount of margin may be reduced. The same is true of personnel. Each service must add a margin of safety in estimating its requirements for doctors, nurses, skilled mechanics, and other types of specialists. The total margin is greater if the computations are made separately. Another source of economy will be the pooling of facilities and personnel in localities where at present both services have to operate, but where from the nature of the circumstances, facilities and personnel are not fully used.

Other examples of duplication could be cited. Business men have to deal with separate buyers, who may use separate specifications for items which could as well have the same specifications. Separate inspectors are stationed in their plants. During this war, instances occurred where the purchase of all available quantities of certain items by one service resulted in acute shortages in the other service. Parallel transportation and storage systems required extra overhead.

As the war progressed, it is true that increased cooperation reduced the extent of waste and conflict. But voluntary cooperation in such matters can never be expected to be fully effective. A single authority at the top would inevitably achieve a greater degree of economy than would be obtained under divided direction.

3. *We should adopt the organizational structure best suited to fostering coordination between the military and the remainder of the Government.*

Our military policy and program are only a part of a total national program aimed at achieving our national objectives of security and peace. This total program has many aspects, and many agencies of the Government must participate in its execution.

Our military policy, for example, should be completely consistent with our foreign policy. It should be designed to support and reflect our commitments to the United Nations Organization. It should be adjusted according to the success or lack of success of our diplomacy. It should reflect our fullest knowledge of the capabilities and intentions of other powers. Likewise, our foreign policy should take into account our military capabilities and the strategic power of our Armed Forces.

A total security program has still other major aspects. A military program, standing alone, is useless. It must be supported in peacetime by planning for industrial mobilization and for development of industrial and raw material resources where these are insufficient. Programs of scientific research must be developed for military purposes, and their results woven into the defense program. The findings of our intelligence service must be applied to all of these.

Formulation and execution of a comprehensive and consistent national program embracing all these activities are extremely difficult tasks. They are made more difficult the greater the number of departments and agencies whose policies and programs have to be coordinated at the top level of the Executive Branch. They are simplified as the number of these agencies can be reduced.

The consolidation of the War and Navy Departments would greatly facilitate the ease and speed with which the Armed Forces and the other departments could exchange views and come to agreement on matters of common concern. It would minimize the extent to which inter-service differences have to be discussed and settled by the civilian leaders whose main concern should be the more fundamental job of building over-all national policy.

4. *We should provide the strongest means for civilian control of the military.*

Civilian control of the military establishment—one of the most fundamental of our democratic concepts—would be strengthened if the President and the Congress had but one Cabinet member with clear and primary responsibility for the exercise of that control. When the military establishment is divided between two civilian Secretaries, each is limited necessarily to a restricted view of the military establishment. Consequently, on many fundamental issues where the civilian point of view should be controlling, the Secretaries of the two Departments are cast in the role of partisans of their respective Services, and real civilian control can be exercised by no one except the President or the Congress.

During and since the war, the need for joint action by the Services and for objective recommendations on military matters has led inevitably to increasing the authority of the only joint organization and the most nearly objective organization that exists—the Joint Chiefs of Staff. But the Joint Chiefs of Staff are a strictly military body. Responsibility for civilian control should be clearly fixed in a single full-time civilian below the President. This requires a Secretary for the entire military establishment, aided by a strong staff of civilian assistants.

There is no basis for the fear that such an organization would lodge too much power in a single individual—that the concentration of so much military power would lead to militarism. There is no basis for such fear as long as the traditional policy of the United States is followed that a civilian, subject to the President, the Congress and the will of the people, be placed at the head of this Department. The safety of the democracy of the United States lies in the solid good sense and unshakable conviction of the American people. They need have no fear that their democratic liberties will be imperiled so long as they continue fulfilling their duties of citizenship.

5. *We should organize to provide parity for air power.*

Air power has been developed to a point where its responsibilities are equal to those of land and sea power, and its contribution to our strategic planning is as great. In operation, air power receives its separate assignment in the execution of an over-all plan. These facts were finally recognized in this war in the organizational parity which was granted to air power within our principal unified commands.

Parity for air power can be achieved in one department or in three, but not in two. As between one department and three, the former is infinitely to be preferred. The advantages of a single department are indeed much clearer when the alternative is seen to be three departments rather than the present two. The existence of three departments would complicate tremendously every problem of coordination that now exists between the War and Navy Departments, and between the Services and the rest of the government.

The Cabinet is not merely a collection of executives administering different governmental functions. It is a body whose combined judgment the President uses to formulate the fundamental policies of the administration. In such a group, which is designed to develop team-work wisdom on all subjects that affect the political life of the country, it would be inappropriate and unbalanced to have three members representing three different instruments of national defense.

The President, as Commander-in-Chief, should not personally have to coordinate the Army and Navy and Air Force. With all the other problems before him, the President cannot be expected to balance either the organization, the training or the practice of the several branches of national defense. He should be able to rely for that coordination upon civilian hands at the Cabinet level.

6. *We should establish the most advantageous framework for a unified system of training for combined operations of land, sea and air.*

Whatever the form which any future war may take, we know that the men of our separate Services will have to work together in many kinds of combinations for many purposes. The Pacific campaign of the recent war is an outstanding example of common and joint effort among land, sea, and air forces. Despite its successes, that campaign proved that there is not adequate understanding among the officers and men of any Service of the capabilities, the uses, the procedures, and the limitations of the other Services.

This understanding is not something that can be created overnight whenever a combined operation is planned and a task force organized. The way men act in combat is determined by the sum total of all their previous training, indoctrination, and experience.

What we seek is a structure which can best produce an integrated training program, carry on merged training activities where that is appropriate, and permit officers to be assigned in such a way that an individual officer will learn first-hand of other Services besides the one in which he has specialized. The organizational framework most conducive to this kind of unified training and doctrine is a unified department.

7. *We should allocate systematically our limited resources for scientific research.*

No aspect of military preparedness is more important than scientific research. Given the limited amount of scientific talent that will be available for military purposes, we must systematically apply that talent to research in the most promising lines and on the weapons with the greatest potentiality, regardless of the Service in which these weapons will be used. We cannot afford to waste any of our scientific resources in duplication of effort.

This does not mean that all Army and Navy laboratories would be immediately or even ultimately consolidated. The objective should be to preserve initiative and enterprise while eliminating duplication and misdirected effort. This can be accomplished only, if we have an organizational structure which will permit fixing responsibility at the top for coordination among the Services.

8. *We should have unity of command in outlying bases.*

All military authority at each of our outlying bases should be placed under a single commander who will have clear responsibility for security, who can be held clearly accountable, and whose orders come from a single authority in Washington. Reconnaissance planes, radar sets, and intelligence and counter-intelligence measures at a United States outpost are not intended to serve separate Services for different purposes. Unification of the Services offers a far greater guarantee of continued unity in the field than does our present organization.

9. *We should have consistent and equitable personnel policies.*

There have been differences in personnel policies between the Army and the Navy during the war. They began with competitive recruitment for certain types of persons, and continued in almost every phase of personnel administration. In rates of promotion, in ways of selecting officers, in the utilization of reserve officers, in awards and decorations, in allowances and in point systems for discharge, the two Services have followed different policies.

This inconsistency is highly undesirable. It will be reduced to a minimum under a unified organization.

Any bill which is enacted to carry out these recommendations cannot provide immediately the ultimate organization plan to accomplish unification. It can only prescribe the general organization of the authorities at the top levels of the unified Department.

I recommend that the reorganization of the armed services be along the following broad lines:

(1) There should be a single Department of National Defense. This Department should be charged with the full responsibility for armed national security. It should consist of the armed and civilian forces that are now included within the War and Navy Departments.

(2) The head of this Department should be a civilian, a member of the President's cabinet, to be designated as the Secretary of National Defense. Under him there should be a civilian Under Secretary and several civilian Assistant Secretaries.

(3) There should be three coordinated branches of the Department of National Defense: one for the land forces, one for the naval forces, and one for the air forces, each under an Assistant Secretary. The Navy should, of course, retain its own carrier, ship, and water-based aviation, which has proved so necessary for efficient fleet operation. And, of course, the Marine Corps should be continued as an integral part of the Navy.

(4) The Under Secretary and the remaining Assistant Secretaries should be available for assignment to whatever duties the President and the Secretary may determine from time to time.

(5) The President and the Secretary should be provided with ample authority to establish central coordinating and service organizations, both military and civilian, where these are found to be necessary. Some of these might be placed under Assistant Secretaries, some might be organized as central service organizations, and some might be organized in a top military staff to integrate the military leadership of the department. I do not believe that we can specify at this time the exact nature of these organizations. They must be developed over a period of time by the President and the Secretary as a normal part of their executive responsibilities. Sufficient strength in these department-wide elements of the department, as opposed to the separate Service elements, will insure that real unification is ultimately obtained. The President and the Secretary should not be limited in their authority to establish department-wide coordinating and service organizations.

(6) There should be a Chief of Staff of the Department of National

Defense. There should also be a commander for each of the three component branches—Army, Navy, and Air.

(7) The Chief of Staff and the commanders of the three coordinate branches of the Department should together constitute an advisory body to the Secretary of National Defense and to the President. There should be nothing to prevent the President, the Secretary, and other civilian authorities from communicating with the commanders of any of the components of the Department on such vital matters as basic military strategy and policy and the division of the budget. Furthermore, the key staff positions in the Department should be filled with officers drawn from all the services, so that the thinking of the Department would not be dominated by any one or two of the services.

As an additional precaution, it would be wise if the post of Chief of Staff were rotated among the several services, whenever practicable and advisable, at least during the period of evolution of the new unified Department. The tenure of the individual officer designated to serve as Chief of Staff should be relatively short—two or three years—and should not, except in time of a war emergency declared by the Congress, be extended beyond that period.

Unification of the services must be looked upon as a long-term job. We all recognize that there will be many complications and difficulties. Legislation of the character outlined will provide us with the objective, and with the initial means whereby forward-looking leadership in the Department, both military and civilian, can bring real unification into being. Unification is much more than a matter of organization. It will require new viewpoints, new doctrine, and new habits of thinking throughout the departmental structure. But in the comparative leisure of peacetime, and utilizing the skill and experience of our staff and field commanders who brought us victory, we should start at once to achieve the most efficient instrument of national safety.

Once a unified department has been established, other steps necessary to the formulation of a comprehensive national security program can be taken with greater ease. Much more than a beginning has already been made in achieving consistent political and military policy through the establishment of the State-War-Navy Coordinating Committee. With respect to military research, I have in a previous message to the Congress proposed the establishment of a federal research agency, among whose responsibilities should be the promotion and coordination of fundamental research pertaining to the defense and security of the Nation. The development of a coordinated, government-wide intelligence system is in process. As the advisability of additional action to insure a broad and coordinated program of national security becomes clear, I shall make appropriate recommendations or take the necessary action to that end.

The American people have all been enlightened and gratified by the free discussion which has taken place within the Services and before the committees of the Senate and the House of Representatives. The Congress, the people, and the President have benefited from a clarification of the issues that could have been provided in no other way. But however strong the opposition that has been expressed by some of our outstanding senior officers and civilians, I can assure the Congress that once unification has been determined upon as the policy of this nation, there is no officer or civilian in any Service who will not contribute his utmost to make the unification a success.

I make these recommendations in the full realization that we are undertaking a task of greatest difficulty. But I am certain that when the task is accomplished, we shall have a military establishment far better adapted to carrying out its share of our national program for achieving peace and security.

HARRY S. TRUMAN

NOTE: On July 26, 1947, the President approved the National Security Act of 1947 (Public Law 253, 80th Cong., 61 Stat. 495) which provided for a Secretary of Defense and for a National Military Establishment comprising Departments of the Army, the Navy, and the Air Force, and related staff agencies.

219   Special Message to the Senate Transmitting Nominations
of United States Representatives to the United Nations.
December 19, 1945

To the Senate of the United States:

In conformity with the provisions of S. 1580, I am sending to the Senate herewith for its advice and consent nominations of the American representatives and alternate representatives for the first part of the first meeting of the General Assembly of the United Nations which is to convene in London early in January. I am also sending to the Senate herewith the nomination of the American representative to the Security Council which will also meet in London sometime in January as soon as that body has been established through the election of its nonpermanent members by the General Assembly.

Section 2(d) of the pending bill wisely provides that the President, or the Secretary of State at the direction of the President, may represent the United States at any meeting of the United Nations regardless of those provisions which call for the appointment of representatives by and with the advice and consent of the Senate. At my request the Secretary of State will, for at least a portion of the session, attend the initial session of the General Assembly. For that reason I am sending to the Senate the nominations of only four representatives to the General Assembly. The Secretary of State will, during the period he is present, act as the senior representative of the United States to the General Assembly. The nominations of the Alternates will insure that there will at all times be five representatives of the United States qualified under the provisions of S. 1580.

HARRY S. TRUMAN

NOTE: The President transmitted with the message the following nominations:

U.S. Representative to the United Nations with the rank and status of Ambassador Extraordinary and Plenipotentiary, and U.S. Representative to the Security Council: Edward R. Stettinius, Jr.

U.S. Representatives to the first part of the First Session of the U.N. General Assembly to be held in London, January 1946: Edward R. Stettinius, Jr.; Tom Connally, U.S. Senator from Texas; Arthur H. Vandenberg, U.S. Senator from Michigan; and Mrs. Anna Eleanor Roosevelt.

Alternate U.S. Representatives to the first part of the First Session of the U.N. General Assembly: Sol Bloom, U.S. Representative from New York; Charles A. Eaton, U.S. Representative from New Jersey; Frank C. Walker; John Foster Dulles; and John G. Townsend, Jr.

220 Statement by the President Upon Signing the Reorganization Act of 1945. *December* 20, 1945

I AM PLEASED today to sign the Reorganization Act of 1945, for I believe that in this Act the Congress has established a procedure which should lead to substantial improvements in the organization and management of the Government.

Under the authority of the Act, I shall undertake a systematic review of the Government agencies with a view to regrouping their functions in the most efficient and economical manner and abolishing such functions or agencies as may not be necessary.

The Director of the Bureau of the Budget has been instructed to obtain the recommendations of all departments and establishments covered by the Act and to take the lead in preparing the necessary reorganization plans for my consideration. He will work with the Director of War Mobilization and Reconversion insofar as the reorganization proposals relate to the reconversion of the war agencies.

While I anticipate that this Act will result in some reduction of administrative expenditures in the agencies affected by reorganization plans, I do not consider it probable that we will generally save as much as 25 percent, as suggested in the Act. I wish to point out, also, that administrative expenditures are only a small proportion of the cost of Government. Substantial savings in Government expenditures can come only from reductions in the Governmental programs themselves, and these are made as a rule through the normal budgetary and appropriations processes, not through reorganization action.

The results of reorganization will be evident primarily in the increased effectiveness of Government operations. Regrouping and consolidation to bring together those agencies having related purposes will lead to a greater consistency in the policies of the agencies and better coordination of their programs in operation. This should mean also a simpler and clearer relation between the agencies of the Government and the public. Through these means, the Act will enable us better to adapt the Government for carrying out its responsibility of serving the people.

NOTE: The Reorganization Act of 1945 is Public Law 263, 79th Congress (59 Stat. 613).

221 The President's News Conference of *December* 20, 1945

THE PRESIDENT. [1.] I want to make a statement in connection with the factfinding boards, and this will be available in mimeographed form when you go out.

[*Reading*] "In appointing a factfinding board in an industrial dispute where one of the questions at issue is wages, it is essential to a fulfillment of its duty that the board have the authority, whenever it deems it necessary, to examine the books of the employer. That authority is essential to enable the board to determine the ability of the employer to pay an increase in wages where such ability is in question. Ability to pay is always one of the facts relevant to the issue of an increase in wages.

"This does not mean that the Government or its factfinding board is going to endeavor to fix a rate of return for the employer. It does mean, however, that since wages are paid out of earnings, the question of earnings is relevant.

"The detailed information, obtained from the books of an employer should not be made public. Such a disclosure would place the employer at a disadvantage with respect to his competitors. But the factfinding board should unquestionably have the right to examine the employer's books where it deems it necessary in order to make up its own mind as to whether a demand for an increase is justified, and to make public all findings based on such information, that it deems relevant to the controversy.

"That is one of the things I meant when I stated in my message of December 3, 1945, to Congress, and I quote:

" 'The Board should be . . . directed to make a thorough investigation of all the facts which it deems relevant in the controversy.'

"This is nothing new. There are many instances where the books of corporations are opened for inspection to representatives of the State and Federal Governments and where the information so obtained is used solely by such officials to carry out their functions.

"To confer the right to examine books is one of the main purposes of granting subpoena power to the factfinding boards. I trust that the Congress, which is the only body authorized to grant such power, will do so quickly.

"In view of the public interest involved, it would be highly unfortunate if any party to a dispute should refuse to cooperate with a factfinding board."

[2.] Now, I am going to have for release for you the letter which I sent today—identical letters to Senator Wagner and Representative Carter Manasco, in regard to the full employment bill, which is in conference—those two gentlemen are the Chairmen of the House and Senate conferees—calling attention to the fact that the Senate bill more nearly complies with the message which was sent to the Congress, and expressing the hope that the Senate bill will be adopted by the conferees. The release will speak for itself.[1]

I also want to say while—in that same connection, that I am highly appreciative of the sincere efforts that a large number of Congressmen and Senators put forth in an endeavor to get a full employment bill on the books.

Now then, I am ready for questions.

[3.] Q. Mr. President, oftentimes when you talk about opening up the books of employers, there is a counterproposal made that the unions' books should be opened up. Is there anything you could tell us as to your views on that?

THE PRESIDENT. I think that power applies to everything that is relevant with regard to wages and prices.

[4.] Q. Mr. President, when would you send the message to Congress on the British loan?

---

[1] See Item 222.

THE PRESIDENT. As soon as the State Department has the thing in shape to send down. I told the people who are interested in that, that the message would not go down until after the holidays.

[5.] Q. Mr. President, some people in the Navy seem to think that part of the unification message was intended to muzzle naval officers, and to stop further discussion by them of the whole question of unification. Was that your intention?

THE PRESIDENT. No such intention in view. There has never been any attempt to muzzle anybody. I want everybody to express his honest opinion on the subject, and I want to get the best results that are possible. In order to do that, I want the opinions of everybody. And nobody has been muzzled.

It will be necessary now, though, for all people who are in the services, to make a statement that they are expressing their personal views and not the views of the administration.

I have expressed those views myself.

[6.] Q. Mr. President, have you decided what action you are going to have on the congressional bill returning the employment services to the States?

THE PRESIDENT. I haven't seen that bill as yet. I will very forcibly express my opinion whenever I have seen the bill and had a chance to read it.

[7.] Q. Mr. President, a broadcaster out of Japan today made the assertion that General MacArthur has threatened to resign—is upset about the possibility that Russia might have a part in the occupation of Japan. Could you say anything to bring that back into proper perspective?

THE PRESIDENT. I know nothing about it.

Q. About such a statement?

THE PRESIDENT. About any such statement, and I don't think General MacArthur has made any such statement. I know he has made no such statement to either me or the Secretary of War.

[8.] Q. Mr. President, speaking of resignations, do you expect Secretary Forrestal to resign?

THE PRESIDENT. Well, Secretary Forrestal has been trying to resign ever since I have been here, but I hope he won't resign at a very early date.

[9.] Q. Mr. President, do you care to say what you discussed with Mr. Pelley and Mr. Fort of the Railroad Association?

THE PRESIDENT. They were discussing the Bulwinkle bill.

[10.] Q. Mr. President, there is a report from London that the British Navy rather than the American Navy broke the Japanese code, and the Navy says that anything on that report would have to come from the White House rather than from the Navy Department. Do you have any comment?

THE PRESIDENT. I don't know anything about it.

[11.] Q. Mr. President, have you yet evolved any plan of civil administration of the American Zone in Germany?

THE PRESIDENT. It is under discussion. No plan has been evolved as yet.

Q. No date set as yet?

THE PRESIDENT. No date set. We hope it will be before the 30th of June, however.

[12.] Q. Mr. President, are we to take your further statement about labor unions at the beginning, that you would—you think labor unions should open their books——

THE PRESIDENT. Why certainly—why certainly. It will be a fact-finding board to arrive at its opinion for anything that they deem relevant in the controversy.

[13.] Q. Mr. President, would you care to comment on the progress of the Moscow conference of foreign ministers?

THE PRESIDENT. There is no comment.

[14.] Q. Mr. President, in your reference to the rights of subpoena, on what would that authority or that right be based?

THE PRESIDENT. Well, on the right to get the information that is necessary to settle the controversy. Congress can delegate that power to anybody.

Q. Union books, Mr. President?

THE PRESIDENT. Anything.

Q. There has been talk that the operators—manufacturers—General Motors might walk out of the factfinding board, if the pressure were put on for its books at that time, and we couldn't expect anything further until congressional action?

THE PRESIDENT. Well, I hope they won't take that attitude, because that won't reflect to their credit.

[15.] Q. Mr. President, has Dr. Tugwell asked to be relieved as Governor of Puerto Rico?

THE PRESIDENT. One of the first things I received was the resignation of Dr. Tugwell. I asked him to stay.

Q. Did he renew his request to resign when he was in here?

THE PRESIDENT. Yes, he did.

Q. And you asked him to stay?

THE PRESIDENT. Yes, I still want him to stay.

Q. Mr. President,——

THE PRESIDENT. Let me answer this lady's question.

[16.] Q. Going back to the full employment bill, would you want the House machinery as established in the House bill merged with the Senate bill at all?

THE PRESIDENT. I think the Senate version is the best version of the full employment bill. That is what I wanted to get over.

[17.] Q. Mr. President, Mr. Tugwell is going to stay?

THE PRESIDENT. For a while, yes.

Q. How long is "a while," Mr. President?

THE PRESIDENT. Well, I can't state that. I don't know.

[18.] Q. Mr. President, if—I may have misunderstood the gentleman, but is there any relation between wages and the books of a union, which are merely books of dues collected and expenses——

THE PRESIDENT. Not that I know of. And if they were relevant to investigating, the subpoena power would be there.

[19.] Q. Mr. President, would you care to say anything on the policy of this Government towards Spain and the Franco government?

THE PRESIDENT. It has been expressed at Potsdam. If you will read the Potsdam Declaration, you will find it.

[20.] Q. Mr. President, can you say anything about your discussion with General Gregory this morning?

THE PRESIDENT. No. No comment on that.

[21.] Q. Mr. President, may I ask a question? Do you consider that this present factfinding board in the General Motors case has authority to—they don't have any legislative authority?

THE PRESIDENT. The only authority they have is under the War Powers Act. We have got all the power existing under the War Powers Act.

Q. Mr. President, a spokesman for General Motors said positively today that he would retire the corporation—the corporation would leave the factfinding board. What is the next step under those circumstances?

THE PRESIDENT. I am very sorry to hear that. I hope he will reconsider that and not do it.

[22.] Q. Mr. President, do you have any intentions, or any plans, of going to London at any time during the United Nations Assembly meeting?

THE PRESIDENT. No.

[23.] Q. Mr. President, under the Powers Act—under the War Powers Act, does the panel have power to subpoena books or would that be purely voluntary?

THE PRESIDENT. That would be purely voluntary. They have not got the power, and nobody can give that power but the Congress.

[24.] Q. Another point, going back to the full employment bill. Would you consider the House version of the full employment bill acceptable?

THE PRESIDENT. I would not.

Q. Well, thank you, Mr. President, and a Merry Christmas!

THE PRESIDENT. Thank you.

Voices: Merry Christmas!

THE PRESIDENT. Merry Christmas to all of you. I hope you have a grand Christmas, all of you.

NOTE: President Truman's fortieth news conference was held in his office at the White House at 4 p.m. on Thursday, December 20, 1945.

222   Letter to Senator Wagner and Representative Manasco
      Concerning the Full Employment Bill.
      December 20, 1945

Dear ————— :

The Full Employment Bill adopted by the Senate modified the
language of the original bill but did not remove its essential provisions.

On December 14, 1945, however, the House sent to conference a
wholly new measure lacking the essential features of the Full Employment Bill as passed by the Senate. Many of the Representatives who
voted for the House bill did so, I believe, in the belief that the conferees
would have an opportunity to restore the essentials of the Senate bill.

In my opinion no bill which provides substantially less than the Senate version can efficiently accomplish the purposes intended. I urge
the conferees to support the essential characteristics of the Full Employment Bill as contained in the legislation adopted by the Senate by
a vote of 71 to 10.

The essential characteristics of effective legislation to establish a national policy in respect to employment opportunity, as I see them, were
described in my message to the Congress on September 6, as follows:

"A national reassertion of the right to work for every American
citizen able and willing to work—a declaration of the ultimate duty of
Government to use its own resources if all other methods should fail to
prevent prolonged unemployment—these will help to avert fear and
establish full employment. The prompt and firm acceptance of this
bedrock public responsibility will reduce the need for its exercise.

"I ask that full employment legislation to provide these vital assurances be speedily enacted . . ."

I hope that the Congress will adopt a bill substantially in the form
passed by the Senate.

Very sincerely,

HARRY S. TRUMAN

NOTE: This is the text of identical letters
addressed to the Honorable Robert F.
Wagner, the United States Senate, and
to the Honorable Carter Manasco, the
House of Representatives. Senator
Wagner and Representative Manasco
were the chairmen of the conferees of
the Senate and of the House of Representatives, respectively, on the full employment bill.

223 Letter to Dr. Isaiah Bowman on Federal Assistance for Scientific Research. *December* 20, 1945

[Released December 20, 1945. Dated December 14, 1945]

My dear Doctor Bowman:

Receipt is acknowledged of your letter dated November 24, 1945, on behalf of the newly organized Committee supporting the Bush report, regarding the science legislation now pending before the Congress.

I am keenly interested in the development of research and of appropriate Federal assistance therefor. Brilliant results have been achieved by the scientists during the war. The people deserve these results in peace as well.

My views on the soundest form of Federal assistance have been stated both in my Message to Congress on September 6, 1945, and in the statements made by the Director of War Mobilization and Reconversion and the Director of the Budget.

These views were expressed after the fullest consideration of the best interests of all concerned, after consultation with scientists, with public administrators and with students of Government, after considering the Bush report and the committee reports on which it was based, and after weighing the views expressed in your letter which had previously been called to my attention.

I appreciate the interest taken in this subject by members of your Committee, and feel sure that their basic objectives of freedom of research, and non-partisan administration of a program of aid to scientific research and education, will be attained under such an organization as I have recommended.

I am confident that I can count on them to support scientific research with the same zeal that has made our scientists so eminent.

Very sincerely,

HARRY S. TRUMAN

[Dr. Isaiah Bowman, President, Johns Hopkins University, Baltimore, Maryland]

NOTE: The Bush report, entitled "Science, the Endless Frontier" (Government Printing Office, 1945), was prepared at the request of President Roosevelt and was submitted to President Truman by Dr. Vannevar Bush, Director, Office of Scientific Research and Development. The report was reissued in 1960 by the National Science Foundation as part of the observance of the Foundation's 10th anniversary.

224 Letter to the Administrator, Federal Works Agency, Asking Him To Head a Conference on Traffic Safety. *December 21, 1945*

[Released December 21, 1945. Dated December 18, 1945]

Dear General:

I am deeply concerned by the extent of traffic accidents on the Nation's streets and highways which have increased alarmingly since the end of gasoline rationing. The loss of life, the bodily injuries, and the destruction of property resulting from these accidents are a drain upon the nation's resources which we cannot possibly allow to continue.

It is my intention to call into conference at the White House next spring representatives of the States and municipalities who have legal responsibility in matters of highway traffic, together with representatives of the several national organizations which have a primary interest in traffic safety. I hope that additional means may be devised by such a conference to make our streets and highways safer for motorists and for the public before the beginning of the automobile touring season of 1946.

The Federal Works Agency, through its Public Roads Administration, is the organization that is concerned with matters relating to highway construction and transport.

Therefore, I should like to have you, as Administrator of the Federal Works Agency, head up the conference. I suggest, as a necessary preliminary step, that you call into consultation in the near future appropriate representatives of the interests involved in order to lay the groundwork and prepare the agenda for the conference.

Very sincerely,

HARRY S. TRUMAN

[Major General Philip B. Fleming, Administrator, Federal Works Agency]

NOTE: The White House release of the
President's letter stated that information
supplied to the President showed that
traffic fatalities in the United States
totaled 2,510 during August (the month
in which gasoline rationing ended),
2,839 in September, and 3,440 in October. These figures represented increases of 30, 40, and 50 percent, respectively, over corresponding months
in 1944.

225 Statement and Directive by the President on Immigration
to the United States of Certain Displaced Persons and
Refugees in Europe. *December 22, 1945*

THE WAR has brought in its wake an appalling dislocation of populations in Europe. Many humanitarian organizations, including the
United Nations Relief and Rehabilitation Administration, are doing
their utmost to solve the multitude of problems arising in connection
with this dislocation of hundreds of thousands of persons. Every effort
is being made to return the displaced persons and refugees in the various
countries of Europe to their former homes. The great difficulty is that
so many of these persons have no homes to which they may return.
The immensity of the problem of displaced persons and refugees is
almost beyond comprehension.

A number of countries in Europe, including Switzerland, Sweden,
France, and England, are working toward its solution. The United
States shares the responsibility to relieve the suffering. To the extent
that our present immigration laws permit, everything possible should
be done at once to facilitate the entrance of some of these displaced
persons and refugees into the United States.

In this way we may do something to relieve human misery, and set an
example to the other countries of the world which are able to receive
some of these war sufferers. I feel that it is essential that we do this
ourselves to show our good faith in requesting other nations to open
their doors for this purpose.

Most of these persons are natives of Central and Eastern Europe and
the Balkans. The immigration quotas for all these countries for one
year total approximately 39,000, two-thirds of which are allotted to

Germany. Under the law, in any single month the number of visas issued cannot exceed ten per cent of the annual quota. This means that from now on only about 3900 visas can be issued each month to persons who are natives of these countries.

Very few persons from Europe have migrated to the United States during the war years. In the fiscal year 1942, only ten per cent of the immigration quotas was used; in 1943, five per cent; in 1944, six per cent; and in 1945, seven per cent. As of November 30, 1945, the end of the fifth month of the present fiscal year, only about ten per cent of the quotas for the European countries has been used. These unused quotas however do not accumulate through the years, and I do not intend to ask the Congress to change this rule.

The factors chiefly responsible for these low immigration figures were restraints imposed by the enemy, transportation difficulties, and the absence of consular facilities. Most of those Europeans who have been admitted to the United States during the last five years were persons who left Europe prior to the war, and thereafter entered here from non-European countries.

I consider that common decency and the fundamental comradeship of all human beings require us to do what lies within our power to see that our established immigration quotas are used in order to reduce human suffering. I am taking the necessary steps to see that this is done as quickly as possible.

Of the displaced persons and refugees whose entrance into the United States we will permit under this plan, it is hoped that the majority will be orphaned children. The provisions of law prohibiting the entry of persons likely to become public charges will be strictly observed. Responsible welfare organizations now at work in this field will guarantee that these children will not become public charges. Similar guarantees have or will be made on behalf of adult persons. The record of these welfare organizations throughout the past years has been excellent, and I am informed that no persons admitted under their sponsorship have ever become charges on their communities. Moreover, many of the immigrants will have close family ties in the United States and will receive the assistance of their relatives until they are in a position to provide for themselves.

These relatives or organizations will also advance the necessary visa fees and travel fare. Where the necessary funds for travel fare and visa fees have not been advanced by a welfare organization or relative, the individual applicant must meet these costs. In this way the transportation of these immigrants across the Atlantic will not cost the American taxpayers a single dollar.

In order to enter the United States it is necessary to obtain a visa from a consular officer of the Department of State. As everyone knows, a great many of our consular establishments all over the world were disrupted and their operations suspended when the war came. It is physically impossible to reopen and to restaff all of them overnight. Consequently it is necessary to choose the area in which to concentrate our immediate efforts. This is a painful necessity because it requires us to make an almost impossible choice among degrees of misery. But if we refrain from making a choice because it will necessarily be arbitrary, no choice will ever be made and we shall end by helping no one.

The decision has been made, therefore, to concentrate our immediate efforts in the American zones of occupation in Europe. This is not intended however entirely to exclude issuance of visas in other parts of the world.

In our zones in Europe there are citizens of every major European country. Visas issued to displaced persons and refugees will be charged, according to law, to the countries of their origin. They will be distributed fairly among persons of all faiths, creeds and nationality.

It is intended that, as soon as practicable, regular consular facilities will be reestablished in every part of the world, and the usual, orderly methods of registering and reviewing visa applications will be resumed. The pressing need, however, is to act now in a way that will produce immediate and tangible results. I hope that by early spring adequate consular facilities will be in operation in our zones in Europe, so that immigration can begin immediately upon the availability of ships.

I am informed that there are various measures now pending before the Congress which would either prohibit or severely reduce further immigration. I hope that such legislation will not be passed. This period of unspeakable human distress is not the time for us to close or to narrow our gates. I wish to emphasize, however, that any effort to bring relief to these displaced persons and refugees must and will be strictly within the limits of the present quotas as imposed by law.

There is one particular matter involving a relatively small number of aliens. President Roosevelt, in an endeavor to assist in handling displaced persons and refugees during the war and upon the recommendation of the War Refugee Board, directed that a group of about 1000 displaced persons be removed from refugee camps in Italy and settled temporarily in a War Relocation Camp near Oswego, New York. Shortly thereafter, President Roosevelt informed the Congress that these persons would be returned to their homelands after the war.

Upon the basis of a careful survey by the Department of State and the Immigration and Naturalization Service, it has been determined that if these persons were now applying for admission to the United States most of them would be admissible under the immigration laws. In the circumstances, it would be inhumane and wasteful to require these people to go all the way back to Europe merely for the purpose of applying there for immigration visas and returning to the United States. Many of them have close relatives, including sons and daughters, who are citizens of the United States and who have served and are serving honorably in the armed forces of our country. I am therefore directing the Secretary of State and the Attorney General to adjust the immigration status of the members of this group who may wish to remain here, in strict accordance with existing laws and regulations.

The number of persons at the Oswego camp is, however, comparatively small. Our major task is to facilitate the entry into the United States of displaced persons and refugees still in Europe. To meet this larger problem, I am directing the Secretary of State, the Attorney General, the Secretary of War, the War Shipping Administrator and the Surgeon General of the Public Health Service to proceed at once to take all appropriate steps to expedite the quota immigration of displaced persons and refugees from Europe to the United States. Representatives of these officials will depart for Europe very soon to prepare detailed plans for the prompt execution of this project.

The attached directive has been issued by me to the responsible government agencies to carry out this policy. I wish to emphasize, above all, that nothing in this directive will deprive a single American soldier or his wife or children of a berth on a vessel homeward bound, or delay their return.

This is the opportunity for America to set an example for the rest of the world in cooperation towards alleviating human misery.

DIRECTIVE BY THE PRESIDENT ON IMMIGRATION
TO THE UNITED STATES OF CERTAIN DISPLACED PERSONS AND REFUGEES IN
EUROPE

Memorandum to: Secretary of State, Secretary of War, Attorney General, War Shipping Administrator, Surgeon General of the Public Health Service, Director General of UNRRA:

The grave dislocation of populations in Europe resulting from the war has produced human suffering that the people of the United States cannot and will not ignore. This Government should take every possible measure to facilitate full immigration to the United States under existing quota laws.

The war has most seriously disrupted our normal facilities for handling immigration matters in many parts of the world. At the same time, the demands upon those facilities have increased many-fold. It is, therefore, necessary that immigration under the quotas be resumed initially in the areas of greatest need. I, therefore, direct the Secretary of State, the Secretary of War, the Attorney General, the Surgeon General of the Public Health Service, the War Shipping Administrator, and other appropriate officials to take the following action:

The Secretary of State is directed to establish with the utmost despatch consular facilities at or near displaced person and refugee assembly center areas in the American zones of occupation. It shall be the responsibility of these consular officers, in conjunction with the Immigrant Inspectors, to determine as quickly as possible the eligibility of the applicants for visas and admission to the United States. For this purpose the Secretary will, if necessary, divert the personnel and funds of his Department from other functions in order to insure the most expeditious handling of this operation. In cooperation with the Attorney General, he shall appoint as temporary vice-consuls, authorized to issue visas, such officers of the Immigration and Naturalization Service as can be made available for this program. Within the limits of administrative discretion, the officers of the Department of State assigned to this program shall make every effort to simplify and to hasten the process of issuing visas. If necessary, blocs of visa numbers may be assigned to each of the emergency consular establishments. Each such bloc may be used to meet the applications filed at the consular establishment to which the bloc is assigned. It is not intended however entirely to exclude the issuance of visas in other parts of the world.

Visas should be distributed fairly among persons of all faiths, creeds and nationalities. I desire that special attention be devoted to orphaned children to whom it is hoped the majority of visas will be issued.

With respect to the requirement of law that visas may not be issued to applicants likely to become public charges after admission to the United States, the Secretary of State shall cooperate with the Immigration and Naturalization Service in perfecting appropriate arrangements with welfare organizations in the United States which may be prepared to guarantee financial support to successful applicants. This may be accomplished by corporate affidavit or by any means deemed appropriate and practicable.

The Secretary of War, subject to limitations imposed by the Congress on War Department appropriations, will give such help as is practicable in:

(a) Furnishing information to appropriate consular officers and Immigrant Inspectors to facilitate in the selection of applicants for visas; and

(b) Assisting until other facilities suffice in: (1) transporting immigrants to a European port; (2) feeding, housing and providing medical care to such immigrants until embarked; and

(c) Making available office facilities, billets, messes, and transportation for Department of State, Department of Justice, and United Nations Relief and Rehabilitation Administration personnel connected with this work, where practicable and requiring no out-of-pocket expenditure by the War Department and when other suitable facilities are not available.

The Attorney General, through the Immigration and Naturalization Service, will assign personnel to duty in the American zones of occupation to make the immigration inspections, to assist consular officers of the Department of State in connection with the issuance of visas, and to take the necessary steps to settle the cases of those aliens presently interned at Oswego through appropriate statutory and administrative processes.

The Administrator of the War Shipping Administration will make the necessary arrangements for water transportation from the port of embarkation in Europe to the United States subject to the provision that the movement of immigrants will in no way interfere with the scheduled return of service personnel and their spouses and children from the European theater.

The Surgeon General of the Public Health Service will assign to duty in the American zones of occupation the necessary personnel to conduct the mental and physical examinations of prospective immigrants prescribed in the immigration laws.

The Director General of the United Nations Relief and Rehabilitation Administration will be requested to provide all possible aid to the United States authorities in preparing these people for transportation to the United States and to assist in their care, particularly in the cases of children in transit and others needing special attention.

In order to insure the effective execution of this program, the Secretary of State, the Secretary of War, the Attorney General, War Shipping Administrator and the Surgeon General of the Public Health Service shall appoint representatives to serve as members of an interdepartmental committee under the Chairmanship of the Commissioner of Immigration and Naturalization.

HARRY S. TRUMAN

226   Memorandum of Disapproval of Bill Reducing Certain
       Appropriations and Contract Authorizations for Fiscal
       Year 1946.   *December 23, 1945*

[Released December 23, 1945.   Dated December 22, 1945]

I AM WITHHOLDING my approval of H.R. 4407, "Reducing certain appropriations and contract authorizations available for the fiscal
year 1946, and for other purposes."

It is with sincere regret that I am unable to approve this legislation.
In response to my communication of September 5, 1945, and in conformity with their own careful plans, the Appropriations Committees
of the House and of the Senate held extended hearings and gave mature
consideration to the readjustment of Executive programs and finances
to the problems of the reconversion period. The Congress has acted
expeditiously and considerately to develop the basis for the continuing
peacetime operations of the Government. It has demonstrated a fine
spirit of economy in reducing appropriations without complicating the
delicate adjustment from wartime to peacetime functions, and without
sacrificing the basic progress which has been made during the war years
in the long-term development of Government activity.

So far as the basic purpose of this bill rescinding appropriations is
concerned, I am in thorough agreement with the action of the Congress.
Far from wishing to sacrifice the care and effort which have gone into
its development, I shall by Executive action preserve the full values of
these rescission provisions in the exact terms which the Congress itself
has approved. If these provisions stood alone I should gladly approve
the bill. I have asked the Director of the Bureau of the Budget to place
these rescission amounts in a reserve, non-expendable status, and so to
advise the departments and agencies concerned.

In addition to its effect on appropriations, however, the bill contains
provisions which require our system of public employment offices—
now unified in a single national system—to be broken up within 100
days, and transferred to operation as 51 separate State and territorial
systems.

While I believe such a transfer should be made at the proper time, I am convinced that this bill requires that it be made at the wrong time, and in the wrong way. Such a dispersion and transfer at this time would immeasurably retard our reemployment program. And as the basis for Federal-State cooperation, in a fundamental program of national importance, the provisions of the bill dealing with the public employment offices are unsound and unwise from any point of view.

So far as the timing of the transfer is concerned, the period designated by this bill—the next 100 days—is the most disadvantageous that could have been chosen. It will result in a disrupted and inefficient employment service at the very time when efficient operation is most vitally needed by veterans, workers and employers.

Our local public employment offices are now, and will be during the next several months, in the midst of the peak work load in their history. This is because the offices are now engaged in counseling and placing millions of applicants who require individualized service. These applicants include able-bodied veterans seeking assistance in their readjustment to civilian life, handicapped veterans requiring even more time and guidance in finding the jobs most suitable for them, and unemployed war workers who are confronted by difficult readjustments because of substantial reductions in job opportunities at their wartime skills and wage rates.

At such a time, any change in management and direction is necessarily disruptive to the service. A change which would replace our present single and unified management by 51 separate managements would be very harmful. Even with every effort by the States to promote a smooth transition, the transfer of some 23,000 employees to new conditions of employment, and the adjustment of operations to the requirements of 51 different State agencies, will inevitably cause confusion and delay.

In my reconversion message of September 6 to the Congress, I pointed out our national responsibilities and problems in connection with reemployment during the reconversion period. During this period, displaced war workers, and the veterans who are returning to civilian life at the rate of more than a million per month, will need and have a right to expect from their national government an effective job-counseling

580

and placement service. These problems and responsibilities cannot, in a period when millions of veterans and other workers are moving across State lines, be met adequately through 51 separate and independent public employment service systems, linked only by the necessarily remote and indirect influence of a Federal agency financing the State systems through grants-in-aid.

For these reasons, I now repeat my recommendation that the transfer of our public employment offices to State operation be postponed until June 1947. The Administration is committed to returning the service to State operation, and that commitment will be carried through. But this is not the time.

Apart from the timing of the transfer, the provisions of H.R. 4407 which govern the basis for Federal-State cooperation in the maintenance of public employment offices do not assure that an adequate service will be available in all States.

The bill provides for the operation of public employment offices by the States under rules and regulations prescribed by the Secretary of Labor to carry out the provisions of the Wagner-Peyser Act. Operating costs would be met entirely by the Federal Government. These provisions of the bill would remain in effect for only a few months—the balance of the current year.

The bill precludes the granting of funds to any State which is unable, or unwilling, to comply with the provisions of the bill or any requirement of the Secretary of Labor pursuant to the provisions of the bill.

A Federal-State cooperative program for a national system of public employment offices financed entirely by Federal funds must at least provide assurance as to two basic objectives: The Federal Government must be sure that the essential services are being provided through the States' employment offices, and it must know that the offices are being operated with reasonable efficiency. Under such a program, the Federal Government is not interested in prescribing minute or insignificant details concerning the State operation, but it does have a stake in the preservation of reasonable standards.

H.R. 4407 provides no effective protection for this national interest. If any State, for any reason, cannot or does not meet the minimum requirements, Federal grants cannot be made. But at the same time the Federal Government itself is precluded from continuing the operation of public employment office facilities in the State.

This means, in effect, that when there is a substantial failure to provide essential services or to meet minimum standards of efficiency, the Federal Government must choose between two alternatives which are both unsatisfactory. It must either acquiesce in the substandard operation—or, by withholding funds, it must deprive all of the State's employers, workers, and veterans of a service they need and to which they are entitled.

At a time of such acute emergency—when employment offices are needed to provide veterans with the services with which the Congress has required they be provided, and needed also to assist other unemployed workers in securing peacetime jobs—I cannot approve legislation which, under some conditions, may offer only a choice between a substantially substandard service or no service at all.

It seems clear to me that a matter of such grave importance as our public employment system deserves not only permanent legislation, but legislation carefully and separately considered. Issues of such a difficult and vital nature should not be dealt with as riders to appropriation bills.

The fact is that our present legislation governing the operation of our cooperative Federal-State employment service system, enacted in 1933, needs thorough revision in the light of changed conditions. Several bills now pending before both Houses of the Congress—H.R. 4437, S. 1456, and S. 1510—are designed to accomplish this. Enactment of such permanent legislation is essential before a transfer back to State operation can be achieved in an efficient and orderly manner.

Adequate and uniform standards of service must be maintained and proper security for the personnel of the organization itself must be provided in a permanent way, if it is to keep and attract the calibre of personnel able and eager to perform its important tasks.

Only in this way can we provide a sound and permanent basis for Federal-State cooperation in the maintenance of a postwar system of public employment offices which will meet the needs of veterans, employers, workers, and the nation as a whole.

While I object to the specific measure which this bill proposes to carry out with respect to our employment service, I object even more strongly to the legislative method employed for its enactment. To attach a legislative rider to an appropriation bill restricts the President's exercise of his functions and is contrary to good government.

In view of my past legislative experience, I realize the obligations of the President to the Congress as a coordinate branch of the Government. At the same time, I must be equally aware of the Constitutional responsibility of the President to the people, and of the obligation of the Congress to help him discharge that responsibility.

The Constitution has placed upon the President the duty of considering bills for approval or disapproval. It has always been possible for the Congress to hamper the President's exercise of this duty by combining so many subjects into a single bill that he can not disapprove an objectionable item without holding up necessary legislation.

Partly in order to prevent this practice, it has long been considered a fundamental principle that legislation on a major issue of policy ought not be combined with an appropriation measure. The present bill directly violates that principle. I am obliged to withhold my approval to some very excellent legislation because of the objectionable practice which has been followed by attaching this rider which I cannot possibly approve.

HARRY S. TRUMAN

227 Address at the Lighting of the National Community Christmas Tree on the White House Grounds. *December* 24, 1945

[Broadcast nationally at 5:15 p.m.]

Ladies and gentlemen, and listeners of the radio audience:

This is the Christmas that a war-weary world has prayed for through long and awful years. With peace come joy and gladness. The gloom of the war years fades as once more we light the National Community Christmas Tree. We meet in the spirit of the first Christmas, when the midnight choir sang the hymn of joy: "Glory to God in the highest, and on earth peace, good will toward men."

Let us not forget that the coming of the Saviour brought a time of long peace to the Roman World. It is, therefore, fitting for us to remember that the spirit of Christmas is the spirit of peace, of love, of charity to all men. From the manger of Bethlehem came a new appeal to the minds and hearts of men: "A new commandment I give unto you, that ye love one another."

In love, which is the very essence of the message of the Prince of Peace, the world would find a solution for all its ills. I do not believe there is one problem in this country or in the world today which could not be settled if approached through the teaching of the Sermon on the Mount. The poets' dream, the lesson of priest and patriarch and the prophets' vision of a new heaven and a new earth, all are summed up in the message delivered in the Judean hills beside the Sea of Galilee. Would that the world would accept that message in this time of its greatest need!

This is a solemn hour. In the stillness of the Eve of the Nativity when the hopes of mankind hang on the peace that was offered to the world nineteen centuries ago, it is but natural, while we survey our destiny, that we give thought also to our past—to some of the things which have gone into the making of our Nation.

You will remember that Saint Paul, the Apostle of the Gentiles, and his companions, suffering shipwreck, "cast four anchors out of the stern and wished for the day." Happily for us, whenever the American Ship of State has been storm-tossed we have always had an anchor to the windward.

We are met on the South Lawn of the White House. The setting is a reminder of Saint Paul's four anchors. To one side is the massive pile of the Washington Monument—fit symbol of our first anchor. On the opposite end of Potomac Park is the memorial to another of the anchors which we see when we look astern of the Ship of State—Abraham Lincoln, who preserved the Union that Washington wrought.

Between them is the memorial to Thomas Jefferson, the anchor of democracy. On the other side of the White House, in bronze, rides

Andrew Jackson—fourth of our anchors—the pedestal of his monument bearing his immortal words: "Our Federal Union—it must be preserved."

It is well in this solemn hour that we bow to Washington, Jefferson, Jackson, and Lincoln as we face our destiny with its hopes and fears—its burdens and its responsibilities. Out of the past we shall gather wisdom and inspiration to chart our future course.

With our enemies vanquished we must gird ourselves for the work that lies ahead. Peace has its victories no less hard won than success at arms. We must not fail or falter. We must strive without ceasing to make real the prophecy of Isaiah: "They shall beat their swords into plowshares and their spears into pruning-hooks: nation shall not lift up sword against nation, neither shall they learn war any more."

In this day, whether it be far or near, the Kingdoms of this world shall become indeed the Kingdom of God and He will reign forever and ever, Lord of Lords and King of Kings. With that message I wish my countrymen a Merry Christmas and joyous days in the New Year.

228   Letters to the Members of the Board of Directors on the Termination of the Smaller War Plants Corporation. *December 27, 1945*

[Released December 27, 1945. Dated November 1, 1945]

Dear Maury:

As you know, in line with my reorganization plans, the Smaller War Plants Corporation's functions are being transferred to other agencies. But there is one more job I would like for you to do for small business. It is in connection with little business in world trade.

Sometime ago I authorized you to take a trip to the countries of the Pacific. The purpose of the Mission was to make a report to me concerning the development of small business in these countries and the possibility of stimulating international trade between them and small businesses at home. Particularly, I am interested in the development of American small business in the field of international trade.

585

The countries to be visited by you are the Philippines, China, Korea, Australia, and New Zealand.

It is assumed, of course, that you will work closely with representatives of the Department of State in each country which you visit.

I want to congratulate you on the job that you have done as Chairman of the Smaller War Plants Corporation and for the work you have done for small business.

With best wishes, I am

Sincerely yours,

HARRY S. TRUMAN

[Honorable Maury Maverick, Chairman and General Manager, Smaller War Plants Corporation]

Dear Mr. Howington:

Your excellent service with the War Production Board is well known to me. I, however, am especially mindful of the work you have done as a member of the Board of Directors of the Smaller War Plants Corporation from the very day of its inception.

Small business is the keystone of the free enterprise system. I compliment you particularly on the work that you have done in the matter of war production and in harnessing the small plants of America for that purpose.

In reorganizing the Government, we have concluded that it is appropriate that the duties of the Smaller War Plants Corporation be taken over by other established branches of the Government. I am sure I will have your cooperation in this.

Thanking you for your great service to America, I am

Sincerely yours,

HARRY S. TRUMAN

[Honorable James T. Howington, Vice Chairman, Board of Directors, Smaller War Plants Corporation]

Dear Judge Rowe:

This is to assure you of my appreciation for your work while a member of the Board of Directors of the Smaller War Plants Corporation.

You, as a banker and as a lawyer, know the problems of small organizations.

In reorganizing the Government, we have concluded that it is appropriate that the duties of the Smaller War Plants Corporation be taken over by other established branches of the Government. I am sure I will have your cooperation in this.

I wish to compliment and thank you for your period of service and to assure you that I deeply appreciate it.

With best wishes, I am

Sincerely yours,

HARRY S. TRUMAN

[Honorable C. Edward Rowe, Member, Board of Directors, Smaller War Plants Corporation]

Dear Pat:

We all appreciate very much the fact that you came here to Washington, leaving your heavy duties as President of the McDonough Steel Company, to serve on the Board of Directors of the Smaller War Plants Corporation.

You have worked hard, you have done your duty, and it has been an aid of the first order to war production.

Today I wrote your Chairman, Mr. Maury Maverick, about the study which I wished him to make in China. You are invited to go on this mission also, because of your knowledge of little plants, and because of the fact that you understand industrial production from the smaller business viewpoint.

I would like you to go with Mr. Maverick to assist him in making the report, which I know will be of great value.

Again let me assure you of my appreciation of your great service to the Government of the United States.

Sincerely yours,

HARRY S. TRUMAN

[Honorable Patrick W. McDonough, Member, Board of Directors, Smaller War Plants Corporation]

Dear Larry:

I remember with great pleasure the time we served together in the Congress of the United States.

The Smaller War Plants Corporation, under present plans of reorganization, will have its powers assumed by other organizations. But I cannot fail to say to you that your work with the Smaller War Plants Corporation has been of great benefit to small business and the free enterprise system. I appreciate what you have done for a year as a member of the Board of Directors of the Smaller War Plants Corporation.

With best personal good wishes, I am,

Sincerely yours,

HARRY S. TRUMAN

[Honorable Laurence Arnold, Member, Board of Directors, Smaller War Plants Corporation]

NOTE: Executive Order 9665 (3 CFR, 1943–1948 Comp., p. 480), providing for the transfer of the functions of the Smaller War Plants Corporation to the Reconstruction Finance Corporation and the Department of Commerce, was released with the text of these letters.

229 Statement by the President Upon Signing Bill Extending the Second War Powers Act. *December 28, 1945*

I HAVE TODAY signed H.R. 4780 extending, for six months, certain titles of the Second War Powers Act. The continued exercise of these powers beyond December 31, 1945, although on a steadily decreasing scale, is absolutely necessary in the interests of reconversion.

The extension for only six months of the statute, and especially of those sections creating the priorities and allocations powers, will, however, not meet the full need. We know that our economy will be plagued with major war-born shortages six months from now, and that the Government must have the means of dealing with these shortages. There must, therefore, be further legislation to cover the period after June 30, 1946.

This further legislation should become law at the earliest possible date, so that industry and Government will know as far in advance as possible the laws under which they are to operate, and can plan accordingly. In the absence of specific legislation covering the latter part of 1946, the approach of June 30 will become an unsettling factor in the Nation's economy and may well be accompanied by hoarding and by a tendency to delay production and distribution until the date has passed. Any such tendency would seriously hamper reconversion and would add a new and dangerous inflationary factor to the many already existing.

I request, therefore, that the Congress consider and enact, at the earliest possible time, suitable legislation to extend the Government's power to deal with shortages.

NOTE: As enacted, H.R. 4780 is Public Law 270, 79th Congress (59 Stat. 658). On June 29, 1946, the President approved a bill further extending the Second War Powers Act (Public Law 475, 79th Cong., 60 Stat. 345).

230 Letter to the Chairman, National War Labor Board, on the Establishment of the National Wage Stabilization Board. *December* 31, 1945

Dear Mr. Garrison:

I have your letter of December 27, 1945, pursuant to which, and in accordance with my letter to you of November 6, 1945, I am issuing an Executive Order terminating the existence of the National War Labor Board as of January 1, 1946, and creating a National Wage Stabilization Board to carry on the stabilization functions required under the Stabilization Act of 1942.

I am accepting as of December 31, 1945, the resignations of the members of the National War Labor Board who have heretofore been appointed by the President.

I wish to extend to all members of the National War Labor Board, to the members of its regional agencies and commissions, and to its staff in Washington and in the field, my thanks for the outstanding wartime job they have done in the last four years, under the most difficult circumstances, in helping to maintain industrial peace, maximum production, and wage stabilization. They have earned and thoroughly deserve the gratitude of their fellow citizens.

I deeply appreciate the accomplishments of the Board, as summarized in your letter, and I shall await with interest the submission of your more detailed terminal report.

Very truly yours,

HARRY S. TRUMAN

[Honorable Lloyd K. Garrison, Chairman, National War Labor Board]

NOTE: Mr. Garrison's letter was released with the President's reply. Also released was the text of Executive Order 9672 "Establishing the National Wage Stabilization Board and Terminating the National War Labor Board" (3 CFR, 1943–1948 Comp., p. 488) together with a list of appointments to the newly created Board and a list of resignations from the National War Labor Board.

Appendix A—White House Press Releases, 1945

NOTE: Includes releases covering matters with which the President was closely concerned, except announcements of Presidential personnel appointments and approvals of legislation with which there was no accompanying statement.

Releases relating to Proclamations and Executive Orders have not been included. These documents are separately listed in Appendix B.

For list of Press and Radio Conferences, see subject index under "News Conferences."

April

12 Statement by the President after taking the oath of office

13 Messages to the President on the death of President Roosevelt

14 White House statement on the forthcoming visit of Foreign Secretary Molotov

16 Address before a joint session of the Congress

17 Statement by the President upon signing bill extending the Lend-Lease Act

17 Letter from Mrs. Franklin D. Roosevelt

17 Address broadcast to the Armed Forces

18 Statement by the President on the death of Ernie Pyle

18 Statement by the President on the Senate's approval of the water utilization treaty with Mexico

19 Veto of bill for the relief of Ben Grunstein (Congressional Record, vol. 91, p. 3577)

20 Telegram from James M. Cox requesting the release of Leonard Reinsch from the President's staff

23 White House statement concerning discussions with Foreign Minister Molotov

23 Joint statement with allied leaders warning against mistreatment of prisoners in Germany

24 Special message to the Senate transmitting tax conventions between the United States and the United Kingdom

April

25 Address to the United Nations Conference in San Francisco

26 Letter to Secretary Wallace requesting a study of the patent laws

27 Statement by the President announcing the junction of Anglo-American and Soviet forces in Germany

27 Letter to Edwin W. Pauley appointing him as the President's personal representative on the Reparations Commission

27 Statement by the President on announcing Mr. Pauley's appointment to the Reparations Commission

27 Statement by the President announcing the appointment of Dr. Isador Lubin to the Reparations Commission

27 Statement by Edwin W. Pauley following his appointment to the Reparations Commission

30 White House release of summary of Judge Rosenman's report on the needs of the liberated areas

May

1 Statement by the President commending the Office of Price Administration

1 Letter to the Director, Office of War Mobilization and Reconversion, concerning key personnel of the war agencies

1 Citation accompanying the Medal for Merit presented to Julius A. Krug

2 White House statement on the proposed reduction of funds for ship construction

May

2 White House statement on the proposed reduction of funds for war agencies

2 Statement by the President concerning the termination of the Office of Civilian Defense

2 Statement by the President on the surrender of German forces in Italy

2 Message to Field Marshal Alexander on the surrender of German forces in Italy

2 Message to General Clark on the surrender of German forces in Italy

2 Statement by the President announcing designation of Robert H. Jackson as U.S. Chief of Counsel for the prosecution of war crimes

2 Letter accepting resignation of Frank C. Walker, Postmaster General

3 Veto of bill providing for the deferment of additional agricultural workers

3 White House statement concerning price and distribution controls on meat

3 Text of National War Labor Board order changing terms and conditions of employment at plants of United Engineering Co., Ltd.

4 Letter accepting resignation of Harry D. White, Assistant Secretary of the Treasury

5 Statement by the President concerning Philippine Independence

6 Letter accepting resignation of Lt. Col. Joseph V. Hodgson, U.S. Commissioner on the U.N. War Crimes Commission

7 Statement by the President on the timing of the announcement of German surrender

7 White House announcement of the President's scheduled broadcast on the surrender of Germany

7 Letter, by direction of the President, from the chief administrative assistant to all Governors

8 Broadcast to the American people announcing the surrender of Germany

May

8 Statement by the President calling for unconditional surrender of Japan

8 Messages to Allied leaders and to General Eisenhower on the surrender of Germany

9 Statement by the President upon signing bill extending the Selective Service Act

10 Special message to the Congress transmitting report on work of the District of Columbia Juvenile Court

12 Letter accepting resignation of Donald M. Nelson, Personal Representative of the President to other governments

12 Letter to Edwin A. Locke, Jr., concerning the mission to China established by Donald M. Nelson

15 Statement by the President concerning freedom of the press in Germany

15 Statement by the President on German reparations

15 White House announcement of U.S. members of the Reparations Commission

15 Special message to the Congress transmitting report on War Production Board

18 Statement by the President following a discussion with Foreign Minister Bidault of France

21 Remarks before the Congress on presenting the Medal of Honor to Sergeant Jake W. Lindsey

21 Special message to the Congress transmitting annual report of the Alien Property Custodian

22 Letters to heads of war agencies on the economic situation in the liberated countries of northwest Europe

23 Letter accepting resignation of Francis Biddle, Attorney General

23 Letter accepting resignation of Frances Perkins, Secretary of Labor

23 Letter accepting resignation of Claude R. Wickard, Secretary of Agriculture

23 Letter accepting resignation of Marvin Jones, War Food Administrator

Appendix A

Appendix A

594

July

11 Letter accepting resignation of James M. Barnes, Administrative Assistant to the President

13 Statement by the President: Bastille Day

14 Letter to Secretary Morgenthau concerning the appointment of Fred M. Vinson as his successor

16 Statement by the President on the manpower needs of the western railroads

17 Special message to the Congress on amending the Surplus Property Act to provide for a single administrator

17 Veto of bill for the relief of Philip Kleinman (Congressional Record, vol. 91, p. 7588)

17 Letter to the President of the Senate and to the Speaker of the House of Representatives transmitting reports on foreign war relief activities

19 White House statement concerning report "Science—The Endless Frontier" submitted by the Director, Office of Scientific Research and Development

20 Remarks at the raising of the flag over the U.S. Group Control Council headquarters in Berlin

20 Letter to David K. Niles, Administrative Assistant to the President

24 Veto of bill for the relief of Leo Gottlieb (Congressional Record, vol. 91, p. 8322)

25 Letter read by Secretary Vinson at the Humanitarian Award Dinner of the Variety Clubs of America

26 White House statement concerning wage increases for radio operators and armed guards of certain airlines

27 Letter to Alben W. Barkley on the eighth anniversary of his election as Majority Leader of the Senate

31 Veto of bill authorizing the improvement of certain harbors

August

1 White House announcement concerning the celebration of the 150th anniversary of the Treaty of Green Ville

2 Joint report with Allied leaders on the Potsdam conference

4 Veto of bill for the relief of the Southwestern Drug Company (Congressional Record, vol. 91, p. 8323)

4 Veto of bill for the relief of the Morgan Creamery Company (Congressional Record, vol. 91, p. 8323)

4 Veto of bill conveying certain property to Norwich University

6 Statement by the President announcing the use of the A-bomb at Hiroshima

9 Letter to the Chairman, War Production Board, on measures to speed reconversion

9 Letter to Edward R. Stettinius appointing him U.S. Representative on the Preparatory Commission of the United Nations

9 Radio report to the American people on the Potsdam conference

13 Citation accompanying the Distinguished Service Medal presented to James F. Byrnes

13 White House announcement of the forthcoming visit of President de Gaulle

13 Statement by the President on the 10th anniversary of the Social Security Act

14 Statement by the President announcing the surrender of Japan

14 Text of Swiss note transmitting Japanese surrender message

14 Statement by the President announcing a reduction in the draft

14 Statement by the President commending Federal employees

15 Messages to the President from Gen. Douglas MacArthur, Gen. Henry H. Arnold, and Lt. Gen. Robert C. Richardson, Jr.

15 Statement by the President: the Jewish New Year

Appendix A

Appendix A

Appendix A

October

17 Memorandum on the Community War Fund campaign in the National Capital area

17 White House announcement of appropriations request for the resumption of public works programs

19 White House announcement of the designation of Maury Maverick as the President's Representative to present to San Francisco the flag flown over the Capitol in Washington on the day the U.N. Charter was approved

19 Statement by the President on appointing Fred Smith to head a public relations committee for the Labor-Management Conference

22 Statement by the President on the anniversary of the founding of the Czechoslovak Republic

23 Address before a joint session of the Congress on universal military training

25 Statement by the President following discussions with President Osmeña of the Philippines

25 Letter from William Green, Ira Mosher, Philip Murray, and Eric Johnston concerning the National Labor-Management Conference

26 Letters to the High Commissioner to the Philippines and to the heads of Federal agencies recommending measures for the assistance of the Philippines

27 Address in New York City at the commissioning of the U.S.S. *Franklin D. Roosevelt*

27 Address on foreign policy at the Navy Day celebration in New York City

29 Letter to Dr. Lyman J. Briggs on his retirement as Director of the National Bureau of Standards

30 Radio address to the American people on wages and prices in the reconversion period

31 Letter from Gen. Dwight D. Eisenhower on restoration of civil government in Germany

November

1 Special message to the Senate transmitting agreement on petroleum between the United States and the United Kingdom

1 Statement by the President on announcing the mission to Japan of Ambassador Edwin W. Pauley, personal representative of the President on reparations matters

1 Letter to Edgar F. Puryear on receiving report of the Review Committee on Deferment of Government Employees

1 White House statement concerning the establishment of the Franklin Delano Roosevelt Memorial Foundation

5 Address at the opening session of the Labor-Management Conference

7 Letter to the Chairman, House Appropriations Committee, concerning the need for additional funds for advance planning of public works

8 Message to the Congress transmitting report of the War Production Board covering operations under the Property Requisitioning Act of 1941

8 White House statement concerning the President's flagship U.S.S. *Williamsburg*

12 Message to the Congress transmitting Report of the Commission on the Erection of Memorials and Entombment of Bodies in the Arlington Memorial Amphitheater

12 Veto of bill for relief of Daniel D. O'Connell and Almon B. Stewart (Congressional Record, vol. 91, p. 10609)

13 Special message to the Congress on U.S. participation in the United Nations Relief and Rehabilitation Administration

13 Statement by the President on the problem of Jewish refugees in Europe

13 Letter to Prime Minister Attlee concerning the need for resettlement of Jewish refugees in Palestine

14 Letter to President Osmeña of the Philippines upon approving a bill of the Philippine Congress

599

Appendix A

December

10 Letter accepting resignation of Artemus L. Gates, Under Secretary of the Navy

12 White House statement clarifying news conference reply to question concerning ceiling prices on housing

12 Letter accepting resignation of Michael W. Strauss, Assistant Secretary of the Interior

12 Letter accepting resignation of Harry W. Bashore, Commissioner of Reclamation

12 Citation accompanying the Medal for Merit awarded to Henry Morgenthau

12 Citation accompanying the Medal for Merit awarded to Ralph K. Davies

12 White House announcement of appointment of members of Committee to Coordinate Government Medical Services

12 Memorandum report on housing submitted by the Director of War Mobilization and Reconversion

12 Letter to Wilson Wyatt appointing him Housing Expediter

14 Citation accompanying the Distinguished Service Medal awarded to Fleet Admiral Ernest J. King

15 Statement by the President: United States Policy Toward China

17 Veto of bill concerning claim against the United States of the Eastern Contracting Co. (Congressional Record, vol. 91, p. 12202)

17 Veto of bill raising the rank of chiefs and assistant chiefs of naval bureaus

18 Veto of bill for the relief of Dr. J. D. Whiteside and St. Luke's Hospital (Congressional Record, vol. 91, p. 12266)

18 Veto of bill for the relief of Saunders Memorial Hospital (Congressional Record, vol. 91, p. 12262)

18 White House announcement of emergency board action on wage request for dining car chefs and cooks

December

19 Special message to the Congress recommending the establishment of a Department of National Defense

19 Special message to the Senate transmitting nominations of United States representatives to the United Nations

19 White House announcement concerning forthcoming address by Winston Churchill at Fulton, Mo.

20 Statement by the President upon signing the Reorganization Act of 1945

20 Statement by the President concerning the authority of factfinding boards to examine books of the employer

20 Letter to Dr. Isaiah Bowman on Federal assistance for scientific research

20 Letter to Senator Wagner and Representative Manasco concerning the full employment bill

21 Letter to the Administrator, Federal Works Agency, asking him to head a conference on traffic safety

22 Statement and directive by the President on immigration to the United States of certain displaced persons and refugees in Europe

22 White House announcement concerning award of Legion of Merit to nine officers on duty in the White House map room during the war

22 White House announcement of appointment of Lt. Gen. Edmund B. Gregory as Chairman, War Assets Corporation

23 Memorandum of disapproval of bill reducing certain appropriations and contract authorizations for fiscal year 1946

24 Address at the lighting of the national community Christmas tree on the White House grounds

27 Letters to the members of the Board of Directors on the termination of the Smaller War Plants Corporation

28 Statement by the President upon signing bill extending the Second War Powers Act

Appendix A

Appendix B—Presidential Documents Published in the Federal Register, 1945

PROCLAMATIONS

603

Appendix B

EXECUTIVE ORDERS

604

Appendix B

Appendix B

Appendix B

Appendix B

Appendix B

Appendix B

Appendix B

Appendix B

PRESIDENTIAL DOCUMENTS OTHER THAN PROCLAMATIONS AND EXECUTIVE ORDERS

Appendix C—Presidential Reports to the Congress, 1945

Subject	Published	Sent to the Congress	Date of White House release
Report covering the Juvenile Court for the District of Columbia for fiscal year 1943–1944	H. Doc. 173	May 10	May 10
Report of the War Production Board covering operations under the Property Requisitioning Act, for the period October 16, 1944, through April 15, 1945	H. Doc. 178	May 15	May 15
Report of the Alien Property Custodian under the Trading With the Enemy Act, for the period June 30, 1943, to June 30, 1944	H. Doc. 184	May 21	May 21
Nineteenth Annual Report on Lend-Lease Operations for the period ended March 31, 1945 . . .	H. Doc. 189	May 22 (H) May 24 (S)	. . . .
United States Participation in Operations of UNRRA:			
Third Annual Report	H. Doc. 251	June 30	. . . .
Fourth Annual Report	H. Doc. 309	Oct. 11	. . . .
Report of the American Red Cross and the War Refugee Board reflecting war relief operations for the period July 1940 through April 30, 1945 .	H. Doc. 262	July 17	July 17
Third Annual Report of the National Patent Planning Commission	H. Doc. 283	Sept. 6	Sept. 6
Ninety-third, Ninety-fourth, and Ninety-fifth Annual Reports for the Board of Directors of the Panama Railroad Company for the fiscal years ended June 30, 1942, 1943, and 1944	. . . .	Oct. 9	Oct. 9
Report of the War Production Board covering operations for the period from April 16, 1945, through October 15, 1945	H. Doc. 373	Nov. 8	Nov. 8
Annual Report of the Commission on the Erection of Memorials of the Entombment of Bodies in the Arlington Memorial Amphitheater	H. Doc. 376	Nov. 12 (H) Nov. 13 (S)	Nov. 12 . . . .

Appendix D—Rules Governing This Publication

[Reprinted from the Federal Register, vol. 24, p. 2354, dated March 26, 1959]

TITLE 1—GENERAL PROVISIONS

Chapter I—Administrative Committee of the Federal Register

PART 32—PUBLIC PAPERS OF THE PRESIDENTS OF THE UNITED STATES

PUBLICATION AND FORMAT

Sec.
32.1 Publication required.
32.2 Coverage of prior years.
32.3 Format, indexes, ancillaries.

SCOPE

32.10 Basic criteria.
32.11 Sources.

FREE DISTRIBUTION

32.15 Members of Congress.
32.16 The Supreme Court.
32.17 Executive agencies.

PAID DISTRIBUTION

32.20 Agency requisitions.
32.21 Extra copies.
32.22 Sale to public.

AUTHORITY: §§ 32.1 to 32.22 issued under sec. 6, 49 Stat. 501, as amended; 44 U.S.C. 306.

PUBLICATION AND FORMAT

§ 32.1 *Publication required.* There shall be published forthwith at the end of each calendar year, beginning with the year 1957, a special edition of the FEDERAL REGISTER designated "Public Papers of the Presidents of the United States." Each volume shall cover one calendar year and shall be identified further by the name of the President and the year covered.

§ 32.2 *Coverage of prior years.* After conferring with the National Historical Publications Commission with respect to the need therefor, the Administrative Committee may from time to time authorize the publication of similar volumes covering specified calendar years prior to 1957.

§ 32.3 *Format, indexes, ancillaries.* Each annual volume, divided into books whenever appropriate, shall be separately published in the binding and style deemed by the Administrative Committee to be suitable to the dignity of the office of President of the United States. Each volume shall be appropriately indexed and shall contain appropriate ancillary information respecting significant Presidential documents not published in full text.

SCOPE

§ 32.10 *Basic criteria.* The basic text of the volumes shall consist of oral utterances by the President or of writings subscribed by him. All materials selected for inclusion under these criteria must also be in the public domain by virtue of White House press release or otherwise.

§ 32.11 *Sources.* (a) The basic text of the volumes shall be selected from the official text of: (1) Communications to the Congress, (2) public addresses, (3) transcripts of press conferences, (4) public letters, (5) messages to heads of state, (6) statements released on miscellaneous subjects, and (7) formal executive documents promulgated in accordance with law.

(b) Ancillary text, notes, and tables shall be derived from official sources only.

FREE DISTRIBUTION

§ 32.15 *Members of Congress.* Each Member of Congress shall be entitled to one copy of each annual volume upon application therefor in writing to the Director.

Appendix D

§ 32.16 *The Supreme Court.* The Supreme Court of the United States shall be entitled to twelve copies of the annual volumes.

§ 32.17 *Executive agencies.* The head of each department and the head of each independent agency in the executive branch of the Government shall be entitled to one copy of each annual volume upon application therefor in writing to the Director.

PAID DISTRIBUTION

§ 32.20 *Agency requisitions.* Each Federal agency shall be entitled to obtain at cost copies of the annual volumes for official use upon the timely submission to the Government Printing Office of a printing and binding requisition (Standard Form No. 1).

§ 32.21 *Extra copies.* All requests for extra copies of the annual volumes shall be addressed to the Superintendent of Documents, Government Printing Office, Washington 25, D.C. Extra copies shall be paid for by the agency or official requesting them.

§ 32.22 *Sale to public.* The annual volumes shall be placed on sale to the public by the Superintendent of Documents at prices determined by him under the general direction of the Administrative Committee.

*   *   *   *   *

ADMINISTRATIVE COMMITTEE OF
THE FEDERAL REGISTER,

WAYNE C. GROVER,
Archivist of the United States,
Chairman.

RAYMOND BLATTENBERGER,
The Public Printer,
Member.

WILLIAM O. BURTNER,
Representative of the Attorney
General, Member.

Approved March 20, 1959.

WILLIAM P. ROGERS,
Attorney General.

FRANKLIN FLOETE,
Administrator of General Services.

[F.R. Doc. 59–2517; Filed, Mar. 25, 1959;
8:45 a.m.]

INDEX

[Main references are to items except as otherwise indicated]

617

Index

[Main references are to items except as otherwise indicated]

618

Index

Index

Index

Index

622

Index

[Main references are to items except as otherwise indicated]

Cadet Nurse Corps, United States, 130 n.

Cairo Declaration (1943), 143, 177, 216

Calhoun, David R., 137 n.

California
  Downey, Sen. Sheridan, 147 [15, 18]
  River development, 128, 155
  San Francisco, 1 n., 2, 4 [10, 11, 13], 10, 22 ftn. (p. 36), 26 [3], 31 [4], 33, 52 [15], 60 [1, 10], 64 [1], 66, 67 [1], 68, 96, 97, 157 [13]
  Water resources development, 165

California, University of, 31 [7]

Canada
  Alaska highway, 64 [3]
  Atomic bomb, 97
    Proposed discussion re, 178
  Atomic energy, 156, 164 [1], 181 [3]
    Joint declaration with Prime Ministers of Canada and U.K., 193 [7, 8, 10]
  King, W. L. Mackenzie, 107 ftn. (p. 234), 157 [17]
    Joint declaration, 191
    Joint statement, 209
  News conference remarks, 64 [3], 157 [17], 164 [1], 181 [3], 193 [7, 8, 10]
  Ottawa, 209 n.
  Quebec, 177, 181 [3]
  St. Lawrence River development, 148, 155
  U.S.-U.K.-Canada combined boards, 107 ftn. (p. 234), 198, 209

Cancer, research on prevention, 192

Candidacy for second term, 181 [12]

Cannon, Repr. Clarence, letter, 185

Capital Transit Co. (D.C.), Government operation, 195 n., 208 ftn. (p. 528)

Caroline Islands, U.S. navy operations, World War II, 161

Carr, Albert Z., 151 n.

Caruthersville, Mo., 147 [9], 163

Casablanca, 177

Case, Norman S., 60 [2]

Charleston, S.C., Mayor Edwin Wehman, 147 n.

Chester Springs, Pa., 76 [4]

Chiang Kai-shek, 151 n.
  News conference remarks on, 4 [14], 118 [18], 147 [3], 172 [2]

Chiang Kai-shek, Madame, 118, [6, 18]

Chicago, Ill., 163
  Mayor Edward J. Kelly, 44 [12]

Chief Justice of the United States (Harlan F. Stone), 1 n.

Chiefs of Police, International Association of, 62

Chiefs of Staff, Combined, U.S.-U.K., 197, 198

Chiefs of Staff, Joint. See Joint Chiefs of Staff

Child care centers, Federal aid, 157 [10]
  Letter, 159

Child health programs, 192

Child welfare, 99

Chile, 150 n.
  Rios, Juan Antonio, 56, 170

China, 100, 136, 178
  American Production Mission, termination, statement, 151
  Atomic energy declaration of U.S., U.K., and Canada, reaction to, 193 [8]
  Chiang Kai-shek, 4 [14], 118 [18], 147 [3], 151 n., 172 [2]
  Council of Foreign Ministers, membership, 91, 97
  Mission of General Marshall, 202 [12, 15], 211 [8]
  Mission (U.S.) on development of small business, 228

[Main references are to items except as otherwise indicated]

Index

Index

[Main references are to items except as otherwise indicated]

Index

[Main references are to items except as otherwise indicated]

Index

Index

Index

[Main references are to items except as otherwise indicated]

Index

Index

[Main references are to items except as otherwise indicated]

Index

Index

Index

637

Index

[Main references are to items except as otherwise indicated]

International cooperation, 66
  Atomic energy, 156, 178, 191, 193 [7, 8]
  Connally resolution, 69
  Fulbright resolution, 69
  News conference remarks, 193 [7, 8], 202 [6]
International Court of Justice, Statute of
  Ratification, 69
  Signing at San Francisco conference, 68
International Labor Organization, 132 [11], 181 [10]
International Military Tribunal, 129 [8], 132 [1, 2]
International Monetary Fund. See Bretton Woods agreements
International monetary stabilization, 76 [3]
International trade. See Trade, international
Interstate Commerce Commission
  Freight rate ruling, 208 [3]
  Lee, William E., 202 [2]
  Patterson, William J., 202 [2]
Inventory controls, 128
Investments abroad, 31 [3]
Iowa, Council Bluffs, 149
Iran
  Teheran, 177
  U.S. foreign policy, 208 [12]
Iraq, Prince Abdul Ilah, 47
Irrigation projects, 164 [8]
Isaiah, prophecy of, reference to, 227
Isolationism, 147 [12]
Italy, 91, 97
  Armistice, 40 [3], 175 [16]
  Fascism. See Fascism
  Invasion, World War II, 45, 178
  Mussolini, Benito, 22 [21], 66

Italy—Continued
  News conference remarks, 40 [3], 107 [21], 147 [11], 175 [16]
  Refugees from, 225
  Relief for, 186
  Surrender of German forces, 20, 21
Iwo Jima, 45
  U.S. invasion, 161, 178

Jackson, Andrew, 227
Jackson, Lt. Arthur J., Congressional Medal of Honor award, 160 n.
Jackson, Justice Robert H.
  Appointment as U.S. Chief of Counsel, war crimes trials, statement, 22 [5]
  News conference remarks on, 22 [5, 14], 31 [2], 44 [9], 52 [2, 9], 60 [9], 67 [2], 157 [1]
  War crimes report, 52 [2, 9], 60 [9]
Jackson County, Mo., 163
  President's service as Judge for Eastern District, 68
  Visit, 68
Jacobson, Douglas T., Congressional Medal of Honor award, 160 n.
Japan, 2, 3, 20, 27, 30, 33, 34, 37, 50, 54, 66, 91, 125, 136, 146 n., 161, 186, 190, 216, 218
  Aggression in Manchuria, 139, 216
  Allied Control Commission, question of, 147 [1]
  Allied policy toward, 132 [5], 147 [4]
    Statement, 143
  Atomic bomb targets
    Hiroshima, 93, 97, 156, 178
    Nagasaki, 178
  Demobilization of U.S. forces, 138
  Emperor Hirohito, 100, 143, 145, 172 [2]
  Greece in state of war with Japan, 75

638

Index

Index

[Main references are to items except as otherwise indicated]

Index

641

Index

[Main references are to items except as otherwise indicated]

Index

[Main references are to items except as otherwise indicated]

Index

645

Index

647

Index

Index

Orphans, immigration from Europe, 225

Osmena, Sergio, 24, 157 [2], 176
  Discussions with, statement, 175 [2]
  Letter, 189

Osobka-Morawski, Edward, message, 78

OSS. *See* Strategic Services, Office of

Oswego, N.Y., 225

Ottawa, Canada, 209 n.

Pacific campaign, World War II, 45, 218

Palau Islands, 45

Palestine
  Jewish immigration, 106 [18], 147 [13], 152, 172 [10], 181 [8], 187, 188, 210
  Jewish national state, proposed, 106 [8, 18], 202 [4]
  News conference remarks, 106 [18], 147 [13], 157 [9, 11], 172 [10], 181 [8], 202 [4]

Palestine commission (Anglo-American Committee of Inquiry), 187
  Members, question re, 193 [6], 202 [4, 8], 208 [4]
  Statement, 210

Panama Canal, 70, 128

Paper conservation, statement, 58

Paris, 12 n.

Park police, U.S., jurisdiction over park areas in District of Columbia, 80

Park System, National Capital, 80

Parker, John J., 132 [1]

Parler, J. D., 147 n.

Parran, Dr. Thomas. *See* Surgeon General, Public Health Service

Parten, Jubal R., 31 [7]

Patent laws, letter to Secretary Wallace, 11

Patman (Repr. Wright) bill on housing, 208 [19]

Patterson, Robert P., 116 n.
  Appointment as Secretary of War, 137 [5]
  News conference remarks on, 129 [4], 137 [5]
  See also War, Secretary of (Robert P. Patterson)

Patterson, William J., 202 [2]

Paul, Saint, 227

Pauley, Edwin W., 32, 97
  Letter, 13
  News conference remarks on, 31 [7], 60 [6], 118 [3], 157 [12]
  Personal Representative on Reparations Commission
    Appointment, 13, 15
    Mission to Japan, statement, 182

Pay
  Congressmen, 52 [19], 128
    Letter, 59
  Diplomats, 52 [19]
  Federal judiciary, 128
  Government employees, 128
  See also Wages

Pearl Harbor attack, 45, 51, 93, 97, 122
  Army and Navy reports, 116, 118 [5, 12, 14, 17], 129 [10]
  Congressional investigation, 129 [7, 10], 202 [15]
  News conference remarks, 107 [6], 116, 118 [5, 12, 14, 17], 129 [7, 10], 202 [15]
  Trial of U.S. officers in command, question of, 107 [6], 116, 118 [5, 14]

Pearlstine, Milton, 147 n.

Peleliu Island, U.S. capture of, 161

Pelley, John J., 221 [9]

Pemiscot County (Mo.) Fair, remarks, 163

649

Index

Index

[Main references are to items except as otherwise indicated]

Index

Index

[Main references are to items except as otherwise indicated]

653

Index

[Main references are to items except as otherwise indicated]

Index

Index

Index

[Main references are to items except as otherwise indicated]

657

Index

[Main references are to items except as otherwise indicated]

Index

Index

Index

Index

663

Index

Index

Index

Index

[Main references are to items except as otherwise indicated]

For Reference

Not to be taken from this room